The Enlightenment and the Rights of Man

Oxford University Studies in the Enlightenment – formerly *Studies on Voltaire and the Eighteenth Century* (*SVEC*), is dedicated to eighteenth-century research.

The Enlightenment and the Rights of Man

VINCENZO FERRONE

Translated by

ELISABETTA TARANTINO

Published by Liverpool University Press on behalf of
© 2019 Voltaire Foundation, University of Oxford
ISBN 978 1 78962 036 8
Oxford University Studies in the Enlightenment 2019:11
ISSN 0435-2866

Voltaire Foundation
99 Banbury Road
Oxford OX2 6JX, UK
www.voltaire.ox.ac.uk

A catalogue record for this book is available from the British Library

The correct style for citing this book is
Vincenzo Ferrone, translated by Elisabetta Tarantino
The Enlightenment and the rights of man
Oxford University Studies in the Enlightenment
(Liverpool, Liverpool University Press, 2019)

Cover illustration: Struck bronze medal. Obverse: Representation of the supplicant slave. Reverse: Two hands shaking at the centre.

This translation published 2019 by
Liverpool University Press
4 Cambridge Street
Liverpool
L69 7ZU

Printed and bound by TJ International Ltd, Padstow, Cornwall, PL28 8RW

Oxford University Studies in the Enlightenment

The Enlightenment and the rights of man

The Enlightenment redefined the ethics of the rights of man as part of an outlook that was based on reason, the equality of all nations and races, and man's self-determination. This led to the rise of a new language: the political language of the moderns, which spread throughout the world its message of the universality and inalienability of the rights of man, transforming previous references to subjective rights in the state of nature into an actual programme for the emancipation of man.

Ranging from the Italy of Filangieri and Beccaria to the France of Voltaire, Rousseau and Diderot, from the Scotland of Hume, Ferguson and Smith to the Germany of Lessing, Goethe and Schiller, and as far as the America of Franklin and Jefferson, Vincenzo Ferrone deals with a crucial theme of modern historiography: one that addresses the great contemporary debate on the problematic relationship between human rights and the economy, politics and justice, the rights of the individual and the rights of the community, state and religious despotism and freedom of conscience.

Contents

Acknowledgements

After a decade's work on a project, it is not only a duty but also, and even more so, a pleasure to be able to thank those who helped make it happen. Heartfelt thanks go, first of all, to Margaret Jacob, Lynn Hunt and Geoffrey Symcox for their ongoing friendship and for their encouragement when, in the spring of 2003, they witnessed the early steps of this research under the aegis of the UCLA Department of History's 'European history colloquium'. I am deeply indebted to the librarians of the Fondazione Luigi Einaudi and the Fondazione Luigi Firpo in Turin, and especially to Mrs Anna Maccioni. In helping prepare the final text of the original Italian version Giuseppe Rutto, Franco Motta, Gerardo Tocchini and Alessio Maurini offered invaluable advice. It goes without saying that any remaining errors are entirely my own. Last but not least, my thanks go to the Compagnia di San Paolo, who have long supported my research into the rights of man, starting with my critical edition of Gaetano Filangieri's *Science of legislation*.

A version of chapters 9 and 10 and chapters 14 and 15 was first published in *Rivista storica italiana* and *Studi francesi* respectively. I am grateful to the directors of these journals, Giuseppe Ricuperati and Lionello Sozzi, for allowing republication.

I am also indebted to the translator of this English version, Elisabetta Tarantino, for the patience and competence with which she undertook to render into English an extremely complex text.

Finally I am deeply grateful to Greg Brown, Nicholas Cronk and the Voltaire Foundation for giving the English version of this book a home in their collection, and thus allowing it to reach the wider audience that the subject of the rights of man certainly calls for.

This book strikes a deep chord, and it is a great joy to be able to dedicate it to the later generations: all my students across the years, and my children, Isabella and Daniele.

Preface to the English translation

It is always a great honour and pleasure for someone who believes in the values of cosmopolitanism to be able to present the results of their work to speakers of another language. For this reason, I should like to clarify why both in the title and in the book itself I always use the expression 'rights of man' when referring to its use in the eighteenth century and earlier, rather than the phrase 'human rights', with which anglophone readers are more familiar. Even more than on linguistic criteria, this decision is based on specific historical reasons, since history too has its rights.[1] Lucien Febvre highlighted the crucial importance of historical linguistics.[2] But even without this, it is easy to see that these phrases, which are nonetheless linked together in ways that are still to be fathomed, are symptomatic of two different worlds and two different cultures. They represent styles of thought that can be quite divergent from each other, and that certainly belong to distinct contexts. The phrase 'human rights', according to Lynn Hunt's lucid formulation, 'appeared rarely in French in the second half of the eighteenth century and was mainly used to distinguish between divine right and human right, again with no necessary political connotation'.[3] We know that it only became common usage in international public debate in the second half of the twentieth century, with the end of the Cold War and the decline of old utopian thought systems such as socialist internationalism, communism or the democratic reform

1 See Vincenzo Ferrone, 'The rights of history: Enlightenment and human rights', *Human rights quarterly* 39 (2017), p.130-41.

2 Cf. Lucien Febvre, 'Civilisation: évolution d'un mot et d'un groupe d'idées', in *Pour une histoire à part entière* (Paris, 1962), book 4, part 1, p.670ff.

3 Cf. Lynn Hunt, 'Revolutionary rights', in *Revisiting the origins of human rights*, ed. Pamela Slotte and Miia Halme-Tuomisaari (Cambridge, 2015), p.105-18 (118).

of capitalism, which human rights replaced, becoming a sort of 'last utopia'.[4] This was the new battle cry, a form of morality that embraced the whole of mankind and upheld apolitical universalism against the nationalistic logic of empire and individual states.

It was all quite distant from the language of the 'rights of man'. The latter had different objectives and a different history, which historians of human rights sometimes rather simplistically link back to the French Revolution, the Jacobin Terror and Napoleon's imperialism. As we shall see in what follows, the Enlightenment project was something quite different. Its objective was to safeguard the exercise of rights: Enlightenment thinkers had discovered the existence of these rights and their fascinating double nature as simultaneously a moral and a political issue. The Enlightenment aimed at transforming these into political rights and rights of citizenship, protecting them through their constitutionalisation or the action of new democratic and republican governments. Above all, it would attempt to legitimise these rights by means of a cultural revolution that for the first time foregrounded a new humanism, in which the scientific theory of the monogenesis of all human beings favoured by Buffon, Diderot, Rousseau and the *Encyclopédie* redefined the term 'man' from both the epistemological and the moral point of view in all its polysemy. In this sense – which is the sense applied throughout this book – 'man' denoted an individual without gender specification (the use of the masculine pronoun notwithstanding), who was universally the holder of rights. And this applied to all his *variétés*, this being the actual term used by Buffon, all over the world. This is why it is necessary to keep these two terms – the rights of man and human rights – quite distinct from each other.

The aim of this book, therefore, is to give a detailed account, including in terms of its linguistic origin, of the Enlightenment emancipation project in relation to the rights of man. I believe that this is important, and not only in order to adhere to philological best practice, which enjoins us to avoid anachronisms. Above all, this study upholds history's right to a central role in our contemporary political debate and its ability to put forward solutions to the disturbing crisis of the humanities that we are experiencing at the moment. The search for historical truth may be subject to limitations and illusions, just like the pursuit of any kind of truth. But it is certainly worth our facing those dangers.

4 Cf. Samuel Moyn, *The Last utopia: human rights in history* (Harvard, MA, 2010).

Introduction: why did the Enlightenment in the Western world discover the rights of man, and what are those rights?

The Enlightenment poses an enigma for us, the key to which can be found in its discovery and passionate defence of the rights of man. This is the most important result of the research described in this book.

For far too long, our conception of the Enlightenment has been based on a view that originated with the great philosophers, from Kant to Hegel, and then resonated through every part of Europe, acquiring diverse shapes. Ultimately, however, the Enlightenment has been presented to us either as a disembodied, though important, manifestation of the history of reason and rationality in the Western world, or as an enigmatic phenomenology of the spirit, whereby a spirit unhappily alienated from itself became the main agent of the crisis that led to the French Revolution.[1]

After the Second World War, thanks to Peter Gay, Franco Venturi and others, the historians' point of view began to prevail, and the Enlightenment started to be seen as an autonomous reform movement made up of real people and ideas. However, it is only in the last few decades, with the new focus on cultural history, that we have become increasingly aware of how this movement helped construct a new humanism for the modern world and overturn the *Ancien régime*, profoundly affecting the way in which we live today.[2] The fall of the Berlin Wall in 1989, which brought to an end the tragically

1. On these contrasting points of view, see Vincenzo Ferrone, *The Enlightenment: history of an idea*, translated by Elisabetta Tarantino (Princeton, NJ, 2015).
2. See *Le Monde des Lumières*, ed. Vincenzo Ferrone and Daniel Roche (Paris, 1999; original: *L'Illuminismo: dizionario storico*, Rome and Bari, 1997). On the Enlightenment as a new humanism for the modern world there is a vast bibliography, starting with Alfred Cobban, *In search of humanity: the role of the Enlightenment in modern history* (London, 1960) and including Dan Edelstein, *The Enlightenment: a genealogy* (Chicago, IL, 2010).

unrealistic dream of a communist society, no doubt accelerated this development, which in turn posed new and important questions on the real import of the political and cultural programme of the Enlightenment.

Against this background, one issue that attracted a great deal of attention was that of the eighteenth-century origins of the discourse of the rights of man as a political language of the moderns, a language that in fact began to develop long before the French Revolution. That there should be a special focus on this issue was inevitable, given the understandable interest that the question of the rights of man arouses in politicians, legal experts, sociologists and political scientists all over the world.[3] Several considerations have inevitably presented themselves to historians as a consequence of the Second World War, the Holocaust and the ferociously regular occurrence of genocide. First among these is the fact that the only possible basis for a theory of the rights of man is the value and dignity of human life: a principle that can be – but unfortunately by no means is – universally accepted. These rights must come to be seen as a powerful moral idea available to humanity.[4] They constitute the ethical tenet on which to build liberal political systems and forms of government that are capable of sustaining themselves while respecting democratic principles.

It is not by chance that concepts such as *humanity* and the *dignity of man*, which are not found in the 1789 Declaration, in 1948 became the focus of the Universal Declaration of Human Rights, the first article of which asserts: 'All human beings are born free and equal in dignity and rights.'[5]

Above all, these same ideas resurface in the bitter and moving words of those who denounced the violence and especially the humiliation suffered by the victims of Nazi concentration camps. As Primo Levi incessantly reminds us, 'in order to live, an identity – that is dignity

3. See Kenneth Cmiel, 'The recent history of human rights', *The American historical review* 109 (2004), p.117-35.
4. See Brian Tierney, *The Idea of natural rights: studies on natural rights, natural law, and Church law, 1150-1625* (Atlanta, GA, 1997), p.5.
5. On the importance of the Human Dignity Principle in legal systems and constitutions drawn up after the Second World War, see Stefano Rodotà, *Il diritto di avere diritti* (Rome and Bari, 2012), p.184ff. In the preamble to the UN Declaration we also read that 'recognition of the inherent dignity and of the equal and inalienable rights of all members of the human family is the foundation of freedom, justice and peace in the world.'

– is necessary': without this, the very notion of human existence becomes meaningless.[6]

This is what brought about the growing need to investigate the true nature of this new Enlightenment humanism, which began to develop these values in the course of the eighteenth century. It became important to trace the origins of this movement and the way in which it championed both the individual and mankind as a species. The underlying assumption was that the development of a language of the rights of man ultimately presupposed the invention of 'man' in the modern epistemological sense, to which Michel Foucault famously alluded in *Les Mots et les choses*.[7] This was a civil and intellectual enterprise of enormous magnitude. It found its iconic representation in the image of a black man in chains above the caption 'Am I not a Man and a Brother?' – a question addressed simultaneously to Heaven and to the slave owners. This image circulated widely in paintings and coins commissioned by Enlightenment thinkers such as Condorcet, founder of the Society of the Friends of the Blacks, as part of their campaign to mobilise public opinion in Europe against the slave trade.

In a famous essay on 'Jean-Jacques Rousseau, founder of the sciences of man' Claude Lévi-Strauss upheld the need for a historical investigation into the ancient and modern concepts of humanity.[8] Rousseau's description of the nature of the human was markedly different from Descartes's rationalistic and abstract 'thinking thing'. It departed even more significantly from the distinction made by every culture between 'us' and 'the other', the latter being considered 'barbaric', 'savage' or 'primitive' on the basis of presumed natural differences.

In opposition to this view, Enlightenment culture insisted on the need to identify with 'the other' in order to know ourselves, and on the universal sense of compassion for the suffering of a fellow

6. See Primo Levi, *The Drowned and the saved*, translated by Raymond Rosenthal (London, 1988), p.103.
7. See Michel Foucault, *The Order of things: an archaeology of the human sciences* (London, 2002), p.336.
8. The essay can be found in English in Claude Lévi-Strauss, *Structural anthropology II*, translated by Monique Layton (Chicago, IL, 1976), p.33-43, and in *Jean-Jacques Rousseau: critical assessments of leading philosophers*, ed. John T. Scott (London and New York, 2006), p.198-206 (from which I quote later in this work). It was originally published as 'Jean-Jacques Rousseau, fondateur des sciences de l'homme', in *Jean-Jacques Rousseau*, ed. Samuel Baud-Bovy *et al.*, (Neuchâtel, 1962), p.239-48.

human being. In this way, the Enlightenment effectively affirmed the principle of the fundamental unity of mankind: it recognised the existence of cultures and civilisations different from our own, asserting their full human dignity above and beyond the superficial physiological traits that distinguished the populations of the earth. It brushed aside all those controversial scientific hypotheses that were being produced in the fields of comparative anatomy and physiology, as well as the vociferous clashes between supporters of the theories of the monogenesis or polygenesis of the human species. This created the basis for a new rational and universal ethics founded on the equality of rights. The Enlightenment thus became a great laboratory of modernity, with contrasting visions coexisting side by side, such as those of the good as well as of the bad savage. The study of mankind branched off in every direction. Scientific investigation did not limit itself to the exterior natural features of human beings, but addressed their duty to function as moral beings as well. The Enlightenment embraced the obscure and disturbing aspects revealed by the works of Schiller or Goya, alongside the positive potential of the individual who lives within a community, historically advocated by thinkers like Voltaire and Beccaria.

This attempt to rethink the notion of human dignity in modern terms should not be taken for granted. As Lévi-Strauss wrote:

> We know, in fact, that the concept of humanity as covering all forms of the human species, irrespective of race or civilization, came into being very late in history and is by no means widespread. Even where it seems strongest, there is no certainty – as recent history proves – that it is safe from the dangers of misunderstanding or retrogression. So far as great sections of the human species have been concerned, however, and for tens of thousands of years, there seems to have been no hint of any such idea. Humanity is confined to the borders of the tribe, the linguistic group, or even, in some instances, to the village, so that many so-called primitive peoples describe themselves as 'the men' (or sometimes – though hardly more discreetly – as 'the good', 'the excellent', 'the well-achieved'), thus implying that the other tribes, groups or villages have no part in the human virtues or even in human nature.[9]

Johann Gottfried Herder aptly summed up the way in which Enlightenment circles in Europe revised the concept and the very

9. Claude Lévi-Strauss, *Race and history* (Paris, 1952), p.12.

definition of humanity, from a historical perspective and with reference to the eighteenth-century debate on the rights of man. In 1794, he wrote, with lucid irony: 'You fear that the word "humanity" might not quite pass muster. Might we not then use a different word? How about "mankind", "human nature", "the rights of man", "the duties of man", "the dignity of man", "philanthropy"?' Herder was aware that most people were still forced to live in utterly miserable conditions, and how the term 'humanity' seemed irritatingly rhetorical and inane in the face of the many devastating conflicts that plagued the world. He believed that the main purpose of the *Aufklärung* should be to investigate every aspect of the human condition, through the natural sciences, history, philosophy, poetry, literature, the theatre and the visual arts, and, above all, to practise humanitarian feelings in civil and political life: 'Humanity is the special reward of all human effort. It is the vocation of our species. We must constantly seek to educate ourselves in humanity, otherwise, high or low, we all sink to the level of mere beasts: we revert to brutality.'[10]

Herder's comparative history of the word 'humanity' aimed at highlighting its cosmopolitan and universal character. He pointed out that humanitarianism, compassion and sympathy for the suffering of fellow human beings were feelings that manifested themselves throughout the centuries in every people on earth. The *philanthropia* found in Homer and other Greek authors surfaced just as readily in Islamic culture, the writings of Confucius or the lesser-known Indian religions. The term *humanitas* had been coined by the Romans, who, with Terence, Seneca, Cicero and the Stoics, had advocated the leniency of the law, and the worth and dignity of man. The task of the Enlightenment was to continue this precious moral tradition, while making sure that the new 'sciences of man' were not reduced to a mere branch of the natural sciences.

Herder thus drew a picture that was as favourable towards the ancients as it was critical of contemporary society: the feudal and despotic *Ancien régime*, devoid of true humanitarian spirit, had enslaved man and deprived him of his dignity. The German philosopher,

10. Translated from Johann Gottfried Herder, *Briefe zur Beförderung der Humanität*, ed. Heinz Stolpe with Hans-Joachim Kruse and Dietrich Simon, 2 vols (Berlin and Weimar, 1971), vol.1, p.139 and 140. Heidegger's 'Letter on humanism' is still an important contribution on this subject: see Martin Heidegger, *Basic writings*, ed. David Farrell Krell, translated by Frank A. Capuzzi with J. Glenn Gray (London, 1978), p.193-242.

however, omitted from his picture the role played in Roman society by slavery, the inhuman institution of the gladiators, which lasted down to the time of Emperor Constantine, as well as the total absence of anything resembling the rights of man.[11] Unlike other Enlightenment thinkers, Herder did not place special importance on the legacy of the Italian Renaissance, including Pico della Mirandola's famous 'Oration on the dignity of man', which prepared the way for Cesare Beccaria's role as 'defender of man'. Other philosophers, however, such as Voltaire or Condorcet, outlined a more convincing genealogy for the struggle for the rights of man carried out by the new Enlightenment humanism in the eighteenth century, as they found its roots also in fifteenth-century civic humanism, and in the centuries-old struggle for *libertas philosophandi* and the autonomy and freedom of the individual.

However, it was Diderot who, in the *Encyclopédie* entry for 'Humanité' – which, significantly, was placed in the 'Morality' section – successfully captured both the ancient and the modern, the physical and the moral aspects of all previous discussions of the 'human' character of individuals:

> Humanity is a feeling of good will toward all men. Ordinarily only great and sensitive souls are consumed by it. This noble and sublime enthusiasm is tortured by the sufferings of others and tormented by the need to relieve such suffering; it fills men with the desire to traverse the world in order to do away with slavery, superstition, vice, and misfortune.[12]

In recent years, the aspects highlighted here by Diderot have become the two fundamental questions addressed by the international debate on this subject, i.e. the growing empathy with the past, and the Enlightenment's conscious effort to transform this feeling into a precise political programme of emancipation, which led to its discovery of the language of the rights of man.

11. Cf., by Paul Veyne, '*Humanitas*: Romans and non-Romans', in *The Romans*, ed. Andrea Giardina, translated by Lydia G. Cochrane (Chicago, IL, and London, 1993), p.342-69; 'Païens et charité chrétienne devant les gladiateurs', in *L'Empire gréco-romain* (Paris, 2005), p.545-631.
12. 'Humanity', in *The Encyclopedia of Diderot & D'Alembert: collaborative translation project*, translated by Nelly S. Hoyt and Thomas Cassirer (Ann Arbor, MI, 2003), http://hdl.handle.net/2027/spo.did2222.0000.172 (last accessed 24 April 2019). Originally published as 'Humanité', in *Encyclopédie, ou Dictionnaire raisonné des sciences, des arts et des métiers*, 17 vols (Paris, Briasson, 1751-1772), vol.8 (1765), p.348.

Why did this language arise at this specific time and place, i.e. late-eighteenth-century Europe and America? On what basis could Jefferson assert in the 1776 Declaration of Independence that the truths it stated were 'self-evident'? What role did the nascent public opinion and the new figure of the socially aware writer play in the diffusion of this language? In reply to these questions, cultural historians, and especially the pioneering work carried out by Lynn Hunt, have pointed to the change in sensitivity and in the collective way of thinking brought about by the success of novels such as those by Samuel Richardson and Jean-Jacques Rousseau: what these novels had in common was that they engendered a sense of good will, or *bienveillance*, in their readers, encouraging them to identify with 'the other'.[13]

This volume seeks to qualify this view and extend it in other directions. In this study I show the importance of the Enlightenment's contribution to the discovery of our language of the rights of man. I analyse its political awareness and its determination to confront the dominant logic of the *Ancien régime* with a radical new culture of reform. This culture of reform used every means of communication at its disposal to address public opinion and the various governments. Its goal was to ensure that human beings were protected from the oppressive actions of power and other human beings, and were thus enabled to achieve freedom and happiness. Consequently, this study examines the development of the idea of the rights of man in history within the various European contexts in which it arose. This allows us to see how this idea was profoundly reinterpreted by the Enlightenment in a moral and political sense, by comparison with the first tentative reflections in medieval canon law on the natural rights of the individual.

In Italy, for instance, from the point of view of the history of ideas, we can see the important contribution made first by philosophers such as Giambattista Vico and Antonio Genovesi, and then by Cesare Beccaria and Gaetano Filangieri in juridical and political terms. Thus, in a Late-Enlightenment bestseller such as Filangieri's *Science of legislation*, which was translated into all major European languages, the rights of man and the equality principle became the basis of a new legal system, and indeed of every aspect of society: from devising new

13. See Lynn Hunt, *Inventing human rights: a history* (New York, 2007). For an original take on this subject, see also Dan Edelstein, 'Enlightenment rights talk', *The Journal of modern history* 86 (2014), p.530-65. On the theoretical foundations of this research, see *Beyond the cultural turn: new directions in the study of society and culture*, ed. Victoria E. Bonnell and Lynn Hunt (Berkeley, CA, 1999).

and legally sound forms of state devoted to ensuring that those rights were applied in practice; from education to penal reform and to the drafting of new economic and religious laws capable of safeguarding the dignity of man. Using slightly anachronistic terms, we might say that for the first time in history, in dealing with economic development and the laws that were to govern the new political economy, the rights of man were opposed to the autonomy of the economic market, and the former won. The latter principle, by contrast, remained dominant in the Anglo-Saxon world. This was especially the case with David Hume and Adam Smith in Scotland, who differed radically from their Neapolitan counterparts in advocating a form of political neutralisation of the rights of man, which they saw as a dangerous disturbing element when it came to politics or economics: in their view, those rights should be confined to the administration of justice.

In the eighteenth century, a new theory of rights became widespread in the physiocratic circles in Paris and throughout Northern Europe. It was a theory that described the rights of man as 'duty-based', in accordance with the Stoic and community-based view of society that had been revived and popularised by Samuel von Pufendorf in his 1673 pamphlet *De officio hominis et civis iuxta legem naturalem*. This view of natural law, which was similar to the one upheld by Grotius, was as much backward- as forward-looking: it was imbued with Scholastic rationalism, and was far too ready to assent to the tenet of the absolute power and divine right of kings. Accordingly, already from the start of the century it was opposed by Enlightenment circles in Naples, Milan and Paris, who proclaimed the autonomy and freedom of the individual and assigned to mankind a new role in history: a role characterised by interaction with the community, active participation in the political life of the state, especially in its republican form, and his natural right to the pursuit of happiness.

In France, more than anywhere, thanks to figures such as Rousseau, Voltaire, Diderot and Mercier, the language of rights became an actual 'political formula': a powerful weapon against the *Ancien régime* that appealed to public opinion and the humanitarian feelings of the population through every available means of communication. The result was the rise, in the Late Enlightenment, of the 'politicisation of literature', a radical change in aesthetic perception whereby, in accordance with Diderot's tenets, every art form was expected to appeal to reason as well as to feelings, and to contribute to liberate man from the slavery, inequalities and status-biased judiciary system of the *Ancien régime*.

The debate concerning these themes in Italy, France and America resonated in the heart of Europe with far greater strength than has hitherto been recognised: one need only mention the fortune of Beccaria, Diderot's anti-slavery writings, Voltaire's defence of Calas or the 1776 Declaration. A decisive battle for the history of the rights of man in the Western world was being fought everywhere: from the most prestigious universities to the Berlin and Munich gazettes; at court as well as in the theatre. Since the start of the eighteenth century the rights issue had been thought of in terms of Pufendorf's 'duty-based' version, which had been adopted and popularised by Christian Wolff and by Scottish Enlightenment circles/thinkers. Now, in the second half of the century, it was used especially in opposition to the theory of absolutism that was being applied to modern states, an instance of which was the way in which Frederick II of Prussia was sliding towards despotism.

This process, however, suffered a serious setback with the political machinations of the Order of the Illuminati, a masonic-style secret society set up in 1776 in the German state of Bavaria by Johann Adam Weishaupt. The ensuing scandal, which affected the young Herder, Goethe and Schiller, effectively halted the progress of the movement for the rights of man, as it contributed to the proclamation in 1794 of the General Law Code for the Prussian States (*Allgemeines Landrecht für die Preußischen Staaten*). The Prussian Code transformed into rigid juridical formulae the eighteenth-century debate over the rights issue in the Holy Roman Empire. In so doing, it put an end to German Enlightenment and cosmopolitanism, by upholding a political culture along the lines of Thomas Hobbes' *Leviathan*, whereby only the State, in its modern bureaucratised and legislatively omnipotent version, was capable of creating and maintaining civil society. In such a state, rights were granted from above, rather than existing independently of the State and civil society itself, as argued by John Locke and Late-Enlightenment republican thinkers.

The French Revolution and the ensuing Terror put definitively on hold the Enlightenment's attempt to support man's quest for freedom and happiness through the establishment of inalienable rights. Enlightenment efforts in this respect were hidden from the historians' view. European history undoubtedly took a different course – and the role played in these events by the Enlightenment's attempt to uphold the rights of the individual above all forms of nationalism still remains very much to be ascertained. My research here is mainly devoted to the question of how and why the Enlightenment had discovered the rights of man in the first place.

The answer to this question must lie to a great extent in the terrible civil wars and religiously motivated conflict that devastated Europe for over 200 years, from the sixteenth to the early eighteenth century, with the loss of millions of lives. The merciless strife between Protestants and Catholics had created a permanent rift and destroyed any idea of universal truth within Christianity. Incessant theological disputes had reinforced scepticism and caused unquenchable hatred. Above all, these events had started to call into question the ancient belief that religion was a necessary aspect of civilised society: that God had been invented in order to stop men killing one another. By the late nineteenth century Dostoevsky could contemplate with anguish the thought that, if there is no God, 'everything is permitted.'[14]

The civil and religious conflicts of the sixteenth and seventeenth century had already shown the failure of this invention all over Europe. Far from limiting man's murderous propensities and will to power, God had become a pretext for Christians to wage war against one another. Having come to this bitter conclusion, the founding fathers of modern natural law, including Grotius and Pufendorf, began to work in order to give new foundations to the principle of authority, and to create a new moral science of the duties of man that would be secular and entirely independent of any form of divisive theology.

Thus, the disillusionment caused by these conflicts led to the discovery of the ethical principle of the rights of man as a new instrument capable of limiting the will to power and killer instinct of the so-called *homo necans*.[15] Hobbes and his followers started to uphold the natural right to life; with Barbeyrac, religious freedom became an inalienable right, and so did the pursuit of happiness in the thought of Burlamaqui: all of which was to be achieved thanks to man's own reason, rather than through divine providence. It was from the moral failure and burning embers of this divided Christianity, which threatened man's very existence, that the Enlightenment arose and created the political language of the rights of man.

14. Fyodor Dostoevsky, *The Karamazov brothers*, translated with an introduction and notes by Ignat Avseyp (Oxford, 2008), p.103 and *passim*. In 1762 Jean-Jacques Rousseau had already observed: 'If no Deity exists, the wicked alone can be said to reason, and virtuous men are fools' (Jean-Jacques Rousseau, *Emilius, or an Essay on education, by John James Rousseau, translated from the French by Mr. Nugent, in two volumes*, London, J. Nourse and P. Vaillant, 1763, vol.2, 'The profession of faith made by the vicar of Savoy', p.57).
15. Cf. Walter Burkert, *Homo necans: the anthropology of Ancient Greek sacrificial ritual and myth*, translated by Peter Bing (Berkeley, CA, 1983).

The true objective of the Enlightenment thus lies in the creation of a new rational and universal ethics, based on rights and on man's education in humanity. Its aim was to go beyond the ancient idea that civil society was necessarily based on the nexus between ethics and religion, an idea that Plato uses in the tenth book of his final work, *The Laws*, in opposition to atheism. Even more clearly than in Pierre Bayle's atheist society or in the theses put forward by the 'Radical Enlightenment', these objectives can be seen as the inspiration behind the positions of theists like Voltaire, Filangieri or Rousseau. These thinkers favoured a natural religion common to all nations of the world, with no Churches or theologians, a religion that worshipped a faraway God uninterested in human vicissitudes, whose main purpose was nonetheless, or rather for this very reason, to improve man's living conditions on earth. It was positions such as these that created the bases for the new universal and cosmopolitan theory of the rights of man. This gave rise to the first investigations into religion as natural experience and the answer to man's existential anxieties, as well as to Rousseau's civil religion based on the rights of man.

This view that civil and religious wars played an important role in the discovery of the rights of man is supported by the analogy with the way in which human rights were rediscovered after the Second World War, that is, after mankind experienced the Holocaust and risked annihilating itself through the terrible resurgence of *homo necans* and his will to power. This is why we must gain full awareness of the history of the rights of man. The nature of the Enlightenment is still prone to being misunderstood. In order to understand the real import of the Enlightenment, therefore, we must engage in a reconstruction of the past. We must attempt to explain the contradictory genealogy of the language of rights, and the centuries-old struggle to put that discourse into practice, against all kinds of nationalist and reactionary stances that sought to uphold the *Ancien régime* throughout Europe.

Until we gain full understanding of this, the view of the Enlightenment as intrinsically universalist and internationalist in nature and of its fundamental link with the moral principle of the dignity of man will continue to encounter resistance.[16] This is all the more peculiar in that no one calls into question the universalist character of two

16. A universalist or 'global' view of democracy has been put forward by Amartya Sen in several articles, though my historical analysis differs from his in several respects. See also *Human rights and revolutions*, ed. Jeffrey N. Wasserstrom, Greg Grandin, Lynn Hunt and Marilyn B. Young, 2nd edn (Lanham, MD, 2007).

other offshoots of the same cultural environment: modern science and commercial markets.

In fact, in modern China, with its capitalist and technocratic bias, for instance, democracy and the rights of man can still be described as subversive Western tendencies to be kept at bay.[17] In Vienna in 1993 the governments of countries from the Asiatic continent demanded a new declaration of rights that should take 'Asiatic values' into account.[18] This was peculiarly in line with the hypothesis, put forward in the same year by Samuel P. Huntington, that the future of the world was to be dominated by the clash of civilisations, a view that in the West found special favour with neoconservatives and followers of *Realpolitik*.[19]

All this, however, amounts to a betrayal of Enlightenment values. For the past few decades, some political circles have exploited the rhetoric of rights in order to justify their recourse to war and various forms of imperialism. In fact, this has nothing to do with the Enlightenment, which was a humanitarian and internationalist movement whose adherents, both men and women, fought for 200 years to ensure that human rights would be recognised and implemented all over the world. This project was based on the ethical principle of universal equality: it would never have ratified the idea that those rights are a peculiar 'ethnical' trait of white Western man.

This worryingly skewed perspective already informs the groundwork for the 1948 Universal Declaration of Human Rights. On that occasion, a dedicated UNESCO committee exerted its best efforts in the pursuit of the 'theoretical bases' of those rights. Mixing together the rights of the individual and the rights of nations, the committee traced both back to the Reformation and the rise of capitalism. No mention was made of the Enlightenment and its universalistic principles.[20]

17. On the difficult struggle for the rights of man in China in the last decade of the nineteenth century, cf. Stephen C. Angle, *Human rights and Chinese thought: a cross-cultural inquiry* (Cambridge, 2002), and Marina Svensson, *Debating human rights in China: a conceptual and political history* (Lanham, MD, 2002).
18. Cf. Cmiel, 'Recent history'.
19. Cf. Samuel P. Huntington, *The Clash of civilizations?* (Cambridge, MA, 1993).
20. *Human rights: comments and interpretations*, a symposium edited by UNESCO with an introduction by Jacques Maritain, version dated 25 July 1948 available online at http://unesdoc.unesco.org/images/0015/001550/155042eb.pdf (last accessed 24 April 2019), Appendix I. For an account of the investigation carried out by this committee, cf. Mary Ann Glendon, *A World made new: Eleanor Roosevelt and the Universal Declaration of Human Rights* (New York, 2001), p.73ff.

If this book can help revive the original and authentic principle of the rights of man, as opposed to what passes as such in the warmongering rhetoric of the new masters of the world, then it will have done something worthwhile 'for the sake of life and action', as Nietzsche said of the uses of history.

I

From natural law to the natural rights of the individual

1. The historiographical debate and the discontinuity of the Enlightenment

In 1765 Voltaire found himself involved yet again in a battle against intolerance and superstition. He looked back on his long engagement with the issue of liberty and his personal struggle against the *Ancien régime*, and, with characteristic pithiness and effectiveness, allied his efforts firmly with the cause of the rights of man:

> The more my compatriots look for truth the more they will love their liberty. The strength of spirit that leads us to truth is the same force that makes good citizens of us. What does it actually mean, to be free? It means to reason correctly, to *recognize* the rights of man. And when you *know* these well, you will also want to *defend* them.[1]

Nothing could give a better idea of the increasingly important role that the concept of the rights of man played in the 1760s and 1770s in the cultural overhaul of the *Ancien régime* by the Late Enlightenment. At this crucial moment, all over Europe, the constant reference to the 'rights of man', a phrase that did not even exist before this time, led to the creation of a new and original political discourse as part of the Enlightenment project of reform.[2] This phrase quickly became their battle cry, something not unlike a modern-day political myth. Or rather, it became their 'political formula' *par excellence*, which they used with increasing efficacy in the political struggles of those years.[3] A first

1. Voltaire, *Questions sur les miracles*, in *Œuvres complètes de Voltaire*, ed. Louis Moland, 52 vols (Paris, 1877-1885), vol.25, p.357-450 (413-14); emphasis added. All unattributed translations in this volume are by the present translator.
2. On the rise of the term 'rights of man' see chapters 9 and 10 below.
3. The expression 'political formula' (*formula politica*) was invented at the beginning of the twentieth century by Gaetano Mosca, a pioneer of modern elite theory. Mosca maintained that every social group in history had justified its power by

look at the sources reveals something rather surprising: while the term 'rights of man' spread with remarkable rapidity, this was only rarely accompanied by learned philosophical or juridical discussions on what this theory of the 'rights of man' actually was, what those rights consisted in, and on what bases they were founded. These questions did not seem to elicit any specific interest at the time. For instance, in the American colonies' 1776 Declaration of Independence, Thomas Jefferson further publicised what was already a widely held conviction when he stated quite simply that the truths on which the theory of the rights of man were founded were so obviously self-evident that they needed no definition. In fact, two centuries later the question that Jefferson cunningly bypassed, namely what exactly we mean by 'rights of man', still remains largely unanswered. This is especially true of the search for specific, solid foundations for this concept in theoretical and philosophical terms. Many accused the discourse of the rights of man of being not only revolutionary but irksomely generic and rhetorical, and even went so far as to deny the very existence of these supposed rights. In his *Reflections on the Revolution in France* (1790) Edmund Burke described how the 1628 Petition of Rights had been informed by an awareness of the practical rights of Englishmen, eschewing 'that vague speculative right', 'the rights of men'.[4] Karl Marx devoted some famous pages to this issue in his 1843-1844 essay 'On the Jewish question', only to conclude that the concept of the rights of man was nothing more than an ideological construct and an instrument fashioned by the bourgeoisie for the purposes of class domination.[5] More recently, Alasdair MacIntyre's less original but

---

appealing to 'an abstract principle, something that we might call a "political formula": to say that every magistrate is an instrument of the king's authority, who in turn derives his power from God, is to use a "political formula". The same is true of the opposite belief, that every form of power is founded on the will of the people: this too is a "political formula".' Cf. Gaetano Mosca, *Scritti politici*, ed. Giorgio Sola (Turin, 1982). From a historical point of view, the 'rights of man' too might be interpreted partly as a political formula invented by Enlightenment circles to obtain political and cultural hegemony in late eighteenth-century Europe. But, as we shall see below, the reality is rather more complicated.

4. Edmund Burke, *Reflections on the Revolution in France and on the proceedings in certain societies in London relative to that event*, ed. Conor Cruise O'Brien (London, 1986), p.149ff.
5. Cf. Karl Marx, 'On the Jewish question', translated by Clemens Dutt, in Karl Marx and Frederick Engels, *Collected works*, vol.3: *Karl Marx, March 1843-August 1844* (London, 1975), p.146-74.

nonetheless significant contribution described the idea of the rights of man as a chimera, a dangerous fiction that should be discarded as soon as possible.[6]

After the Second World War, at the time of the 1948 Universal Declaration of Human Rights, UNESCO commissioned Jacques Maritain to gather the opinion of major intellectuals of various nationalities and beliefs, in what turned out to be a vain attempt to define the philosophical bases of those rights. Maritain ended up with a series of interpretations and rational justifications that were in fact entirely incompatible with one another.[7] Things have not changed.[8] In Italy, for instance, figures as ideologically divergent as Benedetto Croce and Norberto Bobbio found themselves in agreement over the objective impossibility – in fact, the total irrelevance – of giving a philosophical foundation to the theory of the rights of man, a pursuit that they denounced as 'a badly formulated problem'. It is obvious that these rights are a purely historical construct and their study, as Bobbio repeatedly maintained, belongs to the historical and social sciences.[9]

The thesis I put forward here mostly follows in the footsteps of these two Italian philosophers. However, I locate the decisive impulse for the rise of the modern discourse of the rights of man in the cultural revolution brought about by the Enlightenment, rather than in individual positions or specific authors. It was the Enlightenment that first sought to clarify certain issues, experimented with them on a practical level, and then publicised their conclusions to the whole world. These conclusions were that we can only properly speak of

6. Cf. Alasdair MacIntyre, *After virtue: a study in moral theory* (1981), 3rd edn (London, New Delhi, New York and Sydney, 2013). According to MacIntyre 'there are no such rights, and belief in them is one with belief in witches and unicorns' (p.73). Michel Villey, *Le Droit et les droits de l'homme* (Paris, 1990) contains a harsh indictment of these rights, which he calls 'unreal' (*irréels*) and considers both a source of anarchy and a 'justification for totalitarian regimes and psychiatric hospitals' (p.153ff.). Villey also lists a series of opponents of the theory of rights, including Burke, Bentham, Marx and every pope before John XXIII. On this subject, see also *Nonsense upon stilts: Bentham, Burke and Marx on the rights of man*, ed. Jeremy Waldron (London, 1987).
7. Cf. UNESCO, *Human rights*. In his introduction, when listing a series of rights to be brought to the attention of member States, Maritain could claim no more than a 'convergence in practice' on these points (p.iii).
8. For the state of the question up to the turn of the century, see Michael Ignatieff, *Human rights as politics and idolatry* (Princeton, NJ, 2001).
9. Specific references can be found in Vincenzo Ferrone, 'Bobbio, l'Illuminismo e l'età dei diritti', *Rivista storica italiana* 118 (2006), p.258-67.

'the rights of man' when several characteristics and conditions are simultaneously present: 1) these rights must be naturally inherent in human beings as such; 2) they must be the same for all individuals, without any distinction of birth, social status, nationality, religion, gender, race; 3) they must be universal, which means that they must apply in every corner of the world; 4) finally, they must be considered inalienable and imprescriptible in the face of any kind of political or religious institution. The emphasis on the principle of the inalienability of these rights was the new element that allowed the Enlightenment to forge a powerful and original political discourse. This new discourse replaced the scattered and ineffectual references to the rights of the individual in the state of nature, as investigated by the school of natural law and its jurists in the previous centuries. Their new and effective political formula led to the overthrow of the *Ancien régime*, as it gave a crucial impulse to the emancipation of man through the practice of rights in the construction of modern civil society.

Voltaire seems to be predicting all this in the 1765 passage quoted at the beginning of this chapter, where he calls for a new civilisation where the arbitrary power of tyrants would find an insurmountable barrier in the defence of the rights of man. In fact, in this passage Voltaire summarises the true originality and the element of discontinuity in the Enlightenment's action, which was directed not only externally, in protecting the individual from the power of others, but also internally, in redefining the whole idea of man's identity and of the human condition in Western culture. For instance: while for Christianity the essence of humanity lay in man's belief that, as God's child, he was the subject of an eschatological design, in Voltaire's words we sense, for the first time, the passionate belief that man's humanity resided wholly within man himself, in the acknowledgement of his dignity and his possession of inalienable rights. In a view that, as we shall see, was widespread in Enlightenment circles throughout Europe, man's historical destiny lay in the elevation of mankind as a whole. The terms 'man' and 'rights' thus became virtually interchangeable, without the need for mediation on the part of any religious system. The one concept defined the other. The issue of finitude and of the limits imposed on human knowledge and action, man's place in the chain of being, his search for truth, his very liberty: everything referred back to the Enlightenment discourse of the natural rights of the individual. Ultimately, in the course of the eighteenth century the new awareness of these rights led, on the one hand, to the 'invention of liberty', with all the new potentials that this opened up. But on the other hand, it nailed man down to the ethical principle of his responsibility towards others, to the momentous acceptance of his finitude, and to an awareness that, as Voltaire would often point out, to be free meant first and foremost to acknowledge and defend the rights of others.

One work that clearly recognises the importance of this new discourse of natural rights within the cultural revolution caused by Enlightenment humanism is Condorcet's *Esquisse d'un tableau historique des progrès de l'esprit humain* (1793). This prophetic text, written in one burst just before the author's death in mysterious circumstances and brimming with civic passion, sums up the whole issue by setting before our eyes a philosophy of history totally centred on man, his intellectual, scientific and material conquests through the centuries, the idea of the perfectibility of the human spirit in its wayward progress towards happiness – i.e. towards the possibility of breaking free, here on earth, from the curse of original sin. In a process typical of the Enlightenment, Condorcet went about solving the ancient problem of what constituted natural law, as opposed to positive law, by looking at the human condition both from a strictly scientific point of view, in relation to actual physical existence, and from the point of view of historical knowledge, of the stadial development of populations. Within the new 'science of man' propounded by the Enlightenment, the individual was thus attributed his rights on the basis, on the one hand, of the belief in the absolute value and dignity of man, and, on the other, of a scientific hypothesis subject to empirical demonstration, concerning the fundamental unity and identity of human nature from a psychological point of view. Above all, these preliminary hypotheses seemed to be confirmed by the Enlightenment's reading of historical fact.

Condorcet was positive about it. The history of the human spirit in the Western world demonstrated beyond any reasonable doubt not only that those natural rights existed in practice, but also that it was vital to progressively acknowledge them if human existence was to attain freedom and dignity. A crisis had occurred in the sixteenth century, when, faced with the terrible wars of religion, the triumph of Machiavellian politics, and such vicious intolerance that every form of life seemed under threat, a handful of free spirits began their struggle for the restoration of some of the natural rights of man. Scientists and intellectuals started searching for 'rights which had been too long forgotten, or, rather, which had never been well known or properly explained'. It started to be generally understood that 'liberty is an inalienable good' and that 'the natural equality of men, the cornerstone of their rights, is the basis of all true morality.'[10] The protagonists of this quest were mostly scientists and literary figures, the new and powerful elite that was transforming the history of modern Europe. The enemy was represented by the jurists, who for centuries had been busy finding in positive law every possible justification for violence and arbitrary power, and denying the dignity of man on the basis of 'curious inequalities', of a political realism totally unconcerned with human nature. A few years later significant progress would be achieved thanks to figures such as Sidney and Locke. However, as Condorcet pointed out, 'if man has not [...] reached a state of perfection, his natural dignity is not degraded; some at least of his rights are recognized; he can no longer be said to be a slave though he can be said to be not truly free.'[11] The crucial step, what might be called the actual invention of the modern theory of the rights of man by the Enlightenment, occurred in the second half of the eighteenth century. It was no longer enough to acknowledge the existence of natural rights, as had in fact been happening for quite a long time: these rights had to be put into practice and transformed into political rights, 'droits politiques', according to the phrase expressly coined by Condorcet: they needed to become constitutional rights guaranteed by law, as part of a radical programme of reform of *Ancien régime* society.

In previous centuries, the school of natural law had recognised that certain rights derived from the objective existence of nature as a pre-political entity. Subsequently, the historical school and the positivist school of law had claimed quite the opposite: that the rights of the individual were the result of legislation and an act of will on the part of the State. The solution put forward by the Enlightenment in the second half of the eighteenth century for the first time merged both positions together.[12] Certain rights were certainly inherent in the nature of man; however, they needed to be historically recognised

10. Antoine-Nicolas de Condorcet, *Sketch for a historical picture of the progress of the human mind*, translated by June Barraclough, with an introduction by Stuart Hampshire (London, 1955), p.111 and 109.
11. Condorcet, *Sketch*, p.125-26.
12. For an overview of these debates, which however, like other studies on this subject, fails to recognise the originality of the Enlightenment solution, cf. Alfred Dufour, *Droits de l'homme, droit naturel et histoire: droit, individu et pouvoir de l'Ecole du droit naturel à l'Ecole du droit historique* (Paris, 1991).

and, above all, put into practice in political life through the rule of law and by becoming part of the constitution. Thus a new, entirely human form of right, constructed by mankind for the benefit of mankind, was set up as an alternative to the old divinely sanctioned right. As Paul Hazard recognised, 'For a civilization founded on Duty – duty towards God, duty towards the sovereign, the new school of philosophers were fain to substitute a civilization founded on the idea of rights – rights of the individual, freedom of speech and opinion, the prerogatives of man as man and citizen.'[13] The 1776 Declaration of Independence on the part of the American colonies became a crucial stage in this historical process. As Condorcet pointed out, after this event the cause of the rights of man took its place once and for all on the international scene.

In fact, Condorcet's own text, which expresses a typically late-eighteenth-century concern for the rights of women and queries the legitimacy of slavery from a declaredly cosmopolitan and universalist point of view, was both a virtual manifesto of the rights of man according to the Enlightenment, and a groundbreaking attempt at tracing the history of this phenomenon.[14] These aspects have not been given due consideration by readers of the *Esquisse*, and especially by historians of the rights of man, and neither has the specific genealogy highlighted by Condorcet. In the twentieth century, Ernst Cassirer was one of the few authors who focused on the important role played by the Enlightenment in forging the new discourse of the rights of man. Cassirer's overview, however, mostly denounced the paradoxical character of the Enlightenment's position in this respect. On the one hand there was the *Encyclopédie*, a bastion of methodological empiricism; on the other, there was the belief in the innate character of the rights of man. On the one hand, the Enlightenment's interest in the world of history inevitably leaned towards relativism; on the other, it claimed universal scientific validity for a moral principle that it presumed was invariably present in every human being on earth.[15]

13. Paul Hazard, *The Crisis of the European mind 1680-1715*, translated by J. Lewis May, with an introduction by Anthony Grafton (New York, 2013), p.xvi.
14. This important text is discussed in further detail at the end of this volume.
15. Cf. Ernst Cassirer, *The Philosophy of the Enlightenment*, translated by Fritz C. A. Koelln and James P. Pettegrove (Princeton, NJ, 1951), p.243ff. (original: *Die Philosophie der Aufklärung*, 1932), and especially his 1932 essay, 'Vom Wesen und Werden des Naturrechts', in *Gesammelte Werke: Hamburger Ausgabe, XVIII, Aufsätze und kleine Schriften (1932-1935)*, ed. Ralf Becker (Hamburg, 2004), p.203-27.

A few scattered references to the issue of the rights of man in the culture of the Enlightenment are also found in lesser-known works by nineteenth-century authors, or in important essays by Paul Hazard and Peter Gay. By contrast, Franco Venturi and Robert Darnton make virtually no allusion to this topic. It is only in this last decade that things have begun to change.[16]

The reasons for this delay are unclear. However, they may have something to do with the tendency to link the Declaration of the Rights of Man directly to the French Revolution, bypassing the role played by the Enlightenment.

A few examples will serve to support this view. As we know, this issue only attracted attention at an international level with the publication of Georg Jellinek's *Die Erklärung der Menschen- und Bürgerrechte* in 1895. Jellinek investigated the historical and juridical significance of the 1789 Declaration, which would reverse the legitimacy criteria of public law in the Western world by positing its justification *ex parte civium*, that is to say on the rights of the citizens rather than of their rulers. Jellinek's thesis was stated in explicit terms: 'The idea of legally establishing inalienable, inherent and sacred rights of the individual is not of political but religious origin. What has been held to be a work of the Revolution was in reality a fruit of the Reformation and its struggles.'[17] According to Jellinek, neither the theorists of natural law, nor Rousseau and his Enlightenment, and least of all the French Revolution had given rise to the modern discourse of rights. The 1789 Declaration was modelled to a great extent on the American Declaration of 1776, and the latter was a direct product of the struggle for religious freedom that had involved the American settlers from the moment they had arrived in the new continent. The

16. For an important contribution on this subject, see for instance Hunt, *Inventing human rights*. On the renewed interest in these topics, see Cmiel, 'Recent history'. This new critical trend is exemplified by my own volume, *The Politics of Enlightenment: republicanism, constitutionalism, and the rights of man in Gaetano Filangieri*, translated by Sophus Reinert (New York, 2012; original: *La società giusta ed equa: repubblicanesimo e diritti dell'uomo in Gaetano Filangieri*, Rome and Bari, 2003).
17. Georg Jellinek, *The Declaration of the Rights of Man and of Citizens: a contribution to modern constitutional history*, translated by Max Farrand (New York, 1901), p.77. Jellinek was equally opposed to Otto von Gierke's thesis that assigned an important role to the schools of natural law in the genesis of the 1789 Declaration; cf. Otto von Gierke, *The Development of political theory*, translated by Bernard Freyd (London, 1939), p.108-109 (original: *Johannes Althusius und die Entwicklung der naturrechtlichen Staatstheorie*, Breslau, 1880).

authoritative but also uncompromising nature of Jellinek's positions caused furious reactions, which eventually undermined the credibility of his arguments.[18] Jellinek was accused of pan-Germanism because of the polemical way in which he linked the concept of human rights with the Germanic and Anglo-Saxon concept of law, as opposed to that developed by imperial Rome, with its tendency towards despotism and absolutism. He was also harshly criticised for assigning spurious historical roots to what was in fact a typically nineteenth-century liberal interpretation of the rule of law, in which the rights of the individual do not come before the State (as maintained by the school of natural law), but arise in the course of history as a form of concession and self-restraint on the part of the State itself.[19]

It was only after the end of the Second World War that historians refuted Jellinek's assertions once and for all. This new perspective began to emerge in 1951 with the early writings of constitutional historian Gerhard Oestreich on social discipline and the rise of the modern State. Though mindful of the question of context, Oestreich ascribed the decisive role in the rise of the modern theory of human rights to the Neo-Stoic positions that had manifested themselves as a reaction to religious conflict in sixteenth-century Europe: 'The Stoic and Christian concepts of natural law were the most powerful cultural factors in the rise of the rights of man and of citizens.'[20] Through his writings, Justus Lipsius had popularised again the works of Cicero, Seneca, Epictetus and Marcus Aurelius, which extolled moderation in a prince, civic virtues in his subjects, and the equality of all human beings in nature on the basis that we all participate in *logos* or universal reason. The idea of an unchangeable natural law provided the foundations for a new *ius gentium* based on the equality of all peoples. A new version of the Stoics' moral philosophy from Ancient Greece and Rome, with its emphasis on personal ethics, was deployed in order to counteract the dissolution of the old social order and the development of modern individuality. According to Oestreich, through the mediation of Lipsius, the Ciceronian emphasis on duty,

18. On this debate, which involved E. Boutmy, E. Troeltsch, G. Del Vecchio and, more recently, G. Oestreich, H. Hofmann and G. Tarello, see Stéphane Rials, *La Déclaration des droits de l'homme et du citoyen* (Paris, 1988), p.356ff.
19. On Jellinek and *Staatsrechtslehre*, cf. Maurizio Fioravanti, *Giuristi e costituzione politica nell'Ottocento tedesco* (Milan, 1980).
20. Gerhard Oestreich, *Geschichte der Menschenrechte und Grundfreiheiten im Umriß* (Berlin, 1968), p.14.

civic virtues and social discipline provided the intellectual framework for the early modern process of secularisation, the formation of the modern absolutist state, with its bureaucracy and large standing armies, and the simultaneous confessionalisation and institutionalisation of the Churches. The renewed popularity of these Ciceronian virtues highlighted the need for peaceful social coexistence, tolerance and freedom of conscience. This foregrounded politics and 'reason of State' over and above the 'reason of the Church' – of *any* Church – and of theological divergences, which had caused the bloody civil wars between Catholics and Protestants. The process of laying the foundations of the theory of human rights was completed by the Jesuits and Dominicans of the 'Second Scholastics', who updated Aquinas' theory of natural law with elements of moral philosophy drawn from Neo-Stoicism, thus opening the way to the theories of Grotius, Pufendorf and Locke, and eventually to the Declaration of 1789.

Oestreich's illuminating survey of the importance of European Neo-Stoicism for the history of human rights gave rise to a vast and interesting research movement, which is still extremely active, especially in the Anglo-Saxon world. However, as we shall see below, the hypothesis that these rights derive from a Ciceronian sense of duty is not entirely borne out by a detailed analysis of the facts. While this theory does throw light on how the language of rights evolved from the Ciceronian discourse of civic duties in the Protestant, i.e. German, English and Scottish, language of natural law, this does not apply to the French and Italian Enlightenment circles. In these countries, an opposite development took place: it was the rise of Neo-Epicureanism that turned the seventeenth-century ethics of duties, first, into an ethics of rights, and then, after the establishment of the natural right to the pursuit of happiness, into the rights of man as 'droits politiques', according to Condorcet's definition.

Nevertheless, Oestreich must be credited with bringing back to the centre of the stage that idea of natural law that had been harshly criticised by authors such as Jellinek. In the past few decades, a considerable amount of research in this field has led to new insights into the changes undergone by the concept of natural law, into the origins of the discourse of natural rights and the discourse of the rights of the individual in general.[21] One aspect that still tends to be neglected,

21. See especially the pioneering study by Ernst Bloch, *Natural law and human dignity*, translated by Dennis J. Schmidt (Cambridge, MA, 1986; original: *Naturrecht und menschliche Würde*, Frankfurt am Main, 1961).

however, is the highly original way in which the Enlightenment departed from the earlier school of modern natural law to create its own discourse on this subject. It is this aspect that will be examined in detail in the present study.[22]

22. In fact, despite his general focus on Neo-Stoicism and his more or less stadial view of Western constitutionalism, Oestreich offered some interesting remarks on this subject, which are not at all incompatible with the discontinuity thesis put forward in the present study: 'The concept of the "rights of man" came down to us especially from the eighteenth century, when the philosophers of the Enlightenment, who had a pre-eminent role in the field of social thought and the theory of the state, fully developed their theory of natural rights. For the first time in its 2000-year history the theory of natural law became a practical philosophy, divided into the three branches of ethics, economy and politics, dealing with the individual, domestic and public spheres respectively. There is a close connection between natural law in this overall practical meaning, the theory of natural rights and, ultimately, the theory of the rights of man. The concept of the "rights of man" implies that there are innate rights that belong to the very essence of man. Such rights are immutable and unconditional. It is on their presence or absence that the existence of the human being as person depends, whose dignity and worth they determine' (Oestreich, *Geschichte der Menschenrechte*, p.11-12).

2. The metamorphosis of ancient natural law

The Enlightenment's critique of the theory of natural law was radical and persistent. Enlightenment philosophers took every opportunity to distance themselves from that centuries-old model and stressed the ways in which their own position differed from it so frequently and thoroughly that they seemed to be ringing its death knell. Their cultural revolution completely transformed the language and practices of the ancient tradition of natural law, opening the way to a general rethinking of what constituted natural rights. By the end of the eighteenth century, a metamorphosis had taken place in this respect. Of course, if was not the first time that significant changes had occurred, but now the Enlightenment swept away the very foundations of natural law as the expression of an ordered universe, and finally placed man, his will and liberty, at the centre of everything. It unmasked the political nature of the *arcana iuris*, the supposedly sacred mystery of the law, that had upheld the juridical order of the *Ancien régime*. It opposed the workings of time and history to the idea of the fixity and immutability of nature. It demystified and relativised all possible interpretations from the point of view of the human being, effectively removing natural models from their exclusive role as legitimising agents. The final revolution, which culminated in the theory of the rights of man, came after centuries of constant transformations. The following overview is necessary if we are to understand what will eventually remain of this ancient model, which had played such an important role in the history of the Western world.

Sophocles' *Antigone* is a much-quoted expression of the ideal of an immutable and eternal justice forever etched in the laws of the universe. From the historical point of view, we know that the idea of 'natural right' (*dikaion physikon*, right according to nature) first appeared in Ancient Greece alongside the concept of nature and alongside philosophy itself.[1] At about this time, man was beginning to question the authority and the ancient laws of the gods. Myth was replaced by reason and philosophy as the principal means through which one could reflect on first things and universal principles, and nature became the main point of reference in the attempt to clarify what was right and to define the concept of justice. A distinction was established between what derived from nature (*dikaion physikon*) and what arose from convention (particularly, from the will of the legislator: *dikaion nomikón*, or positive law).[2] Surrounded by youths, Socrates would critically expatiate on natural law and on the quest for justice on the basis of nature. He would question divinely justified law and the very bases of all authority, traditions and customs, and in the process he laid the foundations for the form of political science that would be applied by Plato in his reflections on wrong and iniquitous laws.[3] Aristotle was overall more conservative in his role as the intellectual founder of natural law, as is shown by his acceptance of inequality and slavery as founded in nature.[4] For all his interest in the issue of justice, Plato believed that the identification of what was right or wrong belonged to the world of ideas rather than to the empirical

1. On this term, see Aristotle, *Nichomachean ethics*, V, 7, 1134b. In Greek the term *dikaion* denotes both what is just and what is lawful, with a revealing overlap that would give rise to significant confusion between the concepts of justice, fairness and right. The *Thesaurus Graecae linguae, ab Henrico Stephano constructus, ediderunt Hase, Sinner et Fix*, 3rd edn (Paris, 1833), col.1475-77, translates this Greek term as ‘aequitas, ius’. We should also note that *dikaion* is a noun derived from the adjective *dikaios*, while in Latin it is the adjective *iustus* that comes from the noun *ius*. This in turn derives from *iubeo*, to issue a command, highlighting the imperative nature of right rather than its conformity to the universal order of things.
2. Cf. ‘The origin of the idea of natural right’, chapter 3 in Leo Strauss, *Natural right and history* (Chicago, IL, and London, 1953): ‘Nature was discovered when man embarked on the quest for the first things in the light of the fundamental distinctions between hearsay and seeing with one’s own eyes, on the one hand, and between things made by man and things not made by man, on the other’ (p.88). See also the precise philological and philosophical distinctions in Carl Schmitt, *The Nomos of the earth in the international law of the jus publicum europaeum*, translated and annotated by G. L. Ulmen (New York, 2003), on the different meanings in time of the term *nomos*, which was at first associated with the measurement and appropriation of land and later came to represent positive law (p.67ff.).
3. Cf. Plato, *Laws*, IV, 715.
4. Cf. Michel Villey, *La Formation de la pensée juridique moderne: cours d’histoire de la philosophie du droit*, 4th edn (Paris, 1975), p.41ff.

study of nature.[5] It was therefore Aristotle who clearly defined both the relationship and the distinction among such key concepts as nature, laws, right. His discussion of 'right by nature' in ethics and politics would remain a standard reference point for centuries to come, along with his theory of *epieikeia*, in which natural law and positive law are engaged in a constant dialogue between equals, leading to the possibility of realising a true form of justice that is based on the nature of things.[6]

In the Roman world, natural law was founded on a view of nature as containing inbuilt rules and regulations capable of guiding men in their search for justice. In fact, this was a philosophical concept that had come from Greece and been transplanted into an entirely different tradition, in whose juridical texts the term 'justice' itself had very little currency. The concept of *ius*, by contrast, arose in the earliest archaic times of Rome, between the eighth and seventh centuries BC, an era dominated by a sense of religious rituality, and continued to develop gradually, with the Law of the Twelve Tables in 450 BC, and then with the role of magistrates and the study of law and legal procedure in the republican age. This was a new and original view of law as a kind of practice and science that was entirely distinct from morality, religion or politics. It was concerned with the formalistic imposition of social discipline and favoured the rise of a class of jurists who acted as 'neutral' or 'impartial' regulators in society.[7]

5. See, however, in Plato's later dialogues, the powerful defence of natural law against the relativism of the Sophists and all those who maintained 'that there is one class of things beautiful by nature, and another class beautiful by convention; while as to things just, they do not exist at all by nature, but men are constantly in dispute about them and continually altering them, and whatever alteration they make at any time is at that time authoritative, though it owes its existence to art and the laws, and not in any way to nature' (Plato, *Laws*, translated by R. G. Bury, 2 vols, *Loeb classical library* 192, Cambridge, MA, 1926, vol.2, X, 889e-890a). On the Sophists' critique of natural law and Plato's position, cf. Bloch, *Natural law*, chapter 4, p.7-9.
6. Cf. Aristotle, *Nicomachean ethics*, translated by H. Rackham, *Loeb classical library* 73 (Cambridge, MA, 1926), V (E), 2, 1130a-b. A little later, Aristotle specifies: 'Political Justice [*politikon dikaion*] is of two kinds, one natural [*physikon*], the other conventional. A rule of justice is natural that has the same validity everywhere, and does not depend on our accepting it or not. A rule is conventional that in the first instance may be settled in one way or the other indifferently, though having once been settled it is not indifferent' (V (E), 7, 1, 1134b).
7. Cf. Aldo Schiavone, *The Invention of law in the West*, translated by Jeremy Carden and Antony Shugaar (Cambridge, MA, 2012).

There are obvious differences between these two modes of thinking, which critics today indicate through the contrasting paradigms of *nomos* and *ius*: the former representing Greek philosophical thought, the latter embodying Roman juridical science. The Greeks privileged a substantive view of justice, linked to ethics and politics, but without any juridical specialism. The Romans, by contrast, created a powerful, highly formalised juridical science, the result of an atavistic concern with ritual and order. As Aldo Schiavone writes: 'Justice (as the respect for a shared and superior moral law, however open it might remain to discussion) and legality (as formal compliance with a scientifically constructed order) were about to diverge along two separate paths in the course of Western history, just like their paradigms of reference: politics and law.'[8] This separation still largely applies today, causing considerable problems.

In the republican period, from Quintus Mucius' *Iuris civilis libri* to the works of Cicero, *ius* became an autonomous discipline. Drawing on a variety of sources, including Greek philosophy, it provided a logical systematisation of a centuries-old experience and everyday practice of the law. In this way, juridical science became a technological discipline, whereby an abstract and formalised *ius civile* was deployed for the preservation of order and discipline. This *ius* was based on abstract, economy-derived patterns of social relationships, on ways of being that were modelled on father–children relationships, on the dualism between form and content. It formalised certain archetypal models that treated juridical concepts – such as those of contract, ownership, inheritance, obligation, slavery and legal protection – as ontological manifestations.

With the rapid expansion of the Roman empire, this formalised concept of law as the study and science of social order, which had been perfectly well equipped to deal with private social affairs in republican Rome, started to reveal its shortcomings both in terms of effectiveness and, especially, in terms of legitimacy, as the new expansionistic political structure brought with it new moral challenges. Jurists then turned to natural law, to nature seen as a source of justice, the ultimate and most important, albeit retroactive, justification for the transformation of *ius* from an act of will into a form of knowledge. Cicero and the moral philosophy of the Stoics took centre stage in this new phase. Cicero's definition of natural law, which came down to later centuries through the Christian writer Lactantius, will resurface

8. Schiavone, *Invention of law*, p.295.

at every significant turning point in the history of this discipline, down to the eighteenth century, and is therefore worth quoting in full:

> True law is right reason in agreement with Nature; it is of universal application, unchanging and everlasting; it summons to duty by its commands, and averts from wrong-doing by its prohibitions. And it does not lay its commands or prohibitions upon good men in vain, though neither have any effect on the wicked. It is a sin to try to alter this law, nor is it allowable to attempt to repeal any part of it, and it is impossible to abolish it entirely. We cannot be freed from its obligations by Senate or People, and we need not look outside ourselves for an expounder or interpreter of it. And there will not be different laws at Rome and at Athens, or different laws now and in the future, but one eternal and unchangeable law will be valid for all nations and for all times, and there will be one master and one ruler, that is, God, over us all, for He is the author of this law, its promulgator, and its enforcing judge.[9]

Cicero's views on natural law can be found mostly in his *De legibus*. This was an important work in several respects: it sought to give universal character to ancient *ius* in line with Rome's new imperial role, and it gave a solid philosophical basis to Roman positive law by founding it on an idea of nature according to which the concept of right and wrong is innate in human reason. However, in this respect, Cicero's work did not substantially alter the politics and culture of the Roman empire: the science and tradition of Roman law were far too strong to give way to the latest philosophical trend imported from Greece.

Professional jurists were never well disposed towards this commingling of the law with moral philosophy. Thus Roman natural law never developed into a separate branch of philosophy. It remained subordinate to positive law, which it justified by detecting the existence of certain rules in the very nature of things and in the exercise of the law itself. Should its conclusions clash with the practice of positive law, Roman natural law would not claim any superiority, as we shall see will happen in later centuries. It simply reinforced the work done by previous jurists who had attempted to bring together *ius*, or what was right from a legal point of view, and *bonum et aequum*, what was morally right and good. The meaning of *ius*, *iustitia*, *aequitas* was given

9. *De republica*, III, 22, 33, cited and commented in Alessandro Passerin d'Entrèves, *Natural law: an introduction to legal philosophy*, 2nd edn (London, 1970), p.25.

a new slant in terms of natural law, which brought together concepts of legality, formalism and ethics but avoided impinging on the professional techniques and practice of the *scientia iuris*. It would have been extremely difficult to transform Ancient Roman juridical science into anything resembling our public ethics. Nowhere is this more apparent than in the question of slavery, where the distance between *ius naturale*, or natural law, and *ius gentium*, the law of nations, appeared in all its magnitude.

The moral philosophy of the Stoics asserted that all men are equal and free in the state of nature, and the Sophists strenuously opposed Aristotle's concept of the 'natural slave'.[10] But for jurists in late republican and imperial Rome the idea of the equality and freedom of all individuals only really existed in terms of *ius naturale*. In actual social living, which was regulated by *ius gentium*, slavery had found universal acceptance, and had given rise to the legal principle of 'manumission'. This meant that slaves were devoid of any rights whatsoever, including to their own lives, and could be freed only by the will of a private citizen, their master.

The 'failure of ancient natural law theory' becomes evident in discussions of slavery at the start of the third century AD. See for instance Ulpian: 'after slavery came in by the law of nations, there followed the boon of manumission. And while by natural law men are all called by a single name, in the law of nations there came to be three classes: free men, and set against those slaves and the third class, freedmen, those who had stopped being slaves.' Similar utterances are found in Tryphoninus ('freedom is the condition of natural law and subjection the invention of the law of nations') and especially in Florentinus ('Slavery is an institution of the law of nations, whereby someone is against nature made subject to the ownership of another.')[11]

Pronouncements such as these attest to the incapability of ancient natural law to alter the course of positive law and achieve anything resembling our human rights: something for which it would have been necessary to move from a focus on the relationship among citizens,

10. Cf. Aristotle, *Politics*, I, 2, 1255a: 'It is manifest therefore that there are cases of people of whom some are freemen and the others slaves by nature, and for these slavery is an institution both expedient and just' (translated by H. Rackham, *Loeb classical library* 264, Cambridge, MA, 1932).

11. See the discussion of this point in Schiavone, *Invention of law*, which includes the texts quoted here (p.453). The reference to the 'failure of ancient natural law theory' (p.458) obviously denotes a point of view favourable to modern attitudes. For a different point of view, see Villey, *Formation de la pensée juridique*, p.81.

with its ostensible ethical and political neutrality, to a focus on subjective rights. What legacy did ancient natural law then bequeath to later centuries?

As far as Ancient Rome is concerned, its obvious legacy is the *Corpus iuris civilis*, assembled by Byzantine jurists by order of Emperor Justinian I and completed in 534 AD. This famous collection has long been the object of careful study, which has highlighted its complex multilayered structure and the consequent difficulty in distinguishing between the true position of its various authors and the exigencies of the gathering and presentation of its constituent texts. One thing that emerges quite clearly, however, is its claim to universal validity. Roman law here posits itself as the common substratum of all human relationships, drawing its legitimacy from both reason and natural law.

While the distinction between nature and convention was never in doubt, including the primacy of the latter over the former in actual social and political life, substantial discrepancies arose when attempting to define the relationship between *ius naturale*, *ius civile* and *ius gentium*. For Ulpian, natural law is what nature teaches all animals, as well as men; the law of nations only applies to relationships among human beings and nations; while civil law took both the former and the latter into account, without depending entirely on either.[12] A generation earlier, Gaius had made only a bipartite distinction, between *ius civile* and *ius gentium*, the latter the direct expression of natural reason, and as such present and active amongst all men and nations of the world.[13] Gaius thus focuses on the role played by historical conditions and by *consensus gentium* in transforming natural law into specific instances of the law of nations. However, Ulpian's views proved more influential in the West down to the early modern period. The separation he advocates between natural law and any form of historicity spoke to the general view of nature as a self-sufficient universe, intrinsically stable and permanent. It was precisely its autonomy from human will that allowed nature to serve as arbiter and universal model in man's quest for what was right. This became the prevalent interpretation among the commentators of the *Corpus iuris civilis*, and led to the theologisation of nature in the so-called Aristotelian-Thomistic universe, and thus became the frame of reference of Christian natural law.

12. Cf. *Digesta* 1.1.1.3-4 and 1.1.6pr, http://www.thelatinlibrary.com/justinian/digest1.shtml (last accessed 26 April 2019).
13. *Digesta* 1.1.9, *ibid.*

For centuries the Western world was dominated by the image of nature put forward by Thomas Aquinas in his *Summa theologiae*: the image of a universe in which – as is sung in the Psalms – the heavens and the earth declare every moment the power and the glory of God. Even today, there are important sections of the Christian community for whom this natural theology, ultimately derived from the Bible, still represents an unassailable dogma, and for whom this is a fundamental point of reference in all bioethical, political and social debates, and in their way of seeing the complex relationship between the will of God and the partial autonomy of man.[14]

In his *Divine comedy*, Dante famously gave literary expression to the ultimate foundations of this view of nature. In his *Paradiso* (cantos 1-3) Dante insists on the concept of order, and of a divine providence constantly at work, and depicts the triumph of beauty and harmony in a universe where everything is in its appropriate place, forever reflecting the will of God and his exact design. As Beatrice explains to the Poet before the astonishing spectacle of the heavenly spheres:

> All things created have an order
> in themselves, and this begets the form
> that lets the universe resemble God.[15]

The downward movement of falling objects, or of 'fire toward the moon' (line 115), indeed the behaviour of all 'created things' (line 118), attested to the ontological perfection of this universe and to what has been rightly defined as a fascinating but 'paroxysmal theology of order'.[16] In Thomas Aquinas' *philosophia mundi* the Church certainly

14. Francesco Remotti discusses how the Church today still appeals to the stabilising and legitimatising effect, in anthropological terms, of this stable and everlasting nature in its polemics against ethical relativism. Cf. Remotti, *Contro natura: una lettera al papa* (Rome and Bari, 2008). On this subject, it is worth quoting a text by Isidore of Seville, incorporated into Gratian's *Decretum*, a foundational work in canon law. In this text, *ius naturale* is defined as 'for instance, the union of man and woman, the generation and rearing of children, the common possession of all things and the one liberty of all, the acquisition of those things which are taken from air and land and sea; also the return of a thing deposited or money loaned, the repulsion of force by force' (*Dist.* 1 c.7, quoted in Tierney, *Idea of natural rights*, p.59).
15. *Paradiso*, canto 1, lines 103-105.
16. Paolo Grossi, *L'ordine giuridico medievale* (Rome and Bari, 1995), p.83. Dante quotations are from *Paradiso*, translated by Robert Hollander and Jean Hollander (New York, 2006).

found the highest and most lasting manifestation of its attempt to 'Christianise' pagan natural law and to bring about a new and significantly different humanism from that of the ancients.

On the basis of important Aristotelian texts that resurfaced after being long lost, Aquinas' *Summa theologiae* presents a more autonomous and lay concept of nature than that of Augustine, the Neoplatonists of the early Middle Ages or the twelfth-century School of Chartres, with their metaphysical search for the organic link between God and his creatures, or *ascensio mentis in Deum per scalas creaturarum.*[17] This is not surprising since the context in which the Church operated, and consequently its historical function, varied significantly across these periods.

Augustine was writing at a moment of profound crisis in late antiquity, pervaded by the fear of the imminent dissolution of civilisation in the Mediterranean area. This reinforced his already pessimistic view of human nature and led to a Christian vision centred around the idea of original sin and of the absolute necessity of salvation through grace, in a universe characterised by the contrast between the city of God and the city of man. Given his belief in the utter dependency of sin-ridden mankind on God, Augustine was not interested in the arduous enterprise of founding an ethical system and new political and social institutions in the *saeculum*, the material world. His *De civitate Dei* shows respect and admiration for Roman *ius* and for the civic virtues that had made the Roman empire great, but these were never part of his concept of Christian life. His *homo viator* was a pilgrim in a hostile world, whose only concern was to testify his faith and his being a creature of the true God, as someone who was fully aware of the provisional character of historical time and the limitations of human truth in the face of the Revelation.[18]

By contrast, the main concern of Aquinas and the medieval Church was something entirely different. The year 1000 had come and gone, the end of the world was not felt to be quite so nigh, and people were attending to the needs of the here and now. The task

17. On this subject, see *La filosofia della natura nel Medioevo: atti del terzo congresso internazionale di filosofia medievale, Passo della Mendola, Trento, 31 agosto-5 settembre 1964* (Milan, 1966), and Marie-Dominique Chenu, *Nature, man, and society in the twelfth century: essays on new theological perspectives in the Latin West*, selected, edited and translated by Jerome Taylor and Lester K. Little (Chicago, IL, 1968; original: *La Théologie au XII*[e] *siècle*, Paris, 1957).

18. See Peter Brown, *Augustine of Hippo: a biography*, 2nd edn (Berkeley, CA, 2000), p.375-76.

in hand was to build the new *Respublica christiana*, to shape life as a Catholic fortress, according to the tenets of a new humanism capable of bringing together faith and reason, philosophy and religion into a harmonious whole, reconciling the individual's dependency on God as a consequence of original sin with man's need to nevertheless pursue justice in this world, to enquire into the furthest recesses of nature, and to obtain the best possible living conditions while waiting for the eschatological design to be fulfilled. Man's relationship with God was no longer exclusively dominated by the enlightening effects of grace, as in Augustine. A new emphasis is now placed on 'natural reason', on man's dignity and rationality; man is no longer simply God's creature and God's subject, but takes upon himself part of the responsibility in the workings of the universe and in the task of distinguishing between good and evil, right and wrong. Thus, in discussing the question posed in Psalms 4:6, *quis ostendit nobis bonum*, Aquinas refers man to 'the light of natural reason'.[19]

The kind of universe described in Aquinas' theologised nature fulfilled a human need that has long been known to psychologists and anthropologists alike: the need to give meaning to our life on earth by eliminating disorder, to make Augustine's *malignum saeculum* less hostile by rationalising space and time.[20] St Thomas' theology presented a unified cosmos that was organised according to a rigid hierarchical order, where even man's partial autonomy from God's

19. 'Now among all others, the rational creature is subject to Divine providence in the most excellent way, in so far as it partakes of a share of providence, by being provident both for itself and for others. Wherefore it has a share of the Eternal Reason, whereby it has a natural inclination to its proper act and end: and this participation of the eternal law in the rational creature is called the natural law. Hence the Psalmist after saying (Ps. 4:6): "Offer up the sacrifice of justice", as though someone asked what the works of justice are, adds: "Many say, Who showeth us good things?" in answer to which question he says: "The light of Thy countenance, O Lord, is signed upon us": thus implying that the light of natural reason, whereby we discern what is good and what is evil, which is the function of the natural law, is nothing else than an imprint on us of the Divine light. It is therefore evident that the natural law is nothing else than the rational creature's participation of the eternal law.' (Thomas Aquinas, *The Summa theologica*, translated by Fathers of the English Dominican Province, first part of the second part, question 91, article 2; www.dhspriory.org/thomas/english/summa/index.html, last accessed 26 April 2019).
20. See, respectively, E. H. Gombrich, *The Sense of order: a study in the psychology of decorative art* (Oxford, 1979), and R. A. Markus, *Saeculum: history and society in the theology of St Augustine* (Cambridge, 1970).

will arose organically from the structure of this well-ordered and interconnected reality.[21] The order imposed by God's knowledge and will reigned everywhere. Not only was it made evident to our senses by the beauty and harmony of the skies and motions: it underlay even the apparent chaos of social phenomena and the clash of particularities. The universe was a network of relationships linking all creatures together and arranged in rigid and exact hierarchical order, from the created to the uncreated, which is the first mover. This attenuated Augustine's implacable sentence, as the theological imperfection and utter dependency of the individual marked by original sin was, to a certain extent, redeemed by his being *part* of a *whole*, of an organic, communitarian system along Aristotelian lines.[22] The individual was subsumed into the ontological and epistemological primacy of the *multitudo*, of the *totalitas*, of the *universitas*, of bodies in general as epistemological paradigm. In practical terms, the individual was acknowledged as an autonomous person only insofar as he or she was part of a family or community made up of many particular *ordines*, each of which was seen as one hierarchically placed element in a single, harmonious and universal order.

21. In reiterating the autonomy of nature, Aquinas writes: 'Contradiction, moreover, is implied in contraries and privative opposites: to be white and black is to be white and not white; to be seeing and blind is to be seeing and not seeing. For the same reason, God is unable to make opposites exist in the same subject at the same time and in the same respect. Furthermore, to take away an essential principle of any thing is to take away the thing itself. Hence, if God cannot make a thing to be and not to be at the same time, neither can He make a thing to lack any of its essential principles while the thing itself remains in being; God cannot make a man to be without a soul. Again, since the principles of certain sciences – of logic, geometry, and arithmetic, for instance – are derived exclusively from the formal principles of things, upon which their essence depends, it follows that God cannot make the contraries of those principles; He cannot make the genus not to be predicable of the species, nor lines drawn from a circle's center to its circumference not to be equal, nor the three angles of a rectilinear triangle not to be equal to two right angles. It is obvious, moreover, that God cannot make the past not to have been, for this, too, would entail a contradiction; it is equally as necessary for a thing to be while it is as to have been while it was.' (*Contra gentiles*, translated by James F. Anderson, II, 25, 12-15, www.dhspriory.org/thomas/english/ContraGentiles.htm, last accessed 26 April 2019.)
22. On the importance of Aristotle's anti-individualistic organicism in Aquinas' view of social order, see Norberto Bobbio, 'Il giusnaturalismo', in *Storia delle idee politiche economiche e sociali*, ed. Luigi Firpo, vol.4.1 (Turin, 1980), p.491-558 (512ff.).

It is on the basis of this idea of universal cosmos, social order and a profoundly theologised nature, in which God was viewed as the supreme legislator, that the Christianisation of pagan natural law was accomplished.[23] There was a rapid and complete change in perspective with comparison to Roman *ius*. Natural law was an expression of divine will, and as such it must take absolute priority over both positive and customary law. Aquinas is very clear on this matter. Appealing to the authority of Augustine, he stresses that it is a precise Christian duty to disobey any legal injunction that is unjust and contrary to natural law.[24] Thus human law was finally superseded by divine law as expressed in the natural order of the universe. As stated in the opening paragraph of the *Decretum Gratiani* (*c.*1140), embodied in the *Corpus iuris canonici*: 'Mankind is ruled by two laws: Natural Law and Custom. Natural Law is that which is contained in the Scriptures and the Gospel.'[25] As Gratian explains, this is the law that teaches us to do as we would be done by (and not to do to others what we would not wish to be done to ourselves). Since *ius naturale* was the original source of all juridical acts and thought, it should always be placed higher on the hierarchical scale than custom.[26]

23. There is a large bibliography on the Christianisation of natural law. However, Ernst Troeltsch's 1912 *Die Soziallehren der christlichen Kirchen und Gruppen* is still a fundamental study on this subject (for the English version, see *The Social teaching of the Christian Churches*, translated by Olive Wyon, 2 vols, London, 1931, and subsequent reprints).
24. 'As Augustine says (*De Lib. Arb.* i, 5) "that which is not just seems to be no law at all": wherefore the force of a law depends on the extent of its justice. Now in human affairs a thing is said to be just, from being right, according to the rule of reason. But the first rule of reason is the law of nature [...] Consequently every human law has just so much of the nature of law, as it is derived from the law of nature.' (Aquinas, *Summa theologica*, first part of the second part, question 95, article 2.) Later on, still on this subject, St Thomas writes: 'Man is bound to obey secular princes in so far as this is required by order of justice. Wherefore if the prince's authority is not just but usurped, or if he commands what is unjust, his subjects are not bound to obey him, except perhaps accidentally, in order to avoid scandal or danger.' (Second part of the second part, question 104, article 6, reply to objection 3.) For a controversial historicist reading of Aquinas' natural law, which distinguishes between a fixed and immovable universe and its knowledge in time, see Jacques Maritain, *The Rights of man and natural law* (London, 1945), p.34ff.
25. Quoted in Passerin d'Entrèves, *Natural law*, p.37.
26. Gratian's *Decretum* was adamant on the primacy of natural law over both 'the laws of princes' or secular authorities and ecclesiastical laws (cf. Harold

In fact, these categorical statements should be considered in light of the Scholastics' Christian humanism, with its balance between faith and reason, and, above all, in light of the historical context. We need to take into account the ongoing clash between papal power and secular states, and the existence of several legal systems at the same time, in order to understand the difference, for instance, between the *scientia iuris* of the Christian West and the strict theological and juridical monism of Islamic Sharia law.[27] To say that God was the source and first cause of everything did not mean equating natural law and Scripture. It meant trying to avoid any contradiction between the use of *recta ratio* and Revelation in the pursuit of what was right according to nature, or in relation to important biblical passages, as indeed happened in the seventeenth century with the word of the Psalms and Galileo's description of the earth's movement around the sun.[28]

We saw above how, in Aquinas' universe, alongside God as first cause, an effectively self-sufficient and self-regulated nature could operate by virtue of its own immanent order and of universal natural law, which functioned as immediate second cause (with miracles being allowed as divinely sanctioned exceptions to the order of things). This reinforced the ontological view of law as something everlasting, above and beyond the everyday and the contingent. This law was not the result of an act of legislation: it was the manifestation of an objective natural order to be sought and found in the conviction that all laws and regulations were ultimately written in the very nature of things.[29] Far from being an expression of human will and power, since man was still limited in his autonomy by original sin, *lex* came to be considered an integral part of reality and of a possible order: a set of rules which were to be actively sought and found in a theologised nature governed

J. Berman, *Law and revolution: the formation of the Western legal tradition*, Cambridge, MA, 1983, p.145).

27. In recent years Catholic historians have paid special attention to the *dualism* between politics and religion and between papacy and empire as a foundational element in modern Western civilisation: see Vincenzo Ferrone, 'La "sana laicità" della Chiesa bellarminiana di Benedetto XVI tra *potestas indirecta* e *parresia*', *Passato e Presente* 26 (2008), p.21-40.

28. On the harmonious concord of faith and reason in Aquinas, for whom divine law does not suppress human law, which is based on natural reason, see Emile Bréhier, *La Philosophie du Moyen Age*, chapter 4.4.13, 'Bien naturel et bien surnaturel' (2nd edn, Paris, 1949; available online).

29. For an illuminating discussion of the ontological nature of law in the Middle Ages, see Grossi, *Ordine giuridico*, p.138ff.

by a universal order, and which were then to be transformed into formal regulations.

In the historical context of the Middle Ages in the Western world, the function of this new *scientia iuris* and of its jurists was necessarily of the utmost importance. This context was characterised by particularism and a multiplicity of legal systems, alongside a lack of a centralised state and a territorial power able to fulfil an autonomous legislative function. In this structure, the prince had the task of administering justice (*iurisdictio*), which he fulfilled not so much by creating a legal system through the proclamation of laws as through judicial experience, by coming face to face with concrete events and giving juridical form to the practical administration of justice (*aequitatem statuere*, as described in Bartolus of Saxoferrato and Cino da Pistoia). The Middle Ages were indeed a golden era for juridical science, which was assigned the essential role of finding in nature and maintaining the very bases of social order.[30] This was a unique situation, in which the *scientia iuris* became the epistemological point of reference for all disciplines devoted to the pursuit of truth in the nascent university system in Europe. It was nothing less than the rational art of identifying what was right in nature and the Gospels on each occasion, giving each their due (*iustitia est constans et perpetua voluntas ius suum cuique tribuendi*; *Digesta* 1.1.1.10). The mission of the jurist in finding what was right, good and just in everyday social conflict turned him into a sort of powerful and mysterious *sacerdos iuris* in the eyes of contemporaries, a figure against whom the Enlightenment would exercise both its iconoclastic fury and its more subtle criticism. It is important to understand the specific characteristics of this new *scientia iuris*, and especially, from our point of view, how the Scholastic theory of natural law provided its ultimate legitimating foundation. *Natura, id est Deus*, is how a medieval commentator succinctly indicated the central role played by the concept of *ordo iuris naturalis* in giving meaning to juridical practice.[31]

30. See, for instance, Grossi (*Ordine giuridico*, p.153): if in medieval society 'law is never created but can instead be sought, read, said, interpreted, found, adapted by an individual intelligence that is capable of reading, interpreting, adapting, then it is easy to see how the scope of juridical science is enormous, and so is the role it plays'.
31. Cf. António Manuel Hespanha, *Panorama histórico da cultura jurídica europeia* (Mem Martins, 1997), p.60. Paolo Grossi stresses the 'ordering' function of the new juridical science and how 'the jurist or master of laws, in his role as a learned man, is more intimately connected to God as the ultimate wisdom and ultimate truth than any other earthly worker. He is seen as an enlightened and

Besides focusing on the customary nature of a law system created from the bottom, from actual social experience as the immediate source for multiple individual legal systems, we should consider the way in which medieval jurists worked, and the world picture that legitimised this work. These jurists have been described as 'glossators' or 'commentators', whose activity was thought to consist mainly in *interpretatio*, which is the defining characteristic of the *scientia iuris* itself. But in fact to 'interpret', in this case, meant more than the exegesis of texts or the use of dialectic and rhetoric in order to understand and bring up to date the texts that provided a universal systematisation of the law, such as Justinian's *Corpus iuris civilis* or the *Corpus iuris canonici*. What these jurists did was much more far-reaching: they created a common European juridical system, a new and unified juridical method and professional knowledge capable of surmounting the multiplicity and particularity of individual legal systems. They did so by interpreting everyday events in a creative way, according to reason and common sense as embodied in ancient conceptual frameworks. In this way, they transformed the Ancient Roman juridical institutions into something that was entirely new.[32]

Again, all this was possible only because of the legitimisation provided by the Aristotelian-Thomistic universe and by the supremacy of natural law, whereby the pursuit and realisation of justice in the here and now was seen first and foremost as the application of divine order, that is as the restoration of the just order of things by giving to each his own. Of course, on the one hand, this widespread and generally accepted view of a theologised nature became synonymous with the preservation of the social and political order that had been created by the prevailing power relations; on the other, its organicistic and communal bias left very little space to the subject as the actual holder of those natural rights and therefore to the rise of modern 'subjective rights' – the concept that is at the basis of the Enlightenment theory of the rights of man.

In recent years there has been a heated debate on when and how subjective rights – and, especially, the idea of natural rights – first

---

enlightening being, a sort of mediator between heaven and earth, placed on a higher plane than any other searcher after truth' (Paolo Grossi, *A History of European law*, translated by Laurence Hooper, Chichester, 2010, p.26).

32. For an example of this interpretation applied to the right to property, see Paolo Grossi, *Locatio ad longum tempus: locazione e rapporti reali di godimento nella problematica del diritto comune* (Naples, 1963).

appeared on the scene.[33] There are obvious reasons for this. This is not simply a question of historical interpretation: it affects whether we view modernity, and its connection with politics and religion from the beginning to the present day, in positive or in negative terms.[34] Research into the relationship between law and modernity has focused on three aspects in particular: the classical notion of natural law that developed over the centuries based on the theories of Aristotle and Aquinas; the influence of Judaism, Christianity and Stoicism on classical natural law, which often led to a concept of *ius* as a set of moral and juridical precepts and as binding *lex* for all individuals;[35] the gradual but unstoppable rise of modern subjective rights, which were based on the acknowledgement of natural rights as virtues, faculties and qualities possessed by the individual subject and around which new legal systems should be built. In the first of these three aspects, as we have already seen, much work has been done on the autonomy and ontological character of classical law as a form of science that studies actual things and communities in order to determine the just and objective relationships among men and particularly in the distribution of wealth.[36] In the latter two cases, religious and philosophical individualism and its influence on legal practice have been the object of a great amount of consistently interesting research, even though

33. Historically, the rights of the individual have been perceived as natural rights, even though they could actually be viewed in different terms since the rights of the individual could arise from the will of the legislator rather than from human nature: see, for instance, Kant's views on this matter.
34. The important ideological and political implications of this debate are especially evident in the work of Catholic historians after the Second Vatican Council, when the Church reopened the dialogue with modernity in positive terms and without its usual tendency to demonise it, but also without abandoning its rationalist view of religion. See my chapter on 'Chiesa cattolica e modernità: la scoperta dei diritti dell'uomo dopo l'esperienza dei totalitarismi', in *Chiesa cattolica e modernità, atti del convegno della Fondazione Pellegrino, Torino, 6 febbraio 2004*, ed. F. Bolgiani, V. Ferrone and F. Margiotta Broglio (Bologna, 2004), p.17-131, subsequently included with changes in *Lo strano Illuminismo di Joseph Ratzinger: Chiesa, modernità e diritti dell'uomo* (Rome and Bari, 2013).
35. See, for instance, Gratian's *Decretum*, which defined natural law first and foremost as the biblical injunction not to do to others what we do not want to be done to ourselves. Another example is the constant appeal to the Ten Commandments by many canon law authors.
36. These issues are addressed in the works by Paolo Grossi, Michel Villey and Leo Strauss cited above. Despite important differences in focus, all three authors are critical of the modern concept of subjective rights, which they view as a distortion of classical law, and as such to be rejected at all costs.

the results themselves have not always been entirely convincing. The pioneering work carried out by Michel Villey still provides essential information on this subject.

Villey studied for decades what he calls 'the repeated assassination of the classical system of natural law and its replacement by the system of subjective rights'.[37] In Villey's opinion, the main culprit for this is Franciscan philosopher William of Ockham. Born in Surrey sometime between 1280 and 1290, Ockham was rebellious against papal authority. He was repeatedly condemned for heresy as a consequence of his nominalist philosophy, which centred on the primacy of the individual and of man's will. For Villey, Ockham typifies the change of perspective that caused the irremediable break and, above all, logical incompatibility between the objective law of classical antiquity and modern subjective rights. Ockham's philosophy was comprehensively opposed to the Scholastics' positions as he preached the irreconcilability of faith and reason, placing the emphasis on the former at the expense of the latter. In line with his Franciscan coreligionists, he also opposed Aquinas' view of the partial autonomy of nature from God's will, which made it possible to seek justice in the nature of things, in the *ordo iuris*, since not even God could oppose certain natural principles, such as the fact that the sum of the angles in a triangle always equals two right angles. For the Franciscan philosopher, instead, it was impossible that God's will should ever know any bounds. God's absolute power triumphed over everything. By analogy, man, who had been created in God's image, was endowed with subjective powers. Especially after the Fall, these powers included the capacity to proclaim laws, to own exterior goods and to create norms that protected these powers. In this way, law became the result of a legitimate act of will by a government of men in defence of divinely conferred rights. The rise of subjective rights was also aided by the fact that, with the Franciscans, Christianity's characteristic emphasis on the individual soul had turned into personal mysticism, the glorification of subjectivity and the negation of universals. Thus, on the epistemological level, in the search for a viable juridical and social order only the individual and his will mattered, as opposed to the Scholastics' emphasis on the needs of the community.[38]

37. Villey, *Formation de la pensée juridique*, p.677.
38. I return to this subject below, since it is of primary importance to explain the rise of the modern concept of 'person' and the difference between the 'rights of man' and 'personal rights'. For the moment, we should note that there is now

In 1320, following a dispute on poverty, Pope John XXII denounced the Franciscans' opinions on this subject as heretical. These opinions are particularly relevant to our discussion because they emphasised how, in order to observe the precept of perfect poverty, Christ and the apostles had renounced all forms of subjective right to the enjoyment and possession of goods – which implicitly recognised the existence of such rights. On this occasion, Ockham's nominalism and voluntarism came into contact with concepts developed by the glossators, such as *dominium*, *usufructus*, *ius utendi*, *simplex usus facti*. According to Villey, this resulted in a semantic revolution that set in motion a long journey to modernity, in the course of which the concept of *ius* would experience a fundamental shift from the objective pursuit of right in the nature of things themselves to the power, faculties and qualities of the individual (*ius utendi est potestas licita utendi re extrinseca*). These theological and juridical discussions on property, or *dominium* – which in Roman law denoted a form of power and control over people or things that was quite different from modern *ius* – gave rise to our modern 'possessive individualism'.[39] Above all, these debates brought up a disturbing question: whether God's power over reality was ultimately the same as man's power over nature.

Villey's discontinuity thesis has attracted much attention in the international scholarly community, and has received some positive comments.[40] However, it has also been subjected to criticism and

---

wide consensus on the essential role played by William of Ockham in the history of Western individualism, and on the political, social and juridical effects of this in later centuries. See, for instance, Louis Dumont, *Essays on individualism: modern ideology in anthropological perspective* (Chicago, IL, and London, 1986), p.63ff., which follows on from Villey's thesis but stresses how this form of Christian individualism can only posit its subject by rejecting the world and anchoring the individual to God in every respect.

39. See C. B. Macpherson, *The Political theory of possessive individualism: Hobbes to Locke* (Oxford, 1962).

40. The most illuminating contribution on this issue is still Paolo Grossi's '*Usus facti*: la nozione di proprietà nella inaugurazione del pensiero giuridico moderno', *Quaderni fiorentini* 1 (1972), p.287-355. Grossi discusses the key documents and moments in the Franciscan controversy on poverty and highlights the paradoxical way in which the Franciscans themselves, who had upheld poverty as a free life choice, because of the mystical and theocratic quality of their voluntarism and individualism eventually transformed the concept of right from that of a 'secret rhythm in things' to 'will imposed onto things'. The Franciscans were opposed to the Thomistic glossators' distinction between property and its enjoyment, since in their view it indicated a separation between will and reality.

qualification, not least by Brian Tierney, one of the greatest authorities on canon law and medieval political thought. Tierney opposed Villey's thesis of the radical incompatibility, in both historical and logical terms, of classical objective law, Judeo-Christian moral and natural law, and modern subjective rights. Tierney studied the texts concerning the Franciscan controversy as well as works by authors belonging to different religious orders, both before and after Ockham. Drawing also on research by scholars such as Jacques Maritain and John Finnis on the thought of Thomas Aquinas, he concluded that these three concepts of *ius* did in fact coexist throughout the centuries in question, and can even be found side by side in juridical writings by one same author, even on the same page.[41] It was not only nominalist philosophers or Franciscan friars who included significant elements of subjective rights in their juridical discussions: many authors from the early Middle Ages did the same, based on their everyday practice of the law. This highlighted the need to finally carry out a historical survey of the various natural law theories, taking into account the vast amount of complex and controversial bibliography on the subject of origins that has alternatively found the beginnings of subjective *ius* in Roman law or the Franciscan order, in Gerson, Grotius, Hobbes or Locke. As Tierney polemically points out:

> When Ockham in turn came to write on subjective rights there was no need for him to inaugurate a 'semantic revolution.' A rich language already existed in which rights theories could be articulated. The doctrine of individual rights was not a late medieval aberration from an earlier tradition of objective right or of natural moral law. Still less was it a seventeenth-century invention of Grotius or Hobbes or Locke. Rather, we shall argue, it was a characteristic product of the great age of creative jurisprudence that, in the twelfth and thirteenth centuries, established the foundations of the Western legal tradition.[42]

Instead, they turned property into a moral value: 'a dimension of the subject, an aspect of his autonomy and of his mastery over reality' (p.35). Along these interesting lines, which link the rise of subjective rights with the Franciscans' dispute over the right to property, see also Richard Tuck, *Natural rights theories: their origin and development* (Cambridge, 1979), p.22ff.

41. On the simultaneous presence of classical natural law and subjective natural rights in Aquinas see Maritain, *Rights of man*, and John Finnis, *Natural law and natural rights* (Oxford, 1980). These positions are critiqued in Paolo Grossi, 'Modernità politica e ordine giuridico', *Quaderni fiorentini* 27 (1998), p.13-39.

42. Tierney, *Idea of natural rights*, p.42. In this volume Tierney reviews the work of a great number of authors, both historians and philosophers, from Strauss

Tierney follows Harold Berman's controversial thesis according to which the 'pontifical revolution' brought about by Gregory VII (1075-1122) is the starting point of Western modernity.[43] Accordingly, Tierney traces the origins of the language of natural rights back to Church law and to a number of medieval Decretists, including Rufinus, Ricardus and Huguccio. Tierney detects a shift in the meaning of *ius* from natural law as objective universal harmony to subjective power and prerogative of the individual, and ascribes this development to two main factors. First of all, there was the struggle over the investiture and the political and social unrest of those years. This period saw the advancement of specific individual claims of a concrete and practical nature, often violently put forward, by emperors, popes and bishops, barons against kings, feudal lords against peasants. All these requests for specific powers demanded appropriate legislation.[44] The other factor in determining the new meaning of *ius* was the new and original way in which canonists interpreted the concept of *ius naturale* itself so as to transform these subjective rights into natural rights. In their glosses, these authors explicitly define natural law as a prerogative or power that is inherent in human beings and link it to free will and the autonomy of the individual. With an amazingly modern outlook, Henry of Ghent even went so far as to theorise an inalienable right to life, self-preservation and sovereignty over one's body and actions in cases of extreme necessity: for instance, how a condemned prisoner might legitimately claim a right to attempt to escape.[45] Tierney shows how the authors involved in the Franciscan controversy, such as Ockham and, in later years, Gerson, Suárez and the Second Scholastics, drew much from

---

to Jones, Miller, De Lagarde and Habermas, who wrote on the origins of subjective rights in Ancient Greece, Roman law, the Judeo-Christian tradition down to modern times. He rejects the conclusions of all those who found these origins in the ancient world, including those who see an implicit, as opposed to explicit, theory of natural rights in the Judeo-Christian idea of the dignity and moral autonomy of every individual.

43. See Berman, *Law and revolution*, p.4: 'One of the purposes of this study is to show that, in the West, modern times – not only modern legal institutions and modern legal values but also the modern state, the modern church, modern philosophy, the modern university, modern literature, and much else that is modern – have their origin in the period 1050-1150.'

44. See Tierney, *Idea of natural rights*, p.54ff. On the specific characteristics of medieval individualism Tierney refers to Colin Morris, *The Discovery of the individual, 1050-1200* (New York, 1972).

45. See Tierney, *Idea of natural rights*, p.79ff.

this discourse, which, deployed alongside previous theories, significantly enriched and complicated the traditional reading of *ius naturale* in terms of objective rights.

In fact, the characteristics and historical function of this new language seem to vary with the different authors and contexts, as can be seen at key moments in European history: from the strife that broke out with the conciliarist movement and the Great Schism of 1378-1417 – a time of profound crisis for papal authority, in which popes were being countered by anti-popes – to the controversies caused by the *descubrimiento* of the New World and the behaviour of the Spanish conquerors towards native populations. Tierney finds great originality in the juridical and theological works of Jean Gerson. While he was not quite the father of natural rights (as he has been described in authoritative works on this matter), Gerson certainly made use of these rights in advocating a reformation of the Church in council terms.[46] Gerson starts from the definition of *ius* as subjective right: a prerogative or power compatible with right reason that is granted by God to every soul to enable it to reach perfection. This enables Gerson to justify the existence and action of collective bodies such as the Church and councils, which he considers fundamental for this purpose, in contrast with the traditional view that the rights of the individual are opposed to the rights of communities and collective bodies.[47]

More recently, discussions on the actual existence and importance of a tradition of natural rights in the Middle Ages have focused on the Second Scholastics movement and its presumed contribution to the origins of modernity. Attention has focused on the School of Salamanca and its debates on the legitimacy of the Spanish conquest of the Americas, and especially on the use of the idea of the 'natural slave' as found in Aristotle's *Politics* after its rediscovery in the twelfth century: faced with the genocide of the original American populations, or their enslavement in Spanish *encomiendas*, European thinkers wondered whether the natives should not in fact be considered fully human, and as such endowed with natural rights to property, liberty and self-government.[48] Above and beyond the economic and

46. For a view of Gerson as the fundamental figure in the rise of natural rights, see Tuck, *Natural rights theories*, p.29ff.
47. See Tierney, *Idea of natural rights*, p.210ff.
48. On the reaction of European thought systems to the geographical discoveries, and how ancient and classical categories were adapted to take into account the new reality and the encounter with the 'barbarous other', see Giuliano Gliozzi,

political implications for Spain's colonial and imperial interests, what was at stake was the universality and equality of rights for all men, including 'barbarians' or 'infidels'. Could a theological concept such as Augustine's *bellum iustum* – these debates asked – be used to justify the violent conquest of those primitive and idolatrous populations, since their cannibalistic and incestuous practices were clearly sins against nature and set them apart from Christian civilisation? Could the *ius praedicandi et annuntiandi evangelium* really legitimise the subjection of entire Maya, Aztec and Inca communities, and the crimes committed against them, on the basis that these populations, albeit clearly further advanced on the road to civilisation than the native 'Indian' tribes, were nevertheless devoted to monstrous practices, such as human sacrifices?

Aristotelian psychology and Thomistic theology were applied to questions such as these. Should American *indios* be considered fully human beings and people like us, despite their ferocious and beastly customs, their obvious psychological inferiority as far as the restraint of instincts and passions was concerned, their apparent mental backwardness? The answers provided were varied and extremely problematic. John Mair, a Scottish theologian who taught in Paris, was the first to classify the American populations definitely as Aristotelian 'natural slaves', in a commentary on Peter Lombard's *Sententiae*. The same opinion was expressed by Juan Ginés de Sepúlveda, the most strenuous defender of the American conquest, who did not hesitate to define the *indios* as 'slaves by nature' and '*homunculi* in whom hardly a vestige of humanity remains'.[49] Sepúlveda does go on to put a more Christian slant on his conclusions, pointing out that nowadays reduction to slavery was no longer meant to serve the interests of the slave owners, as in the classical world. Its main function was to give the wretched populations a better life on earth and procure their salvation by providing them with much needed guidance and instruction. These theories were to be furiously rebutted by Dominican friar Bartolomé de Las Casas, the pious and vocal defender of the American Indians, and *Protector de los Indios*, according to the official title that was conferred on him in 1516. Las Casas wrote several works in which he

---

Adamo e il nuovo mondo: la nascita dell'antropologia come ideologia coloniale: dalle genealogie bibliche alle teorie razziali (1500-1700) (Florence, 1977), and especially Anthony Pagden, *The Fall of natural man: the American Indian and the origins of comparative ethnology*, 2nd edn (Cambridge, 1986).

49. Pagden, *Fall of natural man*, p.117.

defended the native American populations by invoking the principle of the unity of all mankind, whereby all human beings are children of God and created in his own image.[50]

A less straightforward position, which would however lead to important developments in the fields of ethnology and stadial theories, was that of theologian Francisco de Vitoria. In his *Relectio de Indis*, which he read in Salamanca in 1539, Vitoria contested the application of the Aristotelian category of the 'slave by nature' to the American Indian. According to Vitoria, the psychological and mental underdevelopment of these populations was comparable to that of 'children by nature': they were fully grown and endowed with fully developed rational faculties, but these existed only in potency rather than in act. These populations, therefore, should be looked after by benevolent masters and Christian governments who were prepared to respect their fundamental humanity.

This is not the place to examine in detail this important debate, on which there is now an extensive bibliography, and which was ultimately unable to prevent the genocide of millions of *indios*. What we are trying to ascertain, with the help of recent research on this subject, is whether a later manifestation of the Thomistic school of thought, such as the Second Scholastics, adopted a subjective theory of rights in its theological and juridical writings and, if so, whether these authors made use of the language of natural rights that had emerged in the Middle Ages. This would mean that the Second Scholastics were already enquiring in modern terms into the fundamental category of *dominium*, seen in natural law as an intrinsic characteristic of the individual, who retained sovereignty over his body, actions and property. *Utrum barbari essent veri domini ante adventum Hispanorum* – whether these populations exercised true dominium before the arrival of the Spaniards – was one of the questions posed by the Salamanca theologians.

Opinions, once again, diverge widely. And this particular academic debate is often hard to follow because it is based on a painstaking analysis of the relevant texts from a technical point of view. Despite

50. As can be seen, contrary to the description given in Tzvetan Todorov, *La Conquête de l'Amérique: la question de l'autre* (Paris, 1982), p.192ff., Las Casas' arguments are not anachronistically based on a multicultural and 'relativistic' approach similar to that of Montaigne or eighteenth-century deists. For an informative edition of Las Casas' work, including an extensive bibliography, see his *De regia potestate*, ed. Giuseppe Tosi (Rome and Bari, 2007).

their generally different positions, Tierney and Villey seem to agree on the fact that ancient objective natural law and natural rights are to be found side by side in sixteenth-century treatises by Dominican and Jesuit theologians. It was, however, a difficult coexistence, which had to accommodate the inflexible social structure of the *Ancien régime* and the undoubted primacy of a divine law that ruled over the natural order.[51]

This view has gathered wide acceptance, and the Second Scholastics have been seen as a 'bridge' between the Middle Ages and the modern world, through which 'the fundamental principles of natural rights were developed and transmitted to the Enlightenment and the modern schools of natural law'.[52] Several authors, however, have expressed opposite views. Richard Tuck, for instance, has no doubt that the Spanish Scholastics remained within the tradition of objective natural rights.[53] As for the anachronistic, and even hagiographic, attribution of the invention of the rights of man to Las Casas or Vitoria, it has been shown to be incorrect both philologically and historically, and from the point of view of the modern critique of the theory of precursors.[54]

51. On the role of the old social structure, see Pietro Costa, *Civitas: storia della cittadinanza in Europa*, vol.1: *Dalla civiltà comunale al Settecento* (Rome and Bari, 1999), p.116ff.
52. Paolo Prodi, *Una storia della giustizia: dal pluralismo dei fori al moderno dualismo tra coscienza e diritto* (Bologna, 2000), p.210. More convincingly, others have underlined the role of the Second Scholastics in developing a Catholic economic theory as an alternative to modern economics and its emphasis on individual profit and interest: see, for instance, Bartolomé Clavero, *La Grâce du don: anthropologie catholique de l'économie moderne* (Paris, 1996).
53. See Tuck, *Natural rights theories*, p.48ff. For a different opinion, see Annabel S. Brett, *Liberty, right and nature: individual rights in later Scholastic thought* (Cambridge, 1997). A more problematic view is expressed by Paolo Grossi in 'La proprietà nel sistema privatistico della seconda scolastica', in *La seconda scolastica nella formazione del diritto privato moderno*, ed. Paolo Grossi (Milan, 1973), p.117-222, where he describes the 'intrasubjective dimension' of the right to property, whereby objective law is seen as a 'natural social corrective with respect to that form of *potestas iuridica* represented by the concept of *dominium*' (p.221).
54. This 'hagiographic' tendency (on which see the previous note) developed as a result of the new interest in modernity by Catholic historiographers in the wake of the Second Vatican Council. An example of this can be seen in the proceedings of an international conference that took place in March 1985 at the Angelicum University (Pontificia Università degli Studi San Tommaso d'Aquino) in Rome, now gathered in a volume tellingly entitled *I diritti dell'uomo e la pace nel pensiero di Francisco de Vitoria e Bartolomé de Las Casas* (Milan, 1988). One essay within this volume bravely critiques this assumption. In 'La dialectique lascasienne

We now know that in the course of the Middle Ages authors began to make precise references to the idea of natural rights and to a voluntaristic concept of *ius*. Nevertheless, there is still a wide gap between what we see here and the invention of the theory of the 'rights of man' as would be developed by the Enlightenment. Despite the fact that those earlier references occurred within crucially important debates and continued to develop in the course of the years, they remain within the framework of classical natural law. Thus, it is true that in 1612 the Jesuit theologian Francisco Suárez, writing about the nexus between the concepts of liberty and natural rights in his *De legibus ac Deo legislatore*, posited the possibility of interpreting *ius* as 'a certain moral faculty that anyone has either regarding his own thing or something due to him'.[55] However, he hardly meant the same thing as Voltaire did when he equated those rights with the very essence of the human being, or when he singled out liberty as the main right of a fully autonomous individual. In the same way, Las Casas' discussion of the rights of the American Indians does not turn him into a Rousseau *ante litteram*, as some claim with much oversimplification. While investigating the origins of an idea we should not ignore the way in which the meaning of words changes over time. In the same way, we should bear in mind that, as well as through a process of continuous evolution, changes can occur abruptly, new patterns can suddenly emerge, and separate strands, derived from different cultural sources, can merge into one.

The road that links the medieval concept of *natural rights* and the Enlightenment's *rights of man* is therefore much longer and far more meandering than is usually thought, and so are the historical

du droit naturel concret: Las Casas et les droits de l'homme' (p.639-49), the Dominican friar Philippe-Ignace André-Vincent rightly highlights the absence from Las Casas' texts not only of the expression 'droits de l'homme', but also of its equivalents, such as 'droits fondamentaux' or 'droits de la personne humaine'. André-Vincent further points out that Las Casas always writes of Indians in the plural, and shows no interest in the concept of subjective rights that can be attributed to man above and beyond his social relationships by virtue of nature alone. For a discussion of the extensive bibliography on the other author in question, see Carlo Galli's preface to Francisco de Vitoria, *De iure belli* (Rome and Bari, 2005). Galli is especially critical of those who insist on attributing to Vitoria an anachronistic awareness of individual human rights, ignoring how the latter in fact assigned a crucial role to nations and other political communities in the development of a new international law that would be independent of both the pope and the emperor.

55. Quoted in Tierney, *Idea of natural rights*, p.50 and 303.

genealogy and political transformations of these rights. We must think twice before placing our Franciscan friars, the austere theologians from Salamanca and eighteenth-century Enlightenment *salons* side by side along this difficult path. As I will try to show, the modern concept of the rights of man as developed by the Enlightenment, and specifically by Condorcet, is indeed an incommensurable paradigm, in Kuhnian terms, compared to earlier concepts of natural rights, both those from the classical era and, for the most part, those developed by Grotius and Pufendorf.[56] In the course of this study we shall see how the Enlightenment language of rights developed from a profound change in the way people viewed the world and the history of mankind – a change that occurred gradually and was the result of many factors, and which led to a degree of philosophical awareness of the autonomy of the human subject that would have been unthinkable in previous centuries. The Scientific Revolution, the devastating wars of religion, the formation of a 'Republic of Letters' by groups of *philosophes* conscious of their political strength, the rise of a modern critical spirit and of a powerful public opinion, the rebellion against the social hierarchies of the *Ancien régime* all contributed to the development of this utterly new and original worldview.

As we have already seen, for the Enlightenment's language of rights to come into being at least four conditions had to be fulfilled, as these rights had to be recognised as natural, equal, universal and inalienable for all men. In addition, there had to be a precise political programme to give these rights a role in the construction of society and the making of history, once they had been recognised in the state of nature. Nothing comparable can be found in the various medieval theories of natural rights, or even in later interpretations of these rights, which operated still within a theologically founded universe and only arose from changes in the juridical meaning of *dominium*, which came to be viewed as individual power, *proprium*, prerogative or claim as opposed to a society's collective interests.

Condorcet's discussion of the genealogy of these rights in his *Esquisse d'un tableau historique des progrès de l'esprit humain* has very little to say about any distant Christian origins of the idea of natural rights. In fact, he found these origins rather in pagan Stoicism and Epicureanism, and in the way in which authors such as Epicurus, Cicero or Seneca extolled the supreme dignity of the human being.

56. On the 'incommensurable paradigm' see Thomas S. Kuhn, *The Structure of scientific revolutions* (Chicago, IL, 1962).

In this way, Condorcet was foregrounding the radical change of perspective brought about by Enlightenment humanism, as it broke free from any form of providentialism and devoted itself to the rational investigation of what characterised human nature. This gave rise to a new and previously unthinkable 'science of man', without which the 1789 Declaration would probably never have happened.

As for the medieval language of natural rights, it was certainly available and did foster some early discussions in universities and princes' courts. However, it never really went beyond specialist circles. In the fifteenth and sixteenth century we know that it was confined to abstruse and near-illegible tracts on theology or natural law written by fairly minor authors, such as Konrad Summenhart, Jacques Almain or John Mair. No trace of this language is found in the great protagonists of this period, like Thomas More or Machiavelli. In the previous century Lorenzo Valla had denied the very existence of natural rights, taking into account only conventional law that was the result of human will. The Catholic world devoted little attention to this subject, at least until the beginning of the twentieth century, with the work of Jacques Maritain and the intellectuals attached to the journal *Esprit*, which was founded in Paris in 1930.[57] In fact, the Catholic Church attacked the Enlightenment version of these rights when it first appeared on the scene. As Brian Tierney writes: 'The popes of our age, who have embraced so enthusiastically the idea of natural rights, after their predecessors condemned it for many years as an irreligious, Enlightenment aberration, have been returning, *unwittingly, perhaps*, to a tradition rooted in the Christian jurisprudence and philosophy of the Middle Ages.'[58]

Among the early Protestant reformers, the prevalent Augustinian conception of weak and sinful man certainly was not conducive to the study of natural rights or the adoption of the Ciceronian ideal of the dignity of man. We have to wait until 1625 and the publication of Grotius' *De iure belli ac pacis* for the first signs that this important intellectual legacy was finally being transformed into modern natural law, albeit amidst problems and ambiguities. By then, the old view of natural law as the pursuit of what was right within the nature of things, from the objective universe to the discovery of the individual, was undergoing yet another transformation. The result of this would

57. See Daniele Menozzi, *Chiesa e diritti umani: legge naturale e modernità politica dalla Rivoluzione francese ai nostri giorni* (Bologna, 2012).
58. Tierney, *Idea of natural rights*, p.343; emphasis added.

unleash fierce polemics on the part of Enlightenment circles all over Europe, which were keen to assert their own language of the rights of man as the crucial turning point in the history of modern politics.

3. Modern natural law as the 'science of morality'

Why did modern natural law only emerge in the seventeenth century? What are its defining characteristics? Who are the protagonists of this crucial phase in the cultural history of the West? Much research has been carried out on the genesis and importance of a specific interpretative paradigm according to which the history of modern natural law is linked to the effort to construct a rational framework for a new science of morality or, in other words, to establish the natural links that form human society on new and scientific principles. The origin of this paradigm has been traced to the French Huguenot Jean Barbeyrac.[1] Through his work as student and translator of the writings of Grotius, Cumberland and Pufendorf, Barbeyrac ensured that these authors' ideas – which have recently received much attention from contemporary scholars – spread widely in the course of the eighteenth century.[2]

These theories on natural law quickly became the dominant point of view in universities across Europe down to the time of the French Revolution and beyond, and they are now the subject of a vast bibliography. However, as we shall see, they are far from uniform in their intents or in their conclusions.[3] They also interact with a variety of factors: for instance, the religious divide and the wars it occasioned in sixteenth- and seventeenth-century Europe, with their

1. See Richard Tuck, 'The modern theory of natural law', in *The Languages of political theory in early modern Europe*, ed. Anthony Pagden (Cambridge, 1987), p.99-120.
2. Cf. T. J. Hochstrasser, *Natural law theories in the Early Enlightenment* (Cambridge, 2000).
3. Bobbio, 'Il giusnaturalismo', is still a useful overview on this subject, but see now also the volume of essays edited by Knud Haakonssen, *Grotius, Pufendorf and modern natural law* (London, 1999).

consequences in both historical and intellectual terms; or the so-called 'crise pyrrhonienne', whereby scepticism and moral and philosophical relativism became the dominant mood up to the early eighteenth century. This epistemological crisis, in fact, has not received enough critical attention, considering that it led to significant intellectual developments, before it was overcome by the Scientific Revolution brought about by the discoveries of Galileo, Descartes and Newton. Without this crisis, Grotius and Pufendorf might never have written their works. Last but not least, we should take into account the political and religious disputes around Louis XIV's absolute monarchy and the revocation of the Edict of Nantes in 1685, a controversy that is a direct antecedent of the Enlightenment debate on the rights of man.

In Barbeyrac's account, seventeenth-century natural law is presented as a new moral science concerned first and foremost with the duties of modern man. While this view may be slightly reductive, its truth content should not be underestimated. In fact, the *Encyclopédie* implicitly accepted this thesis by placing Diderot's entry on 'Droit naturel' ('Natural rights') in the section on ethics rather than under law or politics: as if to show that *this* was the real legacy that had been bequeathed to the Enlightenment.[4] This ties in with the fact that, as is well known, early modern Western culture was characterised by the need to review the very basis of morality and communal interaction in the face of repeated ruptures of the political and social order. The subsequent rise of a Neo-Stoic movement and the diffusion of practices for social discipline throughout Europe affected all branches of knowledge and every political and religious institution.[5] Another important factor besides social conflict was the discovery of the New World and of new nations and customs on the other side of the Atlantic and in Africa and Asia. Thanks to the invention of print, the experience of diversity reported in travellers' accounts reached a wide audience, while at the same time medieval communitarianism was breaking up under the pressure of modern individualism. The general uncertainty and disorientation that followed made the moral practices

4. This author's importance for the Enlightenment is further confirmed by the entry for 'Morale' in the *Encyclopédie* (vol.10, p.699ff.), which follows closely the history of morality written by Barbeyrac as preface to the 1706 French edition of Pufendorf and subsequently included in Jacob Brucker's *Historia critica philosophiae* (1742-1744).

5. Cf. *Disciplina dell'anima, disciplina del corpo e disciplina della società tra medioevo ed età moderna: atti del convegno internazionale di studi, Bologna, 7-9 ottobre 1993*, ed. Paolo Prodi (Bologna, 1994).

and convictions of the past seem hopelessly outdated. It makes sense, therefore, to see the birth of new forms of natural law as an important chapter in the process described by Michel Foucault in his late works.[6] According to Foucault, in the early modern period society underwent a process of 'governmentalisation', which included the development of new disciplinary powers. This process included the critical reappraisal of the authority principle and of the ancient forms of social bond and individual conduct following the sixteenth-century wars of religion. These wars in fact betokened the failure not only of Christianity, but of the whole idea of religion as a cohesive social element, that *coagulum populorum* described by Augustine in his *De civitate Dei*. The momentous break in the unity of the medieval *Respublica christiana* and the need to contain the disastrous effects of religiously motivated civil war acted as a powerful catalyst in the attempt to find a new ethical basis for social coexistence.

After Luther nailed his ninety-five theses on the door of the Wittenberg Castle church, on 31 October 1517, the process of secularisation of public and private life in Europe accelerated. Arguably, this process started back in the Middle Ages, with the struggle over the investiture (1057-1122) and with Gregory VII's reforms that assigned the Church to the 'spiritual' sphere and the empire to the 'temporal' one.[7] However, it is only with the Protestant Reformation that Christianity in the West broke in two, leading to harsh theological controversies among different Churches and confessions and to nearly two centuries of civil and religious war. The Council of Trent re-established a dualism between political and religious power that has had far-reaching implications in every field down to our day. With the great national States rapidly sliding into absolutism and with princes resorting more and more widely to social disciplinary practices, the Catholic Church accentuated further its character as a separate and autonomous *societas perfecta*, with its rigid ecclesiastical hierarchy aided by the formation of new religious orders, such as the powerful Jesuits, that gathered round the central emerging figure of the sovereign

6. See Michel Foucault, *Society must be defended: lectures at the Collège de France, 1975-76*, ed. Mauro Bertani and Alessandro Fontana, translated by David Macey (London, 2003).
7. See Ernst-Wolfgang Böckenförde, 'Die Entstehung des Staates als Vorgang der Säkularisation' (1967), available in English as 'The rise of the state as a process of secularisation', in his *State, society and liberty: studies in political theory and constitutional law*, translated by J. A. Underwood (New York and Oxford, 1991), p.26-46 (32ff.).

pontiff. In this way, previously universal canon law became restricted to an inward-looking *ius publicum ecclesiasticum.*[8]

With the great European monarchies now able to impose agreements on their own terms and repeal ancient ecclesiastical privileges, the Church of Rome found itself forced to renounce the idea and practice of a unified *Respublica christiana.* Consequently, with the exception of the sacrament of marriage, the Catholic Church restricted its sphere of action from the political and social fields to that of ethics. The Church thus devoted itself exclusively to pastoral care, to the internal space of conscience, and to the censuring of behaviour via the use of confession, which became an instrument of social control over individual customs and consciences.[9] An aspect of this was Cardinal Bellarmino's sophisticated political theory of the *potestas indirecta* of the Church in the ethical sphere.[10] This development also led, on the one hand, to the proliferation of popular catechisms and, on the other, to the establishment of the first university chairs in moral theology, which were inspired by Jesuit 'casuistry' and the Neo-Thomism of the School of Salamanca. Above all, the sacrament of confession and penance acquired significant power in the regulation of consciences in the face of nascent religious individualism.[11]

In fact, the Protestant world also experienced a sense of anguish following the breakup of the *Respublica christiana*, as is evidenced, unsurprisingly, from the writings of the major exponents of the new school of natural law. They too reacted to the shattering of the authority principle and to the disappearance of a single universal spiritual authority, though their answers were of course quite different from those provided by the Catholic Church, with its appeal to the authority of Rome and to the institutional and disciplinary power of the sovereign pontiff. Inevitably, however, Protestant authors also

8. Cf. *Il Concilio di Trento e il moderno*, ed. Paolo Prodi and Wolfgang Reinhard (Bologna, 1996), p.19ff; Paolo Prodi, *The Papal prince, one body and two souls: the papal monarchy in early modern Europe*, translated by Susan Haskins (Cambridge, 1987).
9. Cf. Adriano Prosperi, *Tribunali della coscienza: inquisitori, confessori, missionari* (Turin, 1996).
10. See Franco Motta, *Bellarmino: una teologia politica della Controriforma* (Brescia, 2005), p.35ff.
11. Cf. Prodi, *Storia della giustizia*, p.213ff. On the shift from medieval communitarianism to individual conscience through the social practice of confession see the essays collected in John Bossy, *Dalla comunità all'individuo: per una storia sociale dei sacramenti nell'Europa moderna* (Turin, 1998).

insisted on the refounding of society on a new ethical basis, on the search for new universal forms of civil coexistence and effective social and spiritual bonds: it could not be otherwise, given the widespread religiously motivated conflict and the new dualism between the absolute power of national States on the one hand and mutually opposing Christian Churches on the other.

This is confirmed by Grotius and Pufendorf's description of their motivation for writing their works. In 1678 Pufendorf wrote his *Specimen controversiarum circa ius naturale ipsi nuper motarum* in reply to criticism levied by Lutheran theologians against his main work, *De iure naturae et gentium* (1672). Pufendorf clearly explains that his intent in the earlier work had been to create a system of universal norms that would apply to all men, *non quia christiani sed quia homines* – something that had become necessary in order to counteract the dire consequences of the wars of religion, and, indeed, in order to preserve the very existence of man, of all mankind.[12] His predecessors had been wrong in thinking that the fundamental principles of natural law could be determined on the basis of specific religions, i.e. as John Selden wrote in his 1640 *De iure naturali et gentium iuxta disciplinam Hebraeorum*, based on a specific form of divine revelation, such as the Gospels, the Quran or the Seven Laws of Noah. Instead, while taking into due account the precious indications contained in the sacred books, man must first and foremost use his own reason in order to show the necessary correspondence between these precepts and human nature, on the assumption that all men are equal in their natural rights, regardless of their religious faith.[13] This was the only way out of religious fanaticism and the opposing claims of theologians, Catholic priests and Protestant ministers on moral matters, and to avoid the fierce and bloody 'theological controversies' that afflicted Europe in those years, and that personally affected Pufendorf's life.

12. Accordingly, Pufendorf cites as 'a fundamental Law of Nature' that 'every man ought, as far as in him lies, to promote and preserve a peaceful sociableness with others' (Samuel von Pufendorf, *Of the law of nature and nations: eight books*, translated by Basil Kennett, London, Printed for J. Walthoe, R. Wilkin, J. and J. Bonwicke, S. Birt, T. Ward, and T. Osborne, 1729, II, 3, 15, p.137; archive.org/details/oflawofnaturenat00pufe, last accessed 29 April 2019; I have modernised the spelling and other typographical conventions).
13. See Samuel von Pufendorf, *Specimen controversiarum circa ius naturale ipsi nuper motarum* (Osnabrück, ex officina Johannis Georgii Schwänderi, 1678), chapter 1, 'De origine et progressu disciplinae iuris naturalis', p.3ff.

Coming from a family of Lutheran ministers, faithful to the Protestant cause and a confirmed anti-papist, Pufendorf was writing some twenty years after the Peace of Westphalia (1648) had extended to the Calvinists the principle of *cuius regio eius religio* originally ratified between Catholics and Lutherans at the Diet of Augsburg in 1555 in order to stop the first instances of civil war. In fact, the 1648 Peace left the field open to 'religious cleansing' on the part of individual princes, and failed to support the first few timid attempts at toleration, thus creating the premises for Louis XIV's Catholic revanchism and the revocation of the 1685 Edict of Nantes. The latter event aggrieved Pufendorf so profoundly that in 1687 he wrote a polemical tract entitled *De habitu religionis christianae ad vitam civilem*, in which he argued that religion came before the State and should be granted autonomy from politics.

More than half a century earlier, in 1625, Grotius had written his *De iure belli ac pacis* in the midst of the Thirty Years War, i.e. five years after the Battle of the White Mountain and the ensuing forced re-Catholicisation of Bohemia, which caused thousands of casualties and 150,000 refugees. This could not but be reflected in Grotius' work. He knew that the origins of these civil wars went back a long way, and that they would change the history of Europe for ever. This conflict had engendered terrible episodes of mass violence, like the St Bartholomew's Day massacre in Paris in 1572, which claimed the lives of some 20,000 Huguenots (3000 in Paris alone), or the attacks on the Netherlands by that ferocious beacon of Catholicism, the duke of Alba, during the revolt of the United Provinces against Spanish rule. Grotius knew this conflict well: in 1610 he had written about it in his historico-political tract *De antiquitate reipublicae Batavae.* This seemingly endless war is behind his anguished explanation of why he had written his *De iure belli ac pacis.* This work purported to identify a form of international law that would regulate the relationship among the different nations and governments. It set out a series of basic norms of universal morality and justice that should be observed by all States, especially those that described themselves as Christian, even in the religiously motivated conflicts, which were the fiercest and the ones that were seemingly most difficult to resolve:

> I have had many and weighty reasons for undertaking to write upon this subject. Throughout the Christian world I observed a lack of restraint in relation to war, such as even barbarous races should be ashamed of; I observed that men rush to arms for slight causes, or no

> cause at all, and that when arms have once been taken up there is no longer any respect for law, divine or human; it is as if, in accordance with a general decree, frenzy had openly been let loose for the committing of all crimes.
>
> Confronted with such utter ruthlessness many men, who are the very furthest from being bad men, have come to the point of forbidding all use of arms to the Christian, whose rule of conduct above everything else comprises the duty of loving all men.[14]

At the Synod of Dordrecht, in 1618, the more intransigent Calvinists and their tenet of justification through grace alone gained the upper hand over the more tolerant Arminians. Grotius, who was linked to the latter group, was sentenced to life imprisonment and had his property confiscated. He made an adventurous escape to Paris, but this traumatic experience brought home to him how utterly inadequate the ancient social order and the existing law systems now were. Since they were based on particularistic doctrinal perspectives, these normative systems were now incapable of imposing a unanimously recognised concept of justice over all warring parties. In the wake of the widespread sectarian violence, it was time to recognise that the old natural law established by Aquinas could no longer function as a universal point of reference in the pursuit of what was right. Nobody seemed prepared any more to practise toleration and re-examine their own concept of *truth* and the criteria on which it was founded. While Protestant theologians believed there was still a lot to learn from the Old Testament and the Bible in general on the foundations and the correct interpretation of natural law, Catholics placed council deliberations, papal decrees and traditional canon law above anything else. As for the Scholastics, who had been the main upholders of the Aristotelian-Thomistic tradition of thought on this matter, their constant diatribes over interpretation and their obvious philosophical errors could be explained by saying that they had operated 'in unhappy and ignorant times'.

Grotius was aware that he was putting forward dangerously unconventional views in suggesting that the Gospels in fact had nothing to do with natural law: 'in that most holy law a greater degree of moral perfection is enjoined upon us than the law of nature, alone and by itself, would require.'[15] The remit of natural law, by contrast,

14. Hugo Grotius, *Prolegomena to the law of war and peace*, translated by Francis W. Kelsey (New York, 1957), p.21, §28-29.
15. Grotius, *Prolegomena*, p.31, §50. In the introduction to his 1724 French translation

was simply to determine a minimum but universally recognised element of justice that would be valid for anyone, anywhere and at all times, even in times of war, regardless of beliefs or convictions. The *De iure belli ac pacis* therefore arose, in the first instance, from the momentous realisation that the centuries-old natural law of the Christian and Thomistic tradition was irremediably failing: in other words, an awareness, especially, of the collapse of the metaphysical and religious basis of that tradition following the breakup of the medieval *Respublica christiana* and the ensuing doctrinal conflicts. Hence came the urgent need for a new natural law. This new law would be based on entirely original foundations, the kind of premises that would be universally valid and subject to rational proof, in line with the methods of the Scientific Revolution, which in those crucial decades was rapidly advancing through Europe.

With these objectives clearly in mind Grotius attempted to outline this new juridical science, with its contents, boundaries and methods. He presented natural right as a direct expression of the intrinsic rationality of human nature, a 'rule and dictate of right reason, showing the moral deformity or moral necessity there is in any act according to its suitableness or unsuitableness to a reasonable nature, and consequently that such an act is either forbid or commanded by God, the author of nature'.[16] This 'natural and unchangeable philosophy of law', which defined itself as objective and separate from 'all that has its origin in the free will of man', was not to be confused with the numerous forms of positive law that had developed over the centuries. Natural law was 'always the same'. It followed a fixist and mechanical view of nature that would remain popular down to the mid-eighteenth century, and could therefore be imagined as a 'system'.

---

of the *De iure*, Barbeyrac describes the chaotic state in which natural law had been before Grotius, as it was torn asunder by the warring Catholic and Protestant parties. The former featured a Catholic Church that did not hesitate to legitimise 'the assassination of those kings that it declares heretical', and a Scholastic method that consisted in 'a shocking mixture of aridity, vain subtlety and barbarity'. The representatives of the latter were no less violent and 'too occupied in theological controversies to think seriously about a science' of natural law. Cf. Jean Barbeyrac, 'Préface du traducteur', in Hugo Grotius, *Le Droit de la guerre et de la paix* (Amsterdam, Pierre de Coup, 1724), p.iii.

16. Hugo Grotius, *The Rights of war and peace*, translated by John Morrice *et al.* (from the Barbeyrac edition), ed. Richard Tuck (Indianapolis, IN, 2005), I, 1, 1, p.150-51 (I have slightly modernised the spelling and punctuation, though not the grammatical forms, of the original).

By contrast, 'the elements of positive law, since they often undergo change and are different in different places, are outside the domain of systematic treatment, just as other notions of particular things are.'[17]

In Paris, Grotius was one of the key players, together with his friend Mersenne and alongside Peiresc and Gassendi, in the ideological and cultural struggle for the Scientific Revolution that had just been started by Descartes and Galileo.[18] Grotius' *Prolegomena* place a great deal of emphasis on the new methods of investigation as a symptom of the break with the past. However, he is also attempting the not altogether easy feat of joining together new and old truth criteria, empiricism and rationalism, induction and deduction, experience and logical reasoning. On the one hand, Grotius reiterates the importance of universal consensus as a traditional way of ascertaining truth *a posteriori*. Thus, the study of history provides examples and opinions that can help us determine 'a universal cause' in the points of contact between the law of nations and the 'system' of natural law.[19] On the other hand, Grotius links natural law with the axiomatic deductive method, i.e. with an *a priori* truth criterion borrowed from mathematics and geometry, which starts with self-evident axioms or principles and proceeds through abstractions and generalisations: precisely the kind of pattern that characterises not only the works of Descartes, Galileo and Newton, but also Hobbes' *Leviathan* and, above all, Spinoza's *Ethica more geometrico demonstrata*.[20]

17. Grotius, *Prolegomena*, p.22, §31 and 30.
18. On these Parisian circles, see the important study by Robert Lenoble, *Mersenne, ou la Naissance du mécanisme* (Paris, 1943), p.216ff.
19. Deductive geometry and historical method exist side by side in Grotius' epistemology: 'that any thing is or is not by the law of nature is generally proved either *a priori*, that is by arguments drawn from the very nature of the thing; or *a posteriori*, that is, by reasons taken from something external. The former way of reasoning is more subtle and abstracted; the latter more popular. The proof by the former is by showing the necessary fitness or unfitness of any thing with a reasonable and sociable nature. But the proof by the latter is, when we cannot with absolute certainty, yet with very great probability conclude that to be by the law of nature, which is generally believed to be so by all, or at least the most civilised, nations' (Grotius, *Rights*, I, 12, p.159).
20. On the importance of Euclid's axiomatic deductive method in the Scientific Revolution, seen as the geometrisation of space, see Alexandre Koyré, *Galileo studies*, translated by John Mepham (Hassocks, 1978). For an important study and extensive bibliography on this subject, see Luis Vega Reñon, 'La dimostrazione', in *I Greci: storia, cultura, arte e società*, vol.1: *Noi e i Greci*, ed. Salvatore Settis (Turin, 1996), p.285-318.

Grotius explicitly declares: 'just as mathematicians treat their figures as abstracted from bodies, so in treating law I have withdrawn my mind from every particular fact.'[21] Ultimately, modern natural law derived its methodology mainly from Euclidean logics, being based on correct deductions on which to build an overall 'system':

> First of all, I have made it my concern to refer the proofs of things touching the law of nature to certain fundamental conceptions which are beyond question, so that no one can deny them without doing violence to himself. For the principles of that law, if only you pay strict heed to them, are in themselves manifest and clear, almost as evident as are those things which we perceive by the external senses; and the senses do not err if the organs of perception are properly formed and if the other conditions requisite to perception are present.[22]

This process and this epistemological framework, *more geometrico*, of the school of natural law, with its basis in self-evident principles, became the starting point for all subsequent research all over Europe. It was the dominant rhetorical structure in a way of thinking that would go on to influence Jefferson's 1776 Declaration of Independence. In this Declaration, the rights of man are presented for the first time as 'self-evident' principles and axioms. Through this axiomatic deductive method, modernity would assert its reasons, and build its constitutional and republican politics.[23]

The principles on which Grotius founded his view of natural law, as he considered them self-evident and universal, were not drawn from a preliminary analysis of the cosmos, but rather from having observed the presence of specific characteristics in the nature of man as an individual: his rationality and *appetitus societatis*, the need to live as part of a society in order to preserve his species. However, this was

21. Grotius, *Prolegomena*, p.35, §58.
22. Grotius, *Prolegomena*, p.25, §39.
23. Apparently Jefferson had originally described these principles as 'sacred and undeniable', which Benjamin Franklin later changed to 'self-evident' – a phrase that, after Grotius, would be used with great frequency in the rationalistic Euclidean discourse of natural rights. On the changes to the Declaration, see Pauline Maier, *American scripture: how America declared its independence from Britain* (London, 1999; original: *American scripture: making the Declaration of Independence*, New York, 1997). See also Hunt, *Inventing human rights*, for a different interpretation of 'self-evident', which focuses more on *Ancien régime* culture and psychology than on the history of scientific thought. We shall return to this interpretation in our discussion below.

something different from a simple reprise of the idea of the 'social animal' described in Aristotle's *Politics*. Grotius was not referring to just any form of communal life within a hierarchically arranged universe. What he had in mind was something that he believed should be encouraged at all costs: the natural tendency on the part of every individual to live a 'social life – not of any and every sort, but peaceful, and organized according to the measure of his intelligence, with those who are of his own kind; this disposition the Stoics called "sociableness" [*oikeiosis*]'.[24] Although it was something entirely different from natural law, positive law was also inevitably founded on the individual's innate wish to ensure the 'maintenance of the social order [...] which is consonant with human intelligence'.[25] From this tendency came man's social roots and the contractual element in society, which was founded on respect for mutual undertakings, such as 'the abstaining from that which is another's, the restoration to another of anything of his which we may have, together with any gain which we may have received from it; the obligation to fulfill promises, the making good of a loss incurred through our fault, and the inflicting of penalties upon men according to their deserts'.[26]

A much discussed element of Grotius' concept of natural law is his supposed contribution to the 'secularisation' of seventeenth-century Western culture, represented in particular by the formula *etsi Deus non daretur*: that is, we should live as though there was no God. On first impression this notorious phrase, which is used at the start of an important passage in the *Prolegomena*, has been seen as an indication of the presence in Grotius of that dangerous atheism that was beginning to spread in libertine circles across Europe: 'What we have been saying would have a degree of validity even if we should concede that which cannot be conceded without the utmost wickedness, that there is no God, or that the affairs of men are of no concern to him.'[27] In fact, this is far from the truth. As we saw above, Aquinas and his

24. Grotius, *Prolegomena*, p.6, §6. *Oikeiosis* (Lat. *appetitus socialis*) is an individual's 'social sense', which is an attribute of the species rather than a universal law. On the importance of Stoicism and of Cicero's concept of the dignity of man in Grotius' thought, see *Grotius and the Stoa*, ed. H. W. Blom and Laurens C. Winkel (Assen, 2004).
25. Grotius, *Prolegomena*, p.8-9, §8.
26. Grotius, *Prolegomena*, p.9, §8.
27. Grotius, *Prolegomena*, p.10, §11. See also the *De iure*, where Grotius states that 'the law of nature is so unalterable, that God himself cannot change it' (Grotius, *Rights*, I, 10, 5, p.155).

followers had written very similar and perhaps even weightier things on the autonomy of the universe from God's will, without being misunderstood.[28] It is then a serious anachronism to see in Grotius a precursor of later positions that underestimated or sought to suppress the role of religion in the life of the intellect.

Of course, the troubled historical context of those years could easily give rise to unsettling interpretations of the Scholastics' stereotypes as they were being subsumed into an entirely different cultural horizon. Nonetheless, we cannot call into doubt the religious credentials of someone like Grotius, who in 1627 had published *De veritate religionis christianae*, a theological treatise that was infused with Socinian rationalism. He was not in any way an opponent of religion *per se*, and had certainly nothing in common with the libertines. In fact, he was a fully paid up member of the Paris circle of Father Mersenne, who was engaged in a bitter struggle precisely against all kinds of materialist unbelievers. If anything, his reformist zeal was directed towards the christianisation of emerging forms of knowledge, in line with what was happening in France with the Parisian circles of Mersenne and Gassendi and in Italy with the Accademia dei Lincei, and would happen in England at the beginning of the following century with the Boyle Lectures and Newton's natural theology.[29]

Grotius would certainly have subscribed to the 1615 *Letter to the Grand Duchess Christina of Tuscany*, in which Galileo defends the compatibility between Christianity and modern science. To this effect, the scientist had to distance himself from a view of theology as the 'queen of all the sciences' and arbiter of all forms of knowledge: the kind of theology that, following the Council of Trent, was imposed by the clergy as an instrument of absolute knowledge.[30] In order to uphold his heliocentric theory despite the fact that in the Old Testament Joshua orders *the sun* to stand still, Galileo bravely takes on the powerful guild of the 'holy and learned theologians' (p.186). He asks them to start

28. Formally at least, this would seem to vindicate the opinion of those who maintain that there was nothing drastically new in Grotius' thought, least of all any hint of free thought or atheism. See Tierney, *Idea of natural rights*, p.316ff.
29. On the various, as it turned out rather futile, attempts to link the new science with a renewed Christian spirit in Rome at the time of Galileo see the chapter on 'Galileo tra Paolo Sarpi e Federico Cesi' in my *Una scienza per l'uomo: Illuminismo e Rivoluzione scientifica nell'Europa del Settecento* (Turin, 2007), p.96ff.
30. Cf. Galileo Galilei, *Discoveries and opinions of Galileo, including The Starry messenger (1610), Letter to the Grand Duchess Christina (1615), and excerpts from Letters on sunspots (1613), The Assayer (1623)*, translated by Stillman Drake (New York, 1957), p.191.

opening their minds to *libertas philosophandi*, and to distinguish between theological and scientific truth, i.e. between the dogmatic application of biblical exegesis and the use of new scientific instruments like the telescope: 'I think that in discussions of physical problems we ought to begin not from the authority of scriptural passages, but from sense-experiences and necessary demonstrations' (p.182). As Galileo points out, even if they wanted to,

> it is not in the power of the professors of demonstrative sciences to change their opinions at will and apply themselves first to one side and then to the other. There is a great difference between commanding a mathematician or a philosopher and influencing a lawyer or a merchant, for demonstrated conclusions about things in nature or in the heavens cannot be changed with the same facility as opinions about what is or is not lawful in a contract, bargain, or bill of exchange.[31]

Although in a different field of knowledge, with his *etsi Deus non daretur* Grotius was effectively saying the same as Galileo. He asked for philosophical research to be set free from the dogmatism of theologians either side of the Catholic–Protestant divide: not least in the service of a more liberal and tolerant Christianity, capable of opening up to *libertas philosophandi*. In actual fact, the principles and methods of the Scientific Revolution had created a universal demand for new and demonstrable truth criteria.

There were other obstacles to the spreading of the new scientific method, besides theological fundamentalism. The revival of the ancient sceptical philosophy of Arcesilaus and Carneades had led to a widespread relativism in both the ethical and gnoseological fields, which denied the possibility of achieving any authentic form of knowledge. In fact, this was not the first 'crise pyrrhonienne' in the history of culture: see the debate in Plato's Academy in the third century BC and the attack against Stoicism. In the early modern period, this movement was effectively a result of the Protestant Reformation and the wars of religion: the publication by Henri Estienne of Sextus Empiricus' *Outlines of Pyrrhonism* in 1562 had provided the necessary intellectual tools, but arguably the new scepticism would not have found such fertile ground without the process set in motion by Luther. Luther's protest undermined the Church's centuries-old *regula fidei*, which was founded on the deliberations of the Council and the

31. Galileo, *Discoveries and opinions*, p.194.

opinion of the higher hierarchical levels, as well as on tradition and the *consensus gentium*. It called abruptly into question the old criteria of Christian religious truth by rejecting the authority of the pope, the vicar of Christ on earth, and replacing it with the direct authority of the Holy Scriptures (*sola Scriptura*) as interpreted by the individual conscience with the help of divine grace. This caused spiritual and intellectual uncertainty, anguish and disorientation. Above all, it caused a bitter and lengthy conflict that went far beyond the sphere of religion.[32] An important figure among these 'nouveaux pyrrhoniens' who were spreading the ancient philosophy of doubt was Michel de Montaigne. Montaigne was among the first to realise the significance of this extension of philosophical scepticism to the moral and juridical fields. His essays were suffused with an ethical relativism that could partly be linked to the accounts of the way of living of the New World natives but was also due to his own radical scepticism towards the possibility of attaining any form of certain knowledge. Montaigne's sophisticated and successful writings thus played a decisive role in widening the debate and doing away with received wisdom.

Alongside this widespread scepticism, however, we find in this period a passionate search for new truth criteria and for solid foundations on which to build something resembling a new and universally recognised authority principle. Against this background the Scientific Revolution took shape, and within it modern natural law as demonstrative science. A new rational *system* was being built – the noun itself was new and would characterise this whole intellectual movement for over a century. The new movement assumed a neutral stance towards religious controversy. Its concern was with objective and scientific truths that could provide the theoretical basis for a new social order and a new social discipline of moral behaviour.

Grotius, however, was not a philosopher like Gassendi or Descartes, and neither did he possess the same kind of scientific knowledge as his friend Mersenne, who in 1625 had published an important tract on *La Vérité des sciences contre les sceptiques ou pyrrhoniens*. He was not equipped to tackle the great epistemological challenges of the time. Nevertheless, we should not underestimate his role in helping to

32. For an overall account of these issues, see the important book by Richard H. Popkin, *The History of scepticism from Erasmus to Spinoza* (Berkeley, CA, 1979), p.17ff. See also Gianni Paganini, *Skepsis: le débat des modernes sur le scepticisme* (Paris, 2007).

bring the 'crise pyrrhonienne' to an end.[33] Grotius publicly confuted Carneades' idea of the impossibility of determining truly universal criteria of justice through natural law, an idea that Grotius represents by quoting Horace: 'And just from unjust Nature cannot know.'[34] In doing so, Grotius' purpose was also to delimit and qualify the principle of 'usefulness' as possible 'universal truth' to be used axiomatically in the construction of the 'system'. To this effect, he summarises Carneades' attack against the Stoics thus:

> Carneades, then, having undertaken to hold a brief against justice, in particular against that phase of justice with which we are concerned, was able to muster no argument stronger than this, that, for reasons of expediency, men imposed upon themselves laws, which vary according to customs, and among the same peoples often undergo changes as times change; moreover, that there is no law of nature, because all creatures, men as well as animals, are impelled by nature toward ends advantageous to themselves; that, consequently, there is no justice, or, if such there be, it is supreme folly, since one does violence to his own interests if he consults the advantage of others.[35]

As reported by Lactantius, Cicero in his *Republic* had also defended the Stoics' idea of the absolute necessity of a universal form of justice, that applies in the same way to everyone in every place. Without this kind of justice, no form of social life can exist, not even among brigands.[36] Grotius did not add very much to this. If anything, he was more concerned with discussing Carneades' 'usefulness' principle as natural in man and capable at any time of calling into doubt the concept of universal justice. While acknowledging the importance of this principle as a specifically human trait and, frequently, as the basis of conventional law, Grotius did not believe that a new 'system' of natural law could be founded on it. Other characteristics common to all men, such as rationality and sociability, provided much better guidelines, on a theoretical and axiomatic level, in the modern attempt to ascertain what was right according to the nature of things. Above all, these two qualities seemed to him to provide far more solid

33. This is what seems to me to be the case with Richard Tuck's important essay on 'The modern theory of natural law'.
34. Grotius, *Prolegomena*, p.6, §6. Quoting from Horace, *Satires*, I, iii, 113.
35. Grotius, *Prolegomena*, p.5-6, §5.
36. Cf. Giorgio Del Vecchio, *Justice: an historical and philosophical essay*, ed. and translated by A. H. Campbell (Edinburgh, 1952), p.18.

moral principles on which to build a peaceful human community after the catastrophic wars of religion.

Historians of science tell us that the 'crise pyrrhonienne' continued for a long time after Grotius and Descartes (and we shall return to this later). From a philosophical point of view, it was only with the unquestioned triumph of Isaac Newton and his mechanistic universe in the early eighteenth century that scepticism was defeated by the truth criteria developed by the Scientific Revolution. However, the unassailable opinions of the Pyrrhonists will continue to surface here and there, down to the postmodern nihilists of our century. It was not by chance, therefore, that Barbeyrac's long 'Préface du traducteur' in his 1706 French edition of Pufendorf's *De iure naturae et gentium* gives ample space to Carneades' scepticism, and to how, in Barbeyrac's opinion, it had been successfully refuted by the modern school of natural law, on both the methodological and the epistemological level.

Pufendorf's work was rightly considered to be the main protagonist in this *querelle*. In comparison, Grotius' contribution appeared too vague, as his method alternated between history and axiomatic-deductive reasoning, and between *consensus gentium* and *more geometrico* demonstration as the ultimate truth criteria. However, Barbeyrac does more than simply identify the milestones in this debate up to Pufendorf. He goes as far as his own time, and explains in great detail the main development in the 'crise pyrrhonienne': from the publication of Sextus Empiricus' works, which opened up a new period of philosophical and gnoseological relativism, to the cultural relativism of Charron and Montaigne. Finally, Barbeyrac addresses the difficult questions posed close to his own time by Pierre Bayle's moral and religious relativism, with his theory of the virtuous atheist and of the necessary separation between religion and morality, to which we return below.

For Barbeyrac, modern science provided the invincible argument against modern adherents of Carneades' scepticism. A new positivistic and pragmatic form of knowledge had spread throughout Europe in the wake of a moderate form of scepticism, as opposed to the *scepticisme outré* ('extravagant, and […] most ridiculous scepticism') of those who 'will doubt merely for the sake of doubting'.[37] The natural sciences

37. Cf. Jean Barbeyrac, 'An historical and critical account of the science of morality, and the progress it has made in the world, from the earliest times down to the publication of Pufendorf, *Of the law of nature and nations*: in a prefatory discourse to the said work' (henceforth preface to Pufendorf), translated by George Carew,

provided powerful new knowledge, which abandoned the pursuit of transcendental reality and the ultimate nature of things to focus on what was within reach of individual reason and was useful in the here and now. In this way, the new science was able to describe natural processes in terms of general laws and causal explanations. Hence Barbeyrac's celebration of this new knowledge in the wake of his friend John Locke's critique of substantivalism, seen as the epistemological aspect of the new empirical and mathematical study of actual phenomena and relationships among things. According to Barbeyrac, these arguments supported the view

> of the possibility of reducing the science of morality to a system, as well connected, as those of geometry, for example, or mechanics; and founded on as certain principles. It is no part of the business in morality to know the real essence of substances [...] All that is required here is only to examine and compare with care and diligence certain relations, which we conceive between human actions and certain rule.[38]

Pufendorf had been one of the first and foremost authors who had attempted to define the epistemological foundations of modern natural law as demonstrative science, in open opposition to the Neo-Pyrrhonists.[39] In his *De cive*, Hobbes assumes that because of the work of Bacon, Descartes, Galileo and Gassendi his methodology can simply be taken for granted.[40] For his part Spinoza does not even mention the sceptics' arguments in his *Ethica more geometrico demonstrata*, as though he considers them entirely obsolete in the face of the heuristic power of the geometrical method. Pufendorf, by contrast, devotes the entire second chapter in his major work to the crucially important issue 'Of the certainty of moral science'. Pufendorf's strategy consists in attacking Aristotle's famous postulate that in moral science and in the pursuit of natural right it was impossible to apply a demonstrative method: one had to forsake mathematical certainties and make do with 'a broad outline of the truth' (I, iii; 1094b); at most, a historical

bound with Pufendorf, *Law of nature and nations*, with separately numbered pages, 1-88, section III, p.9.

38. Barbeyrac, preface to Pufendorf, p.4.
39. On the major role played by this epistemological model up until its critique by Gödel, see Gabriele Lolli, *Da Euclide a Gödel* (Bologna, 2004).
40. Hobbes does address the question of methodology in other works, especially his 1655 *De corpore*.

comparative method could be used, applying an *a posteriori* principle such as the *consensus gentium*, whereby '[a] rule of justice is natural that has the same validity everywhere' (V, vii; 1134b) – a concept that is also found in Cicero.[41]

Both Descartes and Hobbes had been opposed to the use of the principle of universal consensus as truth criterion on specific points. In the same way, Pufendorf upholds the application of a demonstrative principle such as is used in geometrical science.[42] This was the only method that was really capable of producing 'science, or a clear and certain knowledge, every way and at all times constant to itself'.[43] Thus the new demonstrative science of natural law became the pursuit of the legal order of things and human relations underneath the actual historical reality of events. As Pufendorf explains, the science, or 'part of knowledge', that is the subject of his treatise 'is chiefly employed in demonstrating what is right and what is wrong, what is good and what is evil, what is just and what unjust in human actions'.[44] This was only possible if one considered those actions in an abstract state, and defined their principles and properties as moral entities, as the equivalent, that is, of those physical entities (for instance, the planets viewed as mathematical points) that just a few years later Newton would posit as the object of study of his *Philosophiae naturalis principia mathematica*.

It is only to these abstracted moral entities that the demonstrative method can be effectively applied.[45] For Pufendorf, '[t]o demonstrate

41. Cf. *Tusculan disputations*, I, 13: 'in every inquiry the unanimity of the races of the world must be regarded as a law of nature' (Cicero, *Tusculan disputations*, translated by J. E. King, *Loeb classical library* 141, Cambridge, MA, 1927).
42. On historical Pyrrhonism in general and its relationship to the claim of the primacy of the geometrical method see Carlo Borghero, *La certezza e la storia: cartesianesimo, pirronismo e conoscenza storica* (Milan, 1983).
43. Pufendorf, *Law of nature and nations*, I, 2, 3, p.15.
44. Pufendorf, *Law of nature and nations*, I, 3, 1, p.24.
45. Pufendorf discusses at length what in Barbeyrac's rendition are called 'Etres Moraux' ('moral entities' in Basil Kennett's eighteenth-century English translation). These entities originate from God's will and are introduced in man's dealings with people, actions and things in order to regulate 'the manners and the actions of men' (*Law of nature and nations*, I, 1, 2, p.2). In opposition to Aristotelian substantivalism and by analogy with the 'natural entities' studied by scientists, Pufendorf defines these 'moral entities' as 'certain modes superadded to natural things and motions by understanding beings, chiefly for the guiding and tempering the freedom of voluntary actions, and for the procuring of a decent regularity in the method of life' (I, 1, 3, p.3). (Interestingly, Barbeyrac's

[...] is syllogistically to deduce the necessary certainty of any matter proposed from such principles as, being its causes, must needs make it known beyond doubt and dispute'.[46] The selection of these principles and their ability to give rise to a coherent system through rigorous *more geometrico* demonstration then became the defining characteristic of the new natural law. To this effect, we should consider the full title of Pufendorf's work, as translated by Barbeyrac: *Le Droit de la nature et des gens, ou Système général des principes les plus importants de la morale, de la jurisprudence et de la politique.* This title makes explicit the transformation undergone by the old natural law, under the auspices of the Scientific Revolution, into a *système général* of geometrically demonstrable principles. Accordingly, the majority of natural law treatises that were published in the course of the eighteenth century, while keeping open the possibility of using an axiomatic-deductive method of scientific investigation, differ only in the basic principles on which they build their *système.*

Pufendorf deals with this important aspect in his *Specimen controversiarum circa ius naturale*, where he points out how Hobbes had founded his whole *De cive* (1647) on Epicurean principles.[47] Richard Cumberland reacted strongly against this in his *De legibus naturae* (1672). Although he too adhered to the new methods of investigation, Bishop Cumberland polemically supported those principles of Stoic philosophy that had also been upheld by Grotius and, in fact, by Pufendorf himself. Barbeyrac returns to this issue in his preface to the translation of Grotius' *De iure*, where he explains that, while the new natural law adopted as its main foundation the Stoic principle of sociability, Hobbes had effectively given an exposition, in the new geometrical system, of the hypotheses of Epicurus, for whom the main principles of society are individual interest and individual self-preservation. This had as its corollary the idea that the state of nature was effectively a perpetual state of war.[48]

For the history of the rights of man that I am outlining here it is not necessary to delve into the differences among the all equally formidable volumes on natural law published by Leibniz, Wolff,

French translation at the end of this sentence reads 'quelque ordre, quelque convenance et quelque beauté'. Maybe the English translator found the element of 'beauty' too frivolous to be mentioned in this context.)

46. Pufendorf, *Law of nature and nations*, I, 2, 2, p.14.

47. Pufendorf, *Specimen*, p.12.

48. Barbeyrac, 'Préface' to Grotius, p.cxvii.

Thomasius and many others throughout the eighteenth century.[49] In terms of this study it is more important to analyse Pufendorf's complex relationship with the work of Thomas Hobbes, and we should do so from the epistemological point of view, rather than in relation to their political and juridical thought, as is more often the case.[50]

Mersenne and Gassendi were both admirers of Hobbes' *Elementorum philosophiae sectio tertia de cive*, in which they saw the beginnings of a new science of man as individual. However, the *De cive* had not been meant as an actual treatise on natural law. Its focus was first and foremost on tracing the origins of the modern State, and on '*men's duties*, first as men, then as citizens and lastly as Christians'.[51] In the long run, however, Hobbes' work had powerful effects. It was a significant departure from the hitherto unquestioned principle of the primacy of natural law over positive law that had come down from the Middle Ages to modern thinkers, including Grotius and Pufendorf themselves. With this treatise Hobbes opened the way for the rise of subjective rights in the modern age, which involved a voluntaristic view of law and especially an overall and almost paradoxical change in the relationship between natural and civil law, and between the law and the sciences of man. In this way Hobbes provided the basis for the Enlightenment's campaign to overturn traditional views and assert the rule of law and the political application of the rights of man.

49. On the differences and polemics within the school of natural law see the still useful study by Philippe Meylan, *Jean Barbeyrac (1674-1744) et les débuts de l'enseignement du droit dans l'ancienne académie de Lausanne: contribution à l'histoire du droit naturel* (Lausanne, 1938). See also Bobbio, 'Il giusnaturalismo', p.497ff.
50. On this subject, see, for instance, Fiammetta Palladini, *Samuel Pufendorf discepolo di Hobbes: per una reinterpretazione del giusnaturalismo moderno* (Bologna, 1990); Richard Tuck, *The Rights of war and peace: political thought and the international order from Grotius to Kant* (Oxford, 1999), p.109ff.; *Natural law and civil sovereignty: moral right and state authority in early modern political thought*, ed. Ian Hunter and David Saunders (Basingstoke, 2002).
51. From the 'Preface to the readers' in Thomas Hobbes, *On the citizen*, ed. and translated by Richard Tuck and Michael Silverthorne (Cambridge, 1998), p.7 (emphasis added). As is well known, Hobbes had intended to write a new philosophy of man in three parts: 'the first Section would discuss [the] body and its general properties; the second, Man and his particular faculties and passions; the third, the Commonwealth and the duties of citizens' (p.13). As Hobbes himself openly states, he had been prompted to give priority to the third section by the horrors of the English civil war and the need to restore peace through absolute obedience to the sovereign.

Hobbes' contemporaries immediately realised that his *De cive* offered a powerful legitimisation of absolute power and obedience to it: a convincing theory that upheld the need to build a modern State on a rational level and, in the process, demonstrated the importance of politics itself. That god on earth that Hobbes would go on to describe in his 1651 *Leviathan* was the only form of institution that could safeguard man's life, preserving it from man's own violent instincts (*homo homini lupus*) and from a state of nature characterised by perpetual conflict: the only means, in fact, to create modern civil life. However, though unassailable on a logical level, by attributing so much power to the sovereign this theory effectively undermined the very foundations of the old natural law. Ultimately, in the *De cive*, politics and positive law were the only measure of good and evil, of what was and was not right. Morality and justice itself were no longer intrinsically present in the nature of things in the form of absolute and universal criteria, but became the direct and legitimate expression of the king's political power, which deprived subjects of the possibility of rebelling by appealing to the law of nature. This is why this work appeared so disconcerting: it purported to be based on the principles of the law of nature, but in fact supported absolutism and positive law.

This was something unprecedented in history. Ever since Sophocles' *Antigone*, natural law had been invoked in order to set limits to human power and laws. For centuries the law of nature represented man's share in the *lex aeterna* and in the divine order of creation. It incorporated the general rules and values of moral and social life in a way that was always set *above* positive law. Hobbes had completely overturned this situation. The rhetorical justification of the principles of natural law in the first part of his work was used as the premise on which to build a new form of contractualism, a *pactum subiectionis* between the king and his subjects. These were the foundations of the new all-powerful Leviathan: for the first time, the civil laws of the State triumphed over all things, and the sovereign's power knew no bounds.

Historians have written extensively on this ostensible paradox, whereby disparate and even contradictory things were yoked together to achieve a new form of law of a subjective and voluntaristic kind.[52] As Hobbes explains in *De cive* I, 7, where he describes the premises of the *pactum subiectionis*, 'precisely what is meant by the term *Right* is the

52. Norberto Bobbio's remarks on this matter are still important and enlightening. See his *Thomas Hobbes and the natural law tradition*, translated by Daniela Gobetti (Chicago, IL, and London, 1993), p.114ff.

liberty each man has of using his natural faculties in accordance with right reason. Therefore the first foundation of natural *Right* is that *each man protect his life and limbs as much as he can*.'[53] In order to achieve this, it was necessary to create the Leviathan. Pufendorf addresses this apparent paradox in his critique of the epistemological model described by Hobbes in the tenth chapter of the *De homine* (1658), by stressing the various aspects that differentiate Hobbes' model from his own, despite the common adherence to the idea of *more geometrico* demonstration. Pufendorf followed what today we might call an *essentialist* concept of nature, while Hobbes saw scientific knowledge in *conventional* terms. For him, natural principles, far from providing an accurate and objective representation of reality, were mere empirical constructs: contingent hypotheses with which to describe phenomena and attempt to determine their prime causes through the use of reason.[54] A classic example of this was provided by the idea of the *state of nature* as hypothesis and mental experiment, which was worthy of Galileo's best work on mechanics. Indeed, Hobbes was a great admirer of Galileo, whom he insisted on meeting while in Italy.

However, to consider the study of phenomena as a rigorous semantic system based on contingent and entirely hypothetical principles was liable to destroy the very foundations of both the old and the new school of natural law. This is something that Pufendorf realised straightaway. This is why he attacked in a thorough and detailed manner Hobbes' contention that 'ethics and politics are [...] capable of a demonstration *a priori*': because this did away with the idea of the self-evident and certain character of specific principles in the nature of things, which Hobbes needed to do in order to claim that what was good or bad depended on the sovereign's will. In Pufendorf's analysis, according to Hobbes

> we ourselves are the authors of the principles of justice and injustice, of right and wrong, by making those laws and compacts whence the measures of justice are to be taken: since before any such laws or compacts were instituted, there was no such thing as justice or injustice, public good or evil, among men, any more than among

53. Hobbes, *On the citizen*, p.27 (emphasis in the original).

54. On Hobbes' nominalistic and conventionalistic epistemological model see Arrigo Pacchi, *Convenzione e ipotesi nella formazione della filosofia naturale di Thomas Hobbes* (Florence, 1965). Karl Popper's thoughts on this topic are interesting not least from a historical point of view; see the excerpts included in the anthology *Il neoempirismo*, ed. Alberto Pasquinelli (Turin, 1969), p.659-96.

beasts. The absolute falseness of which position we shall hereafter have occasion to demonstrate; as there is also a fallacy lurking under the word public.[55]

Thus Pufendorf already thought that, by denying the reality of self-evident principles in nature (those principles that are 'the *first* and the highest that can be, so as to want no further proof'; I, 2, 3, p.15), Hobbes was perilously doing away with the centuries-old idea that what was right could be found within nature itself, independently of human will. Morality and justice – the formal respect of agreements – became a historically determined product dependent on man's liberty and sense of responsibility.

In this way, the glorious tradition that we are tracing here was not so much undergoing yet another metamorphosis as coming close to its end. At the time, however, these subtle epistemological differences were less evident than the points of contact between Pufendorf and Hobbes. The principal aim of both was to uphold the authority principle against the political and religious crises of the time. While they resorted to different legitimating mechanisms, both focused on absolute power and the duties of man, and of subjects in particular. Hobbes developed the idea of the Leviathan as an entirely human construct: an act of will whereby single individuals joined together and submitted to the absolute power of a sovereign (*pactum unionis*) as protection against the state of nature, which was dominated by violent passions, the pursuit of profit and the war of all against all (*bellum omnium erga omnes*). Pufendorf, on his part, developed a new system of natural law as a rational construct, which was liable to *more geometrico* demonstration, and founded on the self-evident truth of the sociability principle.

These two models would continue to exist side by side for a long time. However, Pufendorf's concept of natural law spread quickly across the universities and the salons of the Republic of Letters and even on the other side of the Atlantic. This was partly due to the publication in 1673, i.e. one year after the monumental *De iure naturae et gentium*, of a handy compendium, an extremely effective catechism that carried the significant title *De officio hominis et civis iuxta legem naturalem*. The success of this small volume in propagating the new moral science of duties is attested not only by the great number of editions, including several unauthorised ones, but also by the long series of translations that appeared down to the end of the eighteenth

55. Pufendorf, *Law of nature and nations*, I, 2, 4, p.16.

century (for instance, an Italian translation was still being published in Naples in 1785).[56] Whether or not the theories expounded in the compendium corresponded fully with those in the original *De iure*, its fortune sanctioned the importance of the new natural law as a modern science of morality founded first and foremost on 'the duties of man'. For instance, the first Italian translation of the *De iure*, published in 1757, was made by Catholic author Giovambattista Almici precisely in the light of the *De officio hominis*. The authoritarian and disciplinarian sense in which the tract was interpreted comes immediately across in the translator's opening declaration that this work set out 'all the duties towards God, ourselves and others based on the fundamental principle of sociability, but still in relation to God himself, from whom this principle derives and by whom it is stamped onto our nature'.[57]

In fact, the ultimate message of Pufendorf's 'catechism' was quite clear: it demonstrated with utmost logical clarity the necessity of restoring the authority principle, the centrality of the sovereign and the recourse to a form of divine justification, after decades of scepticism, anarchy and civil and religious wars. The notion of morality distinguished human beings from animals in that it was based principally on a voluntaristic concept of law. According to Pufendorf, his *De iure* demonstrated on the basis of the sociability principle that 'a fundamental law of nature' forced man to be sociable if he wanted to escape the precariousness and violence of the state of nature and create a peaceful and ordered *civil society*: 'Every man ought, as far as in him lies, to promote and preserve a peaceful sociableness with others, agreeable to the main end and disposition of human race in general.'[58] All other laws derive from this single one, and are easily arrived at through the exercise of that natural reason that is common to all human beings. Generally, by its very nature, the principle of 'universal sociability' emphasised above all 'the duties of man' as a member of human communities.

All this foregrounded the question of *obligations* and of the ultimate basis of modern natural law and the new morality of duties. As

56. A reference to the extraordinary success of this small volume and to the numerous pirated editions printed in Amsterdam is found in the translator's preface to Samuel von Pufendorf, *Les Devoirs de l'homme et du citoyen, tels qu'ils lui sont prescrits par la loi naturelle*, translated by Jean Barbeyrac (Amsterdam, Pierre de Coup, 1715), p.xxx.
57. Samuel von Pufendorf, *Il diritto della natura e delle genti o sia sistema generale de' principi li più importanti di morale, giurisprudenza e politica*, translated by Giovambattista Almici, 4 vols (Venice, Pietro Valvasense, 1757), vol.1, p.ix.
58. Pufendorf, *Law of nature and nations*, II, 3, 15, p.137.

Pufendorf explains to European public opinion, for the constitution of laws 'a superior is necessary to be supposed, and that such a one as has actually undertaken the government of the other'. Thus, as he mentions at the start of the paragraph, next to the legitimate sovereignty of the monarch, 'it must necessarily be presupposed that there is a God, who governs all things by his Providence, and that he has enjoined us mortals to observe these dictates of our reason as laws, promulged [*sic*] by him to us by the powerful mediation of that light which is born with us.'[59]

Chased out of the door, theology made its triumphant re-entrance through the window. One cannot help imagining Thomas Aquinas secretly smiling at this development. However, it would be a serious mistake to underestimate the originality of modern natural law. This was far from being a mere rehash of that old theology that had led to endless controversy between the supporters of papal authority and those who placed all their trust in the Bible.

The recent separation between moral theology and natural law as academic disciplines in the major European universities was indeed, as Pufendorf claims in his compendium, an important *fait accompli*. The world was rapidly changing, and the Republic of Letters together with it. Across both the Catholic and the Protestant front, new intellectual issues were being debated outside the fold of the hopelessly fragmented *Respublica christiana*. The fiercest clashes were now those between atheists and believers, deists and freethinkers; between those who, like Pierre Bayle, entertained the scandalous hypothesis of a society of virtuous atheists, and those who wielded modern science and the natural theology of Newton and the Boyle Lectures as the last bastion of God's design against the attacks of sceptics and unbelievers. In this respect, it is all the more significant that Barbeyrac should present Pufendorf's *Duty of man* as a happy synthesis of Euclid's *Elements* and Cicero's *De officiis*.[60]

With its unprecedented conjunction of science, religion and morality, and of ancient and modern, Pufendorf's work was the first

59. Samuel von Pufendorf, *The Whole duty of man according to the law of nature*, translated by Andrew Tooke (1691), ed. Ian Hunter and David Saunders (Indianapolis, IN, 2003), I, 3, 10, p.56-57. On the fortune of this model of reference to God as the ultimate source, see Petter Korkman, 'Civil sovereigns and the King of Kings: Barbeyrac on the Creator's right to rule', in *Natural law and civil sovereignty*, ed. I. Hunter and D. Saunders, p.109-22.
60. Cf. Barbeyrac, preface to Pufendorf, p.5.

in a long series of books on the morality of duties that reviewed Stoic philosophy in light of the Scientific Revolution and its contrasting interpretations. The many books that propounded this moral science of duties, newly revised in its form and language, spanned the whole spectrum of attitudes towards religious belief: from the 1682 *Traité de morale* by French Oratorian priest Nicolas Malebranche, which lists a long series of duties as expression of the divine natural order, to Baron Holbach, the atheist author of a 1776 study on *La Morale universelle, ou les Devoirs de l'homme fondés sur sa nature*, where nature is seen in a deterministic sense as a self-sufficient chemical organism. Through Pufendorf and the modern school of natural rights the 'duties of man' became a constant element in our political language. Sometimes this went hand in hand with the reference to rights as a consequence of those duties. However, the two never quite merged together because, as we will see below, their genealogy and aims were too different in the thought of the authors of the period, and especially in the modern culture of the rights of man that would be developed by the Enlightenment in the course of the eighteenth century.

There is no doubt that, by propounding a morality of duties, the modern school of natural law helped to strengthen the power of the sovereign and the idea of political absolutism, and more generally contributed to the comeback of the authority principle, which was surprisingly facilitated also by the success of the Scientific Revolution against the sceptical movement. Once again, however, the rapid historical developments at the turn of the seventeenth century brought to the fore the inherent contradictions in the obsessive pursuit of a rigidly rational 'system' of universal morality. From being developed with the noble intention of protecting mankind from civil war, this paradigm had ended up suppressing individual liberty of conscience and legitimising all kinds of despotism, especially Louis XIV's attack on religious freedom. As a way out of this impasse, thinkers began to explore again half-forgotten solutions, such as those developed by medieval theories of natural and subjective rights, that acknowledged the autonomy of the individual as a 'person'. Eventually, with the Enlightenment, the focus shifts momentously from the 'duties' imposed by the sociability principle to the 'rights of man': in the moral field, at first, and then, finally, in what Condorcet defines for the first time as 'droits politiques', rights that are constitutionally guaranteed in the name of the new Enlightenment humanism.

4. Natural law and 'the crisis of the European mind': Jean Barbeyrac

Traduttore-traditore! This Italian saying acquires a whole new meaning when applied to the life and work of Jean Barbeyrac. He was born into a Huguenot family in Béziers, Lower Languedoc, in 1674. His father was a Calvinist pastor and they were forced to flee to Switzerland after the revocation of the Edict of Nantes in 1685, after which Barbeyrac was orphaned at the age of seventeen. He lived in Lausanne, Geneva, Berlin and Groningen, where he taught law and died in 1744. As a refugee himself, he got to know some of the main figures of the Protestant diaspora, such as Le Clerc and Limborch, not to mention John Locke. He became familiar with the theories of Hobbes, Spinoza and Bayle, and soon became a well-known member of the Republic of Letters.[1] Barbeyrac was the author of a small number of works, including the 1731 *Traité de la morale des Pères de l'Eglise* and several articles for the *Bibliothèque raisonnée des savants de l'Europe*. His fame rests mostly on his monumental translations of Pufendorf, Grotius and Cumberland, to which he contributed long introductions and a rich apparatus of notes. As a result, he is now rightly considered the main author of the astounding success of modern natural law in the Europe of his time.

However, Barbeyrac's contemporaries repeatedly accused him of Socinianism and Arminianism.[2] We should, therefore, examine in further detail his complex intellectual presence, which went far beyond his work as translator and populariser, important as that may have been, especially from a historical point of view. Barbeyrac was both *traduttore* (translator) and *traditore* (traitor), at least in the sense that he

1. Cf. Meylan, *Jean Barbeyrac*.
2. See Anne Goldgar, *Impolite learning: conduct and community in the Republic of Letters, 1680-1750* (New Haven, CT, and London, 1995), p.131ff.

did not simply *report* the thought of the authors he transmitted to his public. He transformed those works with the addition of a significant interpretative apparatus. In this way, Barbeyrac both witnessed and played an important role in what Paul Hazard called 'the crisis of the European mind' that took place at the turn of the seventeenth century: a crucially important period from our point of view because of the profound influence that the inevitable involvement with the question of religion had at this time on the genesis of the rights of man.

The crisis that began with the revocation of the Edict of Nantes has long been the subject of study because of its manifold significance.[3] This crisis heralded the cultural revolution of the Enlightenment. It concluded the long and violent crisis of Christianity that had begun with the Reformation, and marked the beginning of a new phase, which would develop fully in the course of the eighteenth century and in which the religious question would take on new features. In this context, the concept of natural law itself and of its foundations would undergo significant transformations. In the previous centuries, theologians had debated questions such as the Trinity, transubstantiation, the sovereign pontiff and his power, the primacy of works over faith or of the Scriptures over ecclesiastical hierarchy. Now, public philosophical controversies took place on the nature of religion and its historical and anthropological origins, or whether atheism might be justified from a rational and scientific point of view. All this drew on new arguments that departed significantly from the way in which militant anti-Christian viewpoints had in the past made use of heterodox interpretations of Aristotle in the wake of medieval Averroism, as in the materialist positions of Pomponazzi and Cremonini and their Paduan school.[4] A new rationalist atheism, found mainly in Spinoza and Bayle, spread from Northern Europe to the rest of the Western world. It superimposed itself on previous traditions of free thought, such as libertine naturalism and the sixteenth-century tradition of an autonomous and eternal *natura naturans*, as found in Machiavelli, Aretino, Bruno, Campanella or Vanini, which in the eighteenth century would resurface in the materialist positions of authors such as Diderot and Holbach. This gave new life to that rich

3. Cf. Margaret C. Jacob, 'The crisis of the European mind: Hazard revisited', in *Politics and culture in early modern Europe: essays in honour of H. G. Koenigsberger*, ed. Phyllis Mach and Margaret C. Jacob (Cambridge, 1987), p.251-72.

4. Cf. Edward Muir, *The Culture wars of the late Renaissance: skeptics, libertines, and opera* (Cambridge, MA, 2007).

intellectual substratum that had originally developed in Renaissance Italy, causing contemporaries to exclaim that the country was full of libertines, atheists and unbelievers.[5] This current, however, had been all but crushed by the Inquisition, with Bruno and Vanini ending up burned at the stake and the dramatic example set at the end of the seventeenth century by the nine-year-long trial of Neapolitan atheists, accused of being followers of Spinoza and of the atomistic heresy. But before passing the free-thought baton to the United Provinces, radical philosophers all over Italy, from Venice, Padua and Florence to Rome and Naples, had spread their fundamental tenets all over Europe: concepts such as the natural origin of religious fear, the imposture of religions, the critique of miracles, the existence of uncreated matter and the mortality of the soul, which led to the development of a new morality founded on natural instinct rather than on the prospect of reward or punishment after death. These existing currents notwithstanding, Pierre Bayle's corrosive scepticism and the work of the Dutch philosopher of Jewish origin Baruch Spinoza introduced groundbreaking new concepts into the intellectual scene and gave a major impulse to the rise of the Enlightenment.

Spinoza's thought, in particular, was rather an explosive mixture. It brought together an almost dogmatic faith in the epistemological power of reason and philosophy, in contrast with modern scepticism, an adherence to the geometrical methods of deduction of the Scientific Revolution, as applied in Galileo, Descartes and Hobbes, and the systematic use of textual philology as found in the humanism of Lorenzo Valla, Scaliger and Erasmus. Spinoza's *Tractatus theologico-politicus* (1670) and his contemporaneous, though posthumously published, *Ethics* gave a paradoxical new interpretation of the concept of atheism. It was no longer a matter of denying the existence of God and postulating instead an autonomous and uncreated nature. This new atheism was based on a sacral and pantheistic view of the world: *Deus sive natura*, according to the definition first used by freethinking philosopher John Toland in 1720 that would acquire canonical status in the course of the century. Pantheism was the new atheism.

Spinoza rejected Descartes's mind–body dualism as well as the Judeo-Christian idea of a world created by a transcendent God. In their place, his *Ethics* established the rigorously demonstrated image of a divinity that is identified with the rational and logical being of the

5. As in Gabriel Naudé's remark quoted in Giorgio Spini, *Ricerca dei libertini: la teoria dell'impostura delle religioni nel Seicento italiano*, 2nd edn (Florence, 1983), p.7.

one universal substance. This pantheistic and immanent God was at the same time thought and extension. He did not create matter *ex nihilo*, nor did he govern it through his providence. He was neither free nor the ultimate cause: in fact, he could only be conceived of as one of the infinite effects of matter itself. In this rationally determined order, the concepts of evil and free will lost their traditional meaning. Man's freedom as a modality of being was replaced by the consciousness of belonging to this universal Whole and by the progressive assimilation of individual thought into a substance that understands that it is destined to act only unto itself.

On the one hand, man's need for religiosity thus found new support in philosophy, which became the instrument of a new search for rational truth, and for the intellectual understanding of this *Deus sive natura*. On the other hand, traditional revealed religions were unmasked as being based on entirely false premises. Through a sophisticated critical and philological analysis of the Hebrew text of the Bible, the *Tractatus theologico-politicus* put forward in renewed form the ancient libertine thesis of the imposture of religions, revealing the entirely human nature of prophecy and prophets.

Spinoza denies both the authenticity and Moses' authorship of the Pentateuch. He highlights the obvious contradictions in the assertions of the various apostles and even within those of Christ himself. He explains that the Bible 'accommodates all its words and reasons to the understanding of the common people', and that it was written by many different men, and its ultimate function was 'to instil obedience and devotion in [men's] minds'.[6] Revealed religions, therefore, harboured the demon of political power and the hidden but intransigent logic of the authority principle. Ultimately, the violent theological controversies over the interpretation of the Scriptures had nothing to do with ascertaining the truth: it was simply a question of who should wield that power through religious practices, rites and ceremonies, and exactly how. For Spinoza there is no doubt that universal faith is simply a matter of obedience. Faith means 'to believe in God and to revere him, or, which is the same thing, to obey him […] faith does not lead to salvation in itself, but

6. Benedict de Spinoza, *Theological-political treatise*, translated by Michael Silverthorne and Jonathan Israel, ed. Jonathan Israel (Cambridge, 2007), 5, 16, p.77. In recent years a burgeoning bibliography has developed on this subject: see Steven M. Nadler, *A Book forged in hell: Spinoza's scandalous treatise and the birth of the secular age* (Princeton, NJ, 2011).

only by means of obedience'.[7] This is the source of the fundamental incompatibility between reason and faith, philosophy and theology. The latter is suddenly excluded from the realm of truth, and seen simply as an instrument through which priests exercise their power by illustrating the commandments handed down by revealed religions, be it Hebrew, Christian or Islamic. In contrast with this, Spinoza calls for the simplification of religious language: faith in the one and only *Deus sive natura* will be expressed in just a few, clear and universally valid dogmas. In turn, this leads logically to a showdown between scientists, philosophers and theologians, something that in fact had already begun when Galileo and Grotius claimed autonomous status for their new science. As a philosopher, Spinoza calls for the definitive separation of theology and philosophy. Only the latter can access truth and should therefore be granted total freedom of enquiry and expression: 'We conclude therefore without hesitation that Scripture is not to be accommodated to reason nor reason to Scripture.'[8]

The other key figure in the crisis of the European mind is Pierre Bayle, who would probably have had no problem subscribing to most of the opinions expressed by Spinoza in his *Tractatus*: the imposture of revealed religions, the historically defined character of prophets and holy books, the political function of rites and ceremonies. However, Bayle was not a follower of Spinoza from the epistemological or philosophical point of view. He would not want to be considered one of those thinkers who follow no existing religion, and adhere instead to an 'absurd and monstrous hypothesis' such as the *Deus sive natura* discussed in the *Ethics*.[9] In Bayle's opinion, 'the horrid notion Spinoza gives us of God' (p.208 n.N.90), which denies the idea of creation, not only 'overthrows the foundations of all religions' (p.203 n.D.39): it denies all logic and traditional truth criteria in the use of reason. The hypothesis of an immanent, universal Whole characterised by its own internal dialectics led to the paradox that 'men are modifications of God' (p.210 n.N.III.98), that 'God hates and loves, denies and affirms, the same things, at the same time' (*ibid.*) and that thus

7. Spinoza, *Theological-political treatise*, 14, 3, p.179, and 6, p.180.
8. Spinoza, *Theological-political treatise*, 15, 6, p.191. For Spinoza, theology only deals with revealed religion: it explains its dogmas, the Bible's objectives and the modalities of obedience.
9. Quotations are from the entry on Spinoza in *The Dictionary historical and critical of Mr Peter Bayle*, facsimile of edition printed in London by J. J. and P. Knapton, 2nd edn, 5 vols, 1734-1738 (London, 1997), vol.5, p.199-224 (208; subsequent page references are given within the text).

'there is no other agent, nor other patient but God, with respect to physical and moral evil' (p.208 n.N.90). This immanent idea of reality overthrew Christian philosophy by denying the existence of an immaterial God that ruled over all things in perfect liberty. But in fact it seemed to Bayle that 'the system of Spinoza is not liable to lesser objections than the Christian hypothesis' of a transcendent God who created all things (p.213 n.O.110). Above all, from an epistemological point of view, this idea failed to take into account 'the weakness of our reason' (p.213 n.O.108), with its limits, and human inability to understand the ultimate things, or those ineffable entities such as God, the soul, the spirit.

Bayle, the great modern heir of the epistemological scepticism of Carneades and Montaigne, could not accept the underlying dogmatism in Spinoza's geometrical and dialectical rationalism. He was irked by the assurance of the Dutch-born and culturally Jewish philosopher, Maimonides' spiritual heir, that he had finally attained the truth on the authentic nature of God, as if he had solved the enigma of the world.[10] Bayle, the persecuted refugee, was bound to see any form of dogmatism as the great enemy, whatever its origin. It did not matter to Bayle whether this attitude was encountered in the rationalist metaphysics of Descartes, Spinoza and their followers, whose philosophical novels and, in Spinoza's case, absolute monism anticipated the nineteenth-century philosophy of spirit. Or whether it issued from powerful and intolerant Christian theologians on either side of the divide, like Bossuet or Jurieu, who had grown up spiritually under the influence of Augustine, the spiritual father of modern inquisitorial violence. It was only by accepting the insurmountable limitations of the human mind that we could lay the basis for tolerance and peaceable coexistence, as would later be argued by Voltaire, Bayle's true heir, in his critique of Christianity and all revealed religions.

In the chaotic religious debate of those years, when different positions surfaced across traditional divides, and at times even within one and the same thinker, Bayle's positions became a primary example of the nascent Enlightenment humanism. The author of the *Dictionnaire* furthered a moderate scepticism and the study of the limits and potentialities of reason in an operational sense, as

10. On Spinoza and the tradition of the great Jewish thinker Maimonides see Leo Strauss, *Spinoza's critique of religion*, translated by E. M. Sinclair (Chicago, IL, 1997; original: *Religionskritik Spinozas als Grundlage seiner Bibelwissenschaft*, 1930).

applied to the contents of experience. At first this led him to adopt a sort of ontological indifferentism, where he kept equal distance from believers and Spinozian atheists alike. Eventually, while still very much in favour of the idea of probable knowledge, his positions became quite close to those of the new mechanistic and phenomenological science. They also began to resemble the stance of the many deists and rationalists who, in a sort of crypto-Socinianism or Arminianism, were freely questioning religion as a phenomenon, and in the first instance as natural religion, independently of any Church, dogma or traditional theology. This was the intellectual environment, first of all, of the Huguenot refugees, and of Locke, Le Clerc, Newton's God and the Boyle Lectures. It was the Early Enlightenment of the Italian 'enlightened Catholics' who, in Rome, the very centre of Catholicism, bravely fought the Inquisition under the guide of the monk Celestino Galiani in the name of tolerance and *libertas philosophandi*.[11]

Jean Barbeyrac had much in common with this intellectual milieu, which, from its bases in London, Amsterdam, Paris, Berlin or Rome, was attempting to bring Christianity up to date in light of the new science. It was a question of freeing religion from the primacy of dogmatic theology as well as from superstition. The salvific message of revelation needed to be simplified and redirected towards a rationally argued universal morality, legitimised by God's design that was implicit in Newton's mechanistic universe. The members of this 'reformist International' in fact had to fight on two fronts. On the one side there were the ecclesiastical hierarchies of all Christian Churches. On the other, they were faced with the far more radical thought of those who, like the English 'freethinkers', had initially followed in the tradition of Bruno, Spinoza and Bayle and had ended up adhering to an openly militant atheism, which denied that revealed religion had a necessary role to play as social bond and provider of meaning in human life. The result was a three-way conflict, which has been described as a war of ideas between a 'moderate' Newtonian current within the Enlightenment and a 'radical' current, both of which were strenuously opposed by the conservative and reactionary wings of

11. Cf. Margaret C. Jacob, *The Newtonians and the English Revolution, 1689-1720* (Hassocks, 1976); Vincenzo Ferrone, *The Intellectual roots of the Italian Enlightenment: Newtonian science, religion, and politics in the early eighteenth century*, translated by Sue Brotherton (Atlantic Highlands, NJ, 1995; original: *Scienza, natura, religione: mondo newtoniano e cultura italiana nel primo Settecento*, Naples, 1982).

both the Catholic and Protestant Churches.[12] However, the authors of this neat reconstruction do not take into account the importance in this debate of natural law, in its new form as a demonstrable moral science of duties.

In fact, when one reads the extensive 'Préface du traducteur' and the rich annotations to the 1706 Amsterdam edition of Pufendorf's *Le Droit de la nature et des gens*, it is obvious that Barbeyrac himself belongs to the moderate Enlightenment precisely because he is able to present modern natural law in light of the changed historical context. For instance, he deals with Bayle's attack, in both epistemological and religious terms, on the very foundations of the new moral science. In the 'Préface', Bayle's scepticism is openly the enemy to be fought off at all costs.

Barbeyrac was up against the case laid out by Bayle in entries such as those on Pyrrho, Carneades, Xenophanes or Zeno of Elea in his 1697 *Dictionnaire historique et critique*, where he revives ancient scepticism in order to call into doubt the possibility of finding what is right in nature. In reply to Bayle's powerful argument, Barbeyrac draws on the success of modern science, Galileo and Newton's physical and mathematical empiricism and, especially, the French translation of his friend John Locke's *Essay concerning human understanding.* He is thus able to uphold Pufendorf's thesis of the evident truth of certain moral principles, which are universal and geometrically demonstrable.[13] On one point, however, Barbeyrac takes on Bayle's challenge without resorting to anyone's help, and this is in putting publicly forward, for the first time, the deist concept of natural religion as the ultimate universal foundation in relation to morality or natural law:

> In fact, the fundamental principles of natural religion, which must be the basis of all other religion, are also the most firm, or rather only, foundation of this science of morality. Without a deity, *duty*, *obligation*, *right* are no more, to say the truth, than fine ideas, which may please the mind but can scarce touch the heart, and which of themselves cannot impose an indispensable necessity to act or not to act [...] But to give these ideas their full force and due measure of efficacy, to make them strong enough to maintain their ground against passion

12. See Jonathan Israel, *Radical Enlightenment: philosophy and the making of modernity, 1650-1750*, 2nd edn (Oxford, 2002), p.11ff. This pattern was first highlighted in Margaret C. Jacob, *The Radical Enlightenment: pantheists, freemasons and republicans* (London, 1981), p.87ff.
13. Barbeyrac, preface to Pufendorf, p.9.

> and self-interest, they will require a superior Being, a Being superior to us in power and might, who has subjected us to a strict conformity therewith in our conduct.[14]

Thus Barbeyrac distanced himself from the scandalous idea that there could be peoples without God, that history shows that a godless individual or whole 'societies of atheists' were capable of self-government and of living perfectly moral lives, as Bayle had argued for the first time when the 1682 comet had appeared in European skies.[15] What Bayle understatedly defined as his 'Conjectures on the morals of a society without religion' had started a furious debate that would have a huge bearing on eighteenth-century reflections concerning natural law and the nexus between religion, morality and politics.[16] Sidestepping all the discussions on the origins and nature of religion, and on the ceremonies and rites developed by the various nations, Bayle had produced a sensational wild card: atheism as a social and historical fact that had to be taken into account. While his contemporaries were trying to find the natural origin of religion – whether it be the result of man's ancestral fears, of an imposture and political invention by the holders of political power, of an innate concept of God, or a rational construct – Bayle pointed out that atheism was a legitimate fact, since reason is ultimately unable to demonstrate either the existence of God or his non-existence. Bayle's extreme scepticism thus distanced him clearly from the views propagated by the Boyle Lectures and Newtonian natural theology to which the circles close to Barbeyrac adhered *ad maiorem Dei gloriam*. Its logical consequence, however, was a call for universal tolerance, and the condemnation of the fanaticism and superstition of all those who, across the centuries, continued to believe in miracles and to see comets as harbingers of misfortune. Acknowledging that atheists too could live happily and in a virtuous manner inevitably led to the

14. Barbeyrac, preface to Pufendorf, p.14 and 15 (emphasis in the original).
15. See Gianfranco Cantelli, 'La virtù degli atei nei *Pensieri diversi sulla Cometa* di Pierre Bayle: una premessa per una società tollerante', in *La formazione storica della alterità: studi di storia della tolleranza nell'età moderna offerti a Antonio Rotondò*, ed. Henry Méchoulan *et al.*, 3 vols (Florence, 2001), vol.2, p.679-706. On Bayle in general see Gianluca Mori, *Bayle philosophe* (Paris, 1999); *Pierre Bayle dans la République des Lettres: philosophie, religion, critique*, ed. Antony McKenna and Gianni Paganini (Paris, 2004).
16. Cf. Pierre Bayle, *Various thoughts on the occasion of a comet*, ed. and translated by Robert C. Bartlett (Albany, NY, 2000), §161, p.200.

belief that religion should be kept separate from morality and politics, and to uphold the autonomy of morality as a historically determined human construct.

Barbeyrac could only react in a negative manner to these subversive and scandalous 'conjectures', which undermined the idea of natural law as a moral science of the duties of man that had been slowly developing in those years: 'It is certain that morality is the daughter of religion, that they go hand in hand together, and that the perfection of the latter is the standard of perfection in the former.'[17] For Barbeyrac, leaving aside the question of the *truth* of the many revelations in history, the way in which religion guaranteed the validity of the social bond was an indispensable premise for the modality and legitimacy of individual behaviour within human communities. Of course this did not mean stepping suddenly back into a distant past. As we have repeatedly seen, it was no longer time for theological controversies or confessional arguments over the dogmas of the faith. The new, disturbing idea now facing philosophers and theologians was the possible existence of a *religion naturelle*, i.e. that universalist and rationalist religion that had arisen out of the deists' investigation into religiosity as a natural phenomenon and human emotion, which was found among all peoples of the earth as the common substratum to all revealed religions.

This libertine and Socinian view of religious belief appealed to Barbeyrac as well as to other figures of the time, including Clarke, Bentley, Le Clerc, Limborch, Locke and Celestino Galiani, all of whom opposed the anthropological pessimism tinged with Augustinianism that characterised the positions of Luther, Calvin or Bossuet. Instead, they went back to the ancient Pelagian strand of Christianity, via its modern version represented by Socinian rationalism, which called for a simplification of the religious message – for instance, as advocated by Hobbes first and then by Locke, the idea that all that was necessary was to acknowledge Jesus Christ as the Messiah. This current was anti-Trinitarian, aware of the importance of individual conscience, opposed to religious fanaticism as well as to ecclesiastical hierarchy, ceremonies, rites, superstitions, the belief in miracles and the proliferation of dogmas. These forms of Socinianism, especially in their Arminian, Latitudinarian and enlightened Catholic strands, all tended towards a new kind of Christianity: one that eschewed all

17. Barbeyrac, preface to Pufendorf, p.14.

mystery and could be characterised as sensible.[18] Christianity became in fact a form of moral philosophy, which propagated God's ethical teachings to man through religion, philosophy and modern science.

In the wake of Locke and Le Clerc, Barbeyrac explains all this in his 'Préface', where he traces an original and polemical history of morality. Tracing a pattern that will become famous through Voltaire, this account denounces the degeneration of Christ's original message, which was meant to restore man to that rationality and natural morality that was unavailable to the pagan and Jewish world after the Fall: 'He [Jesus Christ] re-established morality in its utmost purity; he fully laid open the true sources thereof; and he gave forth rules touching *the whole duty* both of mankind in general, and of each person in particular. They were general indeed, but perfect, entirely conformable to right reason, and the true interests of mankind.'[19]

The original message of the Gospels did not simply exhort one to love one's neighbour. It was also an invitation to be sensible and tolerant, and to exercise one's freedom of conscience. Its betrayal had begun soon after the death of the first apostles, as Augustine and the other Church Fathers, infusing the evangelical message with pagan philosophy, had focused instead on the creation of new dogmas, ceremonies and rites that would create the basis for the authoritarian and intolerant structure of modern organised religions and foster a 'vast number of ridiculous superstitions' and 'prodigious and amazing idolatry' among the faithful.[20]

The Protestant Reformation had started off with laudable intents but had soon given way to violence and to sectarian opposition between Lutherans and orthodox Calvinists. Worst of all, it resembled its enemy, the 'papist' Catholic Church, in privileging inane theological discussions over the question of morality. As for the *science of morality* that was implicit in Christ's teachings, it had been misunderstood and banished by the different Churches, where the interests of the ministers and ecclesiastical hierarchies had prevailed, and had been forced to take refuge 'amongst the laicks, or undignified [original: *simples*] men of

18. A still useful account of this movement can be found in H. R. Trevor-Roper's chapter on 'The religious origins of the Enlightenment', in his *Religion, the Reformation and social change, and other essays* (London, 1967), p.193-236.
19. Barbeyrac, preface to Pufendorf, section VIII, p.17 (emphasis added).
20. Barbeyrac, preface to Pufendorf, section X, p.35. On the reception of these theses in the Italian Enlightenment, see Giuseppe Ricuperati, *L'esperienza civile e religiosa di Pietro Giannone* (Milan and Naples, 1970), p.571ff.

letters'.[21] The charismatic figure of the Arminian thinker Grotius was thus hailed as a great sign of God's providence. This great regulator and founder of the new natural law had opened up a new period of religious reform within Christianity, which was finally led back to original natural and rational morality. Thanks to him and to those who followed in his wake, such as Pufendorf and Thomasius, modern natural law became not only a bastion against atheism – which in itself gave it prestige and public importance – but also a milestone in the history of Christianity, which finally stood to regain its primitive purity. In this new approach, a rationalist view of religion and a sincere spirit of reform came together, in a singular mixture of innovation and conservatism.

There were, however, significant risks and ambiguities in the attempt to locate morality within this universalistic natural religion. The main difficulty lay in combining modern scientific reason and ancient Christian revelation in such a way that the latter did not create obstacles for the former, taking into due account the contrasting arguments put forward by the followers of Spinoza and Bayle on one side and of Bossuet and Jurieu on the other.

The only way that seemed feasible, and was therefore widely adopted, was to simplify the message of the Gospels reducing it to just a few tenets, as in John Locke's reasonable Christianity. In this way, it could come as close as possible to universal natural religion, but without turning into a form of deism. It would eschew fanaticism, and avoid providing more ammunition to atheists and freethinkers, and especially to those who, like Irish thinker John Toland, claimed to adhere to Locke's positions while in fact he had been majorly influenced by Bruno and Spinoza, and were now speaking in open terms of a Christianity without mysteries, and of life and movement as inherent in matter.

In his difficult search for a new equilibrium in religious matters, Barbeyrac ended up linking natural law as theory of the duties of man, and the pursuit of solid foundations for religion, with the Huguenot refugees' Socinianism and their struggle to reform Christianity. However, it is worth reiterating that what we see here is not simply an updated form of the old authority principle on a rational and scientific basis, a new Scholasticism this time in the name of Newton and Locke. There was much more to this, and it is still quite difficult to evaluate its results from a historical point of view. Conservatism

21. Barbeyrac, preface to Pufendorf, section XII, p.36.

and radicalism, moderation and the desire to look ahead coexist on every page and at every key moment of this complex enterprise, which involved a considerable number of people all over Europe. In this respect, talking of generic and sometimes anachronistic categories such as a radical or moderate Enlightenment does not really take us very far.[22]

Just to remain within the remit of the present study, for instance, it is undoubtedly true that the heterogeneous group of thinkers around Barbeyrac effectively moved in what appear to be two opposite directions. On the one hand they reinforced the moral science of duties, thus having a moderate and even conservative effect. On the other hand, they opened the way to the rediscovery of the medieval theories on the rights of man, which could have radical and even subversive political implications in limiting the power of the sovereign. The coexistence of duties and rights within this representation of natural law, however, appears contradictory only from a philosophical point of view, and in terms of an abstract history of ideas. It becomes perfectly understandable, however, in historical terms, when we examine the actual documents and events that attest how Barbeyrac and the other Huguenot refugees were affected by the revocation of the Edict of Nantes in October 1685. In this light, the subversive character of their ideas comes across with absolute clarity.

22. On the controversial use of these categories, which belong more to the field of philosophy than to that of history, see *Qu'est-ce que les Lumières 'radicales'? Libertinage, athéisme et spinozisme dans le tournant philosophique de l'âge classique*, ed. Catherine Secrétan, Tristan Dagron and Laurent Bove (Paris, 2007). See also Silvia Berti, *Anticristianesimo e libertà: studi sull'Illuminismo radicale europeo* (Bologna, 2012).

5. The return of Antigone: freedom of conscience and the limits of sovereignty

With the revocation of the Edict of Nantes, Louis XIV – Most Christian King, Bossuet's 'new Constantine', the restorer of France's religious unity – unleashed the final, momentous phase of that civil conflict that had beset Europe since the time of Luther. In the name of 'religious cleansing' and the Catholic 'reconquest', over 200,000 French Huguenots were forced to flee to nearby Protestant countries such as Switzerland, England, Germany or the Netherlands. They had been subjected to all kinds of violence and intimidations, like the infamous *dragonnades*, whereby families who refused to convert to Catholicism were obliged to host military troops under their roof, which left them open to looting, torture, rape and, in cases of extreme resistance, downright murder. These practices had directly affected many French regions, and indirectly the whole of Europe.[1] Ancient oppositions flared up again in several regions, as in the *camisard* guerrilla in the Cévennes, or in the struggle between the Waldensians and Victor Amadeus II in Piedmont. The ensuing Protestant diaspora became the background for the new discussions on tolerance and freedom of conscience, a fascinating debate that would alter the terms of the relationship between political and religious power. From the injunction in Matthew's Gospel to 'Render unto Caesar the things which are Caesar's; and unto God the things that are God's', from the struggle between Church and State and of opposite religious denominations among themselves (an issue sometimes described as that of 'ecclesiastical tolerance'), the focus now shifted onto civil toleration in the modern sense and the relationship between the individual and sovereign power, exemplified by Louis XIV's aggressive militarised

1. Cf. Elisabeth Labrousse, *Essai sur la révocation de l'Edit de Nantes* (Geneva and Paris, 1985).

absolutism. Ultimately this led to the recognition, for the first time in the history of the Western world, of the natural and inalienable right of the individual to religious freedom against any form of power.

As we have already seen, among the first to intervene in this debate was Lutheran thinker Samuel von Pufendorf, with his 1687 *De habitu religionis christianae ad vitam civilem*. Pufendorf was a determined supporter of the separation between religion and political power. He argued that the State was not intended to have a religious role and that, for its part, the Church should not claim any form of political power, nor should its ministers be assigned the role of state officials. In the 1648 treaties of Westphalia the word *tolerantia* itself acquires a new and more technical meaning than the general one of virtuous forbearance towards others whose truth was considered in any case to be inferior to ours, and was now used to ratify the existence of three different religious confessions: the Lutheran, the Catholic and the Calvinist. This is similar to the way in which, after the *dragonnades* of the Most Christian King, it had become necessary to rethink the principle of *cuius regio, illius et religio*. Toleration now became a precious virtue in itself, and the only way to avoid a bloodbath within individual states. It was something like a truce, a suspension of the consequences of hostilities, while the opposition between different religious opinions inevitably remained. Its cause would be embraced by any enlightened sovereign concerned about the economic and political needs of his state.

In fact, Pufendorf followed Hobbes and Spinoza in advocating the primacy of politics and civil power over religion. In order to avoid the negative consequences of the spread of heresies and fanaticism and of the conflict among different religious sects, it would be a good thing, in his view, if the sovereign gave a clear indication of which religion should be considered the official one in his state. This return to an absolutistic view of religious unity within a state, according to a pattern that was typical of the seventeenth century, was deeply obnoxious to many Protestant refugees. Jean Le Clerc, for instance, compared it unfavourably with the far more liberal practice adopted by the Dutch Republic, where religious denominations of every kind, both Christian and non, coexisted peaceably and without discrimination, and even non-believers were effectively tolerated.[2]

Nevertheless, Pufendorf's contribution, with its call for a clear separation between Church and State, remained central to the debate

2. Cf. Fiammetta Palladini, 'Stato, Chiesa e tolleranza nel pensiero di S. Pufendorf', in *Formazione storica della alterità*, ed. H. Méchoulan *et al.*, vol.2, p.751-86.

on tolerance. These ideas found important expression in 1689, in the *Epistola de tolerantia* that John Locke wrote while living as a refugee in Holland. In the same year, in his home country the Toleration Act had granted freedom of religion to dissident Protestants, not as a recognised natural right, but as an administrative measure that lifted the sanctions set by previous legislation. Within this political and institutional framework, Locke devotes large amounts of space to defining the functions and characteristics of the Church as a 'free and voluntary society', an institution that was entirely separate and had entirely different functions from the State.[3] This separation between politics and religion and the rejection of coercion, so that faith could remain an essentially private matter, are presented in this letter as the only viable solution to ensure the peaceable coexistence of various religious denominations within a political community. Locke traces the ultimate foundation of the right to toleration back to the Gospel and to the spirit of charity of ancient Christianity, pointing out that 'there is absolutely no such thing, under the Gospel, as a Christian commonwealth.'[4] Locke could not subscribe to Bayle's alarming vision of a republic of virtuous atheists as the one best suited to guarantee the practice of toleration. For him, a simplified, reasonable religion, which acknowledged the different purposes of Church and State, remained the indispensable premise for peaceable civil coexistence, the very definition, in fact, of a morality of custom. In this respect, both Catholics and atheists were excluded from any treatise on tolerance. The former, insofar as they were slavish followers of the pope's authority, were unable to accept the political power of the sovereign that in fact was the sole guarantee of religious freedom. The latter denied the divine foundation of the social bond, on which all morality, promises and oaths were based: 'The taking away of God, though but even in thought, dissolves all.'[5]

Locke's discussion, then, was still circumscribed within the Church–State dualism, and toleration was in fact still a form of tolerance of the other that was confined to Christian believers. A clear signal of the limitations of tolerance in this sense was the exclusion of atheists, even more than of Catholics. Locke still saw the religious freedom of

3. John Locke, 'A letter concerning toleration', in *Two treatises of government: and a letter concerning toleration*, ed. Ian Shapiro (New Haven, CT, and London, 2003), p.211-54 (224).
4. Locke, 'Letter concerning toleration', p.239.
5. Locke, 'Letter concerning toleration', p.246.

the individual in scriptural terms ('The Truth will set you free') and in the Augustinian sense of being part of God's people and as such being granted the ability to avoid sin: it was the freedom to believe in a superior salvific truth, outside which was only error. There is no room in Locke's vision for the arguments of the deists or those put forward by Pierre Bayle, or for the idea of a universal and natural religion without revelation, churches or formal structure of any kind. Equally extraneous to his thought is the need to free morality from all theological concerns, or the idea of toleration as absolute freedom of conscience and an intrinsic inalienable right of the individual against all forms of sovereignty.

As well as in Jean Barbeyrac's prefaces, we find these concerns in the *Dissertatio de religione ab imperio iure gentium libera* read by Gerard Noodt as rector of Leiden University on 8 February 1706. This oration represents a milestone in the history of toleration both because of the originality of the theses that it puts forward and for its instant success, with it being immediately translated into four languages.[6] The intervention in this debate of an illustrious jurist and historian of Roman law such as Noodt marked a high point in a process that had seen the furious controversies sparked off by the works of Spinoza and Bayle, the rise of the libertine and deist traditions, and the study of the religious experience of many different peoples in order to determine their common and universal values.[7] Noodt's oration shows that this process had now come to the attention of those among the reformers

6. Cf. Antonio Rotondò's entry on 'Tolérance', in *Le Monde des Lumières*, ed. V. Ferrone and D. Roche, p.71-85 (79-80). An illuminating discussion of Noodt and his fortune is found in Fabrizio Lomonaco, *Tolleranza: momenti e percorsi della modernità fino a Voltaire* (Naples, 2005), p.53ff. See also Joris van Eijnatten, *Liberty and concord in the United Provinces: religious toleration and the public in the eighteenth-century Netherlands* (Leiden, 2003), p.259ff.
7. The nascent awareness of these issues in Europe and the new cultural and intellectual climate inaugurated by Noodt are well represented by the popularity of the monumental series of volumes on *Les Cérémonies et coutumes religieuses de tous les peuples du monde*, richly illustrated by Bernard Picart and first published in Amsterdam in 1723 by Jean-Frédéric Bernard. This series presented religion as a historical and anthropological phenomenon to be studied through the means of reason. It devoted whole volumes to the denunciation of *Superstitions anciennes et modernes et préjugés vulgaires qui ont induit les peuples à des usages contraires à la religion*, the universal tendency towards religion, and the possible material origins of religions from every part of the world. See Lynn Hunt, Margaret C. Jacob and Wijnand Mijnhardt, *The Book that changed Europe: Picart and Bernard's religious ceremonies of the world* (Cambridge, MA, 2010).

of Christianity who were open to new developments. In particular, Noodt discusses toleration in terms of the religious freedom of the individual, and with two main tenets in mind: the epistemological relativity of religious truth, and religious pluralism as a positive element in civil society.

Noodt had absorbed from Grotius a Neo-Stoic belief in the *dignitas hominis*, and his main concern was to link *libertas* with rationality and natural rights as part of the very essence of human nature. However, he had also taken on board Bayle's modern brand of scepticism. Hence his stipulation, against dogmatic theologians of all times, that there were no undisputed or absolute truth criteria in religion. Who could establish who was right and who was wrong, when faced with so many different religious experiences, so many revelations in the course of human history? The Hebrew or Muslim God, the deities worshipped in America and Asia – were they 'true' or 'false' compared to the Christian God? How could we disregard the fact that there was no single universally valid religious formula that God had revealed to mankind? Even Descartes's rule of evidence, when applied to religious knowledge, did not produce a single faith in the same way that there was a single arithmetic.[8] When it came to religious knowledge, one must look at what was likely or probable. Things like spirituality, religiosity, faith were best expressed in the intimacy of one's conscience, being deeply subjective inner feelings and a matter of personal choice. Above all, this concerned the ethical responsibility of the individual, who was now aware that the pathway to truth had become extremely confused, difficult and elusive.[9] One thing was certain, however. This emphasis on individual conscience enjoined all forms of absolute sovereignty to respect man's natural right to the free pursuit of religious truth. Thus it became contrary to God's will, and therefore immoral, to persecute those who claimed for all mankind the *ius ad libertatem religiosam*.[10]

8. Cf. the passages from the *Dissertatio* cited in Lomonaco, *Tolleranza*, p.69.
9. Cf. Lomonaco, *Tolleranza*, p.75.
10. The Catholic Church first recognised this right to religious freedom as a natural right of man with the Second Vatican Council (1962-1965) and the declaration *Dignitatis humanae*. On the difficulties inherent in this decision, which went contrary to a centuries-old emphasis on 'Truth' as dogma, see Vincenzo Ferrone, 'Il cristianesimo e i diritti dell'uomo', in *Le religioni e il mondo moderno*, ed. Giovanni Filoramo, vol.1: *Cristianesimo*, ed. Daniele Menozzi (Turin, 2008), p.554-68. See also Silvia Scatena, *La fatica della libertà: l'elaborazione della dichiarazione* Dignitatis humanae *sulla libertà religiosa del Vaticano II* (Bologna, 2003).

It was as if the tragic figure of Antigone had come back onto the stage from Sophocles' Ancient Greece. This time, however, she had acquired a new language, a new consciousness of the natural and inalienable rights of man. What she was defending from the grasp of political power was no longer the ancestral tradition of the cult of the dead, or her blood ties and sibling love – themselves derived from God's command in contrast with the will of the despot. For the first time in history, what was at stake was the power and prerogatives of individual conscience.[11]

As a historian, Noodt draws on the example of those great Roman emperors, such as Valentinian I or Marcus Aurelius, who had brought peace and serenity to Rome by publicly supporting religious pluralism, toleration, freedom of conscience and the fight against fanaticism. Intolerance and the persecution of heretics had first arrived on the scene with the Christians themselves, and especially with Augustine's objectionable interpretation of the Gospel precept *compelle intrare* (Luke 14.23) as an injunction to compel potential believers to accept the *Truth* of the Church, if necessary through the use of violence. Here was the ultimate legitimation for the brutal attacks on other religious currents, from the persecution of the Donatists in Late Antiquity down to the Inquisition, the invectives of theologians either side of the Catholic–Protestant divide and Louis XIV's *dragonnades.*

Barbeyrac agreed with Noodt on many points. He immediately translated his *Dissertatio* as *Du pouvoir des souverains et de la liberté de conscience* (Amsterdam, 1707), thus highlighting from the very title the new claim that would alter forever the traditional discourse on tolerance. Himself a Huguenot refugee, Barbeyrac was perfectly aware of the limits of Pufendorf's discussion, with its absolutist bias, when set against contemporary events. Accordingly, in his notes to the 1706 French translation of the *De iure naturae*, he criticises Pufendorf's failure to deal with the *vexata quaestio* of individual conscience as the link between *lex* and human action, stressing that natural law must address the predicament of the subject faced with an unjust or immoral command from his sovereign. Barbeyrac was also not overly convinced by the way in which Pufendorf and Locke looked to the redefinition of the roles of Church and State as a solution to the problem of toleration. In fact, even the sociability principle in itself did not provide a solid enough basis for modern natural law. Two more issues should be

11. There is a vast bibliography on the figure of Antigone in Western culture. For a particularly effective portrayal, see Bloch, *Natural law*, p.105ff.

taken into account: the autonomous existence of individuals, with their passions and, above all, self-interest, and the observance of a natural religion that indicated the duties of man before God.

According to Barbeyrac, the duty to defend one's God-given life guaranteed an individual's natural right to self-defence, even with recourse to violence. The natural right to freedom of conscience also came within this sphere of the safeguard of life and liberty. This right was absolutely inalienable.[12] Contrary to what Hobbes and Pufendorf claimed in their attempt not to undermine royal power, freedom of religion was guaranteed directly by the natural rights of the individual. It was a private and inviolable sphere, off limits to power, and a moral curb on the autonomy of politics. With reference to Algernon Sidney's 1648 *Discourses concerning government*, with their rather general discussion of the legislation required in order to safeguard the *native rights* of the individual, Barbeyrac appeals to the Gospel and to natural law as a defence against the power of the sovereign for those who want to 'follow the light of [their] own conscience': 'the people have as natural and as unquestionable a right to defend their religion by force of arms against a sovereign who endeavours to compel them to renounce it, or to forbid them the free exercise of it, as to defend their lives, their estates, and liberties against the attempts of a tyrant.'[13]

Noodt had gone down the same dangerous path as Bayle, with his scepticism and relativism: in order to undermine the dogmatic and intolerant view of truth, he had upheld the existence of a subjective natural right to religious freedom from a philosophical point of view. Barbeyrac, by contrast, chooses the much safer Lockean alternative of reasonable Christianity and natural religion as ultimate foundation of the new natural law. As is discussed in a 1731 article in the *Bibliothèque raisonnée des ouvrages des savants de l'Europe* – a journal to which Barbeyrac contributed regularly – the recourse to violence in religious matters was not only an attack on man's most sacred natural rights, but a dishonour for religion itself.[14] It was a betrayal of the Gospel's message, which, if correctly interpreted, spoke of tolerance and freedom.

12. Cf. Petter Korkman, 'Life, liberty and the pursuit of happiness: human rights in Barbeyrac and Burlamaqui', in *Transformations in medieval and early-modern rights discourse*, ed. Virpi Mäkinen and Petter Korkman (Dordrecht, 2006), p.257-83 (264). On these issues in general see also *New essays on the political thought of the Huguenots of the Refuge*, ed. John Christian Laursen (Leiden, 1995).
13. Barbeyrac's notes to VII, 8, 5 (n.2) in Pufendorf, *Law of nature and nations*, p.719.
14. Cf. Rotondò, 'Tolérance', p.81.

In his 'Préface du traducteur' to the 1707 translation of Noodt's work, Barbeyrac demonstrates his awareness of the importance of the new theory of natural rights in moral, religious and political terms.[15] In light of the 'despotic power' of the sovereign and 'persecution for matters of conscience' (p.xviii), he urges his readers to reflect on whether a sovereign's power should indeed be as absolute and all-encompassing as it has been considered hitherto, and on 'what authority one man may have over another' (p.xvi): 'Are the people made for the prince, or the prince for the people? Ought we to worship a divinity we do not acknowledge, or one we do [worship] in a way we believe to be disagreeable to him?' (p.xvi-xvii).

After Noodt, the answer to these questions must necessarily be found in the natural right of every individual to freedom of religion: 'Is there any mortal man', asks Barbeyrac in his introduction to Noodt, 'who has a title to lord it over the consciences of another?' (p.xvii). The dominant political discourse on absolute power, the divine right of kings, and the limits of sovereignty was being subverted by the self-evident idea of the natural rights of all human beings: 'Can we, who are men ourselves, need to be taught what are *the natural rights of men*, and how far each of them would or can renounce them?' (p.xvi; emphasis added).

Of course, this was only a first step in the long journey to the modern theory of the 'rights of man' developed by the Enlightenment in the course of the eighteenth century. There was still much to be clarified in order to obtain an overall picture. Above all, we are still far from an idea of the relationship between man and God that somewhat attenuates the overwhelming presence of the latter in the earthly life of the former. Barbeyrac himself did not fully understand all the elements of this new discourse, in either a philosophical or a political sense. Among the many and sometimes contradictory implications of the autonomy of the individual, he focused exclusively on its moral character as limitation of sovereign power, in line with his idea of natural law as moral science of divinely prescribed duties.

In his 1724 French translation of Grotius, Barbeyrac returns to the subject of the sovereign's violation of the natural rights of human beings. In his preface, the translator upholds in part the political

15. Cf. Jean Barbeyrac, 'A preface to the following discourses', prefixed to Gerard Noodt, *The Power of the sovereign, and the right of liberty of conscience*, translated by John Savage (London, J. Humfreys for Andrew Bell, 1708), p.xv-xxiv (page references given within the text).

theses of his friend John Locke. Above all, he defends Pufendorf and Grotius himself against Fénelon and Ramsay, who had accused them of being too much in favour of absolute power and of subscribing to a crude brand of Machiavellian political realism.[16] His hostility to despotism and its adherents was confined to the religious and moral sphere. It never developed into an actual political choice, a republican spirit that advocated the sovereignty of the people or their widened participation and self-government in defence of natural rights.[17] Nevertheless, Barbeyrac's work represents an important milestone in our reconstruction of the slow but steady emergence, out of its medieval past, of a language of rights that would change the history of the Western world.

The very fact that Barbeyrac translated Grotius was a step in this direction. It was the Dutch thinker who carried over to modern times the few little-known references to natural rights that are found scattered throughout the Middle Ages. Thanks to Grotius, the idea of subjective rights that surfaced here and there within traditional objective law started, briefly but importantly, to move towards the modern construction of the I, of the individual as 'person': a free and autonomous human being among equals, in possession of inalienable rights.

In his *De iure belli ac pacis* Grotius had carefully distinguished among three meanings of *ius*, the ancient word for right or law: 1) according to traditional Thomist natural law, 'what is right' in the cosmos and in the nature of things; 2) the positive meaning of 'law' or 'rule'; 3) in relation to a person, a subjective characteristic or 'faculty' of the individual. The latter point represented the great linguistic as well as conceptual innovation. As Grotius explains, 'in [this] sense *Right* is a moral quality annexed to the person, enabling him to *have, or do*, something justly.'[18] Juridically, this *ius* typically manifested itself as legitimate authority or jurisdiction over something that was due to an

16. Cf. Barbeyrac, 'Préface' to Grotius, p.xxxiii.
17. Cf. T. J. Hochstrasser, 'Conscience and reason: the natural law theory of Jean Barbeyrac', *The Historical journal* 36:2 (1993), p.289-308 (307-308); Helena Rosenblatt, *Rousseau and Geneva: from the First Discourse to the Social Contract, 1749-1762* (Cambridge, 1997), p.165.
18. Grotius, *Rights*, I, 1, 4, p.138. See also the Latin original: 'Quo sensu ius est, qualitas moralis personae competens ad aliquid iuste *habendum vel agendum*' (*De iure belli ac pacis libri tres*, Paris, n.n., 1625, p.4). Emphasis added. For an antecedent of this idea in the Second Scholastics, and especially in Francisco Suárez, see Tierney, *Idea of natural rights*, p.50.

individual by contract. However, it represented above all something that is *proprium* to the subject, a form of 'power [...] over ourselves, which is termed liberty'.[19]

This freedom of the individual to think and do certain things was something that still needed to be properly defined. For instance, in his *Leviathan* Hobbes would gloss it as the absence of external impediments, echoing Galileo's principle of inertia. But what is important is that liberty was now finally placed within the remit of natural law and founded at the same time on self-preservation and on equal respect for others' rights. From the point of view of our investigation, however, Grotius' discourse on rights has several limitations. He does not go far in identifying and defining a subject's right to liberty. Because Grotius was writing at a time of civil and religious war, he tends to circumscribe and qualify this natural right of man to self-determination for the sake of security and peace. Grotius denies some essential characteristics of this right, such as its universality and inalienability, maintaining that there were entire peoples who were naturally inclined to submit themselves to the rule of others (*De iure*, I, 3, 8). As we shall see when we discuss the accusations made by Rousseau, Beccaria and the *philosophes* against Grotius, this led the Dutch thinker to uphold the right of conquest, the absolute and divine right of kings, even the lucrative slave trade, all of which are far removed from the Enlightenment language of the rights of man.

For his part, Pufendorf, for whom the restoration of a strong authority principle was a primary concern, immediately abandoned the idea of subjective right and its connection with individual freedom, insisting instead on sociability and the communal duties of man as part of the creation of a new moral science of natural law. Even though in Pufendorf's work there are significant references to natural rights, including in precise linguistic terms, these are consistently linked to the idea of duties, as a logical consequence of a system that did not take the subject's *proprium* into account.[20] If anything, a significant step forward is taken by Hobbes when he redefines the character and

19. Grotius, *Rights*, I, 1, 5, p.138. On the construct of *proprium*, see Costa, *Civitas*, vol.1, p.152ff.
20. See, for instance, Pufendorf, *Law of nature and nations*, I, 1, 7, p.4ff., where *droits* are presented as a consequence of duties, thus confirming, albeit only in the case of Pufendorf and his numerous followers, the thesis put forward in Knud Haakonssen, 'The moral conservatism of natural rights', in *Natural law and civil sovereignty*, ed. I. Hunter and D. Saunders, p.27-42.

foundations of natural law on an entirely subjective basis, as he asserts in the *Leviathan* that *ius naturale* 'is the liberty each man hath, to use his own power, as he will himself, for the preservation of his own nature; that is to say, of his own life'.[21]

For the first time in history, man's natural and inalienable right to life was publicly recognised and subsumed within a person's *proprium*, as a form of individual power, a subject's freedom to act, which in turn became the cornerstone of the modern State. However, in terms of Hobbes' 'social contract', this right to life and self-preservation became a natural and primary law that brought with it certain obligations. As such, it opened the door to the intervention of absolute sovereignty in all other aspects of individual liberty. This is the reason why Hobbes was attacked by many refugee thinkers, including Barbeyrac, who were ready to defend the autonomy of the religious sphere and the inalienable natural right to religious freedom at all costs and against all despots.

The way in which Spinoza contributed to the progressive rise of the Enlightenment language of natural rights was quite different and, its importance and originality notwithstanding, beset by a number of unresolved issues. Spinoza finally gives a definite shape and an actual philosophical and juridical framework to the struggle for *libertas philosophandi* that had been set in motion by figures such as Bruno, Campanella, Galileo and Grotius, and he does so through the new language of rights. In 1670, the 'natural right' of the individual to freedom of thought and of expression in every field is brought to the attention of public opinion all over Europe by a work that would scandalise the world, and whose title is worth quoting in full: *Theological-political treatise, containing several discourses which demonstrate that freedom to philosophize may not only be allowed without danger to piety and the stability of the republic but cannot be refused without destroying the peace of the republic and piety itself.*[22] Spinoza shared Hobbes' harsh political realism and attention to the world of utilitarian passions. But, unlike the English philosopher, he fervently believed that 'the true purpose of the state is in fact freedom'. A political entity based on reason could not limit itself to the safeguard of security and of the natural and inalienable right to life. As Spinoza writes in chapter 20 of his treatise, 'Where it is shown that in a free state everyone is allowed to think what they wish and to say what they think': 'it is impossible for

21. Thomas Hobbes, *Leviathan*, ed. J. C. A. Gaskin (Oxford, 1998), I, 14, 1, p.86.
22. Spinoza, *Theological-political treatise*, p.1.

one person's mind to be absolutely under another's control. For no one can transfer to another person his natural right, or ability, to think freely and make his own judgments about any matter whatsoever, and cannot be compelled to do so.'[23]

Here again, as in Grotius, we find that what defines the subject's *proprium* and his inalienable quality as human being is determined by the nexus between liberty and property. To be free means first of all to be fully in charge of oneself and of the way in which one reaches out to the outside world. The words used by Spinoza make this absolutely clear: 'everyone, by the supreme right of nature, remains master of their own thoughts' (20, 4, p.251). They have full mastery over themselves and over their right and power of thought and speech. This portion of an individual's 'power' was absolutely inalienable with respect to sovereignty. Spinoza points to the 'democratic state' as the form of government that was closest to natural order and that was therefore among the most apt to safeguard this individual power: 'In a democracy no one transfers their natural right to another [...] but rather to the majority of the whole society of which they are a part' (16, 11, p.202). Unfortunately, Spinoza died before he could finish his *Tractatus politicus*, where he planned to give a more detailed discussion of democracy, which he defines as 'a united gathering of people which collectively has the sovereign right to do all that it has the power to do'.[24]

This original but also dangerously ambiguous thesis will be explored again by Jean-Jacques Rousseau. This omnipotent 'general will' that was meant to safeguard the natural rights of the individual could in fact prove as damaging as the absolute will of the prince. From the point of view of European public opinion, Spinoza's contribution to the rise of the modern language of natural rights consisted first and foremost in his defence of the inalienable right to freedom of thought. With obvious reference to Spinoza's theses, Anthony Collins, in his 1713 *Discourse of free-thinking*, would define freedom of thought uncompromisingly as 'a man's right'.[25] Nevertheless, it is undoubtedly an exaggeration to see Spinoza as the father of the rights of man.[26]

23. Spinoza, *Theological-political treatise*, 20, 6, p.250.
24. Spinoza, *Theological-political treatise*, 16, 8, p.200. Spinoza started writing his *Tractatus politicus* in 1676, the year before he died.
25. Anthony Collins, *A Discourse of free-thinking, occasion'd by the rise and growth of a sect call'd free-thinkers* (London, n.n., 1713), p.12.
26. Cf., by Jonathan Israel, *Democratic Enlightenment: philosophy, revolution and human*

In this sense, John Locke, for instance, played a far more important role. Among his contemporaries and the members of the Republic of Letters the English philosopher was unanimously considered the first great propagator of the language of rights in Europe. Locke's reflections on property as a natural right already show an awareness of the political importance of this language. Barbeyrac considered his treatise on education among the fundamental tools for the introduction of the elites to the 'natural rights of men'.[27] However, there are other respects in which Locke's contribution deserves more attention than it has received so far. As we shall see in the following chapter, without his concept of 'person' the Enlightenment could not have formulated its theory of the rights of man as an integral part of the eighteenth-century 'sciences of man'.[28] This is a complex theme, which is only just beginning to receive the detailed attention that it deserves.

---

rights, 1750-1790 (Oxford, 2011) and 'Philosophy, religion and the controversy about basic human rights in 1789', in *Self-evident truths? Human rights and the Enlightenment*, ed. Kate E. Tunstall (New York, 2012), p.111-25. Israel does not take into account the significant ambiguities in Spinoza's discussion of the universality and equality of the right to freedom for all human beings. For instance, in the *Theological-political treatise* the right to vote in the democratic system does not extend to slaves, or to women, who 'have not by nature equal right with men' (*Benedict de Spinoza's political treatise*, translated by A. H. Gossett, ed. R. H. M. Elwes, Raleigh, NC, 2001; translation originally published in 1883), p.61.

27. Barbeyrac, preface to Pufendorf, section XXXI, p.83.
28. The importance of this aspect was first highlighted in John W. Yolton, *John Locke and the way of ideas* (London, 1956).

6. The person as autonomous and conscious individual: John Locke

When and how did the idea of a 'person' first come into being? What difference did this concept make in the history of the individual in the Western world – a history that is still waiting to be written? Recent anthropological research has highlighted the scientific hypothesis of man's biological incompleteness. According to this thesis, the human being is seriously biologically challenged. We are incomplete and defenceless animals that would have been long extinct if it had not been for our recourse to what, today, we call 'culture', i.e. the profitable interaction between mind and body through the workings of our brain.[1] The 'person' as construct thus comes fully within the sphere of 'culture'. It is an attempt by the human animal to situate itself and its I in relation to its environment and to others in order to ensure its own survival and that of its species. The concept of 'person' was unknown in Ancient Greece. In Heraclitus' discussion of *Logos*, Parmenides on *Being* or Plato on *Idea* there is hardly any reflection on the nature of the individual. Significantly, the term *persona* itself first appeared in Latin. It is found in Phaedrus' fables, where it designates the mask that actors wore during a performance. It was first used in a philosophical sense within the current of Stoicism, as slave-born Epictetus mused on how every individual – here for the first time viewed as a self-sufficient and independent being – must wear with dignity and wisdom whatever mask they have been assigned on the world's stage. The rise of Christianity gave a decisive impulse to the centuries-long process that would lead to the 'cultural' characterisation of the person. This process would include the shift from man's dependency on the biblical God to the progressive attribution to a now autonomous subject of qualities such as liberty and responsibility,

1. See Clifford Geertz, *The Interpretation of cultures* (New York, 1973), p.55ff.

rationality, will or the ability to act and to love. Above all, in the seventeenth and eighteenth centuries, man would be endowed with a series of natural rights.

It all began when the concept of person was applied to the debate on the nature of God. Tertullian was the first to speak of an identity of substance (*homoousía*) and different persons in relation to the Father, the Son and the Holy Spirit.[2] This anticipated a religious tradition and a way of thinking that would be consolidated with the Creed imposed by the Council of Nicea in 325 AD. In the course of the countless theological disputes on the Trinity and Christ's divine nature that followed, the concept of person was progressively adapted and extended from the nature of God as Three in One to man's identity. In a version of the Aristotelian nexus between form and substance, Christian thinkers found in the human soul the *principium individuationis* or essence of the subject created in the image of God. Man's mortal body was its form, and the immortal soul, which was God's seal and whose existence preceded that of the body, became the substance that characterised a specific person. For a Christian, the expression 'to animate' (from *anima* = 'soul') soon took on the meaning of 'to generate' or 'give life' to a person. For centuries scholars discussed at which precise moment the rational soul entered the body and transformed it into a person. Semen was considered to be the vehicle of the soul (as in Tertullian), and the moment had to be within the third day from conception.[3] In 314 AD the Synod of Ancyra condemned the practice of abortion on the basis of the widespread opinion that the foetus, which was God's work, already had a soul. In this way, the right to life at every stage of an individual's existence became a fundamental and inalienable prerogative, while at the same time, as God's right over his creatures, it was removed from the sphere of man's will. This is, of course, a bioethical question that has exercised Church representatives down to our own day. After all, the main mission that Jesus assigned to his Church was to ensure the safety of Christian souls. With Boethius Christianity acquired its first important definition of what constitutes a 'person': 'Persona est naturae rationalis individua substantia.' It is easy to see the theological character of this declaration that a person is an individual embodiment of the rational soul.[4]

2. See J. N. D. Kelly, *Early Christian doctrines*, 5th edn (London, 1977), p.109-15.
3. Cf. Adriano Prosperi, *Infanticide, secular justice, and religious debate in early modern Europe* (Turnhout, 2016), p.272ff.
4. Prosperi, *Infanticide*, p.304.

This idea of person, with its specific foundation in a religious concept of the individual, ended up having contrasting implications. On the historical level, it gave metaphysical legitimacy to a person as the possessor of a God-derived soul, which was destined for eternal life and therefore worthy of the utmost care and protection.[5] However, it also enclosed this very important concept within theological, and therefore ecclesiastical, boundaries. Despite the influence of Stoic natural law and its acknowledgement of the autonomy and moral responsibility of the subject in the here and now, Christian individualism remained unsurprisingly confined to the sphere of a subject's religious consciousness and of their most elevated and spiritual component: the rational soul. It never really became a substantial social or political presence. In fact, it acquired a sectarian and radicalised quality, as an individual's point of reference and the very roots of an individual's identity were situated outside the everyday world, in the constant and all-important communion of the soul with God.[6]

In the fifteenth century, again, the proclamation of the dignity of the human person arose mostly from the religious elements of the *pia philosophia* and its Neo-Platonic and hermetic currents. Man was defined as a *magnum miraculum*, a fragment of the divine. This was the result of the interaction between the idea of the incarnation of Christ, elements of gnostic philosophy and the pagan Stoicism of Cicero, with its emphasis on the dignity of man.[7] However, it was at this time that a more philological view started to loosen the traditional nexus between person and substance. Lorenzo Valla, for instance, initiated a significant shift away from the Christian view by denying that the concept of person could be described entirely in terms of the soul and of a spiritual substance. In linguistic terms, 'person' identified a way of

5. See Marcel Mauss' important 1938 lecture, available as 'A category of the human mind: the notion of person; the notion of self', translated by W. D. Hall, in *The Category of the person: anthropology, philosophy, history*, ed. Michael Carrithers, Steven Collins and Steven Lukes (Cambridge, 1985), p.1-25.
6. See Troeltsch, *Social teaching*, vol.1, p.55ff., on the difference between Christianity's transcendental religious individualism and the modern secular concept of the individual as an autonomous entity. On this subject see also Dumont, *Essays on individualism*; Carrithers, Collins and Lukes, *Category of the person*; Charles Taylor, *Sources of the self: the making of the modern identity* (Cambridge, 1989); *L'Individu dans la pensée moderne, XVIe-XVIIIe siècles / L'individuo nel pensiero moderno, secoli XVI-XVII*, ed. Gian Mario Cazzaniga and Yves Charles Zarka (Pisa, 1995).
7. Cf. Eugenio Garin, 'La "dignitas hominis" e la letteratura patristica' (1938), in his *Interpretazioni del Rinascimento*, ed. Michele Ciliberto (Rome, 2009), p.1-32 (10ff.).

being that distinguished each individual within its species. Montaigne added a psychological dimension to the discussion of the profound nature of the human ego, as he highlighted how one human subject could harbour different persons or characters. In this way, Montaigne gave new impulse to the enquiry into our perception of reality and the function of consciousness and the passions.

Locke's contribution to the reflection on this subject in the second edition of his *Essay concerning human understanding* would radically alter the Christian substantialist view of the person as based on the rational soul. This came at the end of a complex process within modern philosophy in the course of which increasing importance had been attributed to the role of consciousness as the *pincipium individuationis* of the subject and its cognitive mechanisms. This process had begun with philosophers such as René Descartes, but had certainly been facilitated by the weakening of the bond between man and God as a result of the European wars of religion. This remains true notwithstanding the resounding success of the Boyle Lectures and of the intelligent design hypothesis that was implicit in Newton's mechanistic universe: a universe that posited the necessity of a watchmaker God who stood, mathematical calculations in hand, and constantly recharged the world's ever-decreasing energy, as opposed to the idle or absent God of the controversy between Leibniz and Newtonian philosopher Samuel Clarke.[8]

Whether active or idle, for the European intellectual elites this architect God was linked to a new kind of deist religion: a religion with no churches, revelations, dogmas, ecclesiastical hierarchy or priests of any kind. This was a natural religion that saw itself as akin to philosophy and science and that, unlike historic religions, defined the relationship between man and God in universal terms. And not only that: man was now placed at the centre of the relationship and acquired ever more responsibilities, while God receded into the distance. In a new application of Grotius' *etsi Deus non daretur*, this God remained the ultimate foundation of legality in the world, but showed no wish to intervene in the petty lives of human beings. After many centuries, the Irish monk Pelagius was making a comeback at the expense of Augustine in the great debate over tolerance and freedom of conscience. In his determination to uphold the centrality of grace and predestination in view of the fallen state of man after original

8. See Alexandre Koyré, *From the closed world to the infinite universe* (Baltimore, MD, 1957), p.236ff.

sin, Augustine had even condemned all unbaptised children to hell. Pelagius, by contrast, appealed to the examples given by Jesus in the Gospels in order to stress man's free will, and the natural goodness, freedom and autonomy of human beings, who were perfectly capable of saving themselves thanks to their own moral qualities, with no need to resort to grace and the Church, or to baptise newborn infants.

This ostracised view of Christianity had nevertheless been upheld by sixteenth-century Italian heretics as well as by Socinians in the following century. During the seventeenth-century controversy on tolerance important new editions of Pelagius marked the beginning of a revival that would culminate in Voltaire's well-known comments in favour of Pelagius' positions.[9] Locke himself would probably not have developed his thought on this matter without the Socinian revival of Pelagius and his defence of the autonomy of individual consciences. An equally important premise for an understanding of Locke's position is the epistemological change brought about by the Scientific Revolution, with its critique of Aristotle's idea of substance and its decision to focus on the study of phenomena and of empirical mathematical relationships. One is tempted to say that, out of all the possible candidates at this extraordinarily complex and exciting time, Cicero, Pelagius and Newton were the symbolic godfathers not only of Enlightenment culture but also of the new concept of 'person' developed by John Locke.

At this point one might ask: from a theoretical point of view, and in terms of the history of ideas, which is the *principium individuationis* that distinguishes one subject from another within the human species? What is their 'personal identity'? In the crucial chapter 'Of identity and diversity' in *An Essay concerning human understanding*, Locke dismisses outright Boethius' idea that this distinguishing principle resided in man's rational substance, or soul. One should, instead, investigate the nature, consciousness and 'mind' of natural man, which was something quite different from the soul. Locke considered the latter mostly a theological and metaphysical notion, which was rather obscure in philosophical terms and unable to explain man's

9. Cf. Camilla Hermanin, *Samuel Werenfels: il dibattito sulla libertà di coscienza a Basilea agli inizi del Settecento* (Florence, 2003), p.202. On the importance of Pelagius in Voltaire's polemics against Augustine's theory of original sin, see Voltaire's entry on 'Péché originel' in his *Dictionnaire philosophique*, ed. Christiane Mervaud, in *Œuvres complètes de Voltaire* (hereafter *OCV*), vol.35-36 (Oxford, 1994), vol.36, p.423-27.

consistent identity in time and the relationship of this identity with man's body. For instance, a talking parrot could come across as a rational creature, if we disregarded its shape. Yet 'the soul alone in the change of bodies, would scarce to any one, but to him that makes the soul the *man*, be enough to make the same *man*.'[10] In order to define the new identity criteria one must look to experience, to the scientific study of the human body, with its thinking matter and living, organised particles: 'The body too goes to the making the man' (II, 27, 15). It was necessary to investigate a human being's feelings, memory processes, imagination and passions, and to be constantly aware of man's finitude and organic complexity. A new natural history of the human intellect and of the 'mind'–'body' interaction needed to be written, which would go beyond Descartes's dualism between *res cogitans* and *res extensa* in terms of what today we would call cognitive psychology and mind science.[11] Within this paradigm, 'man', 'person' and 'substance' were for Locke three different ideas. However, all three were equally necessary if one were finally to replace the old concept of identity of substance with that of identity of consciousness, and set a form of relational perception as the modern foundation of the concept of person (II, 27, 17):

> *Self* is that conscious thinking thing (whatever substance, made up of whether spiritual, or material, simple, or compounded, it matters not) which is sensible, or conscious of pleasure and pain, capable of happiness or misery, and so is concern'd for it *self*, as far as that consciousness extends [...] That with which the *consciousness* of this present thinking thing can join it self, makes the same *person*, and is one *self* with it, and with nothing else.

Locke defined the personal identity of natural man as a synthesis of memory and the rational consciousness of being constantly the same finite individual: a person 'is a thinking intelligent being, that has reason and reflection, and can consider it self as it self, the same

10. John Locke, *An Essay concerning human understanding*, abridged with an introduction and notes by Pauline Phemister (Oxford, 2008), II, 27, 15, p.212-13 (emphasis in the original; subsequent references, to book, chapter and paragraph only, are given in brackets within the text. As with other eighteenth-century quotations, I have modernised the use of capital letters).
11. Cf. Yolton, *John Locke*, p.30ff. See also Daniela Gobetti, *Private and public: individuals, households, and body politic in Locke and Hutcheson* (London, 1992). On the autonomy of the individual in general, see J. B. Schneewind, *The Invention of autonomy: a history of modern moral philosophy* (Cambridge, 1998).

thinking thing in different times and places' (II, 27, 9). In this way, Locke was moving towards modern Enlightenment humanism, a movement that Kant described as the process of man's emancipation and independence, whereby the individual attained liberty and took on full responsibility towards himself and his fellow human beings. Instead of the Christian soul-person, with its metaphysical and theological foundations, Locke upheld the Enlightenment consciousness-person, which was empirically defined by the monistic and organic mind–body nexus and by relational perceptions. Thus man as person became a moral agent, characterised in equal measure by freedom and responsibility.

The concept of person that Locke developed in Grotius' wake has received less attention than Locke's view of the individual as the subject of rights. Already in Roman *ius* the term 'person' denoted first and foremost a specific juridical concept: 'It is a forensick term appropriating actions and their merit; and so belongs only to intelligent agents capable of a law, and happiness and misery' (II, 27, 26). Locke did not quite identify natural man entirely with the juridical person, holder of both rights and duties: this way of thinking, which went beyond the census-defined structure of the *Ancien régime*, would not fully develop until Late Enlightenment politics. His aim was to establish the person as a free and responsible moral agent, with a shift from natural man to moral man and the person's autonomous responsibility. This was in itself an important achievement in the history of modern subjective rights and the rise of the Enlightenment theory of the rights of man.[12] Claiming this new concept of person as his own original idea, Locke writes: 'In this personal identity is founded all the right and justice of reward and punishment; happiness and misery, being that, for which every one is concerned for himself' (II, 27, 18). Education, morality and politics were assigned the task of building the human person in space and time on the basis of their empirical knowledge of natural man, with no concessions to substantialism or Descartes's innatism. The appropriating consciousness of

12. As we know, in sixteenth- and seventeenth-century legal thought a subject's status determined his privileges and juridical freedom. Every person was a human being, but not all human beings were considered to be persons. In the ancient world, the equality that natural law bestowed on all persons was qualified in civil law by a person's status, as in the Roman sources *de statu hominis*. The Enlightenment extended the juridical status of person to every human being. On this, see Guido Alpa, *La cultura delle regole: storia del diritto civile italiano* (Rome and Bari, 2000), p.14ff.

the person as it developed through experience became a focal point in Locke's political thought in its effort to build a modern civil society of free and responsible persons. This appropriating consciousness was a defining characteristic of a person who was morally aware of his or her actions and natural rights, and who understood the need to act in a responsible way, taking into account the necessities of others.

This said, we should also consider other interpretations of Locke's thought on natural law. For instance, we should rethink the widely accepted view according to which Locke's theory of the natural right to property was the origin of the idea of 'possessive individualism' and thus of liberal and pro-capitalistic thought.[13] The problem with this view is that it does not take into consideration Locke's reference to the need to build the person, or the importance of the discovery of the 'other' in the sixteenth and seventeenth century following the political and religious struggle for toleration and freedom of conscience.[14]

As we have seen, Locke is rightly considered the father of the modern right to property seen as a natural right of man. In this he differed from Grotius and Pufendorf, who accepted the traditional conventionalist view of property. Historically, Locke addresses the questions raised by the Levellers, the radical wing of the English revolutionary movement. As part of the struggle for the right to vote, members of this movement, and especially Richard Overton within it, were the first who, though on a fairly small scale, raised the question of property as a natural right and an aspect of individual liberty.[15] Landowners among Cromwell's followers had denounced the subversive character of the Levellers' theories, which seemed to open the way to indiscriminate appropriation. Gerrard Winstanley's communist solution had done nothing to allay their fear by asking: what about the right to property of non-landowners? How do we establish what is mine and what is yours? Starting from Grotius' idea of a person's *proprium* as part of a subject's freedom of action and of property, Locke replies, in the second of his two treatises on government:

> Though the earth, and all inferior creatures, be common to all men, yet every man has a property in his own person: this nobody has

13. See Macpherson, *The Political theory of possessive individualism*.
14. Antonio Rotondò's legacy on this subject is still very important, as is the three-volume work published in his honour (see Méchoulan *et al.*, *Formazione storica della alterità*).
15. Cf. Giuliano Gliozzi, *Le teorie della proprietà da Lutero a Babeuf* (Turin, 1978), p.18ff.

> any right to but himself. The labour of his body, and the work of his hands, we may say, are properly his. Whatsoever then he removes out of the state that nature hath provided, and left it in, he hath mixed his labour with, and joined to it something that is his own, and thereby makes it his property. It being by him removed from the common state nature hath placed it in, it hath by this labour something annexed to it that excludes the common right of other men. For this labour being the unquestionable property of the labourer, no man but he can have a right to what that is once joined to, at least where there is enough, and as good, left in common for others.[16]

The latter point clearly shows that Locke was concerned about the excessive polarisation of wealth and the inequalities that had increased with the introduction of money: the way in which this development had hugely accelerated the appropriation process was putting individual liberty seriously at risk. This in turn brings out the humanitarian element and the centrality of the person in the definition of the natural right to property.

In this respect, the origin and modalities of this particular right are especially significant. Its roots can be traced back to Locke's attack on despotism, and in particular on Robert Filmer's 1680 *Patriarcha, or the Natural power of kings*. In the first of his treatises on government, Locke argues against Filmer's peroration of authority, in the form both of a father's over his children and of a king's over his subjects. In particular, Locke critiques the claim of the divine ratification for this state of dependency and for the father or sovereign's 'absolute, arbitrary, unlimited, and unlimitable power over the lives, liberties, and estates of his children and subjects' (I, 2, 9).[17] This state of things made a mockery of any idea of autonomy and self-mastery of the subject. For Locke, by contrast, the struggle against absolute power should start with the education of the person as a free and responsible moral human being, through the progressive empirical recognition of an individual's rights as part of that individual's freedom. This process would eventually lead to the construction of a State *ex parte civium*, whose constitutional powers would guarantee man's natural rights. Thus, the right to property as a form of limitation of absolute

16. Cf. John Locke, 'The second treatise: an essay concerning the true original, extent, and end of civil government', in *Two treatises of government: and a letter concerning toleration*, p.100-209 (II, 5, 27).
17. John Locke, 'The first treatise: the false principles and foundation of Sir Robert Filmer', in *Two treatises of government: and a letter concerning toleration*, p.7-99.

sovereignty originated within the sphere of personal liberty, in that anyone who wished to enter a subject's domain would require consent from that subject.

Locke's property-owning citizen was therefore a conscious and responsible person, quite unlike the stereotypical portrait drawn by traditional Marxist criticism, of a selfish, asocial and isolated individual, whose presumed rights and powers were an aspect of the violence of the bourgeoisie. He was the starting point of a complex process that would characterise the eighteenth-century Enlightenment, and which we will discuss in detail with reference to Jean-Jacques Rousseau: a process that would link together the subject and civil society, the individual and the community, morality and politics, freedom and equality, transforming Western political culture from a civilisation of duties to a civilisation of rights.

We can now see, therefore, that the accusations of 'individualism' and 'social atomism' levelled against this social subject are entirely anachronistic, ideologically biased and historically unfounded. These categories were part of Hegel and Marx's indictment of the eighteenth century in an attempt to fit this century into their scheme of things, while in fact their theories of dialectical sublation and of the organicistic character of communities, such as nations and social classes, would only apply to the intellectual debate that took place in later centuries. What characterised the political culture of the Enlightenment was in fact quite the opposite. This culture placed great emphasis on the centrality of the social individual as a conscious and responsible person. It took into account the rights of the other, focused on the sociability principle and the political myth of civil society, and appealed to ancient civic virtues in its attempt to contain modern utilitarianism and its pernicious effects. It saw the rise of public opinion and the attempt to solve the problem of conflicting natural rights.[18]

Something that requires more careful analysis is the issue of the ambiguity, limitations and contradictions within Locke's own thought in relation to natural rights and to the very origins of the discourse of the rights of man. As has often been remarked, there is a solid remnant of traditional theology in his views, such as in his assumptions regarding the necessary divine foundation of that natural law of which the rights of man were part, or the inevitable failure of any attempt

18. For an effective rebuttal of the idea of eighteenth-century individualism from a historical viewpoint, see Costa, *Civitas*, vol.1, p.573ff.

to base ethics on a rationally demonstrable logic.[19] The influence of Aquinas and medieval canon law is also evident in Locke's research into the concept of person. On the one hand, Locke constantly stressed that man was absolute master over his own person, while on the other he qualified this idea by assigning man *dominium utile* only, and reserving *dominium directum* for God.[20] In the debate on the legitimacy of suicide that took place across Europe in the seventeenth and eighteenth centuries Locke sided with those who resolutely denied that the natural right to life was at the disposal of man's will.[21]

We should, however, be wary of pushing too far this idea of continuity with the past. It would be wrong to state that, from a theoretical and philosophical point of view, Locke's position on rights is simply a logical offshoot of the acknowledgement of the presence of rights in natural law, as already found in Pufendorf and his followers. We must also take into account the wars of religion, the results of the ensuing debate on tolerance and freedom of conscience, as well as the changes in outlook brought about by the impetuous rise of Neo-Epicureanism and of the natural right to happiness, which are discussed below. Many theoretical ambiguities and contradictions can also be explained through these rapid changes in the historical context and in contingent circumstances.

By upholding a new humanism that placed the individual at its centre, the Enlightenment would turn everything upside down: now, even the duties of man were a direct result of the rights of the subject and the equality principle. Despite occasional ambiguities, by constructing the idea of a person as a free and responsible moral subject Locke was among the first to embark on this long journey towards a revolutionary new concept of the individual.[22] He determinedly pursued

19. See Carlo Augusto Viano, *John Locke: dal razionalismo all'illuminismo* (Turin, 1960), p.157ff.
20. See Brian Tierney, 'Dominion of self and natural rights before Locke and after', in *Transformations*, ed. V. Mäkinen and P. Korkman, p.173-203 (176ff.).
21. The opposite side (which upheld man's complete self-determination also in the matter of the right to life) included important segments of the radical Enlightenment, who subscribed to pantheistic and vitalistic theories in the wake of Giordano Bruno: cf. Silvia Berti, 'Radicali ai margini: materialismo, libero pensiero e diritto al suicidio in Radicati di Passerano', *Rivista storica italiana* 116 (2004), p.794-811.
22. For the idea of a traditionalist Locke who derives man's rights from man's duties, see Knud Haakonssen, *Natural law and moral philosophy: from Grotius to the Scottish Enlightenment* (Cambridge, 1996). For the opposite view, see M. P. Zuckert, *Natural rights and the new republicanism* (Princeton, NJ, 1998). The debate is still

Grotius' initial vision: a *civitas* based on contracts among individuals who owned a series of rights within the political community. Locke's idea of human consciousness as thinking matter and as the nexus between mind and body set the nascent science of man on the right path. This same idea also caused him to be accused of materialism and his works to be condemned by the Church of Rome.[23]

In any event, the history of the rights of man owes much to John Locke.[24] The same is true of all those figures we have discussed so far, from Spinoza to Bayle and Barbeyrac, who were involved in the crisis of European consciousness and the progressive acknowledgement of the most important natural rights. These thinkers, to whose number we should add Galileo Galilei, who was condemned by the Holy Office because of his science, all fought for *libertas philosophandi* and freedom of conscience, which thanks to them became what distinguished and characterised a human person.[25] The next step in the right direction would be, in the first instance, to shift the focus once and for all from the community to the individual and from duties to rights, which involved redefining their foundations, relationship and priority. Then, it was necessary to reflect on the momentous acknowledgement, for the first time in the history of the West, of man's natural right to the pursuit of happiness in life. This included accepting man's finitude and adopting the equality principle as a fundamental ethical postulate through which the universality of the rights of man would be finally recognised. Only in this way could the harsh reality of the *Ancien régime* be subjected to scrutiny and start to crumble, at first in man's consciousness and then in actual terms, bringing about what I have elsewhere described as the Enlightenment's cultural revolution.[26]

open. It seems to be of special concern to historians of political ideas, while greater attention to changes in the historical context would not come amiss.

23. On the persecution of Locke's supporters in Italy, see Ferrone, *Intellectual roots*, p.276-77.

24. This remains true despite the fact that he made a considerable amount of money from his shares in the Royal African Company, which was involved in the slave trade: cf. Jeremy Waldron, *God, Locke, and equality: Christian foundations of John Locke's political thought* (Cambridge, 2002), p.252ff.

25. On the struggle for *libertas philosophandi* in Italy, for instance, see Luca Addante, *Eretici e libertini nel Cinquecento italiano* (Rome and Bari, 2010).

26. See Ferrone, *The Enlightenment*, p.120ff.

7. From duties to rights: the Enlightenment discovery of the natural right to the pursuit of happiness

Nowadays we cannot talk about 'happiness' without feeling rather self-conscious. We hardly ever utter the word, because it sounds anachronistic, rhetorical, 'literary' in a coy sort of way. Above all, it comes across as unsuitable for describing our human condition today. The twentieth century introduced genocide and totalitarianism in human history, while our current governments, and we as individuals, seem able to obtain only various forms of social and economic insecurity and existential angst through our pursuits. What went under the name of 'eudemonism', i.e. that faith in progress and in the constant improvement of *humanitas* that characterised the eighteenth century, seems now only a distant memory. How can we then claim that the moderns invented (or reinvented) man's natural right to the pursuit of happiness? If anything, our nihilist postmodern philosophers seem rather more attracted to the paradoxical possibility of a natural right to *un*happiness. In the eighteenth century, by contrast, the idea of 'happiness', which is as ancient as mankind, was constantly being invoked: at the theatre and in novels, in polite conversation as well as in formidable philosophical tracts. Happiness became the principal objective of the new Enlightenment morality.[1] It was the key concept for the definition of the nature and destiny of the human being, through which the scattered and ineffective natural rights of the subject that had been put forward in previous centuries became the powerful and subversive language of the rights of man with which we are familiar today.

1. For a now classic study on this subject, see Robert Mauzi, *L'Idée du bonheur dans la littérature et la pensée françaises au XVIIIe siècle* (Paris, 1960). A useful overview of this topic can be found in Philippe Roger, 'Bonheur', in *Le Monde des Lumières*, ed. V. Ferrone and D. Roche, p.49-57.

Several intermediate stages, eventually leading to a radical change in the intellectual frame of reference, were required in the shift from a Neo-Stoic morality of duties, which was founded on the sociability principle and had been authoritatively revived in Grotius' and Pufendorf's theory of natural law, to a morality of the rights of the individual as upheld by the Enlightenment. A particularly important role was played by the new Christian Epicureanism of Gassendi and Locke, which complemented the Stoic revival brought about by the works of Justus Lipsius and the print editions of Cicero and Seneca in the course of the sixteenth century.

Duties and rights seem to coalesce in a work first published by Antoine Court de Gébelin between 1773 and 1782: '*Duties of man.* Man's rights consist in the ability to enjoy the use of his organs or bodily attributes as well as of his faculties or intellectual attributes. The former are needed for his preservation, the latter for his happiness. The duties of man therefore consist in preserving his life and being happy.'[2] This new discourse of happiness changed everything in terms of the objectives of the modern morality of man in the Western world. This was not because happiness was a 'new idea in Europe', as the revolutionary Louis Antoine de Saint-Just maintained at the National Convention in Paris. The idea itself in fact had a long history. What had changed was its meaning and its significance for man's life. Christianity had seldom used this term, and had generally done so in a religious and metaphysical way, as it denied the absolute value of the pursuit of physical wellbeing and of happiness in a daily life that was entirely ruled by providence. This kind of happiness did not depend on man. True happiness was not and could not be a thing of this world. It was a transitory and contingent concept, too vague for the life of sorrowful *homo viator*, with his burden of original sin and his fleeting existence as a pilgrim on this earth, according to Augustine's view. Happiness was essentially an otherworldly element: it was the promise of future beatitude in heaven and of the soul's perfection through the knowledge and contemplation of God.

Christianity had absorbed with ease the ancient ideas of pagan Stoics on happiness. The thinking of the philosopher Seneca, the slave Epictetus and Emperor Marcus Aurelius on this subject spoke to every social class. Their views on the precariousness of life and the body–soul divide, their upholding of duty, self-control and detachment from

2. Antoine Court de Gébelin, *Monde primitif, analisé et comparé avec le monde moderne*, 2nd edn, 9 vols (Paris, Durand, 1777-1796), vol.8 (1787), p.573.

earthly goods, passions and fame had a natural affinity with Christian theology and spirituality. Stoic ethics were founded on the rule of reason over the passions as the way to the only real form of happiness, which consisted in the attainment of wisdom. This was because man was seen both as imbued with *logos* and bearer of a spark of that perennial fire that enabled him to explore the eternal law and nature of the cosmos with his reason: all features that, as we have seen, are at the basis of Aquinas' concept of Christian natural law. In turn, this ethical view inspired Renaissance Neo-Stoicism and related attempts to establish a new order principle and a new morality of duties and of social discipline in the attempt to control the dangerous turmoil caused by unruly passions.

The relationship between Christianity and Epicureanism was from the start rather more complex. The original aim of this ancient philosophical current was a therapeutic attempt to relieve human suffering. However, it soon became a byword for materialism, atheism and hedonism. In any case, the spirituality of Christian culture was in open contrast with the Epicureans' emphasis on the body and its atomistic composition, their view of sensory experience as the only true epistemological criterion, and their exhortation to boldly pursue happiness here on earth by seeking pleasure, living life according to nature and avoiding pain.

In the early, libertine version practised by figures like Saint-Evremond, Renaissance Neo-Epicureanism was limited to a few restricted circles. It was with a religious figure like that of priest Pierre Gassendi that Epicureanism began to be Christianised. Gassendi's philosophy systematically restored the reputation of Epicurus and his thought, allowing its reprise in every part of Europe as an important way of reflecting on man's nature and condition. The Scientific Revolution and its interest in atomism and empiricism also contributed to the diffusion of Epicureanism, first in England at the time of Hobbes, Boyle and Newton, and then in the Netherlands and Germany. In France, the Oratorian priest Malebranche brought renewed attention to the principle of self-love as the decisive impulse behind all human action. Hobbes' most important works were based on the principles of Epicurus. Dodging the censorship of the Inquisition, in 1727 in Florence Celestino Galiani and other enlightened Catholics were even able to print a major edition of the whole of Gassendi's works, with an introductory essay that was in fact an important intellectual manifesto of eighteenth-century Christian Neo-Epicureanism, brought up to date by the addition of references to Galileo and Newton.

The authors of this introductory essay to Gassendi rejected Descartes's dualism and boldly advocated the right to *libertas philosophandi* in the study of man as he appeared in nature, taking into account his passions, and his instinct to pursue pleasure and eschew pain. In fact, Galiani and his collaborators attempted to follow the dictates of the French Jansenists and redirect these long-repressed and neglected passions towards divine grace.[3] It was now time to make the Epicureans' 'natural morality' of man acceptable again. This could be done by upholding the principle of self-love alongside that of the love of others and placing the individual on the same level as that natural communitarian instinct and sociability principle that had enjoyed absolute priority in the Neo-Stoical theory of natural law of Grotius and Pufendorf.[4]

The influence of Epicurus is especially present in Locke's work on the importance of the body, with its sensations, pain and pleasure. This was an entirely new science of man, which helped establish beyond doubt the thesis that saw ethics in empirical terms, as 'the seeking out [of] those rules, and measures of human actions, which lead to happiness, and the means to practise them'.[5] As for happiness itself, Locke had previously defined it as 'the utmost pleasure we are capable of' (II, 21, 42). We saw above how this was not simply a revival of Epicurus, or of sixteenth- and seventeenth-century libertine hedonism. Locke foregrounds happiness and unhappiness as defining aspects of human experience in relation to the self and others. All this was part of a complex theory of the construction of the person in terms of the appropriating consciousness of the natural man, with a view to creating a modern civil society that complied with natural rights. Grotius and Pufendorf, as we saw, in indicating the primary objectives of the new moral science based on natural right had stressed the importance of social order, community life and every man's duty 'to promote and preserve a peaceful sociableness

3. On the background to this Italian edition of Gassendi, see Ferrone, *Intellectual roots*, p.57-58. On the rehabilitation of Epicurean self-love by seventeenth-century writers on natural morality, see Mauzi, *L'Idée du bonheur*, p.636ff.; Corrado Rosso, *Moralisti del bonheur*, 2nd edn (Pisa, 1977); Antonio Trampus, *Il diritto alla felicità: storia di un'idea* (Rome and Bari, 2008), p.96ff.
4. On the important role played in the rise of the European Enlightenment by the 'convergence between Augustinian and Epicurean currents of thinking about the nature of man', see John Robertson, *The Case for the Enlightenment: Scotland and Naples 1680-1760* (Cambridge, 2005), p.8ff.
5. Locke, *Essay concerning human understanding*, IV, 21, 3.

with others'.[6] What Locke did was to shift the focus onto the subject, an individual who is made up of rationality but also of fears, desires and passions. This opened the way to the definitive invention by Barbeyrac and Burlamaqui of the natural and inalienable right to the pursuit of happiness.

Nevertheless, we are not looking as yet at a full-blown ethics of happiness in modern terms, i.e. a morality that is rational, universal, created by man for man, linked to passions, pleasures, man's interests, and now at last founded on the honest evaluation of the human condition in its earthly finitude. This will have to wait until the late eighteenth century, when the new intellectual climate created by the Enlightenment will enable the moral and political practice of rights to take hold as part of the new 'sciences of man' at the turn of the century. In the texts on morality now written by English, French, Scottish or Italian philosophers, the traditional seventeenth-century references to the geometric deductive method or a hypothetical state of nature were mostly superseded by new methods: for instance, ethnographic analyses, the study of the different customs of peoples across the earth, or scientific discussions of the validity as epistemological principles of concepts like that of *consensus gentium* or of a hypothetical common psychological makeup, the latter being supposedly the basis for a universal natural morality that was inscribed in the hearts of all men, regardless of religion or nationality. As we will see in greater detail, the focus was not only on reason, but also on passions, feelings, instinct, consciousness, sensitivity and self-interest. All of these were felt to be essential, and were addressed in treatises that presented in more and more sophisticated terms the results of the new scientific research in the fields of physiology, medicine, history or psychology. This gave rise to a great variety of interpretations of human behaviour, which often clashed with one another. Nevertheless, the new Enlightenment humanism was without doubt a laboratory of modernity, and was mainly responsible for the rise of a new culture based on the principle of the dignity of man. It was this movement that led to the full and momentous rediscovery of the natural right to happiness that belonged to all human beings, a development that was to become the cornerstone of the Enlightenment language of the rights of man.

With his lifelong engagement with questions such as the existence of absolute evil, the human condition or the nature of happiness, Voltaire was one of the spiritual fathers of this new humanism. In fact, his

6. Pufendorf, *The Whole duty of man*, II, 3, 15.

works mark the final break with the old Renaissance humanism, from which his own intellectual roots derived. His views diverged greatly from that idea of man as a 'great miracle', a superior being made of semi-divine substance, thanks to which, for instance, Giovanni Pico della Mirandola had claimed human dignity for a restricted number of *magi* and wise men nourished by hermetic and gnostic doctrines with obvious religious and mystical tendencies. As God says to Adam in Pico's celebrated oration 'On the dignity of man':

> I have placed thee at the center of the world, that from there thou mayest more conveniently look around and see whatsoever is in the world. Neither heavenly nor earthly, neither mortal nor immortal have We made thee. Thou, like a judge appointed for being honorable, art the molder and maker of thyself; thou mayest sculpt thyself into whatever shape thou dost prefer. Thou canst grow downward into the lower natures which are brutes. Thou canst again grow upward from thy soul's reason into the higher natures which are divine.[7]

Voltaire also famously believed that every individual should be told: 'Remember your dignity as a man.'[8] However, this statement, which he borrowed directly from Cicero, meant something completely different from what it meant in Pico. It applied to all human beings, from an entirely earthly point of view, and was based on a concrete idea of the human condition and on the serene and disenchanted acceptance of man's finitude and limitations.

Like the ancient Epicureans and their modern equivalent, the deists and followers of Newton's natural theology, Voltaire took as his starting point the hypothesis of the existence of a God who had created the world and who was the foundation of all laws. This was, however, an idle God, who was hidden away, totally uninterested in human affairs and effectively absent from history – as in fact was the God of Epicurus. Voltaire's theism, while mostly based on an authentic and deeply felt belief, was also often in agreement with the libertine idea of religion as *instrumentum regni*, or political tool.[9] On the one hand, he rebutted the atheists' positions with the famous remark that, if God

7. Giovanni Pico della Mirandola, *On the dignity of man* (translated by Charles Glenn Wallis); *On being and the one; Heptaplus* (Indianapolis, IN, 1998), p.5.
8. 'Souviens-toi de ta dignité d'homme': Voltaire, 'Méchant', in *Dictionnaire philosophique*, vol.36, p.346.
9. On the complex issue of Voltaire's religion and religiosity the most important study is still René Pomeau, *La Religion de Voltaire* (Paris, 1969).

did not exist, it would be necessary to invent him. On the other, he greatly admired Pierre Bayle, and agreed with him on the necessity to separate morality from religion once and for all: 'Those who need religion in order to become "honest men" are to be pitied. They would have to be monsters within society if they could not find in themselves the feelings required by society and had to look elsewhere for what must be found in our very nature.'[10] In this sense, in terms of the potential danger for society, Voltaire had no hesitation in preferring a virtuous atheist over an intolerant and fanatical religious man.

In fact, by Voltaire's time the general disenchantment, the process of secularisation, and the separation between the sacred and the profane in history were now established points of view. New perspectives had opened up with respect to the outrageous existence and inevitability of evil, the promise of happiness, the meaning of life, and the limitations and possibilities of man, as he finally emancipated himself from the will of an ever-present providence. At the same time, man acquired dramatic new responsibilities because of his newly acquired moral and political self-government. In a world that was set to do without God's presence and support, the human being appeared naked and alone in the face of evil. Not only Voltaire, but European Enlightenment culture as a whole had to come to terms with the slow decline of the Augustinian view that absolute evil was a consequence of Adam's fall and original sin. With Spinoza's critique of the idea of the absolute truth of the Bible and the desacralisation of heaven in the work of Dom Calmet, evil was relativised and started to be seen as a natural historical phenomenon. This was a shift from theodicy to anthropodicy. As Bronislaw Baczko remarks: 'Detached from Providence, the human adventure must find its purpose and its own resources within itself.'[11]

Voltaire's reflection was entirely focused on the defining characteristics and existential condition of human nature, and he wrote a number of essays on the need to seek a universal morality made by man for man precisely in light of these brief observations. This involved opposing in equal measure Leibniz's facile eudemonism – *tout est bien* – and Pascal's tragic view of life, as Voltaire constantly strove to achieve a difficult balance and find the correct principle

10. Voltaire, *Traité de métaphysique*, ed. W. H. Barber, in *OCV*, vol.14 (Oxford, 1989), p.481.
11. Bronislaw Baczko, *Job, mon ami: promesses du bonheur et fatalité du mal* (Paris, 1997), p.382.

of action and behaviour. Voltaire confronted once and for all the inevitability of evil and nature's power over mankind in his famous philosophical novel *Candide*, over 25,000 copies of which were printed in 1759, in response to the devastating Lisbon earthquake of 1755. Man suddenly appeared to his eyes as weak and defenceless, a forlorn atom adrift in the universe, a 'most miserable being, who has a few hours' respite, a few moments' satisfaction, and a long series of sorrows in his short life', as he wrote in 1772. This is a far cry from Pico della Mirandola's *magnum miraculum*: 'Those who said that all is for the best are charlatans.'[12] Nevertheless, something had to be done. By reducing evil to a product of nature and of history it was possible to create scope for human intervention to reduce its terrible effects. It was necessary to oppose the view held by Pascal, that brilliant and sublime misanthropist, who thought that we had long ago lost the battle against original sin, and that all men were doomed, 'wicked' or 'wretched'.[13]

From Montaigne and his scepticism Voltaire had learned that man was a prisoner of his own finitude. There were severe limits to his knowledge and scope for action. He was, in fact, 'incomprehensible' (cf. III-IV, p.201-205). However, this did not authorise men to place all hope in the workings of divine providence, or to follow Pascal in placing a wager only on God's existence and mercy. We should, instead, take stock of the realities of the human condition, and stop believing in Augustine's dogma of 'the natural infelicity of our weak, our mortal condition' (XXII, p.225). We should fight back, take things into our own hands and seek to live every moment of this tragedy of life with dignity, freedom and a sense of our responsibility towards ourselves as well as others:

> Why should endeavours be us'd to make us reflect on our Being with horror? Our existence is not so wretched as some persons would make us believe it to be. To consider the universe as a dungeon, and all mankind as so many criminals carrying to execution, is the idea of a madman. (VI, p.209)

12. Voltaire, *Il faut prendre un parti, ou le Principe d'action*, ed. Paolo Casini, in *OCV*, vol.74B (Oxford, 2006), p.40.
13. Voltaire, *Letters concerning the English nation: the second edition, with large additions* (London, C. Davis, 1741), letter 25, 'On Pascal's thoughts concerning religion, & c.,' p.197-255 (198). For subsequent quotations, paragraph and page number are given within the text. Cf. also Voltaire, *Lettres philosophiques*, ed. Nicholas Cronk and Nick Treuherz, in *OCV*, vol.6A-B (Oxford, forthcoming).

> Man is not an aenigma, as you figure him to yourself to be, merely to have the pleasure of unriddling it. Man seems to have his due place in the scale of beings [...] Man is like every thing we see round us, a composition in which good and evil, pleasures and pains are found [...] If man was perfect, he would be God; and those contrarieties, which you call contradictions, are so many necessary ingredients to the composition of man, who is just what he ought to be. (III, p.203)

Man should therefore use every possible means to attain those few moments of happiness that lie within his reach. He must reform society so as to limit the presence of evil and sorrow, 'study himself' within the nascent science of man, and always bear in mind that '[i]t would not be proper to divert man from searching after those things which may be of advantage to him, from this reflection, that it is impossible for him to know all things' (LIV, p.249).

It is in this context that Grotius and Pufendorf's natural law was profoundly modified. The emphasis in the seventeenth-century form of natural law had been on *duties* as a necessary premise for man's safety and preservation. With the recognition of the double component in man's natural and cultural disposition, and the consequent attempt to construct a new morality based on the pursuit of happiness both in the private and in the public sphere, a new movement took shape that had its own logic and purpose. Now, in the course of the eighteenth century, the attention shifted onto the identification and practice of *rights* on a political level, which were the prerequisite for the existence of those moments of individual happiness extolled by Voltaire. The assertion of this natural and inalienable right to the pursuit and realisation of happiness for oneself and for others thus became the focus of a new moral, political and juridical language: something that was at the very heart of the Enlightenment's representation of the human being as mortal, limited and subject to pain, but also as predisposed by nature to the constant pursuit of those precious moments of happiness.

As we mentioned above, Jean Barbeyrac was among the first to realise that a radical shift was taking place. In his notes to his French translation of Pufendorf's 1706 *De iure naturae*, Barbeyrac openly criticises the idea that modern natural law should be founded solely on duties and the sociability principle. By the eighteenth century, the recourse to sociability alone was not enough to impose an unassailable logic of duties or the necessity to practise a social discipline that was in fact a close ally of absolute power. Critics of the time coined the derogatory term 'socialist', which they applied to all those who, like

Pufendorf's followers, placed the community and its social bonds above the needs of the individual.[14] The centrality of the individual, and especially the Epicurean self-love principle, was increasingly seen as the necessary complement to the latest incarnation of natural law. And this time it would be its definitive form: that of the Enlightenment sciences of man and of a morality of rights. In contrast with Pufendorf, Barbeyrac had more or less consciously started that metamorphosis by placing those two principles side by side. However, he had stopped short of situating the pursuit of happiness above all else, and of turning it into the primary objective of any moral treatise. The decisive step in this direction was taken instead by his pupil and heir Jean-Jacques Burlamaqui.

A late exponent of the Huguenot diaspora, Burlamaqui (1694-1748) was born in Geneva into a family with ancient roots in Lucca who had fled to escape the Catholic Inquisition. He held the chair of natural law at the University of Geneva and the position of counsellor of State. In his definition, natural law was no longer simply the search for what was right in nature but became a science and a system of rules that would lead man to a 'véritable et solide bonheur'.[15] His *Principes du droit naturel* (1748) ran to dozens of editions and were translated into several languages. From the very first chapter, this tract embodies the final shift towards that anthropological and Neo-Epicurean view of natural law that characterises the Enlightenment, as we move decidedly from the Stoics' view of the centrality of the cosmos to the modern concept of the individual as holder of rights.

In his tract, Burlamaqui engages in an analysis of the physiological, psychological and historical characteristics of man, with special attention to his natural and cultural components as a being made of both matter and intellect: 'Man is an animal endowed with understanding, and reason; a being composed of an organized body, and a rational soul' (I, 3, p.3). However, he goes beyond this, attempting to redefine the very concept of right: 'The idea of Right, and much more that of Natural Right, are undoubtedly relative to

14. Cf. Franco Venturi, '"Socialista" e "socialismo" nell'Italia del Settecento', *Rivista storica italiana* 75 (1963), p.129-40.

15. Jean-Jacques Burlamaqui, *Principes du droit naturel* (Geneva, Barillot et fils, 1748), p.1; 'true and solid happiness' (*The Principles of natural law: in which the true systems of morality and civil government are established, and the different sentiments of Grotius, Hobbes, Puffendorf, Barbeyrac, Locke, Clark, and Hutchinson, occasionally considered*, translated by Thomas Nugent, London, J. Nourse, 1748, I, 1, p.1 – subsequent references are given within the text, and I have modernised the use of italics).

the nature of man' (I, 2, p.2). Burlamaqui argues that the word 'right' should be interpreted in a new way – which he however believed corresponded to the original meaning of the term in the Aristotelian-Thomistic universe. In his view, 'right' was a subjective act of will: the formulation of rules in order to reach a specific goal. Its origin could be traced back to the Latin *dirigo* and French *diriger*, 'which implies, to conduct a person to some certain end by the shortest road' (*ibid.*). The purpose of these rules could only be the rational pursuit of happiness, both public and private: 'The ultimate end of man is happiness' (V, 4, p.46). The principle of self-love was no less fundamentally important than the sociability principle: 'Self-love is a principle that has nothing vicious in itself' (V, 7, p.48). On the basis of this acknowledgement of man's natural tendency to the pursuit of happiness, Burlamaqui finally brought to the attention of European culture a crucial concept, and gave it its name, as he discusses the 'General foundation of the rights of man' (VII, 4, p.70).

In fact, Grotius had already pointed out that 'right' could be 'taken for a personal quality, for a power of acting, or faculty'. And in this sense a subject's right was conceived of as 'a power that man hath to make use of his liberty and natural strength in a particular manner, either in regard to himself, or in respect to other men' (VII, 2, p.68). What needed to be added, however, was that this power, which was generally seen as 'a physical quality', becomes 'right' and 'a moral quality' (VII, 3, p.69) only when universal reason is applied to the definition of rules and guidelines that serve one specific and self-evident objective, i.e. the pursuit of happiness: 'Every exercise of our faculties, that tends of itself to the perfection and happiness of man, meets with the approbation of reason, which condemns whatever leads to opposite ends' (VII, 4, p.70). For Burlamaqui this was borne out by the very nature of things.

Thus, the pursuit of happiness, once it was approved by universal reason, legitimised the very existence of the rights of man. These were finally acknowledged as a necessary instrument through which it might be possible to accomplish the difficult enterprise of making man a little happier in his existence on earth. Turning an ancient tradition on its head, Burlamaqui's treatise addressed a wide readership with a message that was the opposite of what had characterised the history of natural law for centuries, ever since the revival of Stoic thought on this subject. Rights were now privileged over duties. For the first time man – i.e. a person who had value and dignity *per se*, anywhere and at any time – was acknowledged as the holder of subjective natural rights, such as the right to life, freedom, property and the pursuit of happiness. All these rights came before duties. In fact, those duties based on the sociability principle that had so preoccupied Pufendorf and his followers, especially in Northern Europe, were not a first principle, but themselves derived from the natural and inalienable rights of the individual. As Burlamaqui points out, 'Right produces obligation':

> when reason [...] acknowledges [a man] has a particular right; 'tis requisite, by a very natural consequence, that in order to ensure this right to man, she should acknowledge at the same time, that other people ought not to employ their strength and liberty in resisting him in this point; but on the contrary, that they should respect his right, and assist him in the exercise of it, rather than do him any prejudice. From thence the idea of obligation naturally arises. (VII, 5, p.70-71)

The groundbreaking role in the history of natural law of this focus on the 'rights of man', rather than on his duties, has not been paid enough attention by students of Burlamaqui.[16] This is due mainly to two factors. On the one hand, the originality of the first part of the tract is obscured by the repetition in the following pages of hackneyed definitions of natural law, or of Locke's idea of the social contract and of the limitation of absolute, divinely legitimated power. On the other hand, by the early decades of the eighteenth century widespread attention was devoted in Europe to the language of the natural rights of man, as found in the state of nature: there was thus no need to engage with Burlamaqui's subtle distinctions.

In the American colonies, however, Burlamaqui's work became well known, in Thomas Nugent's translation from which we have been quoting, especially in the revised 1763 edition. It became a set textbook at Harvard and Princeton universities, where it exercised a formative influence on future patriots and revolutionaries.[17] It is

16. There is hardly any reference to Burlamaqui's *droits de l'homme* in Bernard Gagnebin, *Burlamaqui (1694-1748) et le droit naturel* (Geneva, 1944); Rosenblatt, *Rousseau and Geneva*, p.91ff.; Jean-Paul Coujou, 'Droit naturel et humanité chez Burlamaqui: étude critique', appended to Jean-Jacques Burlamaqui, *Principes du droit naturel* (Paris, 2007), p.207-482. Some interesting remarks are found, however, in Korkman, 'Life, liberty and the pursuit of happiness'.
17. Cf. R. F. Harvey, *J.-J. Burlamaqui: a liberal tradition in American constitutionalism* (Chapel Hill, NC, 1937); Morton Gabriel White, *The Philosophy of the American Revolution* (New York, 1978), p.62ff.; and especially Haakonssen, *Natural law and moral philosophy*, p.336ff.

not surprising, therefore, that in 1764 James Otis should specifically invoke the natural right to the pursuit of freedom, or that this right should famously feature in Jefferson's opening lines to the 1776 Declaration of Independence, where the new language of rights was used for the first time to legitimise the colonies' revolution against the English monarchy.[18]

As we shall see in our next chapters, by this time the Enlightenment had accustomed European public opinion to the idea that modern universal morality should be based on man's natural rights, especially the right to the pursuit of happiness – not, as claimed by the French Jacobins in their 1793 constitution, to happiness *tout court*.[19] On the one hand, the acknowledgement of this right established the discourse of morality on an entirely new basis. On the other, it brought new and complex challenges, which deserve to be studied with the utmost attention from the historical point of view.

Assuming that there was the possibility of living happily and of reducing the amount of evil in the world: how could society be reformed in order to achieve these goals? How could one turn the acknowledgement, on a historical level, of the existence of natural rights in the moral sphere into political action and legislation capable of reaching these aims? Above all: if these rights were assumed to be universal, and truly applied to all human beings, with no distinction of gender, race or anything else, what about the contemporary slave trade? What about the privileges and inequalities positively enforced by European society under the *Ancien régime*? It became more and more obvious that the answer to these difficult questions would not be found in the old natural law, despite Grotius' and Pufendorf's attempts to update it and make it more relevant, or in the rhetorical and perfunctory acknowledgement of various natural rights of the individual that surfaced here and there in Spinoza or Locke. By the start of the new century, the old natural law from which we started our discussion was being forced into its final metamorphosis by several new powerful factors: the rise of the concept of a 'science of man', which in the Late Enlightenment would turn into the modern 'sciences of man', in the plural, such as anthropology, sociology or political economy; the discovery of the world in its historical dimension, and of the historicity of reality; the idea of the social contract; new forms of republicanism; the epistemological divergences within the

18. For an overview, see Trampus, *Il diritto alla felicità*, p.190ff.
19. On this important distinction, see Trampus, *Il diritto alla felicità*, p.206ff.

Enlightenment's appropriation of the new representations of nature provided by the Scientific Revolution. The pressure exercised by these new forces led to a final showdown, which was radical and effective to an extent that historians of the period are still to recognise.

II

From natural rights to the rights of man as moral and political rights

8. The epistemological break: Diderot and Hume

In 1741, in a letter to the president of the Berlin Academy of Sciences, Maupertuis, Voltaire came down very harshly on the writings on natural law by Leibniz and Wolff ('ce bavard germanique'), which he saw as a late expression of 'toutes les horreurs de la scolastique'. He was no less critical of the work of Grotius and Pufendorf, which in his view was marked by 'un esprit faux, obscur, confus, incertain'.[1] Equally damning criticism is expressed by the major figures of the European Enlightenment, such as Rousseau, Mably or Diderot.[2] As we shall see, in the Italian journal *Il Caffè*, published in Milan, Beccaria's followers held what amounted to a trial of Grotius, Pufendorf and all those who were considered to be eighteenth-century adherents of Neo-Stoical natural law.

A similar demolition, not least from an epistemological point of view, of seventeenth-century natural law as a supposedly rigorous science of morality based on a geometrical-deductive method was carried out by Denis Diderot in his *Encyclopédie*. In this respect, Diderot's controversial entry on 'Droit naturel' was similar to a modern deconstruction exercise. On the one hand, this marked the beginning of Diderot's long and original reflection on morality, law, politics and, more generally, the nascent sciences of man.[3] On the

1. See Voltaire's letter to Pierre-Louis Moreau de Maupertuis, Brussels, 10 August 1741, D2526, in Voltaire, *Correspondence and related documents*, ed. Theodore Besterman, in *OCV*, vol.85-135 (Oxford, 1968-1977), vol.92, p.95.
2. Cf. Peter Gay, *The Enlightenment: an interpretation*, vol.2: *The Science of freedom* (1969; New York and London, 1977), p.459ff.
3. In his entry Diderot points out that, while it may superficially seem a clear and self-evident concept, 'of all the notions of morality, that of natural rights is one of the most important and most difficult to determine' ('Natural rights', translated by Stephen J. Gendzier, in *The Encyclopedia of Diderot & D'Alembert*).

other hand, it started a controversy with Rousseau, Helvétius and other European intellectuals that in fact remains open to this day. Indeed, we must always bear in mind that the new Enlightenment culture developed different ideas of the universal moral order, which sometimes clashed with one another.[4] This was in fact inevitable, given the epistemological premises of the Enlightenment project of the emancipation of man through man, whose basis was complex, empirical and experimental. As I have shown elsewhere, this project never developed into a clearly defined culture of modernity with its own specific traits, being instead open to multiple solutions. It was a true laboratory of modernity, which today still takes centre stage and which was and is characterised first and foremost by the fact that, for the first time in history, the human being, in all its dimensions, was the privileged subject of study. And this happened regardless of the different points of view or instruments that were applied to its investigation, or of the results that were achieved, the latter being in any case only ever provisional, because they dealt with the human dimension.[5] As Diderot wrote in the entry 'Encyclopédie', 'Man is the sole point from which to begin, and to which all must be brought back.' This perfectly embodies the way in which the *philosophes* aimed at redrafting the map of our knowledge by taking as their starting point the 'discovery' or 'enthronement' of man (to use Foucault's famous metaphor):[6]

On this subject, see Jacques Proust, 'La contribution de Diderot à l'*Encyclopédie* et les théories du droit naturel', *Annales historiques de la Révolution française* 35 (1963), p.257-86; Luigi Luporini, 'Per una lettura della voce "Droit naturel" nell' "Encyclopédie"', *Studi storici* 28:3 (1987), p.679-97; and especially Girolamo Imbruglia, 'Indignation et droits de l'homme chez le dernier Diderot: de l'*Encyclopédie* à l'*Histoire des deux Indes*', in *L'Edition du dernier Diderot: pour un Diderot* électronique, ed. Gianluigi Goggi and Didier Kahn (Paris, 2007), p.125-76.

4. Cf. Michel Delon, 'Morale', in *Le Monde des Lumières*, ed. V. Ferrone and D. Roche, p.41-48.
5. Cf. Ferrone, *The Enlightenment*, p.95ff.
6. Foucault (*Order of things* – page references in bracket) rightly insists on the epistemological break caused by the eighteenth-century discovery of man as subject, who is now situated in 'the place of the king' (p.335) as 'a strange empirico-transcendental doublet' (p.347 and *passim*) and is thinking first and foremost in terms of itself. According to Foucault, in the sixteenth century 'there was no epistemological consciousness of man as such': 'Before the end of the eighteenth century, man did not exist – any more than the potency of life, the fecundity of labour, or the historical density of language. He is a quite recent creature, which the demiurge of knowledge fabricated with its own hands less than two hundred

> [I]f man or the thinking, observing being is banished from the surface of the earth, this moving and sublime spectacle of nature is nothing but a sad and silent scene. The universe is dumb; silence and night overtake it. Everything changes into a vast solitude where unobserved phenomena occur in a manner dark and mute. It is the presence of man that gives interest to the existence of beings; and what could we better have in view in the history of those beings, than to yield to this consideration? Why not introduce man into our opus, as he is placed in the universe? Why not make of him a common center? Is there some point in infinite space from which we could more advantageously originate the immense lines which we propose to extend to all other points? What stirring and agreeable reaction of those beings toward man, and of man toward them, would not result?
>
> This is what has led us to seek in the principal faculties of man the general division to which we have subordinated our labors.[7]

This was a new humanism – an Enlightenment humanism – with radically different features compared to the past: now all knowledge derived empirically through the main faculties of the human being. Nevertheless, this entirely new movement could not and should not overlook all the other dimensions of man's existential condition, especially how in everyday life the powerful voice of nature was present alongside and interacted with the autonomous will of the subject. The complex relationship between mind and body meant that, from the point of view of morality, man, though limited and mortal, was constantly both within and outside nature. He was at the same time part of the great chain of being and an individual with his own originality and creativity, who straddles the realms of nature and culture. In this respect, Diderot and many other Enlightenment thinkers, in their long and difficult search for the principles of natural law, would surely have subscribed to the remarks of a young follower that Immanuel Kant published as part of his 1798 *Conflict of the faculties*, on how philosophy must be, as it was in Kant, 'a science of the human being, of his

years ago' (p.336). In Renaissance humanism, a science of man in modern terms was unthinkable, '[a]nd man, as a primary reality with his own density, as the difficult object of all possible knowledge, has no place in it [...] it was not possible at that time that there should arise, on the boundary of the world, the strange stature of a being whose nature (that which determines it, contains it, and has traversed it from the beginning of time) is to know nature, and itself, in consequence, as a natural being' (p.338).

7. 'Encyclopedia', translated by Philip Stewart, in *The Encyclopedia of Diderot & D'Alembert*.

representations, thoughts and actions'. And this new science of man must finally have as its object of study 'all the components of the human being *both as he is and as he should be* – that is, in terms both of his natural functions and of his relations of morality and freedom'.[8]

However, especially from this point of view, one question that inevitably arose was: is man really a free being? And if he is, what degree of liberty does he enjoy in relation to the 'voice of nature'? Diderot, for instance, understood that without natural freedom, which was not an act of volition, 'there will be neither good nor evil in the moral sense, neither right nor wrong, neither obligation nor privilege.'[9] Nevertheless, he was torn between Spinoza's materialistic determinism and the need to accommodate free will, full liberty of conscience and an individual's full assumption of responsibility towards his peers. This remained for him, as for many Enlightenment intellectuals of the time, an insoluble dilemma.[10]

One need only look at the entries for 'Liberté' in the *Encyclopédie*: for instance, the entry for 'Liberté naturelle', where Louis de Jaucourt

8. From a letter to Kant from C. A. Wilmans, quoted in 'Appendix: on a pure mysticism in religion', as part of *The Conflict of the faculties*, translated by Mary J. Gregor and Robert Anchor, in *Religion and rational theology*, ed. Allen W. Wood and George di Giovanni (Cambridge, 1996), p.233-328 (288). Emphasis added.
9. *The Encyclopedia of Diderot & D'Alembert*, under 'Natural rights'.
10. In a letter to Landois written on 29 June 1756 Diderot makes some remarks of an extremely materialistic nature, claiming that there can be no freedom, only chains of unstoppable events – see Paolo Casini's edition of the *Enciclopedia o dizionario ragionato delle scienze, delle arti e dei mestieri ordinato da Diderot e D'Alembert*, ed. and translated by Paolo Casini (Bari, 1968), n.10, p.153, which includes some more bibliographical references on Diderot's materialism and deterministic monism. In his 1767 *Salon*, Diderot seems to take a milder view: 'What is a man?... An animal?... Without doubt; but dogs are animals, too, and wolves as well, while man is neither a wolf nor a dog [...] How many philosophers, having failed to make these simple observations, have prescribed ethical teachings suitable for wolves to Man, which is as stupid [*bêtes*] as prescribing human ethics to wolves!' (*Diderot on art*, vol.2: *The Salon of 1767*, ed. and translated by John Goodman, New Haven, CT, and London, 1995, p.107). Finally, in the 1773 *Réfutation* of Helvétius's *De l'homme*, Diderot harshly criticises the rigid assimilation of man to nature as well as any form of dogmatic materialism that seeks to deny the originality of the individual and the spontaneity of his feelings. By contrast, Diderot stresses the importance and diversity of the life of the mind and man's consciousness compared to physical and biological phenomena. On these passages, see Denis Diderot, *Opere filosofiche*, ed. Paolo Rossi (Milan, 1967), p.16ff. See also Paolo Quintili, *La Pensée critique de Diderot: matérialisme, science et poésie a l'âge de l'Encyclopédie (1742-1782)* (Paris, 2001).

invokes the natural and inalienable right to freedom in order to attack the slave trade.[11] For his part, Diderot had mixed feelings about Hobbes' theories. He was especially opposed to the idea of the state of nature and of man's fiercely utilitarian individualism. When discussing natural rights, Hobbes bore foremost in mind man's animal nature and violent passions. Diderot, instead, focused on the fact that 'man is not only an animal but an animal who reasons', who created forms of culture, relentlessly pursued happiness and was capable of attaining moral 'truth' by applying Bacon's teachings and administering nature itself accordingly.[12] However, Diderot's original contribution to the debate lies specifically in his exhortation to abandon the idea of the centrality of the individual and his will, and to adopt instead a universalist and cosmopolitan view of mankind:

> But if we take away from the individual the right of deciding about the nature of right and wrong, where shall we place this great question? Where? Before the entire human race; for only they may decide the issue, since the good of all is the only passion they have. Particular wills are suspect; they can be good or evil, but the general will is always good: it is never wrong, it never will be wrong.

Of course, the voice of nature remained an inescapable point of reference: besides shaping human feelings and passions, it was the origin of man's inalienable rights, such as the right to natural

11 In the *Encyclopédie*, 'Natural liberty' is defined as a 'right that nature bestows upon all men to dispose of their persons and their goods in the manner they judge most conducive to their happiness, on the condition that they do so according to the terms of natural law, and that they do not abuse it to the detriment of other men [...] The first state that man acquires through nature, and that we esteem the most precious of all things, is the state of liberty; he can neither be traded for another, nor sold, nor lose his person; because naturally all men are born free, that is to say, they are not subject to the power of a master, and no one else has a proprietary right over them.' Why do 'Christian powers', or nations, then, persist in offending the dignity of man and his natural and inalienable right to freedom by allowing the slave trade? Jaucourt's scathing explanation is 'because they needed them for their colonies, their plantations, and their mines. *Auri sacra fames!*' (translated by Thomas Zemanek). In his entry on 'Liberté' in *Le Monde des Lumières*, ed. V. Ferrone and D. Roche (p.59-69), Furio Diaz rightly stresses the nexus between humanity and freedom, and how it was first established by the Enlightenment, especially with Voltaire and Rousseau.

12. Unless otherwise indicated, Diderot quotations in the following pages are from the 'Natural rights' entry in *The Encyclopedia of Diderot & D'Alembert.*

freedom.[13] However, for Diderot the definition of a new concept of morality is also and especially a matter of collective choice and the general will, and of the free and responsible action exercised by the whole of mankind in the course of its history:

> It is to the general will that the individual must address himself to know up to what point he must be a man, a citizen, a subject, a father, a child, and when it is suitable to live or to die. The general will determines the limits of all duties. You have the most sacred natural rights in everything that is not contested by the entire species. They will enlighten you on the nature of your thoughts and your desires. Everything that you will conceive, everything that you will contemplate will be good, noble, exalted, and sublime if it is in the general and common interest. The only essential quality in your species is what you demand from all your fellow men for your happiness and for theirs. It is this conformity of you with all of them and all of them with you that will mark you when you go beyond or stay within the limits of your species. Therefore never lose sight of it; otherwise you will see the notions of benevolence, justice, humanity, and virtue blurred in your understanding. Say often to yourself: I am a man, and I do not have any other truly inalienable rights than those of humanity.

Diderot entered into a lively conversation with Rousseau, who in those months was writing on the same problems. The result was the resurrection in renewed and more powerful form of that centuries-old idea of *consensus gentium* as the epistemological basis of natural law that had been specifically ruled out by thinkers like Descartes, Spinoza, Leibniz and Pufendorf.[14] Diderot's question in this respect was: 'where is the depository of this general will? Where could I consult it?' On this issue, his position differed from that of Rousseau, who assigned normative value to the general will, and saw the new *lex* as a human construct based on procedure. The law was then the result of the social contract and of the primacy of the general will.[15] Diderot, by

13. Diderot's position comes across even more clearly in his posthumous *Pages contre un tyran*, where he invites his fellow intellectuals to reform *Ancien régime* society through new legislation based on three perpetually interconnected types of law: natural, civil and religious.
14. On this important epistemological aspect, see Sergio Landucci, *I filosofi e i selvaggi 1580-1780* (Bari, 1972), p.30ff.
15. The phrase 'volonté générale' had already been used by Montesquieu – see *De l'esprit des lois*, in Montesquieu, *Œuvres complètes*, ed. Roger Caillois, 2 vols (Paris, 1951), vol.2, p.399 (XI, 6). On the different meanings it takes on in Rousseau

contrast, focused on the historical and universal aspects of this general will, and on its cultural features as manifested in the life of man and society. It was to be found

> [i]n the principles of law written by all civilized nations; in the social practices of savage and barbaric peoples; in the tacit conventions between enemies of mankind among themselves; and even in the feelings of indignation and resentment, these two passions which nature seems to have placed even in animals to compensate for the deficiency of laws in society and the blemish of public vengeance.

The general will was then a crucial element in the new moral science of the Enlightenment. As such, it must be discovered and deferred to. Man must be studied as a whole, taking into account his physiology, social passions, ethnology. Sources to be consulted included travel literature, the history of mankind from the remotest eras, the universal law of peoples, but also, as we shall see, public opinion and the free choices made by contemporaries.

Inevitably, Diderot's innovative reflections on natural law were met with scepticism by his contemporaries. The Church was angered by the thought that the definition of morality and of natural rights themselves, now viewed in a historical dimension, should be centred on man, who was deemed to be free and responsible for his actions, and situated at the same time within and outside nature. It could not accept that mankind's general consensus and the general history of man, as an individual and in his social dimension, should determine what was right and what was wrong. And indeed the conclusions reached by Diderot marked the definitive break between Christian natural law and the natural law of the Enlightenment, as they went far beyond Grotius' and Pufendorf's indications that natural law should be independent of revealed religion: man had finally achieved complete autonomy within society. The inherent subversiveness of Diderot's opinions on this matter was immediately obvious, for instance, to Abraham Chaumeix, a determined opponent of the *philosophes*, who attacked this break with tradition in his multivolume *Préjugés légitimes contre l'Encyclopédie*: 'What is mankind? Mankind does not want anything, does not teach anything, does not prescribe anything. The term "mankind" is only an abstract term.'[16]

---

and Diderot, cf. Arthur M. Wilson, 'The development and scope of Diderot's political thought', *SVEC* 27 (1963), p.1876-900.

16. Abraham-Joseph Chaumeix d'Orléans, *Préjugés légitimes contre l'Encyclopédie et essai de réfutation de ce dictionnaire*, 8 vols (Brussels, n.n., 1758), vol.2, p.69.

A few months later, in February 1759, the Sorbonne censors and the *messieurs* in the Paris parliament stopped the publication of the first volumes of the *Encyclopédie*.

As already stated by Aquinas and reiterated by Pufendorf, besides taking *recta ratio* into account as a constituent part of reality, when seeking what is right in nature one should always start by acknowledging the existence of a 'Superior Being above mankind'. An omnipotent God had established a law to which everyone was subject and through which he had set a natural order that was 'eternal and immutable […] Instead, you believe that the general will is natural law.'[17] How dare the *philosophes* think of 'mankind' as a free agent and the author of its own moral rules? This changed everything compared to seventeenth-century natural law – so much so that, after centuries of being accused of all sorts of iniquities by conservative theologians on both sides of the Protestant–Catholic divide, Grotius and Pufendorf, who had been the founding fathers of the so-called modern school of natural law, had now been enlisted by the opposite side. These seventeenth-century thinkers were now seen as the last of the great *veteres*, to whom one could appeal, alongside Newton's mechanistic universe and the Boyle Lectures, in defence of Christianity and religion in general.

The attempt to think of natural rights in geometrical-deductive terms could not survive Diderot's determination to place natural law among the new sciences of man, highlighting the fundamental role played by the general will and man's historical action in determining what was right in nature. Diderot explains clearly in just a few sentences his opposition, on the one hand, to taking a kind of abstract individualism as the starting point for the search of what was morally right, and, on the other, to the view of a fixed natural order and of the fixity of species as confirmed by the previous century's Scientific Revolution:

> the man who listens only to his particular will is the enemy of the human race […] the general will in each individual is a pure act of understanding that reasons in the silence of the passions about what man can demand of his fellow man and about what his fellow man can rightfully demand of him […] the submission to the general will is the bond of all societies […] that if one were to assume the notion of

17. Chaumeix, *Préjugés légitimes*, vol.2, p.73-74. On this famous debate, see Casini, *Enciclopedia*, p.396, and Furio Diaz, *Filosofia e politica nel Settecento francese*, 2nd edn (Turin, 1973), p.131ff.

the species being in perpetual flux, the nature of natural rights would not change, since it would always be related to the general will and to the common desire of the entire species.

Here we find a mention of the issue of the transformation or transmutation of species, which was much debated at the time. This allows us to see the solid foundations on which Diderot based his rejection of previous ideas of natural law. And indeed he was a major exponent of that epistemological break caused by the culture of the Enlightenment with respect to the investigative modalities developed by the previous century's Scientific Revolution.[18] In this respect, Diderot's 1753 pamphlet *De l'interprétation de la nature* is an important manifesto, a sort of *Novum Organum*, of this radical shift in the view of nature, which also implied a shift in the methods of investigation and in the very meaning of scientific enquiry. Although man came to be placed on the throne, the new methods pointed out his epistemological limitations, while at the same time all knowledge was redefined in terms of his three main faculties: memory, reason and imagination. This is illustrated by the outline drawn in the 'Prospectus' and in the tree of knowledge included in the *Encyclopédie*, with their openly empirical methodology. It is in this groundbreaking figurative representation of all human knowledge that morality is included for the first time among the 'sciences of man'.[19]

Diderot's merit was to have acquainted and familiarised European public opinion with a new representation of nature that diverged radically from relatively recent models such as Descartes's geometric mechanicism, Newton's mechanistic universe, or the fixity of species put forward by Réaumur and Linnaeus: all models that gave scientific justification to the fixed natural order that was part of the creationist theory based on the Bible. Diderot viewed with irony this seventeenth-century idea of natural history, which was all taxonomy and classification. In his *Pensées sur l'interprétation de la nature* he wrote scathingly on this timeless and inanimate nature, which was nothing more than a well-crafted language, a naming of the visible, and on Linnaeus' abstract classifications, which were ultimately unable to distinguish man from ape. Diderot never doubts that nature is still at

18. On the historical significance of this long-overlooked epistemological change, see Ferrone, *Una scienza per l'uomo*, p.viii ff.

19. See the tree of knowledge in the first volume of the *Encyclopédie*, and Robert Darnton, *The Great cat massacre and other episodes in French cultural history* (New York, 1984), p.191-213.

work, in which case '[a]ll our natural sciences become as transitory as the words we utter. What we take for natural history is merely the far-from-complete history of a single instant.'[20] Diderot gives an impassioned description of the decline of the static mechanistic universe and its substitution by a dynamic representation of nature as *natura naturans*: fertile, active, productive and perpetually growing, like 'some great animal' (L, p.67), or forever changing its costume, like 'a woman who likes to dress up' (XII, p.41). In this way, Diderot personally contributed to the rise of a biological view of life, based on evolution and the transmutation of species ('I ask, therefore [...] whether animals always have been, and always will be, as they now are'; LVIII, 'Questions', 1, p.75). But what about the human species? How did it change in time? Diderot rediscovered and updated ancient concepts such as epigenesis and spontaneous generation, alongside new reflections on the need to go beyond Descartes's dualism, finally bringing man and nature, microcosm and macrocosm, mind and body, consciousness and matter together again: 'a man is not a machine', Diderot tells his 'young persons preparing to study Natural Philosophy' (foreword, p.34). His most significant contribution, however, was to clarify and advertise the epistemological break with the previous century, and how futile it was to pursue scientific truth, and even more so natural law, by means such as the geometric deductive method, the exclusive primacy of mathematics, or logical syllogism:

> We are at the dawn of a great revolution in science. To judge from the inclination men's minds would appear to have for ethics, literature, natural history and experimental physics, I would almost go so far as to assert that, within the next hundred years, there will hardly be three great geometricians in Europe. This branch of science will just cease at the point where Bernoulli, Euler, Maupertuis, Clairaut, Fontaine and d'Alembert have left it. It will stand like the Pillars of Hercules and no-one will pass beyond. (IV, p.37)

In fact, Diderot's prophecy was unfounded, or even downright wrong. Its value, however, lies in his rejection of the geometric

20. Denis Diderot, *Thoughts on the interpretation of nature and other philosophical works*, ed. David J. Adams (Manchester, 1999), LVIII, 'Questions', 1, p.75 (subsequent references within the text). On the Europe-wide importance of this shift in the view of nature and its repercussions in all branches of human knowledge, see Vincenzo Ferrone, *I profeti dell'Illuminismo: le metamorfosi della ragione nel tardo Settecento italiano*, 2nd edn (Rome and Bari, 2000), p.77ff.

deductive method inspired by Euclidean demonstrative logic, as well as of Aristotelian syllogism, which had dominated the investigation of natural law throughout the seventeenth century. Diderot upheld empiricism, the primacy of experience and 'experimental philosophy' (II, p.36), and the historicity of nature in opposition to the suddenly outdated geometric methods of the metaphysical and 'abstract sciences' (III, p.36). Accordingly, he pointed out that 'the domain of mathematicians is a world purely of the intellect, where what are taken for absolute truths cease entirely to be so when applied to the world we live in' (II, p.35). He was well aware of the remarkable step forward that had taken place when Newton's analytic inductive method superseded Descartes's geometric deductive approach, which, as we have seen, had been adopted by Spinoza and, above all, Pufendorf, who, in the title of his most important work, defined natural law as a 'système général des principes les plus importants de la morale, de la jurisprudence et de la politique'. In the 'Regulae philosophandi' included in the second edition of Newton's *Principia mathematica* (1713), the English scientist explains that the proper method of investigation in the natural sciences does not start with universal principles on the basis of which a whole system is then derived. Instead, one must always begin from experience and the analytical examination of the phenomena themselves, which will allow one to reconstruct their underlying principles. Based on infinitesimal calculus and finally aware of time as a factor, this new mathematical empiricism was something very different from traditional *more geometrico* demonstration.[21]

Diderot found that it was necessary to go even further in the direction of a total empiricism and of an experimental physics that was even more focused on the true nature of phenomena: 'Man is only the minister or interpreter of nature: he can only understand or act insofar as he has knowledge of the beings that surround him, either by means of experiment or reflection.'[22] After Leibniz and Locke, who had established a difference between rational truth ('truths of reason') and factual truth ('truths of fact'), it was impossible not to acknowledge the limitations of the mathematical method. Accordingly, in his contributions to the entry on 'Certitude' in the *Encyclopédie* Diderot distinguishes between different forms of certainty: mathematical and metaphysical (a conventional and intellectual kind of certainty), that

21. Cf. Alexandre Koyré, *Newtonian studies* (London, 1965), p.262ff.

22. *The Encyclopedia of Diderot & D'Alembert*, under 'Art', translated by Nelly S. Hoyt and Thomas Cassirer.

which pertains to physical phenomena, and a third form of certainty, which applies to moral sciences. Diderot wrote eloquently on this subject, both in order to announce the epistemological crisis of the old geometric deductive model and to engage in an important debate with D'Alembert and other European scientists on the philosophical premises of probability calculation, which was being hailed as the new 'science physico-mathémathique de la vie', a precious new tool of enquiry that was particularly useful in the moral sciences and the new sciences of man.[23] In fact, Diderot was not alone in pointing to the limitations of reason and of the geometric deductive method, or in stressing the importance of probable knowledge in the study of social reality. In this, he was backed up by important work that had been carried out by Maupertuis, Buffon and above all Hume, who were all, like Voltaire and many other Enlightenment thinkers, the heirs at the same time of the scepticism of Montaigne and Bayle and of Isaac Newton's scientific dogmatism.[24]

Indeed, in terms of the history of natural law and of its final metamorphosis, which would open the way to the new language of the rights of man, David Hume is an especially important figure. His 1739-1740 *Treatise of human nature*, described on the title page as 'an attempt to introduce the experimental method of reasoning into moral subjects', demolished the metaphysical basis for the old and modern natural law alike, insofar as they were founded on the centrality of reason. It achieved this by means of what early-twentieth-century logical positivists (such as Carnap or Popper) called 'Hume's paradox' or 'Hume's law', whereby a coherent argument cannot move from descriptive premises to prescriptive conclusions, and, since it is not possible to infer what *ought to be* from what *is*, it is impossible to find moral values and determine what is right through the logical examination of the nature of things, as thinkers had done from Aristotle through Aquinas to Pufendorf.[25]

23. For an overall discussion of this topic, see the chapter on 'Il dibattito su probabilità e scienze sociali nel secolo XVIII', in Ferrone, *Una scienza per l'uomo*, p.66-95.
24. Gianni Paganini rightly insists on the fact that 'while it is considered the century of reason *par excellence*, the eighteenth century was also the time when thinkers became most strongly aware of the limitations of human knowledge.' See his chapter on 'Scetticismo e certezza', in *Illuminismo: un vademecum*, ed. Gianni Paganini and Edoardo Tortarolo (Turin, 2008), p.252-65 (253).
25. Cf. David Hume, *A Treatise of human nature: a critical edition*, vol.1: *Texts*, ed. David Fate Norton and Mary J. Norton (Oxford, 2014), III, 1, 1 ('Moral distinctions

Hume had turned his scepticism and philosophical genius to the attempt to verify the limits of reason and of logical language, which led to a revolutionary analysis of the psychological and empirical foundations of the principle of causality. Given the intellectualistic and conventional character of the geometric deductive method, which created connections among ideas (man's perceptions were something else entirely), Hume directed his criticism of metaphysical intellectualism towards the logical inductive method that was applied in the experiments that formed the basis of modern Newtonian science. The conclusions he reached were to remain part of the history of Western philosophy. He showed once and for all that no necessary logical link could be inferred from the analysis of two sequential events (i.e. 'B always follows A'), because that sequence was always liable to change in future. For Hume, it was not possible, by means of logical reasoning, to infer or prove the existence of a principle of uniformity by virtue of which nature's laws were constant and eternal. He pointed out how all arguments concerning relationships of cause and effect and among facts in general were really based only on experience, habit, beliefs and modes of thinking that had developed over the centuries. Whatever its field of enquiry – whether it studied the movements of the stars or the life of man in society – the new experimental science dealt with concrete facts linked to perceptions rather than with abstract ideas: therefore, it must be placed in the sphere of probable knowledge.[26]

However, this did not imply a wholesale acceptance of the sceptical relativism displayed by the followers of Montaigne. It simply meant

not deriv'd from reason'), §27: 'In every system of morality, which I have hitherto met with, I have always remark'd, that the author proceeds for some time in the ordinary way of reasoning, and establishes the being of a God, or makes observations concerning human affairs; when of a sudden I am surpriz'd to find, that instead of the usual copulations of propositions, *is*, and *is not*, I meet with no proposition that is not connected with an *ought*, or an *ought not*. This change is imperceptible; but is, however, of the last consequence. For as this *ought*, or *ought not*, expresses some new relation or affirmation, 'tis necessary that it shou'd be observ'd and explain'd; and at the same time that a reason shou'd be given, for what seems altogether inconceivable, how this new relation can be a deduction from others, which are entirely different from it. But as authors do not commonly use this precaution, I shall presume to recommend it to the reader; and am perswaded, that this small attention wou'd subvert all the vulgar systems of morality, and let us see, that the distinction of vice and virtue is not founded merely on the relations of objects, nor is perceiv'd by reason.'

26. Cf. Mario Dal Pra, *Hume e la scienza della natura umana*, 2nd edn (Rome and Bari, 1973), p.142ff.

situating reason and its limitations in their correct place, and acknowledging that other human faculties, such as instinct, the passions or imagination, also had a role to play in the sciences of man. In fact, reason could be considered the slave of the passions and of custom, to the extent that Hume declared himself a moralist who would rather follow instinct than reason. The new moral science should no longer be based exclusively on abstract or metaphysical concepts, such as principles or 'exact definitions', as had been the case for centuries and in particular in the work of Pufendorf and, more recently, Wollaston or Clarke. It should develop from 'matter of fact', by applying the experimental method to reality. And indeed, Hume remarks with satisfaction, '[m]en are now cured of their passion for hypotheses and systems in natural philosophy, and will hearken to no arguments but those which are derived from experience.'[27]

In line with this, the third book of the *Treatise of human nature* finally does away with that ethical rationalism that for centuries had been the basis of natural law, both old and new, and replaces it with a new naturalistic and experimental ethics. Hume famously attacks those previous systems that saw virtue as 'nothing but a conformity to reason; that there are eternal fitnesses and unfitnesses of things, which are the same to every rational being that considers them; that the immutable measures of right and wrong impose an obligation, not only on human creatures, but also on the deity himself', as per Grotius' famous precept *etsi Deus non daretur.*[28] Hume argues that moral distinctions 'cannot be deriv'd from reason' (III, 1, 1, 6) or judgement. They must be found through the experimental study, from the psychological point of view, of those passions that are constantly and uniformly present in human nature, and especially of 'sympathy' (III, 3, 1, 7), which has been the true engine and primary principle of social interaction and bonds and of man's moral actions across the centuries. In his writings after the *Treatise*, Hume demonstrated how our values, including the very idea of justice and liberty and the authority principle, were nothing but conventions and modes of thinking. They were the spontaneous result of human initiatives and as such they could be examined and

27. David Hume, 'An enquiry concerning the principles of morals', I ('Of the general principles of morals'), §138, in *Enquiries concerning human understanding and concerning the principles of morals*, ed. P. H. Nidditch, 3rd edn (Oxford, 2014), p.174-75.

28. Hume, *Treatise of human nature*, book III, part 1, section 1, paragraph 4 (further references within the text).

understood only through experience and the analysis of reality. This led him to stress the importance of history and of knowledge *a posteriori* as a precious epistemological tool for the construction of the new sciences of man.

Hume himself was the author of important books on history. He was also fiercely opposed to historical Pyrrhonism, which he considered a subtle and devious enemy, to be fought off using philological inference as a valid falsification criterion in the analysis of evidence.[29] In a variety of works, including a short essay addressed to women readers, Hume explains the relevance of historical knowledge in terms of its being an extension of current experience by modern social scientists, in which 'historical facts' could be considered as 'so many collections of experiments, by which the politician or moral philosopher fixes the principles of his science':[30]

> if we consider the shortness of human life, and our limited knowledge, even of what passes in our own time, we must be sensible that we should be for ever children in understanding, were it not for this invention, which extends our experience to all past ages, and to the most distant nations; making them contribute as much to our improvement in wisdom, as if they had actually lain under our observation. A man acquainted with history may, in some respect, be said to have lived from the beginning of the world, and to have been making continual additions to his stock of knowledge in every century.[31]

It is easy to see the importance for our investigation of this authoritative defence of the epistemological value of history in terms of the new science of man, and especially of moral science. Hume himself did not address the issue of the rights of man: however, he gave a major contribution to the modern view of history that at that time was being developed by authors such as Vico, Montesquieu, Voltaire and other Enlightenment thinkers. Among other things, this powerful new concept would give new foundations and legitimacy to the theory of the rights of man as a crucial element in this new philosophy of history – a history that was entirely earthly and centred on the human being,

29. Cf. Giuseppe Giarrizzo, *David Hume politico e storico* (Turin, 1962), p.119ff.
30. 'An enquiry concerning human understanding', VIII ('Of liberty and necessity'), part 1, §65, in Hume, *Enquiries*, p.83-84.
31. 'Of the study of history', in *Essays: moral, political, and literary*, ed. Eugene F. Miller (Indianapolis, IN, 1985), p.563-68 (566-67). Cf. Dal Pra, *Hume*, p.74.

its happiness and its moral and material progress, in opposition to the biblical and Augustinian view. This justification itself was no longer based on philosophical, logical deductive, *a priori* arguments, but on historical, empirical, *a posteriori* evidence.

As I mentioned at the start of this study, it was Condorcet's *Esquisse d'un tableau historique des progrès de l'esprit humain* that was the definitive Enlightenment manifesto of this new way of thinking about man's rights, from the second half of the eighteenth century right down to our day. And this happened on the basis of those very same observations on the epistemological importance of historical knowledge. According to Condorcet, the 'droits naturels de l'homme' were not something that needed to be justified from the logical or philosophical point of view. Instead, they were something that could be 'recognised' and brought to the fore through the critical analysis of past events: more specifically, they could be seen to rise gradually out of the general consensus of the most civilised European nations following cruel and violent struggles for human emancipation.

Indeed, there can be no doubt that the violence and intolerance generated by the religious crisis of the sixteenth and seventeenth centuries had naturally encouraged human reason to search for 'rights which had been too long forgotten, or, rather, which had never been well known or properly explained', and had subsequently led Enlightenment thinkers to assert 'the belief that these rights are inalienable and indefeasible'.[32]

In conclusion, it is important to realise how behind this *a posteriori* validation of the truth of the rights of man as the foundation of a new moral and political science there was a radically new way of looking at historical knowledge and the chronological dimension of reality. We know that in the course of the eighteenth century a conceptual revolution had taken place that had led to universal history being finally examined as history in its own right. It was now 'history' *tout court*, an autonomous topic of study, without an object or subject, in which the time factor was no longer a simple chronological vessel that contained all the various 'histories' in their cycles, becoming instead a dynamic force in itself, and acquiring its own *historical quality*. In this way, history no longer happened *within time* but *because of time*.[33] The

32. Condorcet, *Sketch*, eighth stage, p.111, and ninth stage, p.140.
33. Cf. Reinhart Koselleck, *Futures past: on the semantics of historical time* (Cambridge, MA, 1985), p.xxiv. Koselleck explains how our modern concept of history only arose in Western culture towards the end of the eighteenth century: 'It is an

Enlightenment's revolutionary concept of history introduced the point of view of man, of philosophy and of critical thinking in the way one looked at the meaning of events, together with the conscious use of new philological techniques such as source and witness criticism.[34] An important element to this effect was its 'discovery of time', something that would literally transform the perception of reality in Western culture.

In the course of the seventeenth and eighteenth centuries, the lively debate among geologists, historians, cosmologists, philosophers and scholars of all kinds brought forward some radical and unexpected hypotheses on the history of the universe, nature and the human species. These theories blew to pieces the hitherto unquestioned tradition according to which the history of nature and the history of man not only ran in parallel but had to both be contained within the 6000-year span allowed by biblical chronology.[35] By contrast, a widely divergent chronology for nature and the human species began to emerge from a variety of sources: from the long chronological times postulated by Giambattista Vico, to Voltaire's study of Ancient China, which went back far more than 6000 years, to the geological times described by Buffon, who in his 1778 *Epoques de la nature* argued that the earth was 75,000 years old. As historical time broke through the theological 6000-year barrier, it became clear that man had 'emerged' from nature far later and with evolutionary rhythms and phases that were very different from the pace of geological mutations. Other important studies focused on how animal species had changed in time. In my discussion of Diderot I mentioned the debate between

outcome of the lengthy theoretical reflections of the Enlightenment. Formerly there had existed, for instance, the history that God had set in motion with humanity. But there was no history for which humanity might have been the subject or which could be thought of as its own subject. Previously, histories had existed in the plural – all sorts of histories which had occurred and which might be used as exempla in teachings on ethics and religion, and in law and philosophy [...] If anyone had said before 1780 that he studied history, he would have at once been asked by his interlocutor: Which history? History of what? Imperial history, or the history of theological doctrine, or perhaps the history of France? [...] [H]istory could only be conceived together with an associated subject that underwent change or upon which change occurred' (p.200-201).

34. Arnaldo Momigliano, *Sui fondamenti della storia antica* (Turin, 1984) is still one of the most important studies on this subject.

35. Cf. Paolo Rossi, *The Dark abyss of time: the history of the earth and the history of nations from Hooke to Vico* (Chicago, IL, 1984).

the supporters of epigenesis and of preformation.[36] This controversy finally dismissed the seventeenth-century theory of the fixity of species and of an immovable universe, which could never diverge from the original form into which it had been shaped by God, as described by the natural theology of the Newtonian Boyle Lectures. All the evidence that was coming in from cosmology, geology, anthropology and the comparative history of nations and civilisations told the same story: that there was a *pre*history, and that the human species had undergone a complex evolution in time which had led it to diverge from nature to a certain extent. The vast amount of travel literature that was produced after the discovery of the American continent was updated to reflect the 'discovery of time' and in the course of the eighteenth century became a veritable storehouse for the Enlightenment science of man. The human being now needed to be studied under many different aspects: physiological, medical, psychological, social. Above all, man was to be studied in his historical development, seeking inductively, *a posteriori*, the evidence for scientific truth within his cognitive processes.

In order to explain the variations in the evolution of the different peoples, the mid-eighteenth century came up with a theory of stadial development, i.e. of the gradual development of mankind linked to changes in forms of subsistence: from primitive hunting populations to animal domestication and sedentary farming down to more evolved trading societies. Rousseau notwithstanding, the idea of the 'bad savage' started to become prevalent in Enlightenment circles over Montaigne's myth of the 'noble savage', since it helped explain certain populations' lack of civilisation.[37] Universal history was rewritten according to stages that were derived from the comparison between savage and civilised societies. In relation to this, Montesquieu investigated the spirit and profound nature of laws, and revealed the nexus between forms of government, legislation and modes of production across time and space by applying his hypotheses to different nations across four continents. His work was continued by the Scottish Enlightenment, whose philosophers studied in universal and rational terms how man could be improved in society. Finally, in his contribution to Raynal's *Histoire des deux Indes*, Diderot had no hesitation in crediting travel

36. On this debate, see Giovanni Solinas, *Il microscopio e le metafisiche: epigenesi e preesistenza da Cartesio a Kant* (Milan, 1967); Ferrone, *I profeti dell'Illuminismo*, p.80ff.
37. See, in particular, Ronald L. Meek, *Social science and the ignoble savage* (Cambridge, 1976).

literature and the new historical approach to the study of savage societies with bringing about all the progress that had been achieved through moral philosophy, at the same time denouncing the limitations of the epistemological choices made by the moral philosophers of the previous century, who had sought the foundations of society only in the social order that was before their eyes.[38]

However, it was above all Jean-Jacques Rousseau, with his witty paradoxes and clever intuitions, who finally introduced historical time into the old and much maligned natural law of the previous century. He thus gave a decisive impulse to the transformation of its abstract and immovable geometric deductive rationalism into the Enlightenment science of man. In turn, on both the epistemological and historical level, this science became the starting point for the rise of the modern political and moral language of the rights of man.

38. Cf. Landucci, *I filosofi e i selvaggi*, p.20.

9. The question of Rousseau

Was Rousseau the father of the rights of man, and of the politics of the moderns? His novels have recently been credited with creating a new empathy between human beings and preparing the ground for the rise of the language of rights in Europe in the second half of the eighteenth century. Rousseau has been called a great populariser and even – with some exaggeration – the 'inventor of the phrase "rights of man"'.[1] This reopened a question that had been much debated by historians at the beginning of the twentieth century: did Rousseau play an important role in the genesis of the 1789 Declaration of rights and, more generally, in the rise of modern politics?[2]

In fact, this is a complex question and still very much to be explored from the point of view of tracing the origin of the language of the rights of man in the West. From the lexical point of view, Rousseau uses the phrase only once in his many writings: in the eighth chapter of book IV of his 1762 *Social contract*, where he discusses civil religion and mentions 'the rights or the duties of men'.[3] In this chapter he is borrowing this concept directly from Burlamaqui and Barbeyrac,

1. Hunt, *Inventing human rights*, p.127.
2. See Rials, *La Déclaration des droits*, p.355ff., on the debate between Georg Jellinek, who ruled out the idea that Rousseau may have had any influence on the 1789 Declaration of Rights, and François Boutmy, who claimed such influence not only for the philosopher from Geneva but for the French Enlightenment as a whole. Important discussions on this issue are still to be found in Giorgio Del Vecchio, *Su la teoria del contratto sociale* (Bologna, 1906), and Cassirer, 'Vom Wesen und Werden des Naturrechts', p.218ff.
3. Cf. Jean-Jacques Rousseau, *An Inquiry into the nature of the social contract, or Principles of political right, translated from the French of John James Rousseau* (London, G. G. J. and J. Robinson, 1791; henceforth *Social contract*), p.368. The French original reads 'les devoirs & les droits de l'homme'.

who – as we have seen – had already made conscious use of it. In *Emile*, published in the same year, Rousseau twice uses the phrase 'rights of humanity'.[4] However, he does not explain his use of these neologisms, which he must have thought were not particularly original and therefore easily comprehensible to his contemporaries. These phrases are part of a shared linguistic and conceptual background that is founded on the persistence of the medieval theory of natural law in universities and among scholars across the centuries. They also testify to that slow but unstoppable transformation that we have described in our previous chapters, which was due to the new importance of history, of man himself and his faculties, and of the study of his physiological and psychological nature.

In using those terms Rousseau obviously did not feel that he was being particularly innovative. He devoted special attention, however, to the new term *droit politique*, which he used instead of the old *droit naturel*. This was part of an explicit effort by Rousseau to shift attention from the natural rights of man in the state of nature to the rights of man in civil society, an effort that would make a major contribution to the definition of the modern individual in anthropological and historical terms by focusing on man's communitarian tendencies and the inevitable dialectics of morality and politics in civil society.

Despite the vast literature on this subject that has accumulated over time, the historical question of Rousseau has only been marginally examined from the point of view of the rights of man.[5] In fact, this overlooked area of study may help us find at least a partial solution to the enigma of the most famous and popular author in eighteenth-century Europe. We must remember that, in his *Esquisse d'un tableau historique*, Condorcet, who was his contemporary, already points out the importance of Rousseau's reflections for the history of the rights of man, thanks to his transformation of the 'droits naturels de l'homme [...] inaliénables et imprescriptibles' into 'droits politiques'. In this way Rousseau was giving wider currency to the Enlightenment's acknowledgement of these rights on the historical level.

4. Cf. Rousseau, *Emilius*, vol.2, p.334 and 366.
5. This question is briefly mentioned in Cassirer's works. For a more detailed analysis, see Jean Starobinski, 'Jean-Jacques Rousseau et les droits de l'homme', *Revue des sciences morales et politiques* 144:1 (1989), p.109-26; Lester G. Crocker, 'Les droits individuels et le corps social: Rousseau et Burlamaqui', *Etudes Jean-Jacques Rousseau* 4 (1990), p.9-29 (18ff.).

In a move of great importance for the rise of the 'sciences morales et politiques', Condorcet places Rousseau alongside Sidney and Locke, who had been the first to point out the link between natural rights and politics. However, Rousseau went further, as he gave a profoundly original account of the relationship between nature and culture, and especially of the rise of 'droit politique', and the consequent need to create new institutions capable of guaranteeing 'l'exercice' or the universal political enforcement of natural rights in modern civil society. Rousseau was the only thinker to have finally found the solution to this problem, thanks to his discovery of the 'volonté générale', and to have openly confronted the theoreticians of natural law from the previous century with the accusation of being bad scientists and faithful servants of the absolute state. He alone focused on those principles that linked together natural rights and republicanism, ultimately denouncing the unlawful power of man over man in all its forms: 'These principles, which the noble Sidney paid for with his blood and on which Locke set the authority of his name, were later developed by Rousseau with greater precision, breadth and energy, and he deserves renown for having established them among the truths that it is no longer permissible to forget or to combat.'[6]

Condorcet was right. Rousseau's 1755 *Discourse upon the origin and foundation of the inequality among mankind* had gone straight to the heart of the matter, laying the foundations of a debate that would spread across Europe in the second half of the eighteenth century. Rousseau's *Second discourse*, as it is also known, addresses a specific question put forward by the Dijon academics: 'Quelle est l'origine de l'inégalité parmi les hommes, et si elle est autorisée par la loi naturelle'. Rousseau's uncompromising answer was that there is nothing in natural law that upholds inequality. He went even further, and called into doubt the very concept of natural law as it had developed in previous centuries, attacking its ideological and political premises, pointing out its epistemological errors, and, especially, the fallacy of any investigation that took the universe rather than man itself as its starting point. In explaining his main thesis, Rousseau pointed out that, in order to 'meditate on the equality nature has established among men, and on the inequality they themselves have introduced', it was necessary to found a new science of man and go beyond the old natural law, which had ignored the centrality of the individual and especially the complex relationship between nature and culture as it had developed over time:

6. Condorcet, *Sketch*, p.130 ('The ninth stage').

> It is this ignorance of the nature of man, that so much perplexes and obscures the genuine definition of natural right: for the idea of right, as Monsieur Burlamaqui says, and still more that of natural right, are ideas evidently relative to the nature of man. It is therefore from this very nature of man [...] from his constitution and his state, that we are to deduce the principles of this study.[7]

Just as much ignorance and as 'little agreement' existed in relation to the fundamental concept of natural law, with a general lack of scientific knowledge being accompanied by divergent opinions on the very meaning of the word 'law'. For the ancient jurists such as Ulpian, who still adhered to the Aristotelian view of the universe, natural law was the unchangeable manifestation of the relationship that nature had established among all living creatures, both men and animals, for their common preservation. For the moderns, this concept only applied to mankind, since the true meaning of the word 'law' was that of 'a rule prescribed to a moral being, that is to say, a being intelligent, free, and considered with a view to his relations to other beings' (p.lii). Over the centuries many definitions had been given of natural law, which were 'constantly at variance' (p.liii), and generally constructed on the basis of 'an almost arbitrary fitness' (p.liv) and a logic of domination. Hence the necessity to do away with all 'inveterate prejudices' (p.87), and really get to know natural man, separating the voice of nature from the exercise of human will: 'without applying ourselves seriously to the study of man, his natural faculties and their successive developments, it is impossible we should ever be able to make these distinctions, and separate, in the actual constitution of things, the operations of the divine will from the pretended improvements of human art' (p.lix).

To this end, however, it was necessary to abandon the geometric deductive method, which had played such an important role in the study of natural law in the previous century. One had to do away with that abstract view of natural history, which was essentially a taxonomy, and with the idea of the state of nature as a kind of mental experiment, something that was entirely to do with reason, logic and rationality. All this would be replaced by the Enlightenment's understanding of the autonomy of the historical world following the discovery of time. The new epistemological methods would emphasise empirical experience and the necessary historicity of man and nature,

7. Jean-Jacques Rousseau, *A Discourse upon the origin and foundation of the inequality among mankind* (London, R. and J. Dodsley, 1761), 'Dedication', p.iv and 'Preface', p.l-li (subsequent references within the text).

as they devoted themselves to the study of man's stages of development: state of nature, primitive, savage, barbarian, down to modern man and his civilisation.

These 'researches' were, of course, 'difficult to make' (p.l). Above all, they had never been attempted with a clear epistemological awareness of the role of the new philosophical reflection on historical knowledge, especially in relation to the most ancient times. In order to finally reconstruct the obscure vicissitudes of 'original man' (p.lviii) and his successive developments, one had to look towards a dark and unknown world and an endless, faraway, seemingly impenetrable time, which extended thousands and thousands of centuries beyond what was implied by the biblical narrative. This meant leaping back to the year zero of mankind, to the origin of a 'pure state of nature' (p.52 and *passim*) that, 'if ever it did, does not now, and in all probability never will exist' (p.xlix), and which in any case was not identical or even comparable to the living conditions of savage people as reported by explorers. To this effect it was necessary to reject those 'historical truths' that had been set up by adherents of the historical philological method against the scepticism of the Pyrrhonists, and proceed only by means of 'hypothetical and conditional reasonings, fitter to illustrate the nature of things, than to show their true origin, like those systems, which our naturalists daily make of the formation of the world' (p.10) – naturalists like Buffon, with his *Théorie de la terre* and *Histoire naturelle de l'homme* (1749), or Maupertuis, with his 1750 *Essai de cosmologie.*

Rousseau himself practised this new hypothetical study of history. However, in formulating his conjectures he shows a pioneering historicist spirit, and is ready to take into account any discontinuities and peculiarities in the contexts and evolutionary ages under investigation, which he always examines *iuxta propria principia*. This led him to develop an important new working hypothesis and postulate the existence of something like a *prehistory* of mankind. Though timeless and unchangeable, this remote era of primitive men was nonetheless part of the flow of universal history, as well as being entirely dominated by nature. Rousseau maintained this in opposition to a *history* of mankind characterised by culture and by a dominance of reason that risked more and more stifling 'the authority of nature' (p.lvi), a history made up of different evolutionary stages and sudden, revolutionary leaps forward.[8]

8. Cf. Alberto Burgio, 'Necessità della storia e storia impossibile: per una analisi metodologica del "Discours sur l'inégalité" di Rousseau', *Studi settecenteschi*

This major distinction underlined the total discontinuity between primitive and civil man. In itself, it provided Rousseau with sufficient evidence to denounce the anachronism and the openly teleological tendency of those who, in examining the foundational stages of contemporary societies, had given tongue-in-cheek descriptions of a fantastical state of nature to which they had artfully assigned the vices, ideas, needs, passions, desires and wish for power that characterised civil man: 'In speaking of savages they described citizens' (p.9). These authors thought that they could trace the foundations of society 'back to a state of nature, but not one of them has ever arrived there' (p.8). Their true purpose was to appeal to nature in order to legitimise the hierarchical structures and disciplinary practices of contemporary governments, the king's despotism and all the injustices of modern civil society.

It was therefore necessary to unmask the obviously ideological character of old natural law and to demolish its logical cathedrals brick by brick. In any case, these were built on deeply unsound ideas of the state of nature: from the fierce state of perpetual war described by Hobbes, to the primacy of the sociability principle in the Neo-Stoics, such as Grotius and Pufendorf. The true 'pure state of nature' was entirely different from all of these, and could only be glimpsed by throwing some light on the darkness that enveloped the most primitive times.

First of all, in that prehistoric state of pure nature man was not at all given to perpetual warfare, partly because he did not live in groups, families, hordes or packs best suited to hunting, as recently reasserted by Buffon, who believed that the human being was an eminently social animal from the very beginning. By contrast, unlike important sectors of the Enlightenment movement, Rousseau rejected the idea of the sociability principle, which had been the basis for all previous discussions of the moral science of duties, as the ultimate foundation of civil society.[9] Rousseau believed instead that men had originally lived in a dispersed and isolated state:

11-12 (1988-1989), p.115-40. On the importance of history and experience in Rousseau's epistemological model compared with the geometric deductive method of the previous school of natural law, see Victor Goldschmidt, *Anthropologie et politique: les principes du système de Rousseau* (Paris, 1974), p.136ff.

9. On the importance of the sociability principle in the Enlightenment, see Daniel Gordon, *Citizens without sovereignty: equality and sociability in French thought, 1670-1789* (Princeton, NJ, 1994).

> Let us conclude that savage man, wandering about in the forests, without industry, without speech, without any fixed residence, an equal stranger to war and every social connection, without standing in any shape in need of his fellows, as well as without any desire of hurting them, and perhaps even without ever distinguishing them individually one from the other, subject to few passions, and finding in himself all he wants, let us, I say, conclude that savage man thus circumstanced had no knowledge or sentiment but such as are proper to that condition. (p.86)

In that 'primitive condition' in which man was undistinguishable from other animals, nature ruled over every aspect of life. It was a big mistake to think, as everyone had done until then, that savage man, in his human condition, was characterised by a natural sociability, the use of language, even rationality. We should be wary of 'confounding savage man with the men, whom we daily see and converse with' (p.29). Primitive man had no knowledge of natural law, of right or wrong, morality, virtue or vice. He was neither good nor bad, nor was he 'as well versed in the art of thinking, as philosophers make him' (p.46). In those dark ages he was as yet incapable of 'forming to himself, by the most abstract arguments, maxims of justice and reason' (p.47). No one had yet investigated 'how many thousand ages must have been requisite to develop successively the operations, which the human mind is capable of producing' (p.48), or, for instance, 'the immense space, which must have separated the pure state of nature from that in which languages became necessary' (p.52).[10]

Being ruled solely by the voice of nature, unlike civilised man primitive man did not speak, uttering only inarticulate sounds. He was essentially body, physicality, instinct, passions. Reason and social institutions like property or the family were unknown to him. The relationship between the sexes was sporadic and 'confined entirely to what is physical in love' (p.82), to the struggle for the possession of women, and to reproduction, 'which renders the sexes necessary to each other' (p.79). Since there was no marriage, they were also free of undesirable products of civilisation such as honour killings, abortion

10. Cf. the 'Essay on the origin of languages', chapter VIII, where Rousseau points out that '[w]hen one wishes to study men, one has to look close by; but in order to study man, one has to learn to cast one's eyes far off' (Jean-Jacques Rousseau, *Essay on the origin of languages and writings related to music*, ed. and translated by John T. Scott, in *The Collected writings of Rousseau*, vol.7, Hanover, NH, 1998, p.289-332, 305).

or adultery. In Rousseau's opinion, it was absurd or misguided to ask which was better, civilised life or the pure state of nature, or whether primitive man was happy. And in any case, as he pointed out with a twist of irony, no savage man, however miserable, was capable of lamenting his condition to the point of committing suicide, as was instead sadly common among civilised men. That was really a distant and incommensurable world: a world in which time did not flow but hung suspended. There was no awareness of change. Primitive man

> was alone sensible of his real necessities, took notice of nothing but what it was his interest to see, and [...] his understanding made as little progress as his vanity. If he happened to make any discovery, he could the less communicate it as he did not even know his children. The art perished with the inventer; there was neither education nor improvement; generations succeeded generations to no purpose; and as all constantly set out from the same point, whole centuries rolled on in the rudeness and barbarity of the first age; the species was grown old, while the individual still remained in a state of childhood. (p.86-87)

Rousseau devoted the entire first part of his *Second discourse* to the detailed description of the immutable true state of nature as something entirely different from the civilised state, which was governed by culture and historical time. He discusses every single aspect, always in open opposition to the previous school of natural law, because he was acutely aware of the fact that what was at stake was not only the political legitimation of contemporary forms of power and social discipline, but something even more important: the very idea of humanity. The concept of person now could and must be redefined in the light of the new science of man and its focus on the historical and empirical dimension of the human condition.

There is no doubt that Rousseau's contribution to the rise of the modern individual and the new Enlightenment humanism lies not so much in his famous autobiographical novel, the *Confessions* – despite this being indeed a literary and philosophical monument to psychological introspection – as to his *Discourse upon the origin and foundation of the inequality among mankind*. It is difficult to disagree with those who locate in this work the starting point of Western ethnology and anthropology, and the very basis on which Rousseau developed his political thought.[11]

11. In his 'Jean-Jacques Rousseau' Lévi-Strauss describes this work as 'the first

In his notes to the *Second discourse* Rousseau makes ample use of travellers' accounts, as well as of the latest research on African tribes and the populations of the Caribbean and the Antilles. It is this information which, though second-hand, provides empirical validation for most of his conjectures – not because these savage populations could be identified with primitive man in the pure state of nature, but because of their residual similarities and greater closeness to that degree zero of mankind which was now irretrievably lost but also of fundamental importance in order to understand the stages of evolution of the species. The *Second discourse* did not fail to take into account recent studies in comparative anatomy, physiology, medicine or what we would now call linguistics. This testified to the scientific rigour of Rousseau's work, with its empirical and experimental basis, as opposed to the abstract geometric deductive method of the previous century's school of natural law. With the *Second discourse*, the epistemological break was well and truly under way, and that prestigious movement of thought was a thing of the past.

Buffon had maintained that man's carnivorous diet gave a biological justification to his living and hunting in packs, which in turn proved his natural sociability. In opposition to this, new studies on the configuration of the teeth and the stomach gave Rousseau strong evidence with which to support his thesis that primitive man was essentially frugivorous, which allowed him to live an autonomous and isolated existence scattered across the bush. Rousseau also tended to blur Buffon's clear-cut distinction between men and animals, which was based on the claim that the former had lived consciously and rationally in history since time immemorial. He pointed out that, in those ages, man had no language, consciousness or memory, which meant that in many ways he was more similar to animals than to modern man. The fact that anthropomorphic creatures often featured in travellers' accounts seemed to provide telling evidence in this respect:

> There are found, says the translator of the *History of Voyages, etc.* in the Kingdom of Congo, a great many of those large animals, called orang-outang, in the East Indies, which form a kind of mean rank of beings between men and baboons. Battel tells us, that in the forests of Mayomba in the Kingdom of Loango [southern Ethiopia], there are two sorts of monsters, the largest of which are called *pongos* and the

treatise of general ethnology' (p.199). See also Michèle Duchet, *Anthropologie et histoire au siècle des Lumières* (Paris, 1971), p.322.

> others *enjokos*. The first exactly resemble man, but are much larger and taller. (*Second discourse*, p.222)[12]

> We cannot discover by these passages, what reasons the writers had for refusing to the animals in question the name of wild men; but we may easily guess, that it was on account of their stupidity and want of speech; weak arguments for those who know, that, though the organs of speech are natural to man, it is otherwise with speech itself. (p.226)

For Rousseau, therefore, the question of what characterised man's humanity in the pure state of nature needed to be completely re-examined. He believed that 'in order to study man, one has to learn to cast one's eyes far off', i.e. never to identify the other with the self without first taking into account any obvious differences and peculiarities.[13] Rousseau pointed out the anachronism of attributing to primitive man distinctive traits that only belonged to civilised man, such as sociability and rationality. Against this he put forward new theories that took into account the fact that, in the historical context, nature inevitably ruled over culture. In denying the relevance of the sociability principle to the earliest stage of man's development, the author finds here 'two principles prior to reason, one of which interests us deeply in our own preservation and welfare, and the other inspires us with a natural aversion to see any other being, but especially any being like ourselves, suffer or perish' (p.lv). Both these principles, self-love and sympathy towards others, were in fact passions: they manifested the instinctive power of nature, which at this stage, before reason and culture asserted themselves, was not simply dominant but unstoppable.

In order to put his argument across, Rousseau insisted on the distinction between 'selfishness' and 'self-love' (p.250). The latter was an entirely natural feeling that aimed at the preservation of the individual. The former was an artificial feeling that had arisen at a later stage, as a cultural product of civil society: this was the source of that sense of honour that would create inequalities and privileges and justify the logic of domination. Rousseau also assigned a crucial role to the natural feeling of sympathy or pity, which was the other important piece in the mosaic that defined the humanity of primitive

12. Here Rousseau is referring to the twenty-volume *Histoire générale des voyages* edited from 1746 by the abbé Antoine Prévost and to the writings of English traveller Andrew Battel.
13. See above, n.10.

man: 'It is therefore certain that pity is a natural sentiment, which, by moderating in every individual the activity of self-love, contributes to the mutual preservation of the whole species' (p.76). Even the defender of individual self-interest as the basis of a new rational and utilitarian ethics had to acknowledge, in his 'Fable of the bees', that man was ultimately a compassionate and sensitive being:

> Mandeville was very sensible that men, in spite of all their morality, would never have been better than monsters, if nature had not given them pity to assist reason: but he did not perceive that from this quality alone flow all the social virtues, which he would dispute mankind the possession of. In fact, what is generosity, what clemency, what humanity, but pity applied to the weak, to the guilty, or to the human species in general? Even benevolence and friendship, if we judge right, will appear the effects of a constant pity, fixed upon a particular object: for to wish that a person may not suffer, what is it but to wish that he may be happy? [...] In fact, commiseration must be so much the more energetic, the more intimately the animal, that beholds any kind of distress, identifies himself with the animal that labours under it. (p.73-75)[14]

This meant that social virtues and social behaviour were not founded on the Neo-Stoics' rational morality, with its basis in the sociability principle. And neither were they founded on the religious morality of the Gospels, even though the latter did urge, through subtly argued theological principles, that we should love one another and not do unto others what we did not want done unto us. What society was founded on were passions and ancestral feelings that in the pure state of nature were common to all men.

We should spend a little more time on Rousseau's rejection of the idea that rationality was an intrinsic characteristic of primitive man. According to the philosopher, our understanding of the earliest stage of mankind, which he had been the first to describe – a stage that was solely ruled by nature – had been obfuscated and forgotten by the rise of culture. The original characteristics of those times had been overwritten with culture's own paradigms of knowledge, especially

14. See also Rousseau, *Emilius*: 'And indeed, how should we be excited to pity, but by being transported beyond ourselves, and identified with the suffering animal; that is, by quitting, in some measure, our own existence, to assume his? We suffer only, inasmuch as we judge he suffers; it is not in ourselves, but in him we suffer. No man therefore feels any sensibility, but when his imagination is warmed, and begins to transport him beyond himself' (chapter IV, vol.1, p.335).

concerning the complex definition of the self and its humanity. This subverted the outlook of modern individualism and Descartes's intellectual subjectivism, according to which existence was guaranteed only through thought, abstract reason and the tenacious identification of the I as the self. Rousseau's revolution in the sciences of man was carried out by insisting that primitive man should be studied through historical and empirical methods and that the 'otherness' of savage man should be fully acknowledged.[15] The field of investigation of the human subject became much vaster in terms of both time and space: Descartes's *cogito* lost its centrality, and humanity's ultimate and most profound essence was identified with man's being rather than his thought, and with his sensibility rather than his rationality. The self was redefined through the flow of sensations, empirical knowledge and respect for the different ways of being of the Other, savage man, compared with civilised man. And Rousseau himself would often ask: 'But who am I?', 'What am I?'[16]

In *Emile* (which in the *Confessions* is described as 'the best, as well as the most important' of his writings) Rousseau repeatedly insists on the primacy of feelings: 'I exist, and have senses by which I am affected. This is the first truth that strikes me, and in which I am obliged to acquiesce.'[17] The contrast with Descartes's 'I think therefore I am' is obvious. It is no wonder that critics have often glossed such passages as: 'I feel therefore I am.' Life comes before thought. Nature precedes and influences culture. Primitive man helps me understand the history of my own species, my ultimate individual identity, precisely because he is at the origin of my own being but also something truly Other. In his *Confessions*, Rousseau obsessively questions his own identity. According to Lévi-Strauss

> the expansion of Rousseau's thought stems from a double principle: firstly, of identification with others and even with the most 'other' of all others, be it an animal; and secondly, of refusal to identify

15. On this 'revolution', see Lévi-Strauss, 'Jean-Jacques Rousseau'.
16. See, for instance, Rousseau, *Emilius*, 'The profession of faith made by the vicar of Savoy', vol.2, p.18, and Lévi-Strauss, 'Jean-Jacques Rousseau', p.200-201.
17. Rousseau, *Emilius*, 'Profession of faith', vol.2, p.18. For the quotation on the importance of *Emilius*, see Jean-Jacques Rousseau, *Confessions*, translated by W. Conyngham Mallory (Auckland, 1903), book XI, p.671. Like Hume, Rousseau openly opposed politicians and moralists alike who believed 'that men conducted themselves by their sagacity rather than by their passions' (Rousseau, *Confessions*, book IX, p.491).

> with oneself – in other words, refusal of all that can make the self 'acceptable'. These two attitudes complement each other, and the latter even forms the basis of the former: in truth, I am not 'me', but the weakest, the most humble of 'others'. Such is the discovery of the *Confessions*.[18]

In fact, the experience of sympathy towards the suffering of others became for Rousseau one of the constituent features of humanity and the ultimate foundation of truly natural morality, something that had nothing to do with the abstract ethical rationalism of the previous century. Rousseau would never equate the history of man with the history of reason, as did other great figures of the European Enlightenment. First among these was Voltaire, who wrote to the author of the *Second discourse*: 'no one has ever been so witty as you are in trying to turn us into brutes: to read your book makes one long to go on all fours.'[19]

Rousseau's aim was to redefine the characteristic features of primitive man's humanity in order to answer a question that Enlightenment circles had been asking throughout Europe: what is man? Obviously, this ambitious project could not limit itself to the study of the physical aspects of primitive man, which made him perilously akin to other animals. Nor was it enough to identify the two natural principles that governed human behaviour, i.e. self-love and sympathy with the suffering of others. Unlike the more radical currents of eighteenth-century materialism, one had to go beyond the study of 'physical man' and investigate his metaphysical and moral side. It is in this respect that the influence of the language of natural rights revived by Calvinist refugees in Rousseau's Geneva makes itself felt in a new and unexpected form and becomes central to the whole discussion.

Rousseau accepted that, compared to that 'ingenious machine', an animal entirely ruled by instinct, man did have many traits in common but was also profoundly different: he was a free agent, and

18. Lévi-Strauss, 'Jean-Jacques Rousseau', p.202-203.
19. Voltaire, letter to Rousseau dated 30 August 1755. Referred to in Luigi Luporini's edition of Rousseau's *Discorsi sulle scienze e sulle arti, sull'origine della disuguaglianza fra gli uomini*, translated by Rodolfo Mondolfo (Milan, 1997), p.20, n.35; quoted here in S. G. Tallentyre's translation from *Voltaire in his letters, being a selection from his correspondence* (New York and London, 1919), available on the Voltaire Society of America website, www.whitman.edu/VSA/letters/8.30.1755.html (last accessed 6 May 2019).

therefore 'perfectible'.[20] He had 'the power of willing'[21] and the ability to create culture, and as such could escape natural determinism and influence the history of his own species:

> All animals must be allowed to have ideas, since all animals have senses; they even combine their ideas to a certain degree, and, in this respect, it is only the difference of such degree, that constitutes the difference between man and beast: some philosophers have even advanced, that there is a greater difference between some men and some others, than between some men and some beasts; it is not therefore so much the understanding that constitutes, among animals, the specifical distinction of man, as his quality of a free agent. Nature speaks to all animals, and beasts obey her voice.[22]

When examined in all his components from a historical and empirical point of view, primitive man in the pure state of nature finally revealed himself as he really was: ruled by the world of passions, by the preservation instinct, but also, at the same time, by sympathy for the other. Above all, he was endowed with two basic natural rights that made his humanity complete and gave him a new dignity, setting him apart from animals: the right to life and the right to freedom.

To the right to freedom in particular Rousseau devoted some memorable pages, making it into the modern Enlightenment right *par excellence* – the right of rights. In the zero degree of mankind, where inequality was not perceived and played no role, as we have already seen, this right made man 'a moral being, that is to say, a being intelligent, free, and considered with a view to his relations to other beings' (p.lii). The presence of this right even in those times outside time, devoid of culture and of all notions of mine or yours, of servitude, poverty or domination, supported its claim to be considered the authentic substance of humanity. In contemporary civil society force and violence had prevailed, annihilating all connection with man's primitive freedom, so that this right had become something entirely different.

Once again, Rousseau resorted to a subtle rhetorical technique of criticism that was typical of the Enlightenment, which consisted in the

20. On the close link between liberty and perfectibility in Rousseau, see Jacques Derrida, *Of grammatology*, translated by Gayatri Chakravorty Spivak, with an introduction by Judith Butler (Baltimore, MD, 2016), p.198.
21. *Emilius*, 'The profession of faith', vol.2, p.36.
22. *Second discourse*, p.35-36.

unmasking of ideological positions. He thus denounces the previous century's school of natural law and all those political thinkers who had neglected the nexus between man and liberty. In this way, they had legitimised that absolute power, despotism and fierce domination of man over man whose nefarious influence was felt throughout the Europe of his time, while it was entirely absent from the pure state of nature: 'Political writers argue in regard to the love of liberty with the same sophistry that philosophers do in regard to the state of nature' (p.146). It was only by projecting an anachronistic logic of domination onto the primitive world that these writers had been able to claim that man was naturally predisposed to slavery: 'It is not therefore by the servile disposition of enslaved nations that we must judge of the natural dispositions of man for or against slavery, but by the prodigies done by every free people to secure themselves from oppression' (p.148). In fact, with the exponential growth of the trade in African slaves towards the American colonies, the issue of slavery was becoming a major issue for European public opinion. And it is to this question that Rousseau linked his struggle to have the natural right to freedom acknowledged as a universal and inalienable political right that should be exercised also in modern civil society.

The Enlightenment's abolitionist struggle and its fight against the 'right of slavery' began with Montesquieu's 1748 *Esprit des lois*.[23] Montesquieu's study drew on juridical arguments, through which he attacked the very basis for Roman civil legislation on this issue. In it he discusses the origin of slavery and how it was linked to specific climatic and geographic conditions in order to refute Aristotle's theory of the slave by nature, which had been reprised by members of the Second Scholastics. Montesquieu's condemnation of this theory was clear and uncompromising, as he successfully rebuts the arguments of those Roman jurists who had cited as sources of slavery capture in war, birth from a mother who was herself in slavery and – erroneously – the so-called voluntary slavery pact.[24] He also attacks the prejudices that

23. An important study on these issues is still Russell Parsons Jameson, *Montesquieu et l'esclavage: étude sur les origines de l'opinion antiesclavagiste en France au XVIIIe siècle* (Paris, 1911). More recently, Jean Ehrard has discussed these themes in *Lumières et esclavage: l'esclavage colonial et l'opinion publique en France au XVIIIe siècle* (Brussels, 2008), p.141ff.

24. See the famous book XV, 'In what manner the laws of civil slavery are relative to the nature of the climate', in Montesquieu, *The Spirit of laws*, 4th edn, 2 vols (Edinburgh, Donaldson, 1768), vol.1, p.308-28. Montesquieu is adamant that it is only through pity that '[t]he law of nations, to prevent prisoners from being

allowed the Spanish *conquistadores* to reduce to slavery entire peoples in the American continent. In this respect, Montesquieu points out the cruel hypocrisy with which large swathes of the Christian world claimed that 'religion gives its professors a right to enslave those who dissent from it' (chapter 4, p.312).

Because of his ironic tone and his absolute reliance on the theory of climatic determinism, Montesquieu's discussions 'Of the slavery of the negroes' (chapter 5) and of 'The true origin of the right of slavery' (chapter 6) are rather more dubious. In his attempt to locate the ultimate explanation for this practice, he refers to supposed traits that would in fact give ammunition to pro-slavery propaganda, such as the natural laziness of Africans and how, because of the extremely hot weather, some peoples had the natural propensity to give in to despotism and fall into slavery.[25] This notwithstanding, Montesquieu explains with the utmost clarity that modern slavery was not in fact economically useful, as famously maintained, for instance, by François Melon.[26] Nor was it morally acceptable, since it corrupted both master and slave. And finally, from the point of view of natural law, ever since the time of Ulpian, slavery had been rightly considered to be against nature, because all men were born free and equal.

In his attacks on the right of slavery in the *Social contract* and, even earlier, in the *Discourse upon the origin and foundation of the inequality among mankind*, Rousseau adopts a very different perspective from Montesquieu. He is far more interested in the political and philosophical implications than in the juridical aspects of the question. In his view the crucial problem was to finally get over a dichotomy that was already clearly there in Roman *ius*: that between natural law, which rejected slavery, and civil law, which authorised and regulated it. In the first pages of the *Social contract*, Rousseau openly declares his

put to death, has allowed them to be made slaves.' He adds that '[i]t is false that killing in war is lawful, unless in a case of absolute necessity' and that '[i]f a prisoner of war is not to be reduced to slavery, much less are his children' (chapter 2, p.309-10).

25. Cf. Carminella Biondi, *Ces esclaves sont des hommes: lotta abolizionista e letteratura negrofila nella Francia del Settecento* (Pisa, 1979), p.134ff.

26. Cf. Jean-François Melon, *Essai politique sur le commerce*, 1736 (*A Political essay upon commerce*, translated by David Bindon, Dublin, Philip Crampton, 1738, chapter V, 'Of slavery', p.77): 'The employing of slaves in our colonies, sheweth, that slavery is not deemed to be contrary either to religion or morality. We are therefore, at liberty to enquire, whether it would be more advantageous or not, to extend it every where' – to Europe as well, in that case.

puzzlement: 'Man is born free, and yet we see him every where in chains: and those who believe themselves the masters of others, cease not to be even greater slaves than the people they govern. How this happens I am ignorant' (p.3). In fact, he knew perfectly well. As we shall see, he devoted many years to finding the solution to this enigma. However, he immediately pointed the finger at the seventeenth-century school of natural law as the chronologically closest and most prestigious cause of this persistent and hateful dichotomy.

In their discussions of the right of slavery, Grotius and Pufendorf had relaunched the thesis of the right of conquest as the source of this juridical institution. Importantly, however, they had also legitimised the nascent monarchical absolutism by likening the pact of submission of the people to the sovereign to a voluntary slavery pact that they presumed was countenanced by Roman *ius*. Rousseau had replied to the former issue simply by adducing Montesquieu's arguments. On the latter issue, which, as was first revealed by Barbeyrac, was based on incorrect historical information, Rousseau's contribution is quite original and of the utmost interest.[27]

First of all, Rousseau denies that there can be any analogy between *imperium* and *potestas dominica*, i.e. between sovereignty and a master's domination. This conception of a contract that was supposed to legitimise slavery or tyranny made no juridical sense, since, among other things, it did not imply any reciprocal obligation. But what Rousseau found most repugnant was the idea that a man could spontaneously renounce his liberty. This went counter to the results of his research into the state of pure nature and mankind's original traits, which manifested themselves not only in feelings of compassion and self-love but also in the acknowledgement of the natural and inalienable rights to life and freedom: two fundamental rights the practice of which one had to find a way to safeguard also in contemporary civil society.

27. The existence of a presumed slavery pact in Roman civil law was adduced again by Grotius and Pufendorf and accepted by Montesquieu himself. For his part, Rousseau is concerned not with ascertaining whether this was true or not but only with its refutation. In fact, the concept of voluntary slavery, as presented in the seventeeth century, was entirely absent from Roman law. This had already been pointed out by Barbeyrac in his notes to Pufendorf, *Law of nature and nations*, VI, 3, 3, n.2, p.614 (VI, 3, 3, n.1, vol.2, p.176 in the French edition, *Le Droit de la nature et des gens*, printed in Amsterdam, n.n., 1706). See the detailed discussion of this question in Robert Derathé, *Jean-Jacques Rousseau et la science politique de son temps*, 2nd edn (Paris, 1970), p.192-205.

Already in the *Second discourse*, in attacking Pufendorf for treating liberty as though it were some goods that were subject to a form of contractual logic in civil law, Rousseau denied that anyone could give up their natural right to freedom: 'Besides, the right of property being of mere human convention and institution, every man may dispose as he pleases of what he possesses: but the case is otherwise with regard to the essential gifts of nature, such as *life* and *liberty*, which every man is permitted to enjoy.'[28]

Freedom was in fact something entirely specific, 'the most noble faculty of man' (p.152), something on which the very dignity and humanity of man were founded. It was what set him apart from animals and their reliance on instinct, and made a moral being of him, and an autonomous protagonist in God's design.

Rousseau discussed once again the meaning of 'liberty' and 'to alienate' in his *Social contract*, this time to engage with Grotius' disquieting question (in Rousseau's words): 'If an individual [...] can alienate his liberty, and become the slave of a master, why may not a whole people alienate theirs, and become the subjects of a king?' (chapter IV, 'Of slavery', p.16). To this Rousseau gave his famous reply:

> To say that a man gives himself gratuitously, is absurd and incomprehensible; such an act would in itself be illegal and void, because the person who performed it could not be in his proper senses. To say the same of a whole nation, is to suppose the multitude are all mad; but still, folly would not confer the right so vainly contended for [...] To renounce our liberty, is to renounce our quality of man, and with it all the rights and duties of humanity; and no adequate compensation can possibly be made for such a sacrifice, as it is in itself incompatible with the nature of man; whose actions, when once he is deprived of his free will, must be destitute of all morality. (p.18-19 and 20)

Rousseau always acknowledges his debt to the ideas put forward by Montesquieu and Locke on the issue of slavery. However, his own position shows many original traits in relation both to the former, who never refers to the language of natural rights, and to the latter, who was mainly reacting to Hobbes' *Leviathan*.[29]

28. Rousseau, *Second discourse*, p.154. Emphasis added. In Rousseau's account, Pufendorf 'says that, as we can transfer our property from one to another by contracts and conventions, we may likewise divest ourselves of our liberty in favour of other men' (p.153).

29. On the absence of the language of the rights of man in Montesquieu, see our

Despite his ambiguous position on slavery by right of conquest, Locke too had denied the presence of a voluntary slavery pact in Roman *ius*, on which the defenders of absolutism and the *pactum subiectionis* between a sovereign and his subjects relied to such an extent. He was concerned with the inalienability of the right to life rather than the right to freedom – and these are two rather different things. According to Locke,

> a man, not having the power of his own life, cannot, by compact, or his own consent, enslave himself to any one, nor put himself under the absolute, arbitrary power of another, to take away his life when he pleases. Nobody can give more power than he has himself: and he that cannot take away his own life, cannot give another power over it.[30]

By focusing on the autonomy of human will as an anthropological element even more than a philosophical or religious one, Rousseau had shifted the whole debate on slavery in the direction of the natural and inalienable right to freedom, which thus became the most important criterion that defined an individual's humanity and morality.[31] This would give a new basis to any future political discussion of the legitimacy of power, as well as providing extremely effective ammunition to the Enlightenment abolitionist movement at the end of the century.

Rousseau's *Second discourse*, i.e. the *Discourse upon the origin and foundation of the inequality among mankind*, thus called into doubt the very foundations of seventeenth-century natural law, not simply its epistemological premises. His overall reconstruction of the state of pure nature allowed one to see that in the history of the species man first appeared as an isolated creature that was clearly endowed with

next chapter. One critic who tends to equate Rousseau's position on this issue to Locke's is Robert Derathé, *Jean-Jacques Rousseau et la science politique*, p.200.

30. Locke, *Second treatise*, chapter IV, 'Of slavery', §23, p.110. More exactly, in Locke's opinion freedom, in the sense that in the state of nature man was 'free from any superior power on earth' (§22, p.109), was organically linked with the life and preservation of the species: 'This freedom from absolute, arbitrary power, is so necessary to, and closely joined with, a man's preservation, that he cannot part with it, but by what forfeits his preservation and life altogether' (§23, p.110). In fact, the right to life for Locke was God's gift and as such was not at man's own disposal. Man, as he repeatedly states, cannot 'destroy' or 'take away' his own life: he has the use of it, but does not own it.
31. Cf. *Emilius*, 'Of travelling', vol.2, p.368-69.

natural rights such as those to life and to freedom, the latter being a prerequisite for the anthropological definition of humanity itself. Only much later, with the slow rise of culture, did social man, with his burden of duties, appear on the scene. The theoretical shift from the seventeenth-century language of duties to the eighteenth-century language of rights was now well and truly accomplished.

It would certainly seem that, as has been remarked, this first part of Rousseau's writings is steeped in 'an unfettered individualism'.[32] This important phase focuses on trying to find an answer to the Enlightenment question *par excellence*: 'what is man?', and thus defines the humanity of a subject in an anthropological as well as historical sense. It could not be otherwise, if the objective was to refute the dominant theses put forward by Grotius and Pufendorf.

Rousseau's conclusions radically changed the traditional view of the history of mankind. They subverted once and for all the relative supremacy of rights and duties and thus the very basis of the theoretical reflection on morality and the politics of *Ancien régime* society. However, despite the large amount of effort devoted to reconstructing the state of pure nature, a few important pieces of the puzzle were still missing. His discussion, therefore, did not quite succeed in transforming natural rights into political rights, founding the very idea of politics on a new basis. It was still not entirely clear what had caused that historical shift by virtue of which 'Man is born free, and yet we see him every where in chains', or how, or even whether, this could be remedied.

Rousseau believed that he had shown how in the pure state of nature, in which men had lived isolated and scattered across the land, there was no scope for the logic of domination of the stronger over the weaker. Natural inequality was hardly perceived and had no effect, while moral inequality could not exist in the absence of any form of communal life. With the rise of civil society everything had changed, and for the worse. Primitive man had receded into something entirely different from modern man. The first momentous change had come with the pernicious invention of the right to property, a symbolic as well as material milestone, and something that, for once diverging decisively from Locke, Rousseau did not consider a natural right. Far from it, he harshly criticised it in another famous passage:

32. See Cassirer's 1932 essay 'Das Problem Jean-Jacques Rousseau', in *The Question of Jean-Jacques Rousseau*, ed. and translated by Peter Gay, 2nd edn (New Haven, CT, and London, 1989), p.51.

> The first man, who, after enclosing a piece of ground, took it into his head to say, *This is mine*, and found people simple enough to believe him, was the true founder of civil society. How many crimes, how many wars, how many murders, how many misfortunes and horrors, would that man have saved the human species, who pulling up the stakes or filling up the ditches should have cried to his fellows: Be sure not to listen to this impostor; you are lost, if you forget that the fruits of the earth belong equally to us all, and the earth itself to nobody![33]

This is not the place to describe in detail the various phases of the rise of civil society in history, especially since much has already been written on this subject. However, it may be worth reminding ourselves of a few key points. The starting point is the pure state of nature, which is timeless and unmovable, and in which '*perfectibility*, the social virtues, and the other faculties, which natural man had received in potentia, could never be developed of themselves' (p.93; emphasis in the original). Things changed only through 'the fortuitous concurrence of several foreign causes, which might never happen, and without which he must have eternally remained in his primitive condition' (*ibid.*). In the intermediate stages of the pure state of nature, man started to compete with other animals in his fight for survival. He began to fish and hunt, invented the bow and arrow, and started to cook his food. He also began to recognise his peers. This was an early sign of a latent predisposition to live in packs (which at this stage manifested itself only as instinctive compassion), though only 'by some kind of free association which obliged none of its members, and lasted no longer than the transitory necessity that had given birth to it' (p.104). These were purely occasional and contingent relationships among beings who hardly ever communicated among themselves except through gestures and inarticulate sounds, in a shouted language similar to 'that of crows and monkeys' (p.106).

It took millennia for that 'first revolution, which produced the establishment and distinction of families', alongside the development of language. In his *Histoire et théorie de la terre*, Buffon had claimed that this revolution was probably due to external factors, such as the possible 'mutation' of the earth's axis, which caused environmental and climatic changes that forced men to live together. Man abandoned his nomadic habits, the first families began to appear, language became the first social institution, hatchets and huts were made and 'a species

33. *Second discourse*, p.97.

of property' was invented (p.107). This was the final stage in the pure state of nature, 'the best for man [...] the real youth of the world' (p.117-18): the stage at which a kind of natural society arose, which was akin to the living conditions that were observed in the savage populations of Africa and the Americas.

Rousseau held an extremely positive view of this stage, which fed into the myth of the good savage that had started to circulate in European culture with Montaigne. At this stage, while the cancer of inequality and the contrast between the strong and the weak were beginning to make their appearance, there was still an overriding balance between natural freedom and social duties. The fierceness of primitive man was attenuated by natural pity, and the drive to distinguish oneself was tempered by the pleasure of finding oneself reflected in the other, 'holding a just mean between the indolence of the primitive state, and the petulant activity of self-love' (p.107).

This happy time had come to an end through another major revolution, this time due to the serendipitous invention of metallurgy and agriculture based on the observation of nature. Together, 'iron and corn [...] have civilized men, and ruined mankind' (p.120). Once over the final threshold of the pure state of nature, man was thrown into history, in a context that challenged him to fully develop his faculties and potentialities, such as reason, imagination or memory. Time rushed into modern civil society, while, from the anthropological point of view, 'the species was grown old' (p.87). The strongest and most intelligent soon upset the delicate balance of exchange between those who forged iron and those who grew corn. The new circumstances amplified the hitherto imperceptible natural inequalities. This gave rise to a culture and to political and social institutions that legitimised and magnified violence and domination, slavery and injustice:

> The rich on their side scarce began to taste the pleasure of commanding, when they preferred it to every other; and making use of their old slaves to acquire new ones, they no longer thought of any thing but subduing and enslaving their neighbours; like those ravenous wolves, who having once tasted human flesh, despise every other food, and devour nothing but men for the future.
>
> It is thus that the most powerful or the most wretched, respectively considering their power and wretchedness as a kind of title to the substance of others, even equivalent to that of property, the equality once broken was followed by the most shocking disorders. It is thus that the usurpations of the rich, the pillagings of the poor, and the

> unbridled passions of all, by stifling the cries of natural compassion, and the as yet feeble voice of justice, rendered man avaricious, wicked and ambitious. There arose between the title of the strongest, and that of the first occupier a perpetual conflict, which always ended in battery and bloodshed. Infant society became a scene of the most horrible warfare: mankind thus debased and harassed, and no longer able to retreat, or renounce the unhappy acquisitions it had made; labouring, in short merely to its confusion by the abuse of those faculties, which in themselves do it so much honour, brought itself to the very brink of ruin and destruction. (p.131-32)

Rousseau pointed out very clearly the negative consequences of the rise of political institutions, i.e. of laws and forms of power that had forgotten natural rights, especially man's right to freedom. These institutions had only served to ratify once and for all the rights of the stronger over the weaker, such as the right of conquest and of slavery, the presumed logic of the domination of man over man, inequality and property. Similarly negative effects for the destiny of the species had resulted from the evolution in social relationships. Man's needs had increased exponentially. He had been trapped into the division of labour and entangled in networks of relationships that were harder and harder to escape, in which both slave and master ended up as prisoners of their asymmetrical dependence on each other. This had created a society that was artificial, unjust, immoral, hopelessly hierarchical and far removed by now from the pure state of nature: a society, moreover, that forced its members to wear a mask and become alienated from themselves; a society in which, in order to survive, people had to hide their real feelings.

Accordingly, Rousseau laments how it became 'requisite for men to be thought what they really were not. To be and to appear became two very different things, and from this distinction sprang pomp and knavery, and all the vices which form their train' (p.128). This perversion of the original traits of the human species, and the irreparable loss of the pure state of nature was, then, what had come out of modern civil society and its sophisticated culture, with its logic of domination and its justification of inequality. This was what Enlightenment circles all over Europe had hailed as 'progress'. As Rousseau points out, '[s]avage man and civilized man differ so much at bottom in point of inclinations and passions, that what constitutes the supreme happiness of the one would reduce the other to despair.' The former sought only 'repose and liberty' (p.178), while the latter toiled, suffered and hankered after honour and privileges, being reduced to flatter the powerful whom he hates and the rich whom he despises: 'In fact, the real source of all those differences, is that the savage lives within himself, whereas the citizen, constantly beside himself, knows only how to live in the opinion of others' (p.180).[34]

These statements by Rousseau will help us form an idea of his determined attack against the hypocrisy of court society and the civil society of the *Ancien régime*, with their dependence on inequality, privilege and status. Rousseau touched a raw nerve in contemporary society. His purpose all along had been to expose the most delicate unresolved questions of modernity, and to denounce how it had extended beyond all bounds the totally immaterial hints of natural inequality in primitive society and justified their existence by systematically falsifying the true history of mankind: 'It is sufficient that I have proved that this is not the original condition of man, and that it is merely the spirit of society, and the inequality which society engenders, that thus change and transform all our natural inclinations' (p.181).

This was an obvious but generally neglected truth: that the true characteristics of natural man had been betrayed by a civilising culture founded on the logic of domination and the oppression of the weaker by the stronger. And it came to Rousseau as a terrible epiphany, which in 1749 led him to draft his *Discourse on the sciences and arts* (or *First discourse*) and thus become a political writer.[35] This was

34. The estrangement of modern man, his dehumanisation and split consciousness, and the way in which he was perpetually forced to wear a mask have always been key issues in readings of Rousseau as a critic of modernity. See, for instance, Jean Starobinski, *Jean-Jacques Rousseau: la transparence et l'obstacle* (Paris, 1957). J. G. A. Pocock, *The Machiavellian moment: Florentine political thought and the Atlantic Republican tradition*, 2nd edn (Princeton, NJ, 2003), discusses the political consequences of this process, which placed society and the development of personality on a collision course with each other, leading to a situation in which 'by its nature society humanized man and by the same processes distracted and alienated him again' (p.504).
35. In book VIII of his *Confessions* Rousseau recounts how the Academy of Dijon had set as a question for its annual prize 'Has the progress of sciences and arts contributed to corrupt or purify morals?' ('To corrupt' here is, revealingly, Rousseau's addition.) As soon as he read this, he writes, 'I seemed to behold another world, and became a different man [...] All the rest of my misfortunes during my life were the inevitable effect of this moment of error. My sentiments became elevated with the most inconceivable rapidity to the level of my ideas. All my little passions were stifled by the enthusiasm of truth, liberty, and virtue, and, what is most astonishing, this effervescence continued in my mind upwards of five years, to as great a degree perhaps as it has ever done in that of any other man' (p.406).

an early work, intentionally paradoxical in tone, and marred by an excessively rhetorical style, with which nevertheless Rousseau won a prize offered by the Academy of Dijon for an essay on the effect of the arts and sciences. Rousseau had polemically chosen to demonstrate that the effect was to *corrupt* morals.

For Rousseau, the objective, already familiar to the classical age, of creating the conditions for living well was definitely what had *not* been achieved by the sciences and arts or, more generally, by the kind of culture that had emerged in Europe in the course of history: in particular, modern society had failed to bring about man's emancipation, the happiness of the species, a strengthening of virtue, civic spirit and patriotism, or an attenuation of natural inequality. Instead, modern culture had fostered vices, luxury and vainglory: 'Ancient politicians always conversed on manners and virtue, the moderns only of commerce and money.' And again: 'We have indeed physicians, geometricians, chemists, astronomers, poets, musicians, and painters; we have every thing but good citizens and patriots.'[36]

The great Scientific Revolution, the academic world, and even literary taste had all yielded to fashion, corporations and the primacy of self-love and the logic of domination.[37] Scientific progress only brought forth more inequality, since it had been hijacked by selfish individuals and groups who used the process of professionalisation to create new and powerful corporations. According to Rousseau, civilisation and the progress of the sciences and art were corrupting mankind, as they gave rise to new and terrible inequalities and caused man's alienation and dehumanisation. In describing these paradoxical new developments, Rousseau could take on a visionary and even

36. Jean-Jacques Rousseau, *The Discourse which carried the præmium at the Academy of Dijon, in MDCCL, on this question, propos'd by the said Academy, whether the re-establishment of arts and sciences has contributed to the refining of manners, by a citizen of Geneva* (London, W. Owen, 1751), p.37 and 49.

37. Rousseau reiterates these ideas in the preface to his 1752 *Narcissus*: 'Our writers all look upon it as a masterpiece of modern policy, that the sciences, arts, luxury, commerce, laws, and our other connections, by drawing closer together the bonds of society by personal interest, lay all under a mutual dependence, and by reciprocal wants unite them in one common interest [...] This notion is, doubtless, a very fine one, and is set forth in its best light: but if we examine it with attention and impartiality, we must deduct from it a number of its apparent advantages' (*Narcissus, or the Self-admirer*, in *The Works of J. J. Rousseau, translated from the French, in ten volumes*, Edinburgh, J. Bell, J. Dickson, and C. Elliot, 1773-1774, vol.8, p.61-119, 76).

vaguely reactionary tone, with its strong nostalgia for the past, and especially for Ancient Greece and Rome.[38]

The discussion of these themes in the *Second discourse* was much deeper than the treatment of the same subject in the *First discourse*. In tracing the origins of the exponential rise in inequality back to modern civil society and its culture of the strongest, it was more mature and open towards the future and man's ability to act freely in history.

Other great figures of the Enlightenment also addressed the eighteenth-century discovery of the autonomy of history, with the attendant need to draft relevant new philosophies of history that would be different from those of pagan or Christian culture.[39] However, Rousseau's position was completely original and subversive. It confirms the need to finally look at the Enlightenment as a complex and exciting laboratory of modernity that gave rise to opposing positions, though always in the attempt to understand man through man, uphold his rights and foster his emancipation – not, as is usually the case, as the expression of a presumed Western modernity with well-defined and uniform traits, whose main purpose was to celebrate the triumphal rise of human progress and reason.

This can be illustrated by comparing Rousseau's position with that of Voltaire. Whereas the latter found the meaning of universal history in the process through which peoples and nations achieved civilisation – a slow and difficult process, which was moreover subject to setbacks and reversals – for Rousseau this same process had caused a tragic degradation in the species. He saw it as a terrible and powerful dialectic, which, at least until his time, had created nothing but violence, alienation and dehumanisation. For Rousseau the terms bandied around in Enlightenment salons – reason, progress, civilisation, civil society – were rhetorical and ambiguous. Their meaning was still to be defined in relation to the true face of history, and this seemed to be far from progressive, especially from a moral point of view. Even the discovery of the autonomy of history and the existence of being in time was subject to the same ambiguity. On

38. For an insightful discussion of Rousseau's interest in the classical age and its political overtones, see Luciano Guerci, *Libertà degli antichi e libertà dei moderni: Sparta, Atene e i 'philosophes' nella Francia del '700* (Naples, 1979), p.45. On the way in which large groups of thinkers in the Late Enlightenment were rereading the Scientific Revolution and its corporative aspects in the wake of Rousseau, see Ferrone, *Una scienza per l'uomo*, p.xviii ff.

39. Cf. Karl Löwith, *Meaning in history: the theological implications of the philosophy of history* (Chicago, IL, 1949).

the one hand, it showed that man could fully realise himself and his humanity only in history. On the other, it revealed that the only 'progress' man had made was towards the degradation of the species, so that history became an unstoppable force that turned time into a fearsome enemy. And towards the end of his life Rousseau would write despondently: 'But human nature does not go backward, and it is never possible to return to times of innocence and equality once they have been left behind.'[40]

It is certainly true, as stated by Starobinski, that in the course of the eighteenth century Rousseau was truly 'the most important witness of the discovery of history and time, not through a theory of progress, but through the horrified awareness of the danger and at the same time the rich possibilities of existence in time.'[41]

Down to our day Rousseau has been accused of primitivism, of inane or downright dangerous nostalgia for the noble savage, an indictment that was first directed at him by Voltaire and other Enlightenment thinkers who rejected his critique of modernity. In vain did he assert that he had never wanted 'to destroy the sciences, the Arts, the theaters, the Academies and to plunge the universe back into first barbarism'.[42] As we will repeatedly highlight below, Rousseau's intellectual experience was based first and foremost on the primacy of politics. What he wanted was a less unjust modernity that would preserve the fundamental features of humanity. He sought to understand how there could be such an obvious 'contradiction' between what he saw as the intrinsic goodness in the true nature of freeborn man and the iniquitous social order of his time.

To this end, he did not hesitate to ask how human wickedness could have arisen and grown in the course of time, a question that he considered of primary importance. The immediate aim was to create a new philosophy of history based on the study of anthropology and to grapple with the eminently eighteenth-century question of theodicy – a term whose origin goes back to Leibniz's 1710 *Essai de théodicée sur la bonté de Dieu, la liberté de l'homme et l'origine du mal*. Only in this way

40. Jean-Jacques Rousseau, *Rousseau, judge of Jean-Jacques: dialogues*, ed. Roger D. Masters and Christopher Kelly, translated by Judith R. Bush, Christopher Kelly and Roger D. Masters, in *The Collected writings of Rousseau*, vol.1 (Hanover, NH, 1990), 'Third dialogue', p.213.

41. Jean Starobinski, introduction to Rousseau, *Discours sur l'origine de l'inégalité*, in *Œuvres complètes*, ed. B. Gagnebin and M. Raymond, vol.3: *Du contrat social, écrits politiques* (Paris, 1964), p.lxviii-lxix.

42. *Rousseau, judge of Jean-Jacques*, p.213.

would it be possible to achieve the most important goals: a new politics that would have the task not of creating a utopian heavenly city on earth but of slowing down the vertiginous descent of the species into corruption and moral and physical decay – a politics that could reduce the inevitable inequalities of civilised society, restore man's link with natural morality, and ensure that the natural rights of man were finally put into practice. As Rousseau wrote in his posthumously published 'Political fragments':

> far from thinking that there is no longer either virtue or happiness for us and that heaven has abandoned us without resources to the depravation of the species; let us attempt to draw from the ill itself the remedy that should cure it [...] let us show him all the misery of the state he believed happy, let us make him see [...] the sweet harmony of justice and happiness in a better understood constitution of things.[43]

Therefore, for Rousseau modern politics must take a completely different course from the past. It must abandon all Machiavellian schemes for the conquest of power. It must stop legitimising existing hierarchies and the actions of the strongest, as was the case with the old natural law of Grotius and Pufendorf. And it must renounce all claim to the divine origin of civil power, a claim that goes back to St Paul's famous pronouncement, 'Let everyone be subject to the governing authorities, for there is no authority except that which God has established' (Romans 13.1). Instead, the new politics of the moderns could and should take on a new task, which might seem more limited in scope but was in fact morally far more complex: that of emancipating man through man, reducing inequalities and promoting the true humanity and liberty of the species, i.e. good living in the ancient sense. These were all ambitious objectives, which were intrinsically connected with the question of theodicy and the construction of a new political theology under the aegis of the Enlightenment.

In our discussion of the invention of the natural right to the pursuit of happiness and of the construction of a new Enlightenment humanism, we saw how Voltaire, in response to Leibniz and Pascal, effectively relativised and secularised the problem of absolute evil, on

43. Jean-Jacques Rousseau, 'Political fragments', II ('On the state of nature'), §12, in *Social contract, Discourse on the virtue most necessary for a hero, Political fragments, and Geneva manuscript*, ed. Roger D. Masters and Christopher Kelly, translated by Judith R. Bush, Roger D. Masters and Christopher Kelly, in *The Collected writings of Rousseau*, vol.4 (Hanover, NH, and London, 1994), p.16-75 (20).

both the ontological and theological levels. In Voltaire's treatment this problem, which Augustine addressed with his theory of original sin, became a product of history and nature. Man was still considered a fragile and limited being: a nondescript mixture of good and evil, of pleasure and pain. Nevertheless, according to Voltaire, he was capable of finding in himself what could bring him those few moments of happiness that it was possible to achieve on earth. In the background to this picture of the human condition, in which man was perpetually caught between the fatality of evil and that precious though slender promise of happiness, Voltaire portrayed a faraway God, whose existence was necessary in order to explain the origin and guarantee the legality of the world, but who in fact showed little interest in human affairs. This was a serious blow to Augustinian theology and its attempt to explain the presence of absolute evil in history through the theory of original sin.

Like many other Enlightenment figures, Rousseau was strongly attracted to this idea of a universal natural religion without churches or dogmas and based on a small number of articles of faith. He not only followed Voltaire along this path, but went far beyond, disregarding all possible accusations of heresy or political radicalism. Whereas Voltaire had argued that evil was a natural feature in life, and therefore God the creator must be responsible for it, Rousseau absolved God from this particular charge. Man was created free and intrinsically good, in the same way that nature was not an essentially evil and murderous source of tragedy on a vast scale, as it would appear when one considered all the gratuitous violence, wars, earthquakes and catastrophes in general.[44] The main responsibility for man's misery lay with history and the perverse and erroneous premises on which civil society was built:

> It is the abuse of our faculties that renders us vicious and unhappy. Our vexations, our cares, our troubles proceed from ourselves. Moral evil is certainly our own work; and physical evil would be nothing at all, were it not for our vices, which render us sensible of it [...] Inquire, O man, no longer into the author of evil; that author is thy self [...]

44. On this question Voltaire and Rousseau held a correspondence that was immediately made public. In the *Confessions* the latter writes: 'Voltaire, while he appeared to believe in God, never really believed in anything but the devil, since his pretended deity is a malicious being, who, according to him, had no pleasure but in evil' (book IX, p.500). For Voltaire evil was an entirely natural element that coexisted with good in both nature and the human being.

> Take away our fatal improvements, take away our errors, and our vices, take away the work of man, and all will go well.[45]

Critics have highlighted the importance of religion in Rousseau's work. The poignant 'Profession of faith of the vicar of Savoy' in *Emile* was a milestone in the history of Western religion. This virtually independent text takes up the idea of a natural religion common to all men. It was an idea that, as we have seen, had been put forward in the seventeenth century on a rationalist basis by the deists as well as by John Locke and, later, by Barbeyrac, with a theist variant being found in Voltaire. Here, this idea becomes a profound feeling that stems from the heart and from man's existential needs, rather than from reason: 'I feel my soul; I know it by sensation and by thought; I know it exists, without having any knowledge of its essence [...] Reason but too often imposes on us, so that we are fully intitled to except against her; but conscience never deceives us; she is the true guide of man' (*Emilius*, 'Profession of faith', vol.2, p.42 and 47).

This equation of feeling, immortal soul, self-consciousness and human nature was a central tenet in Rousseau's belief in man's autonomy and moral freedom of choice. This was the pivotal point around which revolved his faith in a new universal religion that was still waiting to arise and, above all, be put into practice. It was a complex and composite idea of religion. Rousseau made use of the traditional rationalist arguments linked to Newton's mechanistic universe and Samuel Clarke's Boyle Lectures. In addition, he critiqued Spinoza's *Deus sive natura*, Bayle's views on atheist peoples and the freethinkers' idea that motion was intrinsic in matter – all theses that had been relaunched by the French materialists, starting with Diderot and the baron d'Holbach. By contrast, Rousseau subscribed to the accusations levelled by Spinoza and the seventeenth-century libertines at the imposture of revealed religions and the proliferation of dogmas and miracles. Faced with endless rows of prophets and saints and the contrasting truth claims of a multiplicity of religious confessions, Rousseau asks his readers: 'Which is the true religion?' (p.66). All revealed religions claimed this title, but behind them hid only power-crazy clerics: 'if they had paid attention to what God says to the heart of man, there never would have been more than one religion upon earth [...] Let us not confound the externals of religion with religion itself' (p.65).

45. *Emilius*, vol.2, p.38 and 39.

It was not these ideas, however, that forced him to flee, and that caused the public burning of his beloved *Emilius*, the only major work that he had proudly signed. The heresy that unleashed the rage of both the Sorbonne and the Geneva Church against him was above all his rejection of original sin. Rousseau was aware of how the dispute between Pelagius and Augustine on this subject in the second decade of the fifth century had changed the history of Christianity. This difficult and disconcerting debate had ended in 418 with a sentence of heresy against Pelagius, which would be reiterated across the centuries: first at the Council of Trent and, in our day, by Joseph Ratzinger (Pope Benedict XVI) and others.[46]

Pelagius denied the very foundations of St Paul's theology of original sin, in which Jesus Christ was the bearer of redemption, and grace was an absolute necessity – a theology that the Church had adopted in response to Matthew 15.19: 'For out of the heart come evil thoughts – murder, adultery, sexual immorality, theft, false testimony, slander.' In a discussion of how no one in life is without original sin that would greatly influence Martin Luther, Augustine famously quoted Jeremiah 10.23: 'I know, o Lord, that the way of a man is not in his power; nor is it for him to walk and direct his own steps.'[47] By contrast, Pelagius believed that this creature of God retained his original natural goodness and his full liberty and responsibility even after Adam's sin. Man, in Pelagian terms, was truly *emancipatus a Deo*, in that he saw himself as an independent being, untouched by absolute evil, naturally good and fully capable of acting for the good and staying out of sin, even without the help of God.[48] It was up to his own free will to choose between good and evil. In this kind of scenario, the Church inevitably lost its role as an indispensable tutor and guide. There was no longer any need to baptise children as quickly as possible to rid

46. Cf. Cardinal Joseph Ratzinger with Vittorio Messori, *The Ratzinger report: an exclusive interview on the state of the Church*, translated by Salvator Attanasio and Graham Harrison (Leominster, 1985). Under the heading 'Restore a place to original sin' (p.78), we read: 'some theologians have made their own the schema of an enlightenment à la Rousseau, with the dogma that lies at the base of modern culture – capitalist or Marxist – that of the man good by nature who is corrupted only by false education and by social structures in need of reform' (p.79).
47. Cf. Augustine of Hippo, *De peccatorum meritis et remissione et de baptismo parvulorum*, II, 17, 26. Quoted in Brown, *Augustine of Hippo*, p.375-76.
48. The Latin phrase is used by Pelagius himself, who borrows it from Roman family law. See Brown, *Augustine of Hippo*, p.353.

them of original sin. Christ himself lost his divine nature and became first and foremost an example of morality. Most importantly, there was no longer any need for grace or redemption. In this way Western Christianity as a historical institution suffered an irreparable blow, which undermined its very foundations and soteriological function. Man could now redeem himself through his own choices and actions. Thus, in pointing to the good savage as a historical example of man devoid of original sin Rousseau was consciously relaunching the Pelagian heresy in the middle of the eighteenth century. In so doing, he founded a new political theology under the banner of the Enlightenment and of human emancipation and autonomy.

This way of solving the problem of theodicy in anthropological terms, by drawing on the ancient and extremely controversial heresy of Pelagius, was nothing short of revolutionary.[49] The reaction on the part of the Church was inevitable and became a veritable witch-hunt, which included an *Arrêt de la cour de Parlement* on 9 June 1762, the *Mandement de Monseigneur l'archevêque de Paris Christophe de Beaumont*, the author's indictment and the public burning of his *Emile*. Rousseau was forced to flee and abscond. As he records in his *Confessions*, 'I was impious, an atheist, a madman, a wild beast, a wolf' (book XII, p.692). The archbishop of Paris accused him of proclaiming himself the 'précepteur du genre humain', and of debasing man to a beast in his *Discourse* on the origins of inequality. Above all, by rejecting the idea of original sin, Rousseau had made the coming of Christ useless and denied the necessity of God's salvific function. And indeed, Rousseau's idea of an absent and disinterested God, who had nothing to do with man's salvation, brought down the ancient walls of Western Christianity, and with them the centuries-old connection between the throne and the altar.

Rousseau's reply came in the form of a public letter. In his *Lettre à M. de Beaumont* he pointed out that he had in fact upheld the cause of God against atheists and materialists, and gave an entirely political explanation of the motivations and consequences of his Pelagian theology.

Rousseau had stated 'that man is a naturally good being, loving justice and order; that there is no original perversity in the human heart'. He had traced the true 'genealogy' of evil back to its historical and social origins. By so doing, he had finally unveiled the role played

49. See Cassirer, *The Question of Jean-Jacques Rousseau*, p.72-77, which, however, does not mention the obvious Pelagian origins of this position. On this issue, cf. Jacques François Thomas, *Le Pélagianisme de J.-J. Rousseau* (Paris, 1956).

by governments and laws in making man wicked and unhappy. This opened the way to a new and revolutionary concept of politics as a tool that man could use 'in order to reform the world'.[50] This powerful instrument could help transform the minds of populations through education, legislation and new forms of self-government that took into due account man's original freedom and responsibility, rejecting the so-called modern culture of civilisation, with its legitimation of domination and hierarchy.

It was the first time that anyone had proclaimed so strongly and clearly man's responsibility in history, or denounced so bravely the false theological premises, which harked back to St Paul and Augustine, of the pernicious politics that was dominant at the time. For the first time, instead of religious 'Reformation', with its Protestant–Catholic disputes, what was being advocated was political 'Reform' in clearly positive and secular terms, meaning the necessary transformation of political and social institutions.[51] In fact, the kind of philosophy of history described in the *Second discourse* made it clear that it was necessary to change the course of events by altering the way in which the relationship between culture and nature had been viewed up to that point. See the opening of *Emile*:

> Every thing is perfect, coming from the hands of the Creator; every thing degenerates in the hands of man. He forces a spot of ground to nourish the productions of a foreign soil; or a tree to bear fruit by the insition of another: he mixes and confounds climates, elements, seasons: he mutilates his dog, his horse, his slave: he inverts the nature of things, only to disfigure them: he is fond of deformity, and monstrous productions: he is pleased with nothing, as it is framed by nature, not even with man: we must break him to his mind, like a managed horse; we must fashion him to his taste, like the trees or plants of his garden.
>
> Were it not for this culture, things would still be worse; for our species will not bear being fashioned by halves. In the present constitution of things, man abandoned from his birth to his own guidance among the rest of society, would be a most monstrous animal.

50. See Jean-Jacques Rousseau, 'Letter to Beaumont', in *Letter to Beaumont, letters written from the mountain, and related writings*, ed. Christopher Kelly and Eve Grace, translated by Christopher Kelly and Judith R. Bush, in *The Collected writings of Rousseau*, vol.9 (Hanover, NH, and London, 2001), p.16-101 (28 and 34).
51. Benjamin Constant for one expressed fierce opposition to this dangerous new idea of the possibility of reforming human history dreamed up by Rousseau and other Enlightenment thinkers: see Ferrone, *Politics of Enlightenment*, p.182ff.

If a return to the origins was now impossible, one could still take political action 'in order to reform the world' and mitigate the tragic exponential growth of inequality brought about by civil society, so-called progress, and a modern civilising society that seemed to have forgotten its relationship with nature and man's natural rights to freedom.

Much has been written on Rousseau as the inventor of the politics of the moderns. This was a radically new politics from every point of view: its contents, its urgent call for reform and intervention, its very basis – in philosophical, scientific and theological terms – when compared to dominant ideas. It would not be entirely wrong to find in this form of politics the most important unifying feature of Rousseau's work as a whole. With this view Rousseau effectively reprised Aristotle's idea of man as a political animal, *zôon politikón*. Accordingly, in his *Confessions* he explains how he 'had perceived everything to be radically connected with politics, and that, upon whatever principles these were founded, a people would never be more than that which the nature of the government made them' (IX, p.470).

However, it is only fairly recently that we have begun to investigate the motivations that compelled Rousseau to become a political writer, and to direct fierce criticism at *Ancien régime* society, its hierarchies and its justification of inequality as part of the natural order of things. To this effect, more attention has been devoted to the historical context, and especially to Rousseau's painful and humiliating condition of social marginality, including in relation to the nascent guild of writers.[52] Rousseau hated the rich, the powerful, the wicked. As he often wrote, with barely contained anger, he despised and felt true 'indignation' towards the Parisian *grand monde* and 'the vices of that city' (*Confessions*, IX, p.485), and 'was so tired of salons, jets d'eau, groves, parterres, and of more fatiguing persons by whom they were shown' (p.479) – all things beloved instead of other *philosophes*, such as d'Holbach or Diderot. All his life Rousseau considered himself a *déraciné*, the defender of the downtrodden, the avenger of the lower classes, the unarmed prophet who had come to reveal the truth concerning the bad faith of governments, which had been created by the violent and were thus incapable of providing justice for all and especially of protecting the poor 'against the tyranny of the rich'.[53]

52. Cf. Baczko, *Job, mon ami*, p.178ff.

53. Cf. Jean-Jacques Rousseau, 'Political economy' [abridged], translated by Stephen J. Gendzier, in *The Encyclopedia of Diderot & D'Alembert*. This entry

Something that has not yet been explored is the significance of political theology in Rousseau's thought, and especially of the secondary role assigned to religion in relation to politics. There is no doubt about the sincerity of Rousseau's religious belief and his links with the spiritual tradition of the Huguenot refugees and Genevan pietism. Equally clear is his opposition to the temporal power of Churches and the absurd claim that civil power originates from God. What is still unclear is the profound motivation behind his harsh attack against the materialist current of the radical Enlightenment circles in Paris.

Even today we risk misunderstanding Rousseau's struggle against 'the clamors of the Coterie Holbachique'[54] if we apply criteria that are at the same time too narrow and too generic, and confuse philosophical radicalism of a materialist and anti-religious kind with political radicalism. We know that, historically, these two aspects do not always coexist. Quite often those who denounced the imposture of religions were rich aristocrats who had no time for the social claims of the marginalised humbler sectors of the population, or for any subversive social or political theories, such as republicanism or democracy, or for the idea of the equality of rights for all men.[55] As for Rousseau, his undoubted radicalism in politics did go hand in hand with his desire for religious reform, in the sense that he wished for a new natural religion that would foster human emancipation and the rise of a republic of free and equal men.[56]

---

contains a famous description of the pact between the rich and the poor that would later inspire Karl Marx and is quoted in *Capital*: 'You need me because I am rich and you are poor. We can therefore reach an agreement: I will permit you to have the honor of serving me on condition that you give me the little you have left in return for the pains I shall take to command you.'

54. *Confessions*, book IX, p.537.

55. On the *coterie holbachique* and its 'salon atheism', which never caused the authorities any trouble, and especially on how the Revolution brought to a head the contradiction between their philosophical radicalism and political moderation, see chapter IX, 'Salons, Lumières, engagement politique: la coterie d'Holbach dévoilée', in Daniel Roche, *Les Républicains des Lettres: gens de culture et Lumières au XVIIIe siècle* (Paris, 1988), p.242-53. For a study that moves in the opposite direction see Jonathan Israel, *A Revolution of the mind: Radical Enlightenment and the intellectual origins of modern democracy* (Princeton, NJ, 2010). Israel's discussion of the baron d'Holbach is critiqued in Antoine Lilti, 'Comment écrit-on l'histoire intellectuelle des Lumières? Spinozisme, radicalisme et philosophie', *Annales HSS* 1 (2009), p.171-206.

56. On the important role played by Rousseau in the resurgence of the republican

Rousseau's critique of the materialists' positions would split the Enlightenment movement. This critique reached back a long way and drew on specific philosophical and above all political arguments, even more than on a discussion of religion itself and its rational justification. Rousseau shared the serious reservations voiced in the *Encyclopédie* entry on 'Liberté' against the determinism that was implicit in the freethinkers' belief that motion was intrinsic to matter, or in Spinoza's thought ('Spinoza ne dépouille pas seulement les créatures de la liberté; il assujettit encore son Dieu à une obscure et fatale nécessité'). For Rousseau, these reductionist views of matter on the one hand effectively equated man with animals and made him entirely subject to nature, instinct and the passions, on the other hand depriving him of individual spirituality and especially of the freedom and perfectibility that are an original trait of the individual. These were like two sides of the same coin, on whose basis one could imagine a morality and politics capable of enacting the necessary reforms and allowing man to take charge of his own history.

This is why Rousseau was fiercely opposed to those who saw only the satisfaction of physical needs and the principle of utility as the fundamental requirements in human society. Against Rameau's mathematical intellectualism and the rationalist rigidity of Condillac and his sensism, Rousseau argued that the rise of music, writing, painting and language itself was linked to the spiritual dimension of the human being: a creature whose liberty and perfectibility had enabled him to break free of the endless repetition of the same in nature in which the animal was caught due to its pure materiality.[57]

Locke and Helvétius had highlighted the importance of empirical experience in man's cognitive processes, maintaining that there was no such thing as an innate moral instinct present in all men. To this Rousseau replied by upholding the primacy of conscience, and of free will as the original and natural distinguishing feature of each individual. It was this that provided the main point of reference for a truly universal morality that is common to all human beings, within the framework of a new natural law that was now transformed into the modern science of man. Man was the same everywhere, that was the most important discovery. As Rousseau writes in *Emile*, across

---

idea in the eighteenth century, see Franco Venturi, *Utopia e riforma nell'Illuminismo* (Turin, 1970), p.96ff.

57. See Rousseau, *Essay on the origin of languages and writings related to music*, especially chapter 1 of the *Essay on the origin of languages*, p.289-93.

all nations of the world and periods in time, 'among that prodigious variety of manners and characters, you will every where find the same ideas of justice and honesty, the same notions of good and evil [...] There is therefore implanted in the human breast, an innate principle of justice and virtue',[58] a moral instinct whereby 'immediately you are seized with the utmost indignation, and you find yourself inclined to espouse the part of the injured and oppressed' (p.50). On this theoretical basis morality and politics interacted dialectically once again, forming a nexus that in the second half of the eighteenth century would be explored, with different results, by authors such as Genovesi, Mably, Kant.

For Rousseau, this obvious connection between morality and politics effectively meant that the latter could not be independent: 'They who would treat of ethics and politics separately, know nothing of either' (book IV, vol.1, p.360). Conscience was what truly distinguished man from animals, alongside freedom and even more crucially than reason ('we may be men, without being learned'; 'Profession of faith', vol.2, p.55). It made man into a moral and political being who was capable of taking his own decisions. Thus, for Rousseau, it was the cornerstone of natural religion, something that provided the very justification for the necessary existence of God ('If no Deity exists, the wicked alone can be said to reason, and virtuous men are fools'; p.57):

> Conscience! conscience! heaven-born instinct; divine and immortal voice; sure guide of a being ignorant and finite; but free and intelligent; thou infallible judge of good and evil, who renderest man like unto God; it is thou who formest the excellence of his nature, and the morality of his actions; without thee I feel nothing within my breast, that raises me above the brute creation, except the dismal prerogative of wandering through a maze of errors, by the help of an understanding unconfined by rule, and of a reason untutored by principle. (p.55)

In the early 1760s, after the second *Encyclopédie* crisis, the materialist coterie led by the baron d'Holbach and Diderot had started their publishing campaign. A series of anti-religious tracts were published in quick succession and to great acclaim, and through them the new generations became acquainted with the work and ideas of Spinoza, the Italian libertines and the English freethinkers. In *Le Christianisme*

58. *Emilius*, 'Profession of faith', vol.2, p.51-52.

dévoilé, which was published under a pseudonym, d'Holbach set out their intention to create a sort of atheism for all, and denounced the imposture of priests and the covert interest of princes, who used bloody and superstitious religions as a means of subjugating the lower classes.[59] According to d'Holbach, that dark, terrible world that had invented religion in order to legitimise the power of kings and despots was now close to collapsing and being substituted by a new Europe, which would be founded on reason.

While there were differences of opinion among them, D'Alembert, Voltaire and Rousseau were not impressed by this cultural politics, with its attempt to spread materialist ideas and a militant atheism among the people in order to bring the struggle against all forms of religion to its ultimate consequences. Rousseau in particular thought that it would be a serious political error to try and replace religion with philosophy in the life of society. This was instead openly advocated in Diderot's famous 1761 manifesto that appeared as a preface to Nicolas Boulanger's posthumously published *Recherches sur l'origine du despotisme oriental*, which unveiled the historical and political import of religious myths and relaunched the Radical Enlightenment.[60] In Rousseau's view, philosophy, especially of a materialist kind, and most of all militant atheism, was not the right instrument through which one could transmit positive values to the masses, or spread a culture of political emancipation beyond a restricted group of literati and wealthy salon frequenters.

That *grand monde* inhabited by *philosophes* really had no idea of the true desperation experienced by the marginalised sectors of the population. Rousseau's concept of popular sovereignty as actual political practice was something much wider and quite different from the search for concrete institutional solutions. He envisaged a popular democratic republic in which everyone had the opportunity to participate in the exercise of power in a direct way. D'Holbach and Diderot, by contrast, still had an elitist idea of democratic representation as something that in any case should be linked to social and economic status.[61] Finally, Rousseau reacted with distaste to the

59. Cf. Diaz, *Filosofia e politica*, p.208ff.
60. Cf. Franco Venturi, *L'antichità svelata e l'idea del progresso in N. A. Boulanger* (Bari, 1947), p.66ff.
61. See the entry for 'Representatives' in the *Encyclopedia*, which is ascribed to d'Holbach ([abridged], translated by Stephen J. Gendzier, in *The Encyclopedia of Diderot & D'Alembert*). In a work published anonymously in London in 1773

fanatical utilitarianism of certain atheists, who rejected all ideals. These people's frame of mind 'creates an attachment to life [...] and concenters all the passions in the mean principle of private interest, and that abject thing, called self'.[62] Thus virtue is enslaved to the mere dynamics of pleasure and pain, which is why Rousseau asks young Emile to believe in universal justice and in the existence of what is right in nature: 'My child, private interest deceives us; but in the expectation of the righteous alone there is no deception' (p.99). There could be no better representation of the contrast between the two great moral and political souls of the Enlightenment: on the one hand, a new school of natural rights founded on human rights; on the other, various forms of utilitarianism.

In his *Confessions* Rousseau describes the 'Profession of faith of the vicar of Savoy' included in *Emile* as an attempt to find a happy medium between 'atheistical and devout fanaticism' (book XI, p.663). In fact this underestimates the emancipatory and demystifying value of the work that in any case had been done by the *coterie holbachique* in revealing the imposture of religions and the logic of domination that was intrinsic in the alliance between throne and altar. This is because for Rousseau the 'political theology' that was under constant attack by the materialists was not a relict of the past that had been superseded by reason and philosophy.[63] Unlike Bayle, he

(the *Système social, ou Principes naturels de la morale et de la politique, avec un examen de l'influence du gouvernement sur les mœurs*, 3 vols), d'Holbach defends the practice of allowing only landowners to elect political representatives, maintaining that '[c]e droit n'est pas fait pour une populace désœuvrée, pour des âmes viles et mercenaires', and that only 'la terre constitue la base physique et politique d'un Etat' (vol.2, part 1, chapter 4, p.53 and 54). In his extensive introduction to Paul-Henri Thiry d'Holbach, *Il buon senso* (Milan, 1985), Sebastiano Timpanaro points out the 'political and social limitations' of d'Holbach's thought (p.xliii).

62. *Emilius*, vol.2, chapter IV, note on p.96.

63. As far as I know, Rousseau never uses the term 'political theology', rather thinking in terms of 'civil religion'. However, the idea of 'political theology' was already outlined in the ancient world on both the lexical and conceptual levels. It was revived and continued to be discussed in subsequent centuries, from Augustine's severe critique of Varro's *theologia civilis* down to its modern incarnation in Carl Schmitt's 1922 *Politische Theologie* (*Political theology: four chapters on the concept of sovereignty*, translated by George Schwab, Cambridge, MA, 1985). For an extensive discussion of the history of this concept and the state of the question see Giovanni Filoramo, 'La sacralizzazione della politica tra teologia politica e religione civile', in *Pluralismo e religione civile: una prospettiva storica e filosofica, atti del convegno, Vercelli, 24-25 giugno 2001*, ed. Gianni Paganini and Edoardo Tortarolo (Milan, 2004), p.202-12.

believed that the religious sentiment was a natural human need that must be satisfied and that had a strong impact on communal life. If anything, this undeniable nexus between religion and politics should be modified in view of the future construction of a republic of free and equal human beings. The famous last chapter in the *Social contract*, which deals with civil religion, is sometimes considered an incongruous addition, something tacked on to the main picture with no real justification. In fact, it draws together the whole project of founding a new politics of the modern. In terms of our investigation, it provides an essential element, since this new civil religion was what Rousseau hoped would bring about the definitive apotheosis of the political practice of the rights of man.

As Franco Venturi clearly showed, religion was a crucial issue in Enlightenment culture. The new solutions that this great laboratory of modernity produced in opposition to the *Ancien régime* from this point of view had far-reaching effects in the history of the Western world, to an even greater extent than the Protestant Reformation itself.[64] Rousseau's position differed from that of atheist circles in Paris, whose publishing campaign aimed to get rid of religion once and for all, since they considered it an obstacle to civilisation. Nor did he subscribe to the deist solution, advocated, for instance, by Locke and Voltaire, whereby the idea of a natural and universal religion was functional to the call for a clear-cut separation of Church and State with reference to the Gospel ('give back to Caesar what is Caesar's, and to God what is God's'). As already mentioned above, Rousseau's difficult and original solution was based on the reprise of ancient civil religion.

From an anthropological point of view, above and beyond its role in the social bond, religion satisfied man's inborn need to believe in something. This need did not originate from man's fear or ignorance, as d'Holbach maintained.[65] Instead, it was rooted in man's awareness of the limitations of his spirit and his reason when it came to determining the meaning of existence. Above all, it allowed man

64. See the still informative discussion of this issue in Franco Venturi, *Giovinezza di Diderot* (Palermo, 1988; a French version first published in 1939), p.35ff. In his *Le origini dell'Enciclopedia* (Turin, 1970), Venturi points out that 'throughout Europe the Enlightenment was always accompanied and even at times replaced by a movement of reform within the official religion itself' (p.48). Cf. also Ferrone, *The Enlightenment*, p.103ff.

65. Cf. Anna Minerbi Belgrado, *Paura e ignoranza: studio sulla teoria della religione in d'Holbach* (Florence, 1983).

to create unassailable foundations on which to base human justice and the political recognition of human dignity and emancipation. As Rousseau wrote to the Protestant minister Vernes on 18 February 1758: 'I have spent my whole life among unbelievers [...] I believe in God, and God would not be just if my soul were not immortal. This, in my view, is what is essential and useful in religion. As for the rest, we can leave it to those who like to dispute.'

In the *Social contract* Rousseau further clarifies his thought on the relationship between politics and religion, giving a precise historical overview and an account of the state of the question. He found that there were two main theses on this subject, by Pierre Bayle and William Warburton, 'one of whom pretends that no religion is of use to a body politic; while the other, on the contrary, asserts that Christianity is the only certain support of it' (p.366-67). Both were wrong, however: the former did not take into account the fact that historically a nation of atheists had never actually existed; the latter forgot all the disasters and conflicts caused by Christianity.

In Rousseau's historical reconstruction, theocracy had been the natural choice of primitive peoples since the earliest times. Every people had distinguished itself by placing a specific god or deities at the head of its nation 'and therefore the political was also a religious war' (p.356). The Romans had exploited in an especially refined way the fundamental unity between politics and religion present in the ancient polytheist system, as they created an enormous empire that encompassed a great variety of peoples and gods. The way in which after every conquest they allowed the defeated populations to retain their own laws and gods speaks of their tolerance as well as of their political shrewdness: 'a crown, presented to Jupiter in his temple of the Capitol, was frequently the only tribute they imposed' (p.360). The coming of Christ broke up this ancient natural unity of political and religious power, and 'the consequence resulting from the double power, has been a perpetual conflict for jurisdiction' (p.362). This was the same pernicious dualism whose tragic consequences Hobbes had already denounced in his *Leviathan*, outlining what responsibilities lay with Christianity in this respect for limiting the absolute sovereignty of the State. In Rousseau's account: 'While things were in this situation [i.e. under the Roman empire], Jesus Christ came to establish a spiritual kingdom on earth: which separating the theological from the political system, divided what had till then been one; and caused those intestine dissensions, which have never ceased to agitate the professors of Christianity' (p.361). The Christian revolution had begun with great humility and under the precepts of the Gospel but it had quickly turned into an oppressive 'religion of the priests' (p.369): 'the pretended kingdom of heaven soon became a kingdom of this world, under a single chief, who governed with the most unlimited despotism' (p.362).

Rousseau discusses the phenomenon of religion in historical, political and theological terms and from three points of view: 1) the religion of man as individual; 2) that of man as citizen, i.e. civil religion; 3) the 'religion of the priests', or 'the Roman catholic faith' (p.369). There is no doubt that his preference went to the first of these, 'the religion of man' (p.371), which was seen as a private inner feeling that was active in man's heart even 'without the pomp of temples, of altars, or of rites; confined entirely to that adoration which the heart pours forth in secret to the supreme God; and to the discharge of those moral duties which reason alone enjoins' (p.367-68). This was a religion quite similar in its values to primitive Christianity. It was 'Christianity; not such as it is at this day, but such as the Evangelists taught it, which is very different from the present faith' (p.371). This shows that, like other European Enlightenment thinkers, Rousseau detached himself from all existing Christian Churches, to the point of becoming a kind of religious reformer, the prophet of a new religious sensibility never experienced before. The Christianity of the Gospels looked like it might provide the necessary guide to man's private religion and moral action. But in fact when examined with the sort of attention that had been devoted to this issue, for instance, by Machiavelli, an author whom Rousseau read with admiration, this religion turned out to be incapable of creating that civil and social bond that was an essential element in the construction of a political community, the latter being the true objective of any great legislator:

> But this religion, having no connection with the body politic, left the laws possessed of that force only which they drew from themselves. (p.371-72)

> Christianity is a religion entirely spiritual, and employing all its attention on a future state; for this world is not the country of a Christian. (p.373)

> But I am guilty of an error when I speak of a republic of Christians, for there can be no such thing. Christianity preaches up servitude and dependance; and its spirit is too favourable to tyranny not to

> be always taken advantage of. In short, the true Gospel Christian is formed to be a slave; and they are so sensible of it, that they hardly endeavour to avoid slavery. This short life is of too little consequence in their eyes to have any thought bestowed upon it. (p.377-78)[66]

This is why it was necessary to go back to the republican model of ancient civil religion, i.e. that religion of the citizen and of the homeland that had proved such an effective instrument of social and political cohesion in the Rome of Cicero's times. However, this was not to be a religious State. Nor was it to impose a religious orthodoxy at the expense of the now unassailable principle of toleration. What was needed was quite simply 'a profession of faith merely civil, the articles of which it is the business of the sovereign to arrange; not precisely as dogmas of religion, but as sentiments conducive to the well being of society; and without which, it is impossible to be either a good citizen, or a faithful subject' (p.381). Rousseau carefully warns against the dire consequences that would derive from this sacralisation of politics should it be 'founded in error and falsehood' (p.370). In his opinion, the only totally unacceptable dogma was intolerance itself: 'Those who make a distinction between civil and religious intolerance, are certainly, in my opinion, mistaken: they must be inseparable; for it is impossible to live in amity with those whom we believe devoted to damnation' (p.383). This also applied to the relationship among States: conflicts of religion should never be allowed to turn into wars.

But what interests us most here are the principles to be included in this profession of civil faith, which was meant to reinforce sociability and implement its politics. Rousseau describes these as 'an expectation of a future life, where the just will be rewarded, and the wicked punished; and a firm confidence in the sanctity of the social contract, and the laws' (p.383). Above all, for the first time in the history of the West in both semantic and linguistic terms, Rousseau

66. See Géraldine Lepan, *Jean-Jacques Rousseau et le patriotisme* (Paris, 2007), p.177ff., for an insightful discussion of the function of political theology in Rousseau's politics of the modern, including the influence of Plato's *Republic* and *Laws*. However, Rousseau's views on civil religion as a way to bring back social unity and overcome Christian dualism were also linked to the theses put forward by Cicero in *De natura deorum*, II, 72. Rousseau had come into contact with these ideas through the exposition found in Lactantius and Augustine on religion as *religio* or link, which not only binds man to God but also connects men to a community under common laws and worship.

cites respect for the rights of man as the necessary foundation for the citizenship of each individual.[67]

However, Rousseau's contribution to the issue of the exercise of natural rights in civil society was not limited to this sacralisation and popularisation of the rights of man, which not only threw light on the anthropological origins of these rights but also asserted their place in the sphere of religion. In terms of a redefinition of the politics of the moderns, the most important result achieved by Rousseau was establishing a link between the acknowledgement of these rights on a historical and anthropological level, the political practice of inalienable natural rights, and the general will, i.e. the social contract and direct democracy. Whatever success he may have achieved with his theoretical solutions and proposals of institutional reform, the usefulness of this result was still paramount.

Several stages in Rousseau's thought contributed to this outcome, starting with the bold hypothetical reconstruction of the history of mankind in the *Second discourse*, on the origins of inequality. His rejection of the theory of original sin had important repercussions in terms of political theology, as it allowed human action to become independent from divine providence. Man was once again a political animal on the model of the Ancient Greeks' *zôon politikón*: a free and responsible agent, actually capable of 'reforming the world'. Finally, compared to Grotius and Pufendorf's previous views on natural law, Rousseau turned the relationship between the individual and his community completely on its head, placing the individual and his natural rights at the top: society, with its sociability principle and the practice of duties came later, not least in chronological terms.

As we have seen, to begin with Rousseau's theoretical enquiry focuses on determining the human characteristics of isolated man in the 'pure state of nature'. This was the main import of his 'discovery of the social', and of his strikingly harsh critique of modern civil society: a society characterised first and foremost by violence, oppression and, above all, alienation; a society in which even artistic and scientific progress had a dehumanising effect, as it led to ever greater inequalities. All these reflections in Rousseau ultimately highlighted the innermost and most authentic dimension of the individual and the need to defend human beings against cultural conformity and a

67. See the mention, already cited at the start of this chapter, of 'les devoirs & les droits de l'homme' in chapter 8 of book IV ('the rights or the duties of men' in the 1791 translation, p.368).

historical development that placed him in a society in which 'man is born free, and yet we see him every where in chains.'

It is for these reasons, for this dialectical opposition between the subject and the logic of society, that the modern individual has in Rousseau his greatest interpreter and spokesperson.[68] However, he was first and foremost the author of an ambitious critical review of our concept of community. This was no longer seen in purely negative terms, but as a crucial opportunity for man to achieve his complete humanisation.

As we saw above, Rousseau viewed with particular enthusiasm the final stage of the pure state of nature, in which the good savage ruled like a sovereign. This stage embodied a perfect balance between natural freedom and social duties. It was the golden age in which a natural society without any form of dominion was happily free from all gratuitous violence and fatuous but pernicious egotism. This 'happiest and most durable epocha',[69] 'the real youth of the world' (p.118), was now gone forever, swept aside by revolutionary developments in metallurgy and agriculture. However, it was still in the background as a wonderful positive example of what common life could be like. Rousseau knew that man was ultimately destined to live in society: this was the decisive and inevitable development of the history of the human species. But this destiny must be fulfilled by boldly going against the idea of the inevitable degradation brought about by time and holding on instead to every possible opportunity to build a better life in society. Communities were obviously part of God's design and were meant to enhance man's complete humanity: they afforded man the opportunity to express his natural freedom through the exercise of the principle of responsibility. Only social man could balance self-love and sympathy for his fellow beings and thus become a complete moral and political entity capable of autonomous choice: a true *zôon politikón*, the ultimate vocation of the human species.

In any case, the kind of society that Rousseau had in mind was very different from the organicist hierarchical structure envisaged by thinkers such as Thomas Aquinas, the Second Scholastics or

68. On the way in which Rousseau 'discovered' the modern 'social' through his definition of the individual in contextual and dialectical terms, see Hannah Arendt, *The Human condition*, 2nd edn (1958; Chicago, IL, 1998). On the specific originality of Rousseau's individualism see also Luc Vincenti, *Jean-Jacques Rousseau: l'individu et la république* (Paris, 2001).

69. *Second discourse*, p.117.

the modern school of natural law, including Grotius and Pufendorf. The latter was ruled by the natural sociability principle, while the principle for the definition of the individual subject was considered in philosophical terms only as a part of the whole – and therefore still in relation to the class structure of the *Ancien régime*.[70] By contrast, for Rousseau society was a sum of independent individuals who chose to come together in a later phase of historical development with a view to ensuring overall happiness.[71]

Thus, it would be entirely wrong to say that Rousseau upheld what today we would call communitarian theories, or that he focused on the whole at the expense of the individual. And it would be equally wrong to continue to address the 'Rousseau enigma' through an artificial division of his intellectual experience into a destructive part, consisting in his radical critique of contemporary society, and a constructive part. From that point of view, the latter consists in the politics of the social contract, which aimed to create a better society but ended up laying the foundations for future totalitarian regimes, with their emphasis on the primacy of nations and of collective over individual identity.

In fact, the fundamental unity of Rousseau's thought is clearly exemplified by his constant attempt to find the best possible way of linking together the individual and his community – which was indeed the big question addressed by the political culture of the Enlightenment as a whole. This would support the good life, the exercise of natural rights and, above all, that political and moral action that characterised the human species from a historical and anthropological point of view. This is the issue at the heart of the *Social contract*, as clearly defined by Rousseau himself:

70. Costa, *Civitas*, vol.1, p.xiv ff., discusses how throughout the Middle Ages and the early modern period any idea of the individual remained linked to the *Ancien régime* structures of class and census, and was in any case viewed in terms of status or membership of corporations.
71. At the turn of the twentieth century, one of the first to describe, and critique, Rousseau's 'atomistic' view of society as a union of isolated individuals was Emile Durkheim (see his *Montesquieu and Rousseau: forerunners of sociology*, translated by Ralph Manheim, Ann Arbor, MI, 1960, p.137-38). For the founder of modern sociology, society was best seen as something that arose from the very beginning as a coherent system of individuals. This association of separate beings gave rise to something with very specific characteristics. By getting together, individuals created a new collective individuality, and it was this entity, rather than its single components, that brought forth whatever was produced within it.

> 'Where shall we find a form of association which will defend and protect with the whole aggregate force the person and the property of each individual; and by which every person, while united with all, shall obey only himself, and remain as free as before the union?' Such is the fundamental problem, of which the Social Contract gives the solution. (p.34-35)

Thus, on the one hand we have the individual as a person and a holder of natural and inalienable rights such as the right to life, liberty and property – the latter rather surprisingly, given the fierce criticism levelled against this institution in the *Second discourse*.[72] On the other hand we have the pursuit of a form of community and of modern civil society that offered the advantages of communal living. Thanks to these, it would become possible to achieve a state in which all men enjoyed political representation under a republican form of government, with the understanding that man as *zôon politikón* owed allegiance only to himself. Above all, human beings would enjoy that original freedom that distinguished man from animals and made him into a unique moral and political individual. However, in order to achieve this it was necessary to go beyond the old natural law. The latter's epistemological component must be adapted into a new science of man, and the Enlightenment must invent a new concept: the idea of 'political right'. Hence the full title of Rousseau's groundbreaking pamphlet: *Du contrat social, ou Principes du droit politique.*

Although the phrase *droit politique*, 'political right' or 'political law' appears in other authors before Rousseau, such as Hobbes, Burlamaqui or Montesquieu, it has there a very different meaning. Rousseau takes issue openly with Montesquieu's basic definition of 'political law' in his *Esprit des lois* as 'laws relative to the governours and the governed'.[73] In his *Emile*, Rousseau replies that this only dealt with 'the positive law under established governments; and there is nothing in the world more different than these two sciences'.[74] The

72. Much has been written on Rousseau's oscillations on the issue of the right to property. In the *Second discourse* he states uncompromisingly: 'Equality vanished; property started up' (p.119), while his position in the essay on 'Political economy' for the *Encyclopédie* is completely different and much more in line with Locke's theories: 'It is certain that the right of property is the most sacred of all the rights of citizens.' Many more examples could be adduced to illustrate Rousseau's constantly shifting opinion on this subject.
73. Montesquieu, *Spirit of laws*, book I, chapter 3, vol.1, p.6.
74. Rousseau, *Emilius*, book V, vol.2, p.365-66.

principle of legality was indeed important in a context where violence and arbitrary power had the upper hand. However, modern political law could not limit itself to a study of the spirit and the nature of laws in order to reassert the primacy of this principle. Its task was far more complex than this, as it must question the moral and political legitimacy of the laws themselves and the government that issued them. It must go as far as exploring the true nature of power, unveiling the logic of domination that had led to unjust laws being not only promulgated but also described as natural and sanctioned by reason. Above all, it must build a new science of government and of the state in order 'to establish the rights of humanity' (p.366). To this effect, one must go beyond the medieval concept of *scientia iuris*, according to which law, in an ontological sense, was located in nature, or rather, as in the opening words of Montesquieu's work, '[l]aws, in their most general signification, are the necessary relations resulting from the nature of things.'[75] In this way, and aided by the prestige of the mechanistic universe of Descartes and Newton, Montesquieu had revived this ontological conception of natural law in the middle of the eighteenth century.

Thus, the fundamental concept of law needed to be reformulated on the basis of man's natural freedom and his republican right to direct political participation. In order to accommodate man as *zôon politikón*, modern civil society was to be recreated so as to reduce the growing inequalities that had been engendered by so-called progress: 'what is the nature, and what the characteristic of a law? This is altogether a new investigation; for as yet the subject has not been justly defined' (p.372). The principles of the new political right that he was about to describe were based on this new concept of nature and of the moral and political function of law as a precious tool for political action: a free and responsible act of human will. This collection of principles should be a kind of 'scale' (p.367), a device for measuring the legitimacy of positive right within the nation states that would allow us 'to judge of the relative goodness of government' (p.383): 'to form a proper judgment of the present institutions, we should be very well acquainted with the foundation and right of civil power' (p.366).

In *Emile* the young disciple is given a detailed illustration of the purpose of the social contract as part of his preparation for leading a political life worthy of a fully emancipated human being:

75. We shall return to this important point in the following chapters.

> we shall inquire whether men are born in subjection or freedom, in society or independency. (p.367)
>
> Proceeding thence to the right of slavery, we shall inquire whether one man can lawfully dispose of himself to another, without any restriction or reserve? That is, whether he has a right to renounce his person, his life, his reason, *himself*, the whole morality of his actions; in a word, to cease to exist before his death, in opposition to nature, by whom he is immediately entrusted with the care of his preservation, and in spite of his own conscience and reason, by which he is apprised of the actions he ought to perform, and of those from which he is bound to refrain. (p.368-69; emphasis in the original)
>
> If a man therefore cannot unconditionally resign his liberty to his master; how can a whole people have a power of making an unlimited alienation of their persons and properties to their chief? And if a slave remains judge of the observance of the contract on the part of his lord; why should not the nation be judges of the performance of the compact on the part of their leader? (p.369)

The true significance and novelty of the *Social contract* in terms of the political life of the Western world is a moot point. One of the most plausible answers is that Rousseau's work brought to completion the tradition of European liberal Protestantism, with its struggle against the theoretical foundations of the absolute power of popes and kings alike, and its rejection of the Pauline concept of the divine origin of sovereignty, against which it upheld a completely human and democratic idea of civil power.[76] Another promising strand of enquiry that has developed recently investigates the nature of Rousseau's republicanism. According to this interpretation, the *Social contract* upholds the theory of the general will in order to defend the idea of the sovereignty of the people against the monarchy and the illegitimate power of rulers in general.[77] More lines of enquiry could be usefully pursued. As already mentioned, starting from the early

76. See Derathé, *Jean-Jacques Rousseau et la science politique*, on the *Social contract*: 'We see this work as the ultimate manifestation of a current of ideas that originated with the Reformation. From the intellectual point of view, this movement was characterised at one and the same time by the struggle against the absolute power of monarchs and the attempt to break free from the traditional doctrine of the Catholic Church on the divine origin of civil power' (p.62).
77. For a useful overview of recent bibliography on this subject see Gabriella Silvestrini, *Diritto naturale e volontà generale: il contrattualismo repubblicano di Jean-Jacques Rousseau* (Turin, 2010).

twentieth century the complex relationship between the *Social contract* and the 1789 Declaration of the Rights of Man had been the subject of a heated debate among scholars, from Jellinek and Boutmy to Del Vecchio, down to Cassirer. This line of research was unfortunately abandoned and has left few traces in more recent studies. However, it has become strongly relevant again in the light of new research that is now being carried out on the political culture of the Enlightenment in the second half of the eighteenth century.

If, as we have seen, the problem at the origin of the social contract was to find a form of association capable of protecting the natural rights of the individual after the development of civil society, in such a way that 'every person, while united with all, shall obey only himself, and remain as free as before the union', the archetype of a community arisen from an ideal pact among free and equal men seemed to Rousseau the only possible solution. This social pact effectively created a 'political body', a 'public person' and a 'collective body'. Thanks to this agreement and these collective decisions all human actions acquired a moral character. The original natural freedom of the individual became civil liberty, which was protected by law. The violent acquisition of goods by the single individual in the state of nature gave way to a right of property that was sanctioned and respected by the whole community. Individual power became public law. This miraculous transformation of the primitive natural rights into modern citizenship rights was accomplished by restoring politics to the primary role it held in the ancient world and through an understanding of the importance of man's actions in his quality as a *zôon politikón* who governed himself in a free and responsible manner. The fundamental instrument through which the political body expressed its motions and will was at last to be found in the new concept of law. As Rousseau writes at the start of chapter VI in the *Social contract*:

> By the Social Compact we have given existence and life to the body politic; it now remains to give it motion and will for legislation. For the primitive act by which the body is formed determines none of the measures that are necessary for its preservation [...] Justice flows from God: He only is the source of it; and if men could be made sensible of its divine authority, we should require neither government or laws. This principle of justice is also undoubtedly universal and founded on reason; but it can never, without the aid of human institutions, be sufficient for the purposes of society, unless its influence were equal on the minds of all men, and the conduct of all men equally regulated by its dictates [...] There must therefore be conventions

> and laws to combine our *duties* and our *rights*; to render the practice of justice mutual between man and man; and to direct it to its great end. (p.96-97; emphasis added)

In relation to the ancient debate between Plato and Aristotle on the relative primacy of the government of men or the government of laws, the whole of the Enlightenment, and especially Rousseau, opted decidedly for the latter. The world could and should be reformed only through legislation drafted by man for man. We tend to forget that after the *Social contract* the term 'legislation' acquired a new philosophical and political meaning, which it still has. In writing that 'the right of every man is determined by law' (p.98) Rousseau expresses the magic-like power that he attributed to the action of laws and their ability to transform the primitive rights of the individual into citizenship rights. As he painstakingly points out, the purpose of laws is always of a general kind: they are 'the acts of the general will [...] the registers of [people's] own wills' (p.101-102). Through this theory of the primacy of laws and the idea that the essence of political power lay in the power of legislation, the principle of legitimacy and Rousseau's definition of republic became an essential part of the political thought of the Enlightenment: 'I therefore denominate every state a republic which is regulated by laws, under whatever form of administration it may be; for then only the public interest governs, and the affairs of the public obtain a due regard. All lawful governments are republican' (p.103).

It is astonishing how the Enlightenment seemed to believe that the general will would always correctly choose what was right before what was evil since the former was an immediate expression of public good. But this completely fideistic tenet was no doubt supported by Rousseau's defence of the philosophy of history and a positive anthropology that was profoundly influenced by a Pelagian kind of political theology. In order to understand the high expectations that Rousseau placed on democracy and the sovereignty of the people, we must bear in mind the importance of the idea that man was born good and that a bad political system had placed him in chains. In contrast with the utilitarian relativism of Locke or Helvétius, this theory held that the eternal principles of a universal morality were inscribed in the consciousness of every individual and could be called forth through the action of the general will.

This view therefore based the actual construction of future political institutions on the direct democracy and 'republican' ideals of the modern *zôon politikón*. These were the instruments that would ensure the application of natural rights in modern political practice and their transformation into citizenship rights. But in fact these tools would turn out to be quite ineffective in the turbulent years of the Revolution, leading to widespread misunderstandings and recriminations.

By designating an effectively omnipotent sovereign as the source of all political and moral legitimation, Hobbes had done away with all reference to the original rights of man. Locke, by contrast, had upheld these very rights in opposition to the authoritarian tendencies of both the monarchy and the power of legislation. Rousseau's 'third way' devolved the task of acknowledging and defending those rights entirely to the State and its power of legislation, in a move that revealed its theoretical ambiguity in the very premises of his social contract: 'All the articles of the social contract will, when clearly understood, be found reducible to this single point – *the total alienation of each associate, and all his rights, to the whole community*' (p.36; emphasis in the original). These are famous and terrible words: here Rousseau attributes to the popular will, i.e. to the power of legislation, an immense force that is subject to no possibility of appeal. This seems to be in open contradiction with the initial tenets, in which he solemnly stipulates that the individual would in any case be free, even after entering into this new association.

Unsurprisingly, much time and effort has been expended on the analysis of this sentence. Some authors, such as Jellinek and Cassirer, have denied that there could be any link between the 1789 Declaration of the Rights of Man and the *Social contract*. Others, more ideologically prejudiced, have gone so far as to see in Rousseau the father of modern totalitarianism.[78] In fact the question is rather more

78. Among the latter, see especially J. L. Talmon, *The Origins of totalitarian democracy* (London, 1952). On the issue of the effective annihilation of natural rights by the general will, see Jellinek, *The Declaration of the Rights of Man and of Citizens*, and Cassirer, 'Vom Wesen und Werden des Naturrechts'. Jellinek's thesis is opposed by Giorgio Del Vecchio in *La Déclaration des droits de l'homme et du citoyen dans la Révolution française*, translated by Antoinette Pellevant Gini (Rome and Paris, 1968; original: *La Dichiarazione dei diritti dell'uomo e del cittadino nella Rivoluzione francese*, Genoa, 1903), and especially in *Su la teoria del contratto sociale*. Del Vecchio argues that 'for Rousseau the Social contract is simply the idea that can and must ensure the civil co-ordination of the natural rights of individuals' (p.37). By contrast, the 'total alienation' of every right should be intended in the sense of a 'purely regulative and methodological principle, which was to be used only to explain the transition of man's rights from the natural to the civil order' (p.101). Robert Derathé agrees with Del Vecchio's conclusions in *Jean-Jacques Rousseau*

complex. It cannot be adjudicated simply on the basis of the meaning of a single sentence and must be considered in the light of Rousseau's oeuvre as a whole. If the Declaration intended to set clear and strong boundaries to monarchical power, tracing a kind of permanent line of demarcation between the State and the rights of the individual, then Rousseau's *Contract* has nothing in common with this revolutionary document that changed the political history of the Western world.

Rousseau opted for an entirely different way to protect man's rights. In his view, only self-government within a democratic and republican regime could carry off the difficult feat of acknowledging and guaranteeing the exercise of rights in civil society. He devolved to the general will the task of building a legal system that would safeguard the rights that man originally enjoyed in nature once those rights were transposed within society. As we have often remarked, this vision was founded on a Pelagian faith in man's original goodness and on the influence of public interest. For Rousseau, in the politics of the moderns direct democracy and rights are two sides of the same coin.

The French Revolution first and centuries of political and constitutional history since then in the Western world have clearly shown how fragile and ambiguous this solution really was. During this time other and far more effective forms of institutional and constitutional engineering were put forward, as we shall see when we discuss the work of William Blackstone and, above all, Gaetano Filangieri. Nevertheless, the importance of Rousseau's theories for the purpose of our research should not be underestimated. Rousseau was the first to clearly highlight the political transformation that had to be undergone by the ancient language of natural rights in the Enlightenment. Besides this, he also focused on other, equally important problems, which are still being keenly debated today.

The history of rights has encouraged us to think of the theory of the rights of man in a vaguely liberal, nineteenth-century way, as a language that arose first and foremost in order to protect the individual from sovereignty and the power of the State. But in this way we have overlooked the other side of the issue, which had started to be

---

et la science politique, p.171ff.: 'Individual or natural rights are not annihilated by the Social contract. We find them again within the State, but in a form that has been reshaped through reason.' A study that entirely misunderstands Rousseau's positions, which are in fact perfectly in line with the libertarian principles of the Enlightenment, is Graeme Garrard, *Rousseau's counter-Enlightenment: a republican critique of the philosophes* (Albany, NY, 2000).

urgently debated in that great laboratory of modernity that was the Enlightenment: how to defend society from individual egotism, and from an arbitrary concept of natural rights as something that could be exercised without restraint, resulting in excessive claims and abuses of power. These thinkers were asking themselves how to avoid what in the following century would indeed manifest itself as unbounded individualism in the economic, civil and social spheres. On the one hand there was the need to acknowledge the value of the individual and his natural rights, which effectively limited political sovereignty. On the other stood society, public interest and sovereignty, the latter being seen as a necessary curb on individual rights. In his *Social contract* Rousseau repeatedly demonstrates his early awareness of this controversial issue and of the need to establish a harmonious dialectical balance between duties and rights in the name of public interest.

In this sense natural freedom must be curbed and regulated by law so that everyone could enjoy it in its best form as civil freedom, not just the strongest, as was the case in the state of nature. From this derived the revolutionary idea that in modern civil society moral and legal equality must be established as the necessary frame of reference for the whole 'social system' if one was to do away once and for all with the *Ancien régime* hierarchies and logic of domination. Thus, Rousseau concludes the first book of the *Social contract* with the assertion that 'so far from destroying the natural equality of mankind, the fundamental compact substitutes a moral and legal equality, instead of that physical inequality which nature placed amongst men; and that let men be ever so unequal in strength or in genius, they are all equalized by the rights of the convention' (p.60).

Even property, or the 'right of the first occupier' (p.53), was subject to being regulated for the sake of public interest, regardless of its primitive and natural origin: 'In whatever manner the acquisition is made, the right which each individual has over his own property, is always subordinate to the right which the community has over all; without which there would be no solidity in the social bond, or any real force in the sovereign power' (p.59).

A similar eminently social interpretation applied to 'the right of life and death'. What did the right to life actually entail? Certainly not the right to do whatever one wanted with one's life, as was claimed by Radical Enlightenment thinkers like Radicati di Passerano, who went so far as to uphold the right to take one's own life (in a move that for the first time highlighted the conflict between the right to freedom and the right to life). What was meant by the right to life was simply the right to preserve one's life by every possible means. But even this posed no end of problems on a theoretical level, such as how to justify sentencing someone to death, for instance. At the start of book II, chapter V, 'Of the right of life and death', Rousseau posits the question 'how individuals, having no right to dispose of their own lives, can transmit to the sovereign power a right which they do not possess' (p.89). In his view, this is a misguided question, since the *Social contract* only entailed the right of all parties to the preservation of their lives, and not the ability to dispose freely of one's life. This was in fact an extremely reductive interpretation that did not link back to the equally important right of the individual to freedom, which was also upheld by the *Contract*. However, it was used to justify inflicting the death penalty onto anyone who threatened or attacked either single individuals or the integrity of one's country through actions such as murder or treason.

Despite its many ambiguities, Rousseau's work is characterised by extremely brave and radical decisions. Thanks to the debate it initiated, the old language of natural rights started to be transformed into the political language of the moderns and of the entire Enlightenment culture in Europe. Much has been said on how Rousseau contributed to the diffusion of the rights of man through his novels, which created a new culture of empathy among individuals. However, there were other, equally important authors whose work had the same kind of effect. By contrast, one might take exception to the overruling and omnipotent function that Rousseau assigned to the general will or to the primacy of nature. But we should always remember that the modern theory of the rights of man was only possible with the rise of *political law*.

The eighteenth-century discovery of man by the Enlightenment, as described by Michel Foucault, could not have happened without Rousseau's reworking of the myth of the noble savage, who lived in happy isolation in the 'pure state of nature', or his insistence that man in this state was already the holder of rights that certified his full humanity, long before his potential social instinct was fully developed or became subject to the duties that were an essential part of the old form of natural right. The redefinition of the natural right to freedom as an indispensable and inalienable part of human identity was a necessary premise for both the critique of the *Ancien régime* and the call for the political and juridical application of the natural rights of primitive man in modern civil society.

Rousseau was a serious political thinker, not someone who lived in cloud cuckoo land or dreamed of impossible worlds. Like many of his

Enlightenment contemporaries, he constantly oscillated between hope and realism, utopia and reform. It could not have been otherwise, since they placed man, his point of view and his struggle for emancipation and self-government at the centre of every discussion. Rousseau repeatedly declares his awareness that equality and democracy were only frames of reference for a theoretical discussion, or representations of what *ought to be* against which one must measure what *is*, i.e. actual governments and positive laws. As he wrily observes at the end of a chapter on 'Democracy' in the *Social contract*, 'If there were a nation of gods they might be governed by a democracy; but so perfect a government will not agree with men' (book III, chapter IV, p.194).

As we shall see, the rights of man in the political culture of the Enlightenment will undergo the same oscillation between hope and realism. These rights were first conceived of in the realm of utopia and of moral reflection. However, with Rousseau they started to become a concrete political formula in the programme of the reform movement in the second half of the eighteenth century. They quickly transformed into a subtle juridical question and became the moral soul of the struggle against the inequalities of the *Ancien régime*. These rights became the rallying cry in the political rebellion of those who were subject to injustices and violence, once again holding a middle ground between utopia and reform.

10. The politicisation of natural rights: legislation and reform in Montesquieu, Helvétius and Beccaria

With his provocations and paradoxes Rousseau was without doubt an explicit or implicit point of reference in the debate on the rights of man in late-eighteenth-century Europe. As we shall see, his thesis of the noble savage, who lived happily in the authenticity of his being, gave rise, as a reaction, to the rather more common theory of the bad savage in need of being civilised. Many Enlightenment circles in Europe favoured a strong ideology of progress and a view of the constant improvement of mankind against his philosophy of history as the degeneration of humanity. Some responded to his theory of the isolation of the individual in the pure state of nature by denying that such a state ever existed, and upholding instead a view that man's development had occurred in stages from the very beginning. One way or another, the extreme popularity of his work meant that he became the main protagonist in the Late Enlightenment laboratory of modernity. As Mirabeau wrote in the *Courrier de Provence* in 1789, referring to Rousseau's by now ubiquitously translated works,

> he alone, with his study of the natural rights of man, discovered the real foundations of society, sweeping aside the dust and the sand, that is to say those exterior relationships of weakness and power, wealth and poverty, of inequality, and all kinds of aristocracy. He showed how faltering the whole construction was wherever it was not built on the consensus of men and on conventions of reciprocity. Whenever we speak of liberty, we must pay homage to this immortal defender of human nature.[1]

Rousseau had not accomplished all this out of nothing. His most important achievement in relation to the rights of man was the idea

1. Translated from the quotation in Rials, *La Déclaration des droits*, p.310.

that the exercise and daily application of these rights would only become possible by transforming natural rights into citizenship rights through legislation and a concept of the law as the expression of the general will. But this concept arose in the wake of a long history of reactions to the medieval *scientia iuris*, and especially Montesquieu's 1748 work, *L'Esprit des lois*. For the purpose of our investigation, this represents a moment of transition rather than an achievement in itself, but it is still an extraordinarily important work. With its intersection of old and new concepts, its ambiguities and epistemological links with seventeenth-century natural law, it paved the way for the sciences of man and the centrality of the idea of legislation in the political culture of the Late Enlightenment.

In his writings, Montesquieu does not actually use the expression 'rights of man'. Also absent is any explicit reference to the theories of the natural rights of the subject, such as those that had already been put forward by Barbeyrac and Locke.[2] His discussion is dominated by the idea of the scientific study of man in history and society, rather than of the individual as such. As a young man he had devoted a lot of time to writing a long *Traité des devoirs*, based on the principle of natural sociability that had been popularised again by Pufendorf and several new editions of Cicero's *De officiis*. Despite being presented at the Academy of Bordeaux in 1725, this ambitious project was eventually abandoned. In the process, however, Montesquieu had started to question the nexus between duties on the one hand and public and private virtue on the other, a Stoic concept based on a morality and obligations that in turn derived from a natural order of things that directly reflected God's will. In his opinion, things were rather more complex, and this concept needed to also take into account the positions of the Neo-Epicureans and the new politics of the modern, with its emphasis on commerce.[3] Above all, it should encompass a view of human action as the result of multiple empirical causes and legislation, i.e. of governance by law as the main instrument for the organisation of life in human society. There was an apparent contradiction in universal law between the fixity of

2. To the best of my knowledge, Montesquieu never mentions the 'rights of man'. Nor does he refer to the 'natural rights of the individual', as is claimed in M. H. Waddicor, *Montesquieu and the philosophy of natural law* (The Hague, 1970), p.154.
3. Cf. Marco Platania, *Montesquieu e la virtù: rappresentazioni della Francia di Ancien Régime e dei governi repubblicani* (Turin, 2007).

the fundamental laws of nature and the multiplicity of positive laws developed by the different populations. This issue must be rationally investigated in order to throw light on its ultimate causes. *L'Esprit des lois* was fundamentally a scientific attempt to discover the moral and physical origin of laws, their ultimate intent, and the single logical rationale of the common structure underneath the multiplicity and variety of the empirical data.

Montesquieu was politically a realist and an admirer of Machiavelli. He was not interested in the pursuit of what was right in nature that had occupied the school of natural law both in ancient and in modern times. Nonetheless, he obviously positioned himself along the same lines as Pufendorf and Barbeyrac, who, by aspiring to scientific objectivity, had transformed the methodology of this kind of investigation. At the theoretical and epistemological core of *L'Esprit des lois* lies the geometric deductive method, duly supported by the use of historical evidence and the fixity and rationality of the Newtonian universe, the validity of whose laws – 'in their most general signification' as 'the necessary relations resulting from the nature of things' – was guaranteed by the God of the Boyle Lectures and his relationship 'to the universe as creator and preserver'.[4]

God, nature and man each had their own laws. In the case of man, the laws that were truly fundamental and invariable and applied to the whole of mankind were linked to specific causes such as climate, religion, forms of government, modes of production or the material conditions of life. Montesquieu's work was characterised throughout by an uncompromising determinism and deductive methodology, which means that facts were selected on the basis of clearly stated principles and hypotheses. 'Every thing gives way now to my principles', he remarked with obvious satisfaction.[5] As is clearly shown by the concluding paragraph of the first chapter of *L'Esprit des lois*, however, Montesquieu remained fully aware of the specific character of man, with his finitude, his being simultaneously within and outside nature, his status as an animal capable of creating culture, and in any case as a protagonist, thanks to his free will:

> Man, as a physical being, is, like other bodies, governed by invariable laws. As an intelligent being, he incessantly transgresses the laws established by God, and changes those which he himself has

4. Montesquieu, *Spirit of laws*, book I, chapter I, vol.1, p.1-2.
5. Montesquieu, *Spirit of laws*, book XXVIII, chapter VI, vol.2, p.243.

> established. He is left to his own direction, though he is a limited being, subject, like all finite intelligences, to ignorance and errour; even the imperfect knowledge he has, he loses as a sensible creature, and is hurried away by a thousand impetuous passions. Such a being might every instant forget his Creator; God has therefore reminded him of his duty by the laws of religion. Such a being is liable every moment to forget himself; philosophy has provided against this by the laws of morality. Formed to live in society, he might forget his fellow-creatures; legislators have therefore, by political and civil laws, confined him to his duty. (p.4)

In line with the cultural revolution of the Enlightenment, which placed more and more emphasis on a new and radical humanism, these observations were followed by extraordinary descriptions of the common elements and differences among the legal systems of various ancient and modern peoples from Asia, Africa and America. Historical time, geography, climate and the dynamics of stadial evolution of entire civilisations were finally studied with a view to finding the physical and moral causes that determined the deep structure of these systems. A new and unexpected world opened up in front of politicians and jurists all over Europe. And the extent of this break with the past becomes even more obvious if we compare this with what was still being produced by the practitioners of the traditional *scientia iuris*, the so-called *sacerdotes iuris*, entrenched in their powerful positions in the universities or the judicial system of the *Ancien régime.*

In 1689 the famous French jurist Jean Domat had started to publish his monumental work on *Les Lois civiles dans leur ordre naturel.* Ostensibly, the main objectives of this work were similar to those of Montesquieu and many other authors from these years, i.e. to discover the foundations of civil law in the natural order, or 'L'esprit des lois et de leur differentes espèces' ('Of the nature and spirit of laws, and their different kinds'), as is stated in the title of chapter XI in Domat's *Treatise of laws*, contained in volume 1 of his *Civil law.*[6] In fact, beyond some superficial similarities, not least in terms of lexis, Domat's work could not be more different from that of Montesquieu. Domat was a

6. Cf. Jean Domat, *The Civil law in its natural order: together with the publick law*, translated by William Strahan, 2 vols (London, printed by J. Bettenham for E. Bell, J. Darby, A. Bettesworth, G. Strahan, F. Fayram, J. Pemberton, J. Hooke, C. Rivington, F. Clay, J. Batley and E. Symon, 1722). On this aspect of the work of Montesquieu and others, see Italo Birocchi, *Alla ricerca dell'ordine: fonti e cultura giuridica nell'età moderna* (Turin, 2002).

Jansenist and a personal friend of Blaise Pascal. A firm believer in original sin, he was attempting to draft a formal 'treatise of laws' that would give a common rational foundation to all civil law on the basis of natural law.[7] In accordance with the traditional model whereby all obligations ultimately derived from God, Domat tried to preserve at all costs the purity, autonomy and ontology of law as a science. Montesquieu, by contrast, was an Enlightenment thinker. He started from entirely different premises and, above all, aimed at entirely different objectives. He was an offshoot of that libertine culture that, through figures such as Machiavelli, Spinoza or Bayle, had been systematically unmasking the *arcana imperii* and the imposture of religions from both an ideological and a philosophical point of view. Montesquieu's work was immediately placed on the Index of prohibited books by the Catholic Church, and he would have smiled ruefully at Domat's claim that the power of judges came 'originally from God'.[8] By then, criticism of the *arcana iuris* had been taking place for some time, fuelled by new historical research on Roman law and on the legislative systems of ancient peoples. It had steadily chipped away at the jurists' eminently political myth of the supernatural origins of legislation. After all, they would remark, the first laws had been given to Moses by God himself. Or, as Neapolitan author Nicola Toppi wrote with utter conviction in 1655, 'Magistratus a Deo positi sunt, diique vocantur', that is to say, magistrates are akin to God, from whom their power derives.[9] The Enlightenment's corrosive attack on the religious and metaphysical roots of the law had soon shifted its attention from the *arcana religionis* through the *arcana dominationis* to the *arcana iuris*.

L'Esprit des lois was certainly a milestone in this long and difficult, but also necessary, historical process of secularisation of juridical science. Without this process, the rights of man would probably never have attained legal status, and it was after they became part of the laws made by man for man that they metamorphosed into political privileges and citizenship rights. After Montesquieu, it was impossible to deny the strong political element in the law as conceived

7. On Domat, see Nicola Matteucci, *Jean Domat, un magistrato giansenista* (Bologna, 1985); Franco Todescan, *Le radici teologiche del giusnaturalismo laico*, vol.2: *Il problema della secolarizzazione nel pensiero giuridico di Jean Domat* (Milan, 1987).
8. Quoted in the important study by Raffaele Ajello, *Arcana juris: diritto e politica nel Settecento italiano* (Naples, 1976), p.140.
9. Cf. Hespanha, *Panorama histórico*, p.60, n.70.

by the moderns, which compromised the ontological character of the medieval *scientia iuris* in a way that some are still lamenting in our own times.[10]

Montesquieu went even further. He famously described how a democratic and republican government should build a specific legal system with the intent of strengthening public virtues, reducing social inequality, and creating a public education structure for the instruction of its citizens that would prepare them for political participation. This lesson was not lost on the future revolutionaries: indirectly, Montesquieu had created the linguistic and theoretical tools of modern liberal thought, especially in its constitutional and republican manifestations. Among the many revolutionary ideas in *L'Esprit des lois* we find the condemnation of slavery and the call to finally separate justice from religion and the concept of crime from that of guilt within the penal system. Above all, this work led to the definitive assertion of the principle of legality in the political and juridical culture of the West.

A decisive step in this direction was the nexus that Montesquieu established once and for all between law and liberty. A few years before Rousseau based the concept of freedom anthropologically on the language of the rights of man, Montesquieu had already realised that the conditions whereby an individual could enjoy social and political freedom in actual terms depended on a state's constitutional and legislative system: 'We must have continually present to our minds the difference between independence and liberty. Liberty is a right of doing whatever the laws permit; and if a citizen could do what they forbid, he would no longer be possessed of liberty, because all his fellow citizens would have the same power.'[11]

Despite these innovations and the important ways in which Montesquieu's work anticipates future developments, there is no doubt

10. See, for instance, how a great expert of medieval law such as Paolo Grossi constantly stigmatises the law of the moderns and the Enlightenment politicisation of law as deriving from a lack of real knowledge of juridical science: the legal Enlightenment was a politics of law. It 'sought to enact a nakedly political view of the law', and '[b]ehind the figleaf of "natural reason" and the "general will" lies the deposition of the whole mechanism of the production of law in the hands of the politically powerful' (Grossi, *History of European law*, p.65 and 69). For Grossi this is clearly a negative development, which gave rise to a pernicious statism and strengthened bourgeois capitalism and possessive individualism: 'And so begins a long period of legalism, and even of legal idolatry' (p.69).
11. Montesquieu, *Spirit of laws*, book XI, chapter III, vol.1, p.195.

that overall it belonged squarely within the logic of the *Ancien régime*'s social and corporative system, in which the hierarchical structure based on nobility of blood was still unquestionably acknowledged as a reflection of the nature of things. As such it became the target of harsh criticism from the new Enlightenment generation. Voltaire accused Montesquieu of wasting time criticising the Islamic or Chinese penal systems, while the French system itself was in dire need of reform because of its obvious and needless cruelty. Morelly and Mably repeatedly pointed to errors in Montesquieu's way of thinking. The marquis d'Argenson pointed out that he was ultimately uninterested in the definition of what was right or wrong. As we have seen, Rousseau expressed his regret that Montesquieu had neglected the 'ought to be' of legislation and the need to create a new *political law*. Finally, a particularly fierce attack came from Helvétius, in line with the way of feeling of many of the new *philosophes*.

All this criticism shows the irredeemable fracture between the first and second generation of Enlightenment thinkers. The later thinkers were now definitely moving towards the politicisation of the Republic of Letters and the reform of the *Ancien régime*. The rights of man acquired more and more importance in public debate, transforming them in the process from a moral issue into a political and eventually a juridical one.

Without further ado, Helvétius accused Montesquieu of being a conservative in politics and a defender of the *status quo*.[12] He described him as someone who 'compromise[s] with prejudice' (H.5) and with the privileges of the rich, the powerful, the aristocracy and clergy, which are 'at variance with the natural rights of those whom they oppress' (H.6). He was especially opposed to Montesquieu passing off particular interests as a constitutional tool capable of supporting freedom in the face of monarchical despotism. According to Helvétius, this had only helped to spread the poison of corporative interest that already circulated through the organism of the *Ancien régime*, in

12. The quotations that follow are from 'Letters of Helvetius, addressed to President Montesquieu and M. Saurin, on perusing the manuscript of *The Spirit of laws*', www.econlib.org/library/Tracy/ddtMSL28.html (last accessed 8 May 2019). Letter I, 'Letter of Helvetius to President Montesquieu', H.5 and H.6; letter II, 'Helvetius to A. M. Saurin', H.16. These letters are part of Antoine Louis Claude Destutt de Tracy, *A Commentary and review of Montesquieu's 'Spirit of laws', to which are annexed, observations on the thirty-first book, by the late M. Condorcet: and two letters of Helvetius, on the merits of the same work*, translated by Thomas Jefferson (Philadelphia, PA, 1811).

such a way that '[e]ven philosophers wish to form corporate bodies' (H.16) and give themselves juridical systems based on privilege and inequality.

Helvétius was indignant about what he saw as a deterministic view of law that legitimised inequalities, privileges and existing power structures in the name of their supposed function as guarantors of freedom. In his opinion this view neglected to take into account the negative effects on public and collective interests and to consider other possibilities that would lead to a more just legislative process made by man for man.

The underlying reasons for Helvétius's critique of Montesquieu became clearly apparent with the publication in 1758 of his *De l'esprit*, without a doubt one of the great masterpieces of the new Enlightenment humanism in Europe. This volume, which was immediately placed on the Index of forbidden books by Pope Clement XIII and solemnly burned outside the Palais de justice in Paris, added a materialist, Neo-Epicurean and utilitarian dimension to the European debate set in motion by Rousseau with his politicisation of morality. In contrast to the latter, and to the traditional study of morality on a metaphysical, spiritual or transcendental basis, which in any case always referred back to God and religion, Helvétius proposed the development of a new morality that would be similar to an experimental kind of physics. He would carry out an unprejudiced scientific investigation into man's spirit as something that was ultimately built for the pursuit of happiness. He viewed the spirit as the link between mind and body, which made thought possible, and as something that was affected by both physical and moral passions, by interest and self-love, by the sexual impulse and even by the will to power that was unavoidably present in every individual. Helvétius's theoretical framework was provided by Locke and Condillac. His outlook was a radical form of empirical sensism, in which memory, matter, thought and sensibility were inextricably linked. Within this frame of reference, which excluded all reference to religion, the first issue to be addressed was the definition of virtue: 'Some maintain, that we have an idea of virtue absolutely independent of different ages and governments; and that virtue is always one and the same. The others maintain, on the contrary, that every nation forms a different idea of it.'

The former group alluded to here by Helvétius were those who followed Plato in describing virtue in abstract terms (even now, in the eighteenth century) as 'the idea of order, harmony, and essential beauty'.[13] The latter group adhered to Montaigne's moral and cultural relativism, and found that the very idea of virtue was arbitrary. Both were wrong, in Helvétius's opinion. One needed to go beyond surface phenomena and those cultural and historical conditions that kept transforming vices into virtues and vice versa. It was necessary to acknowledge once and for all the presence in the deep structures of history and human nature of the persistent, universal and ineradicable pursuit of individual happiness. This must then become collective happiness, public good, collective interest. For every people of the earth at any moment in time virtue had been nothing other than the hankering after happiness. This had taken the most various and even contradictory forms, according to the challenges posed in each case by the historical context. The new utilitarian morality was scientifically founded on the acknowledgement of the material world of individual feelings and passions. As such, it must necessarily start from these considerations and establish public good – that is to say, a nation's collective interest in the pursuit of happiness – as virtue's ultimate purpose.

In fact, this reassessment of individual good as something that must be transformed into collective interest was not the most original aspect of *De l'esprit*. Helvétius writes that 'the sensation of self-love is the only basis on which we can place the foundations of an useful morality' (p.116). However, already in 1723 Mandeville had gone far beyond this with his 'fable of the bees', in which he created the famous private vices, public virtues trope. For some time now eighteenth-century 'utilitarianism' had been growing into one of the main characteristics of European Enlightenment culture. What made *De l'esprit* such a dangerous work, deserving of being consigned to the flames in the eyes of those who were desperate to safeguard the integrity of the *Ancien régime*, lay in the answers it gave to one crucial question: why no moral theory so far had succeeded in contributing to human happiness by reducing injustice, violence and the presence of evil on earth.

In his famous third essay, 'Whether Genius ought to be considered as a natural gift; or, as an effect of education', Helvétius replied to this question by launching yet another devastating attack on the previous century's idea of natural law and its concept of an unchangeable and fixed nature. Like Rousseau before him in some sense, Helvétius

13. Helvétius, *De l'esprit, or Essays on the mind, and its several faculties, written by Helvetius, translated from the edition printed under the author's inspection* (London, printed for the translator, 1759), p.66-67.

strongly denies that inequality among men is an original and ineradicable trait. It was, instead, the product of history, education and, above all, specific moral decisions: 'The great inequality of mind, observable in mankind [...] only depends on the different education they receive, and the unknown and varied chain of circumstances in which they are placed' (p.220). Helvétius thus gave new impulse to the idea of the fundamental equality of all human minds: the idea that was at the origin of the Scientific Revolution, in which the modern scientist was no longer a Renaissance magus in possession of individual superhuman powers but someone who made use of a publicly verifiable method of investigation.

Individual genius and superior talent were not a natural gift but something that developed in a specific context and derived from the different levels of interest manifested by each person, 'their unequal desire of instruction' (p.145): 'The man of genius is then only produced by the circumstances in which he is placed' (p.239).[14] Helvétius was fiercely opposed to Montesquieu's climatic determinism, which in his view opened up dangerous opportunities for those who believed in racial inequality and the supporters of the *Ancien régime*'s hierarchisation of society. He openly attacked the thesis of the presumed superiority of northern populations, with reference to their subjugation by the Romans. And had not the civilisation of the Greeks and the Romans themselves declined despite the climate remaining the same? For Helvétius 'moral causes [...] give us an explanation of all the phaenomena of the mind' (p.238). In fact, he even took a dim view of Rousseau's crypto-primitivism, which seemed to him to inhibit concrete political reform. How could one seriously deny the positive effect of the arts and sciences, and culture in general? How could one reject a public education schedule that had the specific aim of emancipating man and transforming him from a savage into a civil person?

In Helvétius European political culture finally found a powerful new Enlightenment ideology, which was established on an openly positive evaluation of the modern Western world: an ideology that firmly believed in the possibility of changing human life for the better,

14. Helvétius's theory in this regard would be rejected by his friend Diderot, for whom genius was something exceptional and peculiar in nature. On the democratic and republican character of the scientific method and on the thesis of the equality of intelligence in Bacon's *Novum organum* see Paolo Rossi, *Immagini della scienza* (Rome, 1977), p.93ff.

reducing inequality and increasing welfare, so as to promote both public and private happiness.

Once established that man was the result of moral decisions (since we 'ought […] only to search into morals for the true cause of the inequality observable in various minds', p.222), it was indeed possible to intervene in the history of nations by linking morality with politics and, above all, the law. Did not the latter two both have the attainment of earthly happiness by the population as their ultimate objective? As Helvétius explains, '[t]his being granted, morality is evidently no more than a frivolous science, unless blended with policy and legislation' (p.81). Morality and legislation were for him one and the same science. Therefore, they should be rethought and deployed together in the service of human emancipation. He had a clear message for both the 'hypocritical moralists' of the past, who believed that man was bound by the everlasting laws of nature, and the dangerous supporters of a mean-spirited individualistic utilitarianism, and that message was that 'it is only by an absolute detachment from personal interest, by a profound study of the *science of legislation*, that a moralist can become serviceable to his country' (p.82; emphasis added).

In ideological positions based on Hegel and Marx, Helvétius's utilitarian materialism has been profoundly misrepresented as a manifestation of selfish bourgeois individualism. In fact, Helvétius lay the foundations for modern social utilitarianism, which is based on the primacy of public interest. Man's passions cannot be eradicated ('Passions are in the moral, what motion is in the natural world'; p.149), and the conflicting interests of individuals must be realistically acknowledged and reconciled. Legislation must take all these interests into account and include them in collective interest through gradual reform, without any form of constriction. The law must set boundaries even to the drive to the acquisition of property. Even the struggle against the slave trade and the cruel colonialism of European powers could become effective within the framework of natural law and of international treaties and conventions, which would put an end to 'that kind of robbery which subsists between nations' (p.141), paving the way for new forms of confederation among sovereign states that would bring universal peace and justice.

Helvétius indignantly denounced how the Church and the various sovereigns allowed the slave trade to happen because they thought 'that people are, with respect to each other, in the same situation as man in a state of nature before they entered into society, when they acknowledged no other laws but those of strength and cunning' (p.140). Finally, unlike what Voltaire and Rousseau thought, being in this still rather influenced by the old natural law, justice was not innate in the human soul. It was the objective, empirical result of an entirely human effort to reconcile individual interests, and consisted simply 'in the exact observation of the laws which the common interest, that is, the assemblage of all the interests of the individuals has caused them to make' (*ibid.*).

Helvétius's work was considered scandalous and caused violent reactions especially because, like Diderot, d'Holbach and other thinkers in the Parisian Radical Enlightenment, he denied the usefulness of religion as social bond, frame of reference and best vehicle for universal virtue. Unlike Rousseau, who had theorised a modern civil religion which aimed at the establishment of reforms and the rights of man, Helvétius was an atheist and a materialist. He openly stated that all religious experiences were useless and absurd, and liable to cause criminal and bloody acts. He expounded these views in an even more strongly polemical tone in another work, which was published posthumously in 1772: his *De l'homme*, where the target at which he directs his fiercest criticism is papal, Catholic religion. However, the most powerful message that Helvétius's work transmitted to his contemporaries was the fact that the *Ancien régime* could and should be reformed. It was actually possible to connect *what is* with *what ought to be*, morality with politics and law: 'It is then only by good laws that we can form virtuous men. All the art of the legislator consists in forcing them by *self-love* to be always *just* to each other.'[15]

Thus Helvétius, a militant freemason, put forward the new 'science of legislation' – a favourite expression of his – as the ideal instrument through which to assert the dignity and the natural rights of man while still taking as his starting point the clear acknowledgement of man's interests and passions. Thanks to the circulation of ideas, this seminal thought spread throughout Europe, especially in the masonic lodges. It was particularly well received in Italy, in the crucial 1760s, by thinkers such as Gaetano Filangieri and the Neapolitan Enlightenment (as we shall see below) and before them by Cesare Beccaria and the young intellectuals of the Accademia dei Pugni and of *Il Caffè* in Milan.[16]

This famous journal was published from 1764 to 1765, at the same time as various other works finally linked together Rousseau

15. *De l'esprit*, p.120-21; my emphasis.
16. See the important chapter on 'La Milano del *Caffè*' in Franco Venturi, *Settecento riformatore*, vol.1: *Da Muratori a Beccaria* (Turin, 1969), p.645ff.

and Helvétius, natural rights and the passions, utilitarianism and an idea of natural law based on the social contract. In this context, the theses of Grotius, Pufendorf and all those who were still trying to uphold Neo-Stoic views in Italy in the middle of the eighteenth century were subjected to severe scrutiny. These thinkers were accused of maintaining that 'man's sociability was the source of law', thus upholding the uncompromising primacy of duties and abstract ethical rationalism of the previous century.[17] What is more, they undermined the true republican and libertarian spirit that was implicit in the rediscovered language of the natural rights of man.

In fact at this very time in Italy Catholic culture was undergoing a rapid change in outlook with respect to what until then had been considered as the heretical work of Protestants such as Grotius and Pufendorf. In 1757, Giambattista Almici had finally and with great enthusiasm translated Pufendorf's *Of the law of nature and nations*. In Almici's intentions this became a solid outpost of Christian natural law against Neo-Epicureans, atheists and the followers of Hobbes, Locke and Machiavelli alike. In his introduction Almici asserts once again the idea of the divine foundation of civil authority and the religious premises of natural law. His outlook is not linked to a specific religious denomination, his intent being to fend off the new fearsome enemy that seemed happy to do away with the idea of God altogether in order to focus on morality, politics or law. In the years that followed, many Catholic works attacked Helvétius and Rousseau with the explicit objective of upholding the centrality of natural law, the Stoic sociability principle and Aquinas' rationalism as updated by important sectors of modern science.[18] The Catholic reform movement, which had begun with works such as Ludovico Antonio Muratori's 1742 *Dei difetti della giurisprudenza* (*On the defects of jurisprudence*) and had gained further political strength under Benedict XIV's papacy, now seemed set to gain the upper hand in the renewed struggle for cultural hegemony in Italy. It is against this background that the Milanese thinkers hold Grotius to trial in their *Caffè*.

This famous episode deserves to be retold, even if only briefly, and not only because it marked an important turning point in Italian

17. Cf. Alessandro Verri, 'Di Carneade e di Grozio', in '*Il Caffè' 1764-1766*, ed. Gianni Francioni and Sergio Romagnoli (Turin, 1993), p.705-21 (706).
18. For an exhaustive and richly documented description of this debate cf. Philippe Audegean, 'Passions et liberté: loi de nature et fondement du droit en Italie à l'époque de Beccaria', *Studi settecenteschi* 23 (2003), p.197-278.

culture. It also allows us to clarify once again the main aspects of the Enlightenment's growing opposition to the previous century's abstract natural law. Moreover, it shows how the language of natural rights was now spreading beyond Paris, and how it acquired new characteristics as an aspect of the new sciences of man and of the gradual politicisation of morality and law.

The article that attacked Grotius was by Alessandro Verri, the jurist within the Milan group. He accused the author of the *De iure belli ac pacis* of misunderstanding and misrepresenting Carneades as a kind of 'monster', an 'abominable sophist' who, with philosophical arguments of a subtly sceptical nature, had denied the very existence of natural law and of any 'principles of universal justice', upholding instead an Epicurean and conventionalist view of the latter, according to which 'what is useful is right'. In fact, Verri pointed out, Carneades' theses were not at all so rigid or unusual as Grotius asserted. In rejecting the Stoics' fanaticism and their exclusive focus on duties, Carneades adopted the fuller Epicurean meaning of the word 'usefulness', in the sense of a wise man's control over his passions rather than the mere pursuit of immediate pleasure:

> Carneades never maintained anything as absurd as this [...] The word 'usefulness' here includes passions like the remorse that torments guilty hearts, or our moral feelings of compassion. These too should be considered useful means of pursuing justice. To spare someone this feeling of remorse is useful. Equally useful, or even necessary, is to relieve the suffering of others, in that this suffering brings pain to our own soul – and this is what we call commiseration, the mother of good deeds.[19]

The Milanese thinkers thought that the time had come to put aside these ancient accusations and to finally rethink moral philosophy on a Neo-Epicurean basis, as the balancing of 'sensibility and rationality'.[20] It was time to pursue happiness – as the primary and undisputed objective of any form of the new Enlightenment morality – by controlling one's passions and redirecting individual interests towards the public good or usefulness. This process, which would make no concessions to traditional religions, would transform the abstract, *more geometrico* natural law of Pufendorf and his followers into a new 'science

19. Verri, 'Di Carneade e di Grozio', p.708.
20. See, in the same collection, Verri's article on 'Alcune idee sulla filosofia morale', p.685-95 (689).

of man' based on empirical fact and experiment. This new science studied man in his rational and emotional components, but also from a historical point of view. It investigated the world of the passions, rejecting all 'arbitrary systems based on what ought to or could be rather than what was'. The message was: 'Let us start from man and his principles, let us profit from them, build on them.'[21] In this way *Il Caffè* staked its claim to being considered one of the protagonists in the rise of the new political culture of the Enlightenment in Europe.

Indeed, the most damaging accusations against the seventeenth-century school of natural law were those that unmasked the implicit political meaning of those works by Grotius and Pufendorf that were now feted by the Italian Catholic reformers.[22] With a reprise of the verdict expressed by Rousseau in the *Contrat social* a few years earlier, both these authors were denounced as enemies of man and of popular sovereignty, and defenders of despotism and the absolute power of kings. Grotius was even accused of being involved in the slave trade.

It is true that Grotius had the great merit of being the first in the modern age to uphold 'the rights made sacrosanct by nature'. However, he betrayed the true republican spirit of those rights and their inalienable and universal character by defending absolutism and 'tyranny'. He even used Aristotle's theory of the natural slave to legitimise the idea of the existence in nature of 'slave peoples' and 'serf nations', who readily gave up their sovereignty to a despot on a permanent basis. 'In the same way that a man was allowed to give himself up as a slave, so was a nation': with this uncompromising statement Grotius had meant to 'confute the seditious opinion of those who claimed that a nation could try its sovereign and sentence him to death'. According to his implacable accusers at *Il Caffè*, Grotius had thus legitimised despotism and transformed the social contract and its original republican soul into a pact of absolute domination. And because of this, man 'from a person had become a thing', a slave, a body deprived of its rights and its dignity, just another commodity.[23] The Milanese group denounced as equally hypocritical and in bad faith Grotius' defence of the principle of humanitarian intervention

21. Cf. Alessandro Verri, 'Di alcuni sistemi del pubblico diritto', in *'Il Caffè'*, ed. G. Francioni and S. Romagnoli, p.725-39 (737).
22. On the late-eighteenth-century translations of Pufendorf in Italy see Antonio Trampus, *Storia del costituzionalismo italiano nell'età dei Lumi* (Rome and Bari, 2009), p.182ff.
23. Verri, 'Di Carneade e di Grozio', p.717.

against 'those peoples who violate primitive rights and are therefore enemies of mankind'. This opinion had

> come in very handy for justifying the conquest of America, and can serve equally well in other occasions. One can just go in, conquer a country, and then pay a jurist [...] Which of these two, then, Carneades or Grotius, is really guilty of offending justice? The one who flaunted the rights of nature in order to get to know them and violate them? Or the one who, being much less of a hypocrite and far more humane, seemed to attack these rights but in fact professed them, and the only things he did chase off were chimaeras?[24]

As this debate shows, Milan in the early 1760s was very much acclimatised to the language of natural rights in relation to the redefinition of justice.[25]

These ideas had been stated even more clearly in Pietro Verri's 1763 pamphlet, *Meditazioni sulla felicità* (*Meditations on happiness*). Here the other Verri brother shows how well he had understood the lesson coming from Paris. He was now ready to move further in the development of a new science of legislation that, starting from the modern language of the rights of man and the acknowledgement of the passions, would finally give the Enlightenment the juridical tools it needed in order to reform the archaic society of the *Ancien régime*: 'The most perfect legislation of all is that in which both the duties and the rights of man are clear and unassailable, and happiness is distributed as equally as possible among all its members.'[26]

Cesare Beccaria's short treatise *Dei delitti e delle pene* (*On crimes and punishments*), which was published in 1764, was part of this cultural context, in which both the Accademia dei Pugni and *Il Caffè* made ambitious contributions to the European intellectual debate.

24. *Ibid.*, p.720.
25. See also, for instance, the constant references to natural rights in Giuseppe Gorini Corio, *Politica, diritto e religione per ben pensare* (Milan, Agnelli, 1742), p.240ff.
26. Cf. Pietro Verri, *Meditazioni sulla felicità*, ed. Gianni Francioni (Como, 1996), p.61. On the evolution of this text, which Verri published again in 1778 under the new title *Discorso sulla felicità*, and on this quotation in particular see Gianni Francioni's introductory note in his edition of the *Discorso sulla felicità*, in *Edizione nazionale delle opere di Pietro Verri*, vol.3: *I Discorsi e altri scritti degli anni Settanta*, ed. Giorgio Panizza with Silvia Contarini, Gianni Francioni and Sara Rosini (Rome, 2004), p.174. On Verri's thought in those years, see Carlo Capra, *I progressi della ragione: vita di Pietro Verri* (Bologna, 2002), p.177ff.

Beccaria was fully aware of the significance of his book and of the increasing importance of the new language of the rights of man in the struggle to bring order to the juridical chaos of the *Ancien régime*. This meant tackling archaic and mutually contradictory regulations that served the interests of corporations and of the upper classes (laws that, in his address to the reader, Beccaria defines as 'uno scolo de' secoli i più barbari', or a remnant of the most barbaric ages) and a penal system that was founded on torture, the arbitrary power of magistrates and the negation of what already in 1763 Pietro Verri clearly defined as every human being's 'inalienable natural right to defence'.[27]

Beccaria's work was an openly political text, which sounded a call to arms against the *Ancien régime*. It spoke with feeling and sincere sympathy in defence of a humanity oppressed by absurd and violent laws and all kinds of inequalities.[28] According to some, Morellet's 1766 translation misrepresented the work's true meaning, transforming it into a juridical tract in a way that, in Diderot's indignant opinion, amounted to some kind of assassination.[29] Nevertheless, as we shall see in the following chapters, Beccaria's volume unleashed the first great public opinion campaign throughout Europe in support of the rights of man, a campaign that at the same time demanded a less inhumane penal system, as per the 'general theorem' that concludes *On crimes and*

27. Pietro Verri, 'Orazione panegirica sulla giurisprudenza milanese', in Cesare Beccaria, *Dei delitti e delle pene con una raccolta di lettere e documenti relativi alla nascita dell'opera e alla sua fortuna nell'Europa del Settecento*, ed. Franco Venturi (Turin, 1965), p.132.
28. Alberto Burgio has highlighted Beccaria's denunciation of status-based inequalities in the assignment of punishments, as well as his Rousseau-like criticism of contemporary society: 'Who made these laws? The rich and the great, who never deigned to visit the miserable hut of the poor […] Let us attack injustice at its source.' See Burgio, 'L'idea di eguaglianza tra diritto e politica nel *Dei delitti e delle pene*', in *Cesare Beccaria: la pratica dei Lumi*, ed. Vincenzo Ferrone and Gianni Francioni (Florence, 2000), p.79-98. Here and in what follows, the English translation is quoted from *An Essay on crimes and punishments, by the marquis Beccaria of Milan, with a commentary by M. de Voltaire* (Edinburgh, James Donaldson, 1788), p.110.
29. On the indignant reactions by Grimm, Diderot and many other *philosophes*, see Franco Venturi's commentary in Beccaria, *Dei delitti e delle pene*, p.338ff. There is a faithful and lavishly annotated French edition of *Des délits et des peines*, ed. and translated by Philippe Audegean, based on the Italian text established by Gianni Francioni (Paris, 2009). In the original Italian, the text in *Edizione nazionale delle opere di Cesare Beccaria*, vol.1: *Dei delitti e delle pene*, ed. Gianni Francioni (Milan, 1984), contains an extensive commentary and a wealth of information particularly on the sources.

punishments: 'That a punishment may not be an act of violence, of one or of many, against a private member of society, it should be public, immediate and necessary; the least possible in the case given; proportioned to the crime, and determined by the laws' (p.169).

Beccaria's case was both rigorously documented and passionately argued. He invited his contemporaries to rethink the very foundations of society and of a philosophy of history that had always equated religion and politics, sin and crime, spirit of revenge and sovereignty, with disastrous consequences. Beccaria's discussion gave new meaning to Montesquieu's famous indictment of torture, secrecy, the violence of the inquisitorial process and the systematic disregard of the right to defence. Beccaria re-examined the very roots of Western criminal law. For the first time, the focus was not only on the safety of the State and its citizens but also on 'the rights of humanity', such as the right to freedom and the pursuit of happiness. Man was the ultimate purpose of things, not a thing himself. He was an individual in possession of inalienable natural rights who lived in society and in history, according to a vision that anticipated that of Kant and the Enlightenment struggle for man's emancipation of the end of the century. As Beccaria stressed, condemning without hesitation the barbarous laws that allowed the use of torture, '[l]iberty is at an end, whenever the laws permit, that, in certain cases, a man may cease to be a *person*, and become a *thing*' (p.82; emphasis in the original).[30]

On crimes and punishments truly was the first European masterpiece of the new Enlightenment humanism, a movement characterised by its concern with the rights of man and their application in political practice. It was an ambitious little book, which contained the result of collective discussions and skilfully wove together moral, political and legal questions. Its purpose was to defend the interests of mankind and the rights of the individual in relation to penal justice, which at that time was of paramount importance for starting a modern politics of reform. The author himself explains this with great clarity as well as humility, showing his awareness that with this work he was

30. It is this explicit reference, for the first time in history, to the individual's inalienable right to defence that characterises the Milan circle, with Pietro Verri first and then Cesare Beccaria. This was above and beyond their powerful exposition of the inhuman absurdity of torture, a practice based on the idea 'that pain should be the test of truth, as if truth resided in the muscles and fibres of a wretch in torture', and their belief in the fundamental importance of 'that personal liberty, so dear to mankind and to the wise legislator' (cf. *On crimes and punishments*, p.64 and 154).

staking his claim to be considered everywhere as 'la voix du défenseur de l'humanité', as Morellet calls him:[31] 'if by supporting the *rights of mankind* and of invincible truth, I shall contribute to save from the agonies of death one unfortunate victim of tyranny, or of ignorance, equally fatal; his blessing, and tears of transport, will be a sufficient consolation to me for the contempt of all mankind.'[32]

What gives this book its special interest even today is the important presence of the language of natural rights: a presence that derived substantially from Rousseau's social contract, but with the direct influence of Locke and Burlamaqui, alongside its constant reference to Helvétius's utilitarian philosophy.[33] Like all the Milan group of philosophers, Beccaria was entirely familiar with the language of natural rights. However, he only explicitly used this language when he thought it was absolutely necessary. He did so in specific ways that would become a kind of Italian variant of the modern Enlightenment philosophy of law, in which rights and utilitarianism, what was just and what was useful, were carefully balanced together taking into account the humanity of man as an individual.

In chapter XXX of *On crimes and punishments*, devoted to 'Prosecution and prescription', where he reflects, for instance, on the importance of the certainty of punishment based on the study of the nature of crimes, Beccaria refers to the new science of man that had been invoked by Hume and Rousseau. He illustrates the difference between 'atrocious crimes' (p.119) against the person and 'crimes of an inferior degree' against things, and he does so in terms of rights: 'This distinction is founded in human nature. The preservation of life is a natural right, the preservation of property is a right of society' (p.121). In the case of the former, there was greater need to provide safeguard, with a consequently longer prescription time and faster prosecution than for

31. Cf. Morellet's introduction to Cesare Beccaria, *Traité des délits et des peines*, translated by André Morellet (Lausanne, n.n., 1766), p.6.
32. *On crimes and punishments*, p.50. Emphasis added.
33. On Beccaria's thought see Franco Venturi's edition mentioned above. See also the contributions in *Cesare Beccaria*, ed. V. Ferrone and G. Francioni; Philippe Audegean, *La Philosophie de Beccaria: savoir punir, savoir écrire, savoir produire* (Paris, 2010); *Cesare Beccaria tra Milano e l'Europa, convegno di studi per il 250º anniversario della nascita promosso dal Comune di Milano*, ed. Sergio Romagnoli and Gian Domenico Pisapia (Rome and Bari, 1990). In the latter volume, Gianni Francioni, in 'Beccaria filosofo utilitarista', p.69-87, highlights the important difference between Beccaria and Bentham, whose books would later direct some biting criticism at the theory of the rights of man.

the latter. Beccaria was equally clear on the two fundamental natural rights to life and freedom: these must be protected in every possible way from despotism and anarchy, since they were 'the inalienable and equal patrimony of every citizen' (p.122).

The language of rights, once again linked to a utilitarian philosophy of society and justice, was relaunched especially in Beccaria's argument for the abolition of the death penalty, which was never 'really *just* or *useful* in a well-governed state' (p.104; emphasis added). On this controversial issue, *On crimes and punishments* made some important points that are still debated in our own day. This was the issue that tested to the limits the theoretical framework of the text as a whole: its belief in modern civil society, the fundamental equality, freedom and responsibility of men in nature, and the possibility of a harmonious relationship between the individual and society. It called into question the very definition of justice, sovereign power and legal punishment, unleashing deep feelings and ancestral fears, and asking tough questions of political and religious authorities. Its bravely radical, even utopian stance on capital punishment was greeted with amazement throughout Europe.[34]

Where did the right to punish originate from and what legitimised it? According to what principle, what religious belief or secular science had men adopted the horrifying practice of the death penalty since time immemorial and in every country on earth, and made a show of these executions, even though it 'has never made men better'? 'What *right*, I ask, have men to cut the throats of their fellow-creatures?'[35]

In fact 'crimes are only to be measured by the injury done to society' (p.36). This was true from a utilitarian and secular view of justice as 'that bond, which is necessary to keep the interest of individuals united; without which, men would return to their original state of barbarity' (p.20-21). It was equally true when the law was seen in terms of the general will giving the sovereign the power to punish in order to defend the general good from private abuse. Punishment, Beccaria urged, should be neither the expiation of a sin nor revenge for a crime. Its purpose should be solely 'to prevent others from

34. On the extent of the European debate on the right to punish that followed in the wake of Beccaria's pamphlet see Venturi, *Utopia e riforma*, p.119ff. However, like other Beccaria scholars, Venturi does not address the theme of the rights of man, which in fact plays such an important role in *On crimes and punishments*.

35. *On crimes and punishments*, chapter XXVIII, 'Of the punishment of death', p.104. Emphasis in the original.

committing the like offence. Such punishments, therefore, and such a mode of inflicting them, ought to be chosen, as will make strongest and most lasting impressions on the minds of others, with the least torment to the body of the criminal' (p.51).[36]

On this basis, according to Beccaria, the death penalty was neither useful nor necessary 'in a reign of tranquillity'. It was only admissible in the case of anarchy, civil wars or when the 'security of the nation' was endangered (p.105). Historically, it was proven not to work, since the proliferation of increasingly gruesome means of execution had not deterred any criminals, who were in fact more numerous than ever. In utilitarian terms, a sentence to 'perpetual slavery' (p.108), or hard labour, was a more efficient form of punishment: 'The death of a criminal is a terrible but momentary spectacle, and therefore a less efficacious method of deterring others, than the continued example of a man deprived of his liberty, condemned as a beast of burden, to repair, by his labour, the injury he has done to society' (p.106).

Beccaria's proposals gave rise to a heated debate throughout Europe. Public opinion sided for and against them, and there were authoritative reactions not least among fellow Enlightenment thinkers. Several of the latter pointed out the utopian character of these ideas, or how subjecting a human being to 'perpetual slavery' was an equally cruel and ferocious practice. Jurists and those Enlightenment circles that were most open to the incipient political reform of the *Ancien régime* were especially taken aback by Beccaria's attempt, at the start of the chapter on the death penalty, to deny the legitimacy of the latter also from the point of view of the social contract and the language of rights. On this Beccaria was in open polemic with Rousseau, who had drawn a direct link between the right to the preservation of life by the members of the social contract and the power of the sovereign, who was able to safeguard this right by using the death penalty against murderers and the enemies of society.

Beccaria overturned Rousseau's conclusions by attacking his very premises. He explained that the death penalty could not be justified

36. Michel Foucault offered a different and in fact not always entirely convincing interpretation of Beccaria's thought as evidence of the Enlightenment's creation of the modern prison system as something whose purpose was to redeem and govern civil society. Cf. Michel Foucault, *Discipline and punish: the birth of the prison*, translated by Alan Sheridan (London, 1977; original: *Surveiller et punir: naissance de la prison*, Paris, 1975). Foucault makes no reference to the debate on the death penalty and the rights of man in Beccaria or generally in the eighteenth century in Europe.

with reference to the power of the sovereign or to the laws that resulted from the social contract since the latter only related to a small part of the natural freedom of individuals:

> The laws, as I have said before, are only the sum of the smallest portions of the private liberty of each individual, and represent the general will, which is the aggregate of that of each individual. Did any one ever give to others the right of taking away his life? Is it possible, that in the smallest portions of the liberty of each, sacrificed to the good of the public, can be contained the greatest of all good, life? If it were so, how shall it be reconciled to the maxim which tells us, that a man has no right to kill himself? Which he certainly must have, if he could give it away to another.
>
> But the punishment of death is not authorised by any right; for I have demonstrated that no such right exists. It is therefore a war of a whole nation against a citizen, whose destruction they consider as necessary, or useful to the general good. (p.62)

However, few accepted Beccaria's claim that the crucial issue was the social usefulness (or otherwise) of this form of punishment, and that the modern language of rights did not authorise the use of the death penalty, as had been maintained instead by Locke and Rousseau. In fact, several authors authoritatively spoke out against this theory. With their retaliatory stance on punishment as an ethical issue, both Kant and Hegel, for instance, concluded that the death penalty was in fact necessary. The former believed that only death was an adequate response to murder: 'If he has killed, he *must* die', he wrote in his *Metaphysics of morals*; the latter went so far as to state that only by being put to death could the culprit be redeemed and honoured as a rational person.[37]

In 1783, in reply to Beccaria, Gaetano Filangieri reasserted the legitimacy of the death penalty on the basis of the language of rights itself. This settled the question once and for all, but raised new disturbing issues. For Filangieri, the right to punish did not originate in convention. It should be considered a natural right, which preceded the social contract: something similar to a 'deep feeling', an instinctive need for justice that had been common to all men since time immemorial. It did not make sense to hold certain rights by

37. On Kant and Hegel cf. Norberto Bobbio, *The Age of rights* (Cambridge, 1996), p.131. On eighteenth-century reactions, see Franco Venturi's edition of *Dei delitti e delle pene*.

nature without also having the right to punish anyone who violated those rights. One must abide fully by the logic of this language, both when it referred to single individuals and when it regulated their behaviour towards one another. For instance, the right to self-defence was unquestionable: 'Do I, in this state of natural independence, have the right to kill the unjust aggressor? Nobody doubts it. If I thus have this right to his death, he has lost his right to life, because it would be *contradictory* if these two opposing rights existed at the same time.'[38] The question was how this right to punish was conferred and put into practice in civil society through the social contract. First of all, contrary to what had been maintained by Rousseau and Beccaria among others, Filangieri pointed out that the sovereign's power to inflict the death penalty derived from an individual handing over not the rights 'that each had over himself, but the rights that each had over others'. This allows us to understand the true meaning of natural equality. If we accept that man has rights and that these rights are equal for all living beings, then it is obvious that the right to punish is conferred from below. Therefore, it is necessary to safeguard the application of this right in the republican sense of ensuring everyone's involvement in the exercise of justice.[39]

Contrary to Pufendorf and all supporters of absolutism, who saw the death penalty as an 'act of authority by someone superior over someone inferior', Filangieri finally foregrounded the need to give a correct interpretation of the principle of equality in the language of rights, being aware of its importance also for the justification of the death penalty:

> What do we mean by natural equality, I ask? This can be nothing other than equality of rights. Men are thus equal in the state of nature in that they have equal rights. If therefore one loses a right while others keep it, he who loses it is no longer naturally equal to those who keep it, for they are superior. Now, in the state of nature, he who attacks the right of another, at the same time loses (as one has seen) the corresponding right which he had; in this case, then, he is

38. Cf. Gaetano Filangieri, *La scienza della legislazione*, ed. Vincenzo Ferrone, 7 vols (Venice and Mariano del Friuli, 2003-2004), vol.4: *Delle leggi criminali: de' delitti e delle pene*, ed. Gerardo Tocchini and Antonio Trampus (2004), p.23. English translations from this work are either my own or as quoted in Ferrone, *Politics of Enlightenment*, p.65-66.
39. On the republican interpretation of justice and the right to punish in Filangieri see Ferrone, *Politics of Enlightenment*, p.64ff.

> no longer equal to other men, and as a consequence all the others, who have not lost this right, are superior to him, and as superiors they can punish him. The crime thus transmits the right to punish as it destroys equality.[40]

Filangieri made universally known a momentous paradox that had already presented itself to Locke and Rousseau: that the rights of man, which were meant to safeguard human dignity and existence, could instead be used to rationally justify the death penalty. Despite several theoretical attempts to overturn this disturbing conclusion, the question remains unresolved to this day.[41] Witness the fact that, while almost every nation in the world adheres to the 1948 Universal Declaration of Human Rights and its solemn assertion of the centrality of the right to life, the death penalty is still very widely used.

In fact, Beccaria himself in his essay *On crimes and punishments* seems to have foreseen this unsettling contradiction between human rights and the death penalty that still persists in civilised countries, such as the United States of America. In his most persuasive passages, as he passionately defends the cause of mankind he wonders why the death penalty has continued to have so much currency across the centuries despite the fact that, in his view, it cannot really be justified either in terms of rational juridical expediency or by appealing to tradition, since 'the history of mankind is an immense sea of errors' (p.113). In the final analysis, Beccaria believed that this infamous history could be redeemed only through clemency, tolerance and a profound sense of humanity and love towards one's fellow beings: 'Is it not absurd, that the laws, which detest and punish homicide, should, in order to prevent murder, publicly commit murder themselves?' (p.111-12). We should all confess that, in the bottom of our heart, we are horrified by

40. Filangieri, *Scienza della legislazione*, vol.4, p.28.
41. See, for instance, Luigi Ferrajoli, 'Il fondamento del rifiuto della pena capitale', in *Il diritto di uccidere: l'enigma della pena della morte*, ed. Pietro Costa (Milan, 2010), p.57-68. According to Ferrajoli, the theoretical basis for rejecting the death penalty can be found in Hobbes and in the safeguard of the right to life as something that provides the foundation for the law and the state: 'This is what provides the most solid and incontrovertible philosophical basis for rejecting the death penalty: the idea of the safeguarding of life in the social contract. This is the sole justification for the whole juridical artifice, and as such it cannot be contradicted by whatever justification is adduced for the death penalty' (p.61). This, however, does not really solve all doubts on the theoretical level. Ultimately, the decision to oppose the death penalty can only be a brave and consistent individual ethical stance.

the death penalty. Who does not view the role of the executioner with fear and repugnance? Which one of us is not intimately convinced 'that their lives are not lawfully in the power of any one, but of that necessity only, which with its iron sceptre rules the universe'? (p.112).

Whereas the early Church Fathers, correctly interpreting the message of the Gospels, had been opposed to the death penalty, in the course of the centuries Christian humanism had effectively legitimised it.[42] By contrast, the new Enlightenment humanism of Beccaria and the other Milanese philosophers was surprisingly effective in defending the right to life, for the first time in the history of the West. Under this banner, in our own time, the Vatican hierarchies and many Christians strenuously reject the practice of abortion, while having no qualms in approving of the death penalty.[43] And the glorious stand made by the followers of *Il Caffè* in defence of the rights of man is today all too often forgotten.

42. The Church took a hard stance on Beccaria's proposal to abolish the death penalty – see Trampus, *Storia del costituzionalismo italiano*, p.178. See also Danilo Zolo, 'Il patibolo e la guerra: la pena di morte come supplizio religioso', in *Il diritto di uccidere*, ed. P. Costa, p.30-56, on how as late as 1992 the official catechism of the Catholic Church did not exclude 'the death penalty in cases of extreme gravity'. A useful discussion of these topics can additionally be found in Adriano Prosperi, *Delitto e perdono: la pena di morte nell'orizzonte mentale dell'Europa cristiana, XIV-XVIII secolo* (Turin, 2013).
43. See for instance Finnis, *Natural law and natural rights*, p.229ff.

11. The political neutralisation of rights: Wolff, Hume, Ferguson, Smith, Blackstone

Despite the fact that it did not succeed in abolishing the death penalty, the culture of the Enlightenment, as a laboratory of modernity, had the great merit of finally calling into question the theoretical foundations of that practice. This was made possible not only by the rise of a culture that asserted the centrality of the human being, but also by the widespread use of the language of natural rights in eighteenth-century Europe. In Germany and what was then the Holy Roman empire, the prestigious school of natural law dominated the university system with the works of Grotius, Pufendorf, Leibniz and Thomasius. In 1754 an authoritative German writer, Christian Wolff, drew up a first catalogue of the natural rights that were considered to be innate and instrumental to the pursuit of happiness.[1]

However, the meaning, philosophical roots and function of the idea of natural rights in the work of these philosophers are something quite different from what had gradually emerged from the discussions on the social contract, the autonomy of the individual and subjective rights in Hobbes and Locke first and then in Rousseau and Beccaria. These two currents of thought ran in parallel but along quite distinct lines, and only appeared to use the same language. This was already obvious to thinkers on either side, who harshly criticised the opposing positions. For instance, as we have seen, Voltaire had no qualms in voicing what was in

1. Cf. Christian Wolff, *Institutiones iuris naturae et gentium in quibus ex ipsa hominis natura continuo nexu omnes obligationes et iura omnia deducuntur* (Halle, prostat in officina Rengeriana, 1754), part 1, chapter III, 'De obligatione et iure hominum universali in genere', §74 ('De iure connato'), 75 ('De præcedentia') and 95 ('Iura connata quae sint'), p.38-39 and 49-50, where Wolff distinguishes between *iura connata* (innate rights) and *iura adquisita* (acquired rights).

fact the opinion of numerous Enlightenment thinkers who branded German academia as a den of Neo-Thomists, i.e. of old Scholastics masquerading as modern rationalists, according to a definition that is still found among historians today.[2] Leaving aside the ungenerous nature of Voltaire's view, it is true that the philosophical framework, epistemological model and political and cultural implications of the monumental studies on natural law by Thomasius and Wolff were strongly influenced by the Aristotelian notion of an organic cosmos as presented by Aquinas: a model from which thinkers in Paris and Milan were consciously breaking away.

Behind this fundamental break there was a very different past that continued to influence the present. At the end of the sixteenth century Melanchthon revived Scholastic thought among German Lutherans. After this, the study of natural law in the Protestant world developed as a synthesis between the original new theses of Grotius and Pufendorf and the positions of those who wanted at all costs to build an effective barrier against the anarchy and violence of civil war and the wars of religion, Pyrrhonian scepticism, conflicting utilitarian needs, or the individual self-interest upheld by Hobbes' Neo-Epicurean followers. These thinkers adopted Neo-Stoicism because it offered the means to link the rediscovered issue of natural rights with the far more ancient idea of the primacy of duties.[3]

The ideas of *libertas naturalis* and *dignitas humanae naturae*, which derived from Cicero via Pufendorf, are at the basis of many of the opinions expressed by Thomasius and Wolff: against torture, on the use of reason against any form of superstition, and on the right to defence – the latter being, however, stripped of any political implications that might justify its transformation into a natural right to resistance. In his monumental work on natural law Wolff applied with great sophistication the syllogistic and geometrical-deductive model that had been advocated by Pufendorf and vilified by Voltaire, Rousseau and the Milan circle. His constant point of departure was the conviction that God had instituted a precise natural order, an interactive cosmos, on which depended both the duties and related rights of the subject and the function assigned to the power of the sovereign. Compared to Locke, Burlamaqui or Rousseau, the autonomy of the individual and

2. Knud Haakonssen, for instance, refers to the 'neo-scholastic natural law of Leibniz and Wolff' ('The moral conservatism of natural rights', p.34).

3. As we have seen, these developments are well known. They are described in several studies, and especially in Oestreich, *Geschichte der Menschenrechte*, p.47-53.

the need to create new sciences of man on which to base a new kind of moral, political and juridical reflection became secondary objectives. Man's rights were simply a consequence of natural law. They derived from the observance of duties that arose from the overall rationality of the natural order, which was perfectly built so as to ensure public happiness.[4] This effectively weakened the claim of the language of natural rights to become the independent basis for a new republican political system that would overcome the need for absolute power. At the same time, it reasserted the authority principle and the practice of social discipline, which for centuries had had a central role, especially in Germany. One cannot say that Voltaire was wrong in detecting and denouncing the resurgence of the old Thomistic system of thought in these positions.

Thomasius had separated reflections on innate rights from questions of morality, referring to those rights only in abstract juridical terms, as a limitation of the sovereign's *summa potestas*.[5] Wolff, by contrast, continued to follow the old paradigm in which *perfectio hominis* and the *persona moralis* were a God-given aspect of natural law, which gave a specific meaning to innate rights. But in any case his list of natural rights was still based first and foremost on duties, rigid adherence to the natural order and the primacy of sociability, which prevented their development into individual political rights along the lines of what was happening in Paris and Milan. As we shall see when we discuss the rise of the theory of rights in Germany, this development would take place only in the second half of the eighteenth century. Thanks to the discovery of the importance of the human body and its autonomy, the centrality of the passions in the *Sturm und Drang* movement, and above all the resonance of the American Revolution in the 1780s, the language of rights started to acquire political significance also in the territories of the Holy Roman empire. Finally, the study of man would move from the field of morality to that of law and politics. Its purpose would become that of safeguarding a subject now seen as historically, socially and anthropologically autonomous: an individual who had

4. The extensive bibliography on this subject is reviewed in Costa, *Civitas*, vol.1, p.366ff. In relation to Wolff, Costa remarks that 'one could hardly conceive of a more consistently duty-based theory of rights' (p.372). See also the essays in *Christian Wolff 1679-1754: Interpretationen zu seiner Philosophie und deren Wirkung, mit einer Bibliographie der Wolff-Literatur*, ed. Werner Schneiders (Hamburg, 1983).
5. See Thomas Ahnert, 'The prince and the Church in the thought of Christian Thomasius', in *Natural law and civil sovereignty*, ed. I. Hunter and D. Saunders, p.91-105.

acquired both freedom and responsibility here on earth, in modern terms, and was now ready to address the republican and constitutional issues that were put forward by the moderns.

By contrast, an especially interesting development from the point of view of the history of the rights of man was the way in which the English-speaking world, and especially Protestantism, responded, after Grotius, to the rapid diffusion of the language of natural rights throughout Europe. The latest research on this topic has traced the original character of this development, which appears to have been radically different from what was happening in France and Italy. Its main feature seems to have been the more or less deliberate defusing and political neutralisation of the subversive quality of the language of individual rights.[6] This moderate and even conservative way of dealing with the impetuous rise of natural rights had nothing in common with the academic Neo-Thomism of the German philosophers, with their late-seventeenth-century epistemological model and obvious absolutist bias. Nor can it be described as a backward-looking reaction to the strongly political modernity of the Enlightenment circles in Paris or Milan, since on this side of the Channel we find the same willingness to engage with modernity and the new.

In Britain too we find a compelling need for peace and political stability, after the revolution and civil war. But the important works that were produced in Britain in this period responded most directly, on the theoretical level, to Hume's pioneering attack on the previous century's school of natural law, and on the historical level to the momentous economic and social transformation caused by the Industrial Revolution, which on the whole, despite the important differences among its different regions, had catapulted Britain to a position of pre-eminence in the world economy.

As we have seen, Hume had refuted the epistemological basis of seventeenth-century ethical rationalism, with its reliance on reason and the geometric-deductive method that was still used by Wolff and Pufendorf's many followers. As an empiricist, Hume believed that

6. On this idea of neutralisation, see Carl Schmitt, *The Concept of the political* (1932), translated by George Schwab (Chicago, IL, and London, 1996), where the author describes politics as a dialectic of conflict and neutralisation. With reference to the liberal tradition in particular, Schmitt remarks that '[a]lthough liberalism has not radically denied the state, it has, on the other hand, neither advanced a positive theory of state nor on its own discovered how to reform the state, but has attempted only to tie the political to the ethical and to subjugate it to economics' (p.61).

human existence was guided not by abstract reason but by concrete passions, customs, traditions and history. He did not subscribe to the idea of building the new sciences of man on the study of the individual in the pure state of nature, which had been put forward by Hobbes and Locke and enthusiastically adopted by Rousseau through the use of a variety of disciplines, including history, anthropology and medicine. Hume responded to this project by polemically recycling the ancient Aristotelian, Thomistic and Stoic idea of the social nature of the human being as an empirical fact that should be reviewed in the light of new research findings. The individual as an isolated and autonomous being had never in fact existed in the history of the human species. Nor had there ever been a 'social contract' or a 'pure state of nature' – and indeed the disturbing possibility of ever descending into such a state at a future time was to be avoided at all costs. Thus Hume disposed of all the main tenets on the basis of which Rousseau and others sought to create a politics of the moderns by identifying the humanity of man in the individual subject as an autonomous possessor of rights.[7] For him, the only true and therefore possible sciences of man were those that studied man in society and history. Since time immemorial the natural order had developed around societal living, on the basis of intersubjective relations and society-furthering passions, such as compassion and the reciprocal acknowledgement of collective needs. In this way communities had not only continued to exist, but had gradually achieved a new balance thanks to this interaction, which provided safety and stability by selecting the form of government that was most suited to the times and the challenges posed by history. Political action should derive not from abstract theories but from a concrete knowledge of the history of man in society.[8]

Hume's views thus focused on the autonomy and self-sufficiency of the natural order, with society and social practices at its core as the source of political institutions and the engine of mankind's stadial development. In fact, he unleashed a Europe-wide attack on those theories based on the general will and the social contract that, in the wake of Rousseau, had stressed the importance of politics and active

7. Of course, in attacking the idea of the social contract Hume's targets were mostly Locke and the Whigs, according to whom the contract provided the foundation for political authority. See Haakonssen, *Natural law and moral philosophy*, p.111ff.

8. For a detailed analysis of this issue, including an extensive discussion of the relevant bibliography, cf. Costa, *Civitas*, vol.1, p.349ff.

participation by the wider citizenship.[9] As a conservative close to the Tories, who was firmly convinced that the passions ruled over reason, Hume became the defender of every kind of established regime that was legitimised by its history and public opinion: 'Nature is always too strong for principle', he would point out.[10] For instance, while Locke considered property a natural right, for Hume, in line with his sociocentric perspective, it was a rule of interaction, the result of convention, in the same way as justice itself, which he did not believe to be innate in the human soul. It is hardly surprising, therefore, that Hume never really places the language of natural rights at the centre of his investigation.[11]

Hume found this language ambiguous and ultimately dangerous. It definitely required neutralisation, especially when considered in terms of the individual, as a quality and faculty of the human being, i.e. of an autonomous moral agent on whom political discourse was built, according to one of the possible readings put forward by Grotius himself.[12] This idea of rights as the foundation of the social contract, relaunched by Hobbes, Locke and Rousseau, therefore needed to be swept away as rapidly as possible, together with the idea of the state of nature. Above all, with great acumen, Hume saw in the language of rights something that could potentially lead to modern political fanaticism, that form of zeal – a category as dangerous and disturbing as superstition – that had led to civil and religious war, the actions of the Levellers and, in those very years, the popular uprising in London in support of John Wilkes.[13] It was quite a different matter if the rights were seen as derived from duties and natural law, according to a view

9. Hume's 1748 essay 'Of the original contract' would become the main point of reference for all subsequent critiques of the social contract from both the historical and the theoretical point of view. On this essay, and these issues in general, see Marco Geuna, 'Pufendorf in Scozia: ricezione e critica dell'idea del contratto sociale', in *Dal 'De jure naturae et gentium' di Samuel Pufendorf alla codificazione prussiana del 1794, atti del convegno internazionale, Padova 25-26 ottobre 2001*, ed. Marta Ferronato (Padua, 2005), p.303-61 (349ff.).
10. Quoted in Giarrizzo, *David Hume*, p.98. From *An Enquiry concerning human understanding*, section 12, 'Of the academical or sceptical philosophy', part 2, §128.
11. As Haakonssen remarks, 'Hume hardly used the traditional notions of rights in his moral political philosophy' (*Natural law and moral philosophy*, p.117ff.).
12. This possible reading of Grotius' definition of *ius* as a moral quality linked to the person, however, is convincingly argued against in Haakonssen, 'The moral conservatism of natural rights', p.30ff.
13. See Haakonssen, *Natural law and moral philosophy*, p.119ff.

that, as we have seen, had already been put forward by Pufendorf, Cumberland, Wolff and numerous theoreticians of Thomist natural law, both in the Catholic and in the Protestant camp. In this case, Hume had no qualms in turning these rights into the very foundation of his reflections on justice and private law.[14]

The aim was, therefore, to put forward again, in modern terms, the old Aristotelian-Thomist idea of a self-sufficient natural order similar to the ancient cosmos, in which nature and society were blended harmoniously, i.e. a system that would be capable of neutralising rights from a political point of view while furthering the study of the new sciences of man within society. However, this enterprise was not always successful in brushing aside the alarming versions of the language of natural rights that, as we have seen, had spread through France and Italy. An important case in point is Adam Ferguson's work, especially because of the success encountered all over Europe by his 1767 *Essay on the history of civil society*, which was translated into several languages.

Ferguson's view of the natural order was, like Hume's, predominantly sociocentric and organic. The study of the sciences of man was founded on human society, which in turn was the result of economic and political development above and beyond the will, aspirations or intentions of individuals, who were in any case only considered in their role as social beings. Ferguson had read Montesquieu carefully and developed his own original version of the French thinker's method, which consisted in weaving together the study of the means of production, political institutions, and the influence of climate and location in order to trace the history of nations and civilisations as autonomous entities, a history that was the gradual result of the work of successive generations, rather than of 'legislators' and heroic 'founders of states': 'nations stumble upon establishments, which are indeed the result of human action, but not the execution of any human design.'[15] Against Rousseau and his hypothetical history Ferguson states that '[m]an is, by nature, the member of a community' (p.69).[16]

14. See, again by Knud Haakonssen, *The Science of a legislator: the natural jurisprudence of David Hume and Adam Smith* (Cambridge, 1981), p.30ff, and 'Natural jurisprudence and the identity of the Scottish Enlightenment', in *Philosophy and religion in Enlightenment Britain: new case studies*, ed. Ruth Savage (Oxford, 2012), p.258-77.
15. Adam Ferguson, *An Essay on the history of civil society* (Kitchener, 2001), p.144 and 143.
16. For a discussion of these issues see Marco Geuna, 'Aspetti della critica di Adam Ferguson al contrattualismo', in *Passioni, interessi, convenzioni: discussioni*

There had never been such things as isolated primitive man, a state of nature that preceded society, or a social contract: 'Mankind are to be taken in groups, as they have always subsisted' (p.9). From the beginning man had distinguished himself from animals above all for his propensity to live in common and to progress ('man is susceptible of improvement', p.13), as described in theories of stadial development, from hunting to animal domestication and sedentary farming down to modern trading societies.[17] Thus in its journey towards modernity mankind was destined to attain progress and civilisation in forms that were determined by the means of production: there is no trace here of Rousseau's noble savage, nor of his concerns about the negative effects of property, nor his existential angst in the face of Western civilisation in general. Nevertheless, Ferguson certainly did not subscribe to the same moderate and conservative views as Hume and other British philosophers of his time, who were engaged in what we have defined as the political neutralisation of rights. He agreed with Rousseau insofar as he too addressed the idea of the legitimacy of power and the importance of general consensus and participation. Throughout his *Essay*, Ferguson voices his concerns about the corruption and despotism that spread among the moderns as a consequence of the growing wealth of commercial societies. He was an admirer of the way in which the ancient republican forms of government encouraged political participation, created a community spirit and aroused feelings of patriotism and civic humanism. He lamented that all this was jeopardised by modern selfishness and individualism, and complained that '[t]o the ancient Greek, or the Roman, the individual was nothing, and the public every thing', while to the moderns 'the individual is every thing, and the public nothing' (p.67). It is in relation to this underlying 'republicanism' and focus on the community that the language of the rights of man surfaces here and there in Ferguson's *Essay*, helping to attenuate its social determinism.

Although Ferguson writes that he does not intend 'to carry the notion of a right into its several applications', he engages with Locke, Montesquieu and Rousseau on this issue. He enquires into the political and juridical import of natural rights, with no specific reference to the usual Protestant paradigm of the morality of duties and its interaction

settecentesche su virtù e civiltà, ed. Marco Geuna and Maria Luisa Pesante (Milan, 1992), p.129-80.

17. Cf. Meek, *Social science and the ignoble savage*, p.131ff.

with rights. Instead, he points out the link that had emerged in the course of the centuries between violence and despotism on the one hand, and a disregard for the passions and the 'rights of men' on the other:

> Every peasant will tell us, that a man hath his rights; and that to trespass on those rights is injustice [...] The rights of individuals may relate to a variety of subjects, and be comprehended under different heads. Prior to the establishment of property, and the distinction of ranks, men have a right to defend their persons, and to act with freedom; they have a right to maintain the apprehension of reason, and the feelings of the heart. (p.44)

Ferguson was particularly interested in the foundation and what determined the legitimacy of these rights. In fact this was the crucial question for numerous other Enlightenment thinkers in Europe in the 1760s, a decade that was to have a decisive influence on the political struggles of the Late Enlightenment. While Rousseau had focused on the isolated individual in the state of pure nature, Ferguson opted for a sociocentric anthropology. He started from the premise of the innate quality of the sociability principle, and highlighted the central role played, in a positive sense, by feelings of sympathy, mutual attention and empathy within the community. This was where the solution to the problem lay: in the definition of communities and their natural bonds of reciprocity as a natural fact ('love and compassion are the most powerful principles in the human breast'), with no need to invent the figure of an isolated natural man:

> the sense of a right which we maintain for ourselves, is by a movement of humanity and candour extended to our fellow creatures [...] if we only mean to inquire, why they who are well disposed to mankind, apprehend, in every instance, certain rights pertaining to their fellow-creatures, and why they applaud the consideration that is paid to those rights, we cannot perhaps assign a better reason, than that the person who applauds, is well disposed to the welfare of the parties to whom his applauses refer. (p.44-45)

Only 'a principle of humanity', i.e. empathy and all those mutual feelings that cement the bond among individuals in a community, could explain why everyone adhered to a general idea of rights. However, the acknowledged centrality and self-evidence of these rights inevitably led to the possibility of their politicisation, once it was recognised that the equality principle, when extended to the possession of rights, could not be considered to apply only in the state of nature but must be put into practice also in modern civil society:

> mankind [...] have indeed by nature equal rights to their preservation, and to the use of their talents; but they are fitted for different stations; and when they are classed by a rule taken from this circumstance, they suffer no injustice on the side of their natural rights [...] a right to do justice, and to do good, is competent to every individual, or order of men. (p.75-76)

Ferguson did not expand on these few scattered ideas on the possible politicisation of rights in modern civil society. He made, however, some important remarks on these issues. For instance, on how the concentration of wealth in just a few hands could pose a threat to the rights of man: 'In every commercial state, notwithstanding any pretension to equal rights, the exaltation of a few must depress the many' (p.215). Or where he revives the nexus between rights and the law in the wake of Locke and Rousseau: 'Law is the treaty to which members of the same community have agreed, and under which the magistrate and the subject continue to enjoy their rights, and to maintain the peace of society' (p.180). Or yet again in his attack on the slave trade, where he points out that '[l]iberty is a right which every individual must be ready to vindicate for himself, and which he who pretends to bestow as a favour, has by that very act in reality denied' (p.307). These remarks are enough to make us want to take another look at the general modalities in which eighteenth-century anglophone culture engaged with the language of natural rights.

In recent years, important research has been carried out on this subject. Especially significant is the work that has been done on the question of the Scottish Enlightenment. The latter is quite rightly considered to be a crucial part of this subject, and scholars have extensively discussed the contrasting theoretical positions within this movement on the issue of moral philosophy and its central role for an understanding of the persistent influence of Grotius, Pufendorf and their view of natural law.[18] In this sense, students of the Enlightenment

18. Cf. Duncan Forbes, 'Natural law and the Scottish Enlightenment', in *The Origins and nature of the Scottish Enlightenment*, ed. R. H. Campbell and Andrew S. Skinner (Edinburgh, 1982), p.186-204. See also Knud Haakonssen's abovementioned works, which also discuss recent bibliography on this subject. For a more wide-ranging overview, see Eugenio Lecaldano, 'Paradigmi di analisi della filosofia morale nell'illuminismo scozzese', in *Passioni, interessi, convenzioni,*

are still generally in agreement with the view expressed by Knud Haakonssen. This critic argued that, while the Scottish philosophers' 'natural jurisprudence' made large use of the concept of natural rights, they rejected all individualistic aspects, seeing these rights as directly derived from 'natural duties', natural law and a concept of a community as something that was centred around the sociability principle and an integral part of a 'morally well-ordered universe' – a concept that had already been outlined in the work of Grotius and Pufendorf.[19] There is general agreement on the scenario described by Haakonssen, even though some critics may question the precise position of authors such as Gershom Carmichael or Francis Hutcheson, or the individual way in which these and other thinkers revived natural rights in their moral theories in the first half of the seventeenth century.

In 1729 the Irish thinker Francis Hutcheson began teaching moral philosophy at the University of Glasgow, where he used as a textbook Pufendorf's *De officio* with a commentary by his predecessor, Gershom Carmichael. In Hutcheson's interpretation, natural rights do derive from the individual's moral sense, but in a way that is quite different from the full-blown individualism one finds in Hobbes or Rousseau. Hutcheson's *System of moral philosophy* was published posthumously in 1755, but was probably written towards the end of 1737. This work explicitly addresses the issue of the 'rights of man', including the use of this still fairly new phrase.[20] These rights are seen as deriving their legitimacy and ultimate meaning from other social aspects, such as 'duties', respecting the harmony of the natural order, or the subject's self-discipline, civic spirit and natural social virtues. Attributing a right for Hutcheson involved, first of all, recognising an action's positive social effect on the community. Among other things, this meant that no conflict could arise among different rights. In opposition to Mandeville's harsh utilitarianism, Hutcheson defended Shaftesbury's Neoplatonic pronouncements, and was critical of the theory of the general will, and of the far too many concessions that Pufendorf made to Hobbes, Epicureanism and the violent character of the state of

---

ed. M. Geuna and M. L. Pesante, p.13-40. On the extensive research on the Scottish Enlightenment from recent years see Silvia Sebastiani, *The Scottish Enlightenment: race, gender, and the limits of progress* (New York, 2013), p.1-9.

19. Cf. Haakonssen, *Natural law and moral philosophy*, p.311.

20. Cf. Francis Hutcheson, *A System of moral philosophy*, 2 vols (London, n.n., 1755), vol.1, p.314. In the second volume, in dealing with 'Civil polity', the author devotes an entire chapter to 'Rights and duties of parents and children'.

nature. Within this framework of harmony and self-discipline, of the natural and organic hierarchy of the great chain of being and the subject's love for the whole world, Hutcheson revived Grotius' theory of 'perfect rights' (which were linked to those actions that were absolutely necessary to public good and without which social coexistence would be impossible) and 'imperfect rights' (failure to observe which did not undermine the life of society).[21]

We could mention many more examples of this paradigm, according to which the very existence of rights derives from the undisputed primacy of duties, the sociability principle and a Stoic and Aristotelian-Thomistic view of society as something that depended on the harmony of the natural order being always defended and restored in case of infringement of those duties and rights. Indeed this model is still widely accepted among scholars of Catholic and Protestant natural law, leading in the United Kingdom to a specific interpretation of the Enlightenment and the American Revolution in a conservative sense.[22]

However, there were other ways of politically neutralising natural rights, besides having those rights derive from duties, as we have discussed above. A case in point is Adam Smith, according to whom economic development, commercial sociability and a market founded on moral and social principles were the constitutive parts of mankind's historical destiny of progress and modernity. However, Smith made a clear-cut distinction between rights and trade. For him, the language of the rights of man should be confined to the field of justice and of 'natural jurisprudence'. His positions on this had important consequences in the areas of politics and economics, to an extent that has not yet been fully realised.[23]

21. Hutcheson, *System of moral philosophy*, p.252ff. On Hutcheson's 'natural jurisprudence', see Stephen Buckle, *Natural law and the theory of property: Grotius to Hume* (Oxford, 1991), p.191-233; Geuna, 'Pufendorf in Scozia', p.335ff.
22. Examples of the resurfacing of the Neo-Thomistic interpretation of natural rights in the first half of the twentieth century are found in Emmanuel Mounier's 'personalism' and in Jacques Maritain: cf. Ferrone, 'Chiesa cattolica e modernità', p.70ff. On the persistence of the duty-based interpretation of natural rights down to this day see Ronald Dworkin, *Taking rights seriously* (London, 1978), p.171ff., and Finnis, *Natural law and natural rights*, p.201ff., especially chapter 8, 'Are duties prior to rights?'
23. There are a few references to these issues in Istvan Hont, *Jealousy of trade: international competition and the nation-state in historical perspective* (Cambridge, MA, and London, 2005), p.90ff. Hont asks how it could be possible to apply 'natural jurisprudence (the language of Rights) to the politics of subsistence markets', given that Smith was accused of dismissing any form of 'moral economy' with

Adam Smith was originally, and always remained, a moral philosopher. In 1757 he published an acclaimed study on *The Theory of moral sentiments*, which provided an original take on the debate that had begun with the work of his friends and mentors, Hutcheson and Hume. In the wake of other exponents of the Scottish Enlightenment, Smith immediately attacked the coarse individualistic stance that characterised the 'selfish system' of Hobbes and Mandeville, Locke's form of social contract and state of nature, and Rousseau's primitivism and egalitarianism. The old ethical rationalism, epistemologically based on the geometric-deductive method, had succumbed to Hume's corrosive critique. But now Smith's own points of departure, such as Shaftesbury's idea of an innate social feeling or Hutcheson's theory of an *a priori* moral sense and innate benevolence, seemed to him equally inadequate. It was time to abandon these abstract principles and trace the interaction among subjects on an empirical basis, by studying through concrete experience the manifestations of reciprocal usefulness and the way in which this arose from the relationship between self-love and collective interest. It was necessary to investigate the modalities of mutual interest as the only possible foundation for comparing and articulating any form of moral judgement in society. As Smith writes in his *Theory of moral sentiments*, reiterating an empiricist stance that he shared with the whole of the Scottish Enlightenment, man 'can subsist only in society' and history.[24] As a philosopher, Smith was mostly interested in understanding in practical terms how the subject's passions, interests and faculties became objective rules of behaviour, and how they created and interacted with that harmonious natural order of society that was there for everyone to see. He thought he had reached an explanation when he reflected on the importance of sympathy and especially of imagination in human behaviour, and on how the subject was both selfish and compassionate by nature. Despite his undeniable self-love and stubborn pursuit of his own interests, the subject could nevertheless interact with others in a positive way, which belied Hobbes' negative and violent anthropology. And this was due

'his apparent denial of the ultimate human rights to minimum subsistence'. This accusation was made with especial force in E. P. Thompson's classic essay, 'The moral economy of the English crowd in the eighteenth century', *Past & present* 50 (1971), p.76-136.

24. Adam Smith, *The Theory of moral sentiments*, ed. Knud Haakonssen (Cambridge, 2004), p.134.

to the subject's psychological configuration and the way in which the human brain functions in relation to the existence of others.

The *Theory* revolved around the mechanism of imagination. This faculty allowed the subject to empathise with the mind and passions of others, to exchange roles and even contemplate these exchanges from the outside like an external observer. This whole form of sympathetic interaction thus became the *locus* of social approval or disapproval. Empathy with others, the ability to observe their reactions as a neutral spectator, encouraged positive passions over negative ones, while at the same time curbing subjective claims and the power of self-interest. More importantly, it strengthened the universal character of moral rules, which were only valid insofar as they were acknowledged as such by the sentiments of all men, above and beyond their rationality.[25] Much has been written already on the originality and specific characteristics of Smith's *Theory of moral sentiments*. For our purposes, it is enough to stress the ideal and philosophical continuity between the *Theory* and Smith's most important work: *An Inquiry into the nature and causes of the wealth of nations*, published in 1776.

The anthropological, social and above all moral foundations of trade as described in the *Inquiry* are indeed based on the same model as in the *Theory*. The ethics of 'exchange' were thus based on human sociability. While still presented as an undisputed principle, this is however redefined in commercial and utilitarian terms so as to extend the conceptual categories of the old natural law.[26] An equally important role is again played by the dialectic of sympathy (as empathetic imagination) and self-interest. All this takes as its starting point the natural predisposition of the subject to commercial sociability as a constituent element of a harmonious natural order. The ethical and universal character of trade and of man's natural passion for exchange was also to be found in labour as social mediation and added value embodied in the product.[27] The result was a highly original redefinition of the very humanity of the subject.

25. A useful overview of Smith's moral philosophy can be found, together with an extensive bibliography, in Costa, *Civitas*, vol.1, p.412ff.

26. Pufendorf was the first thinker to add the notion of trade to Hobbes' state of nature and to develop a utilitarian concept of sociability, which gave rise to the stadial theory of development. Cf. Hont, *Jealousy of trade*, p.159ff.

27. On this, see Adelino Zanini's introduction to Adam Smith, *Teoria dei sentimenti morali*, ed. A. Zanini (Rome, 1991), p.v-lxxxix, especially p.lvii ff., which includes an important bibliography.

The hypothesis formulated by Adam Smith was even more innovative than what had been postulated by Rousseau when he defined the humanity of the individual in relation to his natural liberty, which distinguished him from animals, which were subject to natural instinct. By contrast, Smith focused on man's 'propensity to truck, barter, and exchange one thing for another' as one of the most emblematic features of the human character, something that 'is common to all men, and to be found in no other race of animals'. Only man 'has almost constant occasion for the help of his brethren' to be able to live, progress and improve his existence through an important innovation: the division of labour.[28] To the latter, decisive issue Smith devoted the entire first book of his treatise, which bears the significant title 'Of the causes of improvement in the productive powers of labour, and of the order according to which its produce is naturally distributed among the different ranks of the people'. In this famous book Smith set out his optimistic philosophy of history, with its belief in the goodness of natural laws and the active presence of divine providence in the world.

Like Montesquieu before him, Smith believed that the change in modes of production was at the origin of the stadial development of nations from primitive huntsmen to modern civil and commercial societies. While agriculture had remained substantially unchanged, the division of labour had greatly affected manufacture through the introduction of 'a great number of machines which facilitate and abridge labour, and enable one man to do the work of many' (p.22). This in turn had led to the development of international trade, thanks to the availability of the widest possible market, which had entirely changed the life of nations and the history of mankind. In Smith's view, these were undoubtedly positive changes, that brought with them civil progress, economic welfare, and more wealth and happiness for all: 'the great multiplication of the productions of all the different arts, in consequence of the division of labour [...] occasions, in a well-governed society, that universal opulence which extends itself to the lowest ranks of the people' (p.25).

Like Enlightenment thinkers throughout Europe, Smith believed that world trade contributed greatly to progress, civil development and a peaceable disposition.[29] The first real world war in human history

28. Adam Smith, *An Inquiry into the nature and causes of the wealth of nations* (London, 2001), p.29.
29. See Albert O. Hirschman's fundamental study, *The Passions and the interests: political arguments for capitalism before its triumph* (Princeton, NJ, 1977).

was the Seven Years War, fought by the great European powers between 1756 and 1763 for dominion over the colonies and international trade. This war would never have happened if economic and political interests had been tempered with a concern for the passions, and for that harmony of the natural order that derived from trade, commercial sociability, and the ethical defence of a market that was both as wide as possible and 'free' in the sense that it was open equally to all individuals and nations. Smith was sincerely indignant over the commercial wars that arose in the previous century out of the 'spirit of monopoly' and 'jealousy of trade' among the nations: 'Commerce, which ought naturally to be, among nations, as among individuals, a bond of union and friendship, has become the most fertile source of discord and animosity' (p.646).[30] Following Hume in this, Smith attributed the very rise of modern liberty to free trade and the effects of manufacture on contemporary civil society.[31] This unexpected confluence between politics and economics, liberty and trade, was in fact founded on a solid anthropological and moral basis, and constitutes one of the most memorable contributions of the Scottish Enlightenment to the new science of man that Hume and Rousseau hoped for.

It becomes clear, then, that the anachronistic view of Adam Smith that was artfully created by nineteenth-century ideologues of laissez-faire has no basis in fact. This view celebrated Smith as a 'pure' economist and the father of a mythical 'self-regulated market', a market that was 'free' in the sense of being independent of society and autonomously guided by an 'invisible hand'. Thus Smith was seen as openly sympathetic towards a future market society that would turn individuals themselves into commercial goods.[32] But in fact, the

30. See also Smith's indictment of the great Dutch and English companies who monopolised international trade with the Indies, thus constantly giving rise to trade wars and violence of all kinds: 'Such exclusive companies, therefore, are nuisances in every respect; always more or less inconvenient to the countries in which they are established, and destructive to those which have the misfortune to fall under their government' (p.851).
31. See Hont, *Jealousy of trade*, p.80ff. In fact, the debate on the free market as a source of economic emancipation and civil liberty had already begun in England in the previous century: cf. J. O. Appleby, *Economic thought and ideology in seventeenth-century England* (Princeton, NJ, 1978).
32. This was already argued by Karl Polanyi in a work originally published in 1944, where he pointed out that 'the idea of the self-regulation of economic life was utterly beyond the horizon of the age' (*The Great transformation: the political and economic origins of our time*, Boston, MA, 2001, p.74). See also S. J. Pack, *Capitalism*

'invisible hand' that guided the unwitting players in the trade scene in Smith's account was simply that same 'providence' that in the *Theory* transformed interest into a positive passion by means of the imagination, thus ensuring the continuation in time of a harmonious natural order.[33] The market's 'freedom' was first of all an ethical element that gave it legitimacy and enhanced its efficiency. The market was for Smith a 'limit idea', the place in which human subjects exercised their freedom and equality by exchanging products in what was at last 'an open and free market' (p.865).

To guarantee the existence of this free market, the work of the legislator was absolutely essential. The latter must be constantly vigilant in order to prevent its total degradation at the hand of unscrupulous monopolists and manufacturers, who were constantly looking for political ways of limiting equal access to the market. Therefore a good legislator must work hard at thwarting 'the mean rapacity, the monopolizing spirit of merchants and manufacturers, who neither are, nor ought to be, the rulers of mankind'.[34] He must bravely reject the interests of the few in defence of public good and everyone's freedom to trade on absolutely equal terms to others. This was a far cry from laissez-faire. It had nothing to do with a free market that existed autonomously in nature and history, was self-regulated and could be left to run its course. These were complex issues, which Smith, as a moral philosopher, addressed with realism and caution. To begin with, the *Wealth of nations* makes several concessions to the State's fiscal or military interests that limit free trade. Even the Navigation Act, which restricted Dutch trade in favour of English goods, seemed to him a positive thing. Smith always thought in terms of actual

as a moral system: Adam Smith's critique of the free market economy (Aldershot, 1991). More in general, see the bibliography discussed in Zanini, introduction to *Teoria dei sentimenti morali*, p.xx ff.

33. The 'invisible hand' is mentioned in book 4, chapter 2 of *Wealth of nations* (p.593). In part 4 of his *Theory of moral sentiments*, where the phrase is used to describe the force that turned the natural greed of the rich to a good purpose (p.249), this force is alternatively named as 'Providence' (p.250). Much has been written on the true meaning of the three occurrences overall of this phrase in Smith, which has been arbitrarily interpreted as the symbol of a self-regulated market. Emma Rothschild successfully argues against traditional liberalist interpretations of this phrase in her *Economic sentiments: Adam Smith, Condorcet and the Enlightenment* (Cambridge, MA, 2001), p.116ff. Rothschild points out that Smith 'did not especially esteem the invisible hand' and in fact used the phrase in an ironic and sceptical way.
34. Smith, *Wealth of nations*, p.461.

historical reality when he discussed the importance of free trade from an economic and above all ethical point of view. He realised that, even in the case of the most advanced nations, such as Great Britain, there was a utopian element to this vision: 'To expect, indeed, that the freedom of trade should ever be entirely restored in Great Britain is as absurd as to expect that an Oceana [*sic*] or Utopia should ever be established in it' (p.614).

Nevertheless, by indicating in man's innate tendency to barter the element that 'originally gives occasion to the division of labour' (p.31) and designating the market as the natural place of birth of modern freedom, Adam Smith transformed his *Inquiry into the nature and causes of the wealth of nations* into a true Enlightenment manifesto: a manifesto for modernity, progress, economic development and the acquisition of wealth by nations and individuals as the way to achieve, not least from a moral point of view, that greatest happiness for the greatest number of people that had been called for by his mentor, Francis Hutcheson, and relaunched by Beccaria in Milan. This was obviously an entirely different way from that outlined by Rousseau, with his focus on the political practice of the rights of man and on the reforms that had become necessary in order to limit the inequalities that had arisen with economic and scientific progress. In fact, the *Wealth of nations* seems designed to demolish Rousseau's theses, which by then occupied a central position in the European political debate.

Smith publicly attacked those theses from the moment the two discourses were first published, in the 1750s.[35] In the introduction and layout of his 1776 work, even though Rousseau is never mentioned, every one of his tenets is critiqued and even overturned. In contrast with the considerable reservations expressed by Rousseau on the role of the arts and sciences in improving the division of labour, Smith hails this as what had made the civil progress of nations possible. He advocates a positive view of modernity and stadial progress against Rousseau's view of human history as constant degeneration that led to an unhappy human being who was everywhere in chains. The noble savage is uncompromisingly turned into a miserable bad slave, a sad contrast to civil man and the prosperity of modern commercial societies.

In the wake of other Scottish Enlightenment thinkers, Smith draws a tragic and violent picture of savage communities of hunters and fishermen: 'Such nations [...] are so miserably poor that, from

35. On this, see Hont, *Jealousy of trade*, p.91.

mere want, they are frequently reduced, or, at least, think themselves reduced, to the necessity sometimes of directly destroying, and sometimes of abandoning their infants, their old people, and those afflicted with lingering diseases, to perish with hunger, or to be devoured by wild beasts' (p.13).

What most alarmed Smith, however, were Rousseau's much advertised views on inequality as the product of progress and modernity, and source of despotism and growing popular misery. He agreed with Voltaire and D'Alembert that they were a dangerous mystification that had to be unmasked at all costs. For him, social inequality was inevitable and even necessary in order to fuel competition and individual ambition. It was a kind of indispensable prerequisite in an advanced civil society that was able to feed an ever growing number of people precisely thanks to commerce and a market in which all men could and should be considered free and equal protagonists. How dare Rousseau deny that, thanks to economic progress, 'a workman, even of the lowest and poorest order, if he is frugal and industrious, may enjoy a greater share of the necessaries and conveniences of life than it is possible for any savage to acquire' (*ibid.*)? How could he not see that 'the accommodation of a European prince does not always so much exceed that of an industrious and frugal peasant as the accommodation of the latter exceeds that of many an African king, the absolute master of the lives and liberties of ten thousand naked savages' (p.28)?

Nevertheless, it is quite striking that Smith's *Wealth of nations*, which was published in 1776, the year of the American Declaration of Independence, should make no reference to the rights of man. A purely economic approach characterises even his discussion of the slave trade, which was being fiercely debated at the time, with Rousseau denouncing its inhumanity exactly because of those rights. By contrast, Smith simply remarked that 'the work done by slaves, though it appears to cost only their maintenance, is in the end the dearest of any' (p.513). In a chillingly objective way, as an economist thinking only in terms of profit and expenditure, the author explained that a mode of production based on the practice of slavery retained a measure of productivity for the tobacco or sugar plantations in America, but would never work for European corn-based agriculture: 'The planting of sugar and tobacco can afford the expense of slave-cultivation. The raising of corn, it seems, in the present times, cannot' (*ibid.*).

This absence of the language of rights in a discussion of political economy is quite astounding but has not as yet been analysed by historians of the subject. However, as far as Smith is concerned, it confirms the specific intellectual attitude that already informs his *Theory of moral sentiments*, with its clear separation of morality from politics and, especially, from the sphere of law and justice. Morality was a positive social virtue that was related to beneficence and based on the sympathy and imagination of an 'impartial spectator': it was 'always free' and could never be 'extorted by force'. Justice, by contrast, was a negative social virtue, whose violation caused an 'injury', doing 'real and positive hurt'.[36] It was liable to cause a rift that must be healed immediately in order to avoid serious consequences in the life of society: 'Beneficence, therefore, is less essential to the existence of society than justice. Society may subsist, though not in the most comfortable state, without beneficence; but the prevalence of injustice must utterly destroy it' (p.135).

Because of its importance, Smith had meant to devote an entire work to the subject of justice, which he never actually wrote. His theories on the autonomy and specificity of justice with respect to morality and politics can be gleaned from the manuscripts of the *Lectures on jurisprudence* that he delivered in 1763 as professor of moral philosophy in Glasgow. Unlike Hume, who disliked the language of natural rights and avoided using it, Smith addressed justice and its rules only in terms of their violation:

> Iustice is violated whenever one is deprived of what he had a right to and could justly demand from others, or rather, when we do him any injury or hurt without a cause. Let us consider then in how many ways iustice may be violated, that is, in how many respects a man may be injured. – 1st, he may be injured as a man; 2dly, as a member of family; 3dly, as a citizen or member of a State.[37]

Previous authors had followed Grotius and Pufendorf in taking as their starting point the duties–rights nexus in the state of nature to then arrive at its recognition by political power. With great originality, in his lectures Smith applied the method used in civil law, starting from the role of government and the legislator and then discussing the rights. The result is a handbook of positive law joined with a historical overview of 'natural jurisprudence', all to the effect of restating the

36. See Smith, *Theory of moral sentiments*, p.125-27.
37. As quoted in Haakonssen, *Natural law and moral philosophy*, p.132. See also Haakonssen, *Science of a legislator*.

autonomy and specificity of justice with respect to morality.[38] By doing away with any reference to the state of nature or the social contract, Smith effectively relativised and turned into a reassuringly historical product the juridical defence of modern rights. These rights became simply one of the many results of civilisation and the rise of modern commercial society, and of the political institutions that were linked to the stadial development of nations. They were acknowledged and respected in all modern civil societies, while being unsurprisingly non-existent in those nations that had not progressed in history. However, this view entailed numerous contradictions and ambiguities. It was quite hard to infer from this whether the bad savage, who had not gone beyond the first stage of civilisation, and who was enslaved and treated like commercial goods, nevertheless had the same natural rights as civil man. This ambiguous and baffling historical reading of human justice effectively defused both the natural, universal and moral character of the rights of man and their political inalienability.

By historicising 'natural jurisprudence', Smith reiterated his conviction that only economic development and free trade could produce civilisation and rights. He distanced himself entirely from Rousseau's theories that assigned a fundamental role to the universality and the inalienability of the rights of natural man as an individual, and to the social contract within the republic of men. As we have seen, for Rousseau, only in this way would it be possible to create a new politics that would reduce the inequalities created by progress, bring down the *Ancien régime* and build the foundations for a fair and just civil society, regardless of its wealth. Was Smith's solution, then, a particularly appealing and effective way of neutralising the political relevance of the nascent language of the rights of man? Can we really say that he transmuted political discourse into economic discourse once and for all, making the thought of Hobbes, Locke and Rousseau obsolete? Was it not simply a radical new way to rethink that nexus between politics and morality that would be at the heart of the political culture of the Late Enlightenment, by finally taking into account the importance of commerce in modern societies?[39]

38. On the German sources of Smith's historicisation of natural rights see chapter 4, 'Adam Smith out of context: his theory of rights in Prussian perspective', in Haakonssen, *Natural law and moral philosophy*, p.129-53.
39. To my knowledge there has not yet been a thorough study of the political neutralisation of the rights of man in Smith's thought. On the more general theme of the dissolution of the political into the economic sphere through the

What is certain is that these diverging political ideas, which emerged in the second half of the eighteenth century, are still being debated today, and a solution is not in sight. Which is the best way to build a better society: take the rights of man as the main instrument for orientation? Or acknowledge the primacy of the free market as a decisive factor in both ethical and emancipatory terms? As we have seen, Smith would not have hesitated to opt for the latter.

The historicisation of the rights of man is something quite different from the gradual acknowledgement of the existence of natural rights in the history of mankind, as debated in Enlightenment circles throughout Europe, and in particular by Condorcet in his *Esquisse d'un tableau historique*. The historicisation of rights not only removed any real substance or defensibility from the condition of the bad savage, which dominated the works of the Scottish Enlightenment and their progressive thinking on stadial history. It also seriously undermined the universalistic and cosmopolitan view, by supporting instead a reading of 'native rights' in nationalistic and patriotic terms that had been hotly debated in Britain since the previous century.[40]

This attitude went on to determine the history of constitutionalism on both sides of the Atlantic, and still more or less consciously dominates a large part of the political and juridical outlook in the Anglo-American world.[41] It is most famously represented by William Blackstone's four-volume *Commentaries on the law of England*, which were published between 1765 and 1769. This work is a refined and learned treatise aimed at the general public, and exemplifies the way in which

separation and autonomy of economy from morality, see Peter Minowitz, *Profits, priests, and princes: Adam Smith's emancipation of economics from politics and religion* (Stanford, CA, 1993). Smith's *Wealth of nations* is not discussed in Reinhart Koselleck, *Critique and crisis: Enlightenment and the pathogenesis of modern society* (Oxford, 1988; original: *Kritik und Krise: ein Beitrag zur Pathogenese der bürgerlichen Welt*, Freiburg, 1959). However, it was undoubtedly a milestone in that crisis of modernity that arose from the separation of ethics and politics in the political culture of the Enlightenment, as described in Koselleck's book.

40. On the reference to 'natural rights' in England, already before Locke and in the realm of both political action and moral discussion, see Quentin Skinner, *Liberty before liberalism* (Cambridge, 1998), p.19-21; Zuckert, *Natural rights*, p.185ff; Oestreich, *Geschichte der Menschenrechte*, p.54-56.

41. The idea that there is nothing natural about the rights of man, which are in fact the product of a specific historical era and context, was amply debated by historicist thinkers in the nineteenth century and then, in the following century, by Italian idealist philosophers, such as Benedetto Croce: see Ferrone, 'Bobbio, l'Illuminismo e l'età dei diritti'.

the language of natural rights was adopted in Britain. Its aim was to provide some grounding in juridical matters for gentlemen who were expected to play a role in public life and in the service of the nation. While the Enlightenment thinkers in Paris and Milan advocated a policy of reforms that could eliminate the injustices of the *Ancien régime*, Blackstone was himself part of the establishment. In his work he describes the theoretical basis of the English juridical system and how it had a concern for liberty at its core, partly with the intention of celebrating, after the difficult civil war years, Britain's newly achieved political and social stability. This explains the components that can be seen at play in this work. On the one hand, we find a traditional philosophical outlook in line with Protestant natural law, which provides a sophisticated synthesis of the theories of Aquinas, Pufendorf, Locke and Newton. On the other, it celebrated English constitutionalism, Britain's mixed form of government, and the myth of the 'Ancient Constitution', which had been created in the seventeenth century by pro-Parliament jurists such as Edward Coke.[42] A few decades earlier Montesquieu had given this myth a new lease of life in a chapter of the *Esprit des lois* entirely devoted to the English constitution as a bastion of liberty.

With his Thomistic education, Blackstone had no qualms about reiterating the primacy of God-derived natural law over man-made positive law. He modernised the concept, however, by comparing the 'law of nature' that regulated human relationships to the way in which matter obeyed Newton's universal law of gravitation: in both cases the law of nature was nothing other than 'a rule of action dictated by some superior being', and as such it was 'of course, superior in obligation to any other. It is binding over the globe. In all countries, and in all times: no human laws are of any validity, if contrary to this.'[43] Blackstone's position was distinctly different from those of Diderot, Rousseau or Beccaria, who were strongly critical of old natural law and advocated the secularisation and autonomy of will of the human legislator. In contrast with this, Blackstone relaunched the whole system developed by Pufendorf around the centrality of duties and the sociability principle in the formulation of laws that must always guide man's behaviour, starting with 'his duty to God,

42. Cf. J. G. A. Pocock, *The Ancient Constitution and the feudal law: a study of English historical thought in the seventeenth century* (Cambridge, 1957).
43. William Blackstone, *Commentaries on the law of England*, a facsimile of the first edition of 1765-1769 with an introduction by S. N. Katz, 4 vols (Chicago, IL, 1979), vol.1, p.41.

to himself, and to his neighbour'. The natural rights discussed by Locke in relation to the 'original contract' were also connected with this and ultimately derived from 'natural duties' (vol.1, p.60), as in the traditional Protestant view of natural law that we discussed above.

There was, nevertheless, something truly new in Blackstone's *Commentaries* that appealed to his contemporaries just as it does to us today. It was the passionate defence of the 'British Constitution', a matter-of-fact, unwritten guarantor of liberty that Blackstone proudly called 'our free constitution'. Montesquieu had already pointed to it as a powerful and exemplary instrument of freedom for the whole of the Western world, stressing in particular its efficiently balanced mixed government, with power being shared among crown, Commons and House of Lords. Blackstone goes even further, illustrating for the first time the close relationship between the language of natural rights and the Ancient Constitution.

In the first book, when dealing with the 'absolute rights of individuals', i.e. those rights that relate 'to the persons of men and are then called *iura personarum* or the rights of persons' (vol.1, p.118), after the usual reference to how they ultimately derived from 'absolute duties', Blackstone described their earliest manifestation both in the state of nature and after their historical transformation, thanks to the English constitution, into the rights of free civil man.[44] From the beginning and then historically across the centuries, this constitution had been developed in order to allow the shift from natural liberty – 'The absolute right of man considered as a free agent', a right that was innate in man and granted by God at the moment of creation – to the English people's 'liberties':

> this spirit of liberty is so deeply implanted in our constitution, and rooted even in our very soil, that a slave or a negro, the moment he lands in England, falls under the protection of the laws, and with regard to all natural rights becomes *eo instanti* a freeman [...]. The absolute rights of every Englishman (which, taken in a political and extensive sense are usually called their liberties) as they are founded on nature and reason, so they are coeval with our form of government. (vol.1, p.123)

In this way Blackstone effectively provided a different but no less ambitious solution, based on history and the idea of community, to

44. For Blackstone there were ultimately only three rights that needed safeguarding: personal safety, personal liberty and property.

the question that Rousseau had asked in the *Social contract*, where he wondered whether and how it could be possible to ensure the political exercise of the natural rights of man in modern civil and commercial societies. With its emphasis on what today we would call the 'historical constitutionalisation of natural rights', Blackstone's English solution was far removed from continental theories. It had obviously nothing to do with the rethinking of the very concept of law in terms of the general will and man's autonomous action, and least of all with the strategic political function in the promotion of the rights of man and the reforms needed to bring down the *Ancien régime* that Helvétius and the Paris and Milan circles were beginning to assign to the new legislative systems, which were just then being drafted.

It was only at the end of the eighteenth century that 'constitutions' in the modern sense of written digests of a nation's fundamental values and principles began to appear. In the *Ancien régime*, this term referred to a conglomerate of things: customs, traditions, government institutions, unwritten and customary laws that had accumulated in common law across the centuries, alongside the 'statutes, acts or edicts, made by the King's majesty by and with the advice and consent of lords spiritual and temporal and commons in parliament assembled'.[45] The historical constitutionalisation of rights was therefore portrayed as a material fact that had arisen in the British community over hundreds of years. After all kinds of struggles, clashes and civil wars, the British system had finally achieved universally admired serenity and stability. Blackstone described with pride the history of British law: from the rudimentary laws of the Celts, Saxons and Danes, to the earliest forms of 'general immemorial custom or common law', and the struggle for the Magna Carta, the Bill of Rights and all the 'declarations of our rights and liberties' that had started off as a 'residuum of natural liberty' but had finally given rise to the glorious and much admired 'rights of the people of England' (p.125). None of this had anything to do with the presumed anthropological basis of natural rights or their practical political application through democracy and the general will, as in the system put forward by Rousseau.

The Ancient Constitution model had already been extolled by the first Enlightenment generation, starting with Voltaire and Montesquieu

45. Blackstone, *Commentaries*, vol.1, p.85. On the 'natural constitutions' of the *Ancien régime* and their customary basis see Trampus, *Storia del costituzionalismo italiano*, p.13ff.

and ending, in 1771, with Genevan thinker Jean-Louis de Lolme and his *Constitution de l'Angleterre, ou Etat du gouvernement anglais, comparé avec la forme républicaine et les autres monarchies de l'Europe*. In fact, the years in which Blackstone published his *Commentaries* witnessed the deepening crisis of this model.

After the watershed of the Seven Years War (1756-1763), fought across four continents and three oceans by Britain and France for imperial supremacy over the new colonies, the political situation in England had again entered a phase of strong turbulence through the violent riots generated by the 'Wilkes and Liberty' movement. These attacks were directed against King George III's despotism and the crown's attempts to shift the balance of power away from Parliament and towards itself, also as a consequence of the rise of radical politicians, such as John Wilkes himself, who had been jailed for sedition. These developments were reported with both alarm and curiosity by the gazettes of other European countries. Wilkes had first publicised his opinions in a series of sarcastic articles in the *North Britton*. In 1765, as he sought asylum across the major European capitals, from Paris through Milan to Naples, he was easily able to persuade the main Enlightenment thinkers that liberty and personal rights were seriously at risk in the United Kingdom. Although Wilkes' arguments were still based on the Ancient Constitution, whose rules had been violated by George III in his attempt to boost his personal power, intellectuals and gazette writers throughout Europe came to the conclusion that what they were witnessing was in fact the definitive crisis of that ancient constitutional model, which now appeared totally anachronistic.

This feeling was increased by the French debate over the conflict between the monarchy and parliament, which highlighted the limitations of the old status-based constitutionalism of the *Ancien régime* as upheld by Montesquieu, in which 'intermediate bodies' were given the task of controlling the despotism of the sovereign. At the same time, public opinion was deeply affected by the Corsican Revolution (1755-1769), headed by Pasquale Paoli. This event set in motion the first great political and constitutional debate of the Late Enlightenment, on the need to radically rethink the very concept of constitution: a crucial debate in the political history of the West, which would be cut short by the French Revolution.

The Corsican experience influenced the American Revolution in various ways. First of all, for the first time the need arose for an actual written constitution like those in use today, which led to the rediscovery of how these political agreements were based on the popular will and the social contract, which alone could guarantee the liberty, proclaimed independence and constituent power of a newly independent community. Another factor was the rise of a myth of liberty and democracy in the name of Pasquale Paoli in British and, above all, American culture, through the writings on the Corsican events by James Boswell and Catherine Macaulay.[46] European public opinion also followed every phase of the American Revolution, and the Declaration of Independence of July 1776 spread rapidly throughout the continent on the other side of the Atlantic, thanks to its gazettes. Both the Revolution and the ensuing Declaration were important milestones in the history of the rights of man. This text deserves to be cited for its great rhetorical power and momentous contribution to the rise of the political language of the moderns:

> When in the course of human events it becomes necessary for one people to dissolve the political bands which have connected them with another, and to assume among the powers of the earth the separate and equal station to which the laws of nature and of nature's god entitle them, a decent respect to the opinions of mankind requires that they should declare the causes which impel them to the separation.
>
> We hold these truths to be self-evident; that all men are created equal; that they are endowed by their Creator with certain inalienable rights; that among these are life, liberty, and the pursuit of happiness; that to secure these rights, governments are instituted among men, deriving their just powers from the consent of the governed; that whenever any form of government becomes destructive of these ends, it is the right of the people to alter or to abolish it, and to institute new government, laying it's [*sic*] foundation on such principles and organizing it's [*sic*] powers in such form as to them shall seem most likely to effect their safety and happiness.[47]

46. On this, see Trampus, *Storia del costituzionalismo italiano*, p.106ff. Ahead of the events of 1776, the Corsican fighters were acclaimed in Massachusetts, Connecticut, Vermont and the state of New York. The Sons of Liberty patriot society, which was formed after the Stamp Act in order to boycott English products, paid much attention to the Corsican independence struggle from its very beginning. It is not by chance that its meetings were held in 'General Paoli's Tavern'. Six places in the USA are still named after Paoli.
47. For the text, see Maier, *American scripture*, p.236; see also Maier's discussion throughout the book. David Armitage, *The Declaration of Independence: a global history* (Cambridge, MA, 2007), focuses more on the Declaration's role as a foundational text for an independent State than on the issue of the rights of man.

The Declaration not only referred explicitly to the rights of man, but also, for the first time, cited them as the source of the right to resist tyranny and to build the legitimate government of a new community of equal and free men. In this way, it publicly sanctioned the transformation of the ancient language of natural rights into a set of moral and political principles. The reference to the 'self-evident' character of these rights may now sound rather arbitrary and unfounded given the reality of the time. However, it was supported first of all by the persistence of the centuries-old natural law tradition in universities as well as in public debate, and also by its seventeenth-century and then Enlightenment variants that we have described above. Secondly, as we shall see in the following chapters, it was based on the growing political use of the rights of man by Enlightenment circles, literary salons and masonic lodges in their struggle against the *Ancien régime*.

Neapolitan jurist and philosopher Gaetano Filangieri was among those who clearly understood that natural rights had finally mutated into political rights, to the extent that they could even legitimise the use of force and the recourse to rebellion should they be violated by a despot. In 1780 Filangieri firmly declared his support for the American settlers:

> Are colonials perhaps not members of society like the inhabitants of the metropoles are? Are they perhaps not sons of the same mother, brothers of the same family, citizens of the same fatherland, subjects of the same empire? Should they perhaps not have common rights and prerogatives, and among these rights is perhaps that of property and the liberty of disposing of that which is theirs not the most precious one? These rights, which man acquires at birth; which society and the laws must guarantee; which are essential in us, and which form our political existence like the soul and body form our physical existence; these precious rights which cannot be removed without dissolving the knot which unites us to the State; these rights we can never be deprived of, and their exercise can be suspended only by urgent need, inevitable and universal to the entire body politic. But when this cause no longer exists (like in this case), when this divinity which is called the public interest cannot be entirely placated by this violent and frightening sacrifice; when this public interest does not dare to claim it, then merely the suppression, even momentary, of this exercise becomes a frightening injustice, a dangerous attack, a manifest oppression: Could these rights, finally, which must be respected in the person of a private citizen, of a simple individual of

society, be denied to a large part of the body politic? Could they be banished from the colonies of a nation?[48]

After 1776, the political culture of the Enlightenment reached its high point, effectively becoming a brilliant, autonomous political laboratory of modernity. This would come to an end with the events of 1789, but by then the Enlightenment had managed to seek important new answers and reforms on issues such as the rights of man, republicanism and constitutionalism in entirely different terms from the past. From the historiographical point of view, in relation to the American Revolution and the political struggle in Britain we must, of course, also bear in mind that there was undeniably a moderate view of rights as derived from duties, which was an important aspect of Protestant natural law, as we saw above. Equally undeniable is the important role played by groups and individuals who were in favour of the political neutralisation of rights and their historical constitutionalisation – the latter idea having been successfully relaunched with polemical intent by Edmund Burke in his *Reflections on the Revolution in France.*

However, despite the importance of this 'conservative Enlightenment' in English-speaking culture, the politicisation of the rights of man in the Declaration of Independence is undeniable.[49] In the following decades this aspect characterised the rise of the new English working class and the struggle for rights in the United Kingdom, as well as in Western political life in general.[50] In fact, the European Enlightenment had long since started to split in two, giving rise to

48. Filangieri, *Scienza della legislazione*, vol.2: *Delle leggi politiche ed economiche*, ed. Maria Teresa Silvestrini (2004), p.172. Cf. Ferrone, *Politics of Enlightenment*, p.63-64.
49. On this, see the theses put forward by J. G. A. Pocock, 'Clergy and commerce: the conservative Enlightenment in England', in *L'età dei Lumi: studi storici sul Settecento europeo in onore di Franco Venturi*, ed. Lester G. Crocker *et al.* (Naples, 1985), p.523-62, and in Pocock's entry on 'Grande-Bretagne', in *Le Monde des Lumières*, ed. V. Ferrone and D. Roche, p.467-84. For a different view, see Robertson, *The Case for the Enlightenment*, p.4ff. Haakonssen, *Natural law and moral philosophy*, p.317ff., authoritatively links Pocock's theses with the idea of a 'moral conservatism of natural rights' in Protestant natural law. In opposition to this, Zuckert, *Natural rights*, points to Locke's politically innovative language of natural rights. For a useful overview of this debate, which also addresses the issue of the origins and nature of the American Revolution, see Cmiel, 'Recent history', p.120ff.
50. According to E. P. Thompson, '*Pilgrim's Progress* is, with *Rights of Man*, one of the two foundation texts of the English working-class movement' (*The Making of the English working class*, New York, 1966, p.31).

a harsh debate between radicals and moderates, especially on the true nature of the rights of man and the best way to achieve their application in practice.

In the first volume of his monumental *Science of legislation*, which was published starting from 1780, Gaetano Filangieri created the foundations of the new 'Enlightenment constitutionalism' of the end of the century with his implacable critique of the status-based constitutionalism of Montesquieu and the *Ancien régime* as well as of Blackstone's Ancient Constitution, both of which he considered inadequate for the purpose of guaranteeing liberty and the pursuit of happiness.

With renewed republican spirit, this new constitutionalism was built around the idea of rights. One of its aims was to obtain a written constitution that would regulate the balance of power in accordance with the overarching idea of popular sovereignty. Its main purpose, however, was to put together a composite scenario that reformulated the very idea of natural law on the basis of the centrality of man and his history. It gave a detailed outline of a new and original science of legislation that was capable of leading to a modern juridical system: a system that was unprecedentedly founded entirely on the rights of man, the respect of the principle of legality and the equality of rights.[51]

Filangieri's *Science of legislation* was immediately translated into several languages and spread throughout the Western world via masonic circles.[52] Its success was due to the fact that it was a distillation of a century of debates on the metamorphoses of natural law and on the new science of man that had arisen thanks to the Enlightenment. As well as on the work of Hume, Smith and Blackstone, Filangieri capitalised on the unmasking of the *arcana iuris* effected by Montesquieu in his *Esprit des lois*, and on Helvétius's explicit call for a new 'science of legislation'. The *Science of legislation* admirably synthesised morality and politics, thus contributing in an important new way to the politicisation of natural rights that began with Hobbes, Spinoza, Locke, Rousseau and Beccaria.

The *Science of legislation* thus enjoyed huge success among contemporary readers. It not only offered an extremely effective synthesis of the entire political and juridical thought of the European Enlightenment, but could also draw on the Italian background, in which

51. On 'The original character of Enlightenment constitutionalism' see Ferrone, *Politics of Enlightenment*, p.140-52.
52. Cf. *Diritti e costituzione: l'opera di Gaetano Filangieri e la sua fortuna europea*, ed. Antonio Trampus (Bologna, 2005).

the rights of man had been long debated with passion and interesting results – so much so that Filangieri's French translator, Jean-Antoine Gauvin Gallois, was able to write that 'the work whose translation we are offering here began to be published in Italy in 1780. It went through five editions, in Naples, Florence and Milan, which attests to its popularity in the country that pursues the science of the rights and duties of man more fervently and perhaps also more successfully than any other.'[53]

This testimony concerns specifically Beccaria's Milan, and also and especially the Naples of Giambattista Vico and Antonio Genovesi, which for a long time had been home to an important school of natural law that culminated with Gaetano Filangieri and Mario Pagano: this is the subject of our next chapter.

53. 'l'ouvrage, dont nous offrons la traduction au public, a commencé de paraître en Italie en 1780. Cinq éditions, publiées successivement à Naples, à Florence et à Milan, attestent la célébrité dont il jouit dans le pays de la terre où la science des droits et des devoirs de l'homme est cultivée avec le plus d'ardeur et peut-être même avec le plus de succès' ('Préface du traducteur', in Gaetano Filangieri, *La Science de la législation*, 7 vols, Paris, Cuchet, 1786-1791, vol.1, p.v).

12. The Neapolitan school of natural law and the rights of man: Vico and Genovesi

The fact that Italian Enlightenment culture, the heir of the Renaissance and modern humanism, played a protagonist's role in shaping the language of the rights of man in the course of the eighteenth century was something that the Enlightenment's contemporaries were more aware of than more recent historians.[1]

Even a scholar as acute as Franco Venturi always largely ignored the importance of the question of rights in Italian Enlightenment culture. Like many intellectuals of his generation, he probably did so on the back of Croce's idealist prejudice against political language: the latter was considered too abstract and rhetorical and devoid of genuine historical interest, so that it was always successfully opposed and philosophically defeated and 'sublated' in the course of the nineteenth century.[2]

The person who at an early stage flagged up the existence of a 'noble school' of political thought in Naples, based precisely on natural rights and the way these interacted for centuries with the history of nations, was Pierre-Louis Ginguené, author of an *Histoire littéraire*

1. On the importance of Italian humanism in Western history, see Eugenio Garin, *Italian humanism: philosophy and civic life in the Renaissance*, translated by Peter Munz (New York, 1965). For the idea of the Enlightenment's inheritance of Renaissance values, see Vincenzo Ferrone, 'Eugenio Garin: il lungo Illuminismo "da Petrarca a Rousseau"', in *Eugenio Garin: dal Rinascimento all'Illuminismo*, ed. Olivia Catanorchi and Valentina Lepri, with a 'Premessa' by Michele Ciliberto (Rome, 2011), p.269-79.
2. The silence regarding the importance of the Italian contribution to the history of the rights of man persists still, even in the recent book by Hunt, *Inventing human rights*, which mentions only Beccaria and says nothing about the Neapolitan school. On the hostility shown by Italian idealist culture, see Ferrone, 'Bobbio, l'Illuminismo e l'età dei diritti'.

d'Italie in ten volumes and an authoritative political journalist in Paris, before and after the French Revolution. As he wrote in 1807:

> Right from the start of the eighteenth century a great school of political philosophy had emerged in Naples. Giambattista Vico, who had a daring, wide-ranging and deep intellect, but who was also a strange and often obscure writer, in his *New science* sowed the seeds which were then brought to fruition by his pupil Genovesi, with his bright and methodical spirit. The principles of natural law, of the law of nations and of legislation were established in this school on a different basis from that found in Grotius and Pufendorf.[3]

Filangieri and Pagano were the last and most famous interpreters of that school.

It was Pagano himself who sketched out for posterity an admirable profile of that school in relation to the different development of political thought in other European contexts, insisting strongly on the pragmatic value of the first pioneering historical reflections on 'Roman laws' carried out in Naples. In the introduction to the second edition of his *Saggi politici* (*Political essays*) he wrote: 'That shapeless mass where onto the monuments of the most terrible despotisms are grafted maxims of the most enlightened philosophy and the human and moderate sentiments of the most docile principles; in that mass, I say, one finds scattered the seeds of the moral sciences.'[4]

It was the principles contained in the *Institutions* and *Digest* but above all the universalistic and cosmopolitan inspiration of Roman law that had made the jurists of the Neapolitan school think of the 'idea of an eternal law and justice, of the immutable and inalienable rights of man'.

Faithful to Vico's teachings, Pagano clearly distanced himself from Grotius, Pufendorf and Hobbes, denouncing the way they exclusively privileged the rational and geometric-deductive element in natural law. In this way, while acknowledging that Grotius had given 'system and body to the new ideas', he accused him of neglecting in his thoughts on justice the lessons of Roman law and history, the study of

3. See the profile of Filangieri given by Ginguené in Michaud's *Biographie universelle* and translated into Italian in the edition of Filangieri's *La scienza della legislazione* printed in Milan in 1807, vol.1, p.7-20.
4. See Francesco Mario Pagano, *Saggi politici: de' principii, progressi e decadenza delle società, edizione seconda (1791-92)*, ed. Luigi Firpo and Laura Salvetti Firpo (Naples, 1993), p.9-14. (Unattributed translations in this chapter are either my own or from Ferrone, *Politics of Enlightenment*; here from p.74.)

customs and of the forms of power in nations, ultimately privileging rationalistic models: 'He subordinated authority to syllogism, and a thousand passages by poets and orators to reason.' Hobbes took a similar line: 'He favoured reason over memory, and instead of quoting, he demonstrated.' The importance of the author of *Leviathan*, finally, would certainly have been greater if in his researches 'he had not confused facts with rights, if he had linked the idea of order and natural living together with the principles of utility and might'.

In fact it was John Locke, *l'immortale Giovanni Lok*, who earned the title of the real founder of modern political thought for having finally conceived the possibility of the fundamental linking together of 'political bodies and the rights of man'.[5] Montesquieu – according to Pagano – had in fact learned from Locke the idea of the 'temperate monarchical constitution' and of the division of powers without however introducing huge changes of thought. Rousseau's merits were different and no less important and decisive, compared to the English philosopher. 'The first ideas on the equality of the rights of man and the social contract, the origin of the right of property and the right to inflict capital punishment' had to be attributed to Rousseau. In Italy, after Machiavelli, only Giambattista Vico had shown himself capable of standing alongside all these giants of European political and moral thought. He was the only one – in Pagano's eyes – who had tackled with great originality or results the new 'political and moral studies', giving rise to a radical revision of the epistemological method and model that lay at the base of modern natural law and its renaissance in Enlightenment culture at the start of the eighteenth century. Filangieri was his direct heir, since he had followed through to its final conclusions a new political and philosophical understanding of natural law, finally composing a *Science of legislation* of the rights of man where rational method and historical knowledge, the principles of reason and respect for the customs of nations and of their histories, the 'ideal and eternal right' and positive law all went hand in hand.

And that these convictions were very widespread at the time in the Neapolitan intellectual environment is proved by the meeting, and the content of the discussions, between Wolfgang Goethe and Gaetano Filangieri in March 1787, when the German author, who had deliberately come to pay homage to the famous Neapolitan jurist during his masonic journey, reported:

5. Pagano, *Saggi politici*, p.25.

> Soon after we met, [Filangieri] introduced me to the work of an older writer, whose profound wisdom is so refreshing and edifying to all Italians of this generation who are friends of justice. His name is Giambattista Vico, and they rank him above Montesquieu. From a cursory reading of the book, which was presented to me as if it were sacred writ, it seems to me to contain sibylline visions of the Good and the Just which will or should come true in the future, prophecies based on a profound study of life and tradition. It is wonderful for a people to have such a spiritual patriarch.[6]

Vico's works, especially the *New science*, had in fact left a far more profound trace than has generally been thought in intellectual circles in the great capital of the Kingdom of the Two Sicilies. In this context, even though rather slowly, recent studies of the eighteenth century and Enlightenment culture in Italy are realising the importance of Vico's work. Nobody believes any more in the preconceived idealist thesis of Vico the genius, isolated and at the time not topical, but at the same time someone who anticipates the historicism of the nineteenth century and the future contrast between sciences of the spirit and natural sciences, just as Croce and Troeltsch used to do.[7] Nor does it help, and it is historically erroneous, to attribute to the Neapolitan philosopher a capacity for epistemological criticism of modern science on the basis of competences and direct knowledge of the key texts of the Scientific Revolution, by Galileo and Newton, which he did not possess at all.[8] That was certainly not where his greatness and importance for his contemporaries lay. As for the reflections of philosophers on the theoretical importance of Vico's thought, for all their worth, what in fact is emerging is the need for a historical reassessment of his figure in the Italian and European context of the early eighteenth century, going beyond the standard stereotypes devised by Benedetto Croce.

6. Johann Wolfgang von Goethe, *Italian journey*, translated by W. H. Auden and Elizabeth Mayer (Harmondsworth, 1970), p.192. On the meeting between the two men, see Benedetto Croce, *Aneddoti di varia letteratura*, 2nd edn, 4 vols (Bari, 1954), vol.3, p.21-35.
7. See chapter XIX, 'Vico and the tendencies of contemporary culture', in Benedetto Croce, *The Philosophy of Giambattista Vico*, translated by R. G. Collingwood (London, 1913); Ernst Troeltsch, *Der Historismus und seine Probleme*, vol.1: *Das logische Problem der Geschichtsphilosophie* (Tübingen, 1922), p.104ff.
8. On this point one must refer to the polemic between Eugenio Garin ('Postilla vichiana', in *Dal Rinascimento all'Illuminismo*, Florence, 1993) and Paolo Rossi ('Ancora sui contemporanei di Vico', *Rivista di filosofia* 76:3, 1985, p.465-74). For a contribution towards understanding this polemic, see Ferrone, 'Eugenio Garin'.

This reassessment is finally able to place Vico amongst the protagonists of the so-called crisis of the European mind, amongst those who made a significant contribution to the birth of the new Enlightenment cosmopolitan humanism where primitive man, identical everywhere by nature, but having become different through history, made himself 'the rule of the universe'.[9] Vico thus was competing on an equal basis with the greatest European philosophers who in precisely those years were dealing with analogous questions but with different answers.[10]

New science: principles of the new science concerning the common nature of nations of 1744 was a work in which, amongst many other themes, the universal and eternal values of the 'good' and the 'just' amongst peoples were reconsidered, according to Goethe, in the light of 'history and life'. It immediately fascinated those Enlightenment Neapolitans who were committed to giving solid foundations to the language of the rights of man. And it could not have been otherwise, given the urgency of the problem. This came about because this work outlined a science that was considered genuinely 'new' in that it no longer dealt only with the world of nature, the great machinery of the universe, as in the case of Galileo, Descartes, Newton or the thinkers who had revived the natural law tradition, who had been fascinated by the successes of the Scientific Revolution. For the first time, it dealt explicitly with the historical world, the reality constructed by the hands of man, which thus expressed his will and freedom in the course of time: and it did so using a rigorous method of enquiry that was able to lead to important discoveries and principally also to lead to the crucial rediscovery of 'a morality and thence a politics common to all the nations, and on this he bases a jurisprudence of the human race'.[11] In short, this was a highly ambitious attempt to create a genuine science of the historical world of men in the Aristotelian sense of the term 'science' (*scientia debet esse de universalibus et aeternis*) and of this there could now no longer be any doubts.[12]

9. The phrase is Vico's own, quoted and commented on by Garin, *Dal Rinascimento all'Illuminismo*, p.213.
10. This perspective is particularly evident in research from the Anglo-Saxon world. See Israel, *Radical Enlightenment*, p.664ff.; Robertson, *The Case for the Enlightenment*, p.225ff.
11. *The Autobiography of Giambattista Vico*, ed. Max Harold Fisch, translated by Max Harold Fisch and Thomas Goddard Bergin (Ithaca, NY, 1944), p.168.
12. See the important article by Paolo Rossi, 'Che tipo di scienza è la scienza nuova di Vico?', *Rivista di storia della filosofia* 59:2 (2004), p.409-33. Much more sceptical about Vico's originality in reaching new forms of historical epistemology is

This interpretation is confirmed by the very structure of the work, with its 'axioms', its 'postulates' and 'definitions', and its investigation and determining of the 'principles' common to the whole of humanity.[13] This is to be proven *more geometrico*, according to the classic Euclidean geometric-deductive method, adopted by the theorists of modern natural law of the seventeenth century, from Spinoza to Pufendorf, Cumberland, Wolff, to whom we have dedicated many of the foregoing pages. But Vico went far beyond the epistemological model that was the dominant one at the time, completely abstract and rationalistic, which seemed to him, if applied on its own, absolutely inadequate for catching the complexity of human reality in its processes of cognition, ignoring the empirical dimension, and the modifications introduced by the passing of time. Therefore he coupled it with Bacon's experimental method through a decisive and original redefinition of the relationship between philosophy and philology, taking the latter away from the traditional field of literature, from the study of 'writers' to the study of the 'authors of nations'. Bringing together philosophy and philology, the true and the certain, Vico thought it was possible for truth to be certified and for the certain to come true. From a mere collection of facts, a chronicle of events, the knowledge of history became in this way a new, potent *scienza*, thanks to an epistemological process conducted both *a priori* and *a posteriori*, with both an experimental method and a geometric-deductive method, formulating at the outset 'axioms' and 'postulates' thought out philosophically in the mind, and ascertaining later, *a posteriori*, their philological truthfulness in a concrete analysis of the events of peoples.[14] As Vico proudly noted in his 1744 edition of *La scienza nuova*:

> Our Science therefore comes to describe at the same time an ideal eternal history traversed in time by the history of every nation in its rise, development, maturity, decline, and fall. Indeed, we make bold to affirm that he who meditates this Science narrates to himself this ideal eternal history so far as he himself makes it for himself by that proof 'it had, has, and will have to be'. For the first indubitable

---

Arnaldo Momigliano, in the chapter entitled 'Due libri inglesi su Vico', in *Sui fondamenti della storia antica*, p.232ff.

13. Cf. *The New science of Giambattista Vico*, unabridged translation of the 3rd edn (1744) with the addition of 'Practice of the new science', translated by Thomas Goddard Bergin and Max Harold Fisch (Ithaca, NY, and London, 1984), §119 (subsequent paragraph references to this work are given within the text).
14. See Rossi, 'Che tipo di scienza', p.415ff.

> principle posited above is that this world of nations has certainly been made by men, and its guise must therefore be found within the modifications of our own human mind. And history cannot be more certain than when he who creates the things also narrates them. (§349)

Vico goes on to state that

> as geometry, when it constructs the world of quantity out of its elements, or contemplates that world, is creating it for itself, just so does our Science [create for itself the world of nations], but with a reality greater by just so much as the institutions having to do with human affairs are more real than points, lines, surfaces, and figures are.

And this superior cognitive truth or 'reality', continually claimed by him against the sceptics as regards not only the conventional dimension of geometry, but more in general as regards the natural sciences, was in the final analysis guaranteed by the fact that man could know history, as he was its artificer, resorting to the principle of the identity of *verum* and *factum*, and above all, by relaunching into the field of philosophy the ancient criterion of truth which Cicero held dear, of the *consensus gentium*: 'Uniform ideas originating among entire peoples unknown to each other must have a common ground of truth' (§144).[15] And again: there are things on which 'all men agree and always have agreed' (§332) and this agreement holds in 'all nations, barbarous as well as civilised, though separately founded because remote from each other in time and space' (§333). What emerged from this was a cognitive process that was considered capable of making great discoveries, a process that was fruitful and ambitious, which

15. On the *consensus gentium* in Vico, see Ajello, *Arcana juris*, p.130ff. Paradoxically, Vico's claim to have discovered a form of knowledge that was superior to the natural sciences stemmed initially from his substantial unwillingness to engage with the epistemological debate on Isaac Newton's *Principia mathematica* that raged in Naples and in the whole of Europe; or better still it stemmed from his sympathy towards that incredible scientific, Platonic counter-revolution of Paolo Mattia Doria, who liked to reflect on Galileo's laws of motion in anachronistic terms of 'mechanical geometry', ignoring modern analytical geometry, infinitesimal calculus, the concepts of time, speed, acceleration, not to mention the nascent debate on the philosophical foundations of the calculus of probability, all of which finally placed on an original plane the relationship between factual truth and the truth of reason. For the debate in Naples on the laws of motion and Newtonism, see Ferrone, *Intellectual roots*, p.49ff.

oscillated between two points of view which today we would define as historicist and structuralist, sensitive to both the diachronic and synchronic dimensions, to the moments of stability and change in the study of man and of nations.

In the first edition of 1725 this new science was successfully applied first and foremost to the consideration of the vexed question of natural law, and its multiple interpretations in the seventeenth century. This is clearly announced in the full title: *The Principles of a new science of the nature of nations through which the principles of a new system of the natural law of the gentes are discovered.*[16] It came at the end of a long period of consideration by Vico of the themes of universal law and the ultimate foundations of justice. He had carried this out more than anything in order to counteract the continental offensive of the modern followers of Carneades, the sceptics and Pyrrhonists, with the declared aim of 'establishing the fact that there existed a true and eternal law that was accepted by everyone always and everywhere', in such a way as 'to remove from us our miserable whim to cast doubt on justice'.[17]

That 'other system' that was polemically called into question was the one drawn up with great success in Protestant Europe by Grotius, Selden and Pufendorf, who were accused of a 'lack of a critical method applicable to the founders of the nations', which caused them to fail to distinguish 'the natural law of the nations, which was coeval with their customs, from the natural law of the philosophers, which the latter grasped by force of reasoning'.[18]

The three authors had privileged only the geometric-deductive method and abstract philosophical reasoning, ignoring the historical and philological study of the origins of natural right from the dawn of the primitive world, as well as its later developments. Thus they did not realise how religions, languages, customs, institutions and the laws established over time by peoples were a decisive factor for understanding what natural law really was. In that way they had grasped neither the totally human historicity of natural law, nor the providential design that underlay it, nor, finally, the crucial relationship that existed between the discovery of the principles of an ideal, eternal

16. See Giambattista Vico, *The First new science*, ed. and translated by Leon Pompa (Cambridge, 2002).
17. Translated from *De uno universi iuris principio et fine uno*, in Vico, *Opere giuridiche: il diritto universale*, ed. Paolo Cristofolini, with an introduction by Nicola Badaloni (Florence, 1974), p.30.
18. Vico, *Autobiography*, p.172.

law and the concrete philological realisation of these principles in history. But more than anything else the Protestant theoreticians had not understood how crucial for the very definition of natural law was the succession over time

> of three kinds of laws corresponding to the three ages and languages of the Egyptians. The first law was divine, under the government of the true God among the Hebrews and of various false gods among the gentiles. The second was heroic, or peculiar to the heroes who stood midway between gods and men. The third was human, or peculiar to human nature as fully developed and recognized as alike in all men. Not until this last law already holds sway is it possible for philosophers to arise among the nations and perfect it by reasoning from the maxims of an eternal justice. (*idem.*)

Despite the fact that he had been defined respectfully and with sincere admiration as the *iurisconsultus generis humani*, Grotius, on whom Vico and the majority of those involved in Neapolitan juridical and philosophical culture had long meditated, was denounced as the main person responsible for the initial underestimation of the paradigmatic value of Roman law for understanding the real meaning of natural law.[19] This was a very serious error, which had driven all the Protestant scholars off course. Grotius had ignored the history of *ius* over the centuries, which had been investigated in Naples itself by Gianvincenzo Gravina, and its organic involvement with the universal values of an ideal, eternal law valid for all nations of the Empire.[20]

19. On the presence of Grotius in Naples, see Nicola Badaloni's introduction to Giambattista Vico, *Opere giuridiche*, p.5ff. More problematic is the view of Guido Fassò, *Vico e Grozio* (Naples, 1971).
20. Gravina, an important scholar destined to become famous throughout Europe, had the merit of having set in train a completely new tradition of political studies profoundly characterised by historical and more generally philosophical analysis of the links between politics and law. The fame and the European diffusion of his *Originum iuris civilis libri tres* (1701-1708) had quickly imposed everywhere, in the course of the eighteenth century, the necessity of finally reconstructing, on a historical and philological basis, the gradual formation of Roman law, and of critically assessing the political and philosophical components that were implicit in the dramatic shift from the Roman republic to the principate. In his *De romano imperio* and especially his *De imperio et iurisdictione*, like the distinguished jurist and historian of law that he was, Gravina had drawn precisely from the model of the Roman republic the reasons for delineating the salient features of an original juridical order able to limit in the future the power of emperors. This was, of course, very different from the use of that model that Machiavelli

In this way, he had definitely excluded himself from access to a new science of man like the one invented by Vico: a science that, as the latter explicitly pointed out, 'is meditated on the basis of the Roman jurisconsults' idea of the natural law of gentes'.[21]

The centrality of the clash with Grotius and more generally with the studies on natural law that had appeared in Europe in the course of the seventeenth century, although highlighted by many authoritative scholars, has nevertheless been more and more underplayed in recent research. Apart from concentrating their attention particularly on the final 1744 edition of the *Scienza nuova*, scholars have perhaps taken too seriously (forgetting his economic difficulties and frustrations) Vico's bold promotion of himself, in the first edition of 1725, as the champion of a Catholic natural law that was capable of supplying, solely and for the first time in Italy, a complex, different answer that was more sensitive to the rationale of religious orthodoxy against the ambiguities and oscillations that were present in the works of Protestant thinkers.[22]

---

had made famous in his *Discourses on the first decade of Titus Livius*. The great Florentine thinker had gone back to the reconstruction of Livy to investigate in paradigmatic terms the moral nature of civic virtues and the risks of corruption in republics, the public spirit, religious practices and convictions, the art of war, the very destiny of republics in the earthly history of humanity. Gravina, by contrast, concentrated his entire attention on law, institutions, legislation and the political constitution of the Roman republic and later the empire. His learned and sophisticated historical research provided a strong basis for philosophical enquiries into the pact-based nature of political communities in defining rights and duties of citizens and in limiting public powers, questions that would later concern the best European jurists and in particular Montesquieu in his *Esprit des lois*. Drawing a distinction between the *merum imperium* of the emperor and the *iurisdictio* of the magistrates, and insisting on the political and constitutional function of legislation, this Calabrian jurist had actually launched also in Italy the discourse on the sharing and balance of power, and on the priority of the juridical order as a constitutional guarantee to respect that principle of legality and legitimacy that had profoundly animated the history of the Roman republic. For these topics in Gravina see Marcello Capurso, *Accentramento e costituzionalismo: il pensiero italiano del primo Settecento di fronte al problema dell'organizzazione dello Stato* (Naples, 1959); Carlo Ghisalberti, *Gravina giurista e storico* (Milan, 1962).

21. Cf. the heading of book I, chapter 4 in *The First new science*, p.13. On the importance of Roman history for Vico, see Santo Mazzarino, *Vico, l'annalistica e il diritto* (Naples, 1971).

22. Vico wrote about this in his *Autobiography*, p.173: 'By this work, to the glory of the Catholic religion, the principles of all gentile wisdom human and divine have been discovered in this our age and in the bosom of the true Church, and Vico has thereby procured for our Italy the advantage of not envying Protestant

Hence the importance attached to his denunciation of rationalist Socinianism against Grotius, to his accusations against Pufendorf that he paid too little attention to the role of providence, and above all against Bayle for having dared to think that atheist nations could have existed in history. Some have even thought that Vico might have written the *Scienza nuova* just to prove Bayle wrong, but actually he only devotes a few lines to him here and there. As we read at the start of book I, chapter 1 of the 1725 *New science*: 'The natural law of the nations was certainly born with the common customs of the nations. Furthermore, there has never been a nation of atheists in the world because all nations began in some single religion.'[23]

In actual fact Vico's 'religion' was nothing other than the natural and universal religion common to all primitive peoples, the result of the fear and terror felt by the first beings, like Lucretian beasts in their feral wanderings, and fruit also of the desire hidden in the heart of all men to live eternally.[24] Vico paid great attention to the dawn of humanity, to the history of man's distant origins in that feral world where passions, violence, imagination ruled, uncontrolled by reason, as he meditated on the characteristics of human nature and how these changed over time through the historic triadic movement through the animal, heroic and human cycles. And it was this area of his thought that made him a significant protagonist in our history of the rights of man and more broadly in the European debate on natural law.[25]

Holland, England or Germany their three princes of this science', i.e. Grotius, Selden and Pufendorf.

23. *The First new science*, p.9. On his quotations from Bayle see Paolo Rossi, 'Chi sono i contemporanei di Vico?', *Rivista di filosofia* 72:1 (1981), p.51-82 (62), arguing against Gianfranco Cantelli, *Vico e Bayle: premesse per un confronto* (Naples, 1971).

24. On Vico's religion, see the comments by Eugenio Garin to the famous passage in which Vico describes how 'when at last the sky fearfully rolled with thunder and flashed with lightning' over the great forest of the earth, the few primitive giants 'were frightened and astonished by the great effect whose cause they did not know, and raised their eyes and became aware of the sky [...] they pictured the sky to themselves as a great animated body, which in that aspect they called Jove' (*The New science of Giambattista Vico*, §377; cf. Garin, *History of Italian philosophy*, ed. and translated by Giorgio A. Pinton, 2 vols, Amsterdam and New York, 2008, vol.1, p.706).

25. I am not aware of any significant research on Vico and natural rights, whereas, on the question of natural law, see the chapter on Vico in Hochstrasser, *Natural law theories*, p.8ff. On this topic it is still worth reading Gioele Solari, *La scuola del diritto naturale nelle dottrine etico-giuridiche dei secoli XVII e XVIII* (Turin, 1904), p.169ff.

Right from his very first works on universal law, traditionally the opposite of positive law, while he meditated on what is eternally right and what is right by nature, and on what really natural law should mean, Vico had distanced himself from his predecessors, accusing them of having set up philosophical systems that were totally detached from reality, based solely on the principles of utility or sociability. These systems were unable to take in the fact that historical and positive law was nothing other than the concrete realisation of universal law in time. What was 'right' was a genre, an abstraction, an idea, and as such always had to be distinguished from what was 'just', which instead was the idea of what was right translated into fact, into real history. Hence his extraordinary attention to the relationship between *aequitas civilis* and *aequitas naturalis*, his investigation into the profound motives that drove man to obey or to feel strongly within his mind the sense of injustice.[26] That way he finally explained the links between truth (reason) and certainty (authority).

Vico carried this out through his fascinating reconstruction of the 'origin and progress of authority', starting with primitive man who was all senses, violence and imagination, living in a context of individual isolation which meant that 'man *est in solitudine summus* [is supreme in solitude] and by *iure superiori* [superior right] can kill anyone who commits violence', until the final incarnation of authority in reason as displayed by civilised man. In doing this Vico never placed himself within the normal seventeenth-century rationalistic paradigm of contractualism, of the state of nature, of the verification of the consensus and the legitimacy of the sovereign's power. Instead he preferred to elaborate an original definition of '*ius naturale immutabile*', as the perennial aspiration of man in society towards an equal distribution of what is useful amongst all, the *aequum bonum*. He placed in the forefront of the moral and political debate that fundamental equality principle, 'the eternal cause of the just', that had fomented so many conflicts in the past, amongst which was the momentous struggle between the patricians and the plebs, and which was destined to leave a deep mark also on eighteenth-century political debates in every corner of Europe.[27]

26. On the centrality of the concept of *aequitas* in Vico, see Giuseppe Giarrizzo, '*Aequitas* e *Prudentia*; storia di un topos vichiano', in his *Vico, la politica e la storia* (Naples, 1981), p.143ff.
27. Cf. Giambattista Vico, 'Synopsis of universal law', translated by Donald Phillip Verene, in *Giambattista Vico: keys to the 'New science'*, ed. Thora Ilin Bayer and

Writing in the third person in his 'Synopsis of universal law' of 1720, Vico stated:

> Hence he demonstrates that due to their nature there exists among men a truly just society – that is, *aequum bonum*, of equal utility – that consists of *ius naturale immutabile* [immutable natural law]; everyone everywhere concurs about such a society. And that the Skeptics – Epicurus, Machiavelli, Hobbes, Spinoza, Bayle, and others – claim man to be sociable because of utility, brought to it through need or fear, because they were not aware that the causes of things are other than the occasions of them; utilities may themselves change, but the equanimity of them is eternal; and the temporal not being the cause of the eternal, nor the corporeal able to produce the abstract, utility is the occasion through which the idea of equality, which is the eternal cause of the just, is awakened in the mind of man. (p.19-20)

Vico completed his ambitious redefinition of *ius naturale immutabile* by breaking it down into a *ius naturale prius* and a *ius naturale posterius.* The former concerned the individual, his natural right to liberty, to dominion over things and to 'tutelage', meant to ensure self-protection and the exercise of one's will. The latter put centre stage the social bodies to which was extended the binding principle of conservation. The subsequent natural law in its gradual development over time was 'dependent on an eternal reason, which provides just measure to liberty, dominion, and tutelage, and provides them with the eternal form of the just'.[28] The circle of the two natural laws which interacted permanently with and completed each other, bringing about the epistemological mechanism of the ascertaining of truth and the making true of what was certain, entirely contained the course of history, passions, imagination, the social use of language and reason. What took shape and meaning – in a sort of hermeneutic circle – was the natural law of nations in its gradual evolution from the feral, violent stage to the

Donald Phillip Verene (Ithaca, NY, 2009), p.17-38 (20-21). In the 1725 edition of the *New science* the whole of the first part and especially the entirety of book II were dedicated to the historical development of the natural law of peoples (or *gentes*), which was understood as 'an eternal law that proceeds through time' (*The First new science*, p.107). These are extraordinary passages in the context of this phase of 'heroic law', and were applied in this sense to the class struggle between plebs and patricians for the possession of land and for the equality of civil rights. This aspect of his thought has led to a whole Marxist interpretation of Vico, particularly in the works of Nicola Badaloni.

28. Vico, 'Synopsis', p.19 and 20.

heroic phase of dominion and oligarchic hierarchies up until the birth of civil law and the legal recognition of the equality of natural rights. Through the dualism of the two laws, which opened the road to the consideration of the link between reason and authority, between the true and the certain, as well as the definitive formulation of the epistemological principle of *verum ipsum factum*, which was later applied in the *New science*, Vico also provided a decisive contribution, one that has been undervalued for too long, to the theoretical foundation of the modern language of the natural rights of man in Italian Enlightenment culture.[29]

In some extraordinary passages of the *De universi iuris uno principio et fine uno*, dealing with voluntary law and the 'laws born with the aim of ordering human operations in the midst of the corruption of human nature' (chapter CCXIX: *iura pro humanae vitae corruptae ordine nata*), Vico clearly explained the important function of those innate primary rights in man, which made him into a being endowed with volition, desirous of knowledge, a finite power tending towards the infinite (*nosse, velle, posse finitum, quod tendat ad infinitum*). This function fulfilled itself precisely in that circular movement between prior (*prius*) and later (*posterius*) law. The natural rights to liberty, property and tutelage, conferred in their potential state and on all human beings by God in prior (*prius*) law, could reveal themselves completely and testify to their eternal truth only through later (*posterius*) law. As Vico wrote, with uncharacteristic clarity:

> Dominion, liberty, tutelage are innate to man but they arose through occasions and occurrences. Thus, as a special example, liberty existed juridically before wars came about, but once slavery was introduced when enemies were captured, the condition that was opposite to slavery came to be recognised and to obtain a distinctive name. The division of fields equally led to the recognition of the prior ownership of land, and for this reason Vico insists that this division made fields 'distinct' but did not institute them. Similarly tutelage, the protection of oneself, exists potentially in man right from birth; the first signs of it are shown from childhood and it manifests itself gradually with greater force, following the

29. See Guido Fassò, 'Law and the historical origin of the *New science*', in *Giambattista Vico's science of humanity*, ed. Giorgio Tagliacozzo and Donald Phillip Verene (Baltimore, MD, and London, 1976), p.3-14 (Italian version: 'Il problema del diritto e l'origine storica della *Scienza nuova* di G. Vico', *Atti della Accademia Pontaniana* 26, 1977, p.139-48).

development of the senses and the authority they take on as they gradually become better trained.[30]

In short, Vico was right in claiming that he had been the first person in Italy to have treated, and with great originality, the question of natural law, the subject that seemed to have become by then the exclusive prerogative of the Protestant scholars of Northern Europe. His jumbled but nevertheless ingenious research into 'eternal justice' – in a mixture of political realism, implicit in the finite nature of the human being, and the hankering after eternal certainties – had led not only to the discovery of a *New science* or a new way of reflecting on the world of history, but also, and in particular, to his works on universal law which had finally assigned a place of absolute prominence to natural rights in the history of man, seeing them as an essential part of the 'eternal character of every natural right': 'Here man sees, or rather very clearly discerns the distinctive eternal character of every natural right, because those primitive rights of nature, which form the original natural law, receive from what are called consequent rights, which conform with nature, in other words from posterior natural law, that indelible character of immutability that legitimises and authorises them.'[31]

After Vico the language of natural rights became common currency in Neapolitan intellectual circles, where the follower of Newton and Locke, Celestino Galiani, consecrated as head chaplain, in other words the main person responsible for cultural life in the Kingdom of Naples, had for some time now committed himself personally to

30. Translated from Giambattista Vico, *De universi iuris uno principio et fine uno*, in Vico, *Opere giuridiche*, p.91. In chapter LXXV, entitled 'The previous and later natural law of the interpreters is one and the same thing as the Stoics' "first principles of nature" and "consequences of nature"', Vico carried out his umpteenth creative, anachronistic distortion of meaning, attributing to the Stoic concept of *prima naturae* the idea of the potential presence of the natural rights of man already from birth, as is easily confirmed by the overall sense of the pages that follow. In actual fact, the real source was probably Gianvincenzo Gravina and his reflections on the mind–body dualism, which he examined through the selfish individualism of natural man studied by Lucretius and Cicero (*De finibus*, III, V, 19; VI, 20-21), as was acutely noted in Fabrizio Lomonaco's introduction to his edition of Gianvincenzo Gravina, *Originum iuris civilis libri tres* (Naples, n.n., 1713), with a 'Presentazione' by Fulvio Tessitore, 2 vols (Naples, 2004), p.xxiv. On the dualism between prior and posterior law and on Vico's position in his polemic with Grotius for having denied its existence, Nicola Badaloni has written pages that are still useful, in his introduction to Vico, *Opere giuridiche*, p.xxxvi ff.
31. See Vico, *De universi iuris uno principio et fine uno*, in *Opere giuridiche*, p.98.

promoting the study of a new 'moral science'.[32] Amongst those who listened to Vico's last lectures at the university, where he reflected both on the *New science* and on his texts on universal law, there was in particular Antonio Genovesi, who drew great profit from his long-distance comparison with Barbeyrac, Locke, Wolff, Thomasius, Hume, Montesquieu, Burlamaqui, Rousseau, Helvétius and many others.[33] In 1745 Galiani had had him appointed professor of ethics in the public university, hoping for great things. And Genovesi went immediately to work in order to illustrate to the students 'the principles of the just and the unjust', dealing in his lectures with what was actually an 'outline of ethics which', according to what we are told by his pupil and biographer, Giuseppe Maria Galanti, 'turned out to be totally new in Naples'. Nor could it have been otherwise seeing that those lectures, apart from informing students of the best continental work on the topic, were aimed at studying for the first time, alongside the traditional duties, 'the science of rights, in other words the moral faculty to use what belongs to us either by nature or by legitimate concession', and binding together indissolubly – in line with what was happening in the rest of Europe, after Locke, Wolff and Burlamaqui – the science of morality and the pursuit of happiness. 'The aim of this science' – the young professor of ethics explained in his overcrowded lectures – 'is to shape man for happiness, thus its natural object is to let us understand what this man is and what are the rules and the ways through which he can seek and obtain happiness.'[34]

Genovesi was a priest, and at the time was convinced that moral and social regeneration could not be separated in any way from religious renewal and that the moral of the Gospels was the authentic founding cornerstone of Christianity. In this context and those same years

32. In the 1720s Galiani also wrote an unpublished *Scienza morale*: see Ferrone, *Intellectual roots*, p.145ff. Of great interest for the development of the debates on moral science in Naples is the book by Koen Stapelbroek, *Love, self-deceit, and money: commerce and morality in the early Neapolitan Enlightenment* (Toronto, 2008).

33. On the relationship between Vico and Genovesi cf. Paola Zambelli, *La formazione filosofica di Antonio Genovesi* (Naples, 1972), p.239ff.; Giuseppe Galasso, 'Il pensiero religioso di Antonio Genovesi', *Rivista storica italiana* 87 (1970), p.800-23 (822-23).

34. See what is said in [Giuseppe Maria Galanti], *Elogio storico del signor abate Antonio Genovesi* (Naples, n.n., 1772; anastatic edition, Naples, 1977), p.46. In his *Lezioni di etica*, which would later be included in a fourth volume, entitled *Principia legis naturalis*, added to his work *Elementa metaphysicae* (4 vols, Naples, Benedetto Gessari, 1756), Genovesi pointed to Grotius as the father of natural law, which had then been relaunched by Locke and Vico (p.63).

when he undertook amongst other things to translate his beloved John Locke's *The Reasonableness of Christianity*, he had also worked intensely on a major work of theology (*Omnigenae theologiae elementa historico-critico-dogmatica*) in which he discussed the history of Christianity and of the Church, Luther, Calvin, the views of the libertines and deists, of Spinoza, and of freethinkers such as Toland and Collins. In very dense pages he refuted atheism and materialism with rigour and passion, but he also called for tolerance and dialogue, and respect for religious liberty. As the great Lessing in *Nathan the Wise*, Genovesi too was convinced that the best religion was that which made men better and 'the first character of religion is to be useful to the human race', just as 'the first principle of theology is that the true faith must not destroy right reason': it must always 'unite and not divide men'.[35]

With such ideas as these, it is no wonder that he immediately became the object of acute attention by the Inquisition, and by furious clerics and prelates who competed with each other to accuse him of a long list of heresies, and evil and hostile intentions towards the Church. Even before it appeared, the work stirred up such a hornet's nest that it forced Genovesi to immediate surrender. After that 'bitter and cruel persecution,' wrote Galanti, 'he became disgusted with theology; he took back his manuscripts and made a firm resolve not to think any more about such turbulent studies: from now on more interesting subjects occupied his talents.'[36]

Nevertheless, if Italian Enlightenment culture lost a potential great religious reformer, it acquired an even greater one in the moral and economic fields. Genovesi was a reformer and scholar destined to leave his mark on entire generations of southern Italy, and become famous, generating approval in every corner of Europe through the translation of his best works.[37] In December 1754, with the help of

35. See [Galanti], *Elogio storico*, p.61. The best study of these topics and on the events involving the Inquisition is still Paola Zambelli, *La formazione filosofica*, p.421ff.
36. [Galanti], *Elogio storico*, p.76ff. Genovesi always had terrible relations with the Church: just a year before his death, in 1768, he advised the king to abolish the chair of decretals in the University of Naples, maintaining that 'the decretals (according to which the pope was the sole spiritual and temporal ruler of all the earth) were the fundamental basis of the empire of priests, they disunited peoples, subverted the sovereignty of nations, broke all the bonds of society, and destroyed all civil laws' (*Elogio storico*, p.66).
37. For his translations into the most important European languages and in particular in Germany, see what still is the best account of Genovesi: Franco Venturi, 'La Napoli di Antonio Genovesi', in *Da Muratori a Beccaria*, p.636ff.

Bartolomeo Intieri, who put at his disposal money for this purpose, Genovesi became the first university professor of 'civil economy' in Italy.[38] On this topic, critics have insisted on the discontinuity that this event seems to have introduced into Genovesi's thought, and on his change, in terms of research interests, from 'a metaphysician to a merchant', which that chair seems to have drastically imposed on him. However, they unduly neglect the role of chance and personal events, which moved him, also in later years, towards decisions that were only apparently contradictory and in conflict with one another.

In reality, Genovesi remained throughout his life rigorously faithful to his Enlightenment humanism which – as has been stressed several times – had strong and ancient roots in the Italian culture of preceding centuries. Never did he distract his attention from a great, ambitious intellectual project centring on the scientific study of man as such, both as individual and in society, a holder of natural rights given expressly by God in order to pursue happiness on earth and to embody a life that was both dignified, free and responsible. Like Adam Smith and many other Enlightenment scholars working in that crucial decade of the 1760s, Genovesi too before considering himself a modern economist, proud of the presumed scientific autonomy of the new discipline, saw himself primarily as a moral philosopher seeking for the most convenient way to better the human condition. For all these founding fathers of the modern Enlightenment political economy, and as opposed to the opinion of so-called free-marketeers and positivists of later centuries, a new humanity which was finally respectful of human dignity, understood in its entirety, could only come from the preliminary renewal and the reform of ancient ethics. Genovesi explained this very well in the introduction to his *Lezioni di commercio* where he traced his personal encyclopedic tree of knowledge listing all the subjects of study and their hierarchies:

> The principal subject must be the one that the Greeks called Ethics and we call Moral Science. Because either it considers man in general and shows the nature of our natural instincts and affections; and teaches how these can be used so that they become the material of virtue, which is the sole true cause of our happiness, and this is called absolute Ethics; or it considers him as head and ruler of his family and instructs him to govern the family well and procure wealth, power

38. For the meaning of the expression 'civil economy', which was preferred to 'political economy', see Eluggero Pii, *Antonio Genovesi: dalla politica economica alla 'politica civile'* (Florence, 1984).

> and glory for it, and this is called Economics; or lastly it regards him as the head and sovereign of the people and shapes him in such a way as to govern them well, and this is called Politics.[39]

Genovesi never had any doubts about the virtuous circle that connected ethics, economics and politics in the study of man. It is thus no surprise that in the last years of his life he felt the need to write for the students of the University of Naples a work like *Della diceosina o sia della filosofia del giusto e dell'onesto*. Here he provided a synthesis of all of his most authentic ideas and became the founding father of the language of the rights of man in the Italian Enlightenment and one of the first scholars in Europe to conceive of an ethics then an economics and a law that followed on from this, entirely founded on rights and on their political practice in modern civil society.

This manual appeared in 1766 and was an immediate success that also continued into the following century.[40] In this work, the best reflections of continental culture on this subject, duly selected and eclectically combined into a logical and convincing framework, were brought to their ultimate conclusions. From Hume and Rousseau Genovesi drew his cast-iron conviction that ethics had to be placed amidst the new 'sciences of man': that ethics should be researched in the light of the history of man and of nations, examining the works of travellers, medical treatises, physiological studies, works on physics, geology and chemistry. From Locke and his empiricism he learned to value the importance of passions, and the function of pleasure and pain. Lastly, from Newton's *Principia* and from the example of the law of universal gravitation he derived his first considerations on a necessary scientific redefinition of the old Thomist concept of natural law.

Having established that the true aims of the human race were all inscribed within the need to guarantee the conservation and pursuit of individual happiness, Genovesi, using Newtonian language, identified in the two principles of 'love of self and love of the species', present in all human beings, that centripetal and centrifugal force that had to be balanced in order to bring about 'the minimum evil possible'

39. Antonio Genovesi, *Delle lezioni di commercio o sia di economia civile con elementi di commercio*, ed. Maria Luisa Perna (Naples, 2005), p.3.
40. See the introduction by Niccolò Guasti to his new edition of Antonio Genovesi, *Della diceosina o sia della filosofia del giusto e dell'onesto* (Venice and Mariano del Friuli, 2008), p.xliii ff. Henceforth references to this edition will be provided directly in the text.

and to pursue in this way 'our present happiness' (p.52). Nevertheless, the social harmony potentially present in the natural order had to be pursued by studying first the laws of nature concerning man as an individual: 'the natural proprieties of each of us'. In fact, just like Vico with his isolated beasts and prior (*prius*) natural law, and Rousseau, with his primitive people in the 'pure state of nature', the core and Enlightenment originality of Genovesi's work lay in the *Diceosina*: this was his most significant and clear departure from the classical paradigm of Catholic and Protestant natural law that stemmed from the Thomist matrix and was totally built around – as we have seen in the preceding pages – the principle of sociability, the hypothesis that primitive man was born immediately into society, and around the resulting primacy of duties in the definition of ethics.[41]

'Man', Genovesi explained, 'can be considered either alone and isolated, or as a member of a family, or as a citizen of a political body.' Considered in his isolated dimension of a 'finite and limited being', he was 'neither animal nor plant' (p.42), as in the thesis of La Mettrie and the new atheist materialists, nor a prisoner of just his own personal interests and therefore of a rigid law of utility, as Mandeville argued, forgetting the powerful feeling of pity, compassion and the natural sympathy of the subject towards the suffering of others. If anything, the original characters of his individuality had to be rethought in the context of an idea of social harmony, always present in nature, as developed in the works of English Neoplatonists such as Shaftesbury and Hume, combined with the considerations of Maupertuis and Helvétius on the possible use of the passions directed towards the collective interest, and public and private happiness.

The crucial point of the new Enlightenment science of ethics thus became the preliminary study of what is proper (*proprium*) to the individual, the characterisation of his humanity and personality, starting from the so-called properties of the subject. 'What is proper to man, is proper to the individual in other words to the person', Genovesi pointed out with conviction (he had read John Locke's *Thoughts concerning education*, where the concept of person had been particularly well thought through and connected to the individual's reasoning conscience), 'and vice versa the *proprium* of the person is

41. Genovesi uses Vico's concepts regarding the 'bestial state of man', isolated and consisting solely of senses and imagination, against those who upheld an abstract and metaphysical concept of the state of nature commonly found in the theorists of natural law in the preceding century. Cf. *Diceosina*, p.325ff.

proper to man [...] Persons are distinguished through distinct and inseparable natural properties.' Amidst these properties he indicated those natural rights of man of whose existence he had learned reading Grotius, Locke, Vico, Barbeyrac and Burlamaqui:

> Man belongs to the animal kingdom, but being endowed with an immortal mind and an intelligent and reasoning force, which is lord of itself and what belongs to it, he has received certain rights from the law of the world, rights which are proper to him, and he has been placed under certain obligations that are appropriate to such dignity of nature. These rights and obligations do not and cannot exist in other animals [...] Every property of man that he has been born with, whether of mind or body, is an essence (*ousia*), a *ius*, a *right* that is innate in him because *ousia*, *right* and *property* are in ethical terms synonymous. (p.14)

In the context of this strong and explicit characterisation of the humanity of man, with its distinct Enlightenment flavour, Genovesi explained that the function of rights was no longer just the one that had been hypothesised in the previous century by Hobbes and Spinoza, namely that of guaranteeing the preservation of life or of the liberties of the subject against the despotism of sovereigns, but it had by now taken on a new and decisive duty, that of rendering practicable that 'general right' to the pursuit of happiness which was destined to characterise the whole political culture of the European Enlightenment.[42] 'A right', he pointed out on every occasion, 'is always a faculty given to us in order to be happy' (p.15). This shook to its foundations that primacy of duties in the moral sphere that continued to persist and to condition – as we have seen in the foregoing pages – the gradual establishment of the new language of rights in Germany and Anglo-Saxon countries. 'All duties', he would instruct his Neapolitan students with pedagogical passion, 'are founded on the rights' of the subject: 'Duty stems from right and not the other way round', as was believed by Thomasius, Wolff and the Scottish heirs of Pufendorf; and again: 'Our duties are owed to those who have rights' (p.77).

42. On this topic Genovesi specified: 'this word *ius*, *gius*, *right* does not mean anything other than essence, an essential property which we have received through the way the world has been set up', inasmuch as we are reasonable beings (*Diceosina*, p.46). It must be pointed out that Genovesi was teaching such concepts from 1754, as his biographer Galanti testifies (*Elogio storico*, p.59): 'One should note that the rights with which man has been endowed by nature have no other purpose beyond his own preservation and happiness.'

In the *Diceosina* the Stoic concept of sociability, which, according to Pufendorf's teaching, was the element that characterised the humanity of man, and on which the moral science of duties could be constructed, never appears. Genovesi's idea of society, like that of Vico and Rousseau, stemmed from other presuppositions: for him society was made up in the first place of single individuals who held natural rights who over time and for multiple causes built up communities, social bodies according to an order and harmony that had to be investigated and understood. Genovesi understood well that in the eyes of all his contemporaries the cornerstone for examining the possible virtuous relationship between the Self and the Other, between individual and community, lay totally enclosed in the solution to the great eighteenth-century debate on the crucial and highly delicate concept of equality to which Vico, not surprisingly, had already dedicated much space. This was a disturbing debate that had subversive potential for the very fate of the *Ancien régime*, which had been built on the assumed natural and prescriptive character of inequality, a topic which had been noisily launched by Rousseau's paradoxes and had quickly become the nub of political argument in Enlightenment circles, in masonic lodges, in journals and in the best universities of the whole of Europe. The contribution made to the discussion by Neapolitan Enlightenment culture and by Genovesi in particular was extremely important and original. Elsewhere I have reconstructed its main features in some detail.[43] Here I restrict myself to flagging up the most significant moments and conclusions that link with the history of the rights of man.

In the *Diceosina* this question was posed with clarity, starting from the primary objectives of a new ethical science based on Enlightenment values: the security and happiness of the subject in the context of a modern civil society. To this end, Genovesi started from the consideration that in order to guarantee stability and total harmony, nature would never have tolerated the final subjugation and elimination of the human species. Hence the victorious claims of the so-called 'doctrine of the natural equality of man and of the unity of the species', which he upheld with conviction, maintaining it against the most recent propositions that stemmed from the old Aristotelian view that some men are born natural slaves.

That thesis, which outraged the Neapolitan philosopher, cloaked in new scientific garb, was now legitimising in European public

43. Cf. Ferrone, *Politics of Enlightenment*, p.46ff.

opinion the enormous, horrific slave trade. Like Rousseau, Genovesi maintained that all men were born free and equal and that only 'the wickedness of man's brain made them slaves'. He had always explained to his university students that savage peoples had never known slavery: 'Slavery belongs to barbarous and semi-civilised peoples'; it debased human nature, 'forcing men halfway into the condition of animals'; it was also an economic failure since in the end it was not 'in the interests of the human race'; and lastly, the spread of slavery would certainly unleash a legitimate and bloody revolt by those who had to endure it: 'The *ius* to defence is inseparable from our rights!'[44]

Of course the debate on equality in intellectual circles and Neapolitan and European masonic lodges devoted much attention to the subtle difference, already envisaged by the ancients and in Aristotle's *Nicomachean ethics*, between an arithmetical conception of equality (to everyone the same, on the basis of the principle of identity), which always had to be rejected, and an equality of so-called esteem (equality, a fair parity between different people), which had to be supported on all possible occasions. In previous centuries people had long debated the theme of equality in the state of nature without however calling into doubt at any time the legitimacy and natural acceptance of hierarchies in subsequent stages of human evolution and in particular in the contemporary social order of the *Ancien régime*. But halfway through the eighteenth century the question resurfaced in forms that were radically different from those of the past and that were destined to condition our own political thought even today.

Genovesi was well aware of this when he commented on Buffon's theses in his *Histoire naturelle de l'homme* on the different species of men, stigmatising the ambiguous use that was made of it in order to relaunch the theme of the inequality of all human beings, as Buffon confused physical differences with moral ones and proclaimed that 'the equality of men is a chimera in physics and could not be true in ethics' (p.44). On the contrary it was precisely this last link that had to be courageously reconsidered and rejected once and for all. If indeed there were no doubts that men appeared individually and physically different, did it maybe follow then that it was impossible to have the so-called 'equality of rights in general, in other words the faculty of being, of pursuing happiness'? How was it possible to deny – Genovesi

44. The topic of slavery is treated by Genovesi at several points in the *Diceosina*. See the valuable analytical index prepared by Niccolò Guasti for his edition, from which the above quotations come.

asked his students – that the overall structure of the body, arms, legs, was identical for the whole species, that there was the same capacity to suffer and feel joy, that the deep and therefore moral humanity of man was similar everywhere? That humanity was guaranteed not only by the existence of rights, but precisely by their equality, by the ethical postulate of 'the moral equality' of all members of the species. The real cultural and political revolution of the Enlightenment lay here before even the recognition of man's autonomy.

In short, acknowledging man's physical difference should not prevent us from bringing to the fore a new universal and cosmopolitan morality, engraved for all time in the hearts and consciences of all, in order to procure the security and happiness of the species, which was founded ultimately on the 'equality of the rights innate in all men'. That bold and reasoned recognition radically altered the history of ethics in the West, opening the way to a general law that was completely unheard of in the regulation of human behaviour: 'The general law which the just and honest man wants to cling to should only be one, simple law, naturally felt by all, namely *Observe the rights of all men*, and if you have violated them, study how to put them back on their first footing' (p.50). Unlike Rousseau, Genovesi – who had behind him Vico's acute historical-philosophical reflections on the natural law *prius* and *posterius* and on the concept of the *aequum bonum* – did not entrust the social contract, the general will or a political pact with the creation of moral equality in order to legitimise the equal exercise of rights. This came before any convention, it was a pre-political fact: it derived naturally from that deep humanity of man which was consecrated by his being the owner of original rights whose 'truth' had been certified in Vico's terms by universal history, by natural law *posterius*.[45]

The proud awareness of belonging to a great civilisation that had been asking itself these burning questions for some time now, and which for that reason felt it was now able to come to its own conclusions, appears clearly also from the notes that Genovesi added to the first Italian edition of Montesquieu's masterpiece, *L'Esprit des lois*. Still using Vico's *Scienza nuova* as his starting point, Genovesi noted the French writer's lack of understanding of the importance of historical linguistics, of the 'magic of words', of the necessity to rethink

45. A clear example of the use of Vico's theories by Genovesi is found in section 14 of the *Diceosina* (p.82) where he affirms that 'in the case of a conflict, a later right (*diritto posteriore*) in the order of nature is not a right relative to the prior right (*anteriore*).'

in modern terms the intrinsic meaning of the political language of the ancients. As he wrote around 1757:

> I would have liked our author to have defined a bit more precisely, something he has not done before, what he means by 'government'; secondly what we are to understand by the word 'virtue'; third what the word 'honour' means; fourth, what this word 'fatherland' means. These are very complex ideas, nor does he always use them in the same sense. Hence there are often some conclusions that are self-contradictory.[46]

Genovesi directed his strongest attacks on the use of the word 'virtue', which seemed to have become ungraspable. While the old natural law bound moral virtue to duties, Montesquieu had made it the fundamental political principle of republican government, thus excluding it from a monarchical regime, linking it instead to the ancients' love of the fatherland and respect for the *res publica*. This decision had, however, particularly serious consequences inasmuch as it seemed to preclude its political practice in all the governments of contemporary Europe, which were largely oriented towards the monarchical system: in fact it eliminated the universalist moral component, its possible use in the construction (that was becoming ever more necessary) of a modern republican language founded this time on the respect for the rights of men before being based on popular participation and on public interest. Like other Enlightenment supporters of a return to the 'republican spirit' of the eighteenth century, the author of the *Diceosina*, who wanted a new republicanism, one based this time on the recognition of the equality of rights, could not accept Montesquieu's concept in any way:

> This word 'virtue' is highly ambiguous. It can mean Christian humility; it can signify a great love for civil liberty; I call virtue the mind that is not prepared to invade or violate anyone's rights. This virtue is necessary in every state, in those who govern: without it the government dissolves natural society, without which there is no civil society.[47]

46. Cf. *Spirito delle leggi del signore di Montesquieu con le note dell'abate Antonio Genovesi*, 4 vols (Naples, Domenico Terres, 1777), vol.1, p.81. The notes were written around 1757. On this subject see the acute considerations made by Trampus, *Storia del costituzionalismo italiano*, p.74ff.
47. These are Genovesi's words in his notes on Montesquieu's *Spirito delle leggi*, vol.1, p.51.

With these dry and peremptory statements in favour of a new ethics of rights capable of involving every aspect of human reality, including therefore also the legitimacy of the government, Genovesi made his own extraordinary personal contribution to the birth of the modern language of the rights of man as an essential factor in the creation of a modern civil society. And the necessity – reiterated several times – of reformulating with new words ancient concepts and problems becomes even more obvious in all those pages in his manual dedicated to justice, and to its profound link with the new ethics, the economy and the politics of the Enlightenment reformers. The very choice of the manual's title, *Diceosina* (a neologism deriving from Greek *díkaios* meaning 'just' and *dikaiosýne* meaning 'justice': 'the practice of justice, rectitude'), fully revealed Genovesi's plan to redefine ethical thought from its very foundations, embracing every aspect: 'In every country', he wrote, 'where it is believed that men do not all belong to the same species, but some are divine men, others are animal men, others just men, others half-men, only injustice can reign' (p.146). The idea of justice had nothing to do with the might and cunning of the powerful ('might is not a norm for the just'), or with the principle of utility and social interest, as Beccaria theorised in his little book, *On crimes and punishments*.[48] Instead it was based on respect for rights, both the so-called 'innate' natural rights and those acquired through a contract: it was only in this way that the ancient conception of justice in Ulpian could be reborn to new life, reformulated in the eighteenth-century language of rights. To each his own rights! 'The idea of justice has only ever been that of equality of actions and rights [...] There is no justice where there are no rights which are the measure of justice.' Its 'first foundations' were 'all men's similarity in nature and thus the equality of the innate rights of all men'.[49]

48. See Beccaria, *On crimes and punishments*, p.20-21: 'Observe, that by *justice* I understand nothing more than that bond, which is necessary to keep the interest of individuals united; without which, men would return to their original state of barbarity.' On the points of convergence and divergence between Genovesi and Beccaria, see Anna Maria Rao, '*Delle virtù e de' premi*: la fortuna di Beccaria nel Regno di Napoli', in *Cesare Beccaria tra Milano e l'Europa*, ed. S. Romagnoli and G. D. Pisapia, p.534-86.

49. Genovesi defined his thinking thus: 'The word *justice*, *rightness*, *equity*, *equality* is a word of a relationship of fitness between the measure and what is measured [...] The Latins defined *justice* as the constant will to give to each his *ius*. The sense of this definition is deep and marvellous. In the whole of ethics one usually distinguishes three elements: *ius*, *justice* and *law*. *Ius* is the norm of *justice*. *Law*

Once more that principle of equality, now defined in universal, cosmopolitan terms of equality of natural rights, became the new point of reference for reflection in all fields. It was applied in evaluating the possible conflict between natural rights in an ethical or juridical context or for reflecting on the modalities of the right form of political action. For instance, despite his admiration for Beccaria, for his courageous fight against torture and in favour of the separation of crime and sin, Genovesi reached different conclusions on the lawfulness of the death penalty in that he felt that – following the logic of rights – whoever attacked 'unjustly the right of another, was immediately through the law of nature deprived of another right' (p.84). Then, in the case of suicide, although defending the right to life over the right to live it with dignity, he conceded that 'the greatest of rights is our right not be unhappy' (p.115). And one could list many other examples of this kind which demonstrate his commitment to take on all the most burning ethical issues in the light of this new language.

The fact is that in the *Diceosina* the question of the equality of rights really was its beating heart, the unmoved mover, Aristotle would have said, of Genovesi's thought: it was a potential picklock in both moral and political terms, extremely subversive of the unjust, hierarchical logic of the *Ancien régime*. Moreover, was it not perhaps the case that stating that the right to the pursuit of happiness was equal for everyone involved the question of how to guarantee the exercise of this right for all? In the same way – arguing against justice based on social class, which was still accepted by Montesquieu but which had already been rejected by Beccaria – equality before the law could easily be transformed into an entirely legitimate objective, and sweep away, finally, the privileged justice of priests and nobles. Along with Vico, Hobbes and Helvétius, Genovesi also thought that the striking differences between human beings and between peoples were the result of history and culture: 'the great difference between a savage and Archimedes is due not to nature but to art' (p.148). Therefore one had to proceed with the reforms of education, the economy and legislation in order to enhance progress and civilisation: in other words to move from moral reflection to political action, to seize the double nature, both moral and political, implicit in human rights. But what politics?

is the custodian and vindicator of *ius*.' This latter was instead 'all that which is proper and substantial to each of us. Thus every *property* of a man, whether it is born with him or legitimately acquired, is a *ius*' (*Diceosina*, p.147ff.). The italics in this quotation are in the original.

Certainly not the old seventeenth-century politics of Botero's Reason of State, *ex parte principis* (seen from the point of view of the ruler), or the crude realism of the great Machiavelli who – although sensitive to the republican spirit, as Rousseau openly acknowledged in the *Social contract* – knew nothing of rights or the pursuit of happiness, and who taught the separation of ethics from politics. In the Naples of that time, brought to its knees by the terrible famine of 1764, the debate on the legacy of the Florentine writer involved many leading players from Enlightenment circles in the capital. Even in 1779, at the peak of that thorny debate, Galanti wrote his *Elogio di Niccolò Machiavelli*, which would lead to the republication of the Florentine's works, and, going against his mentor Genovesi, he reaffirmed the case for so-called political realism and the clear 'distinction between politics and ethics': the former judged 'what man is in society', while the latter showed men 'how they should be'.[50] In the *Diceosina*, that way of conceiving politics was openly and polemically contested with the help of the works of Rousseau, of Helvétius and in particular of Mably's *Entretiens de Phocion sur le rapport de la morale avec la politique*. Genovesi would probably have subscribed willingly to Kant's famous phrase at the end of the century, which, as if sealing the cultural revolution in the conception of politics carried out by the Enlightenment, peremptorily stated that 'all politics must bend its knee before right.'[51]

Natural right had, in any case, always had in its genetic makeup the vivifying link between morality and politics, even if in the preceding centuries it had always been bound up with religion, which had conditioned its development up to the European wars of religion in the sixteenth and seventeenth centuries. The new eighteenth-century language of natural rights, based on the Enlightenment's science of man, and on the recognition of the autonomy of the thinking subject, with at its centre the ethical postulate of the equality of rights amongst all human beings, and enhanced by the universal right to the pursuit

50. [Giuseppe Maria Galanti], *Elogio di Machiavelli* (n.p. [Naples], n.n., 1779), p.26.
51. Immanuel Kant, 'Toward perpetual peace: a philosophical sketch', in Kant, *Toward perpetual peace and other writings on politics, peace, and history*, ed. and with an introduction by Pauline Kleingeld, translated by David L. Colclasure (New Haven, CT, 2006), p.67-110 (104). On the nature of the new political concepts developed by the Enlightenment and accused of 'hypocrisy' and of an abstract and dangerous utopian moralism, see Koselleck, *Critique and crisis*, p.147ff. For a polemical approach to this interpretation, see below the chapter on the diffusion of the rights of man in Germany.

of happiness, seemed nevertheless to have been created deliberately to exalt and relaunch in new forms that ancient link. Nobody could now doubt any longer that the rights of man were at the same time both a moral and a political fact. Genovesi was totally conscious of this when he distinguished clearly between the 'happiness of that other life [...] the subject of theology more than philosophy' and that 'perfect ethical and political happiness' (p.19), which he intended to discuss in the *Diceosina*. 'All politics and economics', he pointed out, 'that are not based on justice, virtue and honour destroy themselves' (p.174). The ethical postulate of moral equality, rights and the principle of their equality could genuinely become the indispensable linkage to put in relation to one another 'what is' and 'what ought to be', in other words politics and ethics.

As for the utilitarians – the other great aspect of Enlightenment political thought which was becoming established more and more in Northern Europe – the Neapolitan abbot would probably not have shared entirely their programme to pursue the maximum amount of happiness for the greatest number of people. He would perhaps have wanted something more, and for everyone, without any exclusions. Nor would he have accepted that political neutralisation of rights advocated by the Scottish Enlightenment thinkers that in fact confined the language of rights to the moral and juridical spheres, excluding them from the political arena, from the strictly economic discourse about production and the distribution of wealth. That organic, communitarian interpretation that always made rights duty-based, and thus dependent on the sociability principle, was in fact alien to his thought, which was substantially individualistic in its theoretical premises. The 'essential dependence' shared by all human beings did not stem, according to Genovesi, from the natural predisposition to sociability, but from the recognition of the fragility and weakness of the individual, from the duties that a new way of conceiving of culture had to take on (on this topic his golden book, *Del vero fine delle lettere e delle scienze*, written in 1753, is exemplary), as well as from the recognition of the free and responsible choices made by men in the course of time, and in particular from what Genovesi, in a truly original linguistic invention, called the 'right to reciprocal help', the umpteenth right given us in order to be happy: 'Men are similar by nature: they are born with equal *ius*, and are equally weak and in need of help; they are all born with one *ius*, or innate right to receive help, or the obligation of helping one another reciprocally as much as they are able' (p.132).

In order to reinforce the importance of this right, which today we would define as of a social kind, and which his pupil Francesco Mario Pagano would, in the Neapolitan Constitution of 1799, translate as 'right to education, health and work', Genovesi also invoked the moral of the Gospels, as well as the theses of Hume and Rousseau concerning the decisive importance in human relations of empathy, pity and the natural compassion felt towards our fellow men.[52]

This distance from certain crudely economistic aspects of Scottish Enlightenment thought, which was concerned above all with production compared to equal distribution, nevertheless did not send him running into the arms of Rousseau. In the same years that he wrote the *Diceosina*, Genovesi also published a small book entitled *Lettere accademiche* where he attacked head-on the paradoxes of Rousseau's thoughts on the noble savage, on the negative aspects of civilisation, and the presumed goodness of direct democracy. It seemed to him utopian and demagogic to invoke in the *Social contract* the 'general will' as the source of morality and good politics when history had clearly shown the demagogic drift towards plebiscites that that system of government could take on when faced with a populace off the leash, as had regularly happened in the past.[53]

Conscious of representing the almost unanimous view of all the protagonists of the Italian Enlightenment movement, and a proud heir to the intellectual elites of Renaissance humanism, the Neapolitan cleric attacked the Swiss philosopher, accusing him of primitivism, and of undervaluing the emancipatory function of the civilising process carried out through literature, the sciences and educational reform: 'Yes, every people is unhappy where the arts are unknown, where the idea of a civilised existence is unkown.' 'Savage and unhappy are synonymous terms for me, with M. Rossò's permission.'[54] In concrete terms Genovesi also rejected the radical solutions such as communism proposed by Morelly in his *Code de la nature, ou le Véritable Esprit des lois* and the constant pleas for drastic agrarian laws in order to achieve

52. Cf. Ferrone, *Politics of Enlightenment*, p.214ff.

53. Rousseau's democratic political views and his paradoxes about the noble savage were never very acceptable to the Italian Enlightenment. On this topic, see chapter I ('I "velenosi" scritti di Rousseau e le nuove frontiere della politica') in Ferrone, *I profeti dell'Illuminismo*, p.301ff. On the widespread hostility towards the 'democracy' of the ancient world, which was accused of easily degenerating into despotism, see Guerci, *Libertà degli antichi e libertà dei moderni*.

54. See the quotations and comments in the chapter dedicated to 'La Napoli di Genovesi' in Venturi, *Da Muratori a Beccaria*, p.606ff.

by force an egalitarianism that, however, violated the natural right to property. Nor did he subscribe to the fierce criticism of luxury as a source of corruption and the violent dominion of man over man. From his chair of civil economics, he had spent too much time translating the classics of British economic thought and studying the methods for increasing international trade to accept that route of head-on criticism of modernity which had been taken by Rousseau and his followers.[55] Caught between the primacy of wealth and progress championed by the Scottish Enlightenment, and that of the republican virtue of the ancients supported by the Swiss thinker and his followers, Genovesi preferred to focus patiently on a third way, through a programme of reforms that was different but no less ambitious. This way placed equal importance on the new conception of virtue as respect for rights and on wealth, development and distribution, material progress and the civilisation of manners. The language of rights was the cornerstone of this approach, its indispensable method. Only from the new morality of rights was it possible to move towards the Enlightenment policy of the rights of man and really guarantee the exercise of the 'general right' to the pursuit of happiness.

To this end, in the final part of his *Diceosina*, which appeared posthumously in 1777, Genovesi welcomed and relaunched Helvétius's invitation to reflect on the power of legislation as an indispensable tool in modern politics that would finally make a new 'science of laws which is the greatest and most important philosophy'. For only a renewed reform of laws seemed to allow the advocates of reform to overcome the injustices of the *Ancien régime*. It was no longer a time to wonder what was the best form of government between monarchy, republic or democracy, as many followers of Montesquieu were still insisting on doing, but to accept in the first place the profound change that had taken place in the conception of humanity itself and of the living being following the irruption onto the European political scene of the language of rights: there are certain '*ius* that belong to us just as our *ousia*, our human essence does' (p.271), the Neapolitan philosopher continued to repeat to his students in order to flag up the epoch-making change that had come about with the new sciences of man. The crucial point now was to take cognisance of the new theoretical and scientific horizon that people had to refer to, which was to guide the exercise of legislative power and the formulation of laws made by

55. On Genovesi as translator of John Cary, see Sophus A. Reinert, *Translating empire: emulation and the origins of political economy* (Cambridge, MA, 2011), p.231.

man for man, after having gone beyond the old *arcana iuris*, after the *Esprit des lois* and the *Social contract*. Whoever exercised power, in any form or way, had to take stock of the sciences of man, and respect the inalienable and universal rights of man, make laws that were 'guardians of the rights of everyone' (p.361), in order to guarantee public and private happiness.

The *Diceosina* aroused great interest in Naples, including many reactions both for and against. The most important and intelligent response came, however, even though by indirect means, from the three jumbled and sometimes illegible volumes by a great scholar linked to the English tradition of freemasonry, Francescantonio Grimaldi, *Riflessioni sopra l'ineguaglianza tra gli uomini*, which appeared in 1779.[56] A follower of Machiavelli's and Hume's political realism, Grimaldi tackled head-on Rousseau's 'deliriums' with his critical eye directed at the reform movement and the rationalistic utopia outlined by Genovesi with his new moral science. The crucial point to hammer home without the slightest hesitation lay in the ethical postulate of the moral equality of men and thus of the consequent equality of rights.

Grimaldi wrote an appealing and erudite 'moral history of the human species', which was destined to influence a large swathe of conservative thinking also in the following century. For it he made use of his sophisticated scientific background, and drew on history, philosophy, travel literature, medicine, zoology, ethnology, statistics, climatology, physiology, comparative anatomy, the works of Linnaeus, Buffon, Daubenton, Haller, Tyson, Bonnet and De Pauw, and those of Louis Le Cat on the features of black people's blood. He did so denying Rousseau's thesis of primitive, isolated man and emphasising on scientific grounds the physical inequality of all human beings that had been established by new scientific research: this conclusion involved the linked affirmation of moral inequality on the basis of the new theories of Jean Paul Marat and then of the *idéologues* concerning the inextricable links between *physique* and *moral*. But in particular, also on the basis of the works of Hume, Ferguson, Miller, Robertson and Linguet concerning the natural history of man, Grimaldi tried to prove that Western civilisation was the result of elites, of the great aristocracies, of the decisive historical function

56. See Girolamo Imbruglia, 'Una polemica a Napoli sulla *Diceosina* di Genovesi', in *Il Settecento di Furio Diaz*, ed. Carlo Mangio and Marcello Verga (Pisa, 2006), p.121-35.

of the moral and physical inequality of man in the creation of civil society and the great empires.[57]

For Grimaldi, hierarchies, physical and therefore moral differences were definitely the true engine of history: inequality was a natural fact, absolutely indispensable for the birth of a stable social order and a good, civil existence: without inequality there would never have been any modernity nor civilisation in the West. One had therefore to beware of the 'imaginary equality' hypothesised by the new metaphysics: 'accommodate equality to justice, and do not found justice on the maxims of equality', as Genovesi preached, unless one wanted to go back to the traumatic times of Masaniello's revolution, leaving the field ripe for social disorder and civil war. Men certainly had natural rights – indeed Grimaldi did not deny this at all – but these rights were not the same for everyone, just as therefore the right to the pursuit of happiness was different and anything but universal and cosmopolitan. This ingenious father of the Italian conservative Enlightenment, this advocate of a precocious theory of the elites, wrote in melancholy terms:

> I leave to others the pointless outbursts and complaints against either nature or men […] It is not that I am stupid and cannot feel the evils that afflict me and others like me, and I would be excessively sensitive to the remedies that could cure them; but the impossibility that has been proven by fact and confirmed by the experience of several centuries makes me rightly despair of any success. Nor can I find any more effective remedy against inequality than to practise patience as much as I can. An evil that is recognised as irremediable always becomes more bearable. That is perhaps the useful conclusion of my reflections.[58]

The fact is that Grimaldi had been right in fearing the political consequences implicit in the spread of the morality of rights that had been outlined in the *Diceosina*. As we shall see in detail in the following chapters, Genovesi's pupils, such as Francesco Longano, Melchiorre Delfico, Giuseppe Maria Galanti, Filippo Briganti and still others, did not hesitate for a second to make the language of the rights of man

57. See the chapter 'Francescantonio Grimaldi e l'ineguaglianza: le radici scientifiche dell'Illuminismo conservatore', in Ferrone, *I profeti dell'Illuminismo*, p.312ff.

58. Francescantonio Grimaldi, *Riflessioni sopra l'ineguaglianza tra gli uomini*, 3 vols (Naples, Vincenzo Mazzola-Vocola, 1779), vol.1, p.x.

their own, making it common currency in public opinion and political debate in Naples in the final quarter-century, splitting vertically for all time the Enlightenment front between moderates and radicals.

13. The new 'science of legislation' of the rights of man: Filangieri and Pagano

It was only in 1780, with the appearance of the first volume of Gaetano Filangieri's *Scienza della legislazione*, that Genovesi's dream could be said to have been realised at last: the construction of a modern legislation – an organic and complete juridical system, we would term it today – entirely founded on natural rights and on the crucial principle of their equality. That dream, which was destined to promote and give strength to the great reform projects, had in any case surfaced powerfully in Enlightenment circles all over the West, from Paris to Berlin, from London to Madrid, from St Petersburg to Boston. For some time people had only been waiting for a synthesis of all the great political, philosophical, juridical and moral debates developed over the course of the eighteenth century, the definitive emergence of their results in the shape of a modern science of legislation, one that was universal, cosmopolitan and constructed with emancipatory aims. This explains its extraordinary publishing success and the many translations of it into French, German, English, Spanish, Russian, Polish and other languages still: it was a work that truly represented the masterpiece and point of arrival of the political and juridical culture of the late European Enlightenment.[1]

In his 'immense edifice of legislation', Filangieri promised to 'analyse clearly one by one all the links that make up that mysterious chain with which legislation must lead men to happiness'.[2] This had

1. A catalogue of all editions is included in Filangieri, *Scienza della legislazione*, vol.7: *La genesi e le edizioni della 'scienza della legislazione', indice delle fonti, indice analitico, indice dei nomi e dei luoghi*, ed. Antonio Trampus and Gerardo Tocchini (2004).
2. Cf. Filangieri, *Scienza della legislazione*, vol.1: *Delle regole generali della scienza legislativa*, ed. Antonio Trampus (2003), p.38. As usual, henceforth references to this work will be given in the text with the volume and page numbers.

become possible because – as he wrote in the opening pages of his masterwork – in the last quarter of the eighteenth century he believed that a 'peaceful revolution' was under way, which absolutely had to be supported. A great and peaceful cultural and political revolution was indeed promoting European public debate and piloting, through public opinion, the great reforms that were destined to shatter definitively the *Ancien régime*, its injustices, its inequalities and privileges. All this despite the occurrence of very negative events such as: the bloody Seven Years War, the first real world war, which had just ended; European colonialism and the continuing trade wars that were at the origin of the new great empires; the exponential growth of the slave trade; the remarkable wave of rearmament that would bring about what was genuinely a 'military mania', which had led the best scientists to 'find the way to kill the maximum amount of men in the minimum amount of time possible'.

Filangieri perceived lucidly that Enlightenment culture was on the way to becoming hegemonic, conquering the universities, salons and minds of the most important sovereigns on the continent. The revolution of the British colonies in America seemed to him the beginning of a new epoch of great hopes for humanity. 'Philosophy has come to the aid of governments', he claimed optimistically: 'Political ideas themselves have lost that streak of ferocity that made them pernicious.' Amongst intellectuals and in public opinion nobody dared any longer praise the crude political realism outlined in Machiavelli's *Prince*: 'a politician who has obtained the praise of men even though he has compromised their rights' (vol.1, p.15). Filangieri's cosmopolitan *Science of legislation*, written to provide a precise plan and a political outlet for eighteenth-century Enlightenment humanism, seemed to him to be a necessary contribution to help speed up the reform process and to guide it in the right direction, by eliminating juridical chaos and the jungle of different medieval orders of laws and customs which had become stratified in the course of millennia, as he tried to construct, through the work of the new philosophers, that indispensable legislative uniformity, in its principles and its objectives, that would be valid everywhere and for everyone:[3]

> Wise men of the earth, philosophers of all nations, writers and all you who have been entrusted with the sacred safekeeping of knowledge:

3. For a useful outline of the European juridical situation under the *Ancien régime*, see Antonio Padoa-Schioppa, *Italia ed Europa nella storia del diritto* (Bologna, 2003).

> if you wish to live, if you wish your names to be sculpted on the temple of memory, if you want immortality to crown your labours, concern yourselves with those things that over two thousand leagues and after twenty centuries are still of interest. Do not write for a man, but for men; link your glory to the interests of the human race [...] courageously instruct your brothers and defend their rights with freedom [...] and your genius, always useful, will then be contemporary with all ages and will be a citizen of everywhere. (vol.1, p.46)

But the solidity and efficacy of that enterprise were due to the preliminary clarity and courage with which the author had proved himself capable of coping with all the burning questions that had been put in play by Rousseau and Helvétius, by the Scottish Enlightenment thinkers or by characters such as Grimaldi, with his bitter yet, despite that, so penetrating work, *Riflessioni sulla disuguaglianza tra gli uomini*.

Right from the first book, which was entirely devoted to the general rules for the science of legislation, Filangieri did not hesitate to reflect on the origins and history of nations and civil societies, embracing Hume's and Ferguson's theses on progress and civilisation against Rousseau's myth of the noble savage, against abstract contractualism and the seventeenth-century metaphysical idea of a state of nature. Supported by Buffon's researches, the savage was in fact described negatively as the fruit of a derailment from the evolutionary and stadial logic of the species that had been so carefully described in Vico's works.[4] If the savage was akin to one of Vico's beasts, all senses, strength and imagination, his failed historical development made him a 'degenerate man, [a] man who lives against his instinct, against his destination; in short, the ruin and degradation of the human species rather than the simulacrum of its infancy', as 'some misanthropic sophists' held (vol.1, p.47). But the primitive society that Filangieri was thinking of was not assimilable to Hobbes' and Rousseau's state of nature, nor to the representations hypothesised by Grimaldi and those philosophers who made it coincide entirely with civil society, confusing nature with history, and natural law *prius* with natural law *posterius*. As Filangieri pointed out:

4. On the wide-ranging and decisive presence of Vico's works in Filangieri's thought, see the index to the critical edition of his *Scienza della legislazione*, vol.7, p.142. In particular, see vol.1, ch.18; vol.3 (*Delle leggi criminali: della procedura*, ed. Francesco Toschi Vespasiani, 2003), ch.3; vol.5 (*Delle leggi che riguardano l'educazione, i costumi e l'istruzione pubblica*, ed. Paolo Bianchini, 2004), ch.1. On Vico's natural state of wandering like a beast, see Landucci, *I filosofi e i selvaggi*, p.291ff.

> This [primitive society] was to be a purely natural society, a society in which the names of noble and plebs, master and servant, were unknown, as were magistrates, laws, punishments and civic duties. This was a society where no other inequality was known except that which stemmed from the might and strength of the body, no other law except that of nature, no other bond except that of friendship, needs and family relations. This was a society whose members had not given up their natural independence, had not yet placed their strength in the hands of one or more men, had not yet entrusted them with guarding their rights, had not yet put under the protection of the laws their life, their property, their honour. This was a society, I say, where each person was sovereign because he was independent, each was a magistrate because he was a guardian and interpreter of the law which he carried sculpted on his heart, and lastly each one was a judge because he was arbiter of the arguments that arose between him and the other members and was the avenger of the wrongs that were done unto him. (vol.1, p.49)

As Vico had explained, man was born in the state of primary nature as an individual holding natural rights. The latter were aimed at the 'preservation' of the species and were destined to become realised gradually through the course of history, which led nations through different phases before they became modern civil societies. To this end the motor and founding principle of the natural and immutable *ius* was totally contained – as we have seen in the preceding pages – in the idea of equality, which is 'the eternal cause of the just': a principle capable of unleashing wars and fierce struggles between peoples and social classes in the course of the centuries. On this solid theoretical basis the ethical postulate of moral equality formulated by Genovesi in the *Diceosina* also became the crucial linchpin in his *Science of legislation*, the decisive ultimate reason for making law and legislation the very symbol of civilisation, of the overcoming of that primitive stage of humanity, moving it towards the barbarian stage and then towards the final phase of civil society.[5] Referring to the shift from primitive society, where moral equality was totally trampled over by physical inequality among individuals, to civil society, where the state of right and public justice of the modern State ruled, Filangieri thus clarified his thought, indicating

5. On the complex philosophies of history developed by Genovesi's pupils in the context of the Neapolitan Enlightenment at the end of the century, see Ferrone, *I profeti dell'Illuminismo*, p.260ff.

the principles and objectives of the *Science of legislation* as a powerful instrument for civilisation:

> That inequality of strength and might of which we have spoken, this unique kind of inequality that could not be removed from these primitive societies, was destined as time went by and with the development of passions to produce the greatest disturbances. Moral equality, unable to cope with the physical inequality, was doomed to fall before the preponderance of force. The weaker man would necessarily have to be exposed to the whims of the stronger [...] A remedy had to be found to combat this. Only one was found. It was seen that physical inequality could not be destroyed without renouncing moral equality. It was clear that in order to preserve oneself and to preserve peace of mind it was necessary not to be independent. A public force had to be created that was superior to all private force. This public force could only be composed of the aggregate of all private forces. A moral person was needed who could represent the will of all, and who had all these forces in his hands. Finally, it was realised that this public force had to be united with public reason, which interpreting and developing natural law would establish rights, regulate duties, prescribe the obligations of each individual towards the whole of society and towards those that made it up; a reason that would establish a norm, and the citizen who adapted his actions to it would not have anything to fear; a reason that would create and guard an order that was able to maintain equilibrium amongst the needs of each citizen along with the means to satisfy them; finally, a reason that would compensate for the sacrifice of independence and of natural freedom by acquiring the appropriate tools to obtain the *preservation* and the *peace of mind* of those who had stripped themselves of these things for this objective only. This was the origin and reason for civil societies, the origin and reason for laws, and as a consequence this was the sole and universal object of legislation. (vol.1, p.68)

In short, it was precisely through laws that civil society appeared in the natural history of man in order to guarantee the very existence of so-called moral equality, Vico's *aequum bonum*, the respect and practice of the natural rights of man, the preservation and peace of mind of the species. Unlike Vico, Filangieri meant by 'preservation' not only liberty, wellbeing, an equal distribution of wealth, but also the Enlightenment idea of happiness, and by 'peace of mind' he meant above all security and justice.[6] Filangieri's long-distance polemic with Grimaldi

6. It has to be said that also in other passages Filangieri disagreed with Vico in

was thus quite clear, and the same differences from the Scottish Enlightenment thinkers were just as obvious, as the latter had been incapable of grasping the difference, in Vico's terms, between nature and history. At the same time his distancing himself from Rousseau, who saw in modernity the evil and the source of the progressive spread of moral inequality, was not insignificant.

On the basis of the natural law tradition, and in particular of a careful reading of Barbeyrac and Pufendorf, but especially Locke, Filangieri addressed the question of moral equality as equality of rights, adapting the language and structures developed north of the Alps to the continental and Italian debate:[7] 'What is meant by natural equality, I ask? This cannot be anything but equality of rights. Men are therefore equal in the natural state because they have equal rights' (vol.4, p.28). It was from this particular fixed point that the *Science of legislation* had to move to construct the new cosmopolitan juridical order. All the rest seemed superfluous to him and only bound to bring confusion. And again: in order to reflect correctly on the political and social nature of equality it was useful to refer 'not to that metaphysical equality desired in the dreams of politicians, but that equality which is the soul of popular governments, which has as its object not people's *faculties* but their *rights*' (vol.1, p.130).

By analogy with Vico's philosophical theses, which bound together, in a kind of hermeneutic circle, natural law *prius* and natural law *posterius*, as well as ideal eternal history and the concrete history of nations, Filangieri too was convinced that all forms of legislation, in the course of history, always had to contain, as they developed into reality, a 'double character of goodness': a natural goodness defined as 'absolute', and a historical goodness, defined as 'relative'. He went on to clarify: 'I call the absolute goodness of laws their harmony with the universal principles of morality, common to all nations, and all governments and fit for all climates. The law of nature contains the immutable principles of that which is just and fair in all cases' (vol.1, p.61). Relative goodness, by contrast, was the 'relationship between the laws and the state of the nation that receives them' (vol.1, p.75). The

---

some respects. For instance, one must remember that the shift from bestial wandering to civilisation occurred, according to Vico, through the fear of God and thanks to religions (cf. Landucci, *I filosofi e i selvaggi*, p.302), whereas Filangieri attributed the reason for this entirely to legislation.

7. On the European debate concerning the concept of equality, see Robertson, *The Case for the Enlightenment*, p.386-400.

failure to respect the primary natural law, the universal principles of morality, 'by legislators who were not very enlightened or cosmopolitan', had, without exception, produced disasters and tragedies, unleashing homicidal violence and the logic of power.

'Political tyrants, are these your laws?' Filangieri wrote polemically. 'Unhappy men, where are your rights? Would your species have become degraded to this point if it had always consulted nature?' The ancient world, which the Neapolitan jurist knew well thanks to his highly sophisticated classical studies and which he loved profoundly, had stained itself irredeemably with the serious crime of slavery by precisely this, denying the moral equality of men. The Egyptian, Greek and above all Roman legislators had never given credit to natural law as the limit and brake on man's arbitrary rule over other men, a limit based precisely on a common human dignity: 'We will never find in the history of these peoples a legislator who respected the imprescriptible rights of the freedom of man and upheld that inalienability' (vol.1, p.68).

But even modern liberty ran the same risks of repeating the errors of the past. The so-called *libertas americana* claimed with pride by their beloved settlers who were headed by Franklin – with whom Filangieri exchanged letters full of advice and hope, sending him the first volumes of the *Science of legislation* with the intention of helping the revolution provide itself with new legal codes and a written constitution – was staining itself with the same horrendous crime.[8] As Filangieri explained bitterly, 'While humanity is reclaiming its rights everywhere, European America is full of slaves', and this was happening despite the fact that Christianity had denounced at an early stage the injustices and inequalities that lay hidden behind the freedom of the ancients. The modern slave trade, that 'infamous trade', seemed to him absolutely unacceptable on the grounds of human dignity. In 'nature's law-code' there was in fact no clause that could 'render slavery legitimate'. If they really had followed natural law, the principles of universal morals or even just the commands of the Gospels in their authentic meaning

> superstition would not have stained our law-codes with blood, and slavery, outlawed in Europe, would not have gone to establish itself

8. See the letters from Filangieri to Franklin of 24 August and 2 December 1782; 14 July and 23 October 1783; 1 March and 21 April 1784; 24 December 1785, in Eugenio Lo Sardo, *Il mondo nuovo e le virtù civili: l'epistolario di Gaetano Filangieri 1772-1788* (Naples, 1999), p.231, 238, 242, 248, 258, 260, 268.

> in America under the protection of the very laws that had exiled it from us. Senegal's barbarous shores would not be the market where Europeans go to buy at a derisory price the inviolable rights of humanity and reason. (vol.1, p.71)

Whereas the analysis of the absolute good had led Filangieri to his obsession with the rights of man and of moral equality as the inescapable limits and reference points for legislation, his illustration of the concept of relative good opened the way instead to reflection on the epistemological set-up and the very definition of the *science* of legislation. The young Neapolitan jurist wrote, recycling once more Vico's schemes from the *Scienza nuova*: 'I am writing the science of legislation for all peoples and for all time. Let us remind ourselves of the property of a science as established by Aristotle: *Scientia debet esse de universalibus et aeternis*' (vol.1, p.21). Like Voltaire, Mably, Rousseau and Helvétius, Filangieri too considered it now indispensable to follow to the end the high road leading to the birth of a new 'political law' which was respectful at the same time of the proper character of human nature, but also of its will. In this way he went beyond Montesquieu and his Neapolitan followers, Grimaldi and Galanti, beyond the reflections of the Scottish thinkers, Robertson and Ferguson, enriching Blackstone's and Vattel's points of view, laying down the basis for a modern legislative politics that could finally supersede the ancient medieval concept of law as 'rediscovery', where laws were the direct expression of the nature of things, of an eternal natural and social order that the jurists, those powerful *sacerdotes iuris*, 'revealed' to their sovereigns from the heights of their *scientia iuris*.

In fact it was one thing to investigate and get to know the spirit of the laws as they appeared, but quite another to construct a science that was totally operative, identifying 'fixed and secure principles' that were universally valid, the fruit of both natural law and the history of nations. In this context, paraphrasing some famous expressions by Rousseau in *Emile*, Filangieri proudly claimed the philosophical and epistemological originality of his work, its different operative and political intentions compared with the merely cognitive ones of the 'immortal Montesquieu':

> It is a strange thing that amongst the many writers who have devoted themselves to the study of laws – some have dealt with this subject as a mere jurisconsult, some as a philologist, some also as a political writer, but only aiming at just one part of this immense edifice; some, like Montesquieu, have dealt rather with what has been done than

> with what one ought to do; but none has yet reduced this material to a certain, ordered science, uniting means with rules and theory with practice. (vol.1, p.19)

Ultimately, the author's intention was for the *Science of legislation* to become that perfect manual for the Enlightenment legislator that the whole of Europe had been waiting for, and that the great Montesquieu had not written nor wanted to write. And yet, notwithstanding the profound differences in objectives, the analytical model at the outset could only be the same. In identifying the 'general rules for the science of legislation', it was not in any case possible to leave aside the evaluation of the forms of government, of climate, territory, religions, the very 'universal genius of the nations, and the spirit of the times, and the genius and particular character of the people for whom the law is promulgated'. Moreover, the new and original epistemological perspective, the beating heart of the whole work, lay elsewhere, i.e. in

> distinguishing the harmony that the law must have with the principles of nature, from the relationship that it must have with the state of the nation to which it is destined, developing the most general principles that stem from this double character of goodness that every law must have, observing the consequences that follow from this; deducing from this the errors of the laws, the necessary diversity, even the frequent contrasts of legislations, the fates of the legal codes, the need to correct them, the obstacles that render such corrections difficult. (vol.1, p.22)

The detailed plan of the work had envisaged seven books. Only the first five appeared, starting from 1780. The fifth book, devoted to the laws inherent in religion, was printed posthumously by Filangieri's disciples, after the sudden, premature death of the author in 1788. As for the final two, of which there only remain a few indications, Filangieri wanted to devote them to the laws 'to distinguish the sacred rights of property from the secret robbery of usurpation', and to the laws on family rights.

Of all these books, the one that was most innovative and full of suggestions from the point of view of the history of the rights of man – even though this is also perhaps the least studied and understood by critics – is certainly the second one: *Delle leggi politiche ed economiche*.[9]

9. See the recent important contributions by Maria Teresa Silvestrini, 'Free trade,

Right from its title, which indicated the programmatic intention of the author to link organically the political dimension with the economic one, it represented – and represents even today, when it seems to have become fashionable again to study the eighteenth-century topics of 'law and economics' – a sort of distant dialogue, if not an actual settling of scores with the Scottish Enlightenment of Hume, Robertson and Ferguson, and with many conclusions that Adam Smith had reached in his famous *Enquiry* of 1776. This last work was known to Filangieri perhaps directly but in any case it is very present in Italian and Neapolitan debates of the time through accounts in the gazettes.[10]

The common questions faced by Filangieri and Smith are many and significant, their agreement is evident on crucial points, but just as crucial seem to be their profound general divergences, from the epistemological and philosophical point of view, in the very way they conceive of the ethical foundation of the market – a real obsession of the economists who were inspired by Enlightenment humanism – and the treatment of the delicate problem of an efficient 'economic legislation', and of the overall relationship between politics and economics.

We saw in the preceding chapter that the definitive consecration of the autonomy of the market and its laws by Smith as opposed to the primacy of politics in Hobbes' followers, and Smith's reserving the language of rights just to the sphere of jurisprudence, excluding it from the sphere of economics, were founded on a precise ethical basis, i.e. on the modern critical reassessment of the traditional sociability principle, applied to the natural mechanism of exchange, and of the division of labour as the decisive factor in progress. This was on the back of Hume's philosophical and political reflections on the world of passions and more generally on the centrality of human empathy as the fulcrum of relations among human beings, and of the persistent equilibrium of the social order over the centuries. However, in the recent international historiographical debate, we have also discussed

---

feudal remnants and international equilibrium in Gaetano Filangieri's *Science of legislation*', *History of European ideas* 32 (2006), p.502-24; and by Fabrizio Simon, 'Diritti umani, repubblicanesimo dei moderni ed equità sociale: le nuove categorie della storiografia su Gaetano Filangieri', *Storia del pensiero economico* 4:1 (2007), p.141-54.

10. See Franco Venturi, 'Scottish echoes in eighteenth-century Italy', in *Wealth and virtue: the shaping of political economy in the Scottish Enlightenment*, ed. Istvan Hont and Michael Ignatieff (Cambridge, 1983), p.345-62; Gianfranco Tarabuzzi, 'Echi italiani settecenteschi della storiografia inglese', *Archivio storico italiano* 138 (1980), p.391-440.

at length the presence of strong religious and Thomistic roots in the economic thought of the great Scottish thinker: from the centrality of providence to the fundamental distinction, adopted and finely argued by the latter, between retributive justice, which is proper to the political system, and commutative justice, which is instead proper to the market. And in fact, beyond the well-documented and significant presence of scholastic thought in Protestant natural law and later in the Scottish Enlightenment, it is difficult to escape the fact that all these ideas on the common good, on the just price in nature, on the autonomous market, exempted from distributive justice and from politics, are found widely argued actually in Aquinas and later in Grotius and his Protestant followers in Northern Europe.[11]

Filangieri was a disciple of Vico, and of Genovesi the inventor of the concept of 'civil economy', and heir to the great Italian humanist and Renaissance tradition. He had, however, quite different convictions as regards the ethical foundation behind the autonomy of the market and the role of man and his rights throughout history. In his *Science of legislation*, even before empathy and exchange as the natural expression of human sociability, the ideas always in the forefront of his mind were man, his rights, and the principles of moral equality, and of what we ought to be rather than what we are; unlike Smith, he would never have agreed to put the language of rights second behind the language of the markets, with the consequent political 'neutralisation' of rights. His decision to confront the tension between the two fields, the political and the economic, violated the Thomist prejudice of excluding distributive justice from the market, and was in any case part and parcel of the convictions that he had come to through his in-depth study of Vico's *Scienza nuova*, of the epistemological value of this hermeneutic and dialectical circle that had been set up between ideal, eternal history and the concrete history of nations, between primary and secondary natural law, between the truth and facts. This was in just the same way as he had also taken from Vico and the strong humanist traditions that were rooted in Italian culture the certainties regarding the crucial function of the political actions of man in history.

11. See Istvan Hont and Michael Ignatieff, 'Needs and justice in the *Wealth of nations*: an introductory essay', in *Wealth and virtue*, ed. I. Hont and M. Ignatieff, p.1-44 (26ff.). And see especially the fine review of recent books on the Thomistic roots of Smith's work by Paolo Prodi, *Settimo non rubare: furto e mercato nella storia dell'Occidente* (Bologna, 2009), p.307ff.

In this context, we ought to remember that in end-of-century Naples, numerous masonic lodges flourished that were interested in the Renaissance hermetic tradition. As a result, reflections on the meaning and sense of becoming had always been influenced by the presence of a prestigious culture that was sensitive to cyclical, catastrophic conceptions of history, to individual freedom and to the will of man as maker of his own destiny, against the determinism of those who, with a secular version of Thomistic ideas of providence, considered progress as the inevitable future of humanity, and not just a possibility to be seized.[12] In the land of Machiavelli, Michelangelo and Raphael, of highly sophisticated city-dwelling aristocracies, who had a deep influence on Western civilisation, fighting for centuries against Aristotelianism and the Scholasticism of the Holy See, the fascinating challenge of modernity, represented by the Scottish Enlightenment, could not be avoided or mystified.

The fact is that it was one thing to confront the French Enlightenment, to distance oneself from the direct democracy of the ancients, from the myth of the noble savage, from Rousseau's primitivism, his anachronistic refusal to think in modern terms about the economy and his demonisation of production and wealth. It was quite another to propose a different road, an alternative to Adam Smith's convincing theses concerning nature and the causes of the wealth of nations. That Scottish approach, which started from the pre-eminence of the language of the markets and exclusion of the language of rights from the economic and political fields, relegating it solely to the sphere of jurisprudence, almost inevitably weakened and cast doubt upon the whole passionate debate on rights that had been developed by Neapolitan Enlightenment thinkers, throughout the eighteenth century, as an indispensable tool to shape reform and overcome the injustices of the *Ancien régime*.

The so-called 'paradox of modern commercial societies', which were so rich but also so unfair and corrupt, compared to the societies of the ancient world which were poor but virtuous, represented a common challenge for everyone, not just for French and Scottish thinkers, but also for the protagonists of the Italian Enlightenment. And Filangieri was so conscious of this that he immediately rejected any reference to Rousseau's themes of the corruption and decadence

12. On the different kinds of philosophy of history developed in the Enlightenment, and on the Neapolitan version in particular, see Ferrone, *I profeti dell'Illuminismo*, p.278ff.

of modern customs that were caused by wealth, and instead resolutely affirmed, right from his opening pages, that 'wealth and the channels that transmit it have become the primary object of legislation', inasmuch as 'gold has become the measure of everything' and the 'trading and farming nations have established their throne over the warrior nations' (vol.1, p.28).

However, the 'paradox' had to be confronted with a preliminary clarification of the meaning of the words and their change over time. For a start, the wealth of the moderns had nothing to do with that of the ancient world. The nature and shape of wealth had changed radically: it was no longer the result of bloody wars, of booty taken from the defeated, 'the fruit of conquest'. It was now 'the reward of assiduous work and of a life totally devoted' to the cultivation and production and trade of goods. The very concept of 'virtue', as Filangieri had explained in arguing against Montesquieu, had acquired new meanings: it no longer consisted of duties, in the civic republican spirit of the ancients' interest in the *res publica*, but more concretely in the respect for natural rights. As Genovesi had explained in his *Diceosina*, the solution to the 'paradox' had therefore to be sought in the new delicate equilibrium that needed to be established between wealth and virtue, which, translated into the language of the moderns as developed by the Neapolitan Enlightenment, meant the search for a possible and necessary balance between the market and the rights of man. Filangieri explained: 'Everyone believes that virtue cannot take root amid the wealth of a nation. What a woeful idea, and one to which we owe perhaps the unhappy state of present legislation' (vol.1, p.35).

In the chapter on 'The distribution of national wealth' he outlined his personal solution to the 'paradox' as the great 'truth that private interests would want to keep hidden from men and from those who govern them'. This consisted in the fact that a modern economic legislation should deal not only with the production of wealth, but also with its equal distribution, if one wanted to safeguard the true, natural order of things and to guarantee the practice of natural rights in the pursuit of happiness, which was the genuine core of Enlightenment policy:

> Without a fair distribution of wealth, [those who govern] will, instead of creating the happiness of a nation, simply accelerate its decline [...] Public happiness is nothing other than the aggregate of the private happiness of all the individuals that make up that society. When

> wealth is limited to just a few hands, when the wealthy are few and the many are needy, this private happiness of a few members will surely not create the happiness of the whole body of society: on the contrary, as I have said, it will bring about its ruin. (vol.2, p.235)

Filangieri laid out for the first time and with great clarity the Enlightenment right to the pursuit of happiness as a sort of modern social right which was paired with that 'right to reciprocal help' which Genovesi had written about. But he did so in the context of a delicate balance to be sought in the virtuous circle that existed between freedom and property, which had been carefully studied by John Locke and by the Machiavellian tradition. In fact the crucial theoretical point of his deliberations lay in the idea that without a fair distribution of wealth not only did one end up blocking the circulation of goods, the growth of consumption and production, thus reducing the positive efficiency of the exercise of the right to property, but one also seriously undermined the right to freedom of individuals, countenancing the oppression and despotism of the rich and the sharpening of social conflict, and allowing the populace to be 'trampled upon by a hundred despots': 'Today the richest nations are those where the citizens are the most industrious and most free' (vol.2, p.107).

Unlike Smith, who was against the presence of distributive justice in the market, Filangieri, who wanted to rethink the whole economic dimension in the light of the language of rights and of the principle of moral equality, had no doubt that the objective of good legislation should only be 'that of multiplying men and providing for their subsistence, calling upon the wealth that was in the State, preserving it and distributing it with the least possible unfairness' (vol.2, p.262). Only by rigorously respecting all the objectives listed could the new civil society that had been dreamed of by many Enlightenment radicals finally link the economic sphere with the political, the market with the contemporary and balanced exercise of the right to property, the right to liberty and the right to the pursuit of happiness.

The Neapolitan jurist resolutely placed the implementation of the first two rights as the basis for the accumulation of wealth. He did this with such vigour and conviction as to seem even more of a free-marketeer – if that were possible – than Smith himself and the physiocrats. To move in this direction, his *Science of legislation*, rather than proposing new laws, invited the legislator to eliminate the highest number possible of existing laws in order to dismantle, bit by bit, the centuries-old structure of privileges and obligations of the *Ancien régime*. Fully convinced, Filangieri, who hated every form of privilege and despotism, wrote: 'We must begin by removing the obstacles, interfere as little as possible, and let others act as much as possible' (vol.2, p.87). The minimum of state interference and the principle of subsidiarity, as we would say today, seem to be his bywords. To increase agricultural productivity the key lay in the maximum liberty of private citizens in their exercise of the 'imprescriptible' and 'sacred rights to property' (vol.2, p.103).

This created the need to open up landed property to a modern and free market, doing away at last with the 'pernicious and woeful system of fiefdoms' and barons' 'barbarous hunting right', which Filangieri considered as yet another anachronistic 'remnant of feudalism'. It was necessary to reform hereditary law, doing away with the laws on trusts, primogenitures, ecclesiastical tithes and the fact that the immense properties of the Church were off limits to the free market. Conversely, one should encourage the cultivation of abandoned fields. Common land should give way to enclosures, as had happened in England in the previous centuries. Above all, it was imperative to free farmers in Russia, Denmark, Prussia and Poland from the incredible survival of medieval servitude of the glebe as late as the eighteenth century. How was it possible, Filangieri indignantly asked, that 'that philosophy that enlightened the rest of Europe and established the rights of mankind has been unable to annihilate the servitude of the glebe? Who would believe such a thing!' (vol.2, p.103).

In the end his liberalism in agriculture was fully revealed in his denunciation of the 'lack of freedom in the trading of its products' and in particular in the great argument about grain which had exploded in France in the 1770s.[13] In this context his point of reference was not Ferdinando Galiani – his great friend and colleague in government in the Bourbon court – who had fought stridently alongside the Paris *philosophes* against the abstract and sectarian liberalism of the physiocrats, but rather the Milanese Pietro Verri who had allied himself, though with greater realism, alongside the physiocrats, but had worked out an original idea of an active nature, ordered internally by laws that could balance production with needs. Filangieri agreed, lining up in favour of unlimited freedom in the commerce of grains: 'If commerce were free, and furthered nature's designs, it would supply

13. On this topic, see Steven L. Kaplan, *Bread, politics and political economy in the reign of Louis XV*, 2 vols (The Hague, 1976), vol.1, p.90-101.

with the surplus of one country the needs of another and with the law of continuity that would be sufficient to balance periodically needs and abundance' (vol.2, p.90). Most of the time, in fact, it was precisely 'the interference of the government' that produced famine and poverty, giving monopolies carte blanche and favouring distortions of the market.[14]

Filangieri – who did not share at all the physiocrats' prejudices towards industry and commerce – used the same logic that privileged the exercise of the rights of freedom and property in the agricultural world and applied them to industry and commerce, two sectors that had become crucial for increasing the wealth of a modern nation. In this case too the main objective was to create through reforms and the elimination of previous laws which were now obsolete a free modern labour market. 'Competition and rivalry' were his dogmas. Once more one had to remove all types of obstacles to the free production of goods, courageously dismantling the ancient corporations and guilds' privileges. One had to rein in at all costs 'the legislators' ambition in wanting to regulate and control everything': 'Thus the laws that destroy this necessary competition are the curse of the crafts and of manufacture' (vol.2, p.132).

Yet where his contribution to an overall reinterpretation of the economic phenomenon in the light of the language of the rights of man seemed most original was certainly in his treatment – launched by Hume in his 'Of the jealousy of trade' of 1758 – of the irruption into the life and very conception of politics in the West of the modern commercial wars and the new colonial imperialism of the major European states. In chapter 20, 'Of the jealousies of commerce and the rivalries of nations', Filangieri drew a crude, realistic picture of the increasingly violent and bloody clashes between the great continental powers. He denounced their protectionist policies and the monopolies imposed by the great companies, and drew interesting parallels between the commercial jealousy between Carthaginians and Romans and the modern rivalry between the Dutch, English, French and Spanish. The betrayal of the original peaceful spirit of trade relations, which so many Enlightenment thinkers dwelled on, from Montesquieu to Voltaire, Hume and Smith, lay in their having forgotten the 'tight bond that links the interests of each nation with

14. For this see Franco Venturi, 'The position of Galiani between the Encyclopedists and the physiocrats', in his *Italy and the Enlightenment: studies in a cosmopolitan century* (London, 1972), p.180-97; Capra, *I progressi della ragione*, p.338ff.

those of the whole of Europe'.[15] A just and cosmopolitan legislation in the matter of international commerce ought to take account not only of the utilitarian logic of exchange, but also of the universality of rights, of the global interdependence of the protagonists, who were always to be considered free and equal amongst one another in the exercise of their human rights:

> Everything is dependence, everything is related, nothing is isolated. See how this inalterable order of nature has given rise to societies, has caused trade to be born amongst men. Remember that, as far as its destination is concerned, commerce wants all nations to consider themselves as a single society, all of whose members have equal rights to participate in the goods of other societies [...] So abandon this spirit of rivalry and jealousy. Ally your interests and advantages with those of other nations. The general freedom of industry and commerce: this is the sole treaty that an industrious trading nation should establish within itself and seek outside its borders. (vol.2, p.162-63)

It is no surprise, then, that alongside his radical denunciation of the slave trade, Filangieri took a severe stance against the way that the European powers' new, rapacious, eighteenth-century colonialism was developing. It was incomparably more ferocious and unjust than the imperial colonialism of Ancient Rome, which had always aimed, with wisdom and political realism, at establishing respectful and almost egalitarian relationships with her colonies. It was in the context of this topic, which had become one of burning relevance after the Seven Years War, that the reasons for his passionate support for the American colonies' struggle against England also stemmed: a struggle that was immediately transformed into the terms of a political and at the same time economic conflict between the despotism of George III and the practice of the colonists' rights to freedom and property. Was not the violent claim of the English to 'exclusive commerce' perhaps to be seen as a 'very manifest attack on the most sacred rights of the property and freedom of men and citizens?' (vol.2, p.171).

In this perspective, unlike the cautious approach of Smith and Raynal himself, who admitted the possibility of privileged and preferential trade between colonies and the fatherland, Filangieri made no exceptions and considered the claim to exclusive trade a form of

15. On these thinkers' positions, see Hirschman, *The Passions and the interests*, Hont, *Jealousy of trade*, and above all the acute analysis that broadens these themes to the Italian eighteenth century in Reinert, *Translating empire*.

economic exploitation and an unacceptable violation of the principle of equality and of what today we would define as the necessary globalisation and universalisation of rights amongst all the peoples of the earth. In his eyes the American Revolution constituted an epoch-making event, a paradigmatic example of the mistakes and tragedies that the new colonial imperialism was creating with its denial of the rights of man. The rebels were in fact giving 'a terrible lesson to all the colonial powers' in America and in the rest of the world. A lesson that nobody seemed to have yet understood in its real meaning as a warning and alert against inevitable future wars and revolts actually in the name of rights if the work of exploitation and domination continued: 'The fuse is lit [...] The moment when this event will happen is uncertain,' he wrote prophetically, 'but it is inevitable if this flawed system is not reformed' (vol.2, p.176).

Apart from the difference in language and in motivations, the points of convinced consensus with the free-market positions of the physiocrats and, as we have seen, the Scottish Enlightenment, with Hume and Smith in the front rank, ended here. Increase in wealth in fact required, according to Filangieri, not only the abolition of the laws of the *Ancien régime*, in order to remove obstacles to the virtuous and proficient practice of the right to property and liberty, but also the elimination of 'clashes' by governments, which should instead pass laws that were able to promote development. Guaranteeing freedom of exchange and of the division of labour was not enough to increase wealth: what was needed was a proper economic policy by governments to favour the building of new roads, canals, bridges, ports. What was needed was a monetary policy which – precisely in the light of the results of the extraordinary theoretical debate that had developed in eighteenth-century Italy – finally abandoned the always privileged perspective of internal commerce and opened up instead to questions of international trade, and the thorny business of barter, exchanges and the comparison between national currencies in order to guarantee equal and profitable commerce for all the protagonists.[16] Finally there was a need to reform international maritime law. The young Neapolitan jurist, who knew and appreciated Vattel's works, stigmatised his opponents in these terms: 'The sea, the common territory over which all nations have equal rights, but which the preponderance of forces belonging to certain peoples seeks to turn into

16. On the theoretical debate, see the chapter entitled 'Il dibattito sulle monete' in Franco Venturi, *Da Muratori a Beccaria*, p.443ff.

a private patrimony' (vol.2, p.191), had finally to be subject to a new international, cosmopolitan law drawn up in a spirit of fairness and respect for the moral equality of the rights of all nations.

But the key point in his clear divergence from Smith's thought lay above all in the crucial question of the distribution of wealth. And this was a strident clash since it put into direct opposition two different ways of conceiving in positive terms of modernity, progress, wealth and emancipation within the Enlightenment camp itself. This was a radical disagreement, as we have seen, especially about the different way of understanding the ethical foundation of the market and of economic relations: for the Scottish thinker this came about through the principle of sociability, empathy, human benevolence and using the division of labour; for the Neapolitan it was through logic, and the indisputable primacy of the language of the rights of man. The former argued that this distribution came about 'naturally', without any need for intervention by the government, which thus had to restrict itself to the solid protection of the right to property from the indignation of the poor.[17] The latter, however, called for the intervention of legislation and politics in order to attenuate inequalities and to guarantee the exercise of rights for everyone, and particularly amongst these rights there was the fundamental right to the pursuit of happiness.

The fact is that Filangieri had no belief at all in the so-called natural benevolence and empathy of the rich towards the poor. His reasonable utopia had too much of Machiavelli's and Vico's 'political realism' in its makeup to believe in the function of empathy in historical processes. And the main protagonists of the Neapolitan and French Enlightenment thought in exactly the same way: just think of the ferocious polemics by Diderot, Grimm, Mably, during the so-called *Guerre des farines* in Paris, fighting in the name of the party of humanity against the sectarian liberalism of the physiocrats and against the unrestricted use of the right to property by the rich grain merchants.[18] Moreover, it was not only Rousseau who thought that modernity and progress generated, along with an increase in wealth, a heightening of inequalities and social conflict: the concentration of wealth and the

17. See the famous first book 'Of the causes of improvement in the productive powers of labour, and of the order according to which its produce is naturally distributed among the different ranks of the people', in Smith, *Wealth of nations*, p.16, as well as the considerations on the defence of the rich from the indignation of the poor in Hont and Ignatieff, 'Needs and justice', p.25.
18. Hont and Ignatieff, 'Needs and justice', p.13ff. See also my next chapter.

spread of poverty in London, Paris and Naples were by now obvious to everyone and were well documented in history.[19] It was one thing to recognise the existence of natural rights in the state of nature *prius* that Vico had spoken about, but it was quite another to guarantee it being put into practice in the history of humanity: this was the duty of politics in the modern world, according to Filangieri and many Enlightenment thinkers. Was it not also Vico who had recounted in considerable detail the ferocious class struggles between rich and poor in Ancient Rome and successive epochs? Of course certain solutions envisaged by some intellectual circles in Paris on the radical side no longer made any sense in modern civil and commercial society. Communism and the return to the agrarian laws to be imposed just like in Ancient Rome seemed to him – as his master Genovesi had in any case pointed out on several occasions – things that were impossible and anachronistic. For Filangieri knew well that talking of equality of wealth in the modern world was a dangerous 'chimera'. In this area the Scottish Enlightenment thinkers were clearly correct. There was no turning back. But it was quite another thing to try to guarantee the exercise of the natural right of everyone to pursue happiness, reducing wherever possible social and economic inequalities, and increasing the virtuous mechanism between production and consumption.

In any case modern happiness had many aspects on which to reflect without having to resort to the usual myth of Rousseau's noble savage, isolated and happy.[20] Happiness was incarnated in different ways in the peasant, the artisan and the merchant, and it expressed itself above all as a function of people's different needs and individual sensibilities, but it always needed some material starting conditions in its social, collective dimension. As Filangieri explained, 'In order to reach this end [happiness] it is not necessary for all citizens to be equally rich, but that wealth be distributed in an even manner, in other words that wealth should not be entirely restricted to the hands of a few, leaving the rest of society in need.' To this end it was necessary to aim at the equality of 'happiness in all classes, in all social orders, in all families that make up [the State]; an equality that must be the aim of politics and the laws' (vol.2, p.241).[21]

19. See Luciano Guerci, *L'Europa del Settecento: permanenze e mutamenti* (Turin, 1988), p.117ff.
20. On the original socioeconomic reading of the concept of happiness, see Ferrone, *Politics of Enlightenment*, p.209ff.
21. A few months before he died, Filangieri wrote the following, copying with

Instead the modern world was going in the wrong direction, 'dominated [as it was] by the disproportion between the property-owning class and that of non-owners', with grave consequences on consumption, on the growth of wealth, on the lack of growth in populations and particularly on the individual's liberty itself. But how could one avoid the polarisation of wealth, and increase the number of small property-holders ('the multiplicity of proprietors causes the happiness of the state'), without 'damaging the sacred rights of property' (vol.2, p.243)? Once again what returned centre stage – according to a tension that pervades the whole *Science of legislation*, and it could not be otherwise given the inevitable dialectic among different rights – was the inevitable conflict among the different natural rights that had to be harmonised through efficacious laws.[22] The provisions invoked against the monster of feudalism – the laws of primogeniture, mortmain, monopolies, against the creation of big, costly standing armies that were everywhere taking the place of the small soldier-property-owner, a phenomenon which had been relaunched by Machiavelli's republicanism, and in the eighteenth century by Helvétius, Mably, Paine, Jefferson and many others – all these provisions were already moving in the right direction.[23] More generally, in order to avoid a direct attack on the right to property, Filangieri always suggested 'resorting to roundabout ways', incentivising breaking up public lands into

great sympathy a passage from Richard Price's *Observations on the importance of the American Revolution*: 'The idea of perfect equality within society's ranks, although rejected by people of sound sense, because it is impossible for it to exist, has never been entirely banished from the human spirit. It is this that forms the first principle on which the ideas of good, evil and liberty are based, it is this that restrains power and tells them, at least in England, thus far you may go but no further; it is this that makes people abhor what they believe is unjust. It is to this idea that we are beholden for the free constitution that we enjoy' ('Estratto dell'opera di G. Playfair diretto al Marchese D[onato] T[ommasi]', in Filangieri, *La scienza della legislazione con giunta degli Opuscoli scelti*, 6 vols, Milan, 1822, vol.6, p.357-73, on p.366-67).

22. See the acute observations by Pietro Costa on the lack of harmony present in Filangieri's work, in Pietro Costa, Carla De Pascale and Mario Ricciardi, 'La *Scienza della legislazione* di Gaetano Filangieri', *Iride* 19:47 (2006), p.181-202. But Costa does not take due account of the fact that the consistent application of the logic of rights by the Neapolitan jurist is linked to a perennial tension in the analysis of the questions and is actually based on objective oppositions.
23. On the 'republican' reforms of Napoleon's army in Filangieri, see Vincenzo Ferrone, 'Un re, un esercito, una nazione: il riarmo italiano nel '700 tra innovazioni e identità nazionali d'Antico regime', in *Storia d'Italia, Annali 18, Guerra e pace*, ed. Walter Barberis (Turin, 2002), p.383-97.

smaller properties, reforming hereditary rights in order to guarantee equal shares to all male children, even going so far as formulating new laws which would give 'preference to non-property-holders', when it was a question of selling huge private estates, or feudal lands or territory from the immense patrimony of the Church. The important thing was to avoid excessive concentrations of wealth, and the forming of monopolies and economic potentates. Only in this way could the rights to freedom, property and happiness find the right balance and the harmony necessary to increase their positive effects reciprocally.

However, where the modernity of the solutions proposed by Filangieri stood out in particular, again with very different emphases compared to Smith, was certainly on the question of taxation and how its burden should be shared. Apart from attributing many more onerous duties to the State, amongst which, as we shall see, was the crucial one of educating the population to the defence of freedom and political participation, Filangieri actually made taxation the very hinge of a modern civil society that was capable of becoming more and more happy, the fairer and more equal it became. It was in this sense that he asked himself in a polemic against the privileges of the *Ancien régime*, 'Can it possibly be fair that one portion of citizens should profit like another from the benefits of society but without having to pay for them?'

After writing furiously against blood privileges and the hereditary principle of the feudal nobility in the economic field, and in the exercise of justice, Filangieri did not think twice about proposing a sort of moral equality of all citizens when faced with taxes, over and above any differences of class. What sense was there insisting on indirect taxation which fell on rich and poor alike, slowing down the circulation of goods, or on 'capitation', an odious tax which indiscriminately attacked the poor man's right to life, or on the tithes demanded by the Church? Like the physiocrats – and unlike Pietro Verri, who also wanted to tax manufacturing products – Filangieri too thought that the moment had come to push for a single tax that was limited to landed property, paid in proportion to the 'net product', which was understood as 'what was left over from returns once all the expenditure on growing had been deducted'. In this way the rich would finally pay more than the poor and each property owner would be taxed in proportion to his income (vol.2, p.212). Only in this way would distributive justice be able to make the language of rights interact in a virtuous circle with the logic of the markets, and bring the latter onto the side of humanity.

Filangieri died when he was only thirty-seven years old. Here we have focused on volume 2 of his *Science of legislation* because the other volumes have generally been studied by historians and critics in far greater detail. Nevertheless, still too little attention has been paid to those other volumes from the privileged point of view of the history of the rights of man in the West. An exemplary case would be books 3 and 4, which appeared in 1783, and were devoted to substantive criminal law and to procedure: at the end of the century these became the very heart of the European Enlightenment's battle for civil rights through the debate aroused by the publication of Cesare Beccaria's famous work, *On crimes and punishments*, and by the notorious Calas case championed by Voltaire, to which we shall return. Together those two books of Filangieri's work constituted the first attempt to refound the whole system of penal thought by starting from the rights of the individual and from a republican conception of justice as an instrument for overcoming privileges and inequalities before the law. In their original edition the two volumes were widely discussed and often used for modern codifications of the law in France, Germany, Spain and other countries.[24] They would still be at the centre of the debates amongst distinguished jurists in the following century for the technical solutions he proposed; and they would even arouse the unconditional admiration of a great 'enemy' of Filangieri, Benjamin Constant, father of the nascent liberalism and author of a ponderous *Commentaire sur l'ouvrage de Filangieri*, over 400 pages long, written in 1824, with the aim of polemically contesting the Enlightenment legacy that had been summarised in the Neapolitan's work.[25]

In the dense pages of these two volumes Filangieri confronted head-on the theoretical dilemma that had always been at the heart

24. See the many contributions on this subject contained in Trampus, *Diritti e costituzione*, and in *Gaetano Filangieri e l'Illuminismo europeo: atti del convegno tenuto a Vico Equense nel 1982*, ed. Lucio d'Alessandro (Naples, 1991).

25. On Constant's polemic, see Ferrone, *Politics of Enlightenment*, p.176ff. For the admiration of the great German criminal expert Johann Anselm von Feuerbach for Filangieri see Mario Alessandro Cattaneo, 'Alcuni problemi nella dottrina della pena di Gaetano Filangieri', in *Gaetano Filangieri e l'Illuminismo europeo*, ed. L. D'Alessandro, p.262-90. On these topics one should also look at Paolo Becchi, *Vico e Filangieri in Germania* (Naples, 1986); Paolo Becchi and Kurt Seelmann, *Gaetano Filangieri und die europäische Aufklärung* (Frankfurt am Main and Berlin, 2000). There are many references to Filangieri the jurist in Luigi Ferrajoli, *Diritto e ragione: teoria del garantismo penale* (Rome and Bari, 1989). Lastly see the important critical edition of Benjamin Constant, *Commentaire sur l'ouvrage de Filangieri*, ed. Kurt Klocke and Antonio Trampus (Tübingen, 2012).

of the reflections of the entire Enlightenment movement in Europe, namely how to think of the fragile relationship between individual and community in terms of a virtuous balance and of organic composition in the thorny field of justice. In this context, whereas political and economic laws had to be formulated with the aim of increasing wealth and populations, criminal laws, by contrast, had to guarantee above all the safety and tranquillity of citizens, respecting in all possible ways the fundamental balancing of the claims of individuals and those of the community.

In the past, what had been privileged, to the detriment of the rights of individuals, was the security of the State, the peace and order of the community of subjects who obeyed a king/judge against whom there was no appeal. With the cultural revolution brought about by the Enlightenment and the new centrality of man, modern justice could no longer tolerate such an unbalanced and unequal setup. As Filangieri explained: 'If society has to be protected, the rights of man need to be respected, and we are only allowed to sacrifice that portion of rights that is necessary for conserving and defending public safety' (vol.4, p.16). Even the hoary old question of the nature and legitimacy of 'the right to punish', which had so exercised the philosophers and jurists of the entire continent in the wake of the many translations of Beccaria's work, had to be reformulated by paying attention to John Locke's arguments about the natural rights of the individual.

According to Filangieri, that right to punish had no conventional origin from on high, it was not a prerogative of sovereignty, as was thought by the theorists of absolutism, those followers of Hobbes and Pufendorf, who favoured an original pact of irreversible domination between subjects and ruler even in the sphere of justice. Rather it came from below: it was a natural and above all an inalienable right of the individual:

> What was the point of giving man so many obligations without giving him a form of restraint to prevent their violation? What was the point of giving him so many rights and then denying him the one that was absolutely necessary in order to induce others to respect them? The law of nature would have been absurd if it had denied man this right of punishment. (vol.4, p.25)

And in order to clarify further his own thought, he distanced himself from Montesquieu, Beccaria and Rousseau, explaining that the right to punish exercised by society on behalf of individuals drew its legitimacy not from 'the giving up of rights that each one had over himself, as some have believed, but from giving up the right that each one had over the others' (vol.4, p.14).

What emerges clearly from these brief comments is Filangieri's substantially and decisively individualistic conception of the theme of justice. This was destined to influence profoundly his republican idea of a trial and the very redefinition of the relationship between crime and punishment. Like Vico, he always conceived of the right to punish with reference to man in the 'state of natural independence', where, however, the exercise of this power was actually rendered impossible because of the disparity of forces and because of the condition of endemic, irrational violence in primitive man. Only with the evolution towards the social state had the historic actualisation of this right allowed justice to surface in the history of humanity. As for the inalienable nature of the natural right to punish others, there could be no doubts. In the new social state, as Filangieri made clear, it was not that 'a new right' had been created,

> but rather the exercise of the old right had been made more secure. In this social state it is no longer a private individual who arms himself against another private citizen for a crime he has committed, but the whole of society; the repository of public might is the element that exercises this right, of which individuals strip themselves in order to invest the whole of society with it, or the sovereign who represents it. (vol.4, p.16)

The appearance of the law thus became once more the motor, the unmistakable sign that sealed the first move in the process towards the dawn of civilisation. In specific terms, the 'criminal laws', which were understood in Rousseau's terms as 'the formulae that express the social pacts', were to have guarded and guaranteed the exercise of those original natural rights which along with the individual's 'actions' constituted the ingredients of a modern penal legislation, and of that 'great theory of proportionality between crimes and punishments', on which he exercised his sophisticated juridical genius, which was destined to astonish jurists in every corner of Europe.

After examining the evolution of penal rights across the centuries, which had varied according to different governments, and to the historical, geographic and climatic contexts, Filangieri had become convinced that penal procedure was the most urgent and most difficult area to 'correct' if one wanted to create a trial system that was worthy of a modern civil society. On the one hand, the Enlightenment actualisation of the rights of man was now visible to everyone; but on the other, the ruthless logic of domination and class privilege typical of the *Ancien régime* continued to prefer the security of communities and rulers to the detriment of the civil rights and freedom of the individual. This is why book 3 presents itself still today not just as a modern treatise on penal procedure that was technically admirable and innovative, but also as a polemical pamphlet worthy of Voltaire at his best. Filangieri declared his aim from the start: to revive the ancient accusatorial process, modelled on the example of Cicero's republican Rome and of the British world, which he defined succinctly as 'the system of the free Romans and the English'. There were solutions in that trial system that he had admired for some time, such as the *habeas corpus* principle, public debate, people's juries, the figure of a third judge between the prosecution and the defence ('make sure that the judges of law are not the same as the judges of the deed'). These were all principles that chimed with the historic battles to defend the 'sacred rights of humanity', a struggle that had been launched some time previously by Montesquieu, Beccaria and Voltaire against 'the infamous works that provided an apologia for torture', or which had defended the right to arbitrary imprisonment, and unjustified sentences. Along with Beccaria, and against Montesquieu, Filangieri also denounced the illegitimacy and ferocious anachronism of feudal tribunals, and stigmatised the terrible, secret inquisition trials demanded by the Church and the imperial power against the guarantees of the individual's liberty and the republican conception of penal procedure. His crisp conclusions in defence of man deserve to be heard still today for the clarity and civic passion that inspired them:

> Ensure that every inquisitorial mystery disappears from criminal procedure. Replace secret tip-offs with public accusations. Give all citizens the freedom to bring accusations and increase the inspectors of their actions. Create an accusing magistrate in every province of the State, someone who is only to act as accuser in those cases where there is no accuser. Frighten the slanderer and those who abuse power with the punishment of retaliation and of infamy, and safeguard innocence by providing it with all possible means of defence. Do not hide the accusation and the accuser from the accused, but rather make these clear to him in the very instant the accusation is made. Do not let him be treated as a criminal before he is convicted of the crime [...] Do not segregate him from the society of his fellow men before you believe he is worthy of that punishment. Do not force him into a confession which is pointless when it is extracted from him by force, and absurd when it is voluntary. Do not conceal from

> him the witnesses or the testimony of those who will give evidence against him. Allow the judge to hear them in his presence and let him interrupt them, interrogate them, prove the falsity of their words. Do not exclude the witnesses called for by the accused as though only those who give evidence against him are the only bearers of truth. Divide the judicial functions in such a way that each of them amongst whom it is divided has enough power to save the innocent and that no one has enough power to oppress them. Deprive feudal lords of a power that no title can render legitimate and that cannot be left intact without perpetuating the disorders that deprive us of security and freedom. (vol.3, p.234)

In fact, leaving aside the formal aspects and the juridical solutions proposed, Filangieri's two volumes on criminal laws soon appeared to the eyes of his contemporaries as an impressive document against the *Ancien régime* and its injustices. This was so precisely because the work was deeply marked by a republican and participative conception of justice that was founded on the principle of moral equality of rights for all men and thus also on the equality of the right to punish.

Moreover, if one really wanted to redress the scales of justice, in the face of absolutism, which had by now, in the second half of the eighteenth century, degenerated into open 'despotism', the new republican spirit of the Enlightenment and the growing politicisation of the Republic of Letters, which were particularly evident in the pages of the *Science of legislation*, could not but foster the staunch defence of the individual over the security of communities and the whim of sovereign power. And it was for this very reason that, in the long redefinition of 'crimes' and punishments, in the light of the historical conditions of the European nations, amongst which were the 'crimes' against religious and monarchical authority, Filangieri embraced without hesitation the cause of liberty and tolerance. In the former case, in favour of religious freedom and freedom of conscience he courageously denounced the 'monster', the 'terrible and funereal Inquisition', which was guilty of having confused 'the impiety of man' with that of the citizen, thus invading the public sphere: 'Crimes against divinity must not be subject to the sanction of the laws except when they become civil crimes' (vol.4, p.163). It is worth recalling that when the 'monster' was challenged in this way, it replied straightaway by examining the *Science of legislation*, and placing it immediately on the Index.[26] As for the latter case, he

26. On this see Franco Motta, 'Le condanne inquisitoriali della *Scienza della legislazione*', in *Diritti e costituzione*, ed. A. Trampus, p.291-335.

invoked the definitive abolition of crimes of opinion: the so-called *crimen laesae maiestatis*, which in historical terms went back to the famous 'lex Iulia', a law that had been demanded by the 'despotism of the early Caesars', and later revived by the absolutist rulers of modern times in order to attack any form of dissent, without any distinction between concrete subversive actions and simple critiques of power.

In short, the Enlightenment project of a new criminal legislation, based for the first time in the West entirely on the language of the rights of man, seemed to have been created deliberately to sound the death knell for the privileges of the *Ancien régime* and its unjust hierarchies. The subversive and explosive seed hidden in the sophisticated juridical formalism of that legislation, namely the principle of equality of all before the law, constituted a terribly effective and indeed revolutionary formula, which not by chance Filangieri defined with clear consciousness as follows:

> A kind of political liberty which reassures all classes, all conditions, all ranks of civil society. It places a brake on the magistrate and gives the weakest citizen the totality of all the forces of the nation. This voice that says to the powerful 'you are the slave of the law' and reminds the rich that the poor man is his equal, this force that always balances in man's actions the interest that he could have in violating the law with the interest he has in observing it: all this can only be the result of criminal legislation. (vol.1, p.31)

However, it was definitely in book 5, 'On the laws that concern education, customs and instruction', that the now openly political wind blew even more strongly. This wind of change lay in the sense of innovation and emancipation of the modern republican and Enlightenment conception of the rights of man and of the principle of moral equality present in the *Science of legislation*. In this delicate area the real issue at stake was the capacity of the new language of rights to guarantee not only the individual's freedoms, but also those social bonds that were necessary for the survival and emancipation of the community in its totality. It would do this by eliminating at its root any form of dangerous individualism, expanding to the largest number of protagonists the political struggle for reforms and the awareness of rights on an egalitarian and universal basis.

In Filangieri's eyes, ignorance, superstition, poor education and the wicked morals of individuals and of contemporary European nations constituted a worrying threat for the tenor of civil society. With the advent of modern commercial societies, marked as they were by economic liberalism and the overcoming of antique forms of corporativism, and by a sharp polarisation of wealth, regular famines and the explosion of endemic conflicts caused by social fragmentation, he believed that the educator's intervention in the field of education could turn out to be decisive in reinforcing the bonds that were necessary for the future order of society. The lack of an appropriate, up-to-date civic education promoted by governments actually rendered 'all rights uncertain', encouraged rebellion from below and oppression from on high, the fanaticism of inquisitorial burnings at the stake, and the pollution and suppression of public opinion. The individual's new, sacrosanct right of freedom had therefore to find its precise limits in his belonging to a community, in his 'dependence' on others ('man cannot be happy without being free and dependent'), and that could come about solely by educating the populace both in the principle of individual freedom and in the principle of collective interest, thus achieving yet another delicate equilibrium. Hence the need to finally create 'universal' public education, paid for by the State for all social classes, who would be divided up only on the basis of the individual's talent and predispositions, instructing all, from their childhood onwards, in citizenship, in love of the fatherland, in a civic sense, and introducing 'virtue amidst the wealth of the moderns by the same means that classical legislations had introduced it amongst the legions of the ancients' (vol.1, p.36). The high road towards achieving this was that of passing specific laws on the basis of the utilitarian theory of the 'leading passions', illustrated by Helvétius in his *De l'homme*, and relying on the fact that 'education is the fruit of imitation' (vol.5, p.17), of examples, of the efficacy of public opinion when it is correctly guided.

With crude realism and contrary to the *Principes naturels de la morale et de la politique* of the baron d'Holbach, where what dominated was the traditional idea of natural sociability, Filangieri thought it was necessary always to start solely from the individual's passions, his love of self and his 'love of power': the potential predisposition to sociability, love for others, came as a second stage and it was in any case not judged capable of moving history forward. It was thus necessary to direct and lead individuals by the hand towards a reborn eighteenth-century patriotism and a civic sense, enhancing their love for glory and power as a service towards others, and relaunching the honours, prizes and public ceremonies of the ancients for the faithful servants of the community and the public good. All this then had to be further reinforced by a Late Enlightenment cultural policy that was made up of specific programmes of public education: through the educative reading of Voltaire's and Rousseau's philosophical novels, through the establishment of the new political and educative theatre of Diderot, Lessing and Alfieri, through the militant paintings of Goya and David. In short, it was necessary to bring into being with appropriate laws that 'sublime combination' of politics, education, art and literature that was able to give birth to a modern civil society where 'the interest and passions of the individual are so well combined with the interest of society itself, that one cannot pursue its own happiness without contributing to that of the other' (vol.5, p.269).

If ever there was an important work of the Late European Enlightenment from those crucial years that preceded the French Revolution, one that could let us understand clearly how the politics of the Enlightenment thinkers had nothing to do with the succession of violent, revolutionary upheavals that were looming on the horizon, Filangieri's *Science of legislation* was certainly that work. That way of conceiving of politics had always liked expounding its programme of reforms for the *Ancien régime* in terms of construction, piece by piece, of a novel and ambitious cultural hegemony – along Gramscian lines, we would say today – precisely through the education of the people in citizenship and rights, and through the guidance and control of public opinion: this was the sudden great novelty that was radically altering the forms of political struggle in the West.

There is no doubt that Filangieri was one of the major protagonists of that extraordinary politicisation of the Republic of Letters in the last quarter of the century, a politicisation that, founded as it was on the Enlightenment thinkers' consciousness of the birth of public opinion, further explored both the limits and the extraordinary potential of the latter. To this end he openly invited philosophers to make productive use of it, turning it towards political and emancipatory ends: 'What would become of us if public opinion, managed and directed by them [the philosophers], did not besmirch with infamy a monarch who set up an unjust law [...]? What would happen to us if in our monarchies the voice of freedom was never heard by the people and it never reminded them of their precious and inalienable rights?' (vol.5, p.11).

The chapter dedicated to the freedom of the press as embodying man's natural right to criticise and to communicate his own ideas explained very well all the formidable links that bound together the theme of education and the lucid Enlightenment consciousness of the growing importance of public opinion and its immediate political, social and juridical repercussions. Without education for everyone it was not in fact possible to guarantee the individual's equal participation in debates in the public sphere. Without freedom of the press, there was no public opinion, nor respect for popular sovereignty, nor any possible republican participation in the political struggle. As Filangieri wrote: 'Under whatever government, and in whatever nation, public opinion is the strongest element in the State: its influence for good or ill is enormous because it is superior both to action and to the resistance of the public authority, and as a consequence, it is of absolute importance that it should be rectified, directed and corrected' (vol.5, p.19). Public opinion, which was becoming more and more the privileged and unexpected space for political struggle in the modern world, had in short been turned into something close to an actual tribunal of the people:

> This tribunal which is concrete evidence of the fact that sovereignty resides constantly and actually with the people, and which never really relinquishes this sovereignty, even when it deposits some of this authority in the hands of many or of a sole ruler, of a senate or a king: this tribunal, I tell you, is that of public opinion. In an ignorant and corrupt people, this tribunal does not recognise its own interests and with the omnipotence of its decrees perpetuates evil and impedes the good. (vol.5, p.360)

But apart from education for all, the other great necessary condition in order to guarantee the correct and transparent exercise of public opinion was press freedom.[27] Filangieri explained that the legislator 'must then never ignore it. Public interest demands this.' Apart from being a particular natural right that was connected to the critical spirit, that freedom referred back through an organic and indissoluble nexus to another natural right that was no less important, 'which can be neither lost nor alienated as long as one belongs to a society; a right which is superior to and precedes all laws', in other words to the republican right by definition, to participate in the political struggle; to the freedom to 'contribute, as far as each of us can, to the good of the society to which he belongs', articulating his own ideas critically. Of course freedom of the press could adopt defamatory and ambiguous tones, and constitute a danger to public order: for that reason it had

27. The bibliography on freedom of the press and public opinion in the eighteenth century is now huge: see Edoardo Tortarolo, *The Invention of free press: writers and censorship in eighteenth-century Europe* (Dordrecht, 2016); Keith Michael Baker, *Au tribunal de l'opinion: essais sur l'imaginaire politique au XVIIIe siècle* (Paris, 1993).

to be regulated, and the Neapolitan jurist did not draw back from prescribing precise measures. But this 'so precious right', which Kant, in his famous article *Was ist Aufklärung?* from this very period, placed before the very definition of Enlightenment, as a critical and public use of reason in all fields, should never be suppressed. To do so would involve the loss of human dignity and of civic existence.

With Filangieri's *Science of legislation*, which creatively distilled the best ideas produced by political, philosophical and juridical thought in the course of the eighteenth century, Enlightenment humanism really did reach its apex and triumph. At last man had been placed on his throne as Diderot in the *Encyclopédie* had hoped he would be: he had wanted man positioned at the centre of all reflections, making him the principal object of the new sciences. The recognition of his natural rights and of the cosmopolitan, universalistic principle of moral equality even defined his very humanity and the horizon of his earthly existence, as Condorcet had tried to explain – in vain and in desperation – in his *Esquisse d'un tableau historique des progrès de l'esprit humain* before dying in Robespierre's prison.

In order to accentuate the new centrality of Enlightenment humanism, in the fifth book, 'On the laws concerning religion', which appeared posthumously in 1791, Filangieri stressed at every turn the importance and centrality that had now been attained by the human person, and the necessity of guaranteeing the absolute inviolability of his body and conscience. He tried once more to achieve that difficult balance between individual and community, between public and private, that lies at the root of modern civil societies. This was a really crucial question, one that was always at the root of political reflections in the late Enlightenment. To this end, if on the one hand it was necessary to invoke the law to guarantee the increase of wealth, public happiness and the safety of the citizen, and to regulate the public side of relationships, on the other, power and legislation had to give way before individual consciences, that internal forum which debated religious truth, the inner core of the person represented by the private sphere which completely defined one's being and individuality: 'The law should not try to want to know everything, to see everything [...] Authority should stop before the door of the individual's house, should respect that oasis of his peace and freedom, should not try to investigate his inner thoughts and intentions.' In treating that internal forum and in particular the subject's religious beliefs, he argued that one had to move with great caution, never resorting to force, always respecting freedom of conscience. Nevertheless, it was quite another thing dealing with the religious problem from the point of view of the public sphere: it was possible and to a certain extent desirable that religion's duty was to guide 'the secret actions of the citizen', leading him 'to be just, honest and virtuous' (vol.1, p.38), according to that model of modern civic religion proposed by Rousseau in the *Social contract*.

Filangieri was very familiar with the great eighteenth-century debate on the nature of religions and the growing atheist propaganda of important areas of the radical wing of the European Enlightenment. Distant from d'Holbach's and Diderot's materialism, as well as from the Italian libertine tradition, he shared the deistic ideas present in the thought of Locke and Voltaire, as well as the latter's great battles in favour of tolerance and a natural, universal religion without dogmas, priests and churches. With his masonic brothers, first in the lodges that adopted the English rite, and later through contacts with the Bavaria Illuminati, he had personally committed himself to trying to give shape to new forms of religiosity, deriving from the Gnostic-Hermetic tradition, and capable of rethinking and bringing up to date the evangelical basis of primitive Christianity. He was very passionate about the problem of the search for 'Truth'.

Book 5 bears deep and obvious traces of this, making Filangieri appear a sort of restless and sophisticated religious reformer, an aspect that has still to be studied. Referring indirectly to the theses of Lessing's *Nathan der Weise*, Filangieri also wondered about the truthfulness of the revelations of the prophets and the necessity of coming to something like an 'eternal religion of Enlightenment', which would be at the service of the civic education of humanity.[28] From the great German writer he also took the cosmopolitan, universalistic vision regarding the indispensable need for the great monotheistic religions to live together in modern civic societies: 'We are children of the same father, individuals in the same family, so how could I ignore such a sizeable number of my brothers because they did not have the good fortune to share in the best part of our father's inheritance?'[29] He felt that a religious legislation that was valid 'for all peoples and all times' was essential in order to create the basis for a modern civic religion that had already been tried by the Ancient Romans: such a religion would

28. On the religious reforms Filangieri hoped for, see my chapter 'Gaetano Filangieri e l'eterna religione dei Lumi', in Ferrone, *I profeti dell'Illuminismo*, p.338ff.

29. Filangieri, *Scienza della legislazione*, vol.6: *Delle leggi che riguardano la religione*, ed. Gerardo Tocchini (2003), p.13.

be capable of strengthening social bonds, and of educating the people in citizenship and respect for the rights of man. Even before Rousseau, it had been Filangieri's own teacher Vico, in his *De uno universi iuris principio et fine uno*, who taught the Neapolitan Enlightenment thinkers the importance of political theology, the historical and social function of religion in the stages of the civilisation of nations. And Filangieri recalled this fact explicitly and with pride:

> Religion precedes, prepares, works on, accompanies and follows the origin, progress and development of civil societies; in the savage, it is a timid worship that he offers to the unknown cause of his terror and fears in order to restrain or divert its deadly action; in barbarian societies, it is the principle of that *authority* that man can no longer tolerate in the hands of men and therefore places willingly in the hands of deities. Under the auspices of *theocracy*, religion arranges, prepares and by stages works through the slow, difficult, gradual passage from *natural independence* to *civil servitude.* In societies where this *passage* has already happened, in other words in societies that have already reached *perfection*, this cult can come to the aid of public authority in order both to extend the sanction of laws and to obtain what they cannot prescribe [...] Could this religion, I say, which is so naturally inherent in man's nature, so necessary to the formation, perfection and conservation of society, and so terrible when it degenerates, not perhaps be considered as one of the most important objectives of *legislative science*? (vol.5, p.12)

The legislator, however, did not have to occupy himself, or only to a small extent, with the theological debate inside and outside the churches, or with the salvific function of religions in the afterlife, or all those questions of conscience and of the individual's innermost forum, questions which were presided over by the individual's rights to freedom. It was in fact only in relation to the public sphere that he had to ask himself questions about the 'true principles by which the confines can be established between the priesthood and the empire' (vol.1, p.40), about how to avoid both the social effects of militant atheism, rejected in Locke's terms as the source of the breakdown of social bonds, and superstitious and bloody 'fanaticism'. In order to prevent terrible religious wars, tolerance and rights to freedom had to be defended at all costs from the invasion by fundamentalists of all religions. To this end, in Catholic Europe the 'monster' of the Inquisition had to be vanquished forever, laws had to be passed against the celibacy of priests, and against the Church's juridical privileges of mortmain and all forms of its economic, political and juridical power. Also conciliarism had to be revived against the absolute power of the popes. Only in this way could man be defended against himself through the laws, and could he be made happy, by placing religion also at his service and at the service of a renewed conception of politics.

In short, there is no doubt that with Filangieri's work the Neapolitan school of jurists really made a huge contribution to the overall construction of the language of the rights of man in the West. But this contribution must be extended also to another question of supreme importance which still today interests scholars working on the will to power, the negative forms of power and of man's dominion over man: how to protect natural rights and to whom one should attribute this crucial role.

We have seen that, compared to Locke and thanks to Vico's philosophy, the historical recognition of the existence of natural rights and of their organic intersection of morality with 'political bodies' had emerged among the Neapolitan Enlightenment thinkers, who went well beyond the earliest reflections on the subject in the seventeenth and eighteenth centuries. This recognition had come to fruition finally in Filangieri's project for a great science of legislation capable of producing a monumental juridical system entirely founded on the rights of man and on the principle of equality. It was in this context that the new Enlightenment constitutionalism of the turn of the century had taken shape. In a polemic against the old, habitual constitutionalism of the *Ancien régime*, which had been wisely updated by Montesquieu, this new constitutionalism now seemed finally capable of guaranteeing the exercise of politics and the protection of natural rights in contemporary societies. Along with Paine, Condorcet and many other intellectuals who, after 1776, the year of the Declaration of Independence by the American colonies, had wondered what link it was necessary to establish between the rights of man and modern written constitutions, Filangieri had in fact outlined, as an expert and sophisticated jurist, the epistemological and formal character of Enlightenment constitutionalism, rejecting both Rousseau's and Blackstone's suggestions about the road to take in order to bring these rights into being and protect them.

Apart from the creeping primitivism incarnated in Rousseau's myth of the noble savage, Filangieri had never appreciated the Genevan philosopher's Pelagian fideism as regards the original goodness of man. This had led Rousseau to connect the fate of the natural rights to direct democracy, to the undisputed and omnipotent primacy of legislative power and of the people's sovereignty, with its abiding certainty that the general will and republican participation would always choose for the better and create the happiness of the individual, respecting his rights in any case. Filangieri, by contrast, was the child of a political culture that was impregnated with realism. He had grown up in the school of Machiavelli and Vico, and thus he feared deeply the possibility of demagogic drift in the popular assemblies, and the appearance of new Masaniellos at the service of despotism: the latter was the real bête noire of the Neapolitan's whole oeuvre. He preferred to entrust to the new science of legislation the duty of finally creating a juridical system worthy of a modern civic society, built on solid respect and on the function of the uncrossable limit of those natural rights certified by Vico in his *ius naturale prius.* To Filangieri's eyes only the laws and judges could in fact guarantee freedom and rights: politics could certainly not do that, at least not alone, without the uncrossable juridical limits imposed by the iron respect for natural rights. Filangieri expressed a similar aversion both to Montesquieu's *Ancien régime* constitutionalism, which conceded too much to privileges and to the inequalities imposed by intermediate bodies, thus actually denying the universality and equality of rights, and to the constitutional plan consecrated in Blackstone's famous *Commentaries.*

Filangieri did not at all like that prestigious model, which organically blended rights and the Ancient Constitution, bringing about a sort of 'historic constitutionalisation of natural rights' thanks to a centuries-old tradition. He disliked it inasmuch as it had ended up reaffirming the existence only of the 'rights of the people of England'. The violent suppression of the 'Wilkes and Liberty' movement against the despotism of George III and above all the revolt of the American colonies had convinced him of the failure and the obvious inability of the Ancient Constitution to guarantee freedom and the exercise of man's universal and cosmopolitan rights. It was no accident that Filangieri's meticulous, harsh criticism of that constitutional model immediately aroused the interest and admiration of English radicals, who enthusiastically translated the *Science of legislation*, where Filangieri denounced the perilous 'inconstancy of the British constitution', which had never been set down in a precise written text, the risks for freedom implicit in the precarious equilibrium of the mixed form of government, as well as the systematic violations of the principle of equality amongst citizens.[30]

30. Cf. Ferrone, *Politics of Enlightenment*, p.142ff.

Unfortunately Filangieri died in the summer of 1788, without being able to see the triumph of his beloved rights of man, which had become immortal in the Declaration of the Rights of Man of 1789, nor was he able to see their tragic mystification and then their bloody violation during the Terror and then in the decade full of convulsions that followed. However, it was to a friend and disciple of his, Francesco Mario Pagano, a lawyer and authoritative professor of law at the University of Naples, that it fell to test to the full the theoretical structure of the *Science of legislation* and of Enlightenment constitutionalism. This he did when considering the harsh replies that had come from historical events against the rights of man, as he faced up to French revolutionary constitutionalism without any reverential fears, but rather with the pride of someone who felt himself to be the heir of a great cultural tradition. Pagano did so as president of the Legislation Committee who had been entrusted by the provisional government to write the *Project for a constitution of the Neapolitan republic* in the winter of 1799.

That work, the fruit of profound meditation, and of great theoretical weight, is still today too often neglected by the experts on constitutionalism.[31] Yet it is really the final masterpiece of the Neapolitan school of natural law, and at the same time the political testament of the Italian Enlightenment, which was destined to end its existence in the bloodshed of the Catholic legitimist repression of 1799. The profound differences are many and highly original compared with the Thermidor Convention's Constitution of 1795 and the other Italian constitutions that appeared in the peninsula in those same years.[32] As was flagged up in the peninsula's gazettes and by Amaury Duval in the pages of the *Décade philosophique* – Duval had amongst other things begun to translate into French Pagano's famous *Saggi politici* after the German version of 1796 by Jonathan Müller – it was above all the Neapolitan Declaration of the Rights of Man that was particularly

31. For instance there is no reference to it in *Le basi filosofiche del costituzionalismo: lineamenti di filosofia del diritto costituzionale*, ed. Augusto Barbera and Gianfrancesco Zanetti (Rome and Bari, 1997).
32. See the arguments put forward by the editors as well as the bibliography on this topic in *Progetto di costituzione della Repubblica napoletana presentato al governo provvisorio dal comitato di legislazione*, ed. Federica Morelli and Antonio Trampus, with an introduction by Anna Maria Rao (Venice and Mariano del Friuli, 2008). On Pagano, besides the classic work by Gioele Solari, *Studi su Francesco Mario Pagano* (Turin, 1963), see now Dario Ippolito, *Mario Pagano: il pensiero giuspolitico di un illuminista* (Turin, 2008).

different from preceding declarations.[33] This text took to heart the conclusions that Italian Enlightenment culture had arrived at in the course of the eighteenth century, and, apart from dealing with the vicissitudes of the Terror and the failure of French constitutional efforts, introduced 'various metaphysical reflections' on the language of the rights of man themselves, their nature, their historical and philosophical legitimacy, their juridical function with respect to the constitution. Above all it asked the question of how to protect them from a popular sovereignty that was out of control, like the one that had been at work in the Jacobin Terror and during the uncontrollable outburst of violence on all sides.

In working out the design of the Neapolitan Constitution, Mario Pagano had in front of him, as a text for comparison, the Thermidor Constitution of 1795 and in particular its *Déclaration des droits et des devoirs de l'homme et du citoyen*, where for the first time in Western history there was a complete symmetry between rights and duties. On closer inspection, in this case too that sudden change of course was nothing other than the umpteenth concession to the political culture of the *Ancien régime*, against which the *philosophes* and the most advanced circles of European Enlightenment had fought. The language of duties – as we have seen in the foregoing pages – actually came from way back: from Cicero's *De officiis*, but above all from the eighteenth-century revival of the Stoic sociability principle, in the modern natural law of Grotius and Pufendorf. In addition to this legacy there was also the ingenious eighteenth-century reinterpretation of natural law made by the physiocrats and in particular by Victor de Mirabeau, the author, in 1772, of a successful catechism of popular education entitled *La Science, ou les Droits et les devoirs de l'homme*, to which we will return later.

Mario Pagano was well aware of these deep cultural roots of the theory of duties that were hidden in the veins of the *Ancien régime*, and above all he had followed through the gazettes the harsh Paris confrontation in the *Commission des Onze*, which tried to tone down the subversive, revolutionary charge of rights by relaunching duties as a moderate antidote to the excesses of the Terror.[34] His *Dichiarazione*

33. For Duval's intervention, see Franco Venturi, 'L'Italia fuori d'Italia', in *Storia d'Italia*, vol.3: *Dal primo Settecento all'Unità*, ed. Ruggiero Romano and Corrado Vivanti (Turin, 1973), p.985-1481 (1141ff.).

34. See the reconstruction of the debate in Marcel Gauchet, *La Révolution des droits de l'homme* (Paris, 1989), p.70ff. In general on the Thermidor Constitution, see Michel Troper, *Terminer la Révolution: la Constitution de 1795* (Paris, 2006).

dei diritti e doveri dell'uomo, del popolo e de' suoi rappresentanti, published in Naples, appears from its title onwards very different from the Thermidor Constitution and seems to have been written deliberately to reply polemically to the Paris jurists on several fundamental points. His aim was that of restating in this field and with specific merit the claims of Enlightenment constitutionalism, which had been laboriously put together in the preceding decades by figures such as Genovesi, Filangieri, Condorcet and Paine with the sole aim of protecting and bringing into being the rights of man.

In the preliminary report accompanying the *Progetto di Costituzione*, Pagano clarified his point of view regarding the absolute centrality and organic nature of the *Dichiarazione* in relation to the actual constitutional text: 'The most excellent thing found in modern constitutions is the declaration of the rights of man. This solid and *immutable basis* is missing from the legislations of antiquity.'[35] Pagano was the heir of Genovesi and Filangieri, and he himself was a great connoisseur and scholar of the language of rights – on the basis of which he had written the *Considerazioni sul processo criminale* of 1787, which was immediately translated and implemented north of the Alps for reform of the penal code.[36] He crisply explained to the French jurists that their Declaration contained theoretical errors of considerable importance for how to conceive of rights:

> We have availed ourselves of the Declaration that the French Constitution promotes at the outset. But we have also noticed that according to the aforementioned Declaration equality is not yet a right of man, but only the basis for all rights and the principle on which they are established and founded. Equality is a relationship and rights are faculties. These are the faculties of taking action which is given to each of us by the law of nature, in other words invariable reason, and the knowledge of natural relationships, which is positive social law. From this relationship of equality of nature that exists among men derive the existence and the equality of rights. Since men are for that reason equal amongst themselves, they have the same physical and moral faculties: and one man has the same amount of reason to avail himself of his natural might as another. Hence it follows that

35. Cf. Pagano, *Progetto di costituzione*, p.122. Emphasis added. Henceforth page references will be given in the text.
36. See the reconstruction of the diffusion of this work in Francesco Mario Pagano, *Considerazioni sul processo criminale*, ed. Filippo Maria Paladini (Venice and Mariano del Friuli, 2009), p.123ff.

> natural faculties, which are undefined by nature, have to be defined beforehand by reason, since each person has to make use of them in such a way that others can also use theirs. This then is how all the rights of man and the equality of such rights stem from the similarity and equality of nature. (p.122)

Already from these few lines it is clear that Pagano, unlike his French colleagues, felt sharply the need not just to *declare* the 'eternal truths of the rights of man', but to found them, to set them up, to defend them in every way and against everything: to turn these rights into the beating heart, 'the unmovable base of all free constitutions [...] the principal objective of all regular constitutions' (p.131).

The particular hierarchical structure and formal symmetries with which he constructed the Neapolitan Declaration do not leave us in any doubt regarding his intention to reiterate the supremacy of the rights of the individual from which everything else derives. As the primary source for all the rights of man Pagano pointed to man's right 'to conserve and improve his being'. From this last right derived the right to freedom, understood as 'the right of man to avail himself of all his moral and physical forces just as he pleases, with the sole limitation that he not prevent others from doing the same'. There then followed the right to hold an opinion, the right of volition, 'the right to display orally or in writing and in any way his opinions and desires'. This last right was particularly dear to Filangieri and to other European Enlightenment circles. After that was the right to property, and finally the right of resistance: this last right had disappeared from the Thermidor Declaration of 1795 and was here stated in different terms also from the Declaration of 1793. For Pagano this sacred right, which had been given by nature to man to defend all the other rights, did not in fact belong to the people, to the whole nation as the Jacobins believed, but to the individual, and it had to be exercised only against the despot and the tyrant.

In the rigid but extremely eloquent hierarchical structure of the Naples Declaration the rights of the citizen came immediately after those of man and they began with the blunt affirmation that 'every citizen has the right to have all his natural and civil rights guaranteed by the powers of the state' (p.132). The rights of the people only came in third place, and not by chance. Neapolitan Enlightenment culture had in fact long debated throughout the eighteenth century the theme of collective identities, of the concept of fatherland, nation, people and more generally of the political community and civil society.[37] Pagano had learned from Genovesi and Vico to appreciate the so-called 'middle class' or 'civic class' and to specify clearly the meaning of those terms, which were causing such confusion in France. As he made clear in the preliminary report:

> When we say the people, we mean that class of people who are clear about their true interests, and are not a plebs who are asleep in ignorance and degraded in slavery, or the gangrenous aristocratic faction. Both these extremes are diseased tumours in the social body, which corrupt its health. It is regrettable that we do not have in modern languages a word to express the notion that we would like to communicate. Therefore, not being able to be precise about the notion of people, we have predefined its faculty, saying that it can rise up in order to give itself a new constitution, but only one that is free. (p.124)

This business of the entitlement of the constituting power, of its nature and above all of its limits, is a crucial point which clearly separates Enlightenment constitutionalism from the revolutionary version that had emerged in reality in France.

Pagano had no doubts about the legitimacy of the new popular sovereignty, which had taken the place of that of the monarch. Despite this, like the good Enlightenment thinker he was, he had pondered this topic for a long time, and was afraid that it might be misunderstood, and might become omnipotent compared with its original character in the *ius naturale prius*. Nobody in Naples contested the basic right of the people to have a constitution, but this had to come about while maintaining respect for the individual and his rights: 'as long as it was a free constitution' (p.133). The people could indeed 'change their ancient constitution and establish a new one that was more consonant with its current interests, but it always had to be a democratic constitution!' On this question he explained that at the base of this new 'political law, which had been noticed first by the Neapolitan Gravina, then adopted by the famous French public law experts Montesquieu and Rousseau', lay in the first place the principle of equality and then the consideration that 'society is formed by the union of the wills of

37. See chapter 7, 'Nation or fatherland? The republican and constitutional patriotism of Italian Enlightenment thinkers', in Ferrone, *Politics of Enlightenment*, p.100-38. On the theme of collective identities in general, see *Identità collettive tra Medioevo ed età moderna: convegno internazionale di studi*, ed. Paolo Prodi and Wolfgang Reinhard (Bologna, 2002).

men who wish to live together for the reciprocal guarantee of their rights' (p.124). Hence the rigid structure outlined in the Neapolitan Declaration, which always put the rights of man before the rights of the people, thus placing an unbreachable limit on sovereignty.

Within this logic of priorities, duties were illustrated, with great interpretative originality, in the second part of the Declaration, amongst the final articles. There duties derived not from the sociability principle or the communitarian conception of the human being, as the physiocrats and many French constitutionalists still loved to stress in the heated debates that preceded the 1795 Constitution, but solely from respect for the principle of equality amongst individuals. Duties were nothing other than the subject's obligations towards society and towards what today we would call the social rights of the individual. As was to be expected, after the Terror and the violence of the Revolution, Pagano and even the Thermidorians, when reflecting on reciprocal social obligations, no longer dared to appeal to that natural right to the pursuit of happiness that had been so dear to the whole of Enlightenment culture, to Jefferson and Filangieri. Too much blood had been shed. Happiness again seemed an almost ungraspable state of mind. Political realism now dominated the scene. The articles of the Neapolitan *Dichiarazione*, in polemic with the French Declaration, put it like this:

> Man's duties are obligations or moral necessities that come from the moral force of a principle of reason. This principle is the same one whence we derived all rights, in other words the similarity and equality of men. 17. The fundamental duty of man is to respect the rights of others. Equality means that our own rights are worth as much as those of others. 18. Every man must help other men and force himself to protect and to improve the essence of his fellow men, because thanks to the similarity of nature each man must be affected towards others as he is to himself. 19. Thus it is a sacred duty of man to feed the needy. 20. Every man is obliged to enlighten and instruct the others.

However, it was not only the Thermidor Declaration overall that contained lacunae and incongruities and highlighted the elements of strong divergence from Enlightenment constitutionalism, but its whole theoretical backbone. Apart from the obvious differences regarding the organisation of justice, and the bicameral system of representation, about which much has been written, what was really clear was the French jurists' rejection of the constitutionalisation of public education inspired by that 'republican spirit' which was at the centre of the *Science of legislation*.[38] Similarly obvious was the French reluctance to defend to the hilt the rights of man from the excesses of popular sovereignty. It was immediately evident that the thorny question of the balance of power and protection of a constitution founded on the respect of the rights of man had emerged as a complex problem that was very difficult to solve. Already in the course of the eighteenth century attempts at a solution had been tried both in the American colonies and in France with Sieyès's project to create a *jury constitutionnaire*.[39] In the latter case, on closer inspection, this turned out to be an institution with unclear duties and in any case it was an umpteenth variant of legislative power which had specific obligations that were very distant from those of a modern constitutional tribunal.[40] However, this was precisely the direction taken by Pagano's idea of placing as a guardian 'to protect the laws of the constitution and freedom' a supreme, independent tribunal, with powers very close to those of modern constitutional courts.

Behind this extraordinary intuition and piece of constitutional engineering – which encapsulated and typified eighteenth-century Enlightenment constitutionalism – lay decades of reflections on the centrality of the rights of man, on the necessity to defend them from the dangers of an absolute sovereignty that was perilously prone to degenerating into a despotism or tyranny of one or more rulers. In Naples in particular Masaniello's revolution, the recurrent fears aroused by the absolute, despotic powers of the monarchies, of a fanatical and superstitious clergy, of a populace that was easy to manipulate for demagogues who were ready to do anything, all this had inoculated Enlightenment culture so that it could deal with these topics. Deep reflections on them are present in the works of Vico, Genovesi and Filangieri. Already in the second edition of his *Saggi politici* (1792) Pagano had dedicated critical passages to this question, advancing the solution of entrusting the protection of freedom to judges, to a neutral and superior magistracy.[41]

38. On the issues of the organisation of justice and bicameral representation see Antonio Trampus' views and his bibliography in Pagano, *Progetto di costituzione*, p.40ff.
39. For the American colonies, see Mario Einaudi, *Le origini dottrinali e storiche del controllo giudiziario sulla costituzionalità delle leggi negli Stati Uniti d'America* (Turin, 1931).
40. See Troper, *Terminer la Révolution*, p.206ff.
41. Cf. Pagano, *Saggi politici*, p.22, 356, 357.

As we have stressed several times before, the constitution, constructed as it was for the sake of the rights of man, had always been conceived in the context of Enlightenment constitutionalism primarily as the law of all laws, which encompassed organically the declaration of rights. It was in this role that its authentic republican spirit – according to Pagano – had to be protected and guarded by a supreme tribunal. Such a body would be able to restrain the various powers and channel them within their rightful limits in order to safeguard a constitution that had been set up precisely to defend individual rights. In France, by contrast, what had immediately prevailed was a conception of constitutionalism that conceded too much to *la Nation* and its general will, forgetting the absolute primacy of the rights that were consecrated in the *Déclaration*. The results had been horrific, and Pagano did not hesitate to denounce them in his report, advising his fellow countrymen not to go down that route:

> Citizen representatives, we propose an addition that we have made to the French Constitution, for that salutary fear that we must have of despotism and of any arbitrary power, to whose whim our nation has unfortunately become accustomed over the course of so many centuries. If the executive power is too dependent on the legislative body, as it was in the French Constitution of 1793, then the Assembly will absorb the executive, and concentrating all powers in itself the Assembly will become despotic. If, however, the two powers are independent of each other, two kinds of disorder can arise: either the political machine becomes inert and sluggish, because of the lack of intelligence of the two bodies, which become rivals of each other; or the usurpation of one power by the other, because of that natural tendency of all power to increase. Hence the necessity for another body of representatives of the people to act as a supreme tribunal, holding in its hands the balance of powers and enclosing them within their rightful boundaries: in other words, a body that keeps guard over the constitution and liberty. It will force the executive power back within its lines if it has superseded them. It will place a veto over the legislative power if in some cases it usurps the executive. At the same time it will encourage both bodies, when necessary, to fulfil their duties, thus counteracting both the excesses of commission and the defects of omission. The power of this tribunal will reside in this body that we have called the Ephors. (p.129)

With this precise and detailed proposal of constitutional engineering, projected prophetically into the future, the Neapolitan Enlightenment concluded its long intellectual adventure dedicated to the construction of a theory of the rights of man as a political language for modern times. Its eclipse was caused by Napoleon's invasion of the peninsula, the harsh and implacable Restoration of the *Ancien régime* and its political, social and religious culture by the Holy Alliance between throne and altar, and then the appearance of a 'Risorgimento without Enlightenment', which paid no attention to the rights of man. This latter point is something that Italian historiography has failed to take into account even today, obsessed as it is with anniversaries to celebrate, renewing the old images of nationalism and the culture of duties invoked by Mazzini. All this has condemned to oblivion that world and its extraordinary contributions to European Enlightenment culture. But this oblivion, of course, need not last forever.

III

The Late Enlightenment: the rights of man and the political struggle against the *Ancien régime*

14. Public opinion and the defence of man: Voltaire, Diderot and physiocracy

Why did the rise of the rights of man only occur in modern Europe? Are these rights really 'one of the great inventions of our civilisation', as Italian philosopher Norberto Bobbio claimed in 1997?[1] Or are they innate in human nature, and as such universally present in all cultures, though in different forms and at different times? While the debate is still open, there is a feeling that Bobbio may have a point.[2] Moses gave the Jewish people the table of the Ten Commandments, not one with a list of rights. There seems to be no trace of the natural rights of the individual in the Quran. And, at least as far as we currently know, the same applies to Indian and Chinese culture. What matters for our present investigation is not the matter of the universality of rights or of Europe's presumed primogeniture in this respect, but the historical issue hinted at in the earlier question: what are the reasons for the momentous rise of these rights in Late Enlightenment culture?

As we have seen, in the American Declaration of Independence Jefferson proclaimed certain truths to be 'self-evident': 'that all men are created equal; that they are endowed by their Creator with certain inalienable rights; that among these are life, liberty, and the pursuit of happiness'. However, as we have also seen, putting aside the rhetoric, the difficult and complex genealogy of those presumed truths if anything highlighted how those tenets were anything but

1. Cf. Norberto Bobbio, *Autobiografia*, ed. Alberto Papuzzi (Rome and Bari, 1997), p.261.
2. On this issue, on which historians, political scientists and philosophers hold different views, see the first few pages of Tierney, *Idea of natural rights*. See also Amartya Sen, *The Idea of justice* (London, 2009), p.5ff., and G. E. R. Lloyd, *Ancient worlds, modern reflections: philosophical perspectives on Greek and Chinese science and culture* (Oxford, 2004).

'self-evident' and easily agreed on by all. It was certainly not enough to appeal to the geometric-deductive logical demonstrations of the traditional language of natural law, as in Grotius or Pufendorf, and as Jefferson himself seemed to be doing when branding these truths as 'self-evident'. Equally insufficient were Rousseau's 'turn' to anthropology or the use of history in Vico's *New science*, which at most spoke to a few restricted elites. The reasons for the sudden popularity of these 'truths' in the eighteenth century must be sought elsewhere. The answer to our question can be found in the cultural history of those tormented years, with some input from the history of ideas.[3]

With good reason, critics have highlighted the widespread change in mentality, characterised by a new-found respect for the human body, and the heightened sense of empathy towards fellow human beings that resulted from the success of the epistolary novels of Rousseau and Richardson. This certainly played a decisive role in the naturalisation of this language at a popular level and in providing rights with their 'emotional basis'.[4] Nevertheless, this is only part of the story. We cannot shed total light on this phenomenon by studying its passive reception, i.e. solely in terms of the influence exerted by the spread of a new way of thinking that was more attentive to human suffering. We must also take into account the long genealogy and intrinsic greatness and originality of the moral idea of natural rights. From its strong roots in university textbooks, its political discourse was transformed when the works of the greatest European thinkers of the eighteenth century turned it into the language of the moderns. This was a conscious act of will by late-eighteenth-century Enlightenment authors, part of their struggle against the *Ancien régime* especially in the last fifteen years before the French Revolution.[5]

3. On the new cultural history of the Enlightenment see Vincenzo Ferrone and Daniel Roche, *L'Illuminismo nella cultura contemporanea: storia e storiografia* (Rome and Bari, 2002), p.83ff.
4. See Hunt, *Inventing human rights*, p.35ff. With reference to Rousseau's *Julie*, Hunt remarks that the novel 'encouraged a highly charged identification with the characters' (p.38). Given that the rise of the epistolary novel 'coincides chronologically with the birth of human rights' (p.40), Hunt argues that this newly developed empathy acted as the rights' emotional basis. We should also bear in mind that the novel as a phenomenon is part of a wider and momentous European historical process of redefinition of authority relationships within the family and affective relationships at the interpersonal level: see Lawrence Stone, *The Family, sex and marriage in England 1500-1800* (New York, 1977), p.270-404; Maurice Daumas, *La Tendresse amoureuse, XVI*[e]*-XVIII*[e] *siècles* (Paris, 1996).
5. Franco Venturi addressed some of the methodological issues raised by this

Indeed, in the final stages of the development of the new language these authors did not hesitate to make conscious use of all the weapons created by the new culture of the Enlightenment: the critical and public use of reason in every field, and the appeal to public opinion via all means of communication in order to establish the discourse of rights in the minds and hearts of all men. This was carried out by asserting the need for and designing new reforms with the explicit objective of attacking despotism, privileges and injustices head-on.

Condorcet's *Esquisse d'un tableau historique des progrès de l'esprit humain* provides us with an early explicit indication that there was a precise political intent in this direction, and shows that the history of the rights of man had quickly gathered pace with the American Declaration of Independence. For the marquis, with the events of 1776 the cause of the rights of man finally broke out of the restricted circle of academia, of occasional references in dusty old volumes on jurisprudence or moral philosophy, or of cryptic debate in select circles of intellectuals, in order to be 'performed' before everybody's eyes. The issue of rights was now openly debated before public opinion through all possible media: novels, the theatre, painting, gazettes, *salons*, the halls of courts. And everywhere it caused a stir, evoking amazement and deep emotions, and profoundly affecting the political debate in that crucial historical period known as the Late Enlightenment:

> the issue was pleaded *at the bar of public opinion* before the whole of Europe, and *the rights of men* were nobly upheld, and expounded without restriction or reserve, in writings that circulated freely from the shores of the Neva to those of the Guadalquivir. Reports of this great debate penetrated to the most oppressed countries and the most isolated settlements, and the men who lived there were *astonished* to hear that they had rights. They learned what they were, and they learned that other men had had the courage to defend them or to win them back.[6]

---

question when he pointed out at a seminar on his *Settecento riformatore* held at the Fondazione Einaudi in Turin that 'the concept of "mentality" as it is used by French historians and their followers is hopelessly static. An atom, a germ of a nascent political consciousness is far more revealing and indispensable for a historian. A consciousness that is always single, individual, often original and maybe a little weird' (Franco Venturi, 'Postilla', *Annali della Fondazione Luigi Einaudi* 19, 1985, p.451-54, on p.453).

6. Condorcet, *Sketch*, p.145. Emphasis added.

It is this that provides the key to the resounding success of the rights of man before the French Revolution: the critical and conscious use of public opinion by Enlightenment authors as a powerful new instrument for political action. Without these two main protagonists, public opinion and the Enlightenment, it is unlikely that the rights of man would have become such an intrinsic part of the identity of the Western world.

Much has been written on the rise of public opinion in the eighteenth century, following Jürgen Habermas' pioneering work of 1962, which was translated into English as *The Structural transformation of the public sphere.* Habermas analyses the economic and social origins of the phenomenon on the basis of Marx's theory of the progressive capitalist autonomy of bourgeois society from the absolutist state and its class-based public sphere. In recent years this scenario has been called into question, especially by historians.[7] This society- and structure-oriented view was felt by many to be too schematic and anachronistic in its distinction between the absolutist state and bourgeois civil society.

Habermas' reading underestimated the persistent way in which *Ancien régime* society was based on census and corporations, which meant that it could give rise to different forms of public spheres beside the traditional one linked to courtly power. He also failed to take into due account the remarkable growth of the publishing market in the course of the eighteenth century, the rise of 'cultural consumption' among ever larger sectors of the population, the diffusion of new individual reading practices, or the profound transformation of the 'Republic of Letters' under the aegis of the Enlightenment. In any case, whatever its causes, the birth of modern public opinion in the course of the eighteenth century was a phenomenon whose impact and novelty was already universally clear at the time. We should therefore take as our starting point what contemporaries wrote on this subject, if we want to understand how the Enlightenment effected its successful and momentous 'performance' of the rights of man.

The Enlightenment was not the only movement or sector of society that hastened to make use of the nascent public sphere in its political

7. For an overview of the debate on Habermas' theory of the public sphere, see Anthony J. La Vopa, 'Conceiving a public: ideas and society in eighteenth-century Europe', *Journal of modern history* 64 (1992), p.89-116; Sandro Landi, *Stampa, censura e opinione pubblica* (Bologna, 2011). On the exponential growth of cultural consumption in the eighteenth century, see John Brewer, *The Pleasures of the imagination: English culture in the eighteenth century* (New York, 1997).

struggle.[8] However, it developed a radically new idea of public opinion and made conscious use of it in the service of its political project of emancipation. It was the Enlightenment that fully realised that the very meaning of 'opinion' had radically changed from mere belief, or an uncertain and unverifiable personal conviction, to an autonomous tribunal for ascertaining the truth – a positive concept that well fitted the rebirth of the republican spirit at the end of the century. As Louis-Sébastien Mercier wrote in 1782 in his popular *Tableau de Paris*, 'in the space of only thirty years a great and important revolution has taken place in our ideas. Public opinion now holds a preponderant and unstoppable power in Europe.' A sentiment that was echoed by Necker when, in his writings on financial administration, he talked of 'an invisible power that without treasury, guards or army imposes its laws over the city, the court, and even inside the palaces of kings'.[9] In completing Raynal's *Histoire philosophique et politique des établissements et du commerce des Européens dans les deux Indes*, Diderot shows his clear awareness of the growing political import of public opinion:

> Public opinion, in a nation that thinks and speaks, is the rule of government: the latter must never attack it without public reasons, or go against it without explaining why it was wrong. Government

8. We now know that the first to make open use of public opinion in a more or less conscious way were the *messieurs* from the French parliaments, who in their struggle against absolutism made constant appeal to the people and nation, proclaiming themselves the legitimate representatives of popular will: cf. Catherine-Laurence Maire, *De la cause de Dieu à la cause de la nation: le jansénisme au XVIIIe siècle* (Paris, 1998), p.563ff. In 1775 the Church itself showed its awareness of the momentous change that had taken place with the rise of the public sphere in the Western world, and how this brought an end to the obsolete logic of control and repression of cultural production and consumption. The power of the Inquisition had in any case been curbed by the absolute power of the State. Now, the only function left for this institution and its *Index librorum prohibitorum* was the task of disciplining clerics within the Church itself, while the external world was now governed by entirely different mechanisms. Now, with his vehement papal bull, *Inscrutabile divinae sapientiae*, Pius VI aimed to unmask the evil nature of the Enlightenment and the way in which it was poisoning an entire continent. This was a large-scale attempt to mobilise and equip all ecclesiastical structures and religious orders in the effort to bring international public opinion over to the positions of the Holy See. On this, see Antonio Trampus, *I gesuiti e l'Illuminismo: politica e religione in Austria e nell'Europa centrale (1773-1789)* (Florence, 2000), p.252ff.; Patrizia Delpiano, *Church and censorship in eighteenth-century Italy: governing reading in the age of Enlightenment* (London, 2017).
9. Translated from the quotations found in Baker, *Au tribunal de l'opinion*, p.225ff.

> must change all its forms in accordance with this opinion [...] Public opinion voices the general dissatisfaction with things, and the general opinion is the rule of government. It is because opinion is the queen of the world that kings are masters over men.[10]

Gaetano Filangieri, by contrast, was interested in the juridical nature of public opinion in relation to the language of the rights of man. He found its basis in the natural right of the individual to political participation in a republican sense, and in the exercise of the right to freedom of dissent and expression, important aspects of which were the freedom of the press and the right to education.[11]

To Enlightenment thinkers this wonderful new public space that had opened up for everyone, allowing one's private observations to be discussed in front of a wider audience, appeared like a close equivalent, in the context of the construction of the modern civil society that they hoped for, of the modalities and structure of the mythical Republic of Letters: a place where the power of ideas and critical thinking could conjure up a new reality simply by imagining it. In such a world, which was tangible and unreal at the same time, and peopled by free and equal individuals who would all be capable of reading and writing, it was possible to apply one's critical thinking in every field and debate in utter freedom with absolutely anyone, even using utopian discourse if necessary to portray the real future that was to come.

Obviously, this idea that the Republic of Letters could serve as a frame of reference for the interpretation of events came across as an entirely abstract construct. Nevertheless, it fully captured the inevitable oppositional aspects of the nascent public space. The Enlightenment was aware from the start of its political and pedagogical potential: it could provide a model that could serve to educate mankind by inviting its imitation, outlining the rise of a new political imagination, and stimulating the widest possible circulation of hitherto little-known

10. As usual, the translation is by the present translator unless otherwise credited. On this passage and on the spread of the idea of democracy as the rule of public opinion in the Late Enlightenment, see Edoardo Tortarolo, '"Opinione pubblica" e Illuminismo italiano: qualche appunto di lettura', in *Cesare Beccaria*, ed. V. Ferrone and G. Francioni, p.127-38. On the debate in France in general, see A. W. Gunn, *Queen of the world: opinion in the public life of France from the Renaissance to the Revolution* (Oxford, 1995); Arlette Farge, *Dire et mal dire: l'opinion publique au XVIIIe siècle* (Paris, 1992).
11. Cf. Ferrone, *Politics of Enlightenment*, p.123ff.

ideas, values, discourses and cultural practices.[12] The Enlightenment had for a long time given rise to militant intellectuals, who were interested in social communication, the renewal of aesthetic production in the literary, artistic and theatrical fields, and the creation of the modern *public* through mechanisms of identification.[13] These thinkers were thus best placed to appreciate the increasingly virtual and abstract character of the world that was inherent in the phenomenon of public opinion. At the same time, they were well aware of its power of evocation, its capacity to stage, or perform, a political or intellectual scenario and thus help it become reality: in short, its ability to influence the public's will through the power of utopia.[14]

These positions were among the principal modalities of the *philosophes*' political action in those important years that saw the *Ancien régime* enter its final stages, and were harshly criticised by Burke, Tocqueville and Taine. It is true that, on the one hand, these Enlightenment practices inevitably tended towards the 'politicisation of literature', with the consequent 'literarisation of politics'.[15] On the other hand, they gave a powerful boost to the Enlightenment project of reform in the latter decades of the eighteenth century.

As Filangieri urged in his *Science of legislation*, it was essential that public opinion should be 'rectified, directed and corrected', if one was to effect the necessary reforms and create at last a fair and just civil society.[16] Diderot made the same point in a 1775 letter to Necker, where he explained that public opinion,

12. On the political as well as abstract and imaginary character of this phenomenon, see the chapter on 'L'opinion publique comme invention politique' in Baker, *Au tribunal de l'opinion*, p.219ff.
13. See James Van Horn Melton, *The Rise of the public in Enlightenment Europe* (Cambridge, 2001). On the new mechanisms of identification and place-switching, see Jean Starobinski, '"Se mettre à la place": la mutation de la critique de l'âge classique à Diderot', *Cahiers Vilfredo Pareto* 14 (1976), p.364-78.
14. See Nicolas Veysman's intriguing book on the *Mise en scène de l'opinion publique dans la littérature des Lumières* (Paris, 2004), p.34ff.
15. See, for instance, the famous title of the first chapter in book 3 of Alexis de Toqueville's *L'Ancien Régime et la Révolution* (1856) on 'how towards the middle of the eighteenth century men of letters became the principal politicians, and the effects thereof'. On this issue, see also Ferrone, *The Enlightenment*, p.81ff.
16. Cf. Filangieri, *Scienza della legislazione*, vol.5, p.19: 'Under whatever government, and in whatever nation, public opinion is the strongest element in the State: its influence for good or ill is enormous because it is superior both to action and to the resistance of the public authority, and as a consequence, it is of absolute importance that it should be rectified, directed and corrected.'

> the power of which we know very well, both *for good* and *for evil*, at origin is nothing but the result of a few men thinking and then expressing their thoughts. These men give rise to constant centres of instruction in different parts of society, from which errors and rationally formed truths irradiate little by little to the furthest reaches of the city, where they establish themselves as articles of faith.[17]

However, the true spiritual father of public opinion in the age of Enlightenment was definitely Voltaire. Without him, the language of the rights of man would never have taken hold. The decisive move by Voltaire in this respect was his intervention in the *affaire Calas*. This notorious trial was the occasion of the first great success by European Enlightenment circles in mobilising public opinion in favour of the rights of man by means of gazettes and periodicals from every part of the continent.

On 12 October 1761 the son of a Protestant merchant from Toulouse was found dead. Was it murder or suicide? At a time of renewed fanatical opposition between Calvinists and Catholics the rumour spread that the young man wished to become a Catholic and that the father had killed him to prevent him doing so. The latter was therefore arrested, tortured and cursorily tried in the customary way by biased judges. Despite the lack of any evidence of his guilt, in 1762 the merchant was sentenced to death by the wheel, which meant that his bones were broken one by one in front of an eager crowd of spectators. After reading the documentation of the trial, Voltaire became convinced of the victim's father's innocence. He was outraged, and unleashed what became the first public opinion campaign in

17. On this letter, see Jean Gabriel de Tarde, *L'Opinion et la foule* (Paris, 1901), p.83. Emphasis added. According to Tarde, the new 'political public' received within itself all other kinds of publics – whether literary, philosophical or scientific – like a river with its tributaries. Although much has been written on the rise of a politicised public opinion in the Late Enlightenment, the importance of Tarde's intelligent study seems to have gone unnoticed. Tarde takes issue with Durkheim and other French neopositivist thinkers of his time, who credited public opinion with a sort of autonomous life independently of the will of individuals. Against these views Tarde put forward a theory of imitation as the basis of all social instruction, insisting that public opinion must be considered and studied simply as the transformation of an individual opinion into a social tenet. As for Diderot, his views were reprised in 1789 by Jacques Peuchet, who, in the *Encyclopédie méthodique*, described public opinion as a historical and social product that is created by enlightened individuals who are capable of interpreting and communicating the popular will. Cf. Baker, *Au tribunal de l'opinion*, p.259.

France, which led to a review of the trial. As part of this offensive, in 1763 Voltaire published his famous *Traité sur la tolérance à l'occasion de la mort de Jean Calas*. After a bitter struggle with the authorities, in 1764 the *arrêt* of the Toulouse parliament was repealed, followed by Calas's complete rehabilitation in 1765.[18]

This case was followed by similar interventions, not always with equal success: the protagonists of the *affaire Sirven*, the *affaire Martin et Montbailli*, the *affaire Lally-Tollendal* were also cursorily tried and horrendously put to death without any evidence, and the victim's final rehabilitation was not even obtained as it had been for Calas.[19] In those years Voltaire worked hard to answer what he called 'the cry of innocent blood', coining a metaphor with which he would mobilise the Enlightenment party. The *philosophes* supported him with particular vigour in the *affaire* concerning the nineteen-year-old chevalier Jean-François de La Barre, whose pitiful case outraged the new Enlightenment humanism in its mission to defend human beings and their rights.

La Barre was accused of defacing a crucifix on a bridge near Abbeville, which amounted to a charge of blasphemy. Once again because of a bigoted judge, he was sentenced to horrifying tortures: his knee bones were to be shattered and his tongue cut out. Following this he was to be beheaded and then burned at the stake. Voltaire wrote eloquently about this to his network of over 1400 correspondents, which included sovereigns, scientists, artists, journalists and the most important members of the elites of the time, in order to mobilise European public opinion.[20] In his *Relation de la mort du chevalier de La Barre à Monsieur le marquis de Beccaria*, Voltaire vividly and indignantly described every minute of the torments inflicted on the young man, boldly accusing the magistrates of the Paris parliament, who had been asked to give a final verdict on the case, of sending an innocent person to a cruel death. La Barre had been sentenced without any evidence, with cruel superficiality, simply on the basis of some witnesses declaring

18. Cf. David D. Bien, *The Calas affair: persecution, toleration and heresy in eighteenth-century Toulouse* (Princeton, NJ, 1960).
19. A complete analysis of all these interventions by Voltaire can be found in Condorcet, *Vie de Voltaire*, with a preface by Elisabeth Badinter (Paris, 1994), p.107ff. See also the texts collected in Voltaire, *L'Affaire Calas et autres affaires* (Paris, 1975), which includes a useful bibliography.
20. See Eric Walter, 'L'affaire La Barre et le concept d'opinion publique', in *Le Journalisme d'Ancien régime*, ed. Jacqueline Giraud, Pierre Rétat and Henri Duranton (Lyon, 1982), p.361-92.

that he had failed to take off his hat before a passing procession. To Voltaire's anger and amazement, on these grounds, and because books by Voltaire himself and other atheist and libertine authors had been found in La Barre's home, Counsellor Pasquier asked the magistrates of the Paris parliament to confirm the death sentence and avenge this sacrilegious violation of God's rights. In May 1768 Voltaire wrote to Cesare Beccaria asking him what he thought of this horrendous crime, the judicial murder of La Barre. Even if the young chevalier had been guilty, which he was not, surely he could have answered for the crime of blasphemy by spending six months in prison, without the need for any bloodshed or torture. With bitter sarcasm, Voltaire concluded his letter to Beccaria by remarking: 'Voilà donc ce qu'on appelle une religion de douceur et de charité!'[21]

Voltaire's epoch-making struggle of those years against the violence of power, the arbitrariness of judges, judicial torture, and the cruel disregard that this betokened for the human body and its dignity turned him in the collective imaginary into the defender of man and his rights *par excellence.* His pupil Condorcet was instrumental in creating this myth, which persists to this day. Condorcet's *Vie de Voltaire* was published in 1787, while France was undertaking yet another attempt to reform its penal system, with all the attendant controversies. In his affectionate account Condorcet describes Voltaire's return to Paris to be 'crowned' at the Comédie-Française in 1778. On that occasion, he was hailed by the common people as 'the saviour of Calas', the hero who had fought 'to give souls their freedom back, and their rights to men'.[22]

According to Condorcet, Voltaire's brave struggle against judiciary power for the *droits de l'humanité* was greatly aided by his international reputation, his civil passion and, above all, by his literary talent, which comes abundantly through in his addresses to public opinion. These texts were 'seductive in style, apt at alternatively exciting pity or public indignation, the latter being too ready to quieten down in a nation that was still not entirely aware of its own interests' (p.107). In fact, the role played by Voltaire in the history of the rights of man is not quite

21. Voltaire's letter is included in Franco Venturi's edition of Beccaria's *Dei delitti e delle pene* (p.451ff.) alongside the *Relation de la mort du chevalier de La Barre* (p.448ff.). A still useful account of the *affaire La Barre* can be found in Marc Chassaigne, *Le Procès du chevalier de La Barre* (Paris, 1920).

22. '[R]endre aux esprits la liberté, aux hommes leurs droits' (Condorcet, *Vie de Voltaire*, p.128).

so easy to define. We need to take into account both philological and chronological aspects.

We know that Voltaire was already well acquainted with the language of natural rights and was using it in those same years.[23] However, he does not seem to have applied this language in his frequent denunciation of miscarriages of justice. Voltaire experienced the *affaire Calas* and presented it to French public opinion not as a violation of the defendant's natural rights, but as yet another instance of the evil effects of fanaticism and religious intolerance: almost as the latest episode in the civil wars that were occasioned by religion in the previous centuries. His famous *Traité sur la tolérance à l'occasion de la mort de Jean Calas* is quite explicit in this respect. It presents itself as a corrosive history of human intolerance from its first appearance in the West with the Christian religion from Constantine onwards down to the more recent struggles between Catholics and Protestants. Voltaire sarcastically remarked that from the pagans to the Jews, the Muslims, Chinese or Japanese, no religious faith had given rise to the same crimes as those perpetrated in the name of Christian truth, as its adherents violently asserted that each religion was the work of man, while the Church alone is the work of God.

Voltaire called for leniency and toleration, and advocated the exercise of religious freedom, quoting Lactantius to the effect that 'Religion cannot be commanded.'[24] He ironically asked his readers whether Jesus had ever preached intolerance: 'Let us now see whether Christ established sanguinary laws, whether he enjoined non-toleration, instituted the horrors of the inquisition, or the butchery of an Auto-da fé [*sic*]' (p.117). After giving a myriad of historical examples of the atrocities perpetrated by Christian priests and pastors, in his 'Address to the Deity' placed towards the end of his treatise Voltaire describes

23. See the precisely argued reference to the rights of man in Voltaire's *Questions sur les miracles* [1765], p.413-14. See also his 1768 pamphlet *Les Droits des hommes et les usurpations des autres* (ed. Simon Davies, in *OCV*, vol.67, Oxford, 2007, p.135-71), which was written at the time of the occupation of Avignon by order of Voltaire's friend, Minister Choiseul, in that same year. This pamphlet, with its references to the 'droits du genre humain', is mentioned also in Bachaumont's 'secret memoirs' (*Mémoires secrets pour servir à l'histoire de la République des Lettres en France depuis 1762 jusqu'à nos jours*, 36 vols, London, n.n., 1784, vol.4, p.115 [9 October 1768]).

24. Voltaire, *A Treatise upon toleration* (Glasgow, Robert Urie, 1765), p.126. For the original text, see *Traité sur la tolérance*, ed. John Renwick, in *OCV*, vol.56c (Oxford, 2000).

a way of solving the problem. In this moving text, he reiterates the new and powerful idea of a *natural religion* of a theist kind, without Churches or priests: a religion that is tolerant, meek, common to all the peoples of the earth; a religion that could demolish the fortress of blood-thirsty revealed religions much more effectively than could be done by Diderot and d'Holbach's materialist propaganda, which only spoke to restricted elites:

> No longer then do I address myself to men, but to thee, God of all beings, of all worlds, and of all ages; if it may be permitted weak creatures, lost in immensity, and imperceptible to the rest of the universe, to presume to petition thee for aught, who has given plenty of all things, and whose decrees are immutable as eternal. Deign to look with an eye of pity upon the errors annexed to our natures! let not these errors prove the sources of misery to us! Thou has [*sic*] not given us hearts to hate, or hands to kill each other; grant then that we may mutually aid and assist each other to support the burden of this painful and transitory life! May the trifling differences in the garments that cover our frail bodies, in the mode of expressing our insignificant thoughts, in our ridiculous customs, and our imperfect laws, in our idle opinions, and in our several conditions and situations, that appear so disproportionate in our eyes, and all are equal in thine; in a word, may the slight variations that are found amongst the atoms called men, not be made use of by us as signals of mutual hatred and persecution! […] May all men remember that they are brethren! may they alike abhor that tyranny which seeks to subject the freedom of the will, as they do the rapine which tears from the arms of industry the fruits of its peaceful labours! And if the scourge of war is not to be avoided, let us not mutually hate and destroy each other in the midst of peace; but rather make use of the few moments of our existence to join in praising, in a thousand different languages, from one extremity of the world to the other, thy goodness, O all-merciful Creator! to whom we are indebted for that existence! (p.155-56)

Voltaire's call for religious toleration was then not really linked to a redefinition of the political relationship between the Church and the State, as in Locke's view, or to man's natural rights and freedom of conscience, as in Noodt, Barbeyrac and other members of the Huguenot diaspora. Voltaire focused first and foremost on human frailty, on the back of the sceptical tradition of Montaigne and Hume, who had constantly stressed the impossibility for man to attain absolute truths: 'What is toleration? It is the prerogative of humanity. We are all steeped in weaknesses and errors: let us forgive one another's follies, it is the first law of nature.'[25]

This remains true despite the occasional reference in Voltaire to the need to restore 'l'humanité dans ses droits' (as in the version of the entry on 'Tolérance' found in the *Questions sur l'Encyclopédie*) or to whether 'non-toleration is agreeable to the law of nature and of society' (as is asked in chapter 1, paragraph VI of the *Traité*). The new language of the rights of man does not appear in the *Traité*. As evidence of this, one may cite the brief premise to the 1784 Kehl edition, published in Alsace. The editors of Voltaire's tract must have worried that it might be out of step with the times, and therefore translated its message into the modern language of rights that was widespread and well received by public opinion in the years preceding the Revolution. Toleration was presented as a question of respecting the 'rights of conscience' and as synonymous with free thought, the latter being 'the most noble and sacred right that man received from nature'.[26] As we shall see, this was not the only attempt from those years to express ancient issues through the modern language of the rights of man.

We know that after the *affaire Calas* Voltaire's tone and framework of reference in his attack on horrific miscarriages of justice underwent a sudden change. Starting with the Martin and Montbailli *affaire*, and more precisely after 1766, his focus shifted from advocating toleration and denouncing religious fanaticism to publicly attacking judicial torture and the arbitrary decisions of magistrates ensconced in their parliaments and calling for a radical reform of the penal system that would finally make the inscrutable cruelty of the old inquisitorial trial a thing of the past. How and why this happened and how it affected the history of the rights of man are still the subject of debate.

In the political struggle between the crown and the local parliaments in France, i.e. between the *messieurs* in judges' togas who had sentenced Calas, Sirven and La Barre to a barbarous death and Chancellor Maupeou, who was determined to curb their powers and privileges in favour of the monarchy, Voltaire cunningly sided with the latter, which effectively gave his interventions a political character.[27] However, his

25. See the first few lines in the entry 'Tolérance: toleration', in Voltaire, *Philosophical dictionary*, ed. and translated by Theodore Besterman, 2nd edn (London, 2004), p.387-94.
26. Quoted in Voltaire, *Trattato sulla tolleranza*, ed. Lorenzo Bianchi (Milan, 1995), p.31.
27. See Diaz, *Filosofia e politica*, p.343ff.

change of approach was also greatly influenced by the publication in the summer of 1764 of Cesare Beccaria's *On crimes and punishments.* This key text of Italian Enlightenment humanism brought about many changes in the approach to justice and the right to punish throughout Europe. Summarising years of discussions at the Accademia dei Pugni in Milan, as we saw, Beccaria finally outlined a clear project of Enlightenment-inspired reforms of the *Ancien régime* penal system that would bring together security and usefulness to society on the one hand and, on the other, man's natural rights, and especially the rights to freedom and defence. This programme had previously been described by Beccaria at the Accademia dei Pugni itself in an impassioned speech against the inquisitorial trial and judicial torture of Pietro Verri.[28]

In reprising these ideas in his booklet, Beccaria accomplished a technical miracle by achieving a difficult balance between the new natural law of rights and the utilitarian needs of the new secular civil society. In this way, he transformed the traditional moral language of rights into a modern political and juridical discourse, thus creating the philosophical basis for the Enlightenment's ambitious rights-based programme of reform of penal law. Which is probably why contemporaries gave credence to what we now regard as the curiously peculiar speculations reported by Linguet in 1779 in his *Annales politiques et littéraires.* In this account, Beccaria's publication had been especially commissioned by the Parisian Enlightenment thinkers in order to provide the conceptual 'artillery' with which they could attack the parliaments' *messieurs* and mobilise public opinion in their effort to change once and for all French penal legislation. This division of labour would continue in the following years with the French translations of the important works on the rights of men by Filangieri and Pagano.[29]

28. Cf. 'Il punto di vista di Pietro Verri', in Beccaria, *Dei delitti e delle pene*, p.132ff.
29. On the wide circulation of the works of the Italian jurists in France see also Daniel Roche, *France in the Enlightenment*, translated by Arthur Goldhammer (Cambridge, MA, 1998), p.314ff. Linguet's text is quoted as follows in Beccaria, *Dei delitti e delle pene*, p.496: 'Quelque temps après l'affaire de Calas, les encyclopédistes armés de son supplice et profitant de la circonstance, mais sans se compromettre, selon leur usage, écrivirent à Milan au P. F. [Frisi] Barnabite, leur banquier de crédit en Italie et mathématicien digne de sa réputation, que c'étoit le moment de lâcher une déclamation sur la rigueur des peines et sur l'intolérance; que la philosophie italienne devoit fournir l'artillerie, et qu'eux à couvert la serviroient à Paris.'

André Morellet's translation of Beccaria indeed seemed to be built around such a purpose. The volume was presented from its very title as a *Traité des délits et des peines*, and the reference to the 'droits des hommes', which in the Italian edition appeared within the text, was moved forward to the 'Introduction et dessein de l'ouvrage'.[30] This made explicit for the French public something that was obviously quite clear to readers in Milan and the rest of Italy: that Beccaria's work had been written to uphold humanity, the natural rights of man and socially useful forms of punishment against a penal system that was mindful only of the security of the prince and the community and still based on the archaic link between crime and sin.

The history of this book's huge fortune in Europe, including its translation into several languages, has been amply traced by Franco Venturi. As its contemporaries realised, it marked an explicitly political turn in the Enlightenment's stance in favour of a lenient and humanitarian justice, and of a fair and just civil society. At the same time, as Calvinist author Daniel Fellenberg wrote to Beccaria from Switzerland in February 1766, it inaugurated a new era in the history of the rights of man.[31]

In France the conjunction of Maupeou's attack on the parliaments, the *philosophes*' campaign for penal reform, and the appeal to public opinion effectively led to the definitive politicisation of the language of rights. In the subsequent two decades these rights became the main

30. See Cesare Beccaria, *Traité des délits et des peines traduit de l'italien d'après la troisième édition, revue, corrigée et augmentée par l'auteur* (Philadelphia, PA, n.n., 1766), p.8. I am not therefore in agreement with Lynn Hunt's evaluation that 'Beccaria himself did not stress the connection between his views on torture and the nascent rights language', and that others did this for him, including especially André Morellet, who moved the reference to the 'rights of men' from the eleventh paragraph of the Italian edition to the introduction of the French version (cf. Hunt, *Inventing human rights*, p.102). In fact, the language of rights was well known in Milan, and Beccaria's whole work is based on the conscious vindication of the natural rights of man, and in particular of the natural and inalienable right to defence. Morellet apologised to Beccaria for modifying the structure of his chapters by explaining that it was important to speak to jurists and judges even before public opinion (see the letters included in Beccaria, *Dei delitti e delle pene*, p.330ff.).

31. See the letter in Beccaria, *Dei delitti e delle pene*, p.xxxv: 'C'est la voix de l'humanité que vous nous aves fait entendre. Puisse-t-elle sortir souvent de votre bouche et répandre par toute l'Italie la noble ardeur qui vous embrase. On verra alors les italiens modernes réparer les crimes de leurs ancêtres. Ceux-ci ont désolé et asservi les hommes et vous, vous défendrés leurs droits, vos droits; vous ferés régner sur la terre la liberté et le bonheur.'

political formula through which the Enlightenment carried out its attack on enlightened absolutism, despotism, and the privileges and injustices of the *Ancien régime* in the name of a modern civil society, a new *respublica* founded on man's rights. It is no wonder, therefore, that these positions caused a negative reaction among the moderate echelons of the school of natural law, with their belief in the centrality of rights. The Enlightenment's new political stance was obviously incompatible with the view that an individual acted morally mostly by fulfilling the duties imposed by natural law, while for the theoreticians of Protestant natural law in Germany and Scotland those rights that had been assertively placed at the centre of the political scene since the late 1760s were simply an instrument for the accomplishment of duties.

The reaction in France was particularly strong among the physiocrats. An essential part of their purported *nouvelle science* of political economy consisted in relaunching the language of natural rights as derived from duties, with a virtuous circularity and symmetry that would be ratified by the Thermidorian Constitution of 1795. This was done on the basis of a new critical reading of the natural law paradigm as popularised by Barbeyrac and the 1758 French translation of Christian Wolff's work, *Principes du droit de la nature et des gens*, according to which the language of rights and duties was an essential aspect of the law of nature calling man to perfectibility and happiness.

As we discussed in a previous chapter, Wolff updated Pufendorf by upholding the construction of a new science of man that would enable us to discover, as stated in the French version, 'toute l'obligation et tous les droits des hommes', according to what political scientists today would call a 'duty-based' model.[32] In this model, the task of safeguarding these rights was assigned exclusively to the absolute power of the sovereign. François Quesnay reprised these theories in his 1765 'Observations sur le droit naturel des hommes réunis en société', after his famous articles in the *Encyclopédie* on 'Fermiers' and 'Grains'. His aim was to provide the new economic science with solid philosophical foundations and moral legitimacy by reiterating the importance of the 'notion naturelle des droits et des devoirs réciproques des hommes'. To

32. Cf. *Principes du droit de la nature et des gens extrait du grand'ouvrage latin de Mr. De Wolff, par Mr. Formey* (Amsterdam, n.n., 1758), p.v, especially chapters II, 'Des devoirs de l'homme envers soi même et des droits qui y sont liés'; III, 'Des devoirs des hommes envers les autres et des droits qui y sont attachés'; IV, 'Des devoirs de l'homme envers Dieu et des droits qui y sont liés'.

this effect, Quesnay gave a new definition of natural right as the right to those things that appertain to man's enjoyment, or 'le droit que les hommes ont aux choses propres à leur jouissance'.[33] In opposition to Rousseau's historical chimera – the isolated individual in the state of pure nature – the father of physiocracy depicted a deterministic natural order, which was created by God before the existence of any society: it was this order that gave man his rights and duties. In Quesnay's view, the free exercise of the sacred right to property was to be practised in society in accordance with the natural laws that were described in the *Tableau économique* and that could be further gathered through the rational study of the physical and mathematical rules that regulate economic processes. In this way, it would finally be possible to progress from mere subsistence to the enjoyment, or *jouissance*, of the riches produced by agricultural labour.

Quesnay's emphasis on the importance of natural law as the basis for the physiocrats' political economy is reprised by Pierre-Samuel Dupont de Nemours in his 1768 pamphlet, *De l'origine et des progrès d'une science nouvelle*:

> the rights that pertain to every man, before what is established by convention, are: the freedom to provide for his subsistence and wellbeing, and ownership of his own person and of the things that he acquires through his labour. His duties are: to provide for his needs through his labour, and to respect other people's liberty, person and property.[34]

This unshakeable belief in the natural order and its deterministic mathematical law, as illustrated in the *Tableau économique*, is what gave philosophical and moral legitimacy, even more than scientific credibility, to the famous physiocratic dogma: *laissez faire, laissez passer*, i.e. absolute freedom in the exercise of the right to property. In the second half of the eighteenth century the physiocrats' political economy presented itself to European governments as the global science of society. In Le Mercier de La Rivière's 1767 work, *L'Ordre naturel et essentiel des sociétés politiques*, this claim was explicitly based on the political and social function of property owners as a new and

33. Quesnay's text can be read in his collection *Physiocratie, ou Constitution naturelle du gouvernement le plus avantageux au genre humain*, ed. Pierre-Samuel Dupont de Nemours (Leiden and Paris, chez Merlin, 1767-1768), p.13ff.

34. Pierre-Samuel Dupont de Nemours, *De l'origine et des progrès d'une science nouvelle* (London [Paris?], chez Desaint, 1768), p.18.

powerful universal class that was capable of gathering society around itself and enriching it:

> PROPERTY, SECURITY, LIBERTY. Together these form the whole of the social order. It is this right to property, in all its natural and primitive expanse, that will necessarily give rise to the institutions that shape our society. The right to property is like a tree, and all social institutions are the branches that it brings forth and nourishes, and that would die as soon as they were detached from the tree itself.[35]

Within the framework of this ambitious political project, whose aim was in any case to transform the society of the *Ancien régime*, sovereignty ultimately drew its legitimacy from the strenuous defence of property as a God-given natural right. The physiocrats did not adhere to theories of mixed government or neorepublican tendencies, and were not impressed by calls for wider representation and the suppression of social inequalities.[36] Instead, they supported the idea of a strong centralised power as found in the absolute state, as long as it was informed by a thorough knowledge of the laws of economy: an agricultural monarchy of landowners ruled by a *despote légal* who were capable of applying and enforcing the laws of nature and the natural constitution of society as described in the *Tableau économique*.

Historians have for too long described the physiocrats above all as members of the Enlightenment, who put forward a pioneering and autonomous form of economic science characterised by total laissez-faire and the specialist formulation of laws of a physical-mathematical kind. This view, however, fails to take into account the contradictions, ambiguities and paradoxes within this movement, which mingled together the old and the new, nostalgia for the past and a modern outlook.[37] From the epistemological point of view, the mathematical formalism of the *Tableau économique* seemed to anticipate the development of economics as a fully autonomous science. Yet the fact that the physiocrats were still founding that science on natural law betrayed their archaic Aristotelian and Thomistic roots, which

35. Cf. Pierre-Paul Le Mercier de La Rivière, *L'Ordre naturel et essentiel des sociétés politiques*, 2 vols (London, n.n., 1767), vol.2, p.441.
36. See how, in the chapter entitled 'De l'inégalité du droit naturel des hommes', Quesnay invites his readers to bear with patience the inequalities established by God (*Physiocratie*, p.13ff.).
37. For a discussion of the vast bibliography on this subject, see Reinert, *Translating empire*, p.177ff. See also Catherine Larrère, *L'Invention de l'économie au XVIIIe siècle: du droit naturel à la physiocratie* (Paris, 1992).

made them decry all forms of individualism, in line with the rationalistic updating of the old concept of an organic cosmos effected by Malebranche and Wolff with their concept of the 'natural order'. We find the old and the new dialectically confronting each other also in the famous physiocratic idea that only agriculture produced real wealth, while commerce and manufacture were seen as sterile activities. This primacy of agriculture was a remnant of the past, deriving as it did from Fénelon's 'Christian agrarianism' and his opposition to Colbert's mercantilism. In a precarious and paradoxical balance, it linked together the nascent economic individualism of landowners with the hierarchy of the natural order.[38]

These kinds of contradictions and ambiguities are also found in other aspects of the physiocrats' ideological project. While they ostensibly went beyond the *Ancien régime*, critiquing its feudal system, aristocratic privileges, and the absence of freedom of the press and public education, they were happy to adopt its organic and communitarian constitutive principle, as they ideologically exalted the landowning class as the necessary hub of a future social order, to which the *nouvelle science* of economics lent scientific legitimacy.

In fact, the very language of the rights and duties of man in society that is incessantly applied in the physiocrats' works belongs to this same logic. It was a strange mixture of past and future, the ancient and the modern, and created an intriguing ideological compromise: a sort of conservative revolution with a distinctively utopian flavour. This is especially borne out by the work on *Les Droits et les devoirs de l'homme* published in 1774 by Victor de Riqueti, marquis de Mirabeau. This was constructed as a kind of lay catechism, with a set of questions and answers aimed at directing public opinion.[39] With its explanation of their deterministic 'ordre circulaire', it answered the need of sovereigns who wanted to impose an 'instruction populaire, générale et perpétuelle sur les droits et les devoirs de l'homme' in their

38. On the link with Fénelon, see Herbert Lüthy, *La Banque protestante en France de la révocation de l'Edit de Nantes à la Révolution* (Paris, 1961), p.121, where physiocracy is described as the final and most important manifestation of traditional Catholic thought on economics. On Christian agrarianism, see Lionel Rothkrug, *Opposition to Louis XIV: the political and social origins of the French Enlightenment* (Princeton, NJ, 1965), p.234ff.

39. On the physiocrats' conscious use of public opinion in these same years see Keith Michael Baker, 'Politics and public opinion under the Old Regime: some reflections', in *Press and politics in pre-revolutionary France*, ed. J. R. Censer and J. D. Popkin (Berkeley, CA, 1987), p.204-46.

countries. In this work Mirabeau cleverly propounded the tenets of the physiocrats' 'science de l'homme', which updated the Thomistic universe and Fénelon's theories, together with Quesnay's mathematical description of economic processes. Its points of departure were man's material needs, the right to property, including enjoying the fruits of the latter, and, above all, the duty of earning a living through one's work:

> Q. Does everything in man's life then come down to a duty? A. Yes, and this duty to work is the root of all his other duties [...] Q. Does man also have a right, then? A. Yes, and this right, to be able to enjoy what he acquires through his labour or his advantages, is the root of all his other rights. Its natural and necessary objective is the discharge of his duty [...] and in this case it is the duty that comes first.[40]

One can think of no better way to illustrate the grimly conservative and disingenuous character of the physiocrats' language of natural rights, especially when compared to the view of those rights that was put forward in those years by Rousseau, Voltaire, Beccaria, Diderot and all those thinkers who wanted to use it as a formidable weapon for the emancipation of man into a free and autonomous human being. For the physiocrats, what came before everything else was the fulfilment of duties and adherence to the sociability principle and God's natural order, with its deterministic laws. This was what legitimised the very existence of rights. The latter had no independent validity. They certainly did not serve to define the very humanity of the individual as an autonomous being, nor were they seen as a precious tool for ensuring his happiness and emancipation. They were simply part of yet another cleverly conceived version of the Thomistic universe: 'The enemy of peace and order among men is the desire to extend one's rights without increasing one's duties. It is the wish to enjoy something without having to work for it' (p.116). This interpretative slant meant that the physiocrats greatly attenuated the power of the political discourse of rights. The contrast between these opposing readings became especially meaningful and apparent during the famous dispute on the free circulation of grain in the 1770s.

As is well known, the physiocrats' intense lobbying for the liberalisation of the grain trade led in France to the famous free-trade edicts

40. Cf. Victor de Riqueti, marquis de Mirabeau, *La Science, ou les Droits et les devoirs de l'homme* (Lausanne, François Grasset & comp., 1774), p.6-8.

of 1763-1764. However, this had unexpected consequences. Instead of the effect on production and distribution that had been predicted by the *Tableau économique* using rigorous mathematical formulae, what ensued was local famine, uprisings and bloody riots that caused widespread panic. These decisions were therefore subject to serious scrutiny. The Neapolitan economist and diplomat Ferdinando Galiani had lived through the terrible famine that had struck his city in 1764. Four years later, in Paris, he began to write his famous *Dialogues sur le commerce des bleds*, in which he publicly attacked the physiocrats' ideas. Carefully revised by Diderot, who published it in January 1770, Galiani's work confuted the thesis of economic laissez-faire from a historical point of view. With subtle irony and biting sarcasm, it denounced the abstract doctrinarian approach, sectarian spirit and epistemological unsoundness of the *nouvelle science*.

Galiani tackled the problem head on, contesting the very idea of a science of political economy as developed by the physiocrats. The term 'political economy', which, according to Aristotle, yoked together two essentially disparate terms, was, in his view 'far more difficult and complex than was generally thought'.[41] Its underlying dangers became fully apparent when the physiocrats' free-market theories were applied to the grain trade. As Galiani explained,

> Grain can be considered as a product of the earth. From this point of view, it pertains to trade and economic legislation. At the same time, it can be considered in terms of a staple good and the first thing that should be safeguarded in the civil order of societies. And from this point of view it pertains to politics and reason of state. (p.385)

Both aspects must always be taken simultaneously into account. At the epistemological level, the true economist should behave like the 'médicin d'un Etat', treating his patient through empirical methods by trying out different remedies, fully aware that diseases are part of nature and cannot be eradicated. This was a far cry from the physical-mathematical model put forward by Quesnay, who had mistaken mere hypotheses and metaphysical beliefs for universal truths. As Galiani points out, the 'object of economic science is not an arbitrary and sublime truth'. All invented theories and solutions

41. We provide here our translation from Ferdinando Galiani, *Dialogues sur le commerce des bleds*, in *Illuministi italiani*, vol.6: *Opere di Ferdinando Galiani*, ed. Furio Diaz and Luciano Guerci (Milan and Naples, 1975), p.345-612 (546). As usual, subsequent references are given within the text.

must be concretely verified on an individual basis, always bearing in mind the fundamental historical truth that 'everything has changed, everything changes, everything will change' (p.376) – and here, above and beyond the empiricism of Machiavelli and Locke, we see the influence of Hume's scepticism and Vico's *New science* and their rejection of the abstract geometric deductive rationalism of Descartes and Malebranche.

If one really wanted to see political economy as a branch of the new science of man, as claimed by the physiocrats, one would need to take fully on board the fact that 'Man! Man himself was an indeterminate quantity.' Man was a free being, with his own will, who in any case acted as a protagonist in history. Therefore, one could not apply what we would now define as reductionist models of an extreme physicist and mathematical kind to economic processes, because 'the equation of the problem' contained too many unknown quantities: 'The equation becomes indeterminate, or it belongs to that class of problems that are termed *de maximis* and *de minimis*. Such are in fact all political problems' (p.546). However, the physiocrats' greatest mistake was to assume that the natural order was 'a necessary, chain-like order' – something akin to the old universe of Aristotle and Aquinas, or the 'great chain of being', with its fixed hierarchies. All this while, in the second half of the eighteenth century, the fixist view of nature was in decline, partly thanks to the work of Diderot and many other Enlightenment thinkers throughout Europe, with scientists adopting more and more the hypothesis of the transmutation of species and rejecting the geometric deductive model and mechanistic universe of Descartes and Newton.

Galiani accepted that in the long term nature tended towards balance ('without any doubt it brings balance back to all things'), and that therefore the price of grain under free trade would eventually stabilise. However, this would take centuries and require uniform historical contexts in order to happen, and in the meantime one may have to face social conflict and catastrophic occurrences. The best course of action, therefore, was to adopt Machiavelli's political realism and pragmatism, being prepared to apply both reason of state and free-market theories as required in each case. The physiocrats' call to 'let nature take its course' disregarded the fact that man was inevitably at the centre of all processes, and that he was both inside and outside nature. In a Baconian sense, 'we fight [...] we carry on a struggle against nature, and we often succeed in defeating and subjugating it by means of its own forces' (p.552) – though it is not immediately obvious to what extent these are Galiani's own words or to what extent they derive from Diderot's editing.

From these considerations Galiani drew the strong and original idea of a political economy at the service of man, rather than the other way round – an idea that was typical of the new Enlightenment humanism in Europe. This new kind of economy would be guided in an empirical and pragmatic manner by politics and by the concrete knowledge of actual historical processes, avoiding all recourse to abstract mathematical models. In this way, it would become a science devoted not only to the preservation and freedom of the individual but also to his 'emancipation' (p.559), and to the increase of wealth as the basis for the progress of civilisation. Displaying a subtly ironic style alongside a thorough command of a rich array of data, Galiani attacks the idea of the complete liberalisation of the grain trade and the primacy of agriculture that had been dogmatically advocated by the physiocrats. He does so with precise reference to what was happening in all the major European states and on the international trade scene. And he does not limit himself to criticising these theories in minute detail. He intelligently takes this opportunity to put forward the Enlightenment economic model *par excellence*: the model that had been defended also by Hume, Genovesi and Smith, and that was founded, even more than on agriculture, on the development of commerce and industry, as theorised in a pioneering way by John Cary and Jean-François Melon.[42]

Galiani's *Dialogues* unleashed a furious debate in periodicals and gazettes both in France and abroad. For the first time, the Enlightenment's front split almost in two. His witty and influential tract was read and appreciated by figures such as Voltaire, Hume and Smith, who had always been in favour of the free market but had come to dislike the scientific fanaticism of the *secte des économistes*. However, the thinker who best understood the truest and deepest political meaning of Galiani's work was Denis Diderot, who linked it to the rise of the language of natural rights. Diderot replied to the *Réfutation de l'ouvrage qui a pour titre Dialogues sur le commerce des bleds* written by the abbé André Morellet with an unpublished *Apologie de l'abbé Galiani*, in which he accused the physiocrats of a lack of a sense of history, 'rigidity of principles', 'dangerous generalisations' and 'unbearable arrogance', despite having in the past entrusted to them several articles for the *Encyclopédie*. Diderot was especially

42. On this important point see Reinert, *Translating empire*, p.272ff.

enraged by the 'scientific' claim that free and unlimited property rights should be applied to the grain trade, even to the detriment of man's obvious vital needs and of his very dignity:

> This principle is worthy of a Tartar, a cannibal. It is certainly unworthy of civilised man. Are we saying that the sense of humanity is less sacred than the right to property, which is constantly infringed in both peace and war, and which our abbé urges us to uphold to the point of being ready to kill one another, or starve to death?[43]

It did not make sense for society to be founded solely on the interests of landowners, regardless of all consequences: 'Agricultural society does not consist chiefly of the well-to-do tenant farmers, but of the masses of farmhands. Do you think that the former, once they have become richer, will allow the latter to receive part of their wealth so as to lift them out of poverty?' (p.195). Like all *philosophes*, Diderot had been hugely impressed by the uncompromising defence of man undertaken by Voltaire in the Calas case.[44] In his mature years, towards the end of the 1760s, he had started to reflect on the importance of political intervention and on the true significance of his own activity as a philosopher and writer at the service of mankind. He had concluded that what really mattered was to gain a fuller understanding of human nature and of the existential condition of the human being in history, and to defend man from himself and from power in all its manifestations, the cruel logic of domination and the violence of tyrants.

In the summer of 1784, just before he died, Diderot wrote, with disenchanted but also serene awareness: 'What do I perceive? Forms. And then what? More forms. I am ignorant of the thing itself. We walk between shades, shades ourselves for others and for us [...] There is only one virtue, justice; only one duty, to be happy; only one corollary, not to overvalue life and not to fear death.'[45] Fifteen years earlier, however, the language of rights had suddenly appeared to him

43. Our English translation follows Albina Maffioli Barsella's Italian translation from the French of the 'Apologia dell'abate Galiani' found in Denis Diderot, *Scritti politici*, ed. Furio Diaz (Turin, 1967), p.190.

44. In August 1762 Diderot wrote to Sophie Volland: 'C'est de Voltaire qui écrit pour cette malheureuse famille. Oh mon amie, le bel emploi du génie!' See Furio Diaz's remarks in Diderot, *Scritti politici*, p.41ff.

45. From the *Eléments de physiologie*. Quoted in A. M. Wilson, *Diderot* (New York, 1972), p.700.

as something that could provide the political solution to the enigma of human existence: it was the indispensable tool with which one could at the same time protect man, foster his love of freedom and put a stop to tyranny.

Those were decisive years in Diderot's human and intellectual experience. He experienced growing hatred and rage towards any form of despotism and logic of domination. In private and in public he gave voice to radical views, which were characterised by a renewed republicanism, a strong democratic spirit and an aversion to the tenets of the divine right of monarchs and absolutism, even of the most just and enlightened kind: in 1771, he had uncompromisingly attacked Frederick the Great as a tyrant who should be fought in the name of freedom.[46] In his poem *Les Eleuthéromanes, ou les Furieux de la liberté*, which he read in 1772 at a celebration in a Parisian salon, he went so far as to paraphrase Jean Meslier's gory invective against priests and kings.[47]

This growing interest in the language of the rights of man as a weapon in the struggle for liberty and the defence of man is already apparent three years earlier, in Diderot's reading of John Dickinson's *Letters from a farmer in Pennsylvania*. In reviewing this work Diderot declared that he knew 'of no other work more calculated to instruct peoples in their inalienable rights and inspire in them a violent love of liberty'.[48] Again, we find ample traces of Diderot's renewed interest in the universal character of rights as a way to fathom the limits and nature of the historically determined individual in his 1772 *Supplément au voyage de Bougainville*: 'If you scan the history of nations, both ancient and modern, across the centuries you will find that men are subject to three codes: those of nature, civil society and religion.'[49] And

46. See Denis Diderot, *Pages inédites contre un tyran*, with an introduction by Franco Venturi (Paris, 1937). On Diderot's turn to politics and his attack on despotism see Furio Diaz's remarks in Diderot, *Scritti politici*, p.125ff.

47. 'Et ses mains ourdiraient les entrailles du prêtre / Au défaut d'un cordon pour étrangler les rois' (Denis Diderot, *Les Eleuthéromanes, ou les Furieux de la liberté*, in *Œuvres complètes*, ed. Jules Assézat, 20 vols, Paris, 1875-1877, vol.9, p.16). See also, by Herbert Dieckmann, 'Three Diderot letters, and *Les Eleuthéromanes*', *Harvard library bulletin* 6 (1952), p.69-91, and 'The abbé Meslier and Diderot's *Eleuthéromanes*', *Harvard library bulletin* 7 (1953), p.231-35.

48. Quoted in Wilson, *Diderot*, p.599.

49. '[L]e code de la nature, le code civile et le code religieux' (Denis Diderot, *Supplément au voyage de Bougainville, ou Dialogue entre A et B*, in *Œuvres complètes*, vol.2, p.241). The *Supplément* remained unpublished until 1796.

this applied to all the peoples of the earth, as the recourse to rights ultimately constituted the true core of universal morality. Thus, in this dialogue, without further ado, the Tahitian speaker Orou was able to explain to his civilised interlocutor that he lived quite happily without even knowing the words for 'marriage', 'State' or 'religion', because in any case he held the firm belief that 'le bien soit préféré au mal, et le bien général au bien particulier', as well as that his first duty was 'd'être homme' – which meant to be free, but also to respect 'les droits des personnes' at all times (p.221). It was, however, in his contribution to Raynal's *Histoire philosophique et politique des deux Indes* that Diderot made ample and skilful use of the language of natural rights, from what was by now a clearly political point of view, as we shall see in the following chapter.

15. The 'performance' of the rights of man in France between art and politics

We now know that Raynal's *Histoire philosophique et politique des deux Indes* was a key text and bestseller of the Late Enlightenment, vying in popularity and importance with the *Encyclopédie* from the previous decade. After its publication in 1770, the first edition of the *Histoire* was reprinted fifteen times, the second edition of 1774 fourteen times. The third and most important edition came out in 1780, and rapidly went through some ten more reprints.[1] Diderot had a hand in all three editions, but especially the third one, to which he contributed literally hundreds of evocative and passionate pages, whose true value has only recently been recognised.[2] Applying a pattern that was commonly found in the eighteenth century, from Vico to Condorcet, Diderot attempted to outline a kind of historical foundation of natural rights: how they had been neglected and every now and then happily rediscovered by the various nations, linking their ups and downs with the history of man's freedom and the struggle against despotism.[3]

In the ancient world, in accordance with the forms appropriate to the time, the appeal to rights had been a constant feature of republicanism and the struggle for liberty against tyranny. But in contemporary society, which had grown rich and developed on the

1. See C. P. Courtney, 'Les métamorphoses d'un best-seller: l'*Histoire des deux Indes* de 1770 à 1820', in *Raynal, de la polémique à l'histoire*, ed. Gilles Bancarel and Gianluigi Goggi (Oxford, 2000), p.109-20. For an overview of the bibliography on this subject, cf. C. P. Courtney and Claudette Fortuny, 'Répertoire d'ouvrages et d'articles (1800-2003) sur Raynal', *SVEC* 2003:08, p.37-113.
2. See Denis Diderot, *Pensées détachées: contributions à l''Histoire des deux Indes'*, ed. Gianluigi Goggi (Siena, 1976); Michèle Duchet, *Diderot et l''Histoire des deux Indes', ou l'Ecriture fragmentaire* (Paris, 1978).
3. For an important discussion of this subject, see Imbruglia, 'Indignation et droits de l'homme'.

back of material progress, those rights seemed to have disappeared and to have been forgotten. A case in point was the revocation of the Edict of Nantes: suddenly, thousands of French Calvinists, who had previously enjoyed 'the rights of men and of citizens', were forced to flee or suffered persecution and even murder. And this happened '[u]nder the most brilliant reign, and at the most fortunate period of that reign'.[4] In modern times tyranny had then acquired a terrible new face. It was no longer a relationship between individuals, such as the prince and the subject, but one which affected the way of being of society as a whole. This had to do with the ambiguous effect on the population of the increase in wealth due to the division of labour and the overwhelming power of the economy, which forced nations to submit to the despotic power of a few wealthy individuals:

> Tyranny, we are told, is the work of the people, and not of kings. But if so, why do they suffer it? Why do they not repel the incroachments of despotism; and while it employs violence and artifice to enslave all the faculties of men, why do they not oppose it with all their powers? [...] The man who should assert the rights of man would perish in neglect and infamy. Must tyranny, therefore, be endured, under the name of authority?[5]

Just like Rousseau, Genovesi, Filangieri or Smith, Diderot too wondered about the paradox of a modernity that fostered wealth and material progress on the one hand, and new and disturbing forms of social inequality and despotism on the other. How could all these things exist side by side: economic progress and modern forms of domination, ancient virtue and the modern claim to freedom? After the *querelle* on the grain trade, Diderot had suddenly seen with great clarity that the correct way forward was that of the rights of man. This meant that every Enlightenment thinker or *philosophe*, 'who knows and respects the rights of mankind', should fight to the hilt to protect and help spread those rights in every part of the world. One ought to proclaim incessantly the right to freedom against all forms of despotism and tyranny: 'Without freedom, or ownership of one's body and enjoyment of one's spirit, one is neither spouse, nor father,

4. Guillaume-Thomas-François, abbé Raynal, *A Philosophical and political history of the settlements and trade of the Europeans in the East and West Indies*, translated by J. O. Justamond, 8 vols (London, Strahan and Cadell, 1788), vol.7, p.52.
5. Raynal, *History*, vol.7, p.155 (I have returned the last sentence to question form, as it is in the original French).

nor relative or friend. One has no homeland, fellow-citizen or God.' As Diderot asserted in the wake of Locke, 'To be free means to have ownership of oneself. There are three kinds of freedom: natural, civil, and political, i.e. the liberty of man, the citizen, and that of a nation [...] Next to reason, the first of these three forms of freedom is the distinguishing characteristic of man'.[6]

In his *Science of legislation* Filangieri was to translate these principles into a precise expression of support for republican self-government, popular sovereignty and a juridical system mindful of individual rights. But in the *Histoire des deux Indes* Diderot focused on the importance of this struggle, and the need to awaken people's indignation and right of resistance in order to rescue the rights of man from centuries of neglect. A clear example in this sense was provided by the American colonies, where the insurgents had invoked the language of rights to justify their armed struggle in order to create a new and free nation, in the same way as the Dutch had done against the Spaniards in the sixteenth century.

Diderot wrote with passion and admiration about the American Revolution both in the *Histoire* and in other works.[7] He knew, however, that, if one was to get public opinion behind the philosophy of history in defence of man as outlined in the *Histoire*, the same kind of support must be universally extended to include another important issue of those years which desperately required the application of the 'political formula' of the rights of man: the Atlantic slave trade.[8] The very credibility and effectiveness of the new political language of the moderns that was being put forward by the Enlightenment depended on this.

After France's defeat in the Seven Years War at the hands of the British, a number of French colonialists went back to Paris, bringing their slaves with them. This inhuman sight soon awakened

6. For these quotations, see Imbruglia, 'Indignation et droits de l'homme', p.172.
7. See Denis Diderot, 'Apostrophe aux insurgents d'Amérique' (1778), in *Textes politiques*, with an introduction and notes by Yves Benot (Paris, 1960), p.213-14.
8. Over 11 million human beings were carried away from the coasts of Africa between 1519 and 1867, the highest number, nearly 2 million, being transported in the years from 1776 to 1800: see Olivier Pétré-Grenouilleau, *Les Traites négrières: essai d'histoire globale* (Paris, 2004). For a critique of Pétré-Grenouilleau's work and relevant bibliography, see Alessandro Tuccillo, 'Schiavi, colonie, rivoluzione: note in margine a due traduzioni recenti', *Studi storici* 1 (2008), p.109-33. A fundamental text for the quantitative analysis of the slave trade is still P. D. Curtin, *The Atlantic slave trade: a census* (Madison, WI, 1969).

the consciences of their fellow citizens, opening up the old question in entirely new terms.[9] The original purpose of the *Histoire des deux Indes* had been to support the French government and the cause of a humanitarian colonialism against the cruel behaviour and monopoly of the English slave drivers. However, with Diderot's intervention, it became a multifaceted and at times even contradictory work, where Diderot's radical theses could be contradicted, a few pages later, by the far more moderate positions of the advertised author, former Jesuit Raynal. In the event, the publication of book XI, with its famous discussion of slavery, rapidly changed the perception of the whole work in the eyes of European public opinion. It became a large-scale manifesto of the political struggle of the Late Enlightenment against imperialism, colonialism and the Atlantic slave trade operated by the new 'lords of all the world'.[10] This eleventh book of the *Histoire* on the one hand celebrates the humane and civilising effect of international trade, but on the other delivers the harshest possible critique of modern European colonialism. These aspects come to the fore especially in the famous chapter 24, 'Origin and progress of slavery. Arguments made use of to justify it. Refutation of them'.[11]

This chapter is built almost like a play. To us today it still seems like an amazing example of printed theatre, with its hugely effective rhetorical resonance, which followed a model that was fairly widespread in the eighteenth century. This skilful 'performance', which was part of an intriguing 'theatrical' view of history, was directed at the tribunal of public opinion throughout Europe. It was truly a *mise en scène* of the cosmopolitan and universalistic idea of natural rights for 'the preservation of man'.[12] The history of slavery was presented as a dramatic

9. Recent bibliography on this subject is discussed in Patrizia Delpiano, *La schiavitù in età moderna* (Rome and Bari, 2009), p.144ff.
10. See Anthony Pagden, *Lords of all the world: ideologies of empire in Spain, Britain and France c.1500-c.1800* (New Haven, CT, 1995); Sankar Muthu, *Enlightenment against empire* (Princeton, NJ, 2003). It is worth noting that on 25 May 1781 the Paris parliament decreed that the *Histoire* should be publicly burned and Raynal imprisoned, which forced the abbé to flee abroad.
11. Cf. Raynal, *History*, vol.5, p.282. In this English version chapters are marked only by headings in the margin.
12. 'The preservation of man' is Diderot's phrase and is found, for instance in Raynal's *History*, vol.5, p.296. Diderot was hugely interested in stage theatre, to the extent of setting himself up as a reformer of stage plays. However, his plays were conceived mostly as closet drama or printed texts, and were in fact considered unsuitable for stage performance by the actors of the Comédie-Française and by professional dramatists such as Palissot or Collé. On the

fragment of the never-ending story of the pursuit of human freedom throughout Europe and the world. Diderot started this performance from the beginning: from the Greeks, the Romans and the struggle for enfranchisement from servitude of the glebe. As we saw above, he defined liberty as ownership of one's body, the inalienable essence of the individual's humanity: 'Will these eternal and immutable truths, the foundation of all morality, the basis of all rational government, be contested?' (p.294). Adducing one argument after another, in this chapter of the *Histoire* Diderot demolishes the views of an imaginary 'panegyrist' of slavery, calling him an 'executioner' of fellow human beings. He denies the legitimacy of the right of the strongest and is fiercely opposed to the revival, on a new 'scientific' basis, of the Aristotelian theory of the natural slave:

> But these Negroes, say they, are a race of men born for slavery; their dispositions are narrow, treacherous, and wicked; they themselves allow the superiority of our understandings, and almost acknowledge the justice of our authority.
>
> The minds of the Negroes are contracted; because slavery destroys all the springs of the soul. They are wicked; but not sufficiently so with you. They are treacherous; because they are under no obligation to speak truth to their tyrants. They acknowledge the superiority of our understandings, because we have perpetuated their ignorance: they allow the justice of our authority, because we have abused their weakness [...]
>
> Barbarians, will you persuade me, that a man can be the property of a sovereign, a son the property of a father, a wife the property of a husband, a domestic the property of a master, a Negro the property of a planter? (p.298)

Diderot writes scathingly about the way in which Church authorities had been willing to countenance all kinds of atrocities as long as this

---

relationship between closet drama and stage theatre see Julie Stone Peters, *Theatre of the book, 1480-1880: print, text and performance in Europe* (Oxford, 2000). On the phenomenal success of drama aimed at reading rather than performance in the French publishing market see also Wallace Kirsop, 'Nouveautés: théâtre et roman', in *Histoire de l'édition française*, vol.2: *Le Livre triomphant: 1660-1830*, ed. Roger Chartier and Henri-Jean Martin, 2nd edn (Paris, 1990), p.269-84. Cf. also Marie-Laurence Netter, *Du théâtre à la liberté* (Paris, 2012). What Diderot is applying here is effectively the same *mise en scène* of philosophical debates that is found also in both *Jacques le fataliste* and *Le Neveu de Rameau*, as well as in the intense dialogue between Orou and the Almoner in the *Supplément au voyage de Bougainville*.

enabled them to convert and baptise new souls. He is indignant towards them for providing theological justifications for slavery by allowing a certain interpretation of the biblical story of Cam to spread freely across the centuries, whereby Noah's black son and all his descendants were the object of God's curse:[13]

> O Beneficent Jesus! how is it possible that thy mild maxims could have been perverted to justify such an infinite number of horrid acts? If the Christian religion did really thus give a sanction to the avarice of empires, its sanguinary tenets ought for ever to be proscribed. It should either be abolished, or it should disavow, in the face of the whole universe, the enormities that are imputed to it. (p.303)

Diderot firmly believed that '[I]n proportion as morality and policy shall be improved, man will recover his rights' (p.302). However, the struggle against slavery could no longer be put off: 'the condition of these unfortunate people is very different from ours' (p.303). It was no longer enough to try and make slavery and its trade more humane and bearable, or to put forward cautious projects of reform that foresaw its gradual disappearance. The chapter ends in a crescendo that voices the desperate cry of millions of Africans who were killed, abused and enslaved for the sake of the so-called civilisation of the Western world. At the same time, its aim is to awaken the indignation of the reader-spectator against the slave trade and to unveil the genocide perpetrated by the Europeans. In a final *coup de théâtre*, Diderot prophesies the imminent revolt of the enslaved masses, at last united under the guidance of a black Spartacus and determined to claim their rights as human beings:[14]

> If then, ye nations of Europe, interest alone can exert its influence over you, listen to me once more. Your slaves stand in no need either of your generosity or your counsels, in order to break the sacrilegious yoke of their oppression [...] the Negroes only want a chief, sufficiently courageous, to lead them on to vengeance and slaughter.

13. On the Church's position through the centuries see Pétré-Grenouilleau, *Traites négrières*.
14. The image of a black Spartacus is found in the utopian novel by Louis-Sébastien Mercier, *L'An deux mille quatre cent quarante: rêve s'il en fût jamais* (Neuchâtel, n.n., 1772), p.113-15. Diderot uses exactly the same words and concepts, which confirms the close link between the two *philosophes* in their common struggle against the slave trade.

> Where is this great man, whom nature owes to her afflicted, oppressed, and tormented children? Where is he? He will undoubtedly appear, he will shew himself, he will lift up the sacred standard of liberty. This venerable signal will collect around him the companions of his misfortunes. They will rush on with more impetuosity than torrents; they will leave behind them, in all parts, indelible traces of their just resentment. Spaniards, Portuguese, English, French, Dutch, all their tyrants will become the victims of fire and sword. The plains of America will suck up with transport the blood which they have so long expected, and the bones of so many wretches, heaped upon one another, during the course of so many centuries, will bound for joy. The Old World will join its plaudits to those of the New. In all parts the name of the hero who shall have restored the rights of the human species, will be blest; in all parts trophies will be erected to his glory (p.309-10).

These impassioned words evoked the myth of rebellion and openly presented the language of the rights of man as effective political discourse, what today we would call a 'political formula', capable of mobilising international public opinion. The Late Enlightenment was thus staking its claim to the role of leader of Europe's nascent abolitionist movement. In 1781 Condorcet, using a pseudonym, published his famous *Réflexions sur l'esclavage des nègres*. In this text, slavery is at last defined as a crime against humanity, and what was really at stake is made clear once and for all: 'Je parlerai non des intérets du commerce, mais des loix de la justice.'[15] To enslave someone was a violation of the universal rights of man: 'Une loi injuste qui blesse le droit des hommes, soit nationaux, soit étrangers, est un crime commis par les législateurs' (p.13). In his pamphlet, Condorcet puts forward some concrete proposals for reform that would gradually lead to the abolition of slavery. He argues his positions reasonably and with moderation, in a very different tone from Diderot's incendiary prophecies. This effectively paved the way for the formation, in February 1788, of the Société des amis des Noirs, which gathered together all the Parisian Enlightenment thinkers, with their emancipatory and abolitionist views.[16] However,

15. [Condorcet], *Réflexions sur l'esclavage des nègres* (Neuchâtel, Société typographique, 1781), p.v.
16. Cf. Jean-Pierre Barlier, *La Société des amis des Noirs: aux origines de la première abolition de l'esclavage, 4 février 1794* (Paris, 2010); Marcel Dorigny and Bernard Gainot, *La Société des amis des Noirs, 1788-1799: contributions à l'histoire de l'abolition*

Diderot's works, with their use of ancient republican techniques of rhetoric, as can be seen in the passages quoted above, are still a fundamental milestone in the history of the rights of man and in their decisive transformation by the Enlightenment into a weapon in the struggle for 'the preservation of man'. Among other things, this implied the radical redefinition of the politics of the moderns, its horizons and the struggle to get public opinion on the side of moral values rather than of blatant individual or class interests.

Despite long investigations and debates, we still do not have a definitive answer to the question of what politics really meant for Enlightenment thinkers in general, and for Diderot in particular. In a pioneering book first published in French in 1939 as *Jeunesse de Diderot*, Franco Venturi took issue with the French tradition that had turned our *philosophe* into an erudite *pantouflard*, insisting instead that his work must be viewed in political rather than literary or philosophical terms. It was, of course, necessary to define what politics meant for Diderot himself. Venturi wrote his work as a young historian who adhered to Croce's idealism and had a confident knowledge of the works of Marx, Lenin and Sorel. He consequently found the characteristic feature of this important new political concept in the centrality of the 'moment of political invention, creation, action', in accordance with a model that in fact had been widely debated at the beginning of the twentieth century. However, with his historicist background Venturi was averse to any form of anachronism, and was not aware of these obvious similarities. In his research on Diderot and the Enlightenment he never used the political language of his own contemporaries, who spoke of elites, public opinion, psychology of the masses, political and cultural hegemony, and political formulae and myths. Venturi's focus was always on 'ideas', which when circulated transformed reality and set historical processes in motion, so that the new intellectual elites were effectively the protagonists in the modern history of the Western world. 'Discovery and creation' were the key words that Venturi used to define Diderot's thought: 'Free conquest and joyous creation, the assertion of a new religious, philosophical and political world. This creation, however, took place not in the world of literary forms or traditional thinking, but in contact and in contrast with the vital aspects of European culture' at the time of the *Ancien régime*.[17]

---

de l'esclavage (Paris, 1999). See also Claude Mazauric's review of Dorigny and Gainot's book in *Annales historiques de la Révolution française* 317 (1999), p.554-56.

17. Cf. Venturi, *Giovinezza di Diderot*, p.11-12.

Venturi's book was reviewed by Lucien Febvre, who praised its original interpretation of Diderot as the father of a new concept of politics: 'He created a new politics full of possibilities and dynamism at a time when traditional politics seemed sterilised. The genesis of this politics can be found in Diderot himself.'[18] In fact, Venturi's insight into the original role played by the Enlightenment in creating the politics of the moderns has not really been developed further. Venturi himself went on to focus on the modalities of eighteenth-century reformism, republicanism and constitutionalism, ignoring both the crucial theme of the rights of man and, specifically, Diderot's decisive contribution to the great aesthetic revolution of the Late Enlightenment and its new and original links with politics: which was ultimately what characterised the human and intellectual experience of the father of the *Encyclopédie*.

It is in the framework of this revolution that the so-called 'politicisation of literature', with which we began our discussion, came into being. By this we mean the surprising transformation of artists, writers and men of letters into the autonomous protagonists of moral and political life in France at the turn of the century, with a modern style of conjunction between political action in all its forms and public opinion. Diderot was the main agent in this change, and the most subtle theoretician of a cultural phenomenon that founded the idea of art and the artist on an entirely new basis. This was well understood by his contemporaries, as was shown by Lessing's remark that 'no more philosophical mind than his has occupied itself with the theater since Aristotle'.[19]

Diderot did not simply go beyond the ancient idea of art as the imitation of nature as is found in Aristotle's *Poetics*. He was profoundly against the purely rationalistic and objective form of representation that had developed in the previous century: a form that focused on the artistic product in a 'manneristic' way, on rational rules and even scientific definitions, at the expense of the creative role of the artist and the importance of reception. Diderot did away with the traditional views on art of those theoreticians who linked a classicist

18. Lucien Febvre, 'La genèse des idées de Diderot', *Annales d'histoire sociale* 2:1 (1940), p.46-47 (46).

19. Quoted in Wilson, *Diderot*, p.328. On the influence of Diderot's aesthetic thought in Europe, and in Germany in particular, see Roland Mortier, *Diderot en Allemagne, 1750-1850* (Paris, 1954); Anne Saada, *Inventer Diderot: les constructions d'un auteur dans l'Allemagne des Lumières* (Paris, 2003).

aesthetics with *Ancien régime* values and a logic of domination. These were replaced by an acute awareness of the importance of public opinion and by the redefinition of knowledge as outlined in the *Encyclopédie*, with its focus on the absolute centrality of man and his faculties: memory, reason and imagination. With his empiricism and refined sense of psychology, he was also dubious about Newton's mechanistic universe, Descartes's geometric-deductive rationalism and the fixist concept of nature.

In Diderot the discipline of aesthetics – the neologism having been coined in 1750 by German philosopher Alexander Gottlieb Baumgarten – took on radical new meaning and was founded, first of all, on the personal representation of nature as something that was finally located in time, a kind of great animal in constant transformation, similar to the *natura naturans* of the Renaissance, with its inexhaustible creative energy.[20] At the same time, Diderot considered aesthetic events in light of the new sciences of man, with their anthropological, historical, psychological character and their profoundly and eminently human significance. When it came to choosing between on the one hand classicist *taste*, in the sense of adhering to a norm and applying time and careful study to produce a conventional form of beauty, and on the other creative *genius*, a pure and immediate gift of nature, Diderot had no hesitations in opting for the latter.[21] In his reflections on aesthetic matters he often referred to the concept of the sublime as formulated by Edmund Burke in his 1756 *Philosophical inquiry into the origin of our ideas of the sublime and beautiful*. This concept was a form of transcendence of the human being out of all given proportion, a breaking of the barriers of finitude – though not their destruction. It was man's true explosion of liberty from nature, and his full artistic emancipation from social conventions. For Diderot, true poetry needed 'something savage, raw, striking, and enormous'.[22]

Diderot saw art as the constant exploration of human potentialities: the free and unfettered pursuit of truth. His Enlightenment creed involved the possibility of constructing a modern and empirical

20. On European neonaturalism, and in particular its manifestations in Diderot and the Late Enlightenment, see Ferrone, *I profeti dell'Illuminismo*, p.81ff.; Michel Delon, *L'Idée d'énergie au tournant des Lumières (1770-1820)* (Paris, 1988).
21. See the article on 'Génie' in the *Encyclopédie*.
22. Cf. Wilson, *Diderot*, p.529. Wilson's extensive bibliography on Diderot's aesthetic thought should be supplemented with Michel Delon's introduction and notes to his edition of Denis Diderot, *Salons* (Paris, 2008).

kind of 'communicative aesthetics', in which a work of art always required the active participation of the spectator in order to be fully complete. In this scenario, the centrality of sentiments, the torrent of tears and passions that were now an objective part of the sensitivity of being, were in any case accompanied by the critical and public use of reason. The purpose was to redefine beauty on the basis of its social function and its ability to create emotions and reality, ethical reflection and political will: ultimately, to shape the present and the future.

In his *Paradoxe sur le comédien* Diderot discussed how even the greatest artistic creation nevertheless required method, preparation, practice and perfect self-control by the protagonist when put on stage. Fantasy must never rule alone, but go hand in hand with communicative reason and critical spirit, since at every instant in man's life the dream could transform into a nightmare.[23] Accordingly, Diderot's poetics is characterised throughout by the constant tension of opposites, the dialectic of situations, the empirical exploration of contrast: see, for instance, in *Le Neveu de Rameau*, the protagonists' tormented introspective reflections on their social situation.

Diderot believed that in the theatre, novels, music or painting it was not enough to seek to move or give pleasure, or to imitate nature with ever new and more precise methods and techniques. Artists should aim at moving their audience in order to make them think, educate them to virtue by awakening their emotions and stirring their souls by creating constantly new and unexpected situations. In his famous 'Eloge de Richardson' (1761), Diderot commented on the amazing power of the imagination as displayed by the author of *Pamela*, and the effect on the reader of those novels, which were as absorbing as they were full of virtuous instruction. This was a perfect example of how literature could activate a psychological mechanism of empathy that could persuade the reader to take action. In his *Salons* Diderot focused instead on the effect of so-called 'moral painting', such as poured out of Jean-Baptiste Greuze's work, or on the republican and anti-tyrannical feelings evoked by the paintings of Jacques-Louis David. In this new sense, painting should not concern itself simply with the world of forms but should strive to reach the soul through

23. See the important remarks by Daniel Arasse in his chapter on 'The artist', in *Enlightenment portraits*, ed. Michel Vovelle, translated by Lydia G. Cochrane (Chicago, IL, and London, 1997), p.226-56.

the eyes so as to speak directly to the public's conscience and fire their critical spirit.[24]

However, it was in discussing the renewal of drama that Diderot's new aesthetics really came into its own, as he unleashed a frontal attack on the *Ancien régime*'s theatre. He saw the latter as the offshoot of a communication system founded on rigid and exact rules, total respect for an absolutistic authority principle, and adherence to rhetorical precepts and communication techniques that dated back to the previous century's âge de l'éloquence.[25] Consequently, he urged authors to bridge the gap between the stage and the audience, and to link performance with the philosophical investigation of the human and social condition of man, so as to involve spectators both rationally and emotionally. Most importantly, Diderot publicly advocated the emancipation of the artist's creative experience from any kind of restraint, tradition or social convention.

In this way the artist became also politician and moralist. His public function was given new value by the communicative aesthetics of the moderns as envisaged by Diderot. He was devoted to the stubborn pursuit of truth, and increasingly aware of his demiurgic role as the creator of new realities. He was, above all, a protagonist in his role as a creator of public-opinion movements, swaying convictions and changing notions, tastes, fashions and history, transforming the very mentality of individuals, to the extent that they could sometimes be pushed to extremes. It is well known how Rousseau's novels completely turned around the general perception of the Alps as an unpleasant and unwelcoming place, giving rise to the modern culture of mountainous places; it is also well known that many young readers committed suicide out of empathy with Goethe's Werther. This vindicated Tocqueville's opinion. In Paris, with the Late Enlightenment disciples of Rousseau and Diderot, the politicisation of literature and its attendant literarisation of politics could

24. See p.401ff. in Michel Delon's edition of Diderot's *Salons*, and the editor's introduction.

25. Important remarks on *Ancien régime* theatre can be found in Gerardo Tocchini, *La politica della rappresentazione: comunicazione sociale e consumo culturale nella Francia di antico regime (1669-1781)*, 2nd edn (Turin, 2012). See also, by the same author, 'L'*Œdipe* del giovane Voltaire alla prova della scena pubblica: canone politico, strategie e autocensure nel teatro tragico della prima età dei Lumi', *Rivista storica italiana* 125 (2013), p.681-763. On this topic, cf. also Marc Fumaroli, *L'Age de l'éloquence: rhétorique et res literaria, de la Renaissance au seuil de l'époque classique* (Paris, 1994), and *Héros et orateurs: rhétorique et dramaturgie cornéliennes* (Geneva, 1996).

be said to have been well and truly accomplished, with momentous consequences for the development of modern communication, and, above all, for the history of the rights of man.

In the case of the Italian Enlightenment, the main protagonists tended to be civil servants or university professors. Consequently, the renewal of the political language of natural rights mostly occurred through works on economics, law or moral philosophy that addressed a small circle of people engaged in the government of the country. By contrast in France it was mainly the artistic and literary representatives of the Enlightenment who exercised a profound influence on politics at the end of the century with works that were directly aimed at public opinion. This led to two different ways of thinking of and popularising the political practice of rights. Thanks to an early understanding of the power of symbolic communication in the construction of social imagination, the *philosophes* not only made the eighteenth century a 'hot' time in the history of utopian thinking and the construction of social dreams capable of anticipating the future: they entrusted all kinds of artistic forms with the task of liaising between the general public and the new Enlightenment politics of the rights for the preservation of man.[26]

In this sense, Diderot's 1771 poem *Les Eleuthéromanes, ou les Furieux de la liberté* was certainly a pioneering effort in explicitly invoking the rights of man as a political formula and battle cry against despotism, pointing to indignation as the crucial passion in any real morally founded political action.[27] However, Diderot's theoretical reflections on the links between art and politics, theatre and rights, were concretely enacted mainly by his disciple Louis-Sébastien Mercier, thanks to whom these theories spread across Europe.

Mercier was an eclectic and successful writer in the medium of both drama and fiction, whose works were frequently reprinted and translated into other languages. Already in the early 1770s Mercier had publicly claimed that a dramatist's political mission and the

26. On the Enlightenment's use of this artistic form see Bronislaw Baczko, *Lumières de l'utopie* (Paris, 1978).

27. 'L'Enfant de la nature abhorre l'esclavage / Implacable ennemi de toute autorité / il s'indigne du joug; la contrainte l'outrage / Liberté, c'est son vœu; son cri, c'est liberté […] / Jamais au public avantage / l'homme n'a franchement sacrifié ses droits' (*Les Eleuthéromanes*, in Diderot, *Œuvres complètes*, vol.9, p.14). On indignation as an essential element in Diderot's political attitude, above and beyond his specific theories on constitutionalism or republicanism see Imbruglia, 'Indignation et droits de l'homme', p.164ff.

principal task of theatre in general lay in the defence of the rights of man and in contributing to his emancipation in accordance with Enlightenment values and ideas.[28] Like Diderot, he firmly believed in the historical and political task that awaited the *hommes de lettres*, who were now enlisted in the struggle to defend and promulgate the rights of man against all tyrants: 'They have for sure taken a direction that can only be to the profit of mankind. They are feared and hated by tyrants because they are considered by them to be friends of truth and defenders of the rights of man.'[29] In his *Bonnet de nuit* Mercier further explained how the theatre should become a true school of morality, and the main tool for communicating with the people:

> Maybe without this powerful art, which shows us all the rights of man, some venal souls would insult generous citizens and force them to smile while they are being abused. And what can persuade man's heart better than the subtle inveigling art of the theatre! Reason is slow and uncertain, while feelings are quick and assured. The former speaks, while the latter subjugate. Reason demands enlightenment, time, debates, while feelings smite with the same force the heart of the rustic as that of the learned man. The language of the theatre is, perhaps, the only language that is really suitable for the multitude.[30]

It is not surprising, therefore, to find constant references to the rights of man in all of Mercier's main works, which were real bestsellers in his time. In the *Tableau de Paris*, those rights were placed firmly at the centre of a political and cultural revolution: 'It is thanks to our *gens de lettres* that the spirit of the capital has become totally opposite to that of the court: the former seeks to re-establish the rights of man, and will allow only the smallest of outlets to the opinions of the great, who used to humiliate the people in every sense.'[31] In his 1771 utopian

28. Cf. Robert Darnton, *The Forbidden best-sellers of pre-revolutionary France* (London and New York, 1995), p.114ff.
29. Translated from Louis-Sébastien Mercier, *Du théâtre, ou Nouvel Essai sur l'art dramatique* (Amsterdam, E. van Harrevelt, 1773), p.2.
30. Louis-Sébastien Mercier, *Mon bonnet de nuit*, 4 vols (Lausanne, Jean-Pierre Heubach, 1785), vol.4, p.150 (only the first two volumes appear to have been translated into English). Similar thoughts are expressed in *Du théâtre*, p.219.
31. [Louis-Sébastien Mercier], *Tableau de Paris*, 2 vols (Hamburg and Neuchâtel, Virchaux et Fauche, 1781), vol.1, p.206 (the *Tableau* was only partially translated into English, hence our translation). In another edition printed in 8 vols in Amsterdam in 1783 the assertion of rights is explicitly linked to the triumph of the Enlightenment: 'C'est en vain que l'on voudroit éteindre aujourd'hui le flambeau de la philosophie. Le fanal est allumé et domine l'Europe. Si l'on

novel *L'An 2440*, which went through dozens of editions in the space of a few years, we are reminded from the outset that respect for the *droits de l'homme* had always been a formidable barrier to superstition. We then watch the protagonist reawaken after seven centuries of progress, in a Paris now ruled by the Enlightenment. He finds himself in a large square with a monument to the black Spartacus who had led the successful revolt against slavery in the name of the *droits imprescriptibles* of universal man. Mercier's historical plays – which were in fact not always enjoyable or successful – often make explicit reference to the rights in issuing warnings and advice to sovereigns.[32] In *Le Juge* (1778), a curious play on the mission of the magistrate, Mercier reminds the enemies of the Enlightenment that 'for the rights of mankind, the man of letters is prepared to risk his freedom and repose' (act 2, scene 10).

Apart from Mercier, several other very famous polygraphs of that century mentioned the rights of man in their works. It is possible to gather references to this issue in the work of Marmontel, especially the 1787 edition of his tragedy *Denys le tyran*.[33] The same applies to Jean-Louis Carra's 1782 philosophical novel, *Odazir, ou le Jeune Syrien*, which engages in fierce polemics against the wealthy and the aristocracy in the name of the equality of rights.[34] In general, the

---

étouffe une voix, vingt autres toutes prêtes réclameront plus hautement les droits de l'homme. Les dominateurs des nations n'ont plus d'autre parti à prendre, que celui d'être justes et modérés' (vol.4, p.303).

32. See, for instance, *Childeric premier, roi de France, drame héroique* (1774), *La Destruction de la Ligue, ou la Réduction de Paris, pièce nationale en quatre actes* (1782) and especially *Portrait de Philippe II, roi d'Espagne* (1785), which would influence Schiller's *Don Carlos*, and in which Mercier denounces Scholastic theology and its use of the Inquisition. For the *Portrait* see the individual edition printed in Amsterdam in 1785. For the other plays, see *Théâtre complet de M. Mercier*, 4 vols (Amsterdam, B. Vlam; Leiden, J. Murray, 1778 [1778-1784]).

33. See Jean-François Marmontel, *Denys le tyran, tragédie* (1748), in *Œuvres complètes*, vol.5 (Paris, Née de la Rochelle, 1787), p.13 (I.i). For other references to the rights in Marmontel, cf. Gerardo Tocchini, 'Politica e letteratura nell'Europa dei Lumi: i romanzi di Marmontel', *Rivista storica italiana* 122:1 (2010), p.41-76 (69ff.). I am grateful to Tocchini for information on many of the works of literature that I mention in this chapter.

34. See [Jean-Louis Carra], *Odazir, ou le Jeune Syrien, roman philosophique, composé d'après les mémoires d'un Turc* (The Hague [Bouillon], [Société typographique de Bouillon], 1782), p.239-40. Also of interest is the abbé Duval-Pyrau's pedagogical novel in the style of *Télémaque*, in which the protagonist urges Themistocles to be just: 'respecte les droits des hommes; mérite et reconnois les bienfaits d'un peuple dont tu tiens ta distinction et ton pouvoir' (abbé Duval-Pyrau, *Aristide*, Yverdon, Société littéraire et typographique, 1777, p.66-67). Finally, in 1784

performance of the rights of man became more and more frequent in both stage theatre and closet drama, in other words in theatre for the stage and theatre for the page.[35] In the same way, after the eminent example provided by Diderot with the *Histoire des deux Indes*, the French publishing industry brought out a raft of new books on what we would now call 'contemporary history': books in which the language of rights helped to measure the degree of civilisation that had been reached by human societies, and to bring before the tribunal of public opinion historical processes that were still in the making.[36]

By the end of the century the language of rights had rapidly become a constant of political discourse. And it was not invoked only against the despotism of the sovereign or the Church of Rome.[37] In

---

one of the most important contributors to the *Histoire des deux Indes*, Jean-Joseph Pechméja, published *Télèphe*, another novel based on Fénelon's model, which was interwoven with masonic themes and whose first part alluded to the rights of man through the lens of ancient slavery: see [Jean-Joseph Pechméja], *Télèphe en XII livres* (London and Paris, Pissot, 1784).

35. Numerous examples could be mentioned, especially from the 1780s. See, for instance: the scene in which the hero, Clodomir, steals away his beloved, who is destined to be sacrificed to the gods, in Antoine Le Blanc de Guillet, *Les Druides, tragédie* (Paris, Louis, [1772]), p.120 (IV.vii); the curious appeal to the rights of man to propagate the use of smallpox vaccination in Claude-Joseph Dorat, *L'Inoculation, ode*, in *Collection complète des œuvres*, 6 vols (Neuchâtel, Société typographique, 1776), vol.1, p.300-301; or their use against slavery in Jean-Antoine Roucher's *Les Mois, poëme en douze chants*, 2 vols (Paris, Quillau, 1779), vol.1, p.91ff.

36. Again, we point here to just a few examples: William Robertson, *Histoire d'Ecosse sous les regnes de Marie Stuart et de Jacques VI jusqu'à l'avènement de ce prince à la couronne d'Angleterre, traduit de l'anglois*, 3 vols (London [Paris], n.n., 1764), vol.1, p.220ff.; William Bolts, *Etat civil, politique et commerçant du Bengale, ou Histoire des conquêtes et de l'administration de la compagnie angloise dans ce pays, ouvrage traduit de l'anglois de M. Bolts*, translated by Jean-Nicolas Démeunier (The Hague, Gosse, fils, 1775); Nicolas-Gabriel Le Clerc and Antoine-François Le Clerc, *Histoire physique, morale, civile et politique de la Russie*, vol.2 (Paris and Versailles, n.n., 1785), p.247ff.; Pierre Poivre, *Voyages d'un philosophe, ou Observations sur les mœurs et les arts des peuples de l'Afrique, de l'Asie et de l'Amérique* (Maastricht, J. E. Dufour & P. Roux, 1779); Gabriel-Henri Gaillard, *Histoire de la rivalité de la France et de l'Angleterre*, 3 vols (Paris, Saillant & Nyon, 1771), vol.3, p.32ff.; [Jacques Accarias de Sérionne], *Situation politique actuelle de l'Europe, considérée relativement à l'ordre moral pour servir de supplément à l'ordre moral* (Augsburg, Conrad Henri Stage, 1781), p.142ff.; Claude-Camille d'Albon, *Discours politiques, historiques et critiques, sur quelques gouvernements de l'Europe* (Neuchâtel, n.n., 1779), p.66ff.

37. This use is found, for instance, in Josef Niklas W. von Windisch-Graetz, *Discours dans lequel on examine les deux questions suivantes: 1º Un monarque a-t-il le droit de*

other, no less significant, cases, it was used in the public ceremonies marking the entry of new members into the great Parisian academic institutions. Necker, for instance, used this language extensively in a speech in praise of Colbert that he read at the Académie française in 1773, in which he outlined the task and defining characteristics of the true man of state.[38] Finally, important translators of ancient authors were not afraid of inserting anachronisms in their versions by inventing the existence of Roman emperors who were improbable defenders of the rights of man – all this with the aim of furthering the understanding and commercial viability of the work in question among contemporaries.[39]

---

changer de son chef une constitution évidemment vicieuse? 2° Est-il prudent à lui, est-il de son intérêt de l'entreprendre? Suivi de réflexions pratiques (n.p., n.n., 1788), p.13-14; or the 'Réflexions impartiales d'un neutre sur le traité éventuel concerté entre la Régence d'Amsterdam et le Congrès américain', in *Correspondance politique sur les affaires présentes de la Hollande: feuille périodique pour servir à l'histoire de ce siècle*, vol.1 (Amsterdam, n.n., 1782), p.23-36 (33ff.). We should add at least two examples of the growing use of the *droits de l'homme, du citoyen et du chrétien* in the Protestant polemic against the Church of Rome: cf. *Les Souffrances de l'Eglise et leur glorieuse issue: sermon sur Michée VII, 8 prononcé dans l'Eglise françoise de Christian-Erlang le 30 octobre 1785, à l'occasion de la commémoration religieuse et du jubilé de la révocation de l'Edit de Nantes, qui a été suivie de l'établissement des réfugiés françois à Christian-Erlang, par Albert Hollard, pasteur* (n.p., n.n., n.d. [1785]), p.27; and [Jean-Paul Rabaut de Saint-Etienne], *Le Roi doit modifier les loix portées contre les protestants; démonstration; avantage que la France tirerait de cette modification* (London [Paris?], n.n., 1784), p.27ff.

38. Cf. [Jacques Necker], *Eloge de Jean-Baptiste Colbert, discours qui a remporté le prix de l'Académie françoise en 1773* (Paris, n.n., 1773), p.6-7, where the author explains that he who administers the finances of a great State 'doit rassembler en sa pensée les droits de l'homme et ceux d'une Nation'. See also the *Discours prononcé dans l'Académie françoise, le lundi IV juin MDCC. LXXXVII à la réception de M. de Rulhiere* (Paris, n.n., 1787), where the new member of the Academy is praised for his 'connoissance plus réfléchie des droits de l'homme & du citoyen' (p.31).

39. See the *Pensées de l'empereur Marc-Aurèle-Antonin, ou Leçons de vertu que ce prince philosophe se faisoit à lui-même: nouvelle traduction du grec, distribuée en chapitres, suivant les matières, avec notes et variantes, par M. de Joly* (Paris, n.n., 1770), p.75 (V, Résignation, vi); *Les Tragédies d'Euripide, traduites du grec par M. [Pierre] Prevost, professeur et membre de l'Académie royale des sciences et belles-lettres de Berlin*, vol.2 (Paris, n.n., 1782), p.45 (*Les Phéniciennes*, II). In the latter case, it was Euripides who was unashamedly transformed into a supporter of equality of rights: 'L'égalité a balancé les droits des hommes; elle mesure et limite leur puissance.' The *droits de l'homme* even make a surprise appearance in *Antiquité d'Herculanum, ou les Plus belles peintures antiques, et les marbres, bronzes, meubles, etc., etc. trouvés dans les excavations d'Herculanum, Stabia et Pompeia, gravés par F. A. David, avec les explications par P. S. Maréchal*, vol.2 (Paris, n.n., 1780), p.98-99.

This notwithstanding, the most obvious signal of the currency acquired by the new language of rights before the French Revolution must surely be how prominently it features in the four volumes entirely devoted to political economy in the *Encyclopédie méthodique*, published in 1786. This is noteworthy in at least two respects. Firstly, its famous predecessor, by Diderot and D'Alembert, made no reference to the *droits de l'homme*, at any level. A few decades on, Panckoucke's *Encyclopédie*, the most important work of the 1780s on the French publishing market, devotes two substantial articles to this topic, 'Droit naturel de l'homme' and 'Droit et devoirs', both by Bordeaux lawyer Guillaume Grivel.[40] Secondly, this was not an inflammatory, anti-despotic reading in the style of Diderot's *furieux de la liberté*, or Mercier's radical theatre, or Condorcet's enlightened claims for the preservation of man. The prevailing interpretation here was the moderate one of the physiocrats as presented in Mirabeau's texts and as it would be bequeathed to the Thermidorian constitutionalists of 1795: an interpretation that, as we have seen, was founded on the primacy of duties and the sociability principle.

The theory of the rights of man as derived from his duties had previously been expounded by Guillaume Grivel from this point of view, with constant reference to the physiocrats, in his three-volume *Théorie de l'éducation, ouvrage utile aux pères de famille et aux instituteurs*, published in Paris by Moutard in 1775. The young lawyer, who is only now beginning to receive some attention from scholars, realised quite early on that a profound change had been taking place on the French social communication scene with the new political theatre and the aesthetic thought of the Enlightenment, with its focus on the moral and political duties of artists. Between 1783 and 1786 Grivel published in Paris an ambitious and rather rambling utopian-psychological novel in six volumes, *L'Isle inconnue, ou Mémoires du chevalier Des Gastines*, in which he sought to popularise the physiocrats' beliefs on the duties and rights of man.[41]

40. On the huge publishing success of the *Encyclopédie méthodique* see Robert Darnton, *The Business of Enlightenment: a publishing history of the 'Encyclopédie' 1775-1800* (Cambridge, MA, 1979).

41. Cf. J. Conan, 'Une utopie physiocratisante: l'*Ile inconnue* de Guillaume Grivel', *Annales historiques de la Révolution française* 265 (1986), p.268-84. The physiocrats' official position was clearly explained in their official journal in 1770: see *Ephémérides du citoyen, ou Bibliothèque raisonnée des sciences morales et politiques*, vol.4 (1770), p.244: 'We believe therefore that any institution that infringes the rights of man, that deprives human beings of their natural freedom to improve

Grivel and the physiocrats were among a number of thinkers who challenged the cultural supremacy of the Enlightenment in the use of the language of rights for political purposes in the two decades prior to the Revolution. And this despite the fact that this cultural hegemony, as built by Voltaire, Rousseau and Diderot in the second half of the eighteenth century, was now virtually unassailable. In 1788 Condorcet was able to recall with justified pride the campaigns that had been fought by the *philosophes* in previous years, how they had finally unleashed the political struggle to defend man and his rights against all forms of despotism, and how this meant occupying a space that no other movement had effectively patrolled before them:

> In every civilised nation with a considerable number of citizens there is no liberty, no enjoyment of natural rights without enlightenment; the enemies of the enlightenment are therefore the enemies of the free rights of man. Now, examine the history of French literature and philosophy since the renaissance of letters, and you will see whether it is with the government or with the aristocracy that the blame lies for the countless obstacles that have been placed in the way of the progress of the enlightenment. By whom were the author of *Emile* and that of the *Histoire philosophique* condemned, or the works on the need to abolish all *corvées* and feudal duties and reform the juridical system? Was it the government who tried to stop the publication of a general dictionary of sciences, a by now indispensable monument to the achievements of reason? […] The more or less strong opposition to the freedom of the press is the true thermometer through which one can judge the intentions of public men or political bodies.[42]

their lot to the best of their ability, provided this does not interfere with the work of others or violate their possessions; that any institution that usurps property, generates and reduces labour, is opposed to mutual help among human beings: any such institution is anti-social, and in contrast with the purpose of sovereignty, harmful to sovereigns themselves and liable to diminish their real power as well as their dignity. Any such institution must, therefore, be reformed' (our translation). The physiocrats' idea that rights derive from duties and the sociability principle, in line with Wolff's theories, is put forward also by d'Holbach in his *Système social*, vol.2, p.56ff.

42. Translated from [Condorcet], *Lettres d'un citoyen des Etats-Unis à un Français, sur les affaires présentes* (Philadelphia, PA, n.n., 1788), p.13-14. After presenting Voltaire and Rousseau as the founding fathers of the rights of man, Condorcet had no qualms in doing the same with D'Alembert (*Eloge de M. D'Alembert, lu dans l'assemblée publique de l'Académie des sciences, le 21 avril 1784*, Paris, n.n., 1784, p.33) and Turgot (*Vie de Monsieur Turgot*, London [Paris], n.n., 1786, p.246).

Although Condorcet does not mention this here, the element that really gave the Enlightenment moral hegemony in the struggle against the *Ancien régime* was the incessant campaign against slavery that had been started twenty years previously by Diderot. The idea of the black Spartacus evoked by the latter and by Mercier seemed to hold the true meaning of the way in which the *philosophes* increasingly identified the political struggle and the practice of rights with the need to direct and mobilise public opinion.

As we saw, Mercier was among the first in this respect, followed by numerous other writers and artists. Among the latter we find playwright Olympe de Gouges, who fought for the rights of women alongside those of the blacks and for the abolition of slavery. Tragically, she ended her life on the guillotine, like many other Enlightenment figures who frequented the *salon* of Mme Helvétius in Auteuil, and who were not much loved by Robespierre.[43]

Thus countless pamphlets, plays and novels appealed to the universal rights of the human being in launching a vigorous attack on modern slavery.[44] It was the gazettes, however, that were most effective in swaying public opinion. In September 1771 Bouillon's *Journal politique* reported on the publication of several pamphlets on the slave trade. The article's author had no qualms in defining this form of commerce as downright 'atroce', also when judged from the political point of view, and asserting

> that all the reasons, pretexts and excuses that have been alleged to explain the abominable transformation of black people into beasts are wrong, empty, iniquitous and unreasonable. Here it is shown that this trade, which is self-destructive, is in every possible way contrary not only to the rights of the men who are being trafficked but also to the interests of the people who carry out this trade in human beings.[45]

43. On the life and death of Olympe de Gouges, see Manfred Geier, *Aufklärung: das europäische Projekt* (Hamburg, 2012), p.307ff.; Olivier Blanc, *Olympe de Gouges: une femme de libertés* (Paris, 1989); Paul Noack, *Olympe de Gouges: 1748-1793 – courtisane et militante des droits de la femme*, translated by Isabelle Duclos (Paris, 1993).
44. This is borne out by the extensive list of pamphlets in the *Liste des ouvrages sur la traite et l'esclavage* that was presented at the National Assembly by Brissot's Société des amis des Noirs and its sister organisation in London: see the microfiche collection under the general editorship of Colin Lucas, *The French Revolution research collection* (Oxford, 1989-).
45. Cf. *Journal politique* (Bouillon, September 1771), p.60. For a general discussion of the journals mentioned in what follows see *Dictionnaire des journaux, 1600-1789*, ed. Jean Sgard, 2 vols (Paris and Oxford, 1991).

Among the replies from the pro-slavery front, it may be worth noting a crude review published in *Nouvelles de la République des Lettres* in which the journalist, in discussing the 'droits des hommes et les différences de ces droits', reiterated the absolute primacy of the right to property, which he had no hesitations in applying to the slaves: 'The owner has the same right over his blacks as over his sugar canes. Property is an absolute right, or the word itself is meaningless.'[46] The popular pro-government paper *Mercure de France* also expressed its opinion. It did so after a positive mention of the translation of Beccaria's work and of 'the multiple editions of this tract, which was undertaken with the express aim of reminding us of the rights of mankind'.[47] In 1783, this authoritative newspaper summarised the whole matter, highlighting the main aspects of the intellectual debate started by the *philosophes*, and especially by Diderot in his contributions to the *Histoire des deux Indes*. The anonymous journalist asked his readers whether Christian morality itself did not legitimise and further the modern slave trade in the same way that the Greek and Roman civilisations of Antiquity legitimised the ancient practice of slavery:

> When truth be told, we do not read in St Paul that slavery is contrary to justice or the rights of men. However, he never mentions the rights of man: his Epistles and the Gospels are not treatises of public law. What we read there is that men are brothers, children of the same father, called to the same legacy. And it does not require a great effort to draw the logical consequence from this: that slavery cannot be legitimate.

Nonetheless, the great Christian nations of the Western world did not hesitate to slaughter or enslave whole peoples: 'Why accuse those who believe slavery to be unjust of being bad Christians and seditious citizens?' And it was at this point in the article that, with biting irony, and with an unidentified but famous quotation that came, unsurprisingly, from Voltaire, the journalist openly reveals his support for the campaign in defence of man unleashed by the *philosophes*:

> Tout au nom de César, et tout au nom des Dieux;
> C'est en ces noms sacrés qu'on fait des Misérables.[48]

46. Cf. *Nouvelles de la République des Lettres*, vol.1 (Lausanne, July 1775), p.317-18.
47. Cf. *Mercure de France*, vol.2 (July 1773), p.79.
48. Cf. *Mercure de France* (Saturday, 5 April 1783), p.136-39. The quotation is taken from the 1769 closet drama *Les Guèbres, ou la Tolérance* (I.v). Another newspaper that sided with the *philosophes* was the *Journal de Paris* – see, for instance,

The abolition of the slave trade was not the only front-line battle in which the *philosophes* were engaged. The merit for starting the latter campaign in the name of the rights of man belongs to Diderot, while it was Condorcet – the main figure and real leader of the Late Enlightenment in France – who relaunched with equal vigour Voltaire's struggle in defence of civil rights and for the reform of the penal system before the Revolution. A crucial battle in this renewed struggle occurred in 1783 around the *affaire des trois roués*, in which three men who were accused of carrying out a theft with the use of violence were sentenced to the wheel without any obvious evidence.[49] In a short pamphlet entitled *Réflexions d'un citoyen non gradué sur un procès très connu*, published anonymously in 1786, Condorcet entered the fray on behalf of the 'amis de l'humanité'. In outlining the general frame of reference for his engagement in this fight, he explicitly cited Voltaire's campaigns for Jean Calas and the defendants' inalienable right to defence, as propounded by Beccaria and the other thinkers of the Milanese Enlightenment.

As in the past, the enemy was the 'despotism of the perpetual, and more or less hereditary, tribunals'. These tribunals were the bastion of *Ancien régime* status-based society, with its privileges and inequalities, and the cruel procedures of its arcane inquisitorial process. Condorcet defended 'the enjoyment of the first rights of mankind' against the magistrates' obvious corporational interests and their willingness to spill innocent blood through their arbitrary sentences, and called for the intervention of the sovereign and public opinion.[50] The 'bitter, ironical and trenchant' tone of this address, as well as its authoritative stance, was immediately recognised by contemporaries as that of 'M. de Condorcet', i.e. 'of a modern *philosophe* who is ready to criticise and subject everything to his scrutiny', in line with the critical and public use of reason that was always the identifying feature of the Enlightenment.[51]

In the same year the *philosophes* had issued another work on this subject written by a disciple of Voltaire: *Mémoire justificatif pour trois hommes condamnés à la roue*, by Charles-Marguerite Dupaty, the famous

---

the references to the rights of man in a review on p.1152 of the issue from Wednesday, 29 September 1784.

49. Cf. Adolphe Wattine, *L'Affaire des trois roués: études sur la justice criminelle à la fin de l'Ancien régime* (Mâcon, 1921).

50. Cf. Condorcet, *Réflexions d'un citoyen non gradué*, in *Œuvres*, ed. Arthur O'Connor and François Arago, 12 vols (Paris, 1847-1849), vol.7, p.141-66 (153).

51. Cf. Bachaumont, *Mémoires secrets*, vol.32, p.131-32.

lawyer who had defended the three men.[52] This text clearly illustrates the transformation that the role of the lawyer itself was undergoing, as well as the growing importance of public opinion, all part of the cultural revolution brought about in France by the Late Enlightenment. In the space of over 200 pages, the author reviews every single aspect of the trial. In the process, this *cause célèbre* turns into something of a literary product, a suspenseful and cleverly constructed narrative, which, as prescribed by Diderot's modern aesthetic, was at the same time greatly affecting and implacably argued from a rational point of view: 'Let sensitive hearts take comfort: these three innocents are still breathing!' Thus the lawyer reassured his readers – and indeed a few years later he would go on to win the trial. There existed in fact neither evidence nor convincing testimonies against the three men, and their defender was able to denounce in great detail the secret procedures on which their case was based, and the openly arbitrary decisions that could only be possible in a legislative system that was a legacy of barbarous ages. Against the stubborn custodians of *Ancien régime* privileges, Dupaty thundered: 'You defend the accusers – and we shall defend the accused. You defend cruelty – and we shall defend mankind. You defend the dark – and we shall defend light [*la lumière*]!'[53]

This work fuelled a heated debate in the Parisian *salons*. The figure of the lawyer was transformed from the representative of a justice that was programmatically deaf to the rights of man into an avenging *philosophe*: a successful writer and man of letters who, with great theatrical skill, was able to relocate the cause of these innocents from the darkness of the law court to the far more open and transparent tribunal of public opinion. In fact, in this way he was simultaneously appealing to two tribunals: a real and a virtual one, which were, however, subtly interconnected. All of a sudden, the power of the magistrates had lost its legitimacy, and the ancient courts of justice, no longer able to resort to the traditional authority principle, were finally called publicly to account for their cruel deeds.

In fact, already from the early 1770s the Enlightenment's work in defence of the rights of man had started to bring about a change not only in the language used by lawyers, but in their hearts and minds, and even in the way they and everyone else who dealt with the

52. See William Doyle, 'Dupaty (1746-1788): a career in the Late Enlightenment', *SVEC* 230 (1985), p.1-125 (102).

53. Cf. Charles-Marguerite Dupaty, *Mémoire justificatif pour trois hommes condamnés à la roue* (Paris, Philippe-Denys Pierre, 1786), p.233.

administration of justice saw themselves before 1789. Even the famous *Causes célèbres*, an important source of information that is already well known to scholars, might be included under this perspective. This collection has been studied, including quite recently, in terms of the traditional historiographical paradigm of the search for the origins of the French Revolution.[54] However, it can help us gauge the radical change that took place in those years in the way of seeing politics as the preservation of man put into practice. This concept is among the most profound and original features of Late Enlightenment culture, which functioned independently of, and at times even in open contrast with, the revolutionary developments to come.

Indeed, any question of some importance in the political and social debate of those crucial years inevitably also turned up in novels and plays, as well as in the *Causes célèbres*, and explicit reference was made to the new language of the rights of man propounded by the *philosophes*. In 1770, judges were examining the delicate issue of *lettres de cachet* and their abuse by the authorities, and were doing so by asking whether 'the rights of man and of the citizen can be temporarily eclipsed by pressing interests of state'.[55] The so-called *mésalliance*, or the obstacles to marriage between people of different social classes, would eventually bring into crisis the values and hierarchical culture of the *Ancien régime*. From an eminently suitable theatrical subject it finally came to be discussed in tribunal courts on the basis of laws that recognised that 'the first right of man was being able to dispose of one's person; that it was right to exert vigilance on the way in which someone exercised this right, but it would be unjust to permanently limit their freedom, no matter what use they wished to make of it'.[56]

In 1780 we find magistrates and public opinion debating the relationship between the universal character of the rights of man and state legislation on the one hand and the rules and traditions that came with belonging to the Jewish community.[57] And in 1777 the

54. See Sarah Maza, *Private lives and public affairs: the 'Causes célèbres' of pre-revolutionary France* (Berkeley, CA, 1993).

55. See Jean-Claude de La Ville, *Continuation des Causes célèbres et intéressantes, avec les jugements qui les ont décidées*, vol.3 (Amsterdam, Chatelain, 1770), p.376.

56. Cf. [Nicolas-Toussaint Le Moyne Des Essarts], *Causes célèbres, curieuses et intéressantes, de toutes les cours souveraines du royaume, avec les jugements qui les ont décidées*, 195 vols (Paris, Simon, 1773-1789), vol.56 (1780), p.107-108 (cause CLX: 'Accusation de rapt de séduction').

57. *Causes célèbres*, vol.65 (1780), p.83-84 (cause CLXXI: 'Question d'état sur les mariages des Juifs. Le divorce est-il admis parmi eux?').

vast repertory of *Causes célèbres* was further augmented by a new trial that dealt with the most sensitive issue of the moment: the slave trade. Two black men who had come to France from the colonies asked and obtained from the judges to be released from slavery. This case caused great sensation, and the public in general concluded that 'these unfortunate men begin to realise how freedom, which is the principal right of man, is also his most precious possession.'[58]

One could go on for a while listing the many trial and tribunal accounts that appeared in print and greatly influenced the collective imaginary and public opinion in favour of the rights, just as the *philosophes* had predicted. In 1784, in attacking Guillaume Grivel's opinion that it was absolutely necessary for man to become finally aware of his rights and duties, *L'Année littéraire* scoffed at the mythical and almost magical character that the phrase had taken on in political debate: 'These are like two magic words through which he deludes himself that he might be able to transform the face of the earth.'[59]

The growing presence of the language of rights in the *Causes célèbres* should not divert our attention away from other issues that are of more pressing importance for our research: for instance, the fundamental role of the freemasons in general, and the Paris Loge des Neuf Sœurs in particular, not only in the attempts to reform French penal law in the course of the 1780s, but in the history of the rights of man as a whole – something that has not yet received sufficient attention from historians of the Enlightenment.[60]

We often forget that among the many *philosophes* who called for judicial reform there were a number of important thinkers, such as Condorcet, Dupaty and Pastoret, who belonged to this famous lodge, which had formed in 1776, three years after the foundation in Paris of the Grand Orient of France. Voltaire received his initiation and *apothéose maçonnique* in Paris to great acclaim on 7 April 1778, a few weeks before he died.[61] This event marked for the first time the more than purely symbolic confluence of important sections of the European Enlightenment into the ancient system of the masonic

58. *Causes célèbres*, vol.35 (1777), p.51.
59. Cf. *L'Année littéraire*, vol.2 (Paris, 1784), p.173-75.
60. No specific reference to the freemasons' contribution to the effort of putting in place a policy of reform of French penal law is found in John A. Carey, *Judicial reform in France before the Revolution of 1789* (Cambridge, MA, 1981); Maza, *Private lives and public affairs*, p.212ff.
61. Cf. Louis Amiable, *Une Loge maçonnique d'avant 1789: la loge des Neuf Sœurs* (1897), ed. Charles Porset (Paris, 1989), p.81ff.

lodges, with their rites, ceremonies and independent culture. Explicitly setting themselves up as the heirs of Helvétius, Diderot and Voltaire, masonic brothers such as Franklin, Condorcet or Dupaty relaunched within the Loge des Neuf Sœurs the militant policy of emancipation and defence of man that was born with the Calas case. In this way, the language of rights was carried into the very heart of freemasonry.

In yet another instance of collaboration between the French and Italian Enlightenment, these thinkers enlisted the help of their masonic brothers from Naples, the jurists Filangieri and Pagano.[62] The brothers of the Loge des Neuf Sœurs ensured that the great theoretical works of the Neapolitans on the right to defence in the modern juridical system became well known in their city, just as Voltaire and Morellet had done decades earlier with the pamphlet on this subject by the Milanese Beccaria.

We thus see an important connection between the work of the Enlightenment and the not-so-secret existence of a huge masonic apparatus throughout Europe: a circuit with some 250,000 adepts, all members of the elites, which Reinhart Koselleck has called 'the strongest social institution of the eighteenth-century moral world'.[63] In those whirlwind years just before 1789, this nexus gave rise to a fascinating though still little-known chapter in the history of the rights of man in the Western world.

A dramatic clash between the radical new militant culture of the Late Enlightenment and the supporters of the *Ancien régime* was to take place in the heart of Europe. In the Holy Roman empire of the German nation, the tragic episode of the Bavarian Illuminati affected the modern relationship between morality and politics, between masonic secret and public opinion, relaunching the positive nexus between emancipation and the rights of man. It is a clash that deserves to be analysed in detail because of its importance and long-term effects on the history of Germany and, above all, the history of rights in the Western world.

62. Cf. Ferrone, *Politics of Enlightenment*, p.177ff.

63. Koselleck, *Critique and crisis*, p.79. The figure 250,000 for the number of freemasons is given in Giuseppe Giarrizzo, *Massoneria e Illuminismo nell'Europa del Settecento* (Venice, 1994), p.346. See also *Le Monde maçonnique des Lumières (Europe-Amériques et colonies): dictionnaire prosopographique*, ed. Charles Porset and Cécile Révauger, 3 vols (Paris, 2013).

16. The politicisation of the Republic of Letters in Germany: freemasonry and the rights of man

The rise of the language of the rights of man in the West is now fairly well understood in terms of the history of ideas, concepts and thought of the great protagonists of intellectual life. However, there is still much to do with respect to the cultural history of rights in every corner of Europe before 1789. We know far too little about the popularity and specific reception of this language in different national contexts, or its political use by institutions, artistic and literary circles, masonic lodges and salons in the major European cities. For other countries, a study along the lines of what we have delineated above for the France of Diderot and Voltaire still remains to be done.

As mentioned at the beginning of the previous chapter, Condorcet outlined the main features of this scenario at quite an early stage, indicating in the 1776 American Revolution the high point of the definitive politicisation of the rights of man as an accomplished fact. The discourse of rights had finally moved out of university classrooms and ethical treatises that were meant for a small number of academics and begun to address the general public through novels and plays. As Condorcet said, 'the issue [of rights] was pleaded at the bar of public opinion before the whole of Europe' in order to justify those momentous events.

The Italian context was among the first to be studied from this point of view. This revealed the existence and characteristics of an 'Enlightenment constitutionalism', which the Neapolitan thinkers developed with a view to safeguarding the rights of man. Much attention has been devoted to the centrality of natural rights both in the constitutional debate that took place in Tuscany under Grand Duke Peter Leopold, which momentously led to the abolition of the death penalty, and in the earlier debate that accompanied the Corsican Revolution. Another line of enquiry has analysed the Italian translations of

Pufendorf's works at the end of the century and how they helped popularise throughout the peninsula Mirabeau's innovative physiocratic project and its new form of symmetry between rights and duties, in which, however, the former were clearly derived from the latter.[1] However, it became immediately apparent that in Italy, as in France, England and the American colonies, the Enlightenment struggle for the rights of man, and against despotism and the slave trade at the end of the century, found fertile ground in the masonic lodges.

The Italian Brotherhood used this language at every opportunity in its attack on *Ancien régime* privileges: for instance in the writings of Enlightenment thinkers such as Delfico, Grimaldi, Longano or Briganti, or in Vittorio Alfieri's tragedies.[2] It is within this scenario that in 1786 Isidoro Bianchi, a friend of Beccaria, Genovesi and Filangieri, and a freemason, brought out a pamphlet on 'the institution of the true freemasons' (*Dell'istituto dei veri liberi muratori*) that would achieve wide distribution. In this brief work, Bianchi explained the real import, from a point of view internal to the Brotherhood, of what was a remarkable phenomenon in the history of freemasonry: the obvious politicisation of lodges in Italy and the rest of Europe after the Seven Years War, and their determined propaganda for the rights of man. Bianchi's discussion is all the more cogent in that the former Camaldolese friar had visited France, Spain, Germany and Denmark. In this way, he built a close masonic network, which allowed him to meet all the most important people and find out what was going on behind the scenes in those troublesome times for European freemasonry.[3]

When he wrote his pamphlet Bianchi knew very well that the extensive circuit of lodges, with its hundreds of thousands of adepts throughout Europe, was undergoing a profound and seemingly irreversible crisis. The movement's three main branches – Baron von

1. For a general overview, cf. Trampus, *Storia del costituzionalismo italiano*. See also Alessandro Tuccillo, *Il commercio infame: antischiavismo e diritti dell'uomo nel Settecento italiano* (Naples, 2013).
2. See Ferrone, *Politics of Enlightenment*, p.134ff. On the propagation of the rights in the English-speaking world see Hunt, *Inventing human rights*, p.113ff. On Alfieri the freemason see Gerardo Tocchini's entry for 'Alfieri, Vittorio' in *Le Monde maçonnique*, ed. C. Porset and C. Révauger, vol.1, p.53-59.
3. On Isidoro Bianchi see Franco Venturi, *Settecento riformatore*, vol.5: *L'Italia dei lumi*. 1. *La rivoluzione di Corsica; Le grandi carestie degli anni sessanta; La Lombardia delle riforme, 1764-1790* (Turin, 1987), p.688ff.; Gerardo Tocchini and Simona Variara, entry for 'Bianchi, Isidoro' in *Le Monde maçonnique*, ed. C. Porset and C. Révauger, vol.1, p.360-65.

Hund's Rite of Strict Observance, the English Rite and the Grand Orient of France – were all trying at that time to inject new meaning and a new sense of purpose into what had been a unique sociability experience when it was launched in England with great success at the start of the century.[4] The substance of this experience was its esoteric knowledge, rites and secrets, its atmospheric initiation ceremonies, and its statutes: all of which went some way towards satisfying a need for both sociability and self-government, as well as the drive towards religiosity of a Christianity in crisis. Now the Brotherhood had begun to feel empty, like a magnificent bottle waiting each time to be refilled with new contents.[5] Two movements had taken advantage of this: the Jesuits, whose Society had been dissolved in 1773 by Pope Clement XIV, and who now joined freemasonry in great numbers, and the Enlightenment, constantly looking for the most effective way of promoting their policy of emancipation and defence of man.

From the mid-1770s, throughout the Western world – from Boston to St Petersburg, from Paris to Berlin, from London to Naples – every Enlightenment figure of some importance joined a masonic lodge. This gave that powerful institution new vitality and emancipatory objectives, though not without causing internal clashes with different components and different cultural and political projects.[6]

In 1782 Pius VI's visit to Vienna marked the beginning of the Catholic Church's final counteroffensive against the Enlightenment.[7] The 'politicisation' of the masonic lodges coincided with a similar development within the Republic of Letters and the world of the Enlightenment in general, since, as we saw, after the beginning of the American Revolution in 1776 the Enlightenment world had stepped up its struggle against the privileges and injustices of the *Ancien*

4. For a general introduction to this phenomenon, with a rich bibliography, see Antonio Trampus, *La massoneria nell'età moderna* (Rome and Bari, 2001).
5. I put forward this historiographical hypothesis of freemasonry as an empty bottle ready to acquire new content according to the different contexts and eras in my article on 'La massoneria settecentesca in Piemonte e nel Regno di Napoli', *Il Vieusseux* 4 (1991), special issue: *La massoneria e le forme della sociabilità nell'Europa del Settecento*, ed. Zefiro Ciuffoletti, p.103-30. The most important recent work on this subject also describes freemasonry as an 'empty box to be filled with new themes and projects' – see Giarrizzo, *Massoneria e Illuminismo*, p.339.
6. On the reasons why Enlightenment thinkers joined freemasonry see Ferrone, *I profeti dell'Illuminismo*, p.251ff.
7. Cf. Trampus, *I gesuiti e l'Illuminismo.*

régime. It was this development that made it almost inevitable that freemasonry should turn from a 'society in possession of secrets' into a 'secret society', i.e. a sect that was able to organise plots and subversive action against the structures of power.[8]

Bianchi was perfectly aware of the transformation that was taking place. He lived for a long time in the Kingdom of Naples and saw how dramatically it had changed in the space of just one decade after the 1760s. These changes affected the lodges' language, objectives, membership and even their names: gone were Les Zélés, La Sécrète, La Constance, La Fidèle, to be replaced by Dell'Eguaglianza (Of Equality), Della Pace (Of Peace), La Philantropia, L'Humanité.[9] Bianchi knew that these changes were not limited to the Kingdom of Naples: the increasingly obvious politicisation of the language of rights and the convergence between the Republic of Letters, the Enlightenment and the Brotherhood in Naples was in no way different from what was happening on the rest of the continent. It was an incredibly rapid transformation. In 1776 the Loge des Neufs Sœurs was founded in Paris under the aegis of the Enlightenment. The American Revolution was openly legitimised through reference to the rights of man, and *libertas americana* became a myth that everywhere helped mobilise members of the Brotherhood in favour of the rebel colonies. Finally, in 1785 the Bavaria Illuminati were accused of plotting to overthrow the government of their country. People were wondering what had happened to the strict masonic prohibition against all forms of political involvement.

The first edition of the *Constitutions* drawn up by James Anderson in 1723 openly warned brothers not to get involved in politics or in conspiracies against governments. It stopped short of recommending the expulsion of any transgressors, however: 'They cannot expel him from the lodge.'[10] In the European states that were under absolutist rule, the numerous translations of the *Constitutions* reiterated the

8. See Giarrizzo, *Massoneria e Illuminismo*, p.420ff.
9. Cf. Eugene Stolper, 'Massoneria settecentesca nel Regno di Napoli', *Rivista massonica* 66 (1975), p.395-432.
10. James Anderson, *The Constitutions of the free-masons, containing the history, charges, regulations, etc. of that most ancient and right worshipful fraternity* (London, printed by William Hunter, for John Senex, and John Hooke, 1723), p.50ff.: 'A mason is a peaceable subject to the civil powers, wherever he resides or works, and is never to be concern'd in plots and conspiracies against the peace and welfare of nations [...] If a brother should be a rebel against the State he is not to be countenanc'd in his rebellion, however he may be pitied as an unhappy man.'

prohibition, without the concession last quoted. Any cause of political strife, any disturbance of the social order must be studiously avoided, and the culprits must be severely punished.[11] The ban on politics was formally reiterated at the great European meeting of the Strict Observance at Wilhelmsbad in 1782.[12] From the very beginning of the movement, freemasons were invited instead to focus on morality and the practice of duties and virtues according to the tenets of seventeenth-century natural law: 'The Mason is oblig'd, by his Tenure, to obey the moral Law.'[13]

Bianchi knew all this, just as he was familiar with the teachings of the Scottish Grand Master Andrew Michael Ramsay, which featured importantly in the rich masonic literature of eighteenth-century Europe. Ramsay clearly indicated the Brotherhood's primary objectives: *philanthropie*, the practice of social virtues as preached by civic humanism and the Enlightenment version of modern natural law, 'l'humanité, la morale pure, le secret inviolable et le goût des beaux arts', as well as an appreciation of the emancipatory potential of science and technology. All this within the cosmopolitan framework of the ancient Stoic tradition. Using expressions that would be perpetuated by masonic texts for years to come, and especially in Lessing's 1778 dialogues, *Ernst und Falk: Gespräche für Freimaurer*, Ramsay attacked 'l'amour de la Patrie mal entendu'.[14] The latter is what today we would call nationalism, something that would shatter social harmony among mankind by pitting nation states against one another according to the logic of domination of absolute monarchy.[15]

The purpose of Bianchi's text was to reassure lay observers and explain to them what was happening with the masonic lodges. For the

11. See, for instance, *Constitutions, histoires, lois* [...] *traduit de l'anglois par Jean Kuenen* (The Hague, Corneille Van Zanten, 1736), p.53: 'C'est pourquoi il faut se défaire de toutes les querelles et de toutes les brouilleries avant que d'entrer dans la loge; d'autant plus si elles sont des disputes sur la Religion ou sur le mérite des Nations et des Gouvernements [...]; nous sommes résolus contre toutes les maximes de la Politique de ne point embrasser des partis qui n'ont jamais fait ni ne feront prospérer la loge.'
12. Cf. *Règle maçonnique, à l'usage des loges réunies et rectifiées, arrêtée au convent général de Wilhelmsbad* (The Hague, J. van Cleef, 1783), p.16.
13. Anderson, *Constitutions of the free-masons*, p.51.
14. Ramsay's famous address to the lodge can be read in Jean Palou, *La Francmaçonnerie* (Paris, 1964), p.317ff. See also Venturi, *Origini dell'Enciclopedia*, p.17ff.
15. On this important question see Pierre-Yves Beaurepaire, *L'Autre et le frère: l'étranger et la franc-maçonnerie en France au XVIIIe siècle* (Paris, 1998).

first time, and with great acumen, certain important questions were being asked: questions on the new relationship that the Enlightenment had established between morality and politics, and on the possible interpretations and effects of the language of the rights of man, which was widely propagated by the Brotherhood and seen from the outside as a powerful political weapon in the hands of the enemies of the *Ancien régime*. Bianchi claims that the ban on politics was still rigorously observed in masonic lodges. Of course, it all depended on what new meanings the term 'politics' was taking on in those years.[16]

One thing this term could indicate is something along the lines of Botero's seventeenth-century reason of State, with all its usual components: the separation of politics and morality, the *arcana imperii* (which included mastery in the Machiavellian art of gaining power through violence), court intrigues and international diplomacy, and the whole logic of domination put into practice as a matter of course by absolutist States and the new colonial empires. In this case, the Brotherhood was and should always remain entirely apolitical. It had nothing to do with that world. All that has been written on how its renewed practice of secrecy was supposed to be considered dangerous for the government of a country is qualified by the fact that every European lodge included kings and princes among its members. Far from being a fearsome political weapon, this secrecy was simply a legitimate way of protecting the new moral truth, which must be propagated only gradually and respecting the opinion of others, as the first Christians had done with pagan values when spreading their Gospel. At the end of the century freemasonry still saw itself as a kind of new civil religion – 'the eternal religion of Enlightenment', as Filangieri wrote, echoing what Lessing was preaching at about the same time.[17] It was a gnostic form of spirituality, without churches, dogmas or clergy. In this sense it was true that its main objectives had not changed: the aim was still to instruct mankind in a 'more perfect morality', 'to bring man back to his original goodness' and, this being the new feature, to teach him to respect his natural rights.

16. On the profound transformation of the meaning of politics in the eighteenth century see Volker Sellin, 'Politik', in *Geschichtliche Grundbegriffe: historisches Lexikon zur politisch-sozialen Sprache in Deutschland*, ed. Otto Brunner, Werner Conze and Reinhart Koselleck, 8 vols (Stuttgart, 1972-1997), vol.4, p.789-874, and especially *The Transformation of political culture: England and Germany in the late eighteenth century*, ed. Eckhart Hellmuth (Oxford and London, 1990).
17. Cf. Ferrone, *I profeti dell'Illuminismo*, p.338ff.

These objectives were hindered by how Western civilisation had developed historically into a society dominated by violence, abuse of power, the 'false and corrupt education, excessive inequalities in rank, the clash of many different interests, the thirst for power and authority'. The task of the freemasons was therefore to improve man by fostering his social instincts and teaching lay persons the rights and cosmopolitanism that were practised within the lodges: 'The members of this honourable society are all brothers. They are distinguished neither through language, habit, opinions, rank or possessions. Equality is their principal law and they view the whole world as a republic in which each nation constitutes a family, of which each individual is a child.'[18]

As a member of the Enlightenment, Bianchi liked to see end-of-century freemasonry as a 'respectable society of philosophers' engaged in the defence and emancipation of man. In fact, the popularity achieved by the language of rights had called into question once and for all the seventeenth-century distinction between morality and politics that was a corollary of reason of state and Machiavellian 'political realism'. Nevertheless, Bianchi considered these rights as just another, valuable element of the 'more perfect morality' derived from natural law. He did not understand, or pretended not to understand, the remonstrances of those who were pointing to the obviously political character taken on by the language of rights with the 1776 American Revolution and the campaigns for judiciary reform and the abolition of the slave trade by Beccaria, Voltaire and Diderot: 'Some may object that the equality and liberty that the freemasons profess are not compatible with maintaining order within the State.' But these were not the Brotherhood's principal aims. The freemasons were concerned with 'the moral sense' and educational aspects of the rights and of concepts such as liberty and equality, which had suddenly flared up with the appearance on the scene of the modern republican spirit. The Brotherhood simply wanted to reiterate the ethical principle of the equality of rights for all human beings – they certainly did not expect to impose 'perfect equality' through political means:

> Of course men are not equal in terms of strength, talent or looks. Besides, we all have this baneful natural inclination to attempt to dominate over others. This being the case, what reasonable being

18. Translated from [Isidoro Bianchi], *Dell'Istituto de' veri liberi muratori*, ed. Giordano Gamberini (Ravenna, 1980), p.28.

> could believe it possible to make all men perfectly equal? Equality among freemasons simply consists in considering one another as brothers, helping one another, sharing all offices with kindness and charity, and respecting the rights of all men with no distinction whatsoever, since these rights were granted to all by beneficent nature in the same measure [...] Who will not accept that good morality is based on this most desirable kind of equality?[19]

Similar problems were posed by the natural right to liberty, which in this case too could be interpreted in both a moral and a political sense:

> Every just and moderate government is founded on liberty, since its real purpose is none other than to guarantee the free and quiet exercise of every citizen's faculties. In this sense liberty is a right that all men received from nature at birth, and everyone must be allowed to make free use of their rights [...]. The freemasons' system is entirely opposed to unruliness and licence: it only allows that freedom which is founded on the most solid principles of healthy morality. (p.49)

In fact, with his stubborn defence of what he claims is the 'apolitical' character of freemasonry and its inability to hatch plots against the State, Bianchi highlighted the fundamental role that the language of the rights of man had played in redefining the relationship between politics and morality, in a way that would shape the moderns' idea of politics. Despite being obvious, the strategic importance of the language of rights in this respect is often underestimated by scholars of freemasonry and the Enlightenment when they investigate the undeniable politicisation of both the lodges and the Republic of Letters in the last quarter of the eighteenth century. This includes Reinhart Koselleck, author of the justly famous, even if now a little dated, *Kritik und Krise: ein Beitrag zur Pathogenese der bürgerlichen Welt* (1959). Koselleck did realise that '[a] morality striving to become political would be the great theme of the eighteenth century.'[20] However, he went on to ignore the very existence of the rights of man, which were at the heart of that 'great theme' as it was being debated in those years throughout Europe and especially in Germany. This is significant in that the origin of this omission must lie in the bias towards political realism that can be seen in the teachings of Koselleck's mentor, Carl Schmitt.

19. *Istituto*, p.48.
20. Koselleck, *Critique and crisis*, p.39.

This did not prevent Koselleck from uncompromisingly condemning the political positions of the Enlightenment.

This movement was accused of giving rise to an ideological kind of philosophy of history seen entirely from the point of view of the civilisation of peoples. Together with its propagation of abstract social utopias, constant but generic reference to morality and virtues, and, last but not least, irresponsible critique of reality, these positions are seen as the causes of the 'pathogenesis' of modern civil society in the Western world, and of a subsequent crisis that is still affecting our society today: the alienation of the spirit in a Hegelian sense, which is now hopelessly divided between 'what is' and 'what ought to be'.[21] Starting in fact from the speeches given by several Enlightenment thinkers at their masonic lodges, Koselleck sought to explain the 'hypocrisy' of the Enlightenment, i.e. its dangerous new concept of politics. He concluded that 'The political secret of the Enlightenment lay in the fact that its concepts, analogous to the indirect assumption of power, were not seen as being political. The political anonymity of reason, morality, nature, and so on, defined their political character and effectiveness. Their political essence lay in being non-political.'[22]

In fact things were quite different from what Bianchi was suggesting. To realise this, one only needed to pay greater attention to the overarching debate that was taking place all over Europe on subjects such as constitutionalism, penal reform and the creation of new governmental institutions that would safeguard the rights of man. The publication of the American Declaration of Independence in every European gazette after 1776 would have sent another extremely clear signal in this respect. All this would have persuaded any unbiased observer of the seriousness and far-sightedness of the Enlightenment political plan: to defend and enfranchise the individual, and to do so by appealing to public opinion in England, France and Italy, and to secret societies in Germany, in order to morally educate mankind towards the respect and practice of rights.

This programme was intentionally played out on two levels: the political and the moral one. In this way, the new language provided the explicit solution to the political enigma of the Enlightenment in its struggle against the *Ancien régime* logic of domination. It was thanks to this double nature that this programme appeared so successful

21. On the political and philosophical origins of this concept, see Ferrone, *The Enlightenment*, p.12ff.
22. Koselleck, *Critique and crisis*, p.147.

in promoting the rights of man across the Republic of Letters and masonic lodges all over Europe. And there was certainly no intention of hiding what was an unstoppable winning feature: if we except the perfunctory excuses put forward by a few freemasons such as Isidoro Bianchi, the Enlightenment pursued openly and with great zeal the *political* outcomes of its new moral programme.[23]

This phenomenon was especially obvious in the territories of the Holy Roman Empire, where the language of natural rights, in the form of *iura connata*, had started to circulate quite early on in the academic environment through the works of Thomasius and Wolff. This was the eventual result of Grotius and Pufendorf's effort to build a renewed science of morality on a scientific and rational basis so that it would be capable of swaying the policy of the monarch and ensuring public happiness.[24] However, if we compare these lists of rights, which were based on the primacy of the moral duties of individuals in society, with the reading of John Locke and the earliest English republican thinkers, we see that they had been politically neutralised from the beginning. These rights had been moved rather in the direction of Hobbes' social contract and Pufendorf's defence of the absolutist state, i.e. of a political sphere that left no scope for the subjects' participation in political life, or for any reference to the right of resistance.

In the early eighteenth century, the authority of the State in German natural law was founded on a form of contractualism consisting in a double pact of association and domination.[25] The latter aspect had been subjected to fierce criticism by Rousseau and the Enlightenment since effectively it placed every power in the hands of the sovereign. The individual lost his original natural liberty to the State, to the extent that, *in statu civili*, not only did he not enjoy any form of political liberty, but whatever freedom he possessed came to him not as an inalienable right but as the sovereign's gracious gift. The *iura connata* previously located in the state of nature became simply

23. For a discussion of this issue with specific reference to the Italian scenario, see Vincenzo Ferrone, 'Il nuovo repubblicanesimo dei diritti dell'uomo nelle logge italiane alla fine del secolo', *Rivista storica italiana* 113 (2001), p.843-58.

24. Cf. Jörn Garber, 'Vom "ius connatum" zum "Menschenrecht": deutsche Menschenrechtstheorie in der Spätaufklärung', in *Rechtsphilosophie der Aufklärung: Symposium Wolfenbüttel 1981*, ed. Reinhard Brandt (Berlin and New York, 1982), p.107-47. See also the works mentioned in Oestreich, *Geschichte der Menschenrechte*, p.50-53.

25. Cf. Gierke, *Development of political theory*, part II, chapter 2, 'The doctrine of the state-contract'.

one of the sovereign's moral duties, and only featured among citizens' private rights as a point of reference. Admittedly, this represented a significant change and a step forward in the way in which absolute sovereignty was legitimised, compared with the previous doctrine of the divine right of kings. However, natural law, as illustrated by Thomasius or Wolff, did not go much further in claiming civil and political liberty for the subject. All it did was to postulate the exercise of moral self-restraint by the sovereign, mindful of the natural rights of his subjects. This is a far cry from the new republican spirit, the political use of the rights of man in the struggle against despotism by Enlightenment circles in Milan or Paris, or the grounds on which the American colonies claimed their Bill of Rights.[26]

Throughout the eighteenth century the inalienability of rights failed to be universally acknowledged, and the sovereignty of the State still dominated over natural rights, which were relegated to the moral sphere. This seems to have characterised German public law in particular, partly because Wolff's theories continued to prevail in the universities of the Holy Roman empire.[27] A case in point is Frederick II's enlightened absolutism and *Polizeiwissenschaft*. In Prussia, economic, civil and military reform was successfully pursued alongside the legitimation of power by a mighty class of public servants and bureaucrats who harboured an unassailable conviction that was typical of German natural law: that the happiness of the people was best served when the natural rights of the individual were administered by the State itself.[28]

The end result was that, while it was understood that the political community and sovereignty itself were based on the acknowledgement of individual rights, an individual could never claim these rights in opposition to the State. Paradoxically, in order to enjoy their

26. As far as the comparison with the American colonies is concerned, this is the indeed quite plausible conclusion reached in what is still the best account of the role of Germany in the history of natural law, i.e. Diethelm Klippel, *Politische Freiheit und Freiheitsrechte im deutschen Naturrecht des 18. Jahrhunderts* (Paderborn, 1976), p.201ff. Among the few attempts to inject Locke's political ideas into German natural law we should mention a 1712 work by Thomasius' pupil Ephraim Gerhard, *Delineatio iuris naturalis.*
27. See Michael Stolleis, *Histoire du droit public en Allemagne: droit public impérial et science de la police 1600-1800* (Paris, 1998; original: *Geschichte des öffentlichen Rechts in Deutschland*, vol.1: *Reichspublizistik und Policeywissenschaft 1600-1800*, Munich, 1988), p.432ff.
28. Cf. Eckhart Hellmuth, *Naturrechtsphilosophie und bürokratischer Werthorizont: Studien zur preußischen Geistes- und Sozialgeschichte des 18. Jahrhunderts* (Göttingen, 1985); Reiner Schulze, *Policey und Gesetzgebungslehre im 18. Jahrhundert* (Berlin, 1982).

rights, subjects were expected to renounce their political practice, relying entirely on the prince's paternalism and ethical obligations.[29] Moreover, by the eighteenth century in German universities, where the cameralist tradition and the natural law of Pufendorf's followers existed side by side, the rise of the 'sciences of the State' had long implanted a fundamental tenet of public law whereby the State and civil society were seen as an organic whole (*societas civilis sive status*).[30]

The idea that the State itself gave rise to civil society, whose economic, political and social development it regulated, had a long pedigree, going back as far as Hobbes' *Leviathan*. In the history of the Holy Roman empire, this was accompanied by the equally important view whereby *Politik*, which was responsible for exercising power and maintaining security within and outside national borders, was a theoretically separate concept from *Policey*, i.e. the administration of the state with a view to ensuring its citizens' wellbeing – though in matter of fact the latter was subsumed within the former.[31] The model propounded by Hobbes in his *Leviathan* and reprised by Pufendorf in his works answered a need for peace and security that pushed aside concerns for individual civil freedoms or the right to political participation. All this as a consequence of the crisis of Christianity that started with the Protestant Reformation and the subsequent massacres and religious strife, which had an especially devastating effect on Germany during the Thirty Years War. Many German states resorted to a powerful new authority principle by building a strong centralised state. Inevitably, this led to the decline of the ancient dualistic system that ruled the late medieval empire, in which the *maiestas realis* of the upper classes effectively delimited the *maiestas personalis* of the elected emperor, thus providing a constitutional guarantee for 'German freedom' and the 'German liberties'.[32] This process

29. See Merio Scattola, *La nascita delle scienze dello Stato: August Ludwig Schlözer (1735-1809) e le discipline politiche del Settecento tedesco* (Milan, 1994), p.29ff.
30. See Edoardo Tortarolo, *La ragione sulla Sprea: coscienza storica e cultura politica nell'Illuminismo berlinese* (Bologna, 1989), p.122.
31. On the specific characteristics of German political thought see Pierangelo Schiera, *Il cameralismo e l'assolutismo tedesco* (Milan, 1968); Emilio Bussi, *Diritto e politica in Germania nel XVIII secolo* (Milan, 1971).
32. In this constitutional form, 'German freedom', which was safeguarded by the power of the upper classes, was still being defended in the course of the eighteenth century as an anti-despotic mechanism, and was famously depicted in Montesquieu's *Esprit des lois*. It is therefore hard to subscribe to the thesis put forward in Leonard Krieger, *The German idea of freedom: history of a political*

had certainly been aided by the confessionalisation of Churches and the extension of social discipline to every field by public institutions as a consequence of the spreading of Neo-Stoicism.[33] All this had undoubtedly strengthened the prestige and authority of the modern State, which was now everywhere set to operate along the lines of an enlightened absolutism, seamlessly incorporating the language of natural rights and directing the moral role of the sovereigns towards the pursuit of public happiness.

Thus in Germany a historical process of statalisation was increasingly transforming the ancient and glorious landowning classes from defenders of liberty into reactionary *Ancien régime* elites. But alongside this, there were new and opposite developments taking place: the growth of an increasingly hard-to-control economic system and civil society, and the individual pursuit of happiness, liberty and emancipation from all forms of authoritarian power. This was what Enlightenment thinkers across Europe were passionately fighting for.[34] Civil society in particular was their battle cry, a political myth that was entering into a deadlock with the idea of the absolute power of the State. In an attempt to evaluate the effects of this increasingly irreconcilable clash, some historians have started to rethink the traditional view of the chronological development of modern Germany. What

tradition (Boston, MA, 1957), which anachronistically assigns an anti-political and authoritarian character to 'German freedom' and traces its origins back to the past. On the constitutional and social function of the Germanic classes in the late Middle Ages, and how these did not 'represent' but 'were' the territory, see the classic works by Otto Brunner, *Land und Herrschaft: Grundfragen der territorialen Verfassungsgeschichte Südostdeutschlands im Mittelalter* (Brünn, 1942), and *The Historical essays of Otto Hintze*, ed. and with an introduction by Felix Gilbert, with the assistance of Robert M. Berdahl (New York, 1975).

33. See Wolfgang Reinhard, 'Disciplinamento sociale, confessionalizzazione, modernizzazione: un discorso storiografico', in *Disciplina dell'anima, disciplina del corpo e disciplina della società tra medioevo ed età moderna*, ed. Paolo Prodi (Bologna, 1994), p.101-23.

34. On the incremental growth of civil society in Germany in the eighteenth century see Horst Möller, *Fürstenstaat oder Bürgernation: Deutschland 1763-1815* (Berlin, 1989). In addition to the way in which the Enlightenment deployed the concept of civil society for propaganda purposes, Jürgen Habermas, relaunching a thesis first put forward by Marx and Engels in *The Holy Family*, suggested that, with its systematic critique of the organic and communal spirit of the *Ancien régime*, the Enlightenment fostered the rise of a modern civil society made up of individuals who were endowed with rights, and that this in turn led to the autonomy of the state and the separation of the public sphere from the private: cf. Ferrone, *The Enlightenment*, p.24ff.

they have found is that a decisive break seems to have occurred in the last three decades of the eighteenth century, which corresponded closely with the rapid politicisation of cultural and institutional life brought about by the cultural revolution of the Late Enlightenment.[35]

It was in the latter part of the century that Germany took the lead in a process that was occurring everywhere in Europe, becoming an extremely noteworthy political laboratory. It is important, however, to define clearly the discontinuous and specific character of its politicisation. For decades historians insisted on a German *Sonderweg*, or specificity in this respect, whereby in this country the Enlightenment was peculiarly apolitical and authoritarian, in a sort of anachronistic prelude to the dark conservatism of the following centuries.[36] In recent times, however, its lodges, reading societies, academies, cultural practices, newspapers, books and campaigns have been studied as part of a common European experience, and the *Aufklärung* has been seen to be interacting creatively with this specific context. It thus revealed a degree of politicisation comparable to what had been taking place in the rest of Europe.[37] This was a kind of politicisation that was no longer limited to the traditional Neo-Stoical use of a language of duties, with its civic application to the *respublica*. This latter tradition was entirely compatible with the enlightened absolutism that for a long time had been the ruling force in that imposing and sclerotic juridical

35. See Horst Möller's important remarks in *Fürstenstaat oder Bürgernation*, p.63ff., on how the end of the Seven Years War in 1763 had greater implications for the history of Germany than the events of 1789. Similar conclusions are reached by Fritz Valjavec, *Die Entstehung der politischen Strömungen in Deutschland 1770 bis 1815* (Munich, 1951), and Koselleck, *Futures past*, p.77. On the Late Enlightenment as an autonomous historical period that affected the whole of Europe in the last quarter of the century, see Ferrone, *The Enlightenment*, p.140ff.
36. Cf. Eckhart Hellmuth, 'Towards a comparative study of political culture: the cases of late eighteenth-century England and Germany', in *Transformation of political culture*, ed. E. Hellmuth, p.1-38 (5ff.). I refer here in particular to Klaus Epstein, *The Genesis of German conservatism* (Princeton, NJ, 1966), and T. C. W. Blanning, *Reform and revolution in Mainz, 1743-1803* (Cambridge, 1974). The idea of the German *Aufklärung* as apolitical and isolated from the rest of Europe is put forward also in Gay, *The Science of freedom*, p.4ff.
37. See the essays in *Aufklärung als Politisierung, Politisierung der Aufklärung*, ed. Hans Erich Bödeker and Ulrich Herrmann (Hamburg, 1987); Horst Möller, *Vernunft und Kritik: deutsche Aufklärung im 17. und 18. Jahrhundert* (Frankfurt am Main, 1986); Richard van Dülmen, *The Society of the Enlightenment: the rise of the middle class and Enlightenment culture in Germany*, translated by Anthony Williams (Cambridge, 1992).

monster that was the Holy Roman empire, with its over 300 States of all sizes. What was emerging now was a form of political action arising from the fact that civil servants and intellectuals were becoming increasingly aware of the despotic tendency that characterised even the enlightened absolutism of sovereigns like Catherine II, Joseph II or Frederick II. It also arose from the need to allow civil society to take charge of itself, and to go beyond the *Ancien régime* logic of privilege and domination.

Within this scenario we can situate Diderot's famous *Pages contre un tyran* – the invective against Frederick II written in the early 1770s – or Lessing's bitter reflections on the climate of censorship and repression in Berlin.[38] These examples are indicative of a clear change of direction towards a renewed republican and cosmopolitan spirit among increasingly wider and important Enlightenment groups across Europe. In the case of German public opinion this feeling was further increased by the news from the American colonies, where the revolution had led to the foundation of a new republican State in the name of the rights of man and the right of resistance.[39] It is no surprise, therefore, that the preservation and emancipation of the individual and the appeal to his rights rapidly became commonplace in public debate. In fact, they are the underlying nexus that can help us find our bearings in the complex political laboratory of late-eighteenth-century Germany.

Among the first to react against the now seemingly prevailing tendency towards despotism were Johann Jacob Moser, Justus Möser and Johann Salomon Brunnquell, who called for the restitution of the ancient German liberties safeguarded by the role played by the landowning classes. The social order they hoped for, however, looked backward to the past rather than forward to a modern civil society of free, equal and politically active citizens.[40] The position of the first German physiocrats was entirely different. Their call for free trade was

38. Cf. Möller, *Fürstenstaat oder Bürgernation*, p.368.
39. See the dated but still useful study by Horst Dippel, *Germany and the American Revolution 1770-1800: a sociohistorical investigation of late eighteenth-century political thinking* (Wiesbaden, 1978).
40. On this issue see Diethelm Klippel, 'The true concept of liberty: political theory in Germany in the second half of the eighteenth century', in *Transformation of political culture*, ed. E. Hellmuth, p.447-66 (454ff.). On the question of liberty in Germany see also Jürgen Schlumbohm, *Freiheit: die Anfänge der bürgerlichen Emanzipationsbewegung in Deutschland im Spiegel ihres Leitwortes, ca. 1760-ca. 1800* (Düsseldorf, 1975).

immediately contested by the cameralists in favour of the traditional practice of protectionism. However, this represented a true turning point in the political theory of the time, as did their defence of the right to property and their idea of a State built according to the laws of political economy and natural order, in which the rights of man could also finally find a place. For the first time, through the physiocrats' works the issue of rights left the rarefied academic world, with its abstract discussions on the sciences of morality, to be discussed, in concrete and real terms, in gazettes, newspapers and German public discourse. Terms like *Rechte der Menschheit* or *Menschenrechte* appeared more and more often and with a very different meaning from the recent past in periodicals such as the *Ephemeriden der Menschheit* – the journal of German physiocrats – or the *Deutsches Museum*, originating harsh debates with the supporters of the old cameralism and of the class-based, corporative system.[41] In 1784 the most important figure among the physiocrats, Johann August Schlettwein, wrote a particularly significant work in this respect, one that dealt with 'the rights of mankind, or the only true foundation of every law, rule and constitution'. In his tract the author urged the State to bear constantly in mind the rights of man, and to acknowledge the importance of civil society, in which lay 'the most complete safeguard of all human rights and their enjoyment'.[42]

There were several aspects of the physiocrats' positions that would have been well received in Germany: the constant references to the natural order, their geometric-deductive rationalism, as found in Wolff and the German tradition in general, deriving rights from duties that in turn drew their legitimacy from natural law and the sociability principle, not to mention their declared support for the 'legal despotism' of the sovereign, which excluded the subjects' political participation in the *res publica*.[43] Equally numerous, however, were the factors that influenced opinion in the opposite direction, including the inevitable nexus between economics, politics and society,

41. See the detailed discussion in Hans Erich Bödeker, '"Menschenrechte" im deutschen publizistischen Diskurs vor 1789', in *Grund- und Freiheitsrechte von der ständischen zur spätbürgerlichen Gesellschaft*, ed. Günter Birtsch (Göttingen, 1987), p.392-433.
42. See Johann August Schlettwein, *Die Rechte der Menschheit oder der einzige wahre Grund aller Gesetze, Ordnungen und Verfassungen* (Giessen, Justus Friederich Krieger, 1784), p.107ff. See the quotation and comments in Möller, *Fürstenstaat oder Bürgernation*, p.291ff.
43. On the importance of the physiocrat movement in Germany see Reinert, *Translating empire*, p.320ff.

the debate on the right to property and its extension to the human body and its functions, and the need for some measure of autonomy of civil society from the State to enable the pursuit of public happiness. All this began to usher in a new liberal idea of the rights of man as an alternative to the old natural law of Wolff and Thomasius and its profoundly absolutist bias.[44]

In the last twenty years before 1789, the major figures of the German Enlightenment took advantage of the new spaces that were opening up towards the self-determination of individuals and the growing politicisation of the Republic of Letters. They bravely engaged in a battle, which was fought first and foremost on the cultural level, against the *Ancien régime* and its most hateful aspects: class and corporational privileges, the servitude of the glebe, religious intolerance, despotism, and a juridical system that was still far too cruel and unjust. In doing so they took as their starting point the new values that were developed across Europe through the critical and public application of reason in every field, following first of all the original kind of humanism that had been outlined from the epistemological point of view in the *Encyclopédie*, and then with the rapid rise also within Germany of the new empirical sciences of man as an autonomous subject. As Moses Mendelssohn wrote in 1784, the task of these sciences was to focus on the 'definition of man as the measure and objective of all our efforts and care'.[45] According to this definition, man's humanity ultimately depended on the acknowledgement of 'human rights', those very rights that are defended by Socrates – the great spiritual father of the European Enlightenment – against the Sophists in Mendelssohn's hugely popular adaptation of Plato, *Phädon, oder Über die Unsterblichkeit der Seele*, published in 1767.[46]

44. As explained in Bödeker, '"Menschenrechte"' (p.399ff.), around 1770 an important debate took place in the German press on the rights of man in relation to concrete proposals of reform of the economy, administration and tax system. A case in point is Isaac Iselin, one of the editors of the *Ephemeriden der Menschheit*, who in 1760 published an 'inquiry into legislation by the editor of philosophical dreams' (*Versuch über die Gesetzgebung von der Verfasser der philosophischen Träume*, n.p., n.n.). In this work Iselin maintained that 'neither the legislator nor the sovereign has any right to violate a man's natural liberty and safety.' In 1768 Iselin publicly praised England for being the first country in the history of the West to abolish personal servitude and guarantee the rights to freedom and property.
45. Quoted in *L'Illuminismo tedesco*, ed. Raffaele Ciafardone (Turin, 1983), p.296-97.
46. For Mendelssohn's references to human rights see Tortarolo, *La ragione sulla Sprea*, p.149ff.

Mendelssohn's public speeches reveal his awareness of the importance of bringing German public opinion round to the new culture of human rights, and of placing before it issues such as the limitations of power and the legitimacy of the State's jurisdiction over individuals. The universal appeal and communicative power of the language of rights, with its capacity to immediately mobilise large groups of people, could in fact be an especially valuable tool in the struggle for the enfranchisement of the Jewish minority. In the preface to his 1782 *Rettung der Juden* Mendelssohn called for the separation between politics and religion that Locke and Voltaire had wanted for the Christian world to be extended to the Jewish community. This was an indispensable precondition for the individual practice of the natural right to religious freedom, and, more generally, for the Jewish claim to equal enjoyment of civil rights. The right to the pursuit of freedom was still the number one Enlightenment objective. However, this objective implied not only specific actions on the part of the government but also, especially, a sustained cultural effort to transform the minds and habits of the population and make them realise that 'the end purpose is the progress not of society but of men.'[47] Christian Wilhelm Dohm similarly upheld the 'natural and sacred rights of men' against the corporative privileges of the *Ancien régime*.[48] Dohm was the founder in 1776 of the *Deutsches Museum* journal. He was an active supporter of the American settlers and translated the pamphlet entitled *Common sense* by Thomas Paine, the future author of *Rights of man*. In 1781, in reply to Lessing's *Nathan der Weise*, Christoph Nicolai, the leading Enlightenment thinker in Berlin, used the language of rights to address the delicate question of religious tolerance, stating without further ado that 'the true reason for tolerance is the innate right of every man to follow his own convictions in matters of faith.'[49]

Another aspect of the struggle against the *Ancien régime* in which German Enlightenment thinkers made use of the language of rights was the denunciation of servitude of the glebe and the particularly harsh living conditions endured by farmers in their country.[50] However, what we have in all these cases is a politically indirect

47. See Tortarolo, *La ragione sulla Sprea*, p.156.
48. Cf. Christian Wilhelm Dohm, *Nachricht von der Neuverfassung der Zünfte in Frankreich* (Kassel, n.n., 1778), p.6.
49. Cf. Möller, *Fürstenstaat oder Bürgernation*, p.322.
50. Cf. Möller, *Fürstenstaat oder Bürgernation*, p.135ff. See especially the discussion of these issues in the *Berlinische Monatsschrift*, vol.1 (1783), p.336-47.

use of this language, which is deployed with great caution, always with an eye to the character and responsibilities of the absolutist government that ruled the country. These thinkers aimed first of all at transforming people's consciousness from the cultural point of view and at influencing public opinion and modifying social behaviour. The supremacy of the State and the sovereign remained unquestioned, and the ultimate objective was to involve them in the process of reform that was necessary in order to put the rights of man concretely into practice. Accordingly, references to the rights often went hand in hand with generic talk of a new philosophy of history, which linked the discovery and practice of the rights themselves with the progress of science and civilisation, meaning that their definitive application was seen as a long-term project. A case in point, which is in fact rather similar to what Condorcet would write in his *Esquisse d'un tableau historique des progrès de l'esprit humain* – is *Aufklärer* Johann Justi's assertion that 'It is the sciences that enlighten the intellect of a people and spread the notions of sociability, the reciprocal behaviour of reasonable creatures and the rights of mankind. It is the sciences, therefore, before anything else, that uproot barbarism and remove peoples from what is uncouth, savage and uncivil.'[51]

The translation and popularity in Germany of Beccaria's *On crimes and punishments* were part of this scenario, in which the propaganda in favour of rights aimed first of all at creating the cultural preconditions for the defence of man and his emancipation. This line is explicitly adopted by the 'German Beccaria' Karl Ferdinand Hommel, an important jurist and follower of Thomasius, who published a translation of *Des Herren Marquis von Beccaria unsterbliches Werk von Verbrechen und Strafen* ('the immortal work by the marquis of Beccaria on crimes and punishments') in Breslau in 1778. In the long and detailed introduction, which traces the history of previous editions, Hommel explains that he himself had argued some of the most important points made by Beccaria in a disputation that had taken place at court in 1765 in the presence of Frederick Augustus, elector of Saxony. This had been favourably received at court, though not by the other jurists present on that occasion. Hommel had explained that 'man, citizen and Christian are three different concepts'. He had pointed out that crime was something that damaged society, and had nothing to do with sin or divine justice: accordingly, the Ancient Roman juridical customs had carefully avoided 'mixing religion

51. See Tortarolo, *La ragione sulla Sprea*, p.137.

and their penal laws together'.[52] The arguments put forward by 'the philosopher' Beccaria in favour of a milder penal law and the natural right to defence, and against judicial torture and the death penalty, are described by Hommel as enhanced by 'the light of eloquence' and expressed in 'words that were worthy of angels' (p.viii). Most importantly, they were a timely attempt 'to defend in a most humane way the nobility of mankind, which until then had been sacrificed to cruel prejudices' (p.xiv-xv).

For Germany too the time had come for a radical reform of penal law in the wake of the Enlightenment culture of the preservation of man that had been inaugurated by Voltaire in France and Beccaria in Italy. This was all the more urgent since the judicial system was such an important measure of a nation's civility, and in Germany this was beset by arbitrary decisions and cruel and unjust sentences. But unsurprisingly the judiciary also seemed particularly hostile to progress, and reluctant to embrace the defence of human rights and review their shameful laws. As Hommel dispiritedly pointed out:

> Apart from what has been done by Christian Thomasius, Montesquieu and our marquis [Beccaria] everything else is a desert. And yet this philosophical century seeks to attain the greatest heights in all other fields. Novels, sermons, the natural sciences, painting and medicine: all boast excellent advances. You alone, Astraea, are lagging behind! In vain would a German Flavius seek to improve the style in which trials are held. It all remains in the hands of the usual barbarians.[53]

As an *Aufklärer*, Hommel was particularly incensed by capital punishment. He understood very clearly what was at stake in Beccaria's astounding proposal to abolish the death penalty. Words such as 'human blood', 'debt of blood' or 'revenge' unleashed incontrollable, ancestral reactions. They called into question the very essence of society, humanity, the right to punish. And yet, it was this that constituted the great challenge that the cultural revolution of the

52. Karl Ferdinand Hommel, 'Hommelische Vorrede' to *Des Herren Marquis von Beccaria unsterbliches Werk von Verbrechen und Strafen* (Breslau, Johann Friedrich Korn, the Elder, 1778), p.iii-li (v-vi). Hommel's introduction can also be read in an Italian translation by Claudio Magris in Franco Venturi's edition of *Dei delitti e delle pene*, p.596-624.
53. 'Hommelische Vorrede', p.xvi-xvii. On the reception of Beccaria's work in Germany see Madeleine van Bellen-Finster, 'Die Rezeption Cesare Beccarias im deutschsprachigen Raum um 1800', *Annali dell'istituto storico italo-germanico in Trento* 11 (1985), p.193-219.

European Enlightenment had taken on: the task of transforming the minds of men and their national customs. Hommel knew 'that the word "blood" has something dreadful about it, which is why it is beloved by poets and rhetoricians, in that it immediately fires our imagination' (p.xxiv). But it was reason that must decide on this issue, leaving aside all traditional preconceived ideas and applying instead moderation and humanity. It was necessary to avoid at all costs a situation where a law that was intended to prevent murders should 'itself become the occasion of new murders' (p.xxvi).

The history of the fortune of Beccaria's ideas in the Holy Roman empire still remains to be written. However, there can be no doubt that it played an important role in creating an environment that was favourable to the rights of man in both government and public opinion. The Europe-wide popularity of the debate on the right to punish is yet another indication that the language of rights developed by the Enlightenment was far more widespread and well known in Germany than historians have believed so far. The problem now is to understand why it all but disappeared in the following century, or rather why it was reviewed and neutralised from a political point of view, as we shall see when we discuss the 1794 *Allgemeines Landrecht für die preussischen Staaten*, which was virtually the tombstone for the Enlightenment concept of the rights of man in this part of Europe.

17. The Bavaria Illuminati, the rights of man and the end of the Late Enlightenment

An important role in the gradual sidelining and transformation of the rights was played no doubt by the bout of arrests and repression unleashed by the governments of the various states, and by the long-term negative consequences of the Bavaria Illuminati scandal, which involved large swathes of the German Republic of Letters. The Illuminati were the first to develop a dangerously subversive project from the language of the rights of man, turning the latter into a political myth to be deployed against the traditional despotic alliance between throne and altar. At the same time, they made use of a new secret society model that became a fearsome instrument for political action.

The rich and constantly growing historical bibliography on this subject tends to overlook the role played by the rights of man in the Illuminati plot.[1] Much more focus has been placed on the secret society itself, its infighting and its generic threat of violent attack – though purely on the verbal level – against all forms of power. Accordingly, the Illuminati have been depicted as atheists, communists, anarchists, heretics and religious reformers. Joseph de Maistre, an important freemason, actively fought their infiltration into lodges throughout Europe, describing them as 'the most criminal of societies', one which was bent on the 'terrible project of extinguishing Christianity and sovereignty in Europe'.[2] In fact, above and beyond their all-encompassing political and cultural intent of subverting all

1. The most important study on this subject is still René Le Forestier, *Les Illuminés de Bavière et la franc-maçonnerie allemande* (Dijon, 1914). For a new interpretation, which I do not quite agree with, see Israel, *Democratic Enlightenment*, p.822ff. For a discussion of the bibliography on this subject see Trampus, *La massoneria*, p.138ff.
2. Quoted in Giarrizzo, *Massoneria e Illuminismo*, p.233.

existing forms of power and order, the Illuminati's most original and enduring legacy is the construction of a complex subversive machinery, which was skilfully organised down to the minutest detail.

The secret society of the Bavaria Illuminati was founded in Munich in May 1776 by Adam Weishaupt, a pupil of Christian Wolff and professor of canon law at Ingolstadt. Its aim was to fight the Society of Jesus, their hated enemy, which was suppressed in 1773 after being accused of conspiring against the Catholic monarchies, and to do so by using their same weapons.[3] The society quickly developed according to a masonic-like pyramidal structure in seven degrees, with ceremonies and initiation rites. The first four degrees (Novice, Minerval, Illuminati minor, Illuminati major) were linked to the recruitment and instruction of adepts. The remaining degrees, which were progressively more secret and inaccessible, served to motivate and organise political action by a very small number of Illuminati. Only the topmost part of the organisation, i.e. the Areopagites and the 'General of Illuminism', were aware of the final objectives and the 'Grand Mysteries' of the 'Mage' and the 'Man King'.[4] This pyramidal structure was held together by strict hierarchical obedience, and the identity of the members and programmes of the higher degrees were hidden from the lower orders. This safeguarded the whole structure and allowed individual members to safely infiltrate masonic lodges, governments, universities, ecclesiastical institutions: in short, every seat of power. In anthropological and sociological terms, this secrecy acted as a vehicle for bringing cohesion to the group and separating the society's adepts from the lay world. Rather than the element of secrecy in itself, it was the dangerous efficiency of this secret society as an institution that alarmed governments. The whole apparatus of

3. On the struggle between Jesuits and Illuminati for control over the masonic network and the momentous suppression of the Society of Jesus see Trampus, *I gesuiti e l'Illuminismo*, p.179ff.

4. There are many works that describe the Illuminati's structure. See, for instance, Pierre-André Bois, *Adolph Freiherr Knigge (1752-1796): de la 'nouvelle religion' aux droits de l'homme* (Wiesbaden, 1990), p.240ff., and especially the second volume of Augustin Barruel's *Mémoires pour servir à l'histoire du jacobinisme*, first published in London in 1797. This matter is found in volume 3 of the four-volume English edition, *Memoirs, illustrating the history of Jacobinism: a translation from the French of the abbé Barruel*, translated by Robert Clifford (London, printed for the author, by T. Burton and Co., and sold by E. Booker, 1797-1798). On the extraordinary fortune of Barruel's work throughout Europe see Dino Carpanetto, 'Augustin Barruel', in *L'albero della Rivoluzione: le interpretazioni della Rivoluzione francese*, ed. Luciano Guerci and Bruno Bongiovanni (Turin, 1989), p.49-56.

rites, initiation ceremonies, precise tasks that were thought out down to the last detail but were kept secret from members lower down the structure – all this could not but exercise a powerful fascination on the mind of contemporaries. But secrecy and organisational ability by themselves are not enough to explain the immediate success of this society, which recruited some 600-700 adepts in a very short time, among whom featured members of the aristocracy, princes and prominent figures from the Republic of Letters. Besides building a credible political project, it was necessary to formulate this project in comprehensible and effective terms, that would strike the collective imaginary and communicate a winning message to the public.

At a time when public opinion was becoming radically politicised, it was no longer enough to invoke the general principles of all European masonic lodges, such as social virtues, philanthropy and the renewal of morality. Hence the Illuminati's deliberate use of the powerful language of the rights of man, through which, as we have seen, morality finally merged into politics and into a new concept of the law, giving rise to the political language of the Enlightenment and of the moderns. The former Jesuit novice Augustin Barruel was quick to realise this, and to denounce the centrality of rights in the subversive project of the Illuminati. Barruel had direct knowledge of this order, having been a tutor in Bavaria and in contact, as a freemason, with some of its important members. For Barruel, the true 'essence' of the Illuminati's subversive programme lay in their intent to restore natural rights, as evidenced by the texts that in 1787 were confiscated in Munich and made publicly known by order of Prince-Elector Charles Theodore. In his *Memoirs* Barruel reports the 'essence' of the Illuminati's creed as being along these lines:

> Liberty and Equality are the essential rights that man in his original and primitive perfection received from nature. Property struck the first blow at Equality; political Society, or Governments, were the first oppressors of Liberty; the supporters of Governments and property are the religious and civil laws; therefore, to reinstate man in his primitive rights of Equality and Liberty, we must begin by destroying all Religion, all civil society, and finish by the destruction of all property.[5]

5. Barruel, *Memoirs, illustrating the history of Jacobinism*, vol.3, p.23-24. Specific reference to the rights of mankind in cosmopolitan terms is also found in the 'Statuten der Illuminaten': '6. Versagt Fremden nicht die Rechte der Menschheit, und Gastfreiheit' (*Einige Originalschriften des Illuminatenordens*, Munich, Joseph

Only in this way was it possible to bring happiness back into the history of human beings. According to Barruel, every aspect of the Order tended to this objective, including its organisation, the degrees of initiation, the instruction of novices and its strategy of taking up government positions. The 'Brother *Insinuator* or *Recruiter*' (p.32) had the task of selecting new adepts among prominent figures in the Republic of Letters or those who had access to the prince, whether they belonged to the aristocracy, the wealthy classes or the bourgeoisie. These potential new members were immediately shown the secret societies' fearsome effectiveness in 'governing those who think they govern us' (p.55). After the initiation, members were supposed to take on a new name that reflected their character. Those who hated tyrants could choose Brutus, Cato or Machiavelli. Those who had an interest in philosophy might opt for Celsus, Porfirius or Tindal. Weishaupt, the leader of the Illuminati, immediately chose the name Spartacus. In fact, as part of the initiation rite the novice's hands were 'loaded with chains, as if he were a slave'. The Provincial then asked the Introducer: 'Who then is it that has reduced him to this state of slavery?' The uncompromising reply was worthy of Rousseau: 'Society, governments, the sciences, and false religion' (p.226-27).

With the second Minerval degree the Illuminati completed the adepts' ideological preparation in line with the tenets of European Enlightenment culture. Their instrument was the Minerval Academy or lodge, the new church of the brothers of Minerva, symbol of Enlightenment. This was something that the Brotherhood itself had been spreading across the continent.[6] They read texts by authors such as Mirabeau, Helvétius, the baron d'Holbach, Adam Smith, Sarpi or

---

Lentner, 1787, p.13). Barruel's citations are generally considered to be accurate, notwithstanding the fact that he is using them in support of his thesis that there was a conspiracy that led to the French Revolution: see Giarrizzo, *Massoneria e Illuminismo*, p.386ff. See also Le Forestier, *Les Illuminés de Bavière*, p.687ff., where we read that 'Barruel a tout lu', and that his quotations from Illuminati texts are 'fidèles'.

6. In Italy the rise of the great State academies in Naples and Turin at the end of the century coincided with the period of activity of the masonic movement: cf. my article 'The Accademia Reale delle Scienze: cultural sociability and men of letters in the Turin of the Enlightenment under Vittorio Amedeo III', *The Journal of modern history* 70 (1998), p.519-60. The *Novizen* were required to read a series of literary works that included *Fiesco's conspiracy at Genoa*, by Friedrich Schiller, Lessing's *Nathan the Wise* and *Emilia Galotti*, Goethe's *Egmont* and Wieland's *Agathon*: cf. *Der Illuminatenorden (1776-1785/87): ein politischer Geheimbund der Aufklärungszeit*, ed. Helmut Reinalter (Frankfurt am Main, 1997), p.22ff.

Epicurus. In the training of the future Illuminati minor and major the library played an important role alongside masonic educational journeys. However, the key transition stage to access the higher degrees was the fourth. There was an important speech that was pronounced by the Hierophant when conferring the degree of 'Epopt or Priest of Illuminism' – as faithfully translated from Barruel's French by his English translator, whereas the original German has 'Anrede auf die neu aufzunehmenden Illuminatos dirigentes', making it sound more like the induction of a new managerial class. In any case, this speech is a very clear expression of the Rousseau- and Lessing-inspired philosophy of history that was the framework of reference for the political action of the Illuminati and its principal objective of winning back the now lost original natural rights:

> As has the individual man (continues the Hierophant) so human nature in the aggregate has its childhood, its youth, its manhood, and its old age. At each of these periods mankind learn and are subject to fresh wants – hence arise their political and moral revolutions. It is at the age of manhood that human nature appears in all its dignity. It is then that, taught by long experience, man conceives at length how great a misfortune it is for him to invade the rights of others. (p.173)[7]

The recovery of these rights and the creation of a new civil society and morality that were prepared to respect them was the main task of secret societies, which were becoming more and more widespread in late-eighteenth-century Germany. As theorised in the Illuminati's form of philosophy of history, this providential task transformed these societies into the privileged means to achieve 'the salvation of human

7. The German original of this passage is somewhat less incisive: 'So, wie also der einzelne Mensch, eben so hat auch das ganze Geschlecht seine Kindheit, Jugend, männliches und graues Alter. Mit jeder dieser Perioden des ganzen Geschlechts lernen die Menschen neue, ihnen vorher unbekannte Bedürfnisse kennen [...] Diese Entwicklung der Bedürfnisse ist die Geschichte der Vervollkommnung des ganzen Geschlechts; denn nach diesen richten sich Kultur, Verfeinerung der Sitten, Entwicklung der schlafenden Geisteskräfte: mit der Entwicklung derselben ändert sich zugleich die Lebensart, der moralische und politische Zustand, die Begriffe von Glückseligkeit, das Betragen der Menschen gegen einander [...] In der Stuffe des männlichen Alters allein erscheint erst das Menschen Geschlecht in seiner Würde, dort allein, nachdem wie vorher durch viele Umwege, durch lange wiederhollte traurige Erfahrungen gelernet, welch ein Unglück es seye, sich die Rechte anderer anzumassen.' Cf. *Nachtrag von weitern Originalschriften, welche die Illuminatensekte* [...] *betreffen*, vol.2: *Dokumenten, Anrede auf die neu aufzunehmenden Illuminatos dirigentes* (Munich, n.n., 1787), p.53-54.

kind', thus legitimising their existence against the profound misgivings that they aroused in governments:

> These means are the secret schools of Philosophy. These schools have been in all ages the archives of nature and of the rights of man. These schools shall one day retrieve the fall of human nature, and Princes and Nations shall disappear from the face of the earth, and that without any violence. Human nature shall form one great family, and the earth shall become the habitation of the man of reason. (p.186-87)

The author of the Hierophant's speech was Baron Knigge (who had assumed the name 'Philo' among the Illuminati). By connecting together secret societies with the rights and universality of mankind into a single political programme of enfranchisement Knigge revived the old struggle for cosmopolitanism in new and original terms. This was a characteristic feature of freemasonry: the constant attempt to avoid fractures, divisions, clashes, and to assert universal brotherhood, social harmony and equality among human beings. It was a programme that was coming increasingly to the fore in the political struggle following the Seven Years War. The *Encyclopédie* had put forward the Enlightenment concept of fatherland as a peaceable political community of free and equal men, who were determined to achieve self-government and exercise it under the banner of the universal equality of rights for all peoples on earth.[8] But this view was seriously undermined by the spirit of conquest and intolerance of the

8. See the entry for 'Patriotisme' in the *Encyclopédie*, by the chevalier de Jaucourt, according to which 'the most perfect patriotism occurs when we are so attuned to the rights of mankind that we respect them in all peoples' (not yet translated in the online project, hence the translation). Diaz, *Filosofia e politica* (p.48ff.), describes the urgent debate that took place in France during the Seven Years War on the concept of patriotism and of fatherland as a political community of self-governing, free and equal men, and on how this led to the *philosophes* who were in favour of Frederick II being accused of treason. On the debate on Enlightenment patriotism in Italy as a new political category see Ferrone, *I profeti dell'Illuminismo*, p.162ff. On the situation in Germany, see Möller, *Fürstenstaat oder Bürgernation*, p.43ff. Möller includes a discussion of Kant's alarmed reaction, quite early on, to the rise of an ethnic idea of nation in German public opinion. In the philosopher's view this 'national folly' must be extinguished and replaced by 'patriotism and cosmopolitanism' (see p.56). On the persistence of these issues in time see the classic study by Friedrich Meinecke, *Cosmopolitanism and the national state*, translated by Robert B. Kimber, with an introduction by Felix Gilbert (Princeton, NJ, 1970; original: *Weltbürgertum und Nationalstaat, Studien zur Genesis des deutschen Nationalstaates*, Munich, 1911).

new nation states, which had resulted in the violent creation of vast colonial empires. While hoping for a society without classes, States or nations, the Hierophant Knigge was forced to admit that everywhere 'Nationalism, or the love for a particular nation' was replacing 'general love' for mankind: 'We really beheld Patriotism generating Localism, the confined spirit of families, and at length Egoism' (p.181). To put a stop to this ruinous and unpredictable process, a new morality and religion were urgently needed, which would be inspired by the ideals of Enlightenment cosmopolitanism and patriotism and propagated through secret societies. In terms of which Kant, the author of *Was ist Aufklärung?*, would certainly have approved, the Hierophant told his epopts that 'true morality' is 'the art of teaching men to shake off their wardship, to attain the age of manhood, and thus to need neither princes nor governments' (p.199).

As for religion, the political theology of the Illuminati blended masonic gnosticism together with the deism of Voltaire and Lessing, and Rousseau's civil religion. Christ became a sort of Grand Master who had come to preach the dogmas of natural religion and show freemasons the way to emancipation. The Gospel's aim was the moral education of mankind so that men would be able to govern themselves and bring back liberty and equality among men, without the use of violence. With this in mind, the Illuminati strove to build a political theology that called into question Augustine's idea of original sin and ultimately redemption itself.[9] Having looked at the documents belonging to the 'Class of the Grand Mysteries', which were restricted to members of the Areopagus only, Barruel was able to uncover and denounce the Order's ultimate objective: to create 'a religion and a morality of the rights of man' (p.254).

9. In his well-informed synthesis Barruel explicitly refers to Knigge's words in the *Anrede auf die neu aufzunehmend Illuminatos dirigentes* (see *Nachtrag*, p.106-107): 'Nun begreift man also, in wie fern Jesus der Erlöser und Heiland der Welt seye. Nun klärt sich die Lehre von der Erbsünde, von dem Fall des Menschen, von der Wiedergeburt auf. Nun weiss man, was der Zustand der reinen Natur, der Zustand der gefallenen Natur, und das Reich der Gnade sey. Da der Mensch aus dem Stande seiner ursprünglichen Freyheit getretten, so hat er den Stand der Natur verlassen, und hat an seiner Würde verlohren; indem er seinen ursprünglichen Leidenschaften und Trieben zu viel nachgegeben, und seinen Gelüsten und sinnlichen Begierden nicht widerstehen konnte. Menschen in Staaten leben also nicht mehr im Stande der reinen, sondern der gefallenen Natur.' I am grateful to Franco Motta for calling my attention to this important illustration of masonic political theology.

On 2 March 1785 Prince Charles Theodore proclaimed the Illuminati traitors of the State and enemies of religion. He also banned all masonic lodges from Bavaria. Perquisitions, arrests and trials followed. Weishaupt and many of the other leaders fled the country. The hunt for the Illuminati soon spread to the other States of the Holy Roman empire. News of the Revolution in France led to a second wave of persecutions in 1790, which aimed to suppress the last surviving remnants of the sect, raising questions about the true motives behind this frenzy of persecution. In Germany there were many other secret societies at the time, including the extremely powerful and equally politicised Rosicrucians in Berlin, who had been extensively infiltrated by the former Jesuits.[10] Why were the Illuminati the only ones to be denounced and persecuted? What was really at stake, apart from the supposed political danger represented by the Order, which in fact is still not quite clear today?

In those years there were also other secret societies that aimed to occupy positions of power and infiltrate institutions, without raising anything like the same degree of alarm. The verbal denunciation of the absolute monarchs' tendency towards despotism was commonplace in public political debate, as was the claim that civil society must be autonomous from and come before the State. The same propaganda in favour of the rights of man and against despotism, feudalism and servitude of the glebe that we have identified as an underlying theme across the various different ideas of the Illuminati was an integral part of late-eighteenth-century masonic language, and as such is found in lodges throughout Europe, especially after the American Revolution.

The oration read at the initiation of Maximilian, duke of Zweibrücken, at the A la Candeur lodge in Strasbourg in 1777 already contained most of what would become the so-called political programme of the Illuminati. The orator articulated a philosophy of history according to which, from time immemorial, freemasonry had defended 'the unacknowledged rights of mankind', devoting itself to the 'defence of the innocent and the weak'. In a very similar way to Knigge the Hierophant with his epopts, he thundered against all forms of despotism, which degraded 'the dignity of man' and enslaved him,

10. On German secret societies, with special reference to the Rosicrucian Order, see Horst Möller, 'Die Bruderschaft der Gold- und Rosenkreuzer', in *Freimaurer und Geheimbünde im 18. Jahrhundert in Mitteleuropa*, ed. Helmut Reinalter (Frankfurt am Main, 1983), p.199-239; see also Manfred Agethen, *Geheimbund und Utopie: Illuminaten, Freimaurer und deutsche Spätaufklärung* (Munich, 1984).

as was still the case in the feudal system and servitude of the glebe. The prince who demanded to be admitted to the lodge was reminded of the importance of social virtues, the nobility of cosmopolitanism and the true nature of power, and was told what his new tasks within the Brotherhood would be. This followed a rhetorical pattern and a language of rights that was increasingly widespread in the European lodges at the end of the eighteenth century:

> Nature only made you a man: everything else is the result of social conventions and abuse of power, which can indeed limit the exercise of primitive rights, but not cancel them. Come to the freemasons' school and you will see the honest and respectable farmer standing beside his lord: the prince reaching out a brotherly hand to his virtuous subject […] You will be judged the same as the last of men, on the basis of your works and […] then the rights of both of you will become absolutely equal once again […] Every step of the way nature instils in you the first law of free men: égalité […] All men have the same right to happiness and almost equal resources for its pursuit […] You will see that freemasonry sets several kinds of merit beside the cry of mankind, and these are separated from one another by accidental and sometimes imaginary distances. You will see it eradicate religious and national hatred. On the one hand, it will reunite the friends of truth and religion, who otherwise would have been separated from one another by subtle dogmas that are not part of custom. On the other hand, it will create this universal monarchy of truth, this perpetual peace, which is the first wish of nature and of a few honest souls, but is ridiculed by our politicians.[11]

These kinds of statements are often found in the documents that were seized from the Illuminati, perhaps at times intermingled with more aggressive expressions of their determination to fight despotism and tyranny. If Lessing's *Dialogues for freemasons* contained 'the true ontology of Freemasonry', as claimed by the author himself, the Illuminati's ideologue, Lessing's faithful disciple Knigge, was keen to accelerate the process towards redemption and was pressing for the immediate politicisation of moral renewal through a direct assumption of government responsibilities by the adepts. He believed that it was no longer enough to preach the cosmopolitan creed and enrol among the freemasons, in Lessing's words, 'every worthy man of the right

11. Translated from the Italian version in Giarrizzo, *Massoneria e Illuminismo*, p.224-26, where this text is described as 'clearly political, brave and in line with Enlightenment ideas'.

disposition, irrespective of nationality, irrespective of religion, and irrespective of social class'.[12] Nor was it enough to continue to lament '[t]he unavoidable evils of the state' (p.198) and of the fragmentation into different nations and religions, as Lessing seemed to have done in his long-term and indefinite project of emancipation through the moral education of humanity. In any case, the political radicalisation of the Order by express wish of its leaders still does not explain – or at least not completely – the extreme vigour with which they were persecuted.

We must also remember that the issue of the Bavaria Illuminati did not affect solely the States that were part of the Holy Roman empire, but sent a strong message across the whole continent. It was a turning point, perhaps the most important battle fought by the Late Enlightenment in Europe and especially in Germany in the struggle for political and cultural hegemony against the Jesuits and those parts of society that were most closely linked to traditional forms of power. This episode is very important also for the history of the rights of man in Germany, and acquires a specific significance especially when seen in the European context of the crisis of freemasonry and the contemporary influx of Enlightenment thinkers into the lodges in order to fight more efficiently for reforms against the *Ancien régime*. This is a historical phenomenon of great importance, which has not yet received the attention that it deserves.

Already in a letter to D'Alembert dating from 1761 Voltaire showed his awareness of freemasonry as a useful instrument in the struggle in which the *philosophes* were engaged.[13] Twenty years later, the majority of Enlightenment thinkers were part of the 250,000-strong masonic system in Europe.[14] However, this was taking place at a time when

12. Cf. Gotthold Ephraim Lessing, 'Ernst and Falk: dialogues for freemasons', in *Philosophical and theological writings*, translated by H. B. Nisbet (Cambridge, 2005), p.184-216 (184 and 201). For instance, Lessing did not at all share the political enthusiasm for the American Revolution harboured by those 'fantasists' among the freemasons who would assert 'that Congress is a lodge, and that it is *there* that the Freemasons are at last establishing their empire by force of arms' (p.209).
13. 'Let all true *philosophes* form a fraternity like the freemasons. Let them meet, support one another, be faithful to their fraternity. In that case, I shall be prepared to go to the stake for them. Such a secret academy would be worth more than the Athenian one and all the ones in Paris' (Voltaire to D'Alembert, Ferney, 20 April 1761, D9743, in Voltaire, *Correspondence and related documents*, vol.107, p.167-68 (167). See also Giarrizzo, *Massoneria e Illuminismo*, p.149.
14. See Giarrizzo, *Massoneria e Illuminismo*, p.346. Figures and a bibliography on

freemasonry was undergoing a profound identity crisis, which had hit in a particularly strong way its most important branch, the Templar Strict Observance. This crisis would eventually give rise to an inter-masonic power struggle. On the one hand there were those who favoured an esoteric and occult approach, like the followers of Saint-Martin and Willermoz in Lyon, who were hoping that freemasonry would help them find theosophic and cabalistic paths towards the universal regeneration of mankind. On the opposite side we find the rationalists, who were closer to the Enlightenment positions that were dominant in the Republic of Letters.

The clash between rationalists and spiritualists within freemasonry in Germany was heightened by the dark action of former Jesuits, who massively infiltrated the masonic lodges. They became especially prominent in the Rosicrucian secret society, which had been born to satisfy the growing need for religiosity in those years. We have important testimony to this effect by Herder (his Illuminati name: Damasus Pontifex), who believed that the visionary *Schwärmer* who were present in great numbers in the German and Austrian lodges all came from the dissolution of the Jesuit order.[15] Herder also thought that the Jesuits were responsible for the clash between *Aufklärung* and *Schwärmerei*, which would have such a profound impact on the political and cultural history of late-eighteenth-century Germany. Their aim was to do away with the world of the Enlightenment by reviving religious spiritualism and esoteric practices as a defining feature of an alternative culture that would give new impulse to the Christian religion.

There was some truth in this. In 1782 the Congress of Wilhelmsbad, in Prussia, was convened to try and find an agreement among all the different rites. It ended instead with the victory of the Lyon members and the defeat of both the Rosicrucians and Bode's rationalist current, marking a turning point in the history of the Bavaria Illuminati. They had begun as a small sect run by the materialist, anti-clerical Weishaupt, who hated the Jesuits, his former teachers, above anything else and wanted to supplant them in the important role of educators of those who were close to the chambers of power.[16] With the

the scenario in Germany can be found in Möller, *Fürstenstaat oder Bürgernation*, p.503ff.

15. Cf. Giarrizzo, *Massoneria e Illuminismo*, p.346. On the considerable Jesuit presence among the Rosicrucians see Freschi, *Dall'occultismo alla politica*, p.54ff.

16. On the controversial figure of the founder of the Illuminati see Martin Mulsow, '"Steige also, wenn du kannst, höher und höher zu uns herauf": Adam

arrival of Adolph von Knigge and Johann Bode the Illuminati had become an actual secret order with far-reaching political and cultural ambitions, whose aim was to relaunch the Enlightenment programme of emancipation on the basis of the rights of man, and to attract the rationalists back within the Strict Observance and to the centre of European masonic power.[17] In fact, the Wilhelmsbad defeat led to increased enrolment of those brothers who were sympathetic towards the Enlightenment and were rather confused as to which way to go. These included state sovereigns, such as the dukes of Saxe-Weimar, Saxe-Gotha and Brunswick, or the earls of Hesse-Kassel and Hesse-Homburg, and famous intellectuals, such as Goethe, Herder, Klopstock, Sonnenfels, Nicolai and others.

The trials and the harsh repression by the Inquisition and the Bavarian government in 1785 were no doubt the result of local issues, malicious allegations and the Rosicrucians' determination to be the most important secret society in Germany.[18] However, they were also due to the attack unleashed by Pius VI on the Enlightenment with his first papal bull, *Inscrutabile divinae sapientiae*, which was clearly seen as nothing short of a declaration of war. All the more so since in 1782, during his visit to Joseph II in Vienna, Pius VI had reiterated the Holy See's intention of winning Europe back for Christianity, especially the strategically important territories of the Holy Roman empire.[19]

Weishaupt als Philosoph', in *Die Weimarer Klassik und ihre Geheimbünde*, ed. Walter Müller-Seidel and Wolfgang Reidel (Würzburg, 2003), p.27-66. Le Forestier, *Les Illuminés de Bavière*, p.563ff, describes Weishaupt's negative traits and intellectual coarseness, something that is indeed borne out by his writings.

17. This was Knigge and Bode's exact plan as described in Leopold Engel, *Geschichte des Illuminatenordens, ein Beitrag zur Geschichte Bayerns* (Berlin, 1906), p.138ff. Their difference in outlook soon led to devastating clashes between Weishaupt and Knigge: see Giarrizzo, *Massoneria e Illuminismo*, p.316ff.
18. See Le Forestier, *Les Illuminés de Bavière*, p.430ff. Interesting information on the repression of the Illuminati is found in recently rediscovered documents that had belonged to Alessandro Savioli, who was one of their leaders under the name of Brutus: cf. Furio Bacchini, *La vita rocambolesca del conte Alessandro Savioli Corbelli (1742-1811)* (Bologna, 2011), p.152ff.
19. Cf. Trampus, *I gesuiti e l'Illuminismo*, p.7ff. On the pope's important visit, see Franco Venturi, *Settecento riformatore*, vol.4: *La caduta dell'Antico Regime, 1776-1789. 2. Il patriottismo repubblicano e gli imperi dell'Est* (Turin, 1984), p.668ff. *Inscrutabile divinae sapientiae* should be read in its integrity. It depicts the world of the Enlightenment as the work of the devil. It accuses it of plotting to spread atheism, overthrow sovereigns and destroy every form of social bond, following a model that is also found, unsurprisingly, in Barruel and, before him, in the verdicts of the Bavarian inquisitors in 1785. On Paul VI's bull see Fulvio De Giorgi,

The Catholic Church feared the unforeseeable consequences of the alliance between the Enlightenment and freemasonry far more than the atheistic and materialistic propaganda by the few scattered circles that drew their inspiration from Helvétius or d'Holbach. It was especially worried by the sudden growth of their ambitious programme of reform, and the way in which it was expanding from the moral and political field and started to pose a threat to religion through the creation of exciting new civil religions that were inspired by gnosticism, deism and the rights of man in lodges in Paris, Naples, Milan, London and Berlin.[20] It was as if with their radicalism and their political use of secret societies the Illuminati were running ahead of time, trying 'to accelerate the revolution of people's minds'.[21] All this, of course, provided the perfect excuse for eradicating every Enlightenment-inspired desire for reform from the lands of the Holy Roman empire.

To this effect, a sort of pre-emptive counter-revolution was put in place by those governments that were the most reactionary and closest to Rome, Bavaria being among these. Barruel's important account in his 1790s *Mémoires pour servir à l'histoire du jacobinisme* is not only an invaluable testimony that allows us to build a picture of these events: it is also probably the final act of revenge by the Jesuits, bringing to completion the demonisation of the Enlightenment programme that had begun with Pius VI.

Some of the interpretations that have been offered of these events in which German freemasons and supporters of the Enlightenment

---

'Correnti e momenti dell'anti-illuminismo nell''800 e '900', in *L'Illuminismo e i suoi critici*, ed. Dante Bolognesi and Sauro Mattarelli (Milan, 2011), p.71-83.

20. On the important issue of religion and its philosophical and political meaning for the late-eighteenth-century Enlightenment see Ferrone, *I profeti dell'Illuminismo*, p.338ff.

21. From a 1781 letter from Friedrich Tieman to Jean-Baptiste Willermoz (see Giarrizzo, *Massoneria e Illuminismo*, p.215): 'I have heard much about the Munich lodge of the Illuminati. I even know some of its members, whom I am forbidden to name. From our meetings so far, I would say that their aim is political rather than religious. One of their leaders did speak of Providence, Revelation and the major points of our doctrine in a way that was entirely contrary to our principles. Their objective is as follows: Bavaria is prey to the most absurd superstition. From the prince down to the Swiss at his door everything is infested with it. It is governed by priests, and it is forbidden to think or speak. Some men, among the most cultured and unwilling to carry this yoke, have secretly got together with the intent of spreading healthier ideas on administration and tolerance. They are trying to educate well-born young men who, once they take up office, must contribute *to accelerate the revolution of people's minds*'. Emphasis added.

found themselves for a while to be uncomfortable bedfellows are therefore rather disingenuous, as well as historically wrong, despite being presented with some degree of rhetorical skill. Although their shared intent to fight the *Ancien régime* and the despotism of the absolutist State caused them to be identified with each other, these were two totally different kinds of cultural experiences, and should be investigated as such. Masonic 'secrets' had very little to do with the 'indirect method' applied by Enlightenment intellectuals in their struggle in those years. There was no 'hypocrisy' comparable to the dark masonic secrecy in those artists and men of letters who, according to Koselleck, in introducing the new morality of the rights of man in their plays, novels or even music failed to address its predictable political consequences.[22] This is all the more obvious if we look at the history of the Republic of Letters in Germany in the last quarter of the eighteenth century from a European point of view, leaving aside the old periodisations and misleading accounts that were produced in the course of the following centuries by a nationalist historiography that was profoundly critical of Enlightenment culture, which was seen as an alien element.

In the previous chapter we looked at the 'performance' or *mise en scène* of the rights in France. We reflected on the nature and forms of this new concept of politics in relation to the aesthetic revolution of

22. Cf. Koselleck, *Critique and crisis*, p.98: 'The stages of the indirect assumption of power recorded in the annals of the lodge followed the analogous pattern of the Republic of Letters.' While disagreeing with those who insist on denying the obvious politicisation that was taking place in Germany at the end of the eighteenth century, Koselleck's own thesis is somewhat different, and still rather biased against the Enlightenment. He accepts that the lodges and the Republic of Letters were obviously politicised, but presents this process in an entirely negative light, denouncing it as abstract in a Hegelian sense, hypocritical and ultimately unwilling to take on real responsibility for their ideas, which in the long term would lead to extremely negative effects from a dialectical point of view. This stereotypical misunderstanding and condemnation was already found in Thomas Mann's 1918 *Reflections of a nonpolitical man*, where Mann described what he considered to be a specifically German view of politics and criticised both 'civilization's literary man', who corresponded to the model of the *philosophe*, and the Enlightenment view of politics: 'belief in politics is belief in democracy, in the *contrat social*. For more than a century and a half, everything that has been understood in a more intellectual sense by politics goes back to *Jean-Jacques Rousseau*: and he is the father of democracy *because* he is the father of the political spirit itself, of political humanity' (translated by Walter D. Morris, New York, 1983, p.16).

the Late Enlightenment. As a matter of fact, thanks to the intensive circulation of ideas these traits were also found in Germany, Italy or Austria. We find everywhere, and in very similar terms, the gradual politicisation of literature and the arts, and a growing awareness of the importance of intellectual power at court and in civil society. These elements were accompanied by theoretical reflection on the strategic function of public opinion, the important role of political communication in shaping people's consciousness, or the new communicative aesthetics that had been developed by figures such as Diderot or Mercier, who credited man and his art with a new creative and emancipatory capability.

In fact, this process had a long genesis. Its roots can be traced back to a significant change in the culture system of the European Enlightenment, to the extent that, in order to understand the events of those years, we must now posit the existence of a Late Enlightenment as an independent historical period, with its own characteristic features, that occupied the final quarter of the eighteenth century and saw the final crisis of the *Ancien régime* being played out in every corner of Europe.[23]

Those were the years of the emergence in the scientific community and the Republic of Letters of a new idea of science as universal experimental knowledge, and of a new representation of nature as *natura naturans*, perpetually changing and in motion. This image and this way of practising science were strongly hostile towards the (then dominant) physical and mathematical form of representation embodied by Newton's mechanistic universe, which was considered too reductionist and elitist. I have discussed elsewhere in greater detail the epistemological implications and social and cultural impact of this epoch-making transformation.[24] It was a momentous development, one that called into doubt the fixity of the natural order, paving the way for the idea of the transformation of the species and the perfectibility of the human being and preparing for the irruption of the concept of history into the nascent science of man. For the first time, scholars acknowledged the importance of feelings and passions, of the imagination, and of a physiology capable of taking psychological aspects into account. Germany too was going in this direction, opening up new horizons for artists and men of letters

23. See Ferrone, *The Enlightenment*, p.140ff. See also the essays in *Il linguaggio del tardo Illuminismo: politica, diritto e società civile*, ed. Antonio Trampus (Rome, 2011).

24. See Ferrone, *I profeti dell'Illuminismo*, p.64ff.; Vincenzo Ferrone and Paolo Rossi, *Lo scienziato nell'età moderna* (Rome and Bari, 1994).

who followed with great attention the continental debate on the new communicative aesthetics.[25]

The literary and theatrical movement of *Sturm und Drang* and the period of 'Weimar classicism' were not specifically a local phenomenon, a polemical pre-Romantic reaction to Enlightenment rationalism, as was claimed by German nationalist historians at the beginning of the twentieth century.[26] In fact, these represented the original and especially interesting German variant of the European Late Enlightenment. The politicisation of Enlightenment literature in Germany also occurred in similar terms to what we find in Italy or France. It was a form of politics that placed the human being as an individual, and all his faculties, at the centre of everything. It examined man scientifically, in both his physiological and his psychological dimension. It studied his capacity for empathy, his self-love, feelings and passions. It explored the public and collective effect of the natural sciences as well as of poetic language. Finally, it investigated the history of man in society and in his intersubjective relationships, and the painful effects of the logic of domination, of the will to power and of despotism in all their historical forms, both individual and collective.

After Locke, Rousseau and Helvétius, the dogma of perfectibility, and especially the representation of an active and vital *natura naturans* as popularised by Diderot's German followers, became the philosophical basis for ambitious educational projects and modern forms of social utopia under the banner of emancipation. Late Enlightenment politics declared as its primary objectives the defence of man and his rights, the emancipation and happiness of the individual, a society of free and equal human beings capable of responsibly governing themselves within a republic, a State governed by laws that were at the service of civil society. The instruments it intended to deploy for this purpose were, first of all, reforms and not revolutions. It was going to make deliberate use of the nascent intellectual power,

25. See *Der ganze Mensch: Anthropologie und Literatur im 18. Jahrhundert*, ed. Hans-Jürgen Schings (Stuttgart, 1994), for some useful essays on the rise of the science of man in Germany and its interaction with the world of letters. On the growing interest in the body in aesthetics and literature see Elena Agazzi, *Il corpo conteso: rito e gestualità nella Germania del Settecento* (Milan, 2000). Cf. also *Die Sachen der Aufklärung*, ed. Frauke Berndt (Halle, 2010).

26. One of the first authors who realised that it was a historical error to contrast the *Sturm und Drang* movement and its rationalistic neonaturalism with the Late Enlightenment was György Lukács in his *Skizze einer Geschichte der neueren deutschen Literatur* (Berlin, 1952).

for which new opportunities had opened up with the discovery of public opinion, and the defeat of the culture of *Ancien régime* society – even more than of its politics and institutions. This had nothing to do with a cunning and hypocritical 'indirect assumption of power' or a covert move 'from self-defence to ruling claim'.[27] Antonio Gramsci, a twentieth-century intellectual with a thorough understanding of politics, saw that this was instead a great political project, lucidly thought out and incredibly modern in outlook. Its aim was to impose values and ideas by achieving a cultural hegemony that would allow them to undermine the *Ancien régime* from its very foundations.[28]

In Germany, as indeed in France, the politicisation of the Late Enlightenment along these lines took into account the aesthetic discussions on the rise of a public sphere open to all. Accordingly, its primary vehicles, even ahead of philosophy and law, were literature and the arts.[29] Lessing was certainly the spiritual father, major theorist and initiator of this form of Enlightenment, being especially aware of the political results that had been achieved through the aesthetic revolution that had been promoted in France by his beloved Diderot. He believed that '[w]hoever reasons rightly, invents, and whoever desires to invent must be able to reason', and, following Diderot, that we should pursue a harmonious balance between empiricism and rationalism in the aesthetic field.[30] Lessing's theories on the ethical and political function of art, as expressed in his *Hamburg dramaturgy* (1767-1769), found a following in, among others, Goethe, Wieland, Mendelssohn, Schiller and Herder. They had a huge influence on the attempt by the German Late Enlightenment to put together its own concrete programme of emancipation based on the virtuous

27. Cf. Koselleck, *Critique and crisis*, p.98.
28. In his early writings, Gramsci describes the cultural revolution of the Enlightenment, especially as it took place in France, as a possible model for socialism as it strove for cultural hegemony in twentieth-century Europe: cf. Antonio Gramsci, 'Socialism and culture', in *The Gramsci reader: selected writings, 1916-1935*, ed. David Forgacs (New York, 2000), p.56-59.
29. This was first pointed out by Ernst Tröltsch in his famous 1897 essay on 'Die Aufklärung': cf. Nicolao Merker, *Die Aufklärung in Deutschland* (Munich, 1982), p.56ff.
30. Cf. Gotthold Ephraim Lessing, 'Dramatic notes (*Hamburg dramaturgy*)', in Lessing, *Selected prose works*, ed. Edward Bell, translated by E. C. Beasley and Helen Zimmern (London, 1890), p.227-493, N.96, p.483 (see Merker, *Die Aufklärung in Deutschland*, p.107). On the huge fortune of Diderot's aesthetic reflections in Europe and especially in Germany see Mortier, *Diderot en Allemagne*; Saada, *Inventer Diderot*.

connection between art and politics: a programme whose complex unity of intents has been rather underestimated.

In order to gain a clearer view of the unique features of this project we must stop defining everything by looking backwards from the vantage point of the French Revolution. This historiographical practice has only resulted in anachronism, ideological bias and historical categories that derive from a nationalist outlook and a facile teleology.[31] By looking at late-eighteenth-century Enlightenment in its own right we can see how greatly this political programme contributed to the exploration of the limits and potentialities of communicative phenomena and of the uses of poetics for the exploration of reality, above and beyond Diderot's pioneering studies. It then becomes clear how its extraordinary results, which always remained in perfect unison with Enlightenment values and ideas, influenced our outlook for centuries to come, and how, through novels, tragedies and musical pieces, they created the necessary context and cultural climate for the 'performance' and rapid diffusion of the language of the rights of man before the great revolution.

Lessing, Goethe and Schiller provide three illustrative examples of the politicisation of the Late Enlightenment in Germany and of the way in which this process merged together a wide range of phenomena: from freemasonry and other secret societies to the political and cultural programme of the Enlightenment, the communicative aesthetics and drive towards the emancipation of the moderns, and the history of the rights of man in the Holy Roman empire. It is therefore extremely important to distinguish among all these strands, which is what we are going to attempt here.

Lessing's *Nathan der Weise* (1779) is an admirable synthesis of the most important elements of Late Enlightenment culture and of the way in which this was giving new meaning to the language of rights: for instance, the pursuit of 'truth' and of a natural religion capable of turning us into better human beings, deism, tolerance, cosmopolitanism and the overarching primacy of a new concept of the humanity of the individual. As for his masonic experience, this finds its most mature expression especially in the *Dialogues*, which set out his philosophy of history. After writing important plays in which

31. See chapter 10, 'The Enlightenment-French Revolution paradigm', in Ferrone, *The Enlightenment*, p.79-86. This persuasive paradigm was reasserted in the field of German studies in Italy by Giuliano Baioni in his important book *Classicismo e rivoluzione: Goethe e la Rivoluzione francese* (Naples, 1969).

he criticised the *Ancien régime*, its prejudices and logic of domination, in the years in which he directed the National Theatre in Hamburg, from 1767 to 1770, Lessing seemed to step up his political struggle even further. He even wrote an 'anti-tyrannical tragedy' with the emblematic title of *Spartacus*, in which he reiterated his republican and anti-despotic zeal, and his aversion to the absolutist State and to those figures whom he considered an obstacle to liberty, such as Frederick II.[32] Lessing's death in 1781 means that he was not involved with the Illuminati. However, his ideas reached the latter through his loyal disciple Knigge. In any case, Lessing would hardly have shared their intent to accelerate political change through secret means in order to restore the natural kingdom of human rights. However, things were rather different in the case of Goethe.

In 1781 Goethe had his initiation in Weimar. He subsequently rose through the lower degrees of the Strict Observance. In 1783, after the rationalists close to the Enlightenment were defeated at the Congress of Wilhelmsbad, he accepted Bode's invitation to join the Bavaria Illuminati, together with Wieland, Herder, Nicolai and Duke Karl August himself. He chose the name of Abaris. His motivations for joining the Order are still the subject of much discussion, especially after the recent discovery of important new documents. In 1991 the American scholar Daniel Wilson suggested that Goethe's intent may have been to spy on the adepts.[33] A more likely interpretation, however, is that at the time the Illuminati appeared as a bastion of the *Aufklärung*, which was then under attack both from the former Jesuits and from the diffusion of *Schwärmerei*. This view is supported by

32. Cf Merker, *Die Aufklärung in Deutschland*, p.54. For an overall discussion of Lessing's intellectual positions, and especially his attempt to reinterpret Spinoza's pantheism in terms of natural religion, see Pierre-Henri Tavoillot, *Le Crépuscule des Lumières: les documents de 'la querelle' du panthéisme (1780-1789)* (Paris, 1995).
33. Cf. by W. Daniel Wilson, *Geheimräte gegen Geheimbunde: ein unbekanntes Kapitel der klassisch-romantischen Geschichte Weimars* (Stuttgart, 1991), *Das Goethe-Tabu: Protest und Menschenrechte im Klassischen Weimar* (Munich, 1999), *Unterirdische Gänge: Goethe, Freimaurerei und Politik* (Göttingen, 1999). Wilson was the first scholar to be able to examine the newly resurfaced *Schwedenkiste*, which contained papers that had belonged to Bode, an important figure in Weimar and one of the leaders of the Illuminati. The papers had been seized by the Gestapo, then taken to Moscow by the Red Army and finally to East Berlin in the 1950s. More information can be found in a review article by Maria Carolina Foi, 'Hans-Jürgen Schings, *Die Brüder des Marquis Posa: Schiller und der Geheimbund der Illuminaten*', *Studi germanici* 37 (1999), p.166-74. Against Wilson's thesis see Müller-Seidel and Reidel, *Die Weimarer Klassik*.

Goethe's correspondence with Lavater between 1781 and 1782, where we read of the former's concern at the impetuous rise of the *Schwärmer*, the so-called visionaries and spiritualists, who saw the anti-mechanistic neonaturalism of Diderot and the *Stürmer* in openly irrational terms. This current gave ample space to occultism, esotericism and fantasies of all kinds, thus effectively fuelling superstition and religious fanaticism, the expectation of miracles and apparitions.

It was a time when 'charlatans' were obtaining considerable success at court and with public opinion. Faced with animal magnetism, Cagliostro's presumed supernatural powers and Lavater's mystical physiognomy, Goethe's alarmed reaction could only be to seek an alternative with the Illuminati.[34] In those difficult years, the new secret order probably appeared as a sort of providential *Ecclesia militans* of the *Aufklärung*, which could finally assert the claims of 'true' rationalist freemasonry and the 'true' Enlightenment in defence of tolerance and the rights of man. The visionaries and their most prestigious figure, Lavater, appeared to them like a real danger to be fought off at all costs. In Goethe's Enlightenment anthropology there was no room for fantasies or an extreme and esoteric religious fanaticism. As he wrote in his poem *The Divine* (1783):

> Only man alone
> Can do the impossible:
> He can distinguish,
> Chooses and judges;
> He can endow
> The moment with permanence.
> He alone may
> Reward the good man,
> Punish the wicked
> Restore and rescue,
> Usefully bind
> All that errs and wanders.

In 1782 he wrote to Charlotte von Stein that in Lavater's works he saw 'the greatest human intelligence joined to the crassest superstition by a thread as fast as it is fine'.[35] This ties in with Gabriel de

34. On these topics cf. Luigi Marino, *I maestri della Germania: Göttingen 1770-1820* (Turin, 1975), p.132ff. (translated into German by Brigitte Szabó-Bechstein as *Praeceptores Germaniae: Göttingen 1770-1820*, Göttingen, 1995). See also Ferrone, *I profeti dell'Illuminismo*, p.91ff.

35. For *The Divine*, see Goethe, *Selected poems*, translated by John Whaley (London,

Mirabeau's evaluation, in a famous letter on Cagliostro and Lavater (Berlin, March 1786), that the latter was all the more dangerous in that 'at home and abroad, in the countryside as in cities, among the brotherhoods and at court, he possessed more authority than Socrates or Plato ever had.'[36]

Again, it is important not to misunderstand this convergence between a great *Aufklärer* and the activity of the Bavaria Illuminati. The objectives and strategy of Weishaupt's conspiracy were one thing, Goethe's masonic experience, and especially his adherence to the Enlightenment, quite another. Nobody denies that there are important masonic elements in several of Goethe's works, and especially in the philosophical novel *Wilhelm Meister's theatrical mission* (which he began in 1777). But this certainly does not imply that the author supported the Illuminati's plots, either actively or simply ideologically. This can be seen in relation to the mysterious Tower Society that seems to covertly manage all the main events in Wilhelm Meister's life. The Society's positive secret activity had nothing to do with political activism, but only with Wilhelm's sentimental and artistic education. Its aim was the legitimate pursuit of a kind of social harmony that would allow men to overcome all differences and violent contrasts, according to the traditional masonic model: that is to say, according to 'true' masonic ideology, as exemplified in Lessing's *Dialogues for freemasons*, to which the Enlightenment thinkers who joined the lodges generally subscribed.[37]

1998), p.47, lines 37-48 (see also Giarrizzo, *Massoneria e Illuminismo*, p.363 and 358ff.). There is a useful account of the interaction between Goethe and Lavater in Giarrizzo's introduction to Goethe, *Il gran Cofto* (Palermo, 1989). For the letter, dated 6 April 1782 from Tiefenort, see *Letters from Goethe*, translated by M. von Herzfeld and C. Melvil Sym, with an introduction by W. H. Bruford (Edinburgh, 1957).

36. Honoré-Gabriel Riqueti, comte de Mirabeau, *Lettre du comte de Mirabeau à *** sur M. M. de Cagliostro et Lavater* (Berlin, François de Lagarde, 1786), p.38 (see also Giarrizzo, *Massoneria e Illuminismo*, p.358-60 and 365; Goethe explicitly mentions 'true freemasonry' in opposition to charlatans like Cagliostro).

37. A more problematic situation is described in Hans-Jürgen Schings, '*Wilhelm Meister* und das Erbe der Illuminaten', in *Die Weimarer Klassik*, ed. W. Müller-Seidel and W. Reidel, p.179-203. Schings believes that Goethe had closer links with the Illuminati than I have outlined, because of the fact that the Tower reappears in *Wilhelm Meisters Lehrjahre* (1794-1796), confirming his sympathy for this world. On Goethe's adherence to both freemasonry and the Enlightenment see also, in the same collection of essays, Hartmut Reinhardt, 'Geheime Wege der Aufklärung: Goethe, der Illuminatenorden und das Epos-Fragment "Die

In 1774, several years before his initiation, the young Goethe, in writing his *Prometheus*, began his complex intellectual and civic reflection along the lines put forward by the Enlightenment. This poem declares war on the presumed, despotic, omnipotence of the gods, in the name of the independence of earthly existence, the fullness of human life, the very possibility of liberating man through man, bravely leaving aside any divine intervention. Prometheus' proud words sound like a manifesto for the *Aufklärung*. They voice the challenge that this movement is now mature enough to speak out loud and clear:

> Here I sit, fashion humans
> In my own image,
> A breed to be my equal,
> To suffer, sorrow,
> To enjoy and be joyful,
> And to ignore you,
> Like me.[38]

Goethe never abandoned his Enlightenment values.[39] Throughout his life and writing career he continued to be interested in the original features, limits and potentialities of the individual in his humanity and his complex and organic relationship with nature, evil, history, power, spirituality. His art – theatre, literature, poetry – was a powerful epistemological tool for the exploration of these issues. His *Iphigenia in Tauris* was a milestone in this respect. It was a kind of gospel of the new *Humanität* that was an important concern of all the main figures of the *Spätaufklärung*, or German Late Enlightenment.[40] Goethe began this tragedy in 1779 and completed it in 1787, which means that it appeared at the same time as Lessing's *Nathan der Weise*. This was

---

Geheimnisse"', p.145-76. Additional discussions of this topic can be found in Marino Freschi, *L'utopia nel Settecento tedesco* (Naples, 1974), p.75ff., and Carla Sabine Kowohl De Rosa, *Storia della cultura tedesca fra 'Ancien régime' e Restaurazione: cronache e personaggi* (Rome and Bari, 2000), p.123ff.

38. Goethe, *Selected poems*, p.21, lines 52-58. For an overview of the transformations undergone by the theme of Prometheus at the turn of the eighteenth century see Raymond Trousson, *Le Thème de Prométhée dans la littérature européenne*, 3rd edn (Geneva, 2001), p.239-371.
39. Cf. Paul E. Kerry, *Enlightenment thought in the writing of Goethe: a contribution to the history of ideas* (Rochester, NY, 2001).
40. See the chapter on 'Die Humanität in Goethes *Iphigenie auf Tauris*', in Thomas Berger, *Der Humanitätsgedanke in der Literatur der deutschen Spätaufklärung* (Heidelberg, 2008), p.173ff.

emblematic of the way in which both authors shared the ideals of the German Late Enlightenment: that is to say, its ambitious transformation of moral values, its opposition to the culture of privilege and inequality of the *Ancien régime*, and its cosmopolitan view of man as a free and responsible human being, who was capable of independently achieving happiness and moral good, and who showed a profound respect for tolerance and the right to life.

In Lessing's *Nathan*, Saladin proves himself a person of great humanity. To immense popular joy he even succeeds in putting an end to the centuries-old conflict among Muslims, Jews and Christians and restores universal tolerance. The barbarian Thoas, king of Tauris, shows analogous magnanimity when faced with the refusal by Iphigenia, Agamemnon's daughter and now Artemis' priestess, to carry out the human sacrifice of the two Greek young men who have landed on his shores. When the king first orders her to proceed with the sacrifice, as is required by a cruel and ancient law of Tauris against strangers, Iphigenia invokes a more powerful law, which speaks directly to human conscience: the law of humanity and respect for each individual's natural right to life:

> Our passions eagerly catch hold of laws
> Which they can wield as weapons. But to me
> Another law, one far more ancient, speaks,
> And doth command me to withstand thee, king!
> That law declaring sacred every stranger.[41]

Iphigenia's determined opposition to the power of the sovereign ('savage mandates of a man') and to cruel and inhuman traditions came as such a shock to contemporary audiences, partly because it was the stand of a woman who was, at the same time, claiming gender parity:

> I am born as free as a man.
> Did Agamemnon's son before thee stand,
> And thou requiredst what became him not,
> His arm and trusty weapon would defend
> His bosom's freedom. I have only words;
> But it becomes a noble-minded man
> To treat with due respect the words of woman. (p.208-209)

41. *Iphigenia in Tauris*, V.iii. Quotations from this play and *Egmont* are from *Dramatic works of Goethe*, translated by Anna Swanwick (London, 1860), here on p.208.

However, where those magic words, capable of making a man change his mind, really strike Thoas and lead him to set the strangers free is by bringing on the sudden realisation of mankind's universal and cosmopolitan character, i.e. according to a principal tenet of the Enlightenment, of our common *Humanität*:

> And dost thou think
> The savage Scythian will attend the voice
> Of truth and of humanity, unheard
> By the Greek Atreus?

To Thoas' incredulous question Iphigenia replies with the same assuredness as any *Aufklärer*:

> 'Tis heard by all,
> Whate'er may be their clime, within whose breast
> Flows pure and free the gushing stream of life. (p.211)

It is hard to imagine a more effective *mise en scène* of the ethical ideas and the new humanitarian universalism of the Enlightenment, whose moral code was forged in order to defend and enfranchise man, seen as a creature with a natural inclination to do good. These moral tenets now revealed themselves as capable of triumphing over religious beliefs and iniquitous and inhuman laws, winning over to their side even kings like Saladin and Thoas.

In the years before the French Revolution, young Goethe took an active part in the politicisation of the Late Enlightenment, that is to say in its transformation into a great political and cultural attack on the *Ancien régime*, by supporting the new republican spirit against absolutism. This is borne out by the conversations that he had in Naples with 'Brother' Filangieri in 1787, when the latter had already become famous in Germany through the translations of his *Science of legislation*. In his travel diary, Goethe records: 'He is also oppressed by his fears of Joseph II. The thought of a despot, even as a phantom possibility, is horrible to noble minds. He told me quite frankly what Naples might expect from this man.'[42] That Goethe shared these fears is something that comes out all too clearly from the final version of his drama on freedom, *Egmont* (1788).

It is surely not a coincidence that Goethe finished writing this play at the time of the republican revolt in Brabant against the absolutist

42. Goethe, *Italian journey*, p.192 (cf. Becchi, *Vico e Filangieri in Germania*, p.109).

reforms imposed by Joseph II. It depicts the ideological and political struggle between Egmont, hero of the sixteenth-century revolt in the Low Countries, and absolute monarchy, in the form of Philip II's Spain and the notorious duke of Alba. The political meaning of this work is concentrated in act 4. Raising the thorny issue of the legitimacy and limitations of the power of the sovereign in relation to the natural and historical rights of the Dutch people, Egmont wonders 'who would deliver us from absolute caprice [...]?'[43] That is to say, who will put a stop to Philip II's despotic will and his determination to subjugate the Dutch people and 'to rob them of their ancient rights, to appropriate their possessions' (p.374)? When the duke of Alba tries to argue for the positive aspects of Philip II's reforms, which were supposed to bring peace and prosperity to the people, Egmont objects: 'these arbitrary changes, these unlimited encroachments of the supreme power, are they not indications that one will permit himself to do what is forbidden to thousands?' (p.376). Ultimately, the duke's position is not only fiercely disdainful but also morally inacceptable: 'Liberty! A fair word when rightly understood. What liberty would they have? [...] Far better is it to circumscribe their power, to control and guide them for their good, as children are controlled and guided. Trust me, a people grows neither old nor wise, a people remains always in its infancy' (p.374-75).

In the years that he spent in Italy, from 1786 to 1788, Goethe completed those tragedies, such as *Iphigenia* and *Egmont*, that display his political engagement against despotism and in favour of freedom and the Enlightenment values that can be summarised under the heading of *Humanität*. At the same time, however, he continued his investigation into the relationship between art and politics, the useful and the beautiful, the history of nature and the history of man. Faced with the amazingly stratified civilisation in the peninsula, the smooth progress of human improvement, without violent interruptions or revolutions, the slow transformation of those worlds, he became more and more persuaded that the political and cultural programme of the Enlightenment as described by Lessing was the best and perhaps the only viable proposition from a political point of view: mankind must be patiently educated to the values of emancipation and human rights. In this sense art and poetry could and should contribute to this project, but always according to their own autonomous and immanent rules.

43. See act 4 (no scene division), *Dramatic works of Goethe*, p.376. Subsequent page numbers given within the text.

These reflections are already evident in the 1789 tragedy *Torquato Tasso*. In it we witness the existential drama of the Italian poet, his frustration born from the inability to acknowledge the limitations of his art and those of his own existence as a poet. This obviously reflects Goethe's own disillusionment, as he vainly strove to compose the inevitable conflict between poetic ideals and the crude and sometimes petty reality of political activism.

As a militant freemason, even during his travels through Italy Goethe must have been aware of what was happening with the Bavaria Illuminati back home. He would have known that enrolment was continuing throughout Europe, and even in Naples, where, for instance, Francesco Mario Pagano joined the Order with the name of Della Porta.[44] And he must have been seriously concerned about the developments in Germany: how the publication in 1787 of the Order's secret papers at the behest of the Bavarian government revealed not only its subversive character, but also the petty infighting between Knigge and Weishaupt, the latter's moral fragility, the rigid hierarchy and reciprocal spying and blackmailing among adepts. Things certainly did not look very reassuring from the point of view of European public opinion. And the struggle for freedom and the rights of man had receded hopelessly into the distance. Worst of all, the ongoing harsh persecution of the Illuminati was now beginning to look like a proper witch hunt, and the formidable propaganda machinery set in motion to terminally discredit the Order was effectively also placing on trial the whole of the values, ideas and political and cultural programme of the *Aufklärung*, which indeed the Illuminati themselves claimed among their explicit objectives. The idea of joining together the activities of secret societies and certain parts of freemasonry with the Enlightenment programme was turning out to be a serious error of judgement, from which urgent lessons must be learned for the future.

Christoph Wieland was among the first to understand what was at stake, as is shown by an article on the 'secret of the Cosmopolitan Order' that he published in the *Teutscher Merkur* in August 1788. Wieland believed that it was imperative to clarify the fundamental difference between the Enlightenment ideals of the Cosmopolitans and the actions of the secret societies.[45] He explained that the end

44. Cf. Giarrizzo, *Massoneria e Illuminismo*, p.350.

45. See Christoph Martin Wieland, 'Das Geheimniss des Kosmopolitenorderns', in Wieland, *Sämmtliche Werke*, ed. Hamburger Stiftung zur Förderung von

could never in any way justify the means. Secret societies and conspiracies were always to be rejected as contrary to the republican spirit of the Enlightenment and its belief in freedom. Wieland was entirely on the side of reforms rather than subversion or revolution. He insisted that no one, for whatever reason, should attempt to accelerate history, altering the natural pace of the education and progress of mankind described by Lessing. Unsurprisingly, the issue of the use of secrecy in the political and civil struggle immediately became the subject of controversy, being rejected by virtually all the most authoritative figures of the Enlightenment in favour of Kant's *Publizität*. Even Knigge, as early as 1788, issued a public apology and openly condemned all forms of secrecy in political activity.[46]

Even before the notorious episode of the Illuminati, in Berlin the debate in defence of the Enlightenment's ideals was unleashed by the growing threat posed by the Rosicrucians. In addition, former Jesuits based in Austria insidiously put forward a new interpretation in a spiritual and Catholic sense of the word *Aufklärung* itself, as an alternative to the religious reading of the Enlightenment suggested by Lessing and by those freemasons who were close to deism and Spinoza's theories. In the wake of this, in 1784 the recently established *Berlinische Monatsschrift* ran a public competition in order to define what should be intended by the word *Aufklärung*, and how to distinguish between 'true' and 'false' Enlightenment. We have already mentioned Kant's famous essay in reply to this question. Another especially interesting response came from Moses Mendelssohn. After pointing out how intricately interconnected the new terms *Aufklärung*, *Kultur* and *Bildung* were, Mendelssohn attempted to identify some boundaries between them. In particular, he highlighted the importance of the third concept, which he defined as a form of collective acculturation accompanied by individual formative processes, the end result being

---

Wissenschaft und Kultur with the Wieland-Archiv [...] and Hans Radspieler, vol.10 (Hamburg, 1984), p.155-203. For this interpretation of Wieland's article, see Giarrizzo, *Massoneria e Illuminismo*, p.366ff. For a different and, in my view, less convincing reading, see Koselleck, *Critique and crisis*, p.96ff.

46. See Bois, *Adolph Freiherr Knigge*, p.271ff. Doubts and even open aversion towards the questionable practice of secrecy and mysteries are also found in Goethe's *Die Mystifizierten*, written in Rome in 1787, and above all in Schiller's *Der Geisterseher* (*The Ghost seer*, 1787-1789). On the public debate around the Illuminati *affaire*, including the intervention of Wieland and Jacobi, see Hans-Jürgen Schings, *Die Brüder des Marquis Posa: Schiller und der Geheimbund der Illuminaten* (Tübingen, 1996), p.163ff.

to bring about significant modifications in the life and history of a nation in a gradual, non-violent way.[47] This was probably the best way to defend the Enlightenment publicly and with some hope of success: by stressing its vocation to *Bildung* and reform against its enemies, whose number could only grow after the Illuminati debacle.

The most complex and intriguing defence of the political and cultural project of the *Spätaufklärung* in Germany, however, was developed by Friedrich Schiller. Unlike Lessing and Goethe he never joined the freemasons' ranks, despite the fact that this movement, as we have seen, had a profound effect on the history of Europe in those years. He did, however, have an in-depth knowledge of their secrets, as is clear from his novel *The Ghost seer*, published in 1789, against the widespread mania of masonic plots, which were to end badly for their protagonists.[48] He knew the coterie of the Illuminati equally well. His esteemed tutor at the Hohe Karlsschule in Stuttgart was Jakob Friedrich Abel, who had put his competence in the fields of physiology, law and psychology to good use in the new science of anthropology.[49] From 1782, Abel was one of the leaders of the Illuminati, under the name of Pythagoras. Several other of Schiller's friends were also members of the Order, and they tried to recruit him even after the Bavarian government ordered the publication of the Illuminati's *Originalschriften* in 1787.[50] After all, Schiller was, in Diderot's words, a 'furieux de la liberté': his loyalty to the rights of man and the Enlightenment's ideals in general, and his proclaimed hatred of all forms of despotism and tyranny, made him a potentially very suitable candidate for the Order, and a formidable interpreter of their subversive project.

In the summer of 1781 the duke's reaction to the production of Schiller's first work, *The Robbers*, forced him to flee from Württemberg. In 1784, he gave a speech at the German-Palatinate Society in Mannheim in which he illustrated his moral and political idea of the new theatre of the Enlightenment as the direct expression of civil

47. Trampus, *I gesuiti e l'Illuminismo*, p.148ff., reconstructs the buildup to the Berlin competition and discusses the meaning of the various entries.
48. Cf. *The Works of Frederick Schiller*, 4 vols, Bohn's standard library series (London, 1854-1865), vol.4: *Early dramas and romances*.
49. On this important aspect of Schiller's education and how it was entirely in line with what was happening in the rest of Europe see Wolfgang Riedel, *Die Anthropologie des jungen Schillers: zur Ideengeschichte der medizinischen Schriften und der philosophischen Briefe* (Würzburg, 1985).
50. Cf. Schings, *Die Brüder des Marquis Posa*.

society and of its values, which placed at its centre the individual, who was free and equal among his peers. This dramatic form was in direct contrast with *Ancien régime* court theatre. For Schiller, every aspect of the aesthetic revolution that had begun with Diderot and Lessing was a great opportunity to defend and liberate man in society, using art and poetry to carry out a critical study of his passions, his history and his rights, and to set out the result of this study freely before the audience, with the aim of involving them emotionally in this project.

It was because Schiller immediately realised the enfranchising power of theatre, and its function as a powerful instrument of political interaction with the nascent public opinion, that he became one of the protagonists in the politicisation of the *Spätaufklärung*. Faced with the crushing censorship of absolutist states and the (more or less) enlightened despotism of late-eighteenth-century monarchs such as Frederick II or Catherine the Great, he conceived of the stage as a bastion of truth. It was a place that allowed an author to be a poet and a political writer at the same time, and to influence the conscience and mind of individuals, mobilising the public in defence of man and his rights against tyranny. A writer could thus contribute to the triumph of what was right and the demise of what was unjust. As Schiller stated, with fittingly juridical language, '[t]he jurisdiction of the stage begins at the point where the sphere of secular laws ends.'[51]

And yet Schiller's idea of the theatre of the Enlightenment was more than a simple form of moral propaganda. It went beyond even a passionate kind of political activism, or a project of cultural hegemony that would place the man of letters at the helm of the new civil society, upsetting the previous balance of power. If his views had been entirely contained within these parameters, then probably he would have accepted the multiple invitations to join the Order of the Illuminati. But as an *Aufklärer* Schiller chose to follow a different path. He remained first and foremost an Enlightenment thinker, determined to explore to its utmost depth the relationship between this original cultural system and reality in all its forms. This reality primarily interested him in its form as human and intellectual experience. In all his greatest works he experimented with the extent and limitations of this new humanism, probing its

51. Quoted in Koselleck, *Critique and crisis*, p.98. Koselleck rightly devotes ample room to Schiller's political and aesthetic thought. See also Israel, *Democratic Enlightenment*, p.751ff.

possible contradictions in his drama. And throughout he maintained a detached and critical attitude towards freemasonry and, indeed, any form of institutional power.

In *The Robbers*, Schiller's passionate belief in individual freedom and hatred for despotism led him to transform the character of Karl Moor into a ringleader, a rebel and a defender of freedom who abhors man's domination over other men in all its guises. In the 1784 drama *Love and intrigue* the clash between the amoral world of the old aristocracy and the morally pure new bourgeoisie, capable of overcoming all social and political differences, inevitably ends in tragedy. And in 1783 *The Conspiracy of Fiesco at Genoa* dissects on stage an especially tormented and heartfelt issue: how liberty itself can be contradictory when it comes into contact with the demonic aspect of power, that will to power that lurks in the heart of every individual, even when they are acting for the common good. Count Fiesco is faced with the alternative of defeating tyranny and bringing the republic back to Genoa, or becoming himself the city's new absolute ruler, thus renewing the old form of domination. Schiller completed this work, after several redactions, in 1786, once again with a tragic ending.

Like Diderot in *Le Neveu de Rameau* or Vittorio Alfieri in *Della tirannide*, Schiller embodied the most restless and original spirit of the Late Enlightenment's aesthetic revolution. For the first time, in placing man decidedly at the centre of things this revolution truly tested his physical and moral humanity. It investigated the most profoundly tragic aspects of the liberty of the moderns, its limits, and the inescapable presence of evil. It sought to make sense of contradictory needs and impulses: on the one hand the claims of natural law; on the other, history, destiny, man's physiological drives that placed self-love on a collision course with the love of others, thus causing other fundamental conflicts, such as those between liberty and responsibility, or the will to power and respect for the rights of man. These dramatic contradictions were indeed inherent in the Enlightenment's project of emancipation. From Hegel onwards they would give rise to a polemical mystification, in the form of the eminently philosophical paradigm of the 'dialectics of the Enlightenment'.[52] In fact, they remained at the core of Schiller's artistic and intellectual experience until his death in 1805.

52. For a critique of the application of Hegel's dialectical paradigm to historical events see Ferrone, *The Enlightenment*, p.16ff.

In *Don Carlos*, first performed in Hamburg in 1787, all these elements come to fruition and are interwoven with the history of the rights of man in Germany and the issue of the Illuminati itself. As Schiller wrote in his 'Letters on Don Carlos' (1788), his tragedy was meant to mirror facts and ideas that were in the common domain at the time, such as 'the sense of freedom in the battle with despotism, the chains of stupidity shattered, thousand-year-old prejudices convulsed, a nation that demands the return of its human rights, republican virtues put into practice, clearer concepts in circulation, minds in ferment, hearts lifted by an inspired concern'.[53]

And so it was. The play was a great success, and the Illuminati in particular saw in it a representation of their own project. And indeed, there could be nothing more apt than the dialogue between the marquis of Posa and Philip II in the famous third act to stir the soul of the audience in favour of liberty and the rights of man in those tumultuous years just before the French Revolution. The king is about to unleash the offensive that was to enslave the Netherlands to absolutism and the Spanish Inquisition, but the marquis is urging him to change course entirely and take on board the widespread new republican spirit based on humanity, universal tolerance and liberty of conscience:

> but grant us liberty of thought [...]
> You can do it, Sire!
> Who else? Devote to your own people's bliss,
> The kingly power, which has too long enrich'd
> The greatness of the throne alone. Restore
> The prostrate dignity of human nature,
> And let the subject be, what once he was,
> The end and object of the monarch's care,
> Bound by no duty, save a brother's love.
> And when mankind is to itself restored,
> Roused to a sense of its own innate worth,
> When freedom's lofty virtues proudly flourish –
> Then, Sire, when you have made your own wide realms
> The happiest in the world, it then may be
> Your duty, to subdue the universe.[54]

53. Friedrich Schiller, 'Letters on *Don Carlos*', translated by Jeanne R. Willson, in Schiller, *Plays: Intrigue and love and Don Carlos*, ed. Walter Hinderer (New York, 1983), p.305-46 (332). See also Schings, *Die Brüder des Marquis Posa*, p.1.
54. Friedrich Schiller, *Don Carlos*, III.x (see vol.3 of *The Works of Frederick Schiller*, p.113-14).

The marquis of Posa, who calls himself 'the world's citizen' (p.107), does not hesitate to ply a disconcerted but intrigued king with flattery and threats in equal measure:

> You would plant
> For all eternity – and yet the seeds
> You sow around you are the seeds of death!
> [...] Man is greater
> Than you esteem him. He will burst the chains
> Of a long slumber, and reclaim once more
> His just and hallow'd rights. With Nero's name,
> And fell Busiris', will he couple yours:
> And – ah! you once deserved a better fate. (p.112-13)

However, as the story develops, as family and political relationships, feelings, friendships and alliances are all swept away by the overriding purpose of bringing about a radical transformation in a very short time, the marquis of Posa, through his contradictory actions, ultimately becomes the most ambiguous and controversial political hero in the history of German theatre. This character, an explicit representation of an Illuminato in action, is Schiller's contribution as an *Aufklärer* to the debates that were taking place in those years. It constitutes a formidable critique of the Order and, more generally, of all those who believed that the course of history could be speeded up by means of secret societies, plots and the violent assumption of power. The true programme of the *Aufklärung* consisted instead, as indicated by Lessing, in gradual reform and the education of mankind in the respect of rights.[55] As Schiller wrote in the 'Letters on *Don Carlos*':

> Give me the name, dear friend [...] give me the name of the founder of an order or even of the order itself that – with the purest designs and most noble impulses – has always kept itself free of arbitrary acts in the application of acts of violence against the freedom of those outside of it, of the essence of secrecy and lust for power. (p.340)

55. See Schings, *Die Brüder des Marquis Posa*, p.23ff., which quotes from the tenth letter on *Don Carlos*, where Schiller writes: 'I am neither an Illuminati nor a Mason, but if both fraternal orders have a moral purpose in common, and if this purpose is the most important one for the society of men, then it must be at least very closely related to the one that Marquis Posa proposed' ('Letters on *Don Carlos*', p.337). An important discussion of this passage can be found in Maria Carolina Foi's 'La buona causa e i mezzi ignobili', introductory essay to her edition of Schiller, *Don Carlos* (Venice, 2004), p.11-47, on p.36.

Thus, the danger for mankind lay not only in the form of tyranny openly practised by sovereigns. The actions of those who proclaimed themselves defenders of the rights of man, with moralistic attitude and ambiguity of intent, could also easily degenerate into fanaticism and despotism. In Schiller's view this distressing realisation was clearly borne out by the case of the Illuminati. One must then be constantly on the alert when it came to the delicate relationship between ends and means in political action. Abstract reason, with its impatience, ideological fanaticism, the untameable logic of the will to power: these could all turn the liberation and emancipation project into hell on earth. Schiller is well aware of this, and in the eleventh of his 'Letters on *Don Carlos*' he writes:

> the most unselfish, purest, and noblest person, because of enthusiastic devotion to his idea of virtue and happiness to be gained, is very often displayed dealing just as arbitrarily with individuals as even the most selfish despot [...] True greatness of mind often leads no less to the violation of the freedom of others than does selfishness and the lust of power, because it acts for the sake of action, not for the sake of the individual subject. (p.339)[56]

With *Don Carlos* and his acute and prophetic reflection on the Bavaria Illuminati, Schiller effectively paved the way for the *Spätaufklärung*'s ideological unmasking of the grand social utopias and logics of power and domination that always lurked at the bottom of human actions. This path has not been sufficiently explored by researchers, whose views are still too often trapped in an oversimplifying dialectic of Enlightenment or in a teleology that sees the French Revolution as the ultimate point of arrival of this process. The Illuminati were a truly important episode in German political history.[57] Being familiar with this, Schiller would have found nothing of what happened with the French Revolution and the ensuing Terror – not even the fact that the latter was incredibly being perpetrated in the name of the rights of man – as entirely a surprise. It is simply not true that he retreated into an astonished silence, falling back onto conservative positions. Like Goethe in fact, he simply continued in his Enlightenment-inspired

56. On this passage, see Maria Carolina Foi, 'Il prezzo dell'amore: incontri pericolosi nel *Don Carlos* di Schiller', in *Cultura e rappresentazione nell'età di Goethe*, ed. Michele Cometa and Luca Crescenzi (Rome, 2003), p.105-40 (132).

57. Cf. Valjavec, *Entstehung der politischen Strömungen*, p.229; Epstein, *Genesis of German conservatism*, p.35ff.

pursuit of the truth about man, by means of art and its independent rules. If anything, he became more and more convinced that the key to human emancipation lay not, as Kant seemed to believe, in the laws of humanity's progress, as described by the new philosophies of universal history, but solely in the daily practice of individual ethical responsibilities in the respect of the rights of man. And an important part of this process would be the full acknowledgement of the role played by art alongside reason in educating humanity and bringing positive results from both the moral and the political point of view.

Schiller's attitude may have acquired a new edge after 1789. He may have felt more keenly the need to rescue and preserve the Enlightenment's values for future generations from the destructive clash between revolutionaries and reactionaries. But he continued his passionately creative research into the rights of man, the tragedy of liberty in its concrete historical development, and the phenomenology of power and domination in history. In 1799 he concluded his Wallenstein trilogy, which explores the disquieting aspects of the psychology of the great man of power. This led him to investigate and discover the pernicious effects of individual self-centredness, the increasingly dominant role played by economic interests in social and political life, as well as the way in which the noblest patriotic or religious ideals could serve as an ideological pretext for the pursuit of wealth and power.

Mary Stuart (1799-1800) again explores the issues of political assassination and the natural rights to life and liberty, this time in relation to the highly dramatic conflict between two queens. It was, however, with *Wilhelm Tell* (1803-1804) that Schiller composed his spiritual will, completing his reflection on the true meaning of rights in the history of humanity. These were meant to be forever the main instrument for the defence of man. The cry of pain and hope that Tell sends forth to his people and to the whole of mankind resonates as strong and clear today as it would have done for his contemporaries:

> Yes! there's a limit to the despot's power!
> When the oppress'd looks round in vain for justice,
> When his sore burden may no longer be borne,
> With fearless heart he makes appeal to Heaven,
> And thence brings down his everlasting rights,
> Which there abide, inalienably his,
> And indestructible as are the stars.[58]

58. Friedrich Schiller, *Wilhelm Tell*, act 2, scene 2 (see vol.2 of *The Works of Frederick Schiller*, p.490). On the idea of human dignity in eighteenth-century Germany,

This was in marked contrast with the propaganda linked to the French Revolution, where the defence of the rights of man had in fact betrayed the Enlightenment's spirit of liberty, as it degenerated into the Terror and then the imperialism of the *Grande Nation*. In *Wilhelm Tell*, Schiller links those rights with the centuries-old history of political communities and their struggle for freedom. This tragedy illustrated very clearly how these rights – the true rights of man – were not something that was bestowed from above or by foreign armies. They were rooted in history and custom. They were the natural and elementary rights of a people who had learned in the course of the centuries to take charge of their own defence, and were entitled to their liberty and human dignity. In fact, their claims resembled those on which the English constitution was based, with its foundations in material conditions and customs. And indeed that constitution, as originally described by Blackstone, was relaunched by Burke as a polemical response to Richard Price in a 1790 work entitled *Reflections on the Revolution in France*, which was translated into German only three years later.

As Schiller knew, the main problem in Germany was no longer simply how to use artistic representation in order to create a public opinion that would support the rights. It was how to protect and concretely apply those rights now that their true political emancipatory meaning had become clear, since this involved a complete overhaul of the State, the only institution that seemed then capable of achieving this within the Holy Roman Empire. But this was not, of course, the kind of despotic State theorised by the supporters of absolutism, against which Schiller fought throughout his life. As he wrote in his essay on 'The legislation of Lycurgus and Solon':

> Everything can be sacrificed for the good of the State, except that for which the State is only a means. The State is never an end unto itself. It is important only insofar as it creates the conditions in which humanity's objective can be fulfilled, and this objective is none other than the development of a person's full strength, i.e. progress.[59]

and especially on the issue of the rights of man in *Wilhelm Tell*, see Bloch, *Natural law*, p.59. See also Maria Carolina Foi, 'Schiller und Erhard: Literatur und Politik in der Weimarer Klassik', *Jahrbuch der Deutschen Schillergesellschaft* 49 (2005), p.193-223. On Schiller in general see also Frederick C. Beiser, *Schiller as philosopher: a re-examination* (Oxford, 2005).

59. Cf. Friedrich Schiller, *Werke: Nationalausgabe*, vol.14: *Bühnenbearbeitungen*, part 2, ed. Hans Heinrich Borcherdt (Weimar, 1949), p.423. These issues show how

This perfectly summarised the Enlightenment idea of the State *ex parte civium*, which was built from the bottom upwards with the purpose of defending the rights of man. This view rediscovered the natural right to resistance and the need for republican self-government, and left no room for enlightened despotism. This was part of a change that took place in the years before and after the Revolution also thanks to the dissemination of Enlightenment values through literature and the theatre in the works of Lessing, Goethe and Schiller. The need to establish a new and different relationship between State and natural rights was now felt as especially urgent in the political laboratory that was represented not only by the *Spätaufklärung*, but more generally by all German political thinkers in the last thirty years of the century.

As we have repeatedly shown, these years were a time of great discontinuity and were rife with consequences in the history of the Holy Roman empire. This included the open critique and dismissal of the old natural law of Pufendorf and Wolff, according to which rights were granted by the sovereign and only existed as duties within an authoritarian and absolutist programme of social discipline. To oppose this, many German thinkers championed a liberal natural law along the lines put forward by John Locke. These authors supported an idea that was gathering increasing consensus in all parts of Europe: that of a civil society that conformed to the state of nature and was populated by free men, all equally endowed with rights. They also looked with approval to the new Enlightenment constitutionalism of Filangieri, Condorcet and Paine, all of whom had greatly profited from the lessons that could be learned from the American Revolution.

Thanks partly to their support for 'legal despotism', German physiocrats rapidly won their struggle for economic freedom, which triumphed everywhere despite the cameralists' opposition. However, they faced a far more complex battle in their attempt to obtain political freedom and transform natural rights into political rights, in the wake of the Enlightenment's campaigns against servitude of the glebe, a census-based juridical system and aristocratic privileges. Their task became all the more arduous in the 1790s with the rise of a small but vocal Jacobin movement, which was inspired by Rousseau's theories, democratic radicalism, and the primacy of legislation and

---

deeply Schiller's theatre engaged with the political and juridical language of the European tradition of the Enlightenment: see Maria Carolina Foi, *La giurisdizione delle scene: i drammi politici di Schiller* (Macerata, 2013).

of the general will in the defence of the rights of man. Soon a third political and cultural movement arose in opposition to both these aspects of nascent German liberalism – one moderate and republican, the other radical and democratic, but both equally inspired by the values and ideals of the European Late Enlightenment. This third player on the scene was the movement led by the Rosicrucians and the Jesuits in defence of the *Ancien régime*, its logic of power, its pervasive community- and hierarchy-based ideal, a movement that was determined to preserve privileges and inequalities, giving a more modern twist, insofar as possible, to ancient forms of domination, but always with a fundamentally reactionary outlook.[60]

What was probably the first important battle in what would become the decades-long struggle for and against the politics of the moderns and its focus on rights was fought in Berlin. From 1783 the intellectual elite close to the Enlightenment had been meeting in the (secret) Berlin Wednesday Society (Mittwochsgesellschaft) in order to ask bold questions concerning the philosophy of history, the reform of the State and how to protect the rights of man.[61] In Frederick's police state, secrecy was obviously a necessary element in a society that discussed issues such as freedom of the press or transparency and openness in government decisions, and that was open to the gradual introduction of republican forms of political representation. In 1785, the *Berlinische Monatsschrift*, which was effectively the unofficial journal of the Mittwochsgesellschaft, published an anonymous project of constitutional reform that was far more advanced than Frederick's absolutism.[62]

Both before and after the Revolution, the *Berlinische Monatsschrift* published several other important contributions to the debate on the rights of man and a new constitutional State. In the autumn of 1790, together with Friedrich von Gentz, Swiss author Eduard von Clauer wrote a number of articles in favour of French revolutionary constitutionalism and the inalienability and equality of rights before the State, arguing against Justus Möser and his census-based view

60. This important historical phase is yet to be studied in all its specific characteristics. For a preliminary bibliography and useful discussion of this heated political and cultural debate in the context of the European Enlightenment in general, thankfully without reference to the myth of a German *Sonderweg*, see Klippel, 'The true concept of liberty', p.459ff.
61. On the Mittwochsgesellschaft see Tortarolo, *La ragione sulla Sprea*, p.165ff.
62. Cf. Karl Otmar von Aretin, *Heiliges Römisches Reich 1776-1806: Reichsverfassung und Staatssouveränität*, 2 vols (Wiesbaden, 1967), vol.1, p.91ff.

of society.[63] In 1792 Wilhelm von Humboldt published his significantly titled *Ideen zu einem Versuch: die Grenzen der Wirksamkeit des Staats zu bestimmen*.[64] In the debates within the Mittwochsgesellschaft it was the civil servant and Enlightenment supporter Christian Dohm who introduced the constitutional ideas of Paine and the American colonies with his contributions and translations. The views thus put forward by Dohm were opposed both to the English mixed-government formula and to Montesquieu's view of the positive function of the intermediate classes and institutions in limiting sovereignty and thus helping ensure liberty, the latter view being supported in Germany by those who were in favour of a census-based system.

Another important political figure in Berlin, the jurist Ernst Ferdinand Klein, brought to members' attention Gaetano Filangieri's constitutionalism, as set out in his *Science of legislation* in opposition not only to the *Ancien régime* logic of power but also to the views propounded by Montesquieu and Blackstone. As a member of the committee instructed by Frederick II in 1780 to draw up the *Allgemeines Landrecht für die Königlich-Preußischen Staaten*, the Prussian civil code, Klein was well placed to appreciate the strongly innovative aspects of Filangieri's work, from its republican spirit, the historical character of legislation, the struggle against feudalism and servitude of the glebe to the denunciation of aristocratic privileges and of a law system based on census, and the call for a written constitution and more generally for a modern and rational juridical system founded on the universal and equal rights of man. However, Klein used Filangieri's work mostly as a pivotal element in his debate with Johann Georg Schlosser, who strenuously defended the ancient German liberties and anachronistic privileges of the feudal system.[65]

In 1789 Schlosser wrote in negative terms about the *Science of legislation*, 'whose eager reception in Italy, France and Germany

63. Cf. Hans Erich Bödeker, 'Zur Rezeption der Menschen- und Bürgerrechte von 1789/1791 in der deutschen Aufklärungsgesellschaft', in *Grund- und Freiheitsrechte im Wandel von Gesellschaft und Geschichte: Beiträge zur Geschichte der Grund- und Freiheitsrechte vom Ausgang des Mittelalters bis zur Revolution von 1848*, ed. Günter Birtsch (Göttingen, 1981), p.258-86 (274ff.).

64. Cf. Wilhelm von Humboldt, *The Limits of state action*, ed. and with an introduction and notes by J. W. Burrow (Cambridge, 1969). I am grateful to Guglielmo Gabbiadini for bringing this text to my attention. It is also interesting to note that the nineteenth-century translation of this text by Joseph Coulthard, Jr, bears the more anodyne title *The Sphere and duties of government* (London, 1854).

65. Tortarolo, *La ragione sulla Sprea*, p.208ff.

certainly does not bode well for the philosophical spirit of our century, at least in this field'. He thus shows his awareness of how important and dangerous this text was in terms of the constitutional debate that was then taking place in Germany for the first time in history.[66] In fact, after a period of huge fortune Filangieri's work was completely forgotten, which raises important questions on the cause of such rapid reversals in those tumultuous years.

We know that Filangieri's work was immediately translated into German, French, Spanish, Russian, Swedish and English, mostly by figures linked jointly to the Enlightenment and the masonic lodges. Three German-language editions were exhibited at the Frankfurt book fair in 1784, printed respectively in Vienna, Switzerland and Ansbach, Franconia, the latter going through three subsequent reprints.[67] This translation included a rich apparatus of notes and was carried out at the behest of jurist and freemason Johann Christian Siebenkees, who was a university professor and edited important journals such as the *Allgemeine Juristische Bibliothek*, the *Juristisches Magazin* and the *Neues Juristisches Magazin*. As if to promote Filangieri's work even further, in 1790 Friedrich Münter, the Danish bishop who had been given by the Bavaria Illuminati the task of recruiting new members in Italy, was responsible for the publication, again in Ansbach, of an impressive edition of the *Elogio storico del cavaliere Gaetano Filangieri*, written by Donato Tommasi, who was also close to the Order. All in all, these factors point to the entire operation being part of the Brotherhood's strategies, especially where the Illuminati are concerned, who, as we know, continued to be present on the political scene despite the climate of tension and persecution.

Münter presented Filangieri as the most important Italian expert in the 'science of the State', a cosmopolitan thinker whose 'heart was inflamed with passion for the rights and liberties of men, and who spoke of despots with unusual fervour'.[68] The influence of Filangieri could then help steer towards the Enlightenment's modern rights-based constitutionalism the debate that had begun in Berlin in 1780 with the drafting of the *Allgemeines Landrecht*. This was indeed his perceived role, and it attracted fierce criticism from many German

66. On Schlosser's attitude to Filangieri see Antonio Trampus, 'Linguaggi della politica e lessico costituzionale: Filangieri e i traduttori tedeschi', in *Diritti e costituzione*, ed. A. Trampus, p.85-126 (89).
67. Cf. Trampus, 'Linguaggi della politica', p.90ff.
68. Cf. Becchi, *Vico e Filangieri in Germania*, p.129.

supporters of the *Ancien régime*. Chief among these was Schlosser, who singled out the Neapolitan jurist for explicit criticism in the title of his 1789 essay against the redaction of a code of law.[69]

Schlosser accused Filangieri of republicanism and of being an enemy of the feudal aristocracy and the ancient German liberties. He was guilty of wanting to replace the ancient and glorious census-based system of political participation, represented by the *Reichsstände* of the empire, with elective popular sovereignty, as in the representative government developed in the American former colonies. Above all, Schlosser criticised Filangieri's idea of law and legislation as an act of will, a form of what 'ought to be'. Schlosser was fiercely opposed to the right of resistance and above all to the new idea of the constitution as a written text, which had a fundamental role to play in safeguarding the rights of man and finally defining the boundaries of legislative, executive and judiciary power. More than in the field of penal law, where his name was increasingly associated with those of Beccaria and Mario Pagano, it was in this respect that Filangieri contributed, to a major extent, to the development of the modern constitutional lexicon in Germany.

This led to a new and original constitutionalism that was distinct from both the traditional material constitution (*Verfassung*) and the codification method with which several European countries experimented in the course of the eighteenth century, which mostly led to mere forms of juridical 'consolidation' and rationalisation of ancient norms.[70] It was through the translations of the *Science of legislation* and the furious reactions of critics such as Schlosser that the German juridical and political lexicon acquired the term *Konstitution*, meaning the fundamental law of the State. Above all this led to the first tentative reflections on the form of constitutionalism put forward by the Enlightenment.[71]

Those reflections were indeed tentative, however, and met with strong opposition. The cause of the new constitutional ideas was

69. See Johann Georg Schlosser, *Briefe über die Gesetzgebung überhaupt und den Entwurf des preussischen Gesetzbuchs insbesondere* (Frankfurt am Main, Fleischer, 1789), p.1-81: 'Erstes Schreiben: Allgemeine Gründe, warum die Verfassung eines Gesetzbuchs zu unsern Zeiten nicht räthlich ist, gegen Filangieri'.

70. On the fundamental difference between eighteenth-century forms of codification and the nascent modern forms of constitutionalism see Giovanni Tarello, *Storia della cultura giuridica moderna*, vol.1: *Assolutismo e codificazione del diritto* (Bologna, 1976).

71. On this see Trampus, 'Linguaggi della politica', p.116ff.

not helped by the intervention of the Bavaria Illuminati or the Brotherhood as a whole, nor by the admiration for Filangieri, their most authoritative spokesperson, expressed by prominent figures with links to the Order, such as Goethe, Nicolai or Wieland.[72] In 1786 Frederick II died and was succeeded by Frederick William II, who was close to the Rosicrucian and anti-Enlightenment environments. This brought about a complete change in the political climate in Berlin. The new sovereign was determined to suppress the Illuminati once and for all, and to quash any attempt at transforming the rights of man into constitutionally guaranteed political rights, or any temptation within the *Gesetzkommission* to replace the code with the 'actual fundamental constitution'.[73] Even a few months before the start of the French Revolution the sovereign was still writing about his intentions in this respect to the prince-elector of Saxony. In his letter he warns the elector that despite having been disbanded and harshly persecuted the Order is still dangerous, and its members are continuing 'to teach their adherents all kinds of extravagant notions, under the name of the rights of mankind'.[74]

It is not surprising, therefore, that there was a shift in balance and mood inside both the *Gesetzkommission* that was to draft the code and the meetings of the Mittwochsgesellschaft. In 1789, Carl Svarez, the main figure within the commission, explained to his colleagues in the secret society that, in accordance with the new sovereign's will, the legal code should be seen as a constitution substitute that could pave the way for the concrete practice of natural rights, but that it should always take into account the juridical tradition of the Holy Roman empire and the social and political model of the ancient German liberties.[75]

Then, the French Revolution and its horrific aftermath completely changed the historical context and heavily influenced the work of the *Gesetzkommission* as indeed political life as a whole in Berlin and throughout Europe. The harsh reaction by the supporters of the *Ancien*

72. Still in 1792 Wieland was writing in positive terms about Filangieri in his journal, *Der Neue Teutsche Merkur*: cf. Antonio Trampus, 'Verfassung und Rechte: Filangieri und die europäische Rezeption der *Scienza della legislazione*', in *Italien in Europa*, ed. Thomas Kroll and Frank Jung (Munich, 2014), p.119-41.
73. Cf. Reinhart Koselleck, *Preussen zwischen Reform und Revolution: Allgemeines Landrecht, Verwaltung und soziale Bewegung von 1791 bis 1848* (Stuttgart, 1967), p.30.
74. Cf. Möller, *Fürstenstaat oder Bürgernation*, p.508.
75. See Tortarolo, *La ragione sulla Sprea*, p.226. On the use of Filangieri's work by the *Gesetzkommission*, and in particular by Christoph Gossler, see p.221ff.

régime, who had always been especially strong in Germany, put serious obstacles in the way of the *Spätaufklärung* as a political laboratory of modernity, the pursuit of a new idea of *Humanität*, and the acknowledgement of the rights of man as constitutionally safeguarded political rights of the individual, as indicated by Condorcet, Filangieri, Price and Paine.

The *Allgemeines Landrecht*, issued in 1794, would continue to play an important role in the social and political history of Prussia up to the turn of the twentieth century. To contemporary observers, it immediately appeared like a two-faced Janus, or rather as a monstrously hybrid juridical creature: a modern head on a gothic body, as Toqueville called it.[76] As was to be expected from the successors of Christian Wolff, from the very beginning, in 1780, the authors of the Prussian code showed great attention towards the language of natural rights. It was this, rather than the old idea of the divine origin of sovereignty, that legitimised the modern State, since the latter was the only institution that was thought to be capable of guaranteeing the exercise of rights, which was impossible in the violent state of nature.[77]

After the episode of the Illuminati and the tensions that arose from the French Revolution, the problem was what kind of relationship should exist between rights and the State. What came first? The Enlightenment's constitutionalism placed rights first. It entrusted a written constitution with their defence, fully in line with Locke's idea of a civil society of free and equal individuals who all held the same inalienable and imprescriptible rights. This society was entirely autonomous from the State, which was a mere instrument for the safeguard of rights. By contrast, the members of the *Gesetzkommission* applied in new ways the principles of Hobbes' *Leviathan*, as developed by the absolutism of Pufendorf and Wolff according to the *societas civilis sive status* formula.[78] Their idea of civil society did not focus on

76. See Kowohl De Rosa, *Storia della cultura tedesca*, p.58.
77. On the preliminary debate within the *Gesetzkommision* see Innocenzo Cervelli, 'Ceti e assolutismo in Germania: rassegna di studi e problemi', *Annali dell'Istituto storico italo-germanico in Trento* 3 (1977), p.431-512; Damiano Canale, 'Dagli stati della persona alle persone dello Stato: Wolff e le origini sistematiche dell'*Allgemeines Landrecht* prussiano del 1794', *Materiali per una storia della cultura giuridica* 28 (1998), p.139-94. On Svarez's *Vorträge* see Emilio Bussi, *Stato e amministrazione nel pensiero di Carl Gottlieb Svarez precettore di Federico Guglielmo III di Prussia* (Milan, 1966).
78. On the Hobbesian character of Frederick's State see Carl Schmitt, *The Leviathan*

the individual, as in the Enlightenment, but consisted in a hierarchy of classes organically shaped and legitimised by the State. In this sense the solemn introduction to the General Code was extremely clear in founding the existence and exercise of natural rights on the State and social status. It did not grant civil society any specific autonomy or make any concessions to natural equality: 'The specific rights and duties of the members of the State are founded only on the personal relationship of each with one another and with the State.'[79]

Thus the defining feature of the Prussian code was the way in which the defence and exercise of rights came to be 'statalised' and linked to birth status, with a paradoxical twist that made them dependent on the limits imposed by the State. While in Rousseau the preservation of individual rights was entrusted to legislation and the general will of the democratic republic, and in Filangieri the rights were constitutionalised and judges made responsible for their protection, in Germany the State proclaimed itself lord and master over the rights of its citizens. In this way, civil society was effectively subsumed into that new omnipotent deity that was the Prussian Leviathan, natural right disappeared entirely from German history, merging into the new state code, and the safeguard of rights and the preservation of man became entirely dependent on the fatherly benevolence of the sovereign, who was the first servant of the State. As in the past, no concession was made to the right of resistance or republican forms of political representation. The State was legitimised by the safeguard of these rights, which was its main purpose, but it could nonetheless suspend their exercise at any time. With a reprise of Kant's famous observations in *Was ist Aufklärung?* Svarez reiterated that the new *Staatsbürger* was indeed allowed to think freely in the privacy of his own conscience, but externally must always obey.[80]

---

in the state theory of Thomas Hobbes: meaning and failure of a political symbol, translated by George Schwab and Erna Hilfstein (Westport, CT, and London, 1996), p.97.

79. See the *Allgemeines Landrecht für die Preussischen Staaten*, *Einleitung*, I, 83: 'Die besonderen Rechte und Pflichten der Mitglieder des Staats beruhen auf dem persönlichen Verhältnisse, in welchem ein jeder gegen den andern und gegen den Staat selbst, sich befindet'. Tortarolo, *La ragione sulla Sprea*, rightly describes this as the 'defeat of a political culture that had been unable to fully develop its identity as an autonomous offshoot of the Enlightenment's concern with reforms and natural law and produce a civil society that, however fragile in itself, was autonomous from the State' (p.324).

80. Cf. Koselleck, *Preussen*, p.27. Koselleck shows how in the final version of the General Code of 1794 'it was significant that citizens' right to natural freedom

Nevertheless, the General Code was obviously modern in several respects. It took important steps forward towards a rational and uniform juridical system that applied to the whole territory, with a view to going beyond medieval juridical pluralism. It cannot be denied that it was the most important and interesting result of a process that had begun centuries earlier, in which the absolutist State attempted to gather all aspects of civil life into its own hands, so that the ancient will to power of divine-right sovereigns became the modern abstract omnipotence of state law. This accomplished the final move from the personal sovereignty of the monarch to the sovereignty of the State, embodied in a total entity in which the rights of the single citizen – including those of the supreme head of state, the king as the first civil servant – were strictly regulated and linked to the relevant duties.

And indeed, picking up on Tocqueville's metaphor, this 'modern head' rested on a body that was quite obviously 'gothic', in the sense that this body was descended from the hierarchical, organicistic and communitarian logics of the *Ancien régime*. The Leviathan that emerged out of the code did attempt to give some uniformity to the old class-based order, assigning a new public role to social classes, but it also preserved their traditional privileges. Effectively, the code had a subsidiary function in relation to statutes and customs, which eventually led to administrators and the bureaucratic apparatus gaining a huge amount of power, in a way that characterised the history of Prussia in the following centuries.[81] These bureaucrats never had much sympathy for the rights of man in the 1789 Declaration, which they considered a negative offshoot of the French Revolution, that is to say something alien to Germanic law and culture rather than a result of the indigenous *Spätaufklärung*.

Quite simply, the *Allgemeines Landrecht* was a significant setback for the Enlightenment in Germany and Europe as a whole. It effectively shipwrecked, or politically neutralised, the republican emancipation project that hinged on the rights of man and aimed to transform natural rights into political rights so as to set limits on the sovereignty

and the safeguard of their individual rights were suppressed […] Despite its reference to fundamental rights, the code failed to go beyond Old Fritz's praxis. The monarch remained the absolute sovereign, and citizens were granted only an inner form of freedom. The true State as depicted by the *Allgemeines Landrecht* did not correspond to the picture of civil society' (p.31).

81. See Hans Rosenberg, *Bureaucracy, aristocracy and autocracy: the Prussian experience, 1660-1815* (Cambridge, MA, 1958).

of the State and defend man from power. This weakened the cause of the preservation of man for centuries. The Enlightenment's constitutionalist project was set brusquely aside and all but forgotten, while the Jacobins' revolutionary constitutionalism was easily demonised and fought off. The 'code' replaced a 'constitution', just as Frederick William II wanted: administration law killed modern constitutional law in its infancy. The only rights advocated by the Enlightenment that maintained their inalienability, and were indeed given a great amount of consideration in the *Allgemeines Landrecht*, were the natural rights to property and economic freedom, i.e. those rights that were successfully supported by the physiocrats.[82] In this respect, there is no doubt that Mirabeau and Smith were more successful as Enlightenment thinkers than Filangieri or Condorcet.

In Germany the history of the rights of man definitely took a different route from the rest of Europe. Some intellectuals, such as Schiller, continued to fight for the rights along the lines of Edmund Burke's historicism, whereby rights were rooted in the history of the peoples rather than in the abstract will of revolutionaries who wanted them to be ratified by a written constitution imposed through violent means. Kant, by contrast, went a different way from most Enlightenment thinkers, advocating instead the separation of ethics and law, and of the internal forum of conscience and the external forum of the State, as summarised in his famous reference, in the *Critique of practical reason*, to 'the starry sky above and the moral law within'. This intriguing and rigorous philosophical position, however, was not a very effective or advanced political tool with which to fight the enlightened absolutism of the Prussian General Code.

Instead of founding the rights in empirical, historical and anthropological terms, as Vico, Rousseau and Condorcet respectively had done, and subsequently asking how these rights could be safeguarded in practice, Kant started from pure reason. He posited *a priori* the autonomy and freedom of the subject and his will, which acquired a positive direction only when it chose as its objective and moral categorical imperative the idea of the person, with its dignity and liberty, i.e. the concept of man not as a means but always as an end in himself. It was a highly noble view in line with Enlightenment humanism. By thus detaching man from nature in transcendental terms, and making him both the legislator and a sovereign's subject in a universally shared legislation, Kant thought that it might be

82. Cf. Koselleck, *Preussen*, p.60.

possible to found the essential rights of the individual simply on Rousseau's idea of natural liberty, whereby the rights are not consubstantial with the human being but nevertheless go back to him, as though they were naturally generated from the realisation of man's liberty in history.[83]

It is true that Kant went far beyond the empirical science of man of other members of the Enlightenment, or the old natural law of Christian Wolff, in that he denied that the objective of morality was public happiness, and thus separated ethics, with its 'internal forum', from law, which was the external task of the State. But in this way in fact he weakened the concrete practice of rights at a political level, scoring another point for the idea of the State as lord and master over rights.[84] Kant followed with interest the new ideas coming from France and was strongly sympathetic towards Rousseau and his defence of cosmopolitanism and of a republican and critical spirit. But he was also a supporter of Frederick II, and a product of Berlin absolutist culture. Crucial ideas in Enlightenment constitutionalism as theorised by Condorcet and Filangieri, such as the democratic concept of a constitution drawn up by the people, or the disquieting possibility of the right to resistance, were obnoxious to him. The latter was in his eye 'the highest and most punishable crime within a commonwealth'.[85] He does not, however, seem to have in any way opposed the idea of the dependence of natural rights on the State or its hierarchical classes, as codified in the *Allgemeines Landrecht.*

83. On the issue of philosophically founding the rights of the individual on the subject and the idea of liberty alone see Leslie A. Mulholland, *Kant's system of rights* (New York, 1989). See also what Kant himself wrote on his attitude towards the rights: 'I learn to honor human beings, and I would feel by far less useful than the common laborer if I did not believe that this consideration could impart a value to all others in order to establish the rights of humanity' (Immanuel Kant, 'Remarks in the *Observations on the feeling of the beautiful and sublime*', in *Observations on the feeling of the beautiful and sublime and other writings*, ed. and translated by Patrick Frierson, Cambridge, 2011, p.63-202, on p.96). On the centrality of man's point of view in Kant's political thought see Emilio Agazzi, *La filosofia della storia e della politica nel pensiero di Emanuele Kant*, ed. Enrico Colombo (1974-1975; Udine, 2012).
84. Ernst Bloch voiced an extremely harsh but intelligent critique of the conservative character and limitations of Kant's view of rights. See *Natural law*, p.67, where he goes so far as to write of the 'political misery of Germany'.
85. Cf. Immanuel Kant, 'On the common saying: that may be correct in theory, but it is of no use in practice', in Kant, *Practical philosophy*, ed. and translated by Mary J. Gregor (Cambridge, 1996), p.276-309 (298), TP 8:299.

In fact, the success of the General Code and its persistence across the centuries cannot be ascribed simply to the defeat of the *Spätaufklärung* and Enlightenment constitutionalism in the last quarter of the century. In the intriguing and in any case modern solution to the issue of rights that was developed in Berlin there was something more profound, which ensured its success in the political and intellectual circles of the Prussian capital. Its roots spread out in various directions, such as the vivid memory of the horrors of civil and religious war that seemed poised to repeat itself with the arrival of the arrogant French, or the perpetual return of Catholic Thomistic organicism in the universities, the Lutheran political theology of the elites and the institutional communitarism that safeguarded the German liberties of the Holy Roman empire. What is certain is that the *Allgemeines Landrecht* put a stop to the Enlightenment's difficult pursuit throughout the eighteenth century of a balance between the construction of individual and collective identities.[86] In the nineteenth century this equilibrium was irremediably shattered in favour of the latter, and the fight among nations and social classes took centre stage. It was as if a new form of *Ancien régime* communitarianism that was only slightly more modern than the old corporations had re-entered the fray.

This tendency towards class status and statalisation arose from, and further strengthened, a new bias towards the collective in German culture, which involved corporations and the whole nation as well as social classes. An aspect of this is the philological and literary rediscovery of ancient Germanic law, with its group and associative organisation, which was polemically opposed to the individualistic and 'foreign' Roman law.[87] This sudden cultural change, which can be observed in both literature and philosophy, soon became irreversible. Everywhere the focus shifted firmly onto the community. Bold new philosophies of spirit were developed, which were hostile to cosmopolitanism and the defence of man as individual, and the primacy of new social and political forms such as nation or people became undisputed. The *Allgemeines Landrecht* was also a greatly effective exercise in political neutralisation. The power of the new Prussian Leviathan effectively smothered the strong conflictuality between morality and politics – or the internal forum and the external one – that was present

86. On these issues, which still need to be studied in more detail, see Prodi and Reinhard, *Identità collettive*.
87. Cf. Maria Carolina Foi, *Heine e la vecchia Germania: le radici della questione tedesca tra poesia e diritto* (Milan, 1990), p.17ff.

in the language of rights, and that Carl Schmitt condemned as a harbinger of violence and crisis in the modern State.[88] All this opened a path that would be followed by Hegel and the historical school down to Gerber, Laband and Jellinek. For these thinkers, subjective rights were never considered primitive or fundamental, as they were for the Enlightenment. They were only seen in their 'organic' public form, as something that existed only by the express will of the State.

The Prussian General Code was really miles away from the new juridical systems that the Paris revolutionaries envisaged would be founded on the rights of man. And it was even further from the Enlightenment constitutionalism of Filangieri, Condorcet or Paine, as can be seen if we compare, for instance, the *Allgemeines Landrecht* with the Neapolitan *Costituzione della Repubblica* drafted in 1799 by Mario Pagano, which we discussed in an earlier chapter. Both the code and the *Costituzione* dealt with the rights of man, but the ways in which they did so had nothing in common with each other. The wide gap between the two should help us reflect on the specific features of the *Spätaufklärung* and examine the historical significance for Germany of the momentous defeat of the *Aufklärung* and its way of seeing the rights as both moral and political entities: a defeat whose effects would be felt for the next two centuries, and that even today could have serious consequences for our common European identity.

88. On the debate on the rights as harmful to the unity of the State, see Schmitt, *Leviathan*, p.73ff. On their political neutralisation presented as a way to go beyond an idea of politics as conflict, violence and *bellum omnium contra omnes* see, again by Carl Schmitt, 'The age of neutralizations and depoliticizations (1929)', *Telos* 96 (summer 1993), p.130-42. Schmitt strongly criticises the political and constitutional views of the Enlightenment, especially the concept of *Humanität*, which he considers an 'instrument of imperialist expansion' (Schmitt, *Concept of the political*, p.54). On the predominance of a State-centred juridical administrative culture in German political culture down to the middle of the twentieth century, see Geminello Preterossi, *Carl Schmitt e la tradizione moderna* (Rome and Bari, 1996), p.24ff.

Conclusion: towards a history of the Enlightenment and the rights of man as an unfinished project and a laboratory of modernity

Francesco Mario Pagano, who was, with Gaetano Filangieri, the father of Enlightenment constitutionalism and of penal reform based on the rights of man, was hanged at dusk on 29 October 1799, on a roughly made scaffold in the market square in Naples.[1] His execution was cheered on by a vast mob roused by servants of Cardinal Ruffo of Calabria, head of the league of the Holy Faith. With Pagano's death, the history of the Italian Enlightenment itself ended in blood. Five years earlier, on 29 March 1794, in Bourg-la-Reine, near Paris, Marie Jean Caritat, marquis of Condorcet, another great figure of the European Late Enlightenment and the struggle for the rights of man, died in unclear circumstances, after being imprisoned for pronouncing a damning speech against the Jacobin constitution. A year earlier his friend Marie Gouze, also known as Olympe de Gouges, the militant defender of the rights of women, had been guillotined after a cursory trial. We could continue for a long time to recite the list of supporters of the Enlightenment and the rights of man who were murdered either by the Jacobin Terror or by the no less ferocious clerical and monarchical restoration of the following years.

In any case, though with different modalities and pace in each context, the European Enlightenment's rights-based emancipatory project that we have examined in this study came to a sudden halt everywhere. It ended up being universally forgotten, incomplete, at least for a long time, its original features unknown to either historians or Western identity memory. For the former, the issue of rights was to remain connected with the 1776 American Declaration of Independence and the 1789 French Declaration of Rights. Dazzled by the powerful Enlightenment–Revolution paradigm and the ensuing

1. Cf. Pagano, *Considerazioni sul processo criminale.*

teleological quest for the intellectual and cultural origins of the French Revolution, scholars failed to pay sufficient attention to this emancipatory project in its autonomous and European character. The same applies to the attempt to outline the equally original and important history of rights in the revolutionary period and ascertain the elements of continuity and difference between the two. The first few pioneering works on the practice of rights in the revolutionary era have only recently begun to appear.[2]

What we have begun to understand is that the Revolution did not unambiguously fulfil its remit of ensuring the actual practice of rights. On the one hand it brought the existence of these rights centre stage for the first time in history, but on the other it crushed all the social dreams and hopes that had become attached to this political language of the moderns, a language that had been so carefully constructed by the Enlightenment over the previous decades. Most of the time, this language became simply a rhetorical tool with which to mask the abuses perpetrated by the army of the *Grande Nation* as it imposed its 'liberty' onto neighbouring countries. Moreover, the Revolution generated infighting among opposing power groups in Paris, as well as violent reactions and cultural and institutional 'antibodies' that in the following two centuries would misrepresent, hinder and ultimately obliterate all over Europe the work carried out by the Enlightenment.

In order to understand who the real enemies of this language were – both old and new – it is useful to look at the French revolutionaries' debates on certain crucial issues: for instance, on how the right of citizenship could be granted to minorities not on the basis of the Enlightenment principle of the equality and universality of the natural rights of all individuals but primarily as part of 'community rights'. The same applies to the old problem of the constitutionalisation of rights as the new legitimising foundation of power, rather than its insurmountable limit, or, of course, to the appalling paradox of a republic that was proclaimed to defend human rights ending in the Terror and its bloodbath. These three questions are indicative of

2. Besides the works mentioned in the preceding chapters, see *The French Revolution and human rights: a brief documentary history*, edited, translated and with an introduction by Lynn Hunt (Boston, MA, 1996); Pietro Costa, *Civitas: storia della cittadinanza in Europa*, vol.2: *L'età delle rivoluzioni (1789-1848)* (Rome and Bari, 2000), p.71ff.; Ladan Boroumand, *La Guerre des principes: les assemblées révolutionnaires face aux droits de l'homme et à la souveraineté de la nation* (Paris, 1999).

both the points of contact and the profound differences between the Enlightenment's project of emancipation and the politics of rights that was put into practice for the first time in history with the French Revolution.

Let us take the case of religious minorities. Calvinists had long been granted full citizenship rights thanks to the campaigns for tolerance and the natural right of individuals to religious freedom promoted by the Enlightenment and by Voltaire in particular. The edict of tolerance promulgated by Louis XVI in November 1787 to cancel the revocation of the Edict of Nantes concerned only civil rights, not political ones, but it nevertheless paved the way for later measures that drew on natural law for their legitimation.[3] But while this undoubted success scored by the Revolution seemed to finally settle a centuries-old conflict, it was far from solving once and for all the problem of religious tolerance in a republican age. In fact, the revolutionaries' radical political decisions only led to new and even more complicated controversies. The same Revolution that had finally granted Calvinists their citizenship rights in those years unleashed fanatical anti-Christian campaigns and attempted to obliterate the ancient ecclesiastical institutions of Catholics, Protestants and Jews alike, its political objective being to conjure up entirely new forms of natural, patriotic and civil religiosity that would give cultural and ideological uniformity to the modern republican *Nation* as one organic block of like-minded individuals.

A complex and especially indicative case in point is the struggle for the emancipation of the over 40,000 Jews who lived mostly in the south of France and Alsace and Lorraine. While the Calvinists were in any case of French origin, in France as in other European countries before 1789 the Jews had enjoyed specific rights as a nation and community with its own ethnic and religious characteristics. A long and arduous debate took place at the National Assembly on this issue. It resulted in the decree of 27 September 1791, which encouraged Jews to become assimilated to the French population, granting citizenship only if they renounced all previous privileges and rights as members of the Hebrew nation.[4] This made it clear that, for the revolutionaries, citizenship meant belonging to the *Grande Nation*

3. Cf. Geoffrey Adams, *The Huguenots and French opinion, 1685-1787: the Enlightenment debate on toleration* (Waterloo, 1991).
4. See the text of the decree and comments in Hunt, *The French Revolution and human rights*, p.99 and 101.

in a full and organic way.[5] There was a fundamental choice to be made, then, before the issue of liberty and the rights of man even arose, and that was whether to remain a Jew or become French. This meant deciding if one wanted to belong to this new France that was still in the process of being built and that, in a kind of continuity with the centralised absolutist state of the *Ancien régime*, would finally be able to go beyond regionalism and speak with a unified voice, despite the Girondins' calls for federalism. What was on offer was a revolutionary citizenship for individuals who were definitely owners of political rights but were constantly expected to participate in a communal civic effort and in duties that bonded all the subjects together within the sacred body of the nation – a nation that was no longer represented by the king's body but by popular sovereignty.[6]

Enlightenment citizenship was something quite different from this revolutionary citizenship informed by the political myth of the *Nation* and thus by the primacy of national community rights. The former was founded on the rights of man, which in turn were meant to defend the individual and further his pursuit of happiness. It was cosmopolitan and universal, and hoped for a political community of free individuals who were all morally equal, holders of rights, capable of self-government in republican and constitutional terms. All this regardless of all ethnic bonds and customs, and looking forward to an open civil society based on merit and virtue, as Enlightenment writers specified in their late-eighteenth-century critique of privileged *Ancien régime* institutions.[7] As a general characteristic, in the political thought of the Enlightenment the fundamental acknowledgement of the primacy of the individual was always accompanied by the attempt to envisage its concrete realisation in the history of peoples. This was to be carried out in harmony with modern civil society, respecting the delicate balance between the subject and the community, while never

5. On citizenship in the revolutionary period as membership of the *Nation* see Costa, *Civitas*, vol.2, p.43ff.
6. On the construction of the *Nation*, see Michel Vovelle, *La Découverte de la politique: géopolitique de la Révolution française* (Paris, 1993), Michel de Certeau, Dominique Julia and Jacques Revel, *Une Politique de la langue: la Révolution française et les patois* (Paris, 1975), and especially David A. Bell, *The Cult of the nation in France: inventing nationalism, 1680-1800* (Cambridge, MA, 2001).
7. Richard Price's 1789 *A Discourse on the love of our country* is a veritable manifesto of these positions (modern edition: Oxford and New York, 1992). On the rise of Enlightenment constitutionalism, which developed especially in Naples, see chapters 12 and 13 above.

forgetting the absolute centrality of the natural rights of the former and the need to protect them.

After the Holocaust, Voltaire was anachronistically accused of anti-semitism because of his critique of how a strong sense of Jewish identity had been liable in the course of the centuries to turn into religious fanaticism.[8] In fact, Voltaire's positions amounted simply to a consistent moral defence of the universal and cosmopolitan character of individual rights against the excessive claims put forward for individual community identities in the course of history. For Enlightenment culture the emancipation of Jews was never an issue of assimilation to one nation or another, as the National Assembly chose to present it. It was simply the concrete acknowledgement of the rights to freedom of every single human being.

This different perspective can be seen clearly also in the struggle against the slave trade. Debates were held at the National Assembly following the violent revolt of some half a million slaves led by mixed-race lawyer Vincent Ogé in Santo Domingo, in the Caribbean – a revolt that, as we saw, was predicted and even publicly hoped for in Diderot, Mercier and Lessing's dramatic references to the advent of a new Spartacus. Despite the need to bear in mind French national interests in the overseas colonies, the day was won in the name of the rights of the individual by the *philosophes* of the Société des amis des Noirs led by Brissot, Mirabeau and Condorcet. This Society was formed specifically for this purpose in 1788, a year after the birth of the sister society in England, the London Committee for the Abolition of the Slave Trade, and it was thanks to the Société's political action that, after a fiery debate, on 4 February 1794 the Assembly passed a resolution that abolished slavery in all the French colonies. Conversely, in 1802, strong economic interests at national level and a renewed politics of domination by the *Grande Nation* led Napoleon to reinstate slavery in the Caribbean, and to suppress the political and civil rights of all black inhabitants, including those who were already free before the rebellion.[9]

8. Lynn Hunt rightly takes issue with Arthur Hertzberg, *The French Enlightenment and the Jews* (New York, 1968), for its 'anachronistic way of reading out of historical context', which 'applies a twentieth-century, post-Holocaust standard of judgment to eighteenth-century writers' (Hunt, *The French Revolution and human rights*, p.31, n.9). On these issues, see also Patrick Girard, *La Révolution française et les juifs* (Paris, 1989).
9. For an overview of the different positions in this debate see Hunt, *The French Revolution and human rights*, p.23-26.

In the case of women's rights of citizenship the revolutionary front was remarkably united in rejecting all universalistic and egalitarian options, and on 30 October 1793 the National Assembly shut down the women's circles that had been created in Paris specifically to lobby for this objective. However, even in this respect it is possible to see some important new elements in these years compared to a recent past in which the attitude of the Enlightenment had still been quite ambiguous and generally unwilling to support the emancipation of women, Rousseau's misogynistic attitude being a case in point.[10] These new elements came from the Cercle social and especially Condorcet, who in 1790 provided a passionate defence of the rights of women in a practical and theoretical sense, arguing for them on the basis of the universalistic principles of the Enlightenment in the militant *Journal de la Société de 1789*.[11]

The different positions on the rights of man held by Enlightenment reformers on the one hand and the radical wing of the Revolution on the other surface most clearly in the constitutional discussions at the National Assembly, a long and difficult negotiation that was obviously affected by the bloodshed that took place during the Jacobin Terror and the Thermidorian Reaction. The language of rights was soon at the centre of the debate. From the very beginning, it was appealed to in the effort to refound politics and legitimise power and sovereignty on a new basis, creating a new political and social order. But the persistence of certain aspects of the *Ancien régime* and traditional political cultures caused tensions and contradictions. In 1792 Necker put before the Assembly Edmund Burke's soon-to-be-famous critique of 'metaphysical rights' as being dangerously utopian and unrealistic, as opposed to the rights of citizenship that had concretely developed in England over the course of the centuries.[12] It was not surprising that, between 1793 and 1795, faced with the upheaval that threatened to

10. For extensive bibliographical references on this subject see Dominique Godineau, 'The woman', in *Enlightenment portraits*, ed. M. Vovelle, p.393-426.
11. Cf. Baczko, *Job, mon ami*, p.358ff.; Gary Kates, '"The powers of husband and wife must be equal and separate": the *Cercle social* and the rights of women, 1790-91', in *Women and politics in the age of democratic revolution*, ed. Harriet B. Applewhite and Darline G. Levy (Ann Arbor, MI, 1990), p.163-80.
12. Cf. Gauchet, *La Révolution des droits de l'homme*, p.iv. In his *Reflections on the Revolution in France*, which were immediately translated into French and German in 1790, Burke pointed out that the *Petition of right* sent to Charles I was not based on 'abstract principles "as the rights of men", but as the rights of Englishmen' (Burke, *Reflections on the Revolution*, p.118).

cause the total dissolution of the social order, the Assembly began to rediscover the seventeenth-century idea of duties, and to consider the need to restore the authority principle and social bond through the physiocrats' version of the language of rights as derived from duties. This authoritarian view of rights was far more reassuring than the libertarian interpretation of Voltaire, Beccaria, Diderot or Condorcet. As we have seen, while it fully belonged within the Late Enlightenment laboratory of political modernity, it also paved the way for the denunciation of the sin of individualism, according to a historically unfounded rhetorical scheme that would nevertheless affect the way the Enlightenment's reform effort has been judged down to this day.[13] Many speeches and texts at the time presented the defence of man from abuses of power or the individual's natural right to the pursuit of happiness as a selfish alternative to virtuous revolutionary citizenship founded on duties and the old sociability principle.[14]

Of course, soon the members of the National Assembly were facing the dramatic scenario of a revolution that was completely out of control and set to devour its children one by one. Robespierre's claim in 1792 that theirs had been 'la première révolution qui ait été fondée sur la théorie des droits de l'humanité' sounded cruelly ironic.[15] The bitter reality was the incessant use of the guillotine and the suspension of the right to freedom in the face of what today we would call, in Carl

13. Two key texts that denounced the Enlightenment along these lines are Hegel's *Elements of the philosophy of right* (ed. Allen W. Wood, translated by H. B. Nisbet, Cambridge, 1991) and especially Karl Marx's 'On the Jewish question', where we read: 'Above all, we note the fact that the so-called *rights of man*, the *droits de l'homme* as distinct from the *droits du citoyen*, are nothing but the rights of a *member of civil society*, i.e., the rights of egoistic man, of man separated from other men and from the community' (p.162; emphasis in the original).
14. See, for instance, Jacques Nicolas Billaud Varenne, *Eléments du républicanisme*: 'Les citoyens sont ceux qui pénétrés des devoirs sociaux, rapportent tout à l'intérêt public et qui mettent leur bonheur et leur gloire à cimenter la prospérité de leur pays […] Les individus, au contraire, sont ceux qui s'isolent, ou plutôt qui savent moins travailler au bien public que calculer leur intérêt particulier: en un mot, ce sont des êtres qui cherchent à rompre l'équilibre de l'égalité pour accroître leur bien-être personnel en usurpant celui des autres' (quoted in Gauchet, *La Révolution des droits de l'homme*, p.246). See also, in Gauchet, the chapters on the return of the 'fantôme des devoirs' onto the political scene with the 1795 Thermidorian constitution.
15. See Maximilien de Robespierre, 'Discours du 26 juillet 1794', in *Œuvres*, vol.10: *Discours, 5e partie: '27 juillet 1793-27 juillet 1794'*, ed. Marc Bouloiseau and Albert Soboul (Paris, 1967), p.544.

Schmitt's synthetic formulation, a state of exception, in which *necessitas legem non habet*. It was difficult to think of another historical situation in which the practical outcome had more tragically contradicted a theory and principles so solemnly announced and rhetorically shared by all. The history of the rights of man would be indelibly affected by this disastrous paradox. Only in recent times have we put sufficient effort into trying to ascertain the true reasons for the Jacobin Terror, also in relation to the so-called triumph of natural right, i.e. of the appeal to nature in the revolutionary age.[16] In this context, the idea of duties as the flipside of rights makes a dramatic reappearance, as in the Thermidorians' significantly titled *Déclaration des droits et des devoirs de l'homme et du citoyen* of 1795. Most importantly, different interpretations are given of the original 1789 *Déclaration des droits de l'homme et du citoyen*, which, having failed to prevent the Terror, now risked sounding ironic and emptily rhetorical: witness what happened to Thomas Paine, the author of a famous reply to Burke actually entitled *Rights of man*, who ended up being jailed in the Luxembourg Palace prison for speaking out against Louis XVI's death sentence.

For decades historians in every part of the world celebrated the universalising and emancipatory character of the 1789 *Déclaration*. Now, the tragic paradox caused by the Terror forced them to reconsider its real meaning and historical function. The profound differences between the 1776 American Declaration of Independence and the 1789 *Déclaration* were already the subject of an important debate between Emile Boutmy and Georg Jellinek at the beginning of the twentieth century, and still pose serious questions for us today.

16. The Terror has been traditionally seen as a state of exception resulting from the wars of aggression against the French Republic. However, for an interesting new reconstruction of its intellectual origins, see Dan Edelstein, *The Terror of natural right: republicanism, the cult of nature and the French Revolution* (Chicago, IL, 2009). According to Edelstein, the Jacobins legitimised the Terror from a cultural point of view on the basis of a disconcerting new interpretation of natural right. This was now no longer seen as a safeguard for liberty that set limits on the arbitrary power of the sovereign. It became instead the natural point of reference for determining not only what is right and virtuous but also mankind's legitimate defence against its enemies, the *hostis humani generis*, i.e. what is against nature. These enemies of mankind could then be swiftly disposed of with no need to abide by conventional laws, or criminal and judicial procedures. The revolutionaries thus developed a form of 'natural republicanism' from their specific reading of seventeenth-century natural right as was found in France, according to a process skilfully reconstructed by Edelstein. It was a reading that always put the safety of the nation and of mankind above individual freedom.

We know that from the very beginning the American Declaration took on an element of sacrality, which further increased in time. In its materiality, it even became, and still is, an object of cult in a lay and civic sense.[17] The French Declaration, by contrast, was soon replaced by new versions, in 1793 and 1795. It disappeared in the nineteenth century, after Napoleon had shamefully reneged on it when he restored legal slavery in 1802.[18] The former Declaration was born to defend the rights of man against George III's despotism, and affected American positive law as far down as the creation of the Supreme Court. The principles of the latter were often overruled by positive law and the primacy of legislation over the rights and natural law, so that some have talked of *légicentrisme*, i.e. the expression of the general will of the sovereign people, according to the model auspicated by Rousseau, which would characterise the history of French revolutionary constitutionalism for decades.[19] This divergence between the two Declarations was due to the limitations imposed not only by the different contexts and the legacy of the past, but also by the varying tasks set by the course of events.

The American Declaration of Independence was first of all a text of international law. It sanctioned the birth of a new State and explained the political and moral reasons for that decision in terms of the rigorous defence of the rights of the individual against power.[20] By contrast, the 1789 *Déclaration des droits de l'homme* was a symbolically significant text but also and especially a political act, which aimed at recreating the foundations of power itself, by using the rights as constitutive and legitimising elements of the new popular sovereignty. Even more than to protect the individual, the purpose of the *Déclaration* was to build a new collective identity: to replace the king's body with that of the nation in the tradition, collective memory and political

17. On this relatively little-known aspect of sacrality see Maier, *American scripture.*
18. Cf. Florence Gauthier, *Triomphe et mort du droit naturel en Révolution 1789-1795-1802* (Paris, 1992); Roger Barny, *Le Droit naturel à l'épreuve de l'histoire: Jean-Jacques Rousseau dans la Révolution: débats politiques et sociaux* (Paris, 1995).
19. Cf. Rials, *La Déclaration des droits*, p.369. Even today the rights of man do not have separate juridical status in France: see, by Blandine Kriegel, *Les Droits de l'homme et le droit naturel* (Paris, 1988), p.10ff., and *Philosophie de la République* (Paris, 1998), p.121ff. On how positive law and the general will soon prevailed over the natural and imprescriptible rights of man see Philippe Raynaud, '*La Déclaration des droits de l'homme* in the political culture of the French Revolution', in *The French Revolution and the creation of modern political culture*, ed. Colin Lucas, 3 vols (Oxford, 1988), vol.2: *The Political culture of the French Revolution*, p.139-49.
20. Cf. Armitage, *Declaration of Independence.*

struggle of those tumultuous years, and to celebrate the general will and legislative power, in line with the persistent as well as inevitable communitarian, corporative and class interests of the centuries-old political culture of the *Ancien régime*.[21]

It is probably true, as some have maintained, that the reason for the 'short circuit' that occurred with the Terror is this fundamental continuity behind the more obvious transformation, according to a pattern highlighted by Tocqueville in *L'Ancien Régime et la Révolution* (1856). This would be at the origin of the general involution that accompanied the Terror itself, with the systematic violation and gradual banalisation of the discourse of the rights of the individual, and the diminished status of natural law in relation to positive law, which represented the general will of the *Grande Nation* within the revolutionaries' constitutionalism. The ultimate result was the victory of the nation and early forms of nationalism over the individual and his natural rights, with dire consequences for the history of the rights of man for centuries to come.[22]

This appears all the more obvious when we look at how the opinions publicly expressed by the true fathers of Enlightenment constitutionalism, such as Filangieri, Paine or Condorcet, were progressively

21. On the persistence not only of the administrative and institutional structure of the *Ancien régime*, as indicated by Tocqueville, but also of its political culture and mentality, see the essays in *The French idea of freedom: the Old Regime and the Declaration of Rights of 1789*, ed. Dale Van Kley (Stanford, CA, 1994), by Keith Michael Baker ('The idea of a Declaration of Rights', p.154-99), David D. Bien ('Old Regime origins of democratic liberty', p.23-71) and Thomas E. Kaiser ('Property, sovereignty, the Declaration of the Rights of Man, and the tradition of French jurisprudence', p.300-42).
22. On the issue of nationalism, see especially François Furet, *Interpreting the French Revolution*, translated by Elborg Forster (Cambridge, 1981). Commenting on Augustin Cochin's work on 'thought societies' and the 'mechanism of the revolution', Furet addressed the way in which 'the French had come to re-invent society under the name of the "people" or the "nation", and of how they came to set it up as the new god of a fictitious community' (p.193). Furet quotes Cochin on how '[l]iving in serfdom under the king in 1789, in freedom under the law in 1791, the people became master in 1793. Now that it governed itself, it did away with the public liberties [...] If the right to vote was suspended it was because the people ruled; the right to legal defence because it did the judging; freedom of the press because it did the writing; freedom of speech because it did the speaking: the doctrine is perfectly clear; the proclamations and laws of the Terror are but an extended commentary on it' (p.193-94). On how the contrast between the rights of the nation and the rights of the individual became insoluble with the French Revolution, see Baker, 'The idea of a Declaration of Rights'; see also the studies mentioned in Costa, *Civitas*, vol.2, p.20ff.

set aside and finally discounted. Those thinkers seriously believed in the cause of the rights of man.[23] It became the prime mover of all their works, which in turn pervaded the political structure of Late Enlightenment culture, to which artists of the calibre of Goya, Schiller or Goethe also gave their contribution. Defending man and protecting the individual's right to liberty against the State and all forms of despotic power always remained their main concern.

In the United States the issue of how to protect the rights was addressed quite early on.[24] The same applies to Naples, where, as we have seen, in 1799 Francesco Mario Pagano invented a tribunal of ephors: something like a modern high court of constitutional justice, which could set limits to legislative power in defence of the constitution and rights. Things were quite different in French revolutionary constitutionalism. In fact, the failure of this crucial objective should have alerted us long ago to the peculiar characteristics of revolutionary constitutionalism and how profoundly it differed from the Enlightenment's version. The proposal put forward by Sieyès to create a *jury constitutionnaire* hardly solved the problem, since the tasks of the latter were far too vague. It ended up being yet another form of legislative power whose purpose differed significantly from that of a modern constitutional tribunal tasked with protecting man's rights.[25] Condorcet was among the first to pose the question. He did so by attempting to draft *déclarations* and projects of constitutions that aimed at setting a clearly defined external limit to the exercise of power by the establishment and the omnipotence of the legislative branch of government and the general will.[26] He not only failed in his attempt: his critique of the Jacobins' form of constitutionalism caused him to be imprisoned and meet with a premature death.[27]

23. In *Taking rights seriously*, Ronald Dworkin correctly identifies the eighteenth-century roots of this mode of thinking.
24. Cf. Einaudi, *Le origini dottrinali*.
25. Cf. Troper, *Terminer la Révolution*, p.206ff. See also Emmanuel Joseph Sieyès, *Les Discours de Sieyès dans les débats constitutionnels de l'An III (2 et 18 thermidor)*, ed. Paul Bastid (Paris, 1939); Pasquale Pasquino, *Sieyès et l'invention de la constitution en France* (Paris, 1998).
26. Cf. Condorcet, *Dichiarare i diritti, costituire i poteri: un inedito sulla dichiarazione dei diritti dell'uomo*, ed. Gabriele Magrin and Mercurio Candela (Milan, 2011). See also Gabriele Magrin, *Condorcet: un costituzionalismo democratico* (Milan, 2001).
27. On Condorcet's death, which happened in unclear circumstances, though probably through suicide, see the moving and intelligent account in Baczko, *Job, mon ami*, p.388ff.

Despite the resounding failure of the defence of rights because of the Terror, that first important *Déclaration* of 1789, on which Condorcet had placed so much hope, nevertheless embodied the entire cultural and political manifesto of the Late Enlightenment: that actual philosophy of the history of the rights of man that we find in Condorcet's *Esquisse d'un tableau historique des progrès de l'esprit humain*. To realise this, we just need to read the Declaration's famous *incipit*:

> Les Représentants du Peuple Français, constitués en Assemblée nationale, considérant que *l'ignorance, l'oubli ou le mépris des droits de l'homme* sont les seules causes des malheurs publics et de la corruption des Gouvernements, ont résolu d'exposer, dans une Déclaration solennelle, les droits naturels, inaliénables et sacrés de l'homme, afin que cette Déclaration, constamment présente à tous les membres du corps social, leur rappelle sans cesse leurs droits et leurs devoirs; afin que les actes du pouvoir législatif, et ceux du pouvoir exécutif pouvant être à chaque instant comparés avec le but de toute institution politique, en soient plus respectés; afin que les réclamations des citoyens, fondées désormais sur des principes simples et incontestables, tournent toujours au maintien de la Constitution, et au bonheur de tous. En conséquence, l'Assemblée nationale reconnaît et déclare, en présence et sous les auspices de l'Etre Suprême, les droits suivants de l'homme et du citoyen.[28]

In the text I have highlighted the reference to 'ignorance, neglect, or contempt of the rights of man'. Condorcet's *Sketch*, which the author began in the early 1780s and completed just before his death, might have been written expressly in order to illustrate the true meaning of these words, which legitimised the rights with recourse to the civil and political history of mankind. As a model this was, in fact, quite similar to the process through which Vico's ideal and eternal right became true in history. It was, in any case, quite far from Jefferson's famous but inconclusive assertion of the 'self-evident' character of rights in the American Declaration of Independence.

Condorcet's *Sketch* is generally studied within the framework of eighteenth-century utopian literature: in fact, it is one of the earliest examples of uchronia, or alternate history.[29] It is especially noteworthy also as the Enlightenment's ultimate political testament and most

28. An English translation can be found, for instance, on the Avalon project website, http://avalon.law.yale.edu/18th_century/rightsof.asp (last accessed 21 May 2019), from which we quote in what follows.

29. Cf. Baczko, *Lumières de l'utopie*, p.192ff.

mature and convincing pronouncement on the matter of rights. This issue is presented here in the form of a passionate, prophetic, future-oriented programme, which speaks convincingly to us to this day. While it has not received much attention from critics, it clearly shows the important function of the rights of man in the Enlightenment's attempt to make sense of the universal history of mankind and the progress of the human spirit. Condorcet's work allows us to see how strongly the rights defined their social dream of a new world, of a previously unheard-of politics at the service of human happiness, and of a civil society that was finally informed by a respect for the citizenship right that is universally granted to all human beings, and which coincides with natural rights.[30]

We know that Condorcet did not intend to write utopian fiction. His *Esquisse* has even been called an 'anti-utopian utopia', i.e. a form of paradoxical uchronia, in which the utopian discourse is projected forward in time, rather than elsewhere in space.[31] This 'historisation' of utopia at the same time argued that social dreams could be concretely realised in rational and scientific terms, according to a model that, in the following century, would pave the way for other philosophies of history, such as that of Karl Marx. As a scientist familiar with the calculus of probability as applied to social issues, who had an empiricist and polemical attitude towards all forms of metaphysics, Condorcet believed that, in light of the consistency of natural laws and the positive verification of the principle of the perfectibility of man in past events, it was possible to make scientific predictions on the future of the human spirit.[32] Hence his important discussion of the tenth and final stage of mankind, a paradigmatic example of social dream based on probable history: 'The time will therefore come when the sun will

30. On civic utopia and citizenship rights in Condorcet, see Bronislaw Baczko, 'Finzioni storiche e congiunture utopiche', in *Nell'anno 2000: dall'utopia all'ucronia, atti del convegno internazionale (Torino 10 marzo 2000)*, ed. Bruno Bongiovanni and Gian Mario Bravo (Florence, 2001), p.9-22 (17ff.).
31. This thesis, put forward by Leszek Kołakowski, is discussed by Baczko in *Lumières de l'utopie*, p.205ff.
32. In his *Sketch*, Condorcet explained that the tenth stage provided an outline 'of our hopes, and of the progress reserved for future generations, which the constancy of the laws of nature seems to assure them' (p.9). Condorcet took it for granted that man could 'with great expectation of success, forecast the future on the basis of his experience of the past' (p.173). On the originality of Condorcet's epistemological model see Keith Michael Baker, *Condorcet: from natural philosophy to social mathematics* (Chicago, IL, and London, 1975); Vincenzo Ferrone, 'Il dibattito su probabilità e scienze sociali nel secolo XVIII', *Physis* 22 (1980), p.27-71.

shine only on free men who know no other master but their reason; when tyrants and slaves, priests and their stupid or hypocritical instruments will exist only in works of history and on the stage.'[33]

The final stage or epoch should lessen inequalities among and within nations. The morality itself of the human being would attain perfection, being founded on the respect of the rights of every man everywhere on earth. Condorcet wrote these moving words as he was about to die a persecuted man because of the Jacobin Terror. What he personally saw as, instead, the probable ultimate outcome of the human experience must have been a great consolation, a worthy and serene conclusion to an existence devoted to the realisation of the Enlightenment's heavenly city on earth:

> These are the questions with which we shall conclude this final stage. How consoling for the philosopher who laments the errors, the crimes, the injustices which still pollute the earth and of which he is often the victim is this view of the human race, emancipated from its shackles, released from the empire of fate and from that of the enemies of its progress, advancing with a firm and sure step along the path of truth, virtue and happiness! It is the contemplation of this prospect that rewards him for all his efforts to assist the progress of reason and the defence of liberty [...] Such contemplation is for him an asylum, in which the memory of his persecutors cannot pursue him; there he lives in thought with man restored to his natural rights and dignity, forgets man tormented and corrupted by greed, fear or envy. (p.201-202)

In fact, the *Esquisse* in its entirety represented something more even than the intellectual testament and the political and social project of the Late Enlightenment. Its author was a great scientist, who loved reason, the sciences and their advancement. With its civic passion, this work is pervaded by the gradual discovery of the new politics of the modern founded on the rights of man. For the first time, the rights were thought of and legitimised as crucial and defining elements of the universal history of mankind and its inevitable progress. At the same time, through a historically verifiable and verified principle of perfectibility, the rights were also legitimately projected into the utopian time of uchronia.[34]

33. *Sketch*, p.179.
34. On the concept of perfectibility, see John Arthur Passmore, *The Perfectibility of man* (London, 1971).

Primitive people had no knowledge of the language of rights, and neither did the Greeks or the Romans. Ancient politics was founded on other principles. Nevertheless, those rights were latently present in human nature from the beginning, and would surface at the right time and in specific contexts throughout the centuries. In order to demonstrate this in scientific terms, it was necessary to investigate universal history from the Enlightenment's viewpoint of the rise of civilisation, so as to clearly ascertain the reasons and links through which 'nature has joined together indissolubly the progress of knowledge and that of liberty, virtue and respect for the natural rights of man' (p.10). For Condorcet the slow realisation of the existence of rights was interwoven with the history of the progress of the human spirit itself at specific key moments: the scientific revolution, the wars of religion, the never-ending conflict between priests and philosophers on the subject of man's autonomy and freedom, the discovery of the printing press, the rise of public opinion, and the emergence of the new culture of the European Enlightenment, with its determination to fight like 'a solid phalanx banded together against all forms of error, against all manifestations of tyranny' (p.141).

Bacon, Descartes, Galileo, the scientific method, the study of the 'book of nature' had all certainly played an important role, paving the way with their ideas for the critique of tradition and of the authority principle on which the old politics was built, with its papal bulls, royal decrees and adherence to custom. Before them, '[i]t was not suspected that the rights of man were written in the book of nature and that to look for them in any other was to misunderstand and outrage them' (p.97). The next stage saw the bloody and horrific civil wars of religion in Europe, which led many intellectuals to fight for liberty of conscience against all forms of religious intolerance: 'But intolerance forced human reason to inquire into those rights which had been too long forgotten, or, rather, which had never been well known or properly explained' (p.110-11). But in fact the modern politics of rights that was to finally transform the long-forgotten natural rights into the universal *droits politiques* of the Enlightenment had started to manifest itself in concrete terms with the earliest medieval statutes, i.e. those charters that formally granted the first, though restricted, citizenship rights. In Condorcet's evaluation, these charters are 'the originals of those declarations of the rights of man which all enlightened men to-day regard as the cornerstones of liberty, but of which the ancients did not and could not have any notion: since domestic slavery sullied their constitutions, since for them citizenship was a merely hereditary or adoptive right' (p.93). But from a theoretical point of view it was only in the following centuries, with the works of Sidney, Locke, Rousseau and Beccaria, that decisive steps forward were taken: 'After long periods of error, after being led astray by vague or incomplete theories, publicists have at last discovered the true rights of man and how they can all be deduced from the single truth, that *man is a sentient being, capable of reasoning and of acquiring moral ideas*' (p.128; emphasis in the original).

However, the crucial shift in the universal history of the rights of man from the enunciation of principles to actual political practice took place mostly in the second half of the eighteenth century. It was the conscious result of the new Enlightenment culture and of the struggles in defence of man in which the *philosophes* engaged by appealing to public opinion, which was the true tribunal, 'independent of all human coercion' (p.100). The *philosophie nouvelle* popularised by Voltaire, Beccaria, Lessing and Diderot, which took for its battle cry '*reason, tolerance, humanity*' (p.137), had thrown in its lot with the acknowledgement of rights, thus laying the foundation for the utopian tenth stage of mankind.

The American Revolution of 1776 was its first victorious experiment. After this event, in every corner of Europe we start to discern the first reforms aimed at subverting the *Ancien régime*, and the Enlightenment starts to obtain its first important results in political and civil terms. Constantly swaying in their political action between history and utopia, between their utopian project of reform and harsh reality, the supporters of the Enlightenment bravely relaunched their ambitious cultural programme, which was based on the public education of mankind in the knowledge and political practice of those inalienable and imprescriptible rights. This would be followed by the incessant struggle 'for liberty of thought and letters, of trade and industry, and for the alleviation of the people's suffering, for the proscription of all penal laws against religious dissenters and the abolition of torture and barbarous punishments' (p.140). No human being was ever again to be excluded from the universal struggle for emancipation, regardless of gender, race or religious belief. In the *Esquisse* the Enlightenment really took on the traits of a great laboratory of modernity, capable of finally going beyond the culture and logic of the *Ancien régime*, on the moral level first, and then in political and juridical terms.

Thus, with Condorcet's uchronia the rights of man became at one and the same time historical certainty and utopian hope, political formula and political myth for the emancipation of man through man by prefiguring his future history. However, the appealing basis of Enlightenment rights outlined by Condorcet, and the emancipatory programme and social dream that gave it strength and vitality, clashed with the reality of the political bloodshed of those years. We know that Condorcet considered the French Revolution as a positive acceleration of the historical process, which opened up new spaces for the progress of the human spirit, rather than as the interruption of the process itself or the radical beginning of a new humanity, as it was for Robespierre.[35] It would never have entered Condorcet's head that this event, which would change the history of the Western world, could give rise to so many excesses and such fanaticism that it would fuel the anti-Enlightenment movement and bring to a sudden halt, and for a very long time, that very programme of political and cultural reforms that was supposed to further the cause of the rights of man.

It is only recently that we have begun to study the true history of the so-called 'Counter-Enlightenment'. Thus, we have started to investigate the social, political, economic and intellectual origins in the eighteenth century of the reactionary culture of the future 'right-wing' Restoration forces and their action in a new century in which national identity and the right to self-determination of whole peoples would always prevail over the rights of the individual.[36] Along this path we have started to study the protagonists and programmes of the cultural war that the late representatives of the *Ancien régime* waged against the values and reforms of the European Enlightenment party, from the end of the Seven Years War onwards. We have started to reflect – or we should in future – on the aggressive, deliberate re-entry of religion into the public sphere instigated by the Catholic Church in the last quarter of the eighteenth century, on the modern organicistic redefinition of the ancient status-based communitarism in the form of new social classes and nations in opposition to one another, on the attack against republican democracy and the individual's rights to liberty, on the creation of a restoration value system and ideology that arranged individuals and peoples into hierarchies, on the God-derived authority principle, on natural inequality and on blood rights, the latter newly legitimised by resorting to tradition and, paradoxically, to that modern science of man that the Enlightenment created for a very different purpose.

35. On these two different conceptions of the revolutionary process, see Baczko, *Job, mon ami*, p.361ff.

36. Cf. Darrin M. McMahon, *Enemies of the Enlightenment: the French Counter-Enlightenment and the making of modernity* (Oxford, 2001).

The pursuit of historical truth and what I have elsewhere described as the historians' point of view on the authentic nature of the Enlightenment and its true role in the definition of modern Western identity came up against a fearsome rival already in the eighteenth century, as is shown by Kant's reply to the question 'Was ist Aufklärung?' asked by the *Berlinische Monatsschrift* in 1784. This was an appealing history of the Enlightenment from an entirely philosophical point of view. In its most powerful form, that of Hegel's dialectics, this interpretation saw the Enlightenment in teleological terms as the main cause of the French Revolution and consequently of the Terror. In its Marxist manifestation, this view blamed the Enlightenment for the rise of merciless and alienating bourgeois individualism. Later representatives of this paradigm, Theodor Adorno and Max Horkheimer, finally accused this movement of causing that open crisis of modernity that led to the Holocaust and the criminal totalitarianism of the twentieth century.[37]

After the Second World War, on the back of this misleading paradigm arose a new and possibly even more sophisticated form of Counter-Enlightenment. This made an especially skilful use of the myth of origins, reading out of context individual statements by Hume or Voltaire that could sound racist or anti-semitic respectively. This highlighted the historical limitations of this world and its undeniable contradictions. It did not, however, warrant the description of the Enlightenment as a cradle of racism.[38] Being in most cases the result of disingenuous anachronism or ideological oversimplification fostered by the acrimonious postmodern polemical stance, the new Counter-Enlightenment accused the *monde des Lumières* of being at the origin of modern racism, sexism, colonialism, genocide, nihilism and any other horror one can think of as being generated by our modernity. For instance, the attempt by the *philosophes* to secularise the world and to brush aside the idea of the literal truth of the Bible has been accused of fostering nineteenth-century racist polygenism in contrast with virtuous Christian monogenism and its idea of the unity of mankind.[39] This was only possible by forgetting that one of the most pervasive and pernicious racist theories against black people, which was commonly referred to in the Protestant world for centuries, was the so-called curse

37. Cf. Ferrone, *The Enlightenment*, p.7ff.

38. For an illuminating analysis, see Sebastiani, *The Scottish Enlightenment*, p.163ff.

39. Cf. Richard H. Popkin's chapter on 'The philosophical basis of modern racism' in his *The High road to Pyrrhonism* (San Diego, CA, 1980), p.79-101.

that had befallen Cam, as narrated in Genesis 9.20-27.[40] In the same way, the Enlightenment's universal Eurocentrism and cosmopolitanism has been linked to their belief in reason, and the latter seen as strongly authoritarian in a Foucauldian sense. Consequently, the Enlightenment has been associated with racism and imperialism because of a presumed hegemonic stance towards the differences, multiculturalism and native cultural traditions of Africa, America and the East.[41] Even the neoclassical appreciation of the Apollo Belvedere by Enlightenment aesthetics as the exemplar of perfect human beauty has been accused of racism and colonialism, since it was presented as a universal paradigm.[42]

The fact is that the eighteenth century saw the rise of the Enlightenment's science of man, with subjects ranging from ethnology, comparative anatomy and physiology to statistics and the social history of peoples.[43] This was bound to open up huge spaces to a myriad possible interpretations of the new discoveries as well as the possibility to reflect like never before on the differences among peoples and their different development. But, as is clearly shown by the redesigning of the tree of knowledge in the *Encyclopédie*, Enlightenment humanism always considered the Scientific Revolution to be at the service of man rather than vice versa, as was instead often the case with nineteenth-century positivism.[44] The terms 'racism' and 'racist' did not exist in the eighteenth century.[45] We should bear in mind the autonomy of

40. Cf. Werner Sollors, 'La maledizione di Cam: ovvero dalla "generazione" alla "razza"', in *Il razzismo e le sue storie*, ed. Girolamo Imbruglia (Naples, 1992), p.183-205.
41. See Edward Said's polemical essay, *Orientalism* (New York, 1978), where the Enlightenment is accused of building an artificial and misleading modern Orientalism in order to establish asymmetrical power relationships of a colonial and imperialistic kind. Against these arguments, their anachronism and ideological mystifications see, by Rolando Minuti, *Oriente barbarico e storiografia settecentesca: rappresentazioni della storia dei Tartari nella cultura francese del XVIII secolo* (Venice, 1994), and *Orientalismo e idee di tolleranza nella cultura francese del primo '700* (Florence, 2006). See also *Le Problème de l'altérité dans la culture européenne: anthropologie, politique et religion aux XVIIIe et XIXe siècles*, ed. Guido Abbattista and Rolando Minuti (Naples, 2006), and especially Muthu, *Enlightenment against empire.*
42. Cf. David Bindman, *Ape to Apollo: aesthetics and the idea of race in the eighteenth century* (Ithaca, NY, 2002).
43. Cf. Sergio Moravia, *La scienza dell'uomo nel Settecento* (Rome and Bari, 1978).
44. On the difference between the Enlightenment and the positivist views of science see Ferrone, *Una scienza per l'uomo.*
45. For a defence of the Enlightenment from the accusation of racism see also Anthony Pagden, *The Enlightenment and why it still matters* (Oxford, 2013), p.vii ff.

science in relation to the use that one might make of it on the basis of ideological presumptions or conflicting interests. It is not enough to discuss the racist use that has been made of Rousseau's description of primitive men as very similar to orangutans (see Tyson), or the doubts raised by Buffon's theories on the human species, or yet again to point to the racist studies that referred to Dutch anatomist Petrus Camper's research on the facial angle – forgetting that Camper himself was strenuously against slavery and a supporter of monogenism. All this still does not authorise us to see the Enlightenment as the cradle of racism or attribute to the *philosophes* any responsibility in defending the slave trade.

If we look at it as we ought to, i.e. as a laboratory of modernity that placed at its centre the investigation of man, the historical phenomenon of the Enlightenment comes across as being characterised by complex tensions between universalism and the hierarchy of nations, individual and community, those who theorised equality and those who saw only differences in nature, the constant pursuit of what was just and the principle of utility. However, in the eighteenth century these tensions never gave rise to anything resembling the racist attitudes of future centuries, the conditions for which were created by unbounded nationalism and misconceived positivism. In fact, in the eighteenth century itself the opposite is the case: the Enlightenment's invention of the language of the rights of man would be the first step on the road to the abolition of the slave trade and in the struggle for equality.

As we saw, in his *Diceosina* Neapolitan thinker Antonio Genovesi understood perfectly well not only what was at stake, but the precise terms in which the question was posed. Genovesi was critical of those who attempted to use Buffon and the results of the new science of man to further the thesis of the natural inequality of men and relaunch the Aristotelian theory of the natural slave. To combat these ideas he invoked, particularly against the slave trade, the ethical principle of the equality of rights for all human beings, regardless of physical differences. In his opinion the new morality of rights could and should set limits on the cultural level to anything in favour of the hierarchy of nations and slavery that might arise from scientific research. Genovesi's reflections are then at the centre of the great debate on the issue of equality that was taking place in the eighteenth century across Europe.[46] In this sense, he put forward the thesis of the 'moral equality'

46. On the debate on equality in European Enlightenment circles see Robertson, *The Case for the Enlightenment*, p.396ff.

of all members of the human species, opposing any notion of natural inequality. It is here, even more so than in the acknowledgement of the autonomy of man, that we can see the true cultural and political revolution caused by the Enlightenment, its strong point, on which rested the universalistic and cosmopolitan bias of its new humanism.

In fact, the history of the rights of man, of which here we have tried to trace the initial phase, in the eighteenth century, still remains to be written in its entirety. There are still too many questions that require an answer, too many pieces missing from the puzzle. For instance, we do not really know why the Enlightenment's idea of rights was virtually abandoned in the following centuries: why they were so crushingly defeated and went unacknowledged in many European States and in the relationship between the West and the rest of the world. Also we know hardly anything about the history of rights, or anything of the kind, among other peoples of the earth. And the very causes of the 'halt' in the Enlightenment programme are still unclear: they certainly do not lie in its own philosophical and theoretical fragility, as some have maintained.[47] If anything, we should look for them in the concrete political and cultural clashes of the nineteenth and twentieth centuries. Only painstaking historical fieldwork will enable us to throw full light on questions such as these, which are of crucial importance for the future of mankind. But this must be carried out with a critical spirit, bearing in mind Nietzsche's acute warning on our constant need for history: 'we need it for life and action, not as a convenient way to avoid life and action, or to excuse a selfish life and a cowardly or base action.'[48] Only in this way will it be possible to really ascertain, beyond all rhetoric and disillusionment, what is still left today of that programme for the emancipation of man through man that was so generously put together by thinkers like Voltaire, Rousseau, Diderot, Condorcet, Paine, Schiller, Beccaria, Filangieri, Goya and many others.

47. See the thesis put forward by Jürgen Habermas in 'Sauver le projet des Lumières', translated by Christian Bouchindhomme, in *Lumières! Un héritage pour demain*, ed. Yann Fauchois, Thierry Grillet and Tzvetan Todorov (Paris, 2006), p.26-27. The German philosopher seems to accuse the Enlightenment of having underestimated the importance of modern social communication as an artistic phenomenon. He detects in this signs of its theoretical fragility, which would lead to a halt in its programme.
48. Friedrich Nietzsche, *The Use and abuse of history*, translated by Adrian Collins, with an introduction by Julius Kraft (Indianapolis, IN, 1957), p.3.

Bibliography

Primary works

[Accarias de Sérionne, Jacques], *Situation politique actuelle de l'Europe, considérée relativement à l'ordre moral pour servir de supplément à l'ordre moral* (Augsburg, Conrad Henri Stage, 1781).

Albon, Claude-Camille d', *Discours politiques, historiques et critiques, sur quelques gouvernements de l'Europe* (Neuchâtel, n.n., 1779).

Alighieri, Dante, *Paradiso*, translated by Robert Hollander and Jean Hollander (New York, 2006).

Anderson, James, *Constitutions, histoires, lois* [...] *traduit de l'anglois par Jean Kuenen* (The Hague, Corneille Van Zanten, 1736).

–, *The Constitutions of the free-masons, containing the history, charges, regulations, etc. of that most ancient and right worshipful fraternity* (London, printed by William Hunter, for John Senex, and John Hooke, 1723).

Aquinas, Thomas, *Contra gentiles* and *Summa theologica* – see 'Online resources'.

Aristotle, *Nicomachean ethics*, translated by H. Rackham, *Loeb classical library* 73 (Cambridge, MA, 1926).

–, *Politics*, translated by H. Rackham, *Loeb classical library* 264 (Cambridge, MA, 1932).

Bachaumont, Louis Petit de, *Mémoires secrets pour servir à l'histoire de la République des Lettres en France depuis 1762 jusqu'à nos jours*, 36 vols (London, n.n., 1784).

Barbeyrac, Jean, 'An historical and critical account of the science of morality, and the progress it has made in the world, from the earliest times down to the publication of Pufendorf, *Of the law of nature and nations*: in a prefatory discourse to the said work', translated by George Carew, bound with Pufendorf, *Of the law of nature and nations: eight books*, translated by Basil Kennett (London, Printed for J. Walthoe, R. Wilkin, J. and J. Bonwicke, S. Birt, T. Ward, and T. Osborne, 1729), with separately numbered pages, 1-88.

–, 'Préface du traducteur', in Hugo Grotius, *Le Droit de la guerre et de la paix* (Amsterdam, Pierre de Coup, 1724).

–, 'A preface to the following discourses', prefixed to Gerard Noodt, *The Power of the sovereign, and the right of liberty of conscience*, translated by John Savage (London, J. Humfreys for Andrew Bell, 1708), p.xv-xxiv.

Barruel, Augustin, *Memoirs, illustrating the history of Jacobinism: a translation from the French of the abbé Barruel*, translated by Robert Clifford, 4 vols (London, printed for the author, by T. Burton and Co., and sold by E. Booker, 1797-1798).

Bayle, Pierre, *The Dictionary historical and critical of Mr Peter Bayle*, facsimile of edition printed in London by J. J. and P. Knapton, 2nd edn, 5 vols, 1734-1738 (London, 1997).

–, *Various thoughts on the occasion of a comet*, ed. and translated by Robert C. Bartlett (Albany, NY, 2000).

Beccaria, Cesare, *Dei delitti e delle pene con una raccolta di lettere e documenti relativi alla nascita dell'opera e alla sua fortuna nell'Europa del Settecento*, ed. Franco Venturi (Turin, 1965).

–, *Des délits et des peines*, ed. and translated by Philippe Audegean, based on the Italian text established by Gianni Francioni (Paris, 2009).

–, *Edizione nazionale delle opere di Cesare Beccaria*, vol.1: *Dei delitti e delle pene*, ed. Gianni Francioni (Milan, 1984).

–, *An Essay on crimes and punishments, by the marquis Beccaria of Milan, with a commentary by M. de Voltaire* (Edinburgh, James Donaldson, 1788).

–, *Des Herren Marquis von Beccaria unsterbliches Werk von Verbrechen und Strafen*, translated by Karl Ferdinand Hommel (Breslau, Johann Friedrich Korn, the Elder, 1778).

–, *Traité des délits et des peines*, translated by André Morellet (Lausanne, n.n., 1766).

–, *Traité des délits et des peines traduit de l'italien d'après la troisième édition, revue, corrigée et augmentée par l'auteur* (Philadelphia, PA, n.n., 1766).

[Bianchi, Isidoro], *Dell'Istituto de' veri liberi muratori*, ed. Giordano Gamberini (Ravenna, 1980).

Blackstone, William, *Commentaries on the law of England*, a facsimile of the first edition of 1765-1769 with an introduction by S. N. Katz, 4 vols (Chicago, IL, 1979).

Bolts, William, *Etat civil, politique et commerçant du Bengale, ou Histoire des conquêtes et de l'administration de la compagnie angloise dans ce pays, ouvrage traduit de l'anglois de M. Bolts*, translated by Jean-Nicolas Démeunier (The Hague, Gosse, fils, 1775).

Burke, Edmund, *Reflections on the Revolution in France and on the proceedings in certain societies in London relative to that event*, ed. Conor Cruise O'Brien (London, 1986).

Burlamaqui, Jean-Jacques, *Principes du droit naturel* (Geneva, Barillot et fils, 1748).

–, *The Principles of natural law: in which the true systems of morality and civil government are established, and the different sentiments of Grotius, Hobbes, Puffendorf, Barbeyrac, Locke, Clark, and Hutchinson, occasionally considered*, translated by Thomas Nugent (London, J. Nourse, 1748).

[Carra, Jean-Louis], *Odazir, ou le Jeune Syrien, roman philosophique, composé d'après les mémoires d'un Turc* (The Hague [Bouillon], [Société typographique de Bouillon], 1782).

Chaumeix d'Orléans, Abraham-Joseph, *Préjugés légitimes contre l'Encyclopédie et essai de réfutation de ce dictionnaire*, 8 vols (Brussels, n.n., 1758).

Cicero, *Tusculan disputations*, translated by J. E. King, *Loeb classical library* 141 (Cambridge, MA, 1927).

Collins, Anthony, *A Discourse of free-thinking, occasion'd by the rise and growth of a sect call'd free-thinkers* (London, n.n., 1713).

Condorcet, Antoine-Nicolas de, *Dichiarare i diritti, costituire i poteri: un inedito sulla dichiarazione dei diritti dell'uomo*, ed. Gabriele Magrin and Mercurio Candela (Milan, 2011).

–, *Eloge de M. D'Alembert, lu dans l'assemblée publique de l'Académie des sciences, le 21 avril 1784* (Paris, n.n., 1784).

[–], *Lettres d'un citoyen des Etats-Unis à un Français, sur les affaires présentes* (Philadelphia, PA, n.n., 1788).

–, *Réflexions d'un citoyen non gradué*, in *Œuvres*, ed. Arthur O'Connor and François Arago, 12 vols (Paris, 1847-1849), vol.7, p.141-66.

–, *Réflexions sur l'esclavage des nègres* (Neuchâtel, Société typographique, 1781).

–, *Sketch for a historical picture of the progress of the human mind*, translated by June Barraclough, with an introduction by Stuart Hampshire (London, 1955).

–, *Vie de Monsieur Turgot* (London [Paris], n.n., 1786).

–, *Vie de Voltaire*, with a preface by Elisabeth Badinter (Paris, 1994).

Constant, Benjamin, *Commentaire sur l'ouvrage de Filangieri*, ed. Kurt Klocke and Antonio Trampus (Tübingen, 2012).

Court de Gébelin, Antoine, *Monde primitif, analisé et comparé avec le monde moderne*, 2nd edn, 9 vols (Paris, Durand, 1777-1796).

Diderot, Denis, 'Apostrophe aux insurgents d'Amérique' (1778), in *Textes politiques*, with an introduction and notes by Yves Benot (Paris, 1960), p.213-14.

–, 'Art', translated by Nelly S. Hoyt and Thomas Cassirer, in *The Encyclopedia of Diderot & D'Alembert: collaborative translation project*, http://quod.lib.umich.edu/d/did/ (last accessed 24 April 2019).

–, *Diderot on art*, vol.2: *The Salon of 1767*, ed. and translated by John Goodman (New Haven, CT, and London, 1995).

–, 'Encyclopedia', translated by Philip Stewart, in *The Encyclopedia of Diderot & D'Alembert: collaborative translation project*, http://quod.lib.umich.edu/d/did/ (last accessed 24 April 2019).

–, 'Natural rights', translated by Stephen J. Gendzier, in *The Encyclopedia of Diderot & D'Alembert: collaborative translation project*, http://quod.lib.umich.edu/d/did/ (last accessed 24 April 2019).
–, *Œuvres complètes*, ed. Jules Assézat, 20 vols (Paris, 1875-1877).
–, *Opere filosofiche*, ed. Paolo Rossi (Milan, 1967).
–, *Pages inédites contre un tyran*, with an introduction by Franco Venturi (Paris, 1937).
–, *Pensées détachées: contributions à l''Histoire des deux Indes'*, ed. Gianluigi Goggi (Siena, 1976).
–, *Salons*, ed. Michel Delon (Paris, 2008).
–, *Scritti politici*, ed. Furio Diaz (Turin, 1967).
–, *Thoughts on the interpretation of nature and other philosophical works*, ed. David J. Adams (Manchester, 1999).
–, and Jean D'Alembert, *Encyclopédie, ou Dictionnaire raisonné des sciences, des arts et des métiers*, 17 vols (Paris, Briasson, 1751-1772) – see also 'Online resources'.
Discours prononcé dans l'Académie françoise, le lundi IV juin MDCC. LXXXVII à la réception de M. de Rulhiere (Paris, n.n., 1787).
Dohm, Christian Wilhelm, *Nachricht von der Neuverfassung der Zünfte in Frankreich* (Kassel, n.n., 1778).
Domat, Jean, *The Civil law in its natural order: together with the publick law*, translated by William Strahan, 2 vols (London, printed by J. Bettenham for E. Bell, J. Darby, A. Bettesworth, G. Strahan, F. Fayram, J. Pemberton, J. Hooke, C. Rivington, F. Clay, J. Batley and E. Symon, 1722).
Dorat, Claude-Joseph, *Collection complète des œuvres*, 6 vols (Neuchâtel, Société typographique, 1776).
Dostoevsky, Fyodor, *The Karamazov brothers*, translated with an introduction and notes by Ignat Avseyp (Oxford, 2008).
Dupaty, Charles-Marguerite, *Mémoire justificatif pour trois hommes condamnés à la roue* (Paris, Philippe-Denys Pierre, 1786).
Dupont de Nemours, Pierre-Samuel, *De l'origine et des progrès d'une science nouvelle* (London [Paris?], chez Desaint, 1768).
Duval-Pyrau, abbé, *Aristide* (Yverdon, Société littéraire et typographique, 1777).

Estienne, Henri, *Thesaurus Graecae linguae, ab Henrico Stephano constructus, ediderunt Hase, Sinner et Fix*, 3rd edn (Paris, 1833).
Euripides, *Les Tragédies d'Euripide, traduites du grec par M.* [*Pierre*] *Prevost, professeur et membre de l'Académie royale des sciences et belles-lettres de Berlin*, vol.2 (Paris, n.n., 1782).

Ferguson, Adam, *An Essay on the history of civil society* (Kitchener, 2001).
Filangieri, Gaetano, 'Estratto dell'opera di G. Playfair diretto al Marchese D[onato] T[ommasi]', in Filangieri, *La scienza della legislazione con giunta degli Opuscoli scelti*, 6 vols (Milan, 1822), vol.6, p.357-73.

–, *La Science de la législation*, 7 vols (Paris, Cuchet, 1786-1791).

–, *La scienza della legislazione*, ed. Vincenzo Ferrone, 7 vols (Venice and Mariano del Friuli, 2003-2004), vol.1: *Delle regole generali della scienza legislativa*, ed. Antonio Trampus (2003); vol.2: *Delle leggi politiche ed economiche*, ed. Maria Teresa Silvestrini (2004); vol.3: *Delle leggi criminali: della procedura*, ed. Francesco Toschi Vespasiani (2003); vol.4: *Delle leggi criminali: de' delitti e delle pene*, ed. Gerardo Tocchini and Antonio Trampus (2004); vol.5: *Delle leggi che riguardano l'educazione, i costumi e l'istruzione pubblica*, ed. Paolo Bianchini (2004); vol.6: *Delle leggi che riguardano la religione*, ed. Gerardo Tocchini (2003); vol.7: *La genesi e le edizioni della 'scienza della legislazione', indice delle fonti, indice analitico, indice dei nomi e dei luoghi*, ed. Antonio Trampus and Gerardo Tocchini (2004).

Francioni, Gianni, and Sergio Romagnoli (ed.), *'Il Caffè' 1764-1766* (Turin, 1993).

Gaillard, Gabriel Henri, *Histoire de la rivalité de la France et de l'Angleterre*, 3 vols (Paris, Saillant & Nyon, 1771).

[Galanti, Giuseppe Maria], *Elogio di Machiavelli* (n.p. [Naples], n.n., 1779).

[–], *Elogio storico del signor abate Antonio Genovesi* (Naples, n.n., 1772; anastatic edition, Naples, 1977).

Galiani, Ferdinando, *Dialogues sur le commerce des bleds*, in *Illuministi italiani*, vol.6: *Opere di Ferdinando Galiani*, ed. Furio Diaz and Luciano Guerci (Milan and Naples, 1975), p.345-612.

Galilei, Galileo, *Discoveries and opinions of Galileo, including The Starry messenger (1610), Letter to the Grand Duchess Christina (1615), and excerpts from Letters on sunspots (1613), The Assayer (1623)*, translated by Stillman Drake (New York, 1957).

Genovesi, Antonio, *Della diceosina o sia della filosofia del giusto e dell'onesto*, ed. Niccolò Guasti (Venice and Mariano del Friuli, 2008).

–, *Delle lezioni di commercio o sia di economia civile con elementi di commercio*, ed. Maria Luisa Perna (Naples, 2005).

–, editorial matter in *Spirito delle leggi del signore di Montesquieu con le note dell'abate Antonio Genovesi*, 4 vols (Naples, Domenico Terres, 1777).

–, *Elementa metaphysicae*, 4 vols (Naples, Benedetto Gessari, 1756).

Goethe, Johann Wolfgang von, *Dramatic works of Goethe*, translated by Anna Swanwick (London, 1860).

–, *Italian journey*, translated by W. H. Auden and Elizabeth Mayer (Harmondsworth, 1970).

–, *Letters from Goethe*, translated by M. von Herzfeld and C. Melvil Sym, with an introduction by W. H. Bruford (Edinburgh, 1957).

–, *Selected poems*, translated by John Whaley (London, 1998).

Gorini Corio, Giuseppe, *Politica, diritto e religione per ben pensare* (Milan, Agnelli, 1742).

Grimaldi, Francescantonio, *Riflessioni sopra l'ineguaglianza tra gli uomini*, 3 vols (Naples, Vincenzo Mazzola-Vocola, 1779).

Grotius, Hugo, *De iure belli ac pacis libri tres* (Paris, n.n., 1625).

–, *Prolegomena to the law of war and peace*, translated by Francis W. Kelsey (New York, 1957).

–, *The Rights of war and peace*, translated by John Morrice *et al.* (from the Barbeyrac edition), ed. Richard Tuck (Indianapolis, IN, 2005).

Helvétius, *De l'esprit, or Essays on the mind, and its several faculties, written by Helvetius, translated from the edition printed under the author's inspection* (London, printed for the translator, 1759).

–, 'Letters of Helvetius, addressed to President Montesquieu and M. Saurin, on perusing the manuscript of *The Spirit of laws*', www.econlib.org/library/Tracy/ddtMSL28.html (last accessed 8 May 2019).

Herder, Johann Gottfried, *Briefe zu Beförderung der Humanität*, ed. Heinz Stolpe with Hans-Joachim Kruse and Dietrich Simon, 2 vols (Berlin and Weimar, 1971).

Hobbes, Thomas, *Leviathan*, ed. J. C. A. Gaskin (Oxford, 1998).

–, *On the citizen*, ed. and translated by Richard Tuck and Michael Silverthorne (Cambridge, 1998).

Holbach, Paul-Henri Thiry, baron d', 'Representatives', translated by Stephen J. Gendzier, in *The Encyclopedia of Diderot & D'Alembert: collaborative translation project*, http://quod.lib.umich.edu/d/did/ (last accessed 20 May 2019).

–, *Systême social, ou Principes naturels de la morale et de la politique, avec un examen de l'influence du gouvernement sur les mœurs*, 3 vols (London, n.n., 1773).

Hollard, Albert, *Les Souffrances de l'Eglise et leur glorieuse issue: sermon sur Michée VII, 8 prononcé dans l'Eglise françoise de Christian-Erlang le 30 octobre 1785, à l'occasion de la commémoration religieuse et du jubilé de la révocation de l'Edit de Nantes, qui a été suivie de l'établissement des réfugiés françois à Christian-Erlang, par Albert Hollard, pasteur* (n.p., n.n., n.d. [1785]).

Hommel, Karl Ferdinand, 'Hommelische Vorrede' to *Des Herren Marquis von Beccaria unsterbliches Werk von Verbrechen und Strafen* (Breslau, Johann Friedrich Korn, the Elder, 1778), p.iii-li.

Humboldt, Wilhelm von, *The Limits of state action*, ed. and with an introduction and notes by J. W. Burrow (Cambridge, 1969).

–, *The Sphere and duties of government*, translated by Joseph Coulthard, Jr (London, 1854).

Hume, David, *Enquiries concerning human understanding and concerning the principles of morals*, ed. P. H. Nidditch, 3rd edn (Oxford, 2014).

–, 'Of the study of history', in *Essays: moral, political, and literary*, ed. Eugene F. Miller (Indianapolis, IN, 1985), p.563-68.

–, *A Treatise of human nature: a critical edition*, vol.1: *Texts*, ed. David Fate Norton and Mary J. Norton (Oxford, 2014).

Hutcheson, Francis, *A System of moral philosophy*, 2 vols (London, n.n., 1755).

[Illuminati], *Einige Originalschriften des Illuminatenordens* (Munich, Joseph Lentner, 1787).

–, *Nachtrag von weitern Originalschriften, welche die Illuminatensekte […] betreffen*, vol.2: *Dokumenten, Anrede auf die neu aufzunehmenden Illuminatos dirigentes* (Munich, n.n., 1787).

Iselin, Isaac, *Versuch über die Gesetzgebung von der Verfasser der philosophischen Träume* (n.p., n.n., 1760).

Jaucourt, Louis de, 'Natural liberty', translated by Thomas Zemanek, in *The Encyclopedia of Diderot & D'Alembert: collaborative translation project*, http://quod.lib.umich.edu/d/did/ (last accessed 24 April 2019).

Kant, Immanuel, *The Conflict of the faculties*, translated by Mary J. Gregor and Robert Anchor, in *Religion and rational theology*, ed. Allen W. Wood and George di Giovanni (Cambridge, 1996), p.233-328.

–, 'On the common saying: that may be correct in theory, but it is of no use in practice', in Kant, *Practical philosophy*, ed. and translated Mary J. Gregor (Cambridge, 1996), p.276-309.

–, 'Remarks in the *Observations on the feeling of the beautiful and sublime*', in *Observations on the feeling of the beautiful and sublime and other writings*, ed. and translated by Patrick Frierson (Cambridge, 2011), p.63-202.

–, 'Toward perpetual peace: a philosophical sketch', in Kant, *Toward perpetual peace and other writings on politics, peace, and history*, ed. and with an introduction by Pauline Kleingeld, translated by David L. Colclasure (New Haven, CT, 2006), p.67-110.

Las Casas, Bartolomé de, *De regia potestate*, ed. Giuseppe Tosi (Rome and Bari, 2007).

La Ville, Jean-Claude de, *Continuation des Causes célèbres et intéressantes, avec les jugements qui les ont décidées*, vol.3 (Amsterdam, Chatelain, 1770).

Le Blanc de Guillet, Antoine, *Les Druides, tragédie* (Paris, Louis, [1772]).

Le Clerc, Nicolas-Gabriel, and Antoine-François Le Clerc, *Histoire physique, morale, civile et politique de la Russie*, vol.2 (Paris and Versailles, n.n., 1785).

Le Mercier de La Rivière, Pierre-Paul, *L'Ordre naturel et essentiel des sociétés politiques*, 2 vols (London, n.n., 1767).

[Le Moyne Des Essarts, Nicolas-Toussaint], *Causes célèbres, curieuses et intéressantes, de toutes les cours souveraines du royaume, avec les jugements qui les ont décidées*, 195 vols (Paris, Simon, 1773-1789).

Lessing, Gotthold Ephraim, 'Dramatic notes (*Hamburg dramaturgy*)', in Lessing, *Selected prose works*, ed. Edward Bell, translated by E. C. Beasley and Helen Zimmern (London, 1890), p.227-493.

–, 'Ernst and Falk: dialogues for freemasons', in *Philosophical and theological writings*, translated by H. B. Nisbet (Cambridge, 2005), p.184-216.

Levi, Primo, *The Drowned and the saved*, translated by Raymond Rosenthal (London, 1988).

Locke, John, *An Essay concerning human understanding*, abridged with an introduction and notes by Pauline Phemister (Oxford, 2008).

–, *Two treatises of government: and a letter concerning toleration*, ed. Ian Shapiro (New Haven, CT, and London, 2003).

Marcus Aurelius, *Pensées de l'empereur Marc-Aurèle-Antonin, ou Leçons de vertu que ce prince philosophe se faisoit à lui-même: nouvelle traduction du grec, distribuée en chapitres, suivant les matières, avec notes et variantes, par M. de Joly* (Paris, n.n., 1770).

Maréchal, Sylvain, *Antiquité d'Herculanum, ou les Plus belles peintures antiques, et les marbres, bronzes, meubles, etc., etc. trouvés dans les excavations d'Herculanum, Stabia et Pompeia, gravés par F. A. David, avec les explications par P. S. Maréchal*, vol.2 (Paris, n.n., 1780).

Marmontel, Jean-François, *Œuvres complètes*, vol.5 (Paris, Née de la Rochelle, 1787).

Melon, Jean-François, *A Political essay upon commerce*, translated by David Bindon (Dublin, Philip Crampton, 1738).

Mercier, Louis-Sébastien, *L'An deux mille quatre cent quarante: rêve s'il en fût jamais* (Neuchâtel, n.n., 1772).

–, *Du théâtre, ou Nouvel Essai sur l'art dramatique* (Amsterdam, E. van Harrevelt, 1773).

–, *Mon bonnet de nuit*, 4 vols (Lausanne, Jean-Pierre Heubach, 1785).

–, *Portrait de Philippe II, roi d'Espagne* (Amsterdam, n.n., 1785).

–, *Tableau de Paris, nouvelle édition*, 2 vols (Hamburg and Neuchâtel, Virchaux et Fauche, 1781).

–, *Tableau de Paris, nouvelle édition corrigée et augmentée*, 8 vols (Amsterdam, n.n., 1783).

–, *Théâtre complet de M. Mercier*, 4 vols (Amsterdam, B. Vlam; Leiden, J. Murray, 1778 [1778-1784]).

Mirabeau, Honoré-Gabriel Riqueti, comte de, *Lettre du comte de Mirabeau à *** sur M. M. de Cagliostro et Lavater* (Berlin, François de Lagarde, 1786).

Mirabeau, Victor de Riqueti, marquis de, *La Science, ou les Droits et les devoirs de l'homme* (Lausanne, François Grasset & comp., 1774).

Montesquieu, Charles de Secondat, baron de, *Œuvres complètes*, ed. Roger Caillois, 2 vols (Paris, 1951).

–, *Spirito delle leggi del signore di Montesquieu con le note dell'abate Antonio Genovesi*, 4 vols (Naples, Domenico Terres, 1777).

–, *The Spirit of laws*, 4th edn, 2 vols (Edinburgh, Donaldson, 1768).

Morellet, André, introduction to Beccaria, *Traité des délits et des peines* (Lausanne, n.n., 1766).

[Necker, Jacques], *Eloge de Jean-Baptiste Colbert, discours qui a remporté le prix de l'Académie françoise en 1773* (Paris, n.n., 1773).

Pagano, Francesco Mario, *Considerazioni sul processo criminale*, ed. Filippo Maria Paladini (Venice and Mariano del Friuli, 2009).

–, *Progetto di costituzione della Repubblica napoletana presentato al governo provvisorio dal comitato di legislazione*, ed. Federica Morelli and Antonio Trampus, with an introduction by Anna Maria Rao (Venice and Mariano del Friuli, 2008).

–, *Saggi politici: de' principii, progressi e decadenza delle società, edizione seconda (1791-92)*, ed. Luigi Firpo and Laura Salvetti Firpo (Naples, 1993).

Pechméja, Jean-Joseph, *Télèphe en XII livres* (London and Paris, Pissot, 1784).

Pico della Mirandola, Giovanni, *On the dignity of man* (translated by Charles Glenn Wallis)*; On being and the one; Heptaplus* (Indianapolis, IN, 1998).

Plato, *Laws*, translated by R. G. Bury, 2 vols, *Loeb classical library* 192 (Cambridge, MA, 1926).

Poivre, Pierre, *Voyages d'un philosophe, ou Observations sur les mœurs et les arts des peuples de l'Afrique, de l'Asie et de l'Amérique* (Maastricht, J. E. Dufour & P. Roux, 1779).

Price, Richard, *A Discourse on the love of our country* (1789; Oxford and New York, 1992).

Pufendorf, Samuel von, *Les Devoirs de l'homme et du citoyen, tels qu'ils lui sont prescrits par la loi naturelle*, translated by Jean Barbeyrac (Amsterdam, Pierre de Coup, 1715).

–, *Il diritto della natura e delle genti o sia sistema generale de' principi li più importanti di morale, giurisprudenza e politica*, translated by Giovambattista Almici, 4 vols (Venice, Pietro Valvasense, 1757).

–, *Le Droit de la nature et des gens* (Amsterdam, n.n., 1706).

–, *Of the law of nature and nations: eight books*, translated by Basil Kennett (London, Printed for J. Walthoe, R. Wilkin, J. and J. Bonwicke, S. Birt, T. Ward, and T. Osborne, 1729), archive.org/details/oflawofnaturenat00pufe (last accessed 29 April 2019).

–, *Specimen controversiarum circa ius naturale ipsi nuper motarum* (Osnabrück, ex officina Johannis Georgii Schwänderi, 1678).

–, *The Whole duty of man according to the law of nature*, translated by Andrew Tooke (1691), ed. Ian Hunter and David Saunders (Indianapolis, IN, 2003).

Quesnay, François, *Physiocratie, ou Constitution naturelle du gouvernement le plus avantageux au genre humain*, ed. Pierre-Samuel Dupont de Nemours (Leiden and Paris, chez Merlin, 1767-1768).

Rabaut de Saint-Etienne, Jean-Paul, *Le Roi doit modifier les loix portées contre les protestants; démonstration; avantage que la France tirerait de cette modification* (London [Paris?], n.n., 1784).

Raynal, Guillaume-Thomas-François, abbé, *A Philosophical and political history of the settlements and trade of the Europeans in the East and West Indies*, translated by J. O. Justamond, 8 vols (London, Strahan and Cadell, 1788).

'Réflexions impartiales d'un neutre sur le traité éventuel concerté entre la Régence d'Amsterdam et le Congrès américain', in *Correspondance politique sur les affaires présentes de la Hollande: feuille périodique pour servir à l'histoire de ce siècle*, vol.1 (Amsterdam, n.n., 1782), p.23-36.

Règle maçonnique, à l'usage des loges réunies et rectifiées, arrêtée au convent général de Wilhelmsbad (The Hague, J. van Cleef, 1783).

Robertson, William, *Histoire d'Ecosse sous les regnes de Marie Stuart et de Jacques VI jusqu'à l'avènement de ce prince à la couronne d'Angleterre, traduit de l'anglois*, 3 vols (London [Paris], n.n., 1764).

Robespierre, Maximilien de, 'Discours du 26 juillet 1794', in *Œuvres*, vol.10: *Discours, 5e partie: '27 juillet 1793-27 juillet 1794'*, ed. Marc Bouloiseau and Albert Soboul (Paris, 1967).

Roucher, Jean-Antoine, *Les Mois, poëme en douze chants*, 2 vols (Paris, Quillau, 1779).

Rousseau, Jean-Jacques, *Confessions*, translated by W. Conyngham Mallory (Auckland, 1903).

–, *Discorsi sulle scienze e sulle arti, sull'origine della disuguaglianza fra gli uomini*, translated by Rodolfo Mondolfo, ed. Luigi Luporini (Milan, 1997).

–, *Emilius, or an Essay on education, by John James Rousseau, translated from the French by Mr. Nugent, in two volumes* (London, J. Nourse and P. Vaillant, 1763).

–, *Essay on the origin of languages and writings related to music*, ed. and translated by John T. Scott, in *The Collected writings of Rousseau*, vol.7 (Hanover, NH, 1998).

–, [*First discourse*] *The Discourse which carried the præmium at the Academy of Dijon, in MDCCL, on this question, propos'd by the said Academy, whether the re-establishment of arts and sciences has contributed to the refining of manners, by a citizen of Geneva* (London, W. Owen, 1751).

–, 'Letter to Beaumont', in *Letter to Beaumont, letters written from the mountain, and related writings*, ed. Christopher Kelly and Eve Grace, translated by Christopher Kelly and Judith R. Bush, in *The Collected writings of Rousseau*, vol.9 (Hanover, NH, and London, 2001), p.16-101.

–, *Narcissus, or the Self-admirer*, in *The Works of J. J. Rousseau, translated from the French, in ten volumes* (Edinburgh, J. Bell, J. Dickson, and C. Elliot, 1773-1774), vol.8, p.61-119.

–, 'Political economy' [abridged], translated by Stephen J. Gendzier, in *The Encyclopedia of Diderot & D'Alembert: collaborative translation project*, http://quod.lib.umich.edu/d/did/ (last accessed 24 April 2019).

–, 'Political fragments', in *Social contract, Discourse on the virtue most necessary for a hero, Political fragments, and Geneva manuscript*, ed. Roger D. Masters and Christopher Kelly, translated by Judith R. Bush, Roger D. Masters and Christopher Kelly, in *The Collected writings of Rousseau*, vol.4 (Hanover, NH, and London, 1994), p.16-75.

–, *Rousseau, judge of Jean-Jacques: dialogues*, ed. Roger D. Masters and Christopher Kelly, translated by Judith R. Bush, Christopher Kelly and Roger D. Masters, in *The Collected writings of Rousseau*, vol.1 (Hanover, NH, 1990).

–, [*Second discourse*] *A Discourse upon the origin and foundation of the inequality among mankind* (London, R. and J. Dodsley, 1761).

–, [*Social contract*] *An Inquiry into the nature of the social contract, or Principles of political right, translated from the French of John James Rousseau* (London, G. G. J. and J. Robinson, 1791).

Schiller, Friedrich, 'Letters on *Don Carlos*', translated by Jeanne R. Willson, in Schiller, *Plays: Intrigue and love and Don Carlos*, ed. Walter Hinderer (New York, 1983), p.305-46.

–, *Werke: Nationalausgabe*, vol.14: *Bühnenbearbeitungen*, part 2, ed. Hans Heinrich Borcherdt (Weimar, 1949).

–, *The Works of Frederick Schiller*, 4 vols, Bohn's standard library series (London, 1854-1865).

Schlettwein, Johann August, *Die Rechte der Menschheit oder der einzige wahre Grund aller Gesetze, Ordnungen und Verfassungen* (Giessen, Justus Friederich Krieger, 1784).

Schlosser, Johann Georg, *Briefe über die Gesetzgebung überhaupt und den Entwurf des preussischen Gesetzbuchs insbesondere* (Frankfurt am Main, Fleischer, 1789).

Sieyès, Emmanuel Joseph, *Les Discours de Sieyès dans les débats constitutionnels de l'An III (2 et 18 thermidor)*, ed. Paul Bastid (Paris, 1939).

Smith, Adam, *An Inquiry into the nature and causes of the wealth of nations* (London, 2001).

–, *The Theory of moral sentiments*, ed. Knud Haakonssen (Cambridge, 2004).

Spinoza, Benedict de, *Benedict de Spinoza's political treatise*, translated by A. H. Gossett, ed. R. H. M. Elwes (Raleigh, NC, 2001; translation originally published in 1883).

–, *Theological-political treatise*, translated by Michael Silverthorne and Jonathan Israel, ed. Jonathan Israel (Cambridge, 2007).

Tracy, Antoine Louis Claude Destutt de, *A Commentary and review of Montesquieu's "Spirit of laws", to which are annexed, observations on the thirty-first book, by the late M. Condorcet: and two letters of Helvetius, on the merits of the same work*, translated by Thomas Jefferson (Philadelphia, PA, 1811).

Verri, Alessandro, 'Alcune idee sulla filosofia morale', in *'Il Caffè' 1764-1766*, ed. Gianni Francioni and Sergio Romagnoli (Turin, 1993), p.685-95.

–, 'Di alcuni sistemi del pubblico diritto', in *'Il Caffè' 1764-1766*, ed. Gianni Francioni and Sergio Romagnoli (Turin, 1993), p.725-39.

–, 'Di Carneade e di Grozio', in *'Il Caffè' 1764-1766*, ed. Gianni Francioni and Sergio Romagnoli (Turin, 1993), p.705-21.

Verri, Pietro, *Discorso sulla felicità*, in *Edizione nazionale delle opere di Pietro Verri*, vol.3: *I Discorsi e altri scritti degli anni Settanta*, ed. Giorgio Panizza with Silvia Contarini, Gianni Francioni and Sara Rosini (Rome, 2004).

–, *Meditazioni sulla felicità*, ed. Gianni Francioni (Como, 1996).

Vico, Giambattista, *The Autobiography of Giambattista Vico*, ed. Max Harold Fisch, translated by Max Harold Fisch and Thomas Goddard Bergin (Ithaca, NY, 1944).

–, *The First new science*, ed. and translated by Leon Pompa (Cambridge, 2002).

–, *The New science of Giambattista Vico*, unabridged translation of the 3rd edn (1744) with the addition of 'Practice of the new science', translated by Thomas Goddard Bergin and Max Harold Fisch (Ithaca, NY, and London, 1984).

–, *Opere giuridiche: il diritto universale*, ed. Paolo Cristofolini, with an introduction by Nicola Badaloni (Florence, 1974).

–, 'Synopsis of universal law', translated by Donald Phillip Verene, in *Giambattista Vico: keys to the 'New science'*, ed. Thora Ilin Bayer and Donald Phillip Verene (Ithaca, NY, 2009), p.17-38.

Vitoria, Francisco de, *De iure belli*, with preface by Carlo Galli (Rome and Bari, 2005).

Voltaire, *L'Affaire Calas et autres affaires* (Paris, 1975).

–, *Correspondence and related documents*, ed. Theodore Besterman, in *Œuvres complètes de Voltaire*, vol.85-135 (Oxford, 1968-1977).

–, *Dictionnaire philosophique*, ed. Christiane Mervaud, in *Œuvres complètes de Voltaire*, vol.35-36 (Oxford, 1994).

–, *Les Droits des hommes et les usurpations des autres*, ed. Simon Davies, in *Œuvres complètes de Voltaire*, vol.67 (Oxford, 2007), p.135-71.

–, *Il faut prendre un parti, ou le Principe d'action*, ed. Paolo Casini, in *Œuvres complètes de Voltaire*, vol.74B (Oxford, 2006).

–, *Letters concerning the English nation: the second edition, with large additions* (London, C. Davis, 1741).

–, *Lettres philosophiques*, ed. Nicholas Cronk and Nick Treuherz, in *Œuvres complètes de Voltaire*, vol.6A-B (Oxford, forthcoming).

–, *Philosophical dictionary*, ed. and translated by Theodore Besterman, 2nd edn (London, 2004).

–, *Questions sur les miracles*, in *Œuvres complètes de Voltaire*, ed. Louis Moland, 52 vols (Paris, 1877-1885), vol.25, p.357-450.

–, *Traité de métaphysique*, ed. W. H. Barber, in *Œuvres complètes de Voltaire*, vol.14 (Oxford, 1989).

–, *Traité sur la tolérance*, ed. John Renwick, in *Œuvres complètes de Voltaire*, vol.56C (Oxford, 2000).

–, *Trattato sulla tolleranza*, ed. Lorenzo Bianchi (Milan, 1995).

–, *A Treatise upon toleration* (Glasgow, Robert Urie, 1765).

–, *Voltaire in his letters, being a selection from his correspondence*, translated by S. G. Tallentyre (New York and London, 1919).

Wieland, Christoph Martin, 'Das Geheimniss des Kosmopoliten-orderns', in Wieland, *Sämmtliche Werke*, ed. Hamburger Stiftung zur Förderung von Wissenschaft und Kultur with the Wieland-Archiv […] and Hans Radspieler, vol.10 (Hamburg, 1984), p.155-203.

Windisch-Graetz, Josef Niklas W. von, *Discours dans lequel on examine les deux questions suivantes: 1º Un monarque a-t-il le droit de changer de son chef une constitution évidemment vicieuse? 2º Est-il prudent à lui, est-il de son intérêt de l'entreprendre? Suivi de réflexions pratiques* (n.p., n.n., 1788).

Wolff, Christian, *Institutiones iuris naturae et gentium in quibus ex ipsa hominis natura continuo nexu omnes obligationes et iura omnia deducuntur* (Halle, prostat in officina Rengeriana, 1754).

–, *Principes du droit de la nature et des gens extrait du grand'ouvrage latin de Mr. De Wolff, par Mr. Formey* (Amsterdam, n.n., 1758).

Secondary works

Abbattista, Guido, and Rolando Minuti (ed.), *Le Problème de l'altérité dans la culture européenne: anthropologie, politique et religion aux XVIII*e *et XIX*e *siècles* (Naples, 2006).

Adams, Geoffrey, *The Huguenots and French opinion, 1685-1787: the Enlightenment debate on toleration* (Waterloo, 1991).

Addante, Luca, *Eretici e libertini nel Cinquecento italiano* (Rome and Bari, 2010).

Agazzi, Elena, *Il corpo conteso: rito e gestualità nella Germania del Settecento* (Milan, 2000).

Agazzi, Emilio, *La filosofia della storia e della politica nel pensiero di Emanuele Kant*, ed. Enrico Colombo (1974-1975; Udine, 2012).

Agethen, Manfred, *Geheimbund und Utopie: Illuminaten, Freimaurer und deutsche Spätaufklärung* (Munich, 1984).

Ahnert, Thomas, 'The prince and the Church in the thought of Christian Thomasius', in *Natural law and civil sovereignty: moral right and state authority in early modern political thought*, ed. Ian Hunter and David Saunders (Basingstoke, 2002), p.91-105.

Ajello, Raffaele, *Arcana juris: diritto e politica nel Settecento italiano* (Naples, 1976).

Alpa, Guido, *La cultura delle regole: storia del diritto civile italiano* (Rome and Bari, 2000).

Amiable, Louis, *Une Loge maçonnique d'avant 1789: la loge des Neuf Sœurs* (1897), ed. Charles Porset (Paris, 1989).

Angle, Stephen C., *Human rights and Chinese thought: a cross-cultural inquiry* (Cambridge, 2002).

Appleby, J. O., *Economic thought and ideology in seventeenth-century England* (Princeton, NJ, 1978).

Arasse, Daniel, 'The artist', in *Enlightenment portraits*, ed. Michel Vovelle, translated by Lydia G. Cochrane (Chicago, IL, and London, 1997), p.226-56.

Arendt, Hannah, *The Human condition*, 2nd edn (1958; Chicago, IL, 1998).

Aretin, Karl Otmar von, *Heiliges Römisches Reich 1776-1806: Reichsverfassung und Staatssouveränität*, 2 vols (Wiesbaden, 1967).

Armitage, David, *The Declaration of Independence: a global history* (Cambridge, MA, 2007).

Audegean, Philippe, 'Passions et liberté: loi de nature et fondement du droit en Italie à l'époque de Beccaria', *Studi settecenteschi* 23 (2003), p.197-278.

–, *La Philosophie de Beccaria: savoir punir, savoir écrire, savoir produire* (Paris, 2010).

Bacchini, Furio, *La vita rocambolesca del conte Alessandro Savioli Corbelli (1742-1811)* (Bologna, 2011).

Baczko, Bronislaw, 'Finzioni storiche e congiunture utopiche', in *Nell'anno 2000: dall'utopia all'ucronia, atti del convegno internazionale (Torino 10 marzo 2000)*, ed. Bruno Bongiovanni and Gian Mario Bravo (Florence, 2001), p.9-22.

–, *Job, mon ami: promesses du bonheur et fatalité du mal* (Paris, 1997).

–, *Lumières de l'utopie* (Paris, 1978).

Badaloni, Nicola, introduction to Vico, *Opere giuridiche: il diritto universale*, ed. Paolo Cristofolini (Florence, 1974).

Baioni, Giuliano, *Classicismo e rivoluzione: Goethe e la Rivoluzione francese* (Naples, 1969).

Baker, Keith Michael, *Au tribunal de l'opinion: essai sur l'imaginaire politique au XVIIIe siècle* (Paris, 1993).

–, *Condorcet: from natural philosophy to social mathematics* (Chicago, IL, and London, 1975).

–, 'The idea of a Declaration of Rights', in *The French idea of freedom: the Old Regime and the Declaration of Rights of 1789*, ed. Dale Van Kley (Stanford, CA, 1994), p.154-99.

–, 'Politics and public opinion under the Old Regime: some reflections', in *Press and politics in pre-revolutionary France*, ed. J. R. Censer and J. D. Popkin (Berkeley, CA, 1987), p.204-46.

Barbera, Augusto, and Gianfrancesco Zanetti (ed.), *Le basi filosofiche del costituzionalismo: lineamenti di filosofia del diritto costituzionale* (Rome and Bari, 1997).

Barlier, Jean-Pierre, *La Société des amis des Noirs: aux origines de la première abolition de l'esclavage, 4 février 1794* (Paris, 2010).

Barny, Roger, *Le Droit naturel à l'épreuve de l'histoire: Jean-Jacques Rousseau dans la Révolution: débats politiques et sociaux* (Paris, 1995).

Baud-Bovy, Samuel, *et al.* (ed.), *Jean-Jacques Rousseau* (Neuchâtel, 1962).

Beaurepaire, Pierre-Yves, *L'Autre et le frère: l'étranger et la franc-maçonnerie en France au XVIIIe siècle* (Paris, 1998).

Becchi, Paolo, *Vico e Filangieri in Germania* (Naples, 1986).

–, and Kurt Seelmann, *Gaetano Filangieri und die europäische Aufklärung* (Frankfurt am Main and Berlin, 2000).

Beiser, Frederick C., *Schiller as philosopher: a re-examination* (Oxford, 2005).

Bell, David A., *The Cult of the nation in France: inventing nationalism, 1680-1800* (Cambridge, MA, 2001).

Bellen-Finster, Madeleine van, 'Die Rezeption Cesare Beccarias im deutschsprachigen Raum um 1800', *Annali dell'istituto storico italo-germanico in Trento* 11 (1985), p.193-219.

Berger, Thomas, *Der Humanitätsgedanke in der Literatur der deutschen Spätaufklärung* (Heidelberg, 2008).

Berman, Harold J., *Law and revolution: the formation of the Western legal tradition* (Cambridge, MA, 1983).

Berndt, Frauke (ed.), *Die Sachen der Aufklärung* (Halle, 2010).

Berti, Silvia, *Anticristianesimo e libertà: studi sull'Illuminismo radicale europeo* (Bologna, 2012).

–, 'Radicali ai margini: materialismo, libero pensiero e diritto al suicidio in Radicati di Passerano', *Rivista storica italiana* 116 (2004), p.794-811.

Bianchi, Lorenzo, editorial matter in Voltaire, *Trattato sulla tolleranza*, ed. Lorenzo Bianchi (Milan, 1995).

Bien, David D., *The Calas affair: persecution, toleration and heresy in eighteenth-century Toulouse* (Princeton, NJ, 1960).

–, 'Old Regime origins of democratic liberty', in *The French idea of freedom: the Old Regime and the Declaration of Rights of 1789*, ed. Dale Van Kley (Stanford, CA, 1994), p.23-71.

Bindman, David, *Ape to Apollo: aesthetics and the idea of race in the eighteenth century* (Ithaca, NY, 2002).

Biondi, Carminella, *Ces esclaves sont des hommes: lotta abolizionista e letteratura negrofila nella Francia del Settecento* (Pisa, 1979).

Birocchi, Italo, *Alla ricerca dell'ordine: fonti e cultura giuridica nell'età moderna* (Turin, 2002).

Blanc, Olivier, *Olympe de Gouges: une femme de libertés* (Paris, 1989).

Blanning, T. C. W., *Reform and revolution in Mainz, 1743-1803* (Cambridge, 1974).

Bloch, Ernst, *Natural law and human dignity*, translated by Dennis J. Schmidt (Cambridge, MA, 1986; original: *Naturrecht und menschliche Würde*, Frankfurt am Main, 1961).

Blom, H. W., and Laurens C. Winkel (ed.), *Grotius and the Stoa* (Assen, 2004).

Bobbio, Norberto, *The Age of rights* (Cambridge, 1996).

–, *Autobiografia*, ed. Alberto Papuzzi (Rome and Bari, 1997).

–, 'Il giusnaturalismo', in *Storia delle idee politiche economiche e sociali*, ed. Luigi Firpo, vol.4.1 (Turin, 1980), p.491-558.

–, *Thomas Hobbes and the natural law tradition*, translated by Daniela Gobetti (Chicago, IL, and London, 1993).

Böckenförde, Ernst-Wolfgang, 'Die Entstehung des Staates als Vorgang der Säkularisation' (1967), available in English as 'The rise of the state as a process of secularisation', in *State, society and liberty: studies in political theory and constitutional law*, translated by J. A. Underwood (New York and Oxford, 1991), p.26-46.

Bödeker, Hans Erich, '"Menschenrechte" im deutschen publizistischen Diskurs vor 1789', in *Grund- und Freiheitsrechte von der ständischen zur spätbürgerlichen Gesellschaft*, ed. Günter Birtsch (Göttingen, 1987), p.392-433.

–, 'Zur Rezeption der Menschen- und Bürgerrechte von 1789/1791 in der deutschen Aufklärungsgesellschaft', in *Grund- und Freiheitsrechte im Wandel von Gesellschaft und Geschichte: Beiträge zur Geschichte der Grund- und Freiheitsrechte vom Ausgang des Mittelalters bis zur Revolution von 1848*, ed. Günter Birtsch (Göttingen, 1981), p.258-86.

–, and Ulrich Herrmann (ed.), *Aufklärung als Politisierung, Politisierung der Aufklärung* (Hamburg, 1987).

Bois, Pierre-André, *Adolph Freiherr Knigge (1752-1796): de la 'nouvelle religion' aux droits de l'homme* (Wiesbaden, 1990).

Bonnell, Victoria E., and Lynn Hunt (ed.), *Beyond the cultural turn: new directions in the study of society and culture* (Berkeley, CA, 1999).

Borghero, Carlo, *La certezza e la storia: cartesianesimo, pirronismo e conoscenza storica* (Milan, 1983).

Boroumand, Ladan, *La Guerre des principes: les assemblées révolutionnaires face aux droits de l'homme et à la souveraineté de la nation* (Paris, 1999).

Bossy, John, *Dalla comunità all'individuo: per una storia sociale dei sacramenti nell'Europa moderna* (Turin, 1998).

Bréhier, Emile, *La Philosophie du Moyen Age*, 2nd edn (Paris, 1949).

Brett, Annabel S., *Liberty, right and nature: individual rights in later Scholastic thought* (Cambridge, 1997).

Brewer, John, *The Pleasures of the imagination: English culture in the eighteenth century* (New York, 1997).

Brown, Peter, *Augustine of Hippo: a biography*, 2nd edn (Berkeley, CA, 2000).

Brunner, Otto, *Land und Herrschaft: Grundfragen der territorialen Verfassungsgeschichte Südostdeutschlands im Mittelalter* (Brünn, 1942).

Buckle, Stephen, *Natural law and the theory of property: Grotius to Hume* (Oxford, 1991).

Burgio, Alberto, 'L'idea di eguaglianza tra diritto e politica nel *Dei delitti e delle pene*', in *Cesare Beccaria: la pratica dei Lumi*, ed. Vincenzo Ferrone and Gianni Francioni (Florence, 2000), p.79-98.

–, 'Necessità della storia e storia impossibile: per una analisi metodologica del "Discours sur l'inégalité" di Rousseau', *Studi settecenteschi* 11-12 (1988-1989), p.115-40.

Burkert, Walter, *Homo necans: the anthropology of Ancient Greek sacrificial ritual and myth*, translated by Peter Bing (Berkeley, CA, 1983).

Bussi, Emilio, *Diritto e politica in Germania nel XVIII secolo* (Milan, 1971).

–, *Stato e amministrazione nel pensiero di Carl Gottlieb Svarez precettore di Federico Guglielmo III di Prussia* (Milan, 1966).

Campbell, R. H., and Andrew S. Skinner (ed.), *The Origins and nature of the Scottish Enlightenment* (Edinburgh, 1982).

Canale, Damiano, 'Dagli stati della persona alle persone dello Stato: Wolff e le origini sistematiche dell'*Allgemeines Landrecht* prussiano del 1794', *Materiali per una storia della cultura giuridica* 28 (1998), p.139-94.

Cantelli, Gianfranco, *Vico e Bayle: premesse per un confronto* (Naples, 1971).

–, 'La virtù degli atei nei *Pensieri diversi sulla Cometa* di Pierre Bayle: una premessa per una società tollerante', in *La formazione storica della alterità: studi di storia della tolleranza nell'età moderna offerti a Antonio Rotondò*, ed. Henry Méchoulan *et al.*, 3 vols (Florence, 2001), vol.2, p.679-706.

Capra, Carlo, *I progressi della ragione: vita di Pietro Verri* (Bologna, 2002).

Capurso, Marcello, *Accentramento e costituzionalismo: il pensiero italiano del primo Settecento di fronte al problema dell'organizzazione dello Stato* (Naples, 1959).

Carey, John A., *Judicial reform in France before the Revolution of 1789* (Cambridge, MA, 1981).

Carpanetto, Dino, 'Augustin Barruel', in *L'albero della Rivoluzione: le interpretazioni della Rivoluzione francese*, ed. Luciano Guerci and Bruno Bongiovanni (Turin, 1989), p.49-56.

Carrithers, Michael, Steven Collins and Steven Lukes (ed.), *The Category of the person: anthropology, philosophy, history* (Cambridge, 1985).

Casini, Paolo, editorial matter to *Enciclopedia o dizionario ragionato delle scienze, delle arti e dei mestieri ordinato da Diderot e D'Alembert*, ed. and translated by Paolo Casini (Bari, 1968).

Cassirer, Ernst, *The Philosophy of the Enlightenment*, translated by Fritz C. A. Koelln and James P. Pettegrove (Princeton, NJ, 1951; original: *Die Philosophie der Aufklärung*, 1932).

–, *The Question of Jean-Jacques Rousseau*, ed. and translated by Peter Gay, 2nd edn (New Haven, CT, and London, 1989).

–, 'Vom Wesen und Werden des Naturrechts', in *Gesammelte Werke: Hamburger Ausgabe, XVIII, Aufsätze und kleine Schriften (1932-1935)*, ed. Ralf Becker (Hamburg, 2004), p.203-27.

Cattaneo, Mario Alessandro, 'Alcuni problemi nella dottrina della pena di Gaetano Filangieri', in *Gaetano Filangieri e l'Illuminismo europeo: atti del convegno tenuto a Vico Equense nel 1982*, ed. Lucio d'Alessandro (Naples, 1991), p.262-90.

Cazzaniga, Gian Mario, and Yves Charles Zarka (ed.), *L'Individu dans la pensée moderne, XVIe-XVIIIe siècles / L'individuo nel pensiero moderno, secoli XVI-XVII* (Pisa, 1995).

Certeau, Michel de, Dominique Julia and Jacques Revel, *Une Politique de la langue: la Révolution française et les patois* (Paris, 1975).

Cervelli, Innocenzo, 'Ceti e assolutismo in Germania: rassegna di studi e problemi', *Annali dell'Istituto storico italo-germanico in Trento* 3 (1977), p.431-512.

Chassaigne, Marc, *Le Procès du chevalier de La Barre* (Paris, 1920).

Chenu, Marie-Dominique, *Nature, man, and society in the twelfth century: essays on new theological perspectives in the Latin West*, selected, edited and translated by Jerome Taylor and Lester K. Little (Chicago, IL, 1968; original: *La Théologie au XIIe siècle*, Paris, 1957).

Ciafardone, Raffaele (ed.), *L'Illuminismo tedesco* (Turin, 1983).

Clavero, Bartolomé, *La Grâce du don: anthropologie catholique de l'économie moderne* (Paris, 1996).

Cmiel, Kenneth, 'The recent history of human rights', *The American historical review* 109 (2004), p.117-35.

Cobban, Alfred, *In search of humanity: the role of the Enlightenment in modern history* (London, 1960).

Conan, J., 'Une utopie physiocratisante: l'*Ile inconnue* de Guillaume Grivel', *Annales historiques de la Révolution française* 265 (1986), p.268-84.

Costa, Pietro, *Civitas: storia della cittadinanza in Europa*, vol.1: *Dalla civiltà comunale al Settecento* (Rome and Bari, 1999).

–, *Civitas: storia della cittadinanza in Europa*, vol.2: *L'età delle rivoluzioni (1789-1848)* (Rome and Bari, 2000).

– (ed.), *Il diritto di uccidere: l'enigma della pena della morte* (Milan, 2010).

–, Carla De Pascale and Mario Ricciardi, 'La *Scienza della legislazione* di Gaetano Filangieri', *Iride* 19:47 (2006), p.181-202.

Coujou, Jean-Paul, 'Droit naturel et humanité chez Burlamaqui: étude critique', in Jean-Jacques Burlamaqui, *Principes du droit naturel* (Paris, 2007), p.207-482.

Courtney, C. P., 'Les métamorphoses d'un best-seller: l'*Histoire des deux Indes* de 1770 à 1820', in *Raynal, de la polémique à l'histoire*, ed. Gilles Bancarel and Gianluigi Goggi (Oxford, 2000), p.109-20.

–, and Claudette Fortuny, 'Répertoire d'ouvrages et d'articles (1800-2003) sur Raynal', *SVEC* 2003:08, p.37-113.

Croce, Benedetto, *Aneddoti di varia letteratura*, 2nd edn, 4 vols (Bari, 1954).

–, *The Philosophy of Giambattista Vico*, translated by R. G. Collingwood (London, 1913).

Crocker, Lester G., 'Les droits individuels et le corps social: Rousseau et Burlamaqui', *Etudes Jean-Jacques Rousseau* 4 (1990), p.9-29.

Curtin, P. D., *The Atlantic slave trade: a census* (Madison, WI, 1969).

D'Alessandro, Lucio (ed.), *Gaetano Filangieri e l'Illuminismo europeo: atti del convegno tenuto a Vico Equense nel 1982* (Naples, 1991).

Dal Pra, Mario, *Hume e la scienza della natura umana*, 2nd edn (Rome and Bari, 1973).

Darnton, Robert, *The Business of Enlightenment: a publishing history of the 'Encyclopédie' 1775-1800* (Cambridge, MA, 1979).

–, *The Forbidden best-sellers of pre-revolutionary France* (London and New York, 1995).

–, *The Great cat massacre and other episodes in French cultural history* (New York, 1984).

Daumas, Maurice, *La Tendresse amoureuse, XVIe-XVIIIe siècles* (Paris, 1996).

De Giorgi, Fulvio, 'Correnti e momenti dell'anti-illuminismo nell''800 e '900', in *L'Illuminismo e i suoi critici*, ed. Dante Bolognesi and Sauro Mattarelli (Milan, 2011), p.71-83.

Delon, Michel, *L'Idée d'énergie au tournant des Lumières (1770-1820)* (Paris, 1988).

–, introduction and notes to Diderot, *Salons* (Paris, 2008).

–, 'Morale', in *Le Monde des Lumières*, ed. Vincenzo Ferrone and Daniel Roche (Paris, 1999; original: *L'Illuminismo: dizionario storico*, Rome and Bari, 1997), p.41-48.

Delpiano, Patrizia, *Church and censorship in eighteenth-century Italy: governing reading in the age of Enlightenment* (London, 2017).

–, *La schiavitù in età moderna* (Rome and Bari, 2009).

Del Vecchio, Giorgio, *La Déclaration des droits de l'homme et du citoyen dans la Révolution française*, translated by Antoinette Pellevant Gini (Rome and Paris, 1968; original: *La Dichiarazione dei diritti dell'uomo e del cittadino nella Rivoluzione francese*, Genoa, 1903).

–, *Justice: an historical and philosophical essay*, ed. and translated by A. H. Campbell (Edinburgh, 1952).

–, *Su la teoria del contratto sociale* (Bologna, 1906).

Derathé, Robert, *Jean-Jacques Rousseau et la science politique de son temps*, 2nd edn (Paris, 1970).

Derrida, Jacques, *Of grammatology*, translated by Gayatri Chakravorty Spivak, with an introduction by Judith Butler (Baltimore, MD, 2016).

Diaz, Furio, *Filosofia e politica nel Settecento francese*, 2nd edn (Turin, 1973).

–, 'Liberté', in *Le Monde des Lumières*, ed. Vincenzo Ferrone and Daniel Roche (Paris, 1999; original: *L'Illuminismo: dizionario storico*, Rome and Bari, 1997), p.59-69.

Dieckmann, Herbert, 'The abbé Meslier and Diderot's *Eleuthéromanes*', *Harvard library bulletin* 7 (1953), p.231-35.

–, 'Three Diderot letters, and *Les Eleuthéromanes*', *Harvard library bulletin* 6 (1952), p.69-91.

Dippel, Horst, *Germany and the American Revolution 1770-1800: a sociohistorical investigation of late eighteenth-century political thinking* (Wiesbaden, 1978).

Dorigny, Marcel, and Bernard Gainot, *La Société des amis des Noirs, 1788-1799: contributions à l'histoire de l'abolition de l'esclavage* (Paris, 1999).

Doyle, William, 'Dupaty (1746-1788): a career in the Late Enlightenment', *SVEC* 230 (1985), p.1-125.

Duchet, Michèle, *Anthropologie et histoire au siècle des Lumières* (Paris, 1971).

–, *Diderot et l''Histoire des deux Indes', ou l'Ecriture fragmentaire* (Paris, 1978).

Dufour, Alfred, *Droits de l'homme, droit naturel et histoire: droit, individu et pouvoir de l'Ecole du droit naturel à l'Ecole du droit historique* (Paris, 1991).

Dülmen, Richard van, *Der Geheimbund der Illuminaten: Darstellung, Analyse, Dokumentation*, 2nd edn (Stuttgart, 1977).

–, *The Society of the Enlightenment: the rise of the middle class and Enlightenment culture in Germany*, translated by Anthony Williams (Cambridge, 1992).

Dumont, Louis, *Essays on individualism: modern ideology in anthropological perspective* (Chicago, IL, and London, 1986).

Durkheim, Emile, *Montesquieu and Rousseau: forerunners of sociology*, translated by Ralph Manheim (Ann Arbor, MI, 1960).

Dworkin, Ronald, *Taking rights seriously* (London, 1978).

Edelstein, Dan, *The Enlightenment: a genealogy* (Chicago, IL, 2010).

–, 'Enlightenment rights talk', *The Journal of modern history* 86 (2014), p.530-65.

–, *The Terror of natural right: republicanism, the cult of nature and the French Revolution* (Chicago, IL, 2009).

Ehrard, Jean, *Lumières et esclavage: l'esclavage colonial et l'opinion publique en France au XVIIIe siècle* (Brussels, 2008).

Eijnatten, Joris van, *Liberty and concord in the United Provinces: religious toleration and the public in the eighteenth-century Netherlands* (Leiden, 2003).

Einaudi, Mario, *Le origini dottrinali e storiche del controllo giudiziario sulla costituzionalità delle leggi negli Stati Uniti d'America* (Turin, 1931).

Engel, Leopold, *Geschichte des Illuminatenordens, ein Beitrag zur Geschichte Bayerns* (Berlin, 1906).

Ephémérides du citoyen, ou Bibliothèque raisonnée des sciences morales et politiques, vol.4 (1770).

Epstein, Klaus, *The Genesis of German conservatism* (Princeton, NJ, 1966).

Farge, Arlette, *Dire et mal dire: l'opinion publique au XVIIIe siècle* (Paris, 1992).

Fassò, Guido, 'Law and the historical origin of the *New science*', in *Giambattista Vico's science of humanity*, ed. Giorgio Tagliacozzo and Donald Phillip Verene (Baltimore, MD, and London, 1976), p.3-14 ('Il problema del diritto e l'origine storica della *Scienza nuova* di G. Vico', *Atti della Accademia Pontaniana* 26, 1977, p.139-48).

–, *Vico e Grozio* (Naples, 1971).

Febvre, Lucien, 'La genèse des idées de Diderot', *Annales d'histoire sociale* 2:1 (1940), p.46-47.

–, *Pour une histoire à part entière* (Paris, 1962).

Ferrajoli, Luigi, *Diritto e ragione: teoria del garantismo penale* (Rome and Bari, 1989).

–, 'Il fondamento del rifiuto della pena capitale', in *Il diritto di uccidere: l'enigma della pena della morte*, ed. Pietro Costa (Milan, 2010), p.57-68.

Ferronato, Marta (ed.), *Dal 'De jure naturae et gentium' di Samuel Pufendorf alla codificazione prussiana del 1794, atti del convegno internazionale, Padova 25-26 ottobre 2001* (Padua, 2005).

Ferrone, Vincenzo, 'The Accademia Reale delle Scienze: cultural sociability and men of letters in the Turin of the

Enlightenment under Vittorio Amedeo III', *The Journal of modern history* 70 (1998), p.519-60.
–, 'Bobbio, l'Illuminismo e l'età dei diritti', *Rivista storica italiana* 118 (2006), p.258-67.
–, 'Chiesa cattolica e modernità: la scoperta dei diritti dell'uomo dopo l'esperienza dei totalitarismi', in *Chiesa cattolica e modernità, atti del convegno della Fondazione Pellegrino, Torino 6 febbraio 2004*, ed. F. Bolgiani, V. Ferrone and F. Margiotta Broglio (Bologna, 2004), p.17-131.
–, 'Il cristianesimo e i diritti dell'uomo', in *Le religioni e il mondo moderno*, ed. Giovanni Filoramo, vol.1: *Cristianesimo*, ed. Daniele Menozzi (Turin, 2008), p.554-68.
–, 'Il dibattito su probabilità e scienze sociali nel secolo XVIII', *Physis* 22 (1980), p.27-71.
–, *The Enlightenment: history of an idea*, translated by Elisabetta Tarantino (Princeton, NJ, 2015; original: *Lezioni illuministiche*, Rome and Bari, 2010).
–, 'Eugenio Garin: il lungo Illuminismo "da Petrarca a Rousseau"', in *Eugenio Garin: dal Rinascimento all'Illuminismo*, ed. Olivia Catanorchi and Valentina Lepri, with a 'Premessa' by Michele Ciliberto (Rome, 2011), p.269-79.
–, *The Intellectual roots of the Italian Enlightenment: Newtonian science, religion, and politics in the early eighteenth century*, translated by Sue Brotherton (Atlantic Highlands, NJ, 1995; original: *Scienza, natura, religione: mondo newtoniano e cultura italiana nel primo Settecento*, Naples, 1982).
–, 'La massoneria settecentesca in Piemonte e nel Regno di Napoli', *Il Vieusseux* 4 (1991), special issue: *La massoneria e le forme della sociabilità nell'Europa del Settecento*, ed. Zefiro Ciuffoletti, p.103-30.
–, 'Il nuovo repubblicanesimo dei diritti dell'uomo nelle logge italiane alla fine del secolo', *Rivista storica italiana* 113 (2001), p.843-58.
–, *The Politics of Enlightenment: republicanism, constitutionalism, and the rights of man in Gaetano Filangieri*, translated by Sophus Reinert (New York, 2012; original: *La società giusta ed equa: repubblicanesimo e diritti dell'uomo in Gaetano Filangieri*, Rome and Bari, 2003).
–, *I profeti dell'Illuminismo: le metamorfosi della ragione nel tardo Settecento italiano*, 2nd edn (Rome and Bari, 2000).
–, 'Un re, un esercito, una nazione: il riarmo italiano nel '700 tra innovazioni e identità nazionali d'Antico regime', in *Storia d'Italia, Annali 18, Guerra e pace*, ed. Walter Barberis (Turin, 2002), p.383-97.
–, 'The rights of history: Enlightenment and human rights', *Human rights quarterly* 39 (2017), p.130-41.
–, 'La "sana laicità" della Chiesa bellarminiana di Benedetto XVI tra *potestas indirecta* e *parresia*', *Passato e Presente* 26 (2008), p.21-40.
–, *Una scienza per l'uomo: Illuminismo e Rivoluzione scientifica nell'Europa del Settecento* (Turin, 2007).

–, *Lo strano Illuminismo di Joseph Ratzinger: Chiesa, modernità e diritti dell'uomo* (Rome and Bari, 2013).

–, and Gianni Francioni (ed.), *Cesare Beccaria: la pratica dei Lumi* (Florence, 2000).

–, and Daniel Roche, *L'Illuminismo nella cultura contemporanea: storia e storiografia* (Rome and Bari, 2002).

–, and Daniel Roche (ed.), *Le Monde des Lumières* (Paris, 1999; original: *L'Illuminismo: dizionario storico*, Rome and Bari, 1997).

–, and Paolo Rossi, *Lo scienziato nell'età moderna* (Rome and Bari, 1994).

Filoramo, Giovanni, 'La sacralizzazione della politica tra teologia politica e religione civile', in *Pluralismo e religione civile: una prospettiva storica e filosofica, atti del convegno, Vercelli, 24-25 giugno 2001*, ed. Gianni Paganini and Edoardo Tortarolo (Milan, 2004), p.202-12.

La filosofia della natura nel Medioevo: atti del terzo congresso internazionale di filosofia medievale, Passo della Mendola, Trento, 31 agosto-5 settembre 1964 (Milan, 1966).

Finnis, John, *Natural law and natural rights* (Oxford, 1980).

Fioravanti, Maurizio, *Giuristi e costituzione politica nell'Ottocento tedesco* (Milan, 1980).

Foi, Maria Carolina, 'La buona causa e i mezzi ignobili', introductory essay to Friedrich Schiller, *Don Carlos*, ed. Maria Carolina Foi (Venice, 2004), p.11-47.

–, *La giurisdizione delle scene: i drammi politici di Schiller* (Macerata, 2013).

–, 'Hans-Jürgen Schings, *Die Brüder des Marquis Posa: Schiller und der Geheimbund der Illuminaten*', *Studi germanici* 37 (1999), p.166-74.

–, *Heine e la vecchia Germania: le radici della questione tedesca tra poesia e diritto* (Milan, 1990).

–, 'Il prezzo dell'amore: incontri pericolosi nel *Don Carlos* di Schiller', in *Cultura e rappresentazione nell'età di Goethe*, ed. Michele Cometa and Luca Crescenzi (Rome, 2003), p.105-40.

–, 'Schiller und Erhard: Literatur und Politik in der Weimarer Klassik', *Jahrbuch der Deutschen Schillergesellschaft* 49 (2005), p.193-223.

Forbes, Duncan, 'Natural law and the Scottish Enlightenment', in *The Origins and nature of the Scottish Enlightenment*, ed. R. H. Campbell and Andrew S. Skinner (Edinburgh, 1982), p.186-204.

Foucault, Michel, *Discipline and punish: the birth of the prison*, translated by Alan Sheridan (London, 1977; original: *Surveiller et punir: naissance de la prison*, Paris, 1975).

–, *The Order of things: an archaeology of the human sciences* (London, 2002).

–, *Society must be defended: lectures at the Collège de France, 1975-76*, ed. Mauro Bertani and Alessandro Fontana, translated by David Macey (London, 2003).

Francioni, Gianni, 'Beccaria filosofo utilitarista', in *Cesare Beccaria tra Milano e l'Europa, convegno di studi per il 250° anniversario della nascita promosso dal Comune di Milano*, ed. Sergio Romagnoli and Gian Domenico Pisapia (Rome and Bari, 1990), p.69-87.

–, introductory note to Verri, *Discorso sulla felicità*, in *Edizione nazionale delle opere di Pietro Verri*, vol.3: *I Discorsi e altri scritti degli anni Settanta*, ed. Giorgio Panizza with Silvia Contarini, Gianni Francioni and Sara Rosini (Rome, 2004).

Freschi, Marino, *Dall'occultismo alla politica: l'itinerario illuministico di Knigge (1752-1796)* (Naples, 1979).

–, *L'utopia nel Settecento tedesco* (Naples, 1974).

Fumaroli, Marc, *L'Age de l'éloquence: rhétorique et res literaria, de la Renaissance au seuil de l'époque classique* (Paris, 1994).

–, *Héros et orateurs: rhétorique et dramaturgie cornéliennes* (Geneva, 1996).

Furet, François, *Interpreting the French Revolution*, translated by Elborg Forster (Cambridge, 1981).

Gagnebin, Bernard, *Burlamaqui (1694-1748) et le droit naturel* (Geneva, 1944).

Galasso, Giuseppe, 'Il pensiero religioso di Antonio Genovesi', *Rivista storica italiana* 87 (1970), p.800-23.

Garber, Jörn, 'Vom "ius connatum" zum "Menschenrecht": deutsche Menschenrechtstheorie in der Spätaufklärung', in *Rechtsphilosophie der Aufklärung: Symposium Wolfenbüttel 1981*, ed. Reinhard Brandt (Berlin and New York, 1982), p.107-47.

Garin, Eugenio, *Dal Rinascimento all'Illuminismo* (Florence, 1993).

–, *History of Italian philosophy*, ed. and translated by Giorgio A. Pinton, 2 vols (Amsterdam and New York, 2008).

–, *Interpretazioni del Rinascimento*, ed. Michele Ciliberto (Rome, 2009).

–, *Italian humanism: philosophy and civic life in the Renaissance*, translated by Peter Munz (New York, 1965).

Garrard, Graeme, *Rousseau's counter-Enlightenment: a republican critique of the philosophes* (Albany, NY, 2000).

Gauchet, Marcel, *La Révolution des droits de l'homme* (Paris, 1989).

Gauthier, Florence, *Triomphe et mort du droit naturel en Révolution 1789-1795-1802* (Paris, 1992).

Gay, Peter, *The Enlightenment: an interpretation*, vol.2: *The Science of freedom* (1969; New York and London, 1977).

Geertz, Clifford, *The Interpretation of cultures* (New York, 1973).

Geier, Manfred, *Aufklärung: das europäische Projekt* (Hamburg, 2012).

Geuna, Marco, 'Aspetti della critica di Adam Ferguson al contrattualismo', in *Passioni, interessi, convenzioni: discussioni settecentesche su virtù e civiltà*, ed. Marco Geuna and Maria Luisa Pesante (Milan, 1992), p.129-80.

–, 'Pufendorf in Scozia: ricezione e critica dell'idea del contratto sociale', in *Dal 'De jure naturae et gentium' di Samuel Pufendorf alla codificazione prussiana del 1794, atti del convegno internazionale, Padova 25-26 ottobre 2001*, ed. Marta Ferronato (Padua, 2005), p.303-61.

–, and Maria Luisa Pesante (ed.), *Passioni, interessi, convenzioni: discussioni settecentesche su virtù e civiltà* (Milan, 1992).

Ghisalberti, Carlo, *Gravina giurista e storico* (Milan, 1962).

Giarrizzo, Giuseppe, *David Hume politico e storico* (Turin, 1962).

–, introduction to Wolfgang Goethe, *Il gran Cofto* (Palermo, 1989).

–, *Massoneria e Illuminismo nell'Europa del Settecento* (Venice, 1994).

–, *Vico, la politica e la storia* (Naples, 1981).

Gierke, Otto von, *The Development of political theory*, translated by Bernard Freyd (London, 1939; original: *Johannes Althusius und die Entwicklung der naturrechtlichen Staatstheorie*, Breslau, 1880).

Girard, Patrick, *La Révolution française et les juifs* (Paris, 1989).

Glendon, Mary Ann, *A World made new: Eleanor Roosevelt and the Universal Declaration of Human Rights* (New York, 2001).

Gliozzi, Giuliano, *Adamo e il nuovo mondo: la nascita dell'antropologia come ideologia coloniale: dalle genealogie bibliche alle teorie razziali (1500-1700)* (Florence, 1977).

–, *Le teorie della proprietà da Lutero a Babeuf* (Turin, 1978).

Gobetti, Daniela, *Private and public: individuals, households, and body politic in Locke and Hutcheson* (London, 1992).

Godineau, Dominique, 'The woman', in *Enlightenment portraits*, ed. Michel Vovelle, translated by Lydia G. Cochrane (Chicago, IL, and London, 1997), p.393-426.

Goldgar, Anne, *Impolite learning: conduct and community in the Republic of Letters, 1680-1750* (New Haven, CT, and London, 1995).

Goldschmidt, Victor, *Anthropologie et politique: les principes du système de Rousseau* (Paris, 1974).

Gombrich, E. H., *The Sense of order: a study in the psychology of decorative art* (Oxford, 1979).

Gordon, Daniel, *Citizens without sovereignty: equality and sociability in French thought, 1670-1789* (Princeton, NJ, 1994).

Gramsci, Antonio, *The Gramsci reader: selected writings, 1916-1935*, ed. David Forgacs (New York, 2000).

Grossi, Paolo, *A History of European law*, translated by Laurence Hooper (Chichester, 2010).

–, *Locatio ad longum tempus: locazione e rapporti reali di godimento nella problematica del diritto comune* (Naples, 1963).

–, 'Modernità politica e ordine giuridico', *Quaderni fiorentini* 27 (1998), p.13-39.

–, *L'ordine giuridico medievale* (Rome and Bari, 1995).

–, 'La proprietà nel sistema privatistico della seconda scolastica', in *La seconda scolastica nella formazione del diritto privato moderno*, ed. Paolo Grossi (Milan, 1973), p.117-222.

–, '*Usus facti*: la nozione di proprietà nella inaugurazione del pensiero giuridico moderno', *Quaderni fiorentini* 1 (1972), p.287-355.

Guerci, Luciano, *L'Europa del Settecento: permanenze e mutamenti* (Turin, 1988).

–, *Libertà degli antichi e libertà dei moderni: Sparta, Atene e i 'philosophes' nella Francia del '700* (Naples, 1979).

Gunn, A. W., *Queen of the world: opinion in the public life of France from the Renaissance to the Revolution* (Oxford, 1995).

Haakonssen, Knud (ed.), *Grotius, Pufendorf and modern natural law* (London, 1999).

–, 'The moral conservatism of natural rights', in *Natural law and civil sovereignty: moral right and state authority in early modern political thought*, ed. Ian Hunter and David Saunders (Basingstoke, 2002), p.27-42.

–, 'Natural jurisprudence and the identity of the Scottish Enlightenment', in *Philosophy and religion in Enlightenment Britain: new case studies*, ed. Ruth Savage (Oxford, 2012), p.258-77.

–, *Natural law and moral philosophy: from Grotius to the Scottish Enlightenment* (Cambridge, 1996).

–, *The Science of a legislator: the natural jurisprudence of David Hume and Adam Smith* (Cambridge, 1981).

Habermas, Jürgen, 'Sauver le projet des Lumières', translated by Christian Bouchindhomme, in *Lumières! Un héritage pour demain*, ed. Yann Fauchois, Thierry Grillet and Tzvetan Todorov (Paris, 2006), p.26-27.

Harvey, R. F., *J.-J. Burlamaqui: a liberal tradition in American constitutionalism* (Chapel Hill, NC, 1937).

Hazard, Paul, *The Crisis of the European mind 1680-1715*, translated by J. Lewis May, with an introduction by Anthony Grafton (New York, 2013).

Hegel, G. W. F., *Elements of the philosophy of right*, ed. Allen W. Wood, translated by H. B. Nisbet (Cambridge, 1991).

Heidegger, Martin, 'Letter on humanism', in *Basic writings*, ed. David Farrell Krell, translated by Frank A. Capuzzi with J. Glenn Gray (London, 1978), p.193-242.

Hellmuth, Eckhart, *Naturrechtsphilosophie und bürokratischer Werthorizont: Studien zur preußischen Geistes- und Sozialgeschichte des 18. Jahrhunderts* (Göttingen, 1985).

–, 'Towards a comparative study of political culture: the cases of late eighteenth-century England and Germany', in *The Transformation of political culture: England and Germany in the late eighteenth century*, ed. Eckhart Hellmuth (Oxford and London, 1990), p.1-38.

– (ed.), *The Transformation of political culture: England and Germany in the late eighteenth century* (Oxford and London, 1990).

Hermanin, Camilla, *Samuel Werenfels: il dibattito sulla libertà di coscienza a Basilea agli inizi del Settecento* (Florence, 2003).

Hertzberg, Arthur, *The French Enlightenment and the Jews* (New York, 1968).

Hespanha, António Manuel, *Panorama histórico da cultura jurídica europeia* (Mem Martins, 1997).

Hintze, Otto, *The Historical essays of Otto Hintze*, ed. and with an introduction by Felix Gilbert, with the assistance of Robert M. Berdahl (New York, 1975).

Hirschman, Albert O., *The Passions and the interests: political arguments for capitalism before its triumph* (Princeton, NJ, 1977).

Hochstrasser, T. J., 'Conscience and reason: the natural law theory of Jean Barbeyrac', *The Historical journal* 36:2 (1993), p.289-308.

–, *Natural law theories in the Early Enlightenment* (Cambridge, 2000).

Hont, Istvan, *Jealousy of trade: international competition and the nation-state in historical perspective* (Cambridge, MA, and London, 2005).

– (ed.), *Wealth and virtue: the shaping of political economy in the Scottish Enlightenment* (Cambridge, 1983).

–, and Michael Ignatieff, 'Needs and justice in the *Wealth of nations*: an introductory essay', in *Wealth and virtue: the shaping of political economy in the Scottish Enlightenment*, ed. Istvan Hont and Michael Ignatieff (Cambridge, 1983), p.1-44.

Hunt, Lynn (ed.), *The French Revolution and human rights: a brief documentary history*, edited, translated and with an introduction by Lynn Hunt (Boston, MA, 1996).

–, *Inventing human rights: a history* (New York, 2007).

–, 'Revolutionary rights', in *Revisiting the origins of human rights*, ed. Pamela Slotte and Miia Halme-Tuomisaari (Cambridge, 2015), p.105-18.

–, Margaret C. Jacob and Wijnand Mijnhardt, *The Book that changed Europe: Picart and Bernard's religious ceremonies of the world* (Cambridge, MA, 2010).

Hunter, Ian, and David Saunders (ed.), *Natural law and civil sovereignty: moral right and state authority in early modern political thought* (Basingstoke, 2002).

Huntington, Samuel P., *The Clash of civilizations?* (Cambridge, MA, 1993).

Ignatieff, Michael, *Human rights as politics and idolatry* (Princeton, NJ, 2001).

Imbruglia, Girolamo, 'Indignation et droits de l'homme chez le dernier Diderot: de l'*Encyclopédie* à l'*Histoire des deux Indes*', in *L'Edition du dernier Diderot: pour un Diderot électronique*, ed. Gianluigi Goggi and Didier Kahn (Paris, 2007), p.125-76.

–, 'Una polemica a Napoli sulla *Diceosina* di Genovesi', in *Il Settecento di Furio Diaz*, ed. Carlo Mangio and Marcello Verga (Pisa, 2006), p.121-35.

Ippolito, Dario, *Mario Pagano: il pensiero giuspolitico di un illuminista* (Turin, 2008).

Israel, Jonathan, *Democratic Enlightenment: philosophy, revolution and human rights, 1750-1790* (Oxford, 2011).

–, 'Philosophy, religion and the controversy about basic human rights in 1789', in *Self-evident truths? Human rights and the Enlightenment*, ed. Kate E. Tunstall (New York, 2012), p.111-25.

–, *Radical Enlightenment: philosophy and the making of modernity, 1650-1750*, 2nd edn (Oxford, 2002).

–, *A Revolution of the mind: Radical Enlightenment and the intellectual origins of modern democracy* (Princeton, NJ, 2010).

Jacob, Margaret C., 'The crisis of the European mind: Hazard revisited', in *Politics and culture in early modern Europe: essays in honour of H. G. Koenigsberger*, ed. Phyllis Mach and Margaret C. Jacob (Cambridge, 1987), p.251-72.

–, *The Newtonians and the English Revolution, 1689-1720* (Hassocks, 1976).

–, *The Radical Enlightenment: pantheists, freemasons and republicans* (London, 1981).

Jameson, Russell Parsons, *Montesquieu et l'esclavage: étude sur les origines de l'opinion antiesclavagiste en France au XVIIIe siècle* (Paris, 1911).

Jellinek, Georg, *The Declaration of the Rights of Man and of Citizens: a contribution to modern constitutional history*, translated by Max Farrand (New York, 1901).

Kaiser, Thomas E., 'Property, sovereignty, the Declaration of the Rights of Man, and the tradition of French jurisprudence', in *The French idea of freedom: the Old Regime and the Declaration of Rights of 1789*, ed. Dale Van Kley (Stanford, CA, 1994), p.300-42.

Kaplan, Steven L., *Bread, politics and political economy in the reign of Louis XV*, 2 vols (The Hague, 1976).

Kates, Gary, '"The powers of husband and wife must be equal and separate": the *Cercle social* and the rights of women, 1790-91', in *Women and politics in the age of democratic revolution*, ed. Harriet B. Applewhite and Darline G. Levy (Ann Arbor, MI, 1990), p.163-80.

Kelly, J. N. D., *Early Christian doctrines*, 5th edn (London, 1977).

Kerry, Paul E., *Enlightenment thought in the writing of Goethe: a contribution to the history of ideas* (Rochester, NY, 2001).

Kirsop, Wallace, 'Nouveautés: théâtre et roman', in *Histoire de l'édition française*, vol.2: *Le Livre triomphant: 1660-1830*, ed. Roger Chartier and Henri-Jean Martin, 2nd edn (Paris, 1990), p.269-84.

Klippel, Diethelm, *Politische Freiheit und Freiheitsrechte im deutschen Naturrecht des 18. Jahrhunderts* (Paderborn, 1976).

–, 'The true concept of liberty: political theory in Germany in the second half of the eighteenth century', in *The Transformation of political culture: England and Germany in the late eighteenth century*, ed. Eckhart Hellmuth (Oxford and London, 1990), p.447-66.

Korkman, Petter, 'Civil sovereigns and the King of Kings: Barbeyrac on the Creator's right to rule', in *Natural law and civil sovereignty: moral right and state authority in early modern political thought*, ed. Ian Hunter and David Saunders (Basingstoke, 2002), p.109-22.

–, 'Life, liberty and the pursuit of happiness: human rights in Barbeyrac and Burlamaqui', in *Transformations in medieval and early-modern rights discourse*, ed. Virpi Mäkinen and Petter Korkman (Dordrecht, 2006), p.257-83.

Koselleck, Reinhart, *Critique and crisis: Enlightenment and the pathogenesis of modern society* (Oxford, 1988; original: *Kritik und Krise: ein Beitrag zur Pathogenese der bürgerlichen Welt*, Freiburg, 1959).

–, *Futures past: on the semantics of historical time* (Cambridge, MA, 1985).

–, *Preussen zwischen Reform und Revolution: Allgemeines Landrecht, Verwaltung und soziale Bewegung von 1791 bis 1848* (Stuttgart, 1967).

Kowohl De Rosa, Carla Sabine, *Storia della cultura tedesca fra 'Ancien régime' e Restaurazione: cronache e personaggi* (Rome and Bari, 2000).

Koyré, Alexandre, *From the closed world to the infinite universe* (Baltimore, MD, 1957).

–, *Galileo studies*, translated by John Mepham (Hassocks, 1978).

–, *Newtonian studies* (London, 1965).

Kriegel, Blandine, *Les Droits de l'homme et le droit naturel* (Paris, 1988).

–, *Philosophie de la République* (Paris, 1998).

Krieger, Leonard, *The German idea of freedom: history of a political tradition* (Boston, MA, 1957).

Kuhn, Thomas S., *The Structure of scientific revolutions* (Chicago, IL, 1962).

Labrousse, Elisabeth, *Essai sur la révocation de l'Edit de Nantes* (Geneva and Paris, 1985).

Landi, Sandro, *Stampa, censura e opinione pubblica* (Bologna, 2011).

Landucci, Sergio, *I filosofi e i selvaggi 1580-1780* (Bari, 1972).

Larrère, Catherine, *L'Invention de l'économie au XVIIIe siècle: du droit naturel à la physiocratie* (Paris, 1992).

Laursen, John Christian (ed.), *New essays on the political thought of the Huguenots of the Refuge* (Leiden, 1995).

La Vopa, Anthony J., 'Conceiving a public: ideas and society in eighteenth-century Europe', *Journal of modern history* 64 (1992), p.89-116.

Lecaldano, Eugenio, 'Paradigmi di analisi della filosofia morale nell'illuminismo scozzese', in *Passioni, interessi, convenzioni: discussioni settecentesche su virtù e civiltà*, ed. Marco Geuna and Maria Luisa Pesante (Milan, 1992), p.13-40.

Le Forestier, René, *Les Illuminés de Bavière et la franc-maçonnerie allemande* (Dijon, 1914).

Lenoble, Robert, *Mersenne, ou la Naissance du mécanisme* (Paris, 1943).

Lepan, Géraldine, *Jean-Jacques Rousseau et le patriotisme* (Paris, 2007).

Lévi-Strauss, Claude, 'Jean-Jacques Rousseau, founder of the sciences of man' (1962), translated by Monique Layton, in *Jean-Jacques Rousseau: critical assessments of leading philosophers*, ed. John T. Scott (London and New York, 2006), p.198-206.

–, *Race and history* (Paris, 1952).

Lilti, Antoine, 'Comment écrit-on l'histoire intellectuelle des Lumières? Spinozisme, radicalisme et philosophie', *Annales HSS* 1 (2009), p.171-206.

Lloyd, G. E. R., *Ancient worlds, modern reflections: philosophical perspectives on Greek and Chinese science and culture* (Oxford, 2004).

Lolli, Gabriele, *Da Euclide a Gödel* (Bologna, 2004).

Lomonaco, Fabrizio, introduction to Gianvincenzo Gravina, *Originum iuris civilis libri tres* (Naples, n.n., 1713), with a 'Presentazione' by Fulvio Tessitore, 2 vols (Naples, 2004).

–, *Tolleranza: momenti e percorsi della modernità fino a Voltaire* (Naples, 2005).

Lo Sardo, Eugenio, *Il mondo nuovo e le virtù civili: l'epistolario di Gaetano Filangieri 1772-1788* (Naples, 1999).

Löwith, Karl, *Meaning in history: the theological implications of the philosophy of history* (Chicago, IL, 1949).

Lucas, Colin (ed.), *The French Revolution research collection* (Oxford, 1989- ; microfiches).

Lukács, György, *Skizze einer Geschichte der neueren deutschen Literatur* (Berlin, 1952).

Luporini, Luigi, 'Per una lettura della voce "Droit naturel" nell'Encyclopédie', *Studi storici* 28:3 (1987), p.679-97.

Lüthy, Herbert, *La Banque protestante en France de la révocation de l'Edit de Nantes à la Révolution* (Paris, 1961).

MacIntyre, Alasdair, *After virtue: a study in moral theory* (1981), 3rd edn (London, New Delhi, New York and Sydney, 2013).

McKenna, Antony, and Gianni Paganini (ed.), *Pierre Bayle dans la République des Lettres: philosophie, religion, critique* (Paris, 2004).

McMahon, Darrin M., *Enemies of the Enlightenment: the French Counter-Enlightenment and the making of modernity* (Oxford, 2001).

Macpherson, C. B., *The Political theory of possessive individualism: Hobbes to Locke* (Oxford, 1962).

Magrin, Gabriele, *Condorcet: un costituzionalismo democratico* (Milan, 2001).

Maier, Pauline, *American scripture: how America declared its independence from Britain* (London, 1999; original: *American scripture: making the Declaration of Independence*, New York, 1997).

Maire, Catherine-Laurence, *De la cause de Dieu à la cause de la nation: le jansénisme au XVIII*[e] *siècle* (Paris, 1998).

Mäkinen, Virpi, and Petter Korkman (ed.), *Transformations in medieval and early-modern rights discourse* (Dordrecht, 2006).

Mann, Thomas, *Reflections of a nonpolitical man*, translated by Walter D. Morris (New York, 1983).

Marino, Luigi, *I maestri della Germania: Göttingen 1770-1820* (Turin, 1975). German version: *Praeceptores Germaniae: Göttingen 1770-1820*, translated by Brigitte Szabó-Bechstein (Göttingen, 1995).

Maritain, Jacques, *The Rights of man and natural law* (London, 1945).

Markus, R. A., *Saeculum: history and society in the theology of St Augustine* (Cambridge, 1970).

Marx, Karl, 'On the Jewish question', translated by Clemens Dutt, in Karl Marx and Frederick Engels, *Collected works*, vol.3: *Karl Marx, March 1843-August 1844* (London, 1975), p.146-74.

Matteucci, Nicola, *Jean Domat, un magistrato giansenista* (Bologna, 1985).

Mauss, Marcel, 'A category of the human mind: the notion of person; the notion of self', translated by W. D. Hall, in *The Category of the person: anthropology, philosophy, history*, ed. Michael Carrithers, Steven Collins and Steven Lukes (Cambridge, 1985), p.1-25.

Mauzi, Robert, *L'Idée du bonheur dans la littérature et la pensée françaises au XVIIIe siècle* (Paris, 1960).

Maza, Sarah, *Private lives and public affairs: the 'Causes célèbres' of pre-revolutionary France* (Berkeley, CA, 1993).

Mazauric, Claude, review of Marcel Dorigny and Bernard Gainot, *La Société des amis des Noirs, 1788-1799: contributions à l'histoire de l'abolition de l'esclavage*, *Annales historiques de la Révolution française* 317 (1999), p.554-56.

Mazzarino, Santo, *Vico, l'annalistica e il diritto* (Naples, 1971).

Méchoulan, Henry, *et al.* (ed.), *La formazione storica della alterità: studi di storia della tolleranza nell'età moderna offerti a Antonio Rotondò*, 3 vols (Florence, 2001).

Meek, Ronald L., *Social science and the ignoble savage* (Cambridge, 1976).

Meinecke, Friedrich, *Cosmopolitanism and the national state*, translated by Robert B. Kimber, with an introduction by Felix Gilbert (Princeton, NJ, 1970; original: *Weltbürgertum und Nationalstaat, Studien zur Genesis des deutschen Nationalstaates*, Munich, 1911).

Melton, James Van Horn, *The Rise of the public in Enlightenment Europe* (Cambridge, 2001).

Menozzi, Daniele, *Chiesa e diritti umani: legge naturale e modernità politica dalla Rivoluzione francese ai nostri giorni* (Bologna, 2012).

Merker, Nicolao, *Die Aufklärung in Deutschland* (Munich, 1982).

Messori, Vittorio – see 'Ratzinger, Cardinal Joseph'.

Meylan, Philippe, *Jean Barbeyrac (1674-1744) et les débuts de l'enseignement du droit dans l'ancienne académie de Lausanne: contribution à l'histoire du droit naturel* (Lausanne, 1938).

Minerbi Belgrado, Anna, *Paura e ignoranza: studio sulla teoria della religione in d'Holbach* (Florence, 1983).

Minowitz, Peter, *Profits, priests, and princes: Adam Smith's emancipation of economics from politics and religion* (Stanford, CA, 1993).

Minuti, Rolando, *Orientalismo e idee di tolleranza nella cultura francese del primo '700* (Florence, 2006).

–, *Oriente barbarico e storiografia settecentesca: rappresentazioni della storia dei Tartari nella cultura francese del XVIII secolo* (Venice, 1994).

Möller, Horst, 'Die Bruderschaft der Gold- und Rosenkreuzer', in *Freimaurer und Geheimbünde im 18. Jahrhundert in Mitteleuropa*, ed. Helmut Reinalter (Frankfurt am Main, 1983), p.199-239.

–, *Fürstenstaat oder Bürgernation: Deutschland 1763-1815* (Berlin, 1989).

–, *Vernunft und Kritik: deutsche Aufklärung im 17. und 18. Jahrhundert* (Frankfurt am Main, 1986).

Momigliano, Arnaldo, *Sui fondamenti della storia antica* (Turin, 1984).

Moravia, Sergio, *La scienza dell'uomo nel Settecento* (Rome and Bari, 1978).

Mori, Gianluca, *Bayle philosophe* (Paris, 1999).

Morris, Colin, *The Discovery of the individual, 1050-1200* (New York, 1972).

Mortier, Roland, *Diderot en Allemagne, 1750-1850* (Paris, 1954).

Mosca, Gaetano, *Scritti politici*, ed. Giorgio Sola (Turin, 1982).

Motta, Franco, *Bellarmino: una teologia politica della Controriforma* (Brescia, 2005).

–, 'Le condanne inquisitoriali della *Scienza della legislazione*', in *Diritti e costituzione: l'opera di Gaetano Filangieri e la sua fortuna europea*, ed. A. Trampus (Bologna 2005), p.291-335.

Moyn, Samuel, *The Last utopia: human rights in history* (Harvard, MA, 2010).

Muir, Edward, *The Culture wars of the late Renaissance: skeptics, libertines, and opera* (Cambridge, MA, 2007).

Mulholland, Leslie A., *Kant's system of rights* (New York, 1989).

Müller-Seidel, Walter, and Wolfgang Reidel (ed.), *Die Weimarer Klassik und ihre Geheimbünde* (Würzburg, 2003).

Mulsow, Martin, '"Steige also, wenn du kannst, höher und höher zu uns herauf": Adam Weishaupt als Philosoph', in *Die Weimarer Klassik und ihre Geheimbünde*, ed. Walter Müller-Seidel and Wolfgang Reidel (Würzburg, 2003), p.27-66.

Muthu, Sankar, *Enlightenment against empire* (Princeton, NJ, 2003).

Nadler, Steven M., *A Book forged in hell: Spinoza's scandalous treatise and the birth of the secular age* (Princeton, NJ, 2011).

Netter, Marie-Laurence, *Du théâtre à la liberté* (Paris, 2012).

Nietzsche, Friedrich, *The Use and abuse of history*, translated by Adrian Collins, with an introduction by Julius Kraft (Indianapolis, IN, 1957).

Noack, Paul, *Olympe de Gouges: 1748-1793 – courtisane et militante des droits de la femme*, translated by Isabelle Duclos (Paris, 1993).

Oestreich, Gerhard, *Geschichte der Menschenrechte und Grundfreiheiten im Umriß* (Berlin, 1968; 2nd edn 1978).

Pacchi, Arrigo, *Convenzione e ipotesi nella formazione della filosofia naturale di Thomas Hobbes* (Florence, 1965).

Pack, S. J., *Capitalism as a moral system: Adam Smith's critique of the free market economy* (Aldershot, 1991).

Padoa-Schioppa, Antonio, *Italia ed Europa nella storia del diritto* (Bologna, 2003).

Paganini, Gianni, 'Scetticismo e certezza', in *Illuminismo: un vademecum*, ed. Gianni Paganini and Edoardo Tortarolo (Turin, 2008), p.252-65.

–, *Skepsis: le débat des modernes sur le scepticisme* (Paris, 2007).

Pagden, Anthony, *The Enlightenment and why it still matters* (Oxford, 2013).

–, *The Fall of natural man: the American Indian and the origins of comparative ethnology*, 2nd edn (Cambridge, 1986).

–, *Lords of all the world: ideologies of empire in Spain, Britain and France c.1500-c.1800* (New Haven, CT, 1995).

Palladini, Fiammetta, *Samuel Pufendorf discepolo di Hobbes: per una reinterpretazione del giusnaturalismo moderno* (Bologna, 1990).

–, 'Stato, Chiesa e tolleranza nel pensiero di S. Pufendorf', in *La formazione storica della alterità: studi di storia della tolleranza nell'età moderna offerti a Antonio Rotondò*, ed. Henry Méchoulan *et al.*, 3 vols (Florence, 2001), vol.2, p.751-86.

Palou, Jean, *La Francmaçonnerie* (Paris, 1964).

Pasquinelli, Alberto (ed.), *Il neoempirismo* (Turin, 1969).

Pasquino, Pasquale, *Sieyès et l'invention de la constitution en France* (Paris, 1998).

Passerin d'Entrèves, Alessandro, *Natural law: an introduction to legal philosophy*, 2nd edn (London, 1970).

Passmore, John Arthur, *The Perfectibility of man* (London, 1971).

Peters, Julie Stone, *Theatre of the book, 1480-1880: print, text and performance in Europe* (Oxford, 2000).

Pétré-Grenouilleau, Olivier, *Les Traites négrières: essai d'histoire globale* (Paris, 2004).

Pii, Eluggero, *Antonio Genovesi: dalla politica economica alla 'politica civile'* (Florence, 1984).

Platania, Marco, *Montesquieu e la virtù: rappresentazioni della Francia di Ancien Régime e dei governi repubblicani* (Turin, 2007).

Pocock, J. G. A., *The Ancient Constitution and the feudal law: a study of English historical thought in the seventeenth century* (Cambridge, 1957).

–, 'Clergy and commerce: the conservative Enlightenment in England', in *L'età dei Lumi: studi storici sul Settecento europeo in onore di Franco Venturi*, ed. Lester G. Crocker *et al.* (Naples, 1985), p.523-62.

–, 'Grande-Bretagne', in *Le Monde des Lumières*, ed. Vincenzo Ferrone and Daniel Roche (Paris, 1999; original: *L'Illuminismo: dizionario storico*, Rome and Bari, 1997), p.467-84.

–, *The Machiavellian moment: Florentine political thought and the Atlantic Republican tradition*, 2nd edn (Princeton, NJ, 2003).

Polanyi, Karl, *The Great transformation: the political and economic origins of our time* (Boston, MA, 2001).

Pomeau, René, *La Religion de Voltaire* (Paris, 1969).

Pontificia Studiorum Universitas a Sancto Thoma Aquinate in Urbe, *I diritti dell'uomo e la pace nel pensiero di Francisco de Vitoria e Bartolomé de Las Casas* (Milan, 1988).

Popkin, Richard H., *The High road to Pyrrhonism* (San Diego, CA, 1980).

–, *The History of scepticism from Erasmus to Spinoza* (Berkeley, CA, 1979).

Porset, Charles, and Cécile Révauger (ed.), *Le Monde maçonnique des Lumières (Europe-Amériques et colonies): dictionnaire prosopographique*, 3 vols (Paris, 2013).

Preterossi, Geminello, *Carl Schmitt e la tradizione moderna* (Rome and Bari, 1996).

Prodi, Paolo (ed.), *Disciplina dell'anima, disciplina del corpo e disciplina della società tra medioevo ed età moderna: atti del convegno internazionale di studi, Bologna, 7-9 ottobre 1993* (Bologna, 1994).

–, *The Papal prince, one body and two souls: the papal monarchy in early modern Europe*, translated by Susan Haskins (Cambridge, 1987).

–, *Settimo non rubare: furto e mercato nella storia dell'Occidente* (Bologna, 2009).

–, *Una storia della giustizia: dal pluralismo dei fori al moderno dualismo tra coscienza e diritto* (Bologna, 2000).

–, and Wolfgang Reinhard (ed.), *Il Concilio di Trento e il moderno* (Bologna, 1996).

–, and Wolfgang Reinhard (ed.), *Identità collettive tra Medioevo ed età moderna: convegno internazionale di studi* (Bologna, 2002).

Prosperi, Adriano, *Delitto e perdono: la pena di morte nell'orizzonte mentale dell'Europa cristiana, XIV-XVIII secolo* (Turin, 2013).

–, *Infanticide, secular justice, and religious debate in early modern Europe* (Turnhout, 2016).

–, *Tribunali della coscienza: inquisitori, confessori, missionari* (Turin, 1996).

Proust, Jacques, 'La contribution de Diderot à l'*Encyclopédie* et les théories du droit naturel', *Annales historiques de la Révolution française* 35 (1963), p.257-86.

Quintili, Paolo, *La Pensée critique de Diderot: matérialisme, science et poésie a l'âge de l'Encyclopédie (1742-1782)* (Paris, 2001).

Rao, Anna Maria, '*Delle virtù e de' premi*: la fortuna di Beccaria nel Regno di Napoli', in *Cesare Beccaria tra Milano e l'Europa, convegno di studi per il 250º anniversario della nascita promosso dal Comune di Milano*, ed. Sergio Romagnoli and Gian Domenico Pisapia (Rome and Bari, 1990), p.534-86.

Ratzinger, Cardinal Joseph, with Vittorio Messori, *The Ratzinger report: an exclusive interview on the state of the Church*, translated by Salvator Attanasio and Graham Harrison (Leominster, 1985).

Raynaud, Philippe, '*La Déclaration des droits de l'homme* in the political culture of the French Revolution', in *The French Revolution and the creation of modern political culture*, ed. Colin Lucas, 3 vols (Oxford, 1988), vol.2: *The Political culture of the French Revolution*, p.139-49.

Reinalter, Helmut (ed.), *Der Illuminatenorden (1776-1785/87): ein politischer Geheimbund der Aufklärungszeit* (Frankfurt am Main, 1997).

Reinert, Sophus A., *Translating empire: emulation and the origins of political economy* (Cambridge, MA, 2011).

Reinhard, Wolfgang, 'Disciplinamento sociale, confessionalizzazione, modernizzazione: un discorso storiografico', in *Disciplina dell'anima, disciplina del corpo e disciplina della società tra medioevo ed età moderna*, ed. Paolo Prodi (Bologna, 1994), p.101-23.

Reinhardt, Hartmut, 'Geheime Wege der Aufklärung: Goethe, der Illuminatenorden und das Epos-Fragment "Die Geheimnisse"', in *Die Weimarer Klassik und ihre Geheimbünde*, ed. Walter Müller-Seidel and Wolfgang Reidel (Würzburg, 2003), p.145-76.

Remotti, Francesco, *Contro natura: una lettera al papa* (Rome and Bari, 2008).

Reñon, Luis Vega, 'La dimostrazione', in *I Greci: storia, cultura, arte e società*, vol.1: *Noi e i Greci*, ed. Salvatore Settis (Turin, 1996), p.285-318.

Rials, Stéphane, *La Déclaration des droits de l'homme et du citoyen* (Paris, 1988).

Ricuperati, Giuseppe, *L'esperienza civile e religiosa di Pietro Giannone* (Milan and Naples, 1970).

Riedel, Wolfgang, *Die Anthropologie des jungen Schillers: zur Ideengeschichte der medizinischen Schriften und der philosophischen Briefe* (Würzburg, 1985).

Robertson, John, *The Case for the Enlightenment: Scotland and Naples 1680-1760* (Cambridge, 2005).

Roche, Daniel, *France in the Enlightenment*, translated by Arthur Goldhammer (Cambridge, MA, 1998).

–, *Les Républicains des Lettres: gens de culture et Lumières au XVIIIe siècle* (Paris, 1988).

Rodotà, Stefano, *Il diritto di avere diritti* (Rome and Bari, 2012).

Roger, Philippe, 'Bonheur', in *Le Monde des Lumières*, ed. Vincenzo Ferrone and Daniel Roche (Paris, 1999; original: *L'Illuminismo: dizionario storico*, Rome and Bari, 1997), p.49-57.

Romagnoli, Sergio, and Gian Domenico Pisapia, *Cesare Beccaria tra Milano e l'Europa, convegno di studi per il 250[o] anniversario della nascita promosso dal Comune di Milano* (Rome and Bari, 1990).

Rosenberg, Hans, *Bureaucracy, aristocracy and autocracy: the Prussian experience, 1660-1815* (Cambridge, MA, 1958).

Rosenblatt, Helena, *Rousseau and Geneva: from the First Discourse to the Social Contract, 1749-1762* (Cambridge, 1997).

Rossi, Paolo, 'Ancora sui contemporanei di Vico', *Rivista di filosofia* 76:3 (1985), p.465-74.

–, 'Che tipo di scienza è la scienza nuova di Vico?', *Rivista di storia della filosofia* 59:2 (2004), p.409-33.

–, 'Chi sono i contemporanei di Vico?', *Rivista di filosofia* 72:1 (1981), p.51-82.

–, *The Dark abyss of time: the history of the earth and the history of nations from Hooke to Vico* (Chicago, IL, 1984).

–, *Immagini della scienza* (Rome, 1977).

Rosso, Corrado, *Moralisti del bonheur*, 2nd edn (Pisa, 1977).

Rothkrug, Lionel, *Opposition to Louis XIV: the political and social origins of the French Enlightenment* (Princeton, NJ, 1965).

Rothschild, Emma, *Economic sentiments: Adam Smith, Condorcet and the Enlightenment* (Cambridge, MA, 2001).

Rotondò, Antonio, 'Tolérance', in *Le Monde des Lumières*, ed. Vincenzo Ferrone and Daniel Roche (Paris, 1999; original: *L'Illuminismo: dizionario storico*, Rome and Bari, 1997), p.71-85.

Saada, Anne, *Inventer Diderot: les constructions d'un auteur dans l'Allemagne des Lumières* (Paris, 2003).

Said, Edward, *Orientalism* (New York, 1978).

Savage, Ruth (ed.), *Philosophy and religion in Enlightenment Britain: new case studies* (Oxford, 2012).

Scatena, Silvia, *La fatica della libertà: l'elaborazione della dichiarazione* Dignitatis humanae *sulla libertà religiosa del Vaticano II* (Bologna, 2003).

Scattola, Merio, *La nascita delle scienze dello Stato: August Ludwig Schlözer (1735-1809) e le discipline politiche del Settecento tedesco* (Milan, 1994).

Schiavone, Aldo, *The Invention of law in the West*, translated by Jeremy Carden and Antony Shugaar (Cambridge, MA, 2012).

Schiera, Pierangelo, *Il cameralismo e l'assolutismo tedesco* (Milan, 1968).

Schings, Hans-Jürgen, *Die Brüder des Marquis Posa: Schiller und der Geheimbund der Illuminaten* (Tübingen, 1996).

– (ed.), *Der ganze Mensch: Anthropologie und Literatur im 18. Jahrhundert* (Stuttgart, 1994).

–, '*Wilhelm Meister* und das Erbe der Illuminaten', in *Die Weimarer Klassik und ihre Geheimbünde*, ed. Walter Müller-Seidel and Wolfgang Reidel (Würzburg, 2003), p.179-203.

Schlumbohm, Jürgen, *Freiheit: die Anfänge der bürgerlichen Emanzipationsbewegung in Deutschland im Spiegel ihres Leitwortes, ca. 1760-ca. 1800* (Düsseldorf, 1975).

Schmitt, Carl, 'The age of neutralizations and depoliticizations (1929)', *Telos* 96 (summer 1993), p.130-42.

–, *The Concept of the political* (1932), translated by George Schwab (Chicago, IL, and London, 1996).

–, *The Leviathan in the state theory of Thomas Hobbes: meaning and failure of a political symbol*, translated by George Schwab and Erna Hilfstein (Westport, CT, and London, 1996).

–, *The Nomos of the earth in the international law of the jus publicum europaeum*, translated and annotated by G. L. Ulmen (New York, 2003).

–, *Political theology: four chapters on the concept of sovereignty*, translated by George Schwab (Cambridge, MA, 1985).

Schneewind, J. B., *The Invention of autonomy: a history of modern moral philosophy* (Cambridge, 1998).

Schneiders, Werner (ed.), *Christian Wolff 1679-1754: Interpretationen zu seiner Philosophie und deren Wirkung, mit einer Bibliographie der Wolff-Literatur* (Hamburg, 1983).

Schulze, Reiner, *Policey und Gesetzgebungslehre im 18. Jahrhundert* (Berlin, 1982).

Sebastiani, Silvia, *The Scottish Enlightenment: race, gender, and the limits of progress* (New York, 2013).

Secrétan, Catherine, Tristan Dagron and Laurent Bove (ed.), *Qu'est-ce que les Lumières 'radicales'? Libertinage, athéisme et spinozisme dans le tournant philosophique de l'âge classique* (Paris, 2007).

Sellin, Volker, 'Politik', in *Geschichtliche Grundbegriffe: historisches Lexikon zur politisch-sozialen Sprache in Deutschland*, ed. Otto Brunner, Werner Conze and Reinhart Koselleck, 8 vols (Stuttgart, 1972-1997), vol.4, p.789-874.

Sen, Amartya, *The Idea of justice* (London, 2009).

Sgard, Jean (ed.), *Dictionnaire des journaux, 1600-1789*, 2 vols (Paris and Oxford, 1991).

Silvestrini, Gabriella, *Diritto naturale e volontà generale: il contrattualismo repubblicano di Jean-Jacques Rousseau* (Turin, 2010).

Silvestrini, Maria Teresa, 'Free trade, feudal remnants and international equilibrium in Gaetano Filangieri's *Science of legislation*', *History of European ideas* 32 (2006), p.502-24.

Simon, Fabrizio, 'Diritti umani, repubblicanesimo dei moderni ed equità sociale: le nuove categorie della storiografia su Gaetano Filangieri', *Storia del pensiero economico* 4:1 (2007), p.141-54.

Skinner, Quentin, *Liberty before liberalism* (Cambridge, 1998).

Solari, Gioele, *La scuola del diritto naturale nelle dottrine etico-giuridiche dei secoli XVII e XVIII* (Turin, 1904).

–, *Studi su Francesco Mario Pagano* (Turin, 1963).

Solinas, Giovanni, *Il microscopio e le metafisiche: epigenesi e preesistenza da Cartesio a Kant* (Milan, 1967).

Sollors, Werner, 'La maledizione di Cam: ovvero dalla "generazione" alla "razza"', in *Il razzismo e le sue storie*, ed. Girolamo Imbruglia (Naples, 1992), p.183-205.

Spini, Giorgio, *Ricerca dei libertini: la teoria dell'impostura delle religioni nel Seicento italiano*, 2nd edn (Florence, 1983).

Stapelbroek, Koen, *Love, self-deceit, and money: commerce and morality in the early Neapolitan Enlightenment* (Toronto, 2008).

Starobinski, Jean, introduction to Rousseau, *Discours sur l'origine de l'inégalité*, in *Œuvres complètes*, ed. B. Gagnebin and M. Raymond, vol.3: *Du contrat social, écrits politiques* (Paris, 1964), p.lxviii-lxix.

–, 'Jean-Jacques Rousseau et les droits de l'homme', *Revue des sciences morales et politiques* 144:1 (1989), p.109-26.

–, *Jean-Jacques Rousseau: la transparence et l'obstacle* (Paris, 1957).

–, '"Se mettre à la place": la mutation de la critique de l'âge classique à Diderot', *Cahiers Vilfredo Pareto* 14 (1976), p.364-78.

Stolleis, Michael, *Histoire du droit public en Allemagne: droit public impérial et science de la police 1600-1800* (Paris, 1998; original: *Geschichte des öffentlichen Rechts in*

Deutschland, vol.1: *Reichspublizistik und Policeywissenschaft 1600-1800*, Munich, 1988).

Stolper, Eugene, 'Massoneria settecentesca nel Regno di Napoli', *Rivista massonica* 66 (1975), p.395-432.

Stone, Lawrence, *The Family, sex and marriage in England 1500-1800* (New York, 1977).

Strauss, Leo, *Natural right and history* (Chicago, IL, and London, 1953).

–, *Spinoza's critique of religion*, translated by E. M. Sinclair (Chicago, IL, 1997; original: *Religionskritik Spinozas als Grundlage seiner Bibelwissenschaft*, 1930).

Svensson, Marina, *Debating human rights in China: a conceptual and political history* (Lanham, MD, 2002).

Talmon, J. L., *The Origins of totalitarian democracy* (London, 1952).

Tarabuzzi, Gianfranco, 'Echi italiani settecenteschi della storiografia inglese', *Archivio storico italiano* 138 (1980), p.391-440.

Tarde, Jean Gabriel de, *L'Opinion et la foule* (Paris, 1901).

Tarello, Giovanni, *Storia della cultura giuridica moderna*, vol.1: *Assolutismo e codificazione del diritto* (Bologna, 1976).

Tavoillot, Pierre-Henri, *Le Crépuscule des Lumières: les documents de 'la querelle' du panthéisme (1780-1789)* (Paris, 1995).

Taylor, Charles, *Sources of the self: the making of the modern identity* (Cambridge, 1989).

Thomas, Jacques François, *Le Pélagianisme de J.-J. Rousseau* (Paris, 1956).

Thompson, E. P., *The Making of the English working class* (New York, 1966).

–, 'The moral economy of the English crowd in the eighteenth century', *Past & present* 50 (1971), p.76-136.

Tierney, Brian, 'Dominion of self and natural rights before Locke and after', in *Transformations in medieval and early-modern rights discourse*, ed. Virpi Mäkinen and Petter Korkman (Dordrecht, 2006), p.173-203.

–, *The Idea of natural rights: studies on natural rights, natural law, and Church law, 1150-1625* (Atlanta, GA, 1997).

Timpanaro, Sebastiano, introduction and editorial matter to Paul-Henri Thiry d'Holbach, *Il buon senso* (Milan, 1985).

Tocchini, Gerardo, 'Alfieri, Vittorio', in *Le Monde maçonnique des Lumières (Europe-Amériques et colonies): dictionnaire prosopographique*, ed. Charles Porset and Cécile Révauger, 3 vols (Paris, 2013), vol.1, p.53-59.

–, 'L'*Œdipe* del giovane Voltaire alla prova della scena pubblica: canone politico, strategie e autocensure nel teatro tragico della prima età dei Lumi', *Rivista storica italiana* 125 (2013), p.681-763.

–, *La politica della rappresentazione: comunicazione sociale e consumo culturale nella Francia di antico regime (1669-1781)*, 2nd edn (Turin, 2012).

–, 'Politica e letteratura nell'Europa dei Lumi: i romanzi di Marmontel', *Rivista storica italiana* 122:1 (2010), p.41-76.

–, and Simona Variara, 'Bianchi, Isidoro', in *Le Monde maçonnique des Lumières (Europe-Amériques et colonies): dictionnaire prosopographique*, ed. Charles Porset and Cécile Révauger, 3 vols (Paris, 2013), vol.1, p.360-65.

Todescan, Franco, *Le radici teologiche del giusnaturalismo laico*, vol.2: *Il problema della secolarizzazione nel pensiero giuridico di Jean Domat* (Milan, 1987).

Todorov, Tzvetan, *La Conquête de l'Amérique: la question de l'autre* (Paris, 1982).

Tortarolo, Edoardo, *The Invention of free press: writers and censorship in eighteenth-century Europe* (Dordrecht, 2016).

–, '"Opinione pubblica" e Illuminismo italiano: qualche appunto di lettura', in *Cesare Beccaria: la pratica dei Lumi*, ed. Vincenzo Ferrone and Gianni Francioni (Florence, 2000), p.127-38.

–, *La ragione sulla Sprea: coscienza storica e cultura politica nell'Illuminismo berlinese* (Bologna, 1989).

Trampus, Antonio (ed.), *Diritti e costituzione: l'opera di Gaetano Filangieri e la sua fortuna europea* (Bologna 2005).

–, *Il diritto alla felicità: storia di un'idea* (Rome and Bari, 2008).

–, *I gesuiti e l'Illuminismo: politica e religione in Austria e nell'Europa centrale (1773-1789)* (Florence, 2000).

–, 'Linguaggi della politica e lessico costituzionale: Filangieri e i traduttori tedeschi', in *Diritti e costituzione: l'opera di Gaetano Filangieri e la sua fortuna europea*, ed. A. Trampus (Bologna 2005), p.85-126.

– (ed.), *Il linguaggio del tardo Illuminismo: politica, diritto e società civile* (Rome, 2011).

–, *La massoneria nell'età moderna* (Rome and Bari, 2001).

–, *Storia del costituzionalismo italiano nell'età dei Lumi* (Rome and Bari, 2009).

–, 'Verfassung und Rechte: Filangieri und die europäische Rezeption der *Scienza della legislazione*', in *Italien in Europa*, ed. Thomas Kroll and Frank Jung (Munich, 2014), p.119-41.

Trevor-Roper, H. R., *Religion, the Reformation and social change, and other essays* (London, 1967).

Troeltsch, Ernst, *Der Historismus und seine Probleme*, vol.1: *Das logische Problem der Geschichtsphilosophie* (Tübingen, 1922).

–, *The Social teaching of the Christian Churches*, translated by Olive Wyon, 2 vols (London, 1931; original: *Die Sozialleheren der christlichen Kirchen und Gruppen*, Tübingen, 1912).

Troper, Michel, *Terminer la Révolution: la Constitution de 1795* (Paris, 2006).

Trousson, Raymond, *Le Thème de Prométhée dans la littérature européenne*, 3rd edn (Geneva, 2001).

Tuccillo, Alessandro, *Il commercio infame: antischiavismo e diritti dell'uomo nel Settecento italiano* (Naples, 2013).

–, 'Schiavi, colonie, rivoluzione: note in margine a due traduzioni recenti', *Studi storici* 1 (2008), p.109-33.

Tuck, Richard, 'The modern theory of natural law', in *The Languages of political theory in early modern Europe*, ed. Anthony Pagden (Cambridge, 1987), p.99-120.

–, *Natural rights theories: their origin and development* (Cambridge, 1979).

–, *The Rights of war and peace: political thought and the international order from Grotius to Kant* (Oxford, 1999).

UNESCO (ed.), *Human rights: comments and interpretations*, with an introduction by Jacques Maritain, version dated 25 July 1948 available online at http://unesdoc.unesco.org/images/0015/001550/155042eb.pdf (last accessed 24 April 2019).

Valjavec, Fritz, *Die Entstehung der politischen Strömungen in Deutschland 1770 bis 1815* (Munich, 1951).

Van Kley, Dale (ed.), *The French idea of freedom: the Old Regime and the Declaration of Rights of 1789* (Stanford, CA, 1994).

Venturi, Franco, *L'antichità svelata e l'idea del progresso in N. A. Boulanger* (Bari, 1947).

–, *Giovinezza di Diderot* (Palermo, 1988; a French version first published in 1939).

–, 'L'Italia fuori d'Italia', in *Storia d'Italia*, vol.3: *Dal primo Settecento all'Unità*, ed. Ruggiero Romano and Corrado Vivanti (Turin, 1973), p.985-1481.

–, *Italy and the Enlightenment: studies in a cosmopolitan century* (London, 1972).

–, *Le origini dell'Enciclopedia* (Turin, 1970).

–, 'Postilla', *Annali della Fondazione Luigi Einaudi* 19 (1985), p.451-54.

–, 'Scottish echoes in eighteenth-century Italy', in *Wealth and virtue: the shaping of political economy in the Scottish Enlightenment*, ed. Istvan Hont and Michael Ignatieff (Cambridge, 1983), p.345-62.

–, *Settecento riformatore*, vol.1: *Da Muratori a Beccaria* (Turin, 1969).

–, *Settecento riformatore*, vol.4: *La caduta dell'Antico Regime, 1776-1789. 2. Il patriottismo repubblicano e gli imperi dell'Est* (Turin, 1984).

–, *Settecento riformatore*, vol.5: *L'Italia dei lumi*. 1. *La rivoluzione di Corsica; Le grandi carestie degli anni sessanta; La Lombardia delle riforme, 1764-1790* (Turin, 1987).

–, '"Socialista" e "socialismo" nell'Italia del Settecento', *Rivista storica italiana* 75 (1963), p.129-40.

–, *Utopia e riforma nell'Illuminismo* (Turin, 1970).

Veyne, Paul, *L'Empire gréco-romain* (Paris, 2005).

–, '*Humanitas*: Romans and non-Romans', in *The Romans*, ed. Andrea Giardina, translated by Lydia G. Cochrane (Chicago, IL, and London, 1993), p.342-69.

Veysman, Nicolas, *Mise en scène de l'opinion publique dans la littérature des Lumières* (Paris, 2004).

Viano, Carlo Augusto, *John Locke: dal razionalismo all'illuminismo* (Turin, 1960).

Villey, Michel, *Le Droit et les droits de l'homme* (Paris, 1990).

–, *La Formation de la pensée juridique moderne: cours d'histoire de la philosophie du droit*, 4th edn (Paris, 1975).

Vincenti, Luc, *Jean-Jacques Rousseau: l'individu et la république* (Paris, 2001).

Vovelle, Michel, *La Découverte de la politique: géopolitique de la Révolution française* (Paris, 1993).

– (ed.), *Enlightenment portraits*, translated by Lydia G. Cochrane (Chicago, IL, and London, 1997).

Waddicor, M. H., *Montesquieu and the philosophy of natural law* (The Hague, 1970).

Waldron, Jeremy, *God, Locke, and equality: Christian foundations of John Locke's political thought* (Cambridge, 2002).

– (ed.), *Nonsense upon stilts: Bentham, Burke and Marx on the rights of man* (London, 1987).

Walter, Eric, 'L'affaire La Barre et le concept d'opinion publique', in *Le Journalisme d'Ancien régime*, ed. Jacqueline Giraud, Pierre Rétat and Henri Duranton (Lyon, 1982), p.361-92.

Wasserstrom, Jeffrey N., Greg Grandin, Lynn Hunt and Marilyn B. Young (ed.), *Human rights and revolutions*, 2nd edn (Lanham, MD, 2007).

Wattine, Adolphe, *L'Affaire des trois roués: études sur la justice criminelle à la fin de l'Ancien régime* (Mâcon, 1921).

White, Morton Gabriel, *The Philosophy of the American Revolution* (New York, 1978).

Wilson, Arthur M., 'The development and scope of Diderot's political thought', *SVEC* 27 (1963), p.1876-900.

–, *Diderot* (New York, 1972).

Wilson, W. Daniel, *Geheimräte gegen Geheimbunde: ein unbekanntes Kapitel der klassisch-romantischen Geschichte Weimars* (Stuttgart, 1991).

–, *Das Goethe-Tabu: Protest und Menschenrechte im Klassischen Weimar* (Munich, 1999).

–, *Unterirdische Gänge: Goethe, Freimaurerei und Politik* (Göttingen, 1999).

Yolton, John W., *John Locke and the way of ideas* (London, 1956).

Zambelli, Paola, *La formazione filosofica di Antonio Genovesi* (Naples, 1972).

Zanini, Adelino, introduction to Adam Smith, *Teoria dei sentimenti morali*, ed. Adelino Zanini (Rome, 1991), p.v-lxxxix.

Zolo, Danilo, 'Il patibolo e la guerra: la pena di morte come supplizio religioso', in *Il diritto di uccidere: l'enigma della pena della morte*, ed. Pietro Costa (Milan, 2010), p.30-56.

Zuckert, M. P., *Natural rights and the new republicanism* (Princeton, NJ, 1998).

Online resources

Aquinas, Thomas, *Contra gentiles*, translated by James F. Anderson, www.dhspriory.org/thomas/english/ContraGentiles.htm (last accessed 26 April 2019).

–, *The Summa theologica*, translated

by Fathers of the English Dominican Province, www.dhspriory.org/thomas/english/summa/index.html (last accessed 26 April 2019).

The Avalon project: documents in law, history and diplomacy, http://avalon.law.yale.edu/18th_century/rightsof.asp (last accessed 21 May 2019).

The Bible, New International Version, www.biblegateway.com (last accessed 21 May 2019).

Eighteenth century collections online, https://www.gale.com/intl/primary-sources/eighteenth-century-collections-online (last accessed 21 May 2019).

Electronic Enlightenment, www.e-enlightenment.com (last accessed 21 May 2019).

The Encyclopedia of Diderot & D'Alembert: collaborative translation project, http://quod.lib.umich.edu/d/did/ (last accessed 24 April 2019).

Library of economics and liberty, http://www.econlib.org (last accessed 21 May 2019).

The Making of the modern world, https://www.gale.com/intl/primary-sources/the-making-of-the-modern-world (last accessed 21 May 2019).

Voltaire Society of America, www.whitman.edu/VSA/index.html (accessed January 2018).

Index